ARCHAEOLOGY
Down to Earth

Second Edition

ARCHAEOLOGY
Down to Earth

Second Edition

David Hurst Thomas
American Museum of Natural History

Harcourt Brace College Publishers

Fort Worth   Philadelphia   San Diego   New York   Orlando   Austin   San Antonio
Toronto   Montreal   London   Sydney   Tokyo

Publisher	Earl McPeek
Acquisitions Editor	Brenda Weeks
Market Strategist	Kathleen Sharp
Project Editor	Angela Williams Urquhart
Art Director	Don Fujimoto
Production Manager	Andrea A. Johnson

Cover images provided by the author.

ISBN: 0-15-505189-X

Library of Congress Catalog Card Number: 98-87431

Address for Orders
Harcourt Brace College Publishers, 6277 Sea Harbor Drive, Orlando, FL 32887-6777
1-800-782-4479

Address for Editorial Correspondence
Harcourt Brace College Publishers, 301 Commerce Street, Suite 3700, Fort Worth, TX 76102

Web Site Address
http://www.hbcollege.com

Printed in the United States of America

8 9 0 1 2 3 4 5 6 7   016   10 9 8 7 6 5 4 3 2 1

Harcourt Brace College Publishers

Preface

◻ ◻ ◻

People who like this sort of thing will find this the sort of thing they like.
BOOK REVIEW BY ABRAHAM LINCOLN (1809–1865),
16TH PRESIDENT OF THE UNITED STATES

This brief book is gleaned from my 700+ page text *Archaeology* (Harcourt Brace, 1998). I have tried to write a user-friendly overview of contemporary Americanist archaeology: what it is, who does it, and why anybody should care about archaeology. By *contemporary,* I mean right now, today. By *Americanist archaeology,* I mean the brand of archaeology currently taught and practiced at major American universities and museums. Americanist archaeology is, of course, practiced around the globe, as scholars will always reflect their intellectual origins, regardless of where they ply their trade.

This book departs, in a few ways, from the standard textbook. In most archaeology texts, the approach is fairly encyclopedic and dispassionate. The author usually assumes an all-knowing voice of authority and attempts to maintain an objective, impersonal, detached style. This mode of presentation is just fine. Most textbook writers use it, and most textbook readers are quite familiar with it.

But I can't do it that way. Little about archaeology is impersonal to me, and my biases are clearly reflected here (as they were in the previous edition of this book).

To be sure: Modern archaeology is a specialized and complicated academic discipline. Today's archaeology has plenty of concepts, several bodies of theory, and a huge array of analytical methods—and these are things I'd like you to understand. But archaeology is more than method and theory. It's also dust and discouragement, and I want you to know something about that part as well.

Many (perhaps most) archaeologists tend to write about their lifework in narrative as dry and stuffy as the caves they often excavate. I don't see why this is necessary. Archaeologists don't talk like that in real life, and many even enjoy what they do (although you'd never know it from the "literature"). Doing archaeology should be fun and satisfying; throughout these pages, we'll try to keep things on a more relaxed and relatively personal level.

You'll find that this book will reflect something of my own personality (and you should be aware of these biases). In the first chapter, for instance, I narrate the history and development of Americanist archaeology. Because the lives and interests of individual archaeologists can be as revealing as their archaeology, I'll give you a brief life history of eight well known American archaeologists. The selection is personal, reflecting my own mind-set and background. Other archaeologists would doubtless choose other examples to personify different values. This is what I mean about the largely personal slant.

Don't be humble. You're not that great.
GOLDA MEIR (1898–1978), ISRAELI POLITICIAN

You'll also find that the text proceeds largely by example, several of which are drawn from my own archaeological experience. I discuss how Gatecliff Shelter was discovered and take you along as we search for a lost sixteenth-/seventeenth-century Franciscan mission in Georgia's fabled Sea Islands. This search not only illustrates the growing importance of high-tech remote sensing approaches, but it also tries to impart something of the flavor of getting out there and actually doing the archaeology.

So now you're forewarned: This is not an encyclopedia. It's a personalized and admittedly idiosyncratic interpretation of what's up in contemporary Americanist archaeology.

> *Scientists are not mere knowledge-acquisition machines; they are guided by emotion and intuition as well as by cold reason and calculation.*
> PAUL HORGAN, STAFF WRITER, *SCIENTIFIC AMERICAN*

How This Book Evolved

My first archaeology textbook was *Predicting the Past: An Introduction to Anthropological Archaeology* (1974), followed by a much larger text called simply *Archaeology* (1979). Both described what was then called the "new archaeology" (and today is better termed the "processual agenda"). This approach was unusual in a couple of ways. For one thing, it was written from a first-person perspective (we talked about this above). I just couldn't see why archaeology needed to be presented as deadly dull and lifeless.

> *I may have my faults, but being wrong ain't one of them.*
> JIMMY HOFFA (1913–1975?), AMERICAN LABOR LEADER

Beyond this, these books reflected the times in which they were written. The 1970s and 1980s were at once stimulating and confusing—not unlike today. Many archaeologists could see little but conflict and chaos: loud arguments about how best to understand the past, with little agreement on much of anything.

I bluntly disagree with this position. The "new archaeologists" had an unfortunate habit of rejecting what had gone before. I believed (and still believe) that the discipline of archaeology develops by selective accretion—adding newer developments in method and theory to the solid base of what our predecessors accomplished. I saw my role as textbook writer to be one of cutting through the hype and self-serving bluster, to demonstrate how the various pieces—"new" and traditional—fit together into a workable discipline of archaeology.

> *Archaeology was not practiced exclusively by idiots before 1962 (or 1950 or 1935).*
> ALBERT SPAULDING (1914–1990), ARCHAEOLOGIST

The processual agenda had three sequential goals. Archaeologists must first *establish cultural chronology*—define the spatial and temporal framework with which to organize the specifics of the archaeological record. The intermediate goal was to *reconstruct past lifeways,* to define the recoverable aspects of past human existence: settlement pattern, population density, technology, economy, organization of domestic life, kinship, maintenance of law and order, social stratification, ritual, art, and religion. In effect, archaeologists working at this intermediate goal were pursuing "the anthropology of the dead." Archaeology's ultimate goal was to transcend the specifics of chronology and lifeway to *define the cultural processes* behind past and present behaviors. So-called *processual archaeology* sought to uncover the timeless and spaceless law-like generalizations that would help us understand modern society and how it came to be. Explaining this sequential, overarching framework in processual archaeology was my major objective in the 1970s.

But after nearly a decade, this approach started to fray around the edges. The discipline had changed, and something new was clearly in order. In *Archaeology II,* published in 1989, I replaced out-of-date and "moribund" sections with fresher examples which, I hoped, demonstrated current archaeology in action.

Although maintaining the basic processual agenda as an organizing framework, I made several significant additions, upgrading the discussions of historical archaeology and cultural resource management ("applied archaeology"), explicitly confronting the changing roles of women in archaeology, and adding a new emphasis on archaeological field methods. I retained the personal (often first-person) tone and many examples were drawn from my own experiences and interests, grounded in the mainstream processual agenda. But I did note that some archaeologists had begun framing alternatives to the processual agenda. The so-called *postprocessual critique* attacked the basic premises of processual archaeology.

For one thing, the postprocessual critics rejected the processual search for universal laws, arguing instead that such "laws" supposedly governing human behavior simply do not exist. Postprocessual critics also pointed out the inadequacies of "an explicitly scientific approach," emphasizing the subjectivity involved in all archaeological interpretation. Some of the more extreme postprocessualists even argued that there is no real past at all: The past is merely a subjective construction in the present. Ecological and "systemic" views of the past were similarly rejected as a "robotic view of the human past." Postprocessual critics favored developing more empathetic and humanistic approaches, which give priority to human thoughts, decisions, and other highly subjective elements.

Archaeology's postprocessual critique rejected the evolutionary, antihistorical, objective, science-based, and ethical neutrality of the processual agenda. Instead, postprocessual archaeologists emphasized empathetic approaches, multiple pathways of belief. They questioned how "value-free" archaeology really is: Do archaeologists discover "a real past" or do they "construct" that past based on present-day experiences and biases? What political purposes underlie archaeological interpretations of the past?

These postprocessual approaches seemed particularly appropriate within the growing field of historical archaeology (where the presence of documentary evidence made the subjective, humanistic approaches more productive). The processual agenda continued to provide a relatively consistent and relatively coherent framework for understanding the past. I continued to argue that "archaeology is anthropology or it is nothing." I still believed that the diverse archaeological approaches fit into the single set of three stepwise and sequential objectives mentioned before: construct cultural chronology, reconstruct extinct lifeways, and define cultural processes. I continued to teach that "the canons of established scientific methods" provide the best way to understand the human past.

In the late 1980s, the processual agenda remained intact, but the postprocessual critique had clearly begun to make inroads.

Why a New Edition?

Any jackass can kick down a barn, but it takes a good carpenter to build one.
SAM RAYBURN (1882–1961), SPEAKER OF THE HOUSE

Today, the field of Americanist archaeology has changed so dramatically that it is difficult to know where to begin. This time around, I found my basic approach required modification from top to bottom. Neither the original processual agenda nor the subsequent postprocessual critique were sufficient to explain what's going on in modern Americanist archaeology. Although it's not an easy story to tell, I'm enjoying the diverse and yet eclectic theoretical blend that characterizes contemporary archaeology.

The "processual agenda" and "postprocessual critique" stand as important historical milestones in a complex dialogue about how to encounter the human past. Both were historical events, firmly grounded in specific places and particular times. But most of the underlying issues—science and humanism, objectivity and empathy—have concerned thoughtful archaeologists for more than a century. For years, archaeology has been buffeted by a number of "theoretical schools," each claiming for itself a privileged status in defining what constitutes adequate explanation in archaeological research.

Archaeology is about facts; if you want the Truth, go next door to the Philosophy Department.
INDIANA JONES, HOLLYWOOD ARCHAEOLOGIST (IN THE MOVIE
INDIANA JONES AND THE LAST CRUSADE)

It is no longer useful—nor even possible—to pick Americanist archaeology apart into such tidy subdivisions. Americanist archaeology is today neither processual nor postprocessual: It employs modified versions of both. The vast majority of those practicing Americanist archaeology fall somewhere toward the middle: There are very few hard-core processualists or die-hard postprocessualists around these days. The surviving parts of processual and postprocessual archaeologies comprise what is today our approach to the past.

Archaeology, history, and anthropology appear as increasingly arbitrary partitions of the necessary elements of comprehensive understanding.

ANDREW SHERRATT, ARCHAEOLOGIST (ASHMOLEAN MUSEUM, OXFORD UNIVERSITY)

So it is that today's Americanist archaeology is best characterized as multiple paths leading toward an understanding of the past. Archaeologists today wrestle with several important questions: To what extent do we "discover" an objective past? Or are we "creating" alternative pasts from the same data? What is the proper mix of humanism and science in archaeology? What social responsibilities does the archaeologist have to properly use the past in the present? Each of these questions has been around for a century, and no clear-cut resolution appears on the horizon.

This is a strength, not a weakness. Learning to live with mutually irreconcilable views about the past is not an easy thing, but it's the only way that archaeology will survive in the upcoming millennium.

So What's New Here?

Here are some of the features that have been added in this edition:

- *New emphasis on the rapidly evolving relationship between archaeologists and Native American people.* These discussions illustrate the dynamic (if sometimes contentious) relationships between native people and the archaeologists who wish to study them. Evolving linkages highlight the increasing importance of newer, multicultural modes of explaining and understanding America's recent and remote past.
- *New integration of scientific and humanistic approaches in archaeology.* Although some believe that it's necessary to choose sides—either be a scientist or be a humanist—I hope to convince you that the choice isn't really necessary. Modern archaeology spans a broad philosophical spectrum, with both scientific and humanistic strategies contributing significantly to modern archaeological theory.
- *Emphasis on the increased importance of cognitive archaeology.* In recent years, a so-called "cognitive revolution" has swept across Americanist archaeology. Concerned with defining an "archaeology of the human mind," cognitive archaeologists pursue a broad agenda, seeking to understand the importance of ritual and religion, symbolism and iconography, and the development of human consciousness.
- *Focus on the increased participation by women in archaeology.* We attempt here to demolish misleading Hollywood stereotypes—to illustrate how the fallacies of Indiana Jones are being replaced by the realities of Indiana Joans. In several places, we demonstrate how feminist archaeology is changing our perception of gender in the past.

- *Accent on the importance of applied archaeology.* America has come to recognize that her common cultural heritage is under threat from the demands of contemporary life. Here, we emphasize the role of archaeologist as manager of cultural and heritage resources, informing students about the broad range of employment possibilities in archaeology and stressing the role of conservation archaeology as a practical extension of the more traditional academic and museum-oriented archaeologies.

- *A new section on the archaeology of African America.* This important addition (1) shows the factual and theoretical basis for a rapidly developing new direction in archaeology (especially in urban America), (2) details how local communities are actively participating in archaeology to learn about their own past, and (3) emphasizes how the new brand of "grassroots" archaeology is available to anybody interested in participating—even avocational archaeologists and kids.

- *Emphasis on the importance of remote sensing as a nondestructive way of learning about the past.* We examine in detail that increasingly sophisticated technology that is enabling archaeologists to find where sites are, what they contain, and how the remains are articulated—all without disturbing the site. Remote sensing technology is rapidly becoming a cost-effective way of doing archaeology in a noninvasive, nondestructive manner.

- *Emphasis on new developments in archaeology at the molecular level,* showing how human diets are being reconstructed from human bones through the analysis of isotope levels and the extraction analysis of ancient DNA.

- *Several "In His/Her Own Words" boxed features.* These first-person excerpts broaden the focus of my own largely first-person approach and also emphasize the importance of seeking multiple voices and explanations about the past.

- *The graphics have been significantly upgraded.* We've spent considerable time and effort gathering photographs of *real people doing real archaeology.* Although some archaeologists do indeed look like movie actors, most don't. As you look through these pictures, you might be surprised to see what real archaeologists look like.

- *Everything is explicitly tied into the Internet.* At the end of each chapter, you'll find a listing of "Archaeology on the Internet," which provides on-line amplification of subjects I'm discussing in the text—"virtual tours" of sites being considered in the text, FAQs (Frequently Asked Questions) about theoretical or methodological advances, more complete discussions and/or bibliographies, relevant professional and avocational groups, and places to find the newest developments in Americanist archaeology.

- *Each chapter now begins with a Preview and ends with a comprehensive Summary.*

- *A new focus on ethical concerns in archaeology.* The final chapter looks in depth at the complex issue of "Who Owns the Past?"—a theme developed throughout this book. It also focuses on the profound implications of the Native American Graves Protection and Repatriation Act—"NAGPRA" for short.

Who Helped Out?

Despite the personal flavor of these pages, don't think that the book was com-pleted by a single pair of hands—no book is. Many people have helped out and I must include several words of thanks.

The overall presentation was vastly improved by a contingent of top-notch colleagues and friends who provided advice and critical reviews of the manuscript. I am particularly grateful to Paul Goldstein, Steve Lekson, and Janet Spector, each of whom slogged through the full-length manuscript and contributed measurably to the final product. For input on the various Internet links, I thank Joelle Clark (Network Subcommittee e-mail coordinator for the Public Education Committee of the Society for American Archaeology).

I also gratefully acknowledge timely and sometimes detailed assistance from Larry Babits, Mary Beaudry, Richard Berger, Lewis Binford, Michael Blakey, Ama Badu Boakyewa, Rob Bonnichson, Bruce Bradley, Jane Buikstra, Robert Carneiro, Catherine Cameron, Margaret Conkey, Cheryl Claassen, C. William Clewlow, the late Don Crabtree, Jay Custer, Phil Da Vita, William Davis, Kathleen Dea-gan, Jeffrey Dean, Rob DeSalle, Robert Elston, Clark Erickson, T. J. Ferguson, Kent V. Flannery, Don Fowler, Anne Fox, George Frison, Ervan Garrison, Joan Gero, Diane Gifford-Gonzalez, Dean Goodman, Martha Graham, Donald K. Grayson, David Grimaldi, Marvin Harris, Christine Hastorf, William Haviland, Brian Hayden, Richard Holmer, Robert L. Humphrey, the late Cynthia Irwin-Williams, Gregory Johnson, William Kelso, Thomas King, Stephen Kowalewski, Charles Lange, Clark Spencer Larsen, Robert Leonard, Mark Leone, Randall McGuire, Frank McManamon, Scotty MacNeish, David B. Madsen, the late William Maples, Joyce Marcus, Alexander Marshack, George Miller, Paul Min-nis, Craig Morris, Michael J. O'Brien, James O'Connell, Christopher Peebles, Kathy Place, Stephen Plog, William Rathje, Elizabeth Reitz, Thomas Riley, John Rick, Anibal Rodriguez, Nan Rothschild, Irwin Rovner, Michael Schiffer, Enid Schildkrout, Payson Sheets, Theresa Singleton, Stanley South, Janet Spector, Charles Spencer, the late William Tallbull, Anya Taylor, Mark Taylor, the late W. W. Taylor, Ian Tattersall, Ruth Tringham, Donald Tuohy, Patty Jo Watson, John Weymouth, the late Joe Ben Wheat, and Mary Whelan. Each contributed worthwhile suggestions, which I often followed. Although the finished product re-mains my own, I gratefully acknowledge the help of these people for improving the ideas and sharpening the focus.

Several others in the American Museum of Natural History also deserve thanks. Margot Dembo handled innumerable editing chores, and my confrere Lo-rann S. A. Pendleton spent endless hours helping with the background research. Rachel Goddard, and Jason Sherman read the full-length draft. Niurka Tyler cheer-fully helped out with dozens of details. I also thank the newer members of our research staff, Eric Powell and Cheryl White, who also contributed their advice and assistance.

In the AMNH Library, the incomparable director, Nina Root, and Mary De-Jong. In Special Collections, the director, Tom Baione, Lisa Stock, Daryl Gammons, Arthur Cook, and Kathy Burek. Our thanks to the AMNH Photography Studio staff, including Craig Chesek, Jackie Beckett, and Denis Finnin.

I also thank the crew at Harcourt Brace, particularly Brenda Weeks and Angela Williams Urquhart. Dennis O'Brien generated much of the artwork illustrating this volume, and I also gratefully acknowledge the contributions of the late Nicholas Amorosi and Diana Salles, both of the American Museum of Natural History.

D. H. T.
Santa Fe, New Mexico

Contents

□ □ □

Chapter 6. Middle-Range Research: Ethnoarchaeology and Experimental Archaeology   157

What Is Archaeology?

❏ ❏ ❏

PREVIEW

Today, there are dozens of ways to do good archaeology. To define the range of acceptable archaeological methods, we will at times emphasize the extremes. One extreme is largely scientific, the other is largely humanistic. One extreme is pretty objective, the other is quite subjective. One extreme values ecology, the other prizes the role of ideas. Sometimes these approaches can coexist, sometimes they clash.

This book will explore today's archaeology and explain why there are multiple views about the past. To understand where such multiple perspectives come from, we must, quite naturally, examine the past. Where else could an archaeologist turn? This first chapter looks at how contemporary archaeology evolved and how the surviving parts fit together.

> *I just like the challenge that prehistory seemed to give, the mystery of it, and finding out about people—why they think the way they do, and what makes history.*
>
> MARGORIE F. LAMBERT, ARCHAEOLOGIST
> (SCHOOL OF AMERICAN RESEARCH)

Archaeological objects vary. So do archaeological contexts. Deciphering meaning from objects in context is the business of **archaeology.** In fact, today we have so many complex techniques for doing so that it has become impossible for anyone to know and understand them all. No matter how hard we might study, we will never learn all there is to know about archaeological theory and technique. New techniques appear each year, and—alas—with each advance, each individual archaeologist becomes relatively less knowledgeable. In truth, archaeologists are learning more and more about less and less.

The same is true of field techniques. Archaeological fieldwork is becoming so refined that many of us now regret portions of our earlier research: We threw too much away. This is nothing new. Archaeologists in 1923 did not save charcoal. Why should they have? Who knew that in 1949 a physicist named Libby would perfect a method of dating lumps of charcoal? Archaeologists did not collect pollen samples in the 1930s because nobody knew how to reconstruct extinct past environments from microscopic pollen grains. In my first field class, I was told to chuck out all the animal bone that was not "identifiable" (whatever that meant). Today, by trying to save all bone, we are learning about hunting strategies, butchering patterns, seasonality, and even the sex and age characteristics of bygone animal populations. Soil from archaeological sites is now a gold mine of information. Traces of blood, sometimes thousands of years old, can now be detected on stone tools. We had always thoroughly scrubbed our artifacts before cataloging them in the laboratory. We now realize that important clues—such as blood residues—can literally go down the drain. Today's archaeologists are beginning to settle for studying dirty artifacts.

Archaeologists are justly proud of their microscopic techniques. No clue from the past is too minor to disregard. We are afraid to throw anything away; indeed, entire sites are occasionally brought back to the laboratory and actually "excavated" under a microscope.

But there is a danger lurking in these minute procedures, and that danger is *myopia,* losing sight of the forest for the trees. This book does not view archaeology through a microscope. It does just the opposite. Instead of magnifying the minutiae of archaeology, our macroscopic perspective will merge particulars in search of overall patterning. Archaeology consists of hundreds, maybe thousands, of tiny pieces. Sometimes the pieces seem so varied that they no longer fit together. Viewed another way, they seem to define a single picture. What you see depends largely on where you stand.

That is one problem: How do we fit the diversified techniques, concepts, and strategies of archaeology into a meaningful whole? There is also a second problem: What does this framework tell us? Can it stand alone, or does it somehow tie into a yet larger whole?

So we are left with this: What are archaeologists? What are scientists? What are humanists? What are anthropologists? When each question has been answered, we will be in a position to assess what contemporary archaeologists are up to. Then we shall find out how they do it. But first, a word about archaeology's past.

The Western World Discovers Its Past

Most historians ascribe the honor of "first archaeologist" to Nabonidus (who died in 538 B.C.), the last king of the neo-Babylonian Empire. A sincerely pious man, Nabonidus's zealous worship of his gods compelled him to rebuild the ruined temples of ancient Babylon and to search among their foundations for the inscriptions of earlier kings. For this reason, Nabonidus is known to modern history more as an antiquarian than an administrator. In fact, we are indebted to the research of his scribes and the excavations by his subjects for much of our modern picture of the Babylonian Empire. Though nobody would call Nabonidus an "archaeologist" in the modern sense of the term, he remains an important figure for one simple reason: *Nabonidus looked to the physical residues of antiquity to answer questions about the past.* This may seem like a simple step, but it contrasted sharply with the beliefs of his contemporaries, who regarded tradition, legend, and myth as the only clues to the past.

Archaeology's family tree has an unsavory branch as well, because the looters and grave robbers of antiquity contributed greatly to the archaeological legacy. In contrast to Nabonidus, untold generations of mercenaries were attracted by the promise of easy riches through the looting of tombs and other ancient storehouses.

Too often, the early-twentieth-century Egyptologists found, to their dismay, that they had been "beaten to the punch" by looters and vandals. Sometimes the bodies were barely cold before the grave goods were purloined. H. E. Winlock, then director of New York's Metropolitan Museum expedition to Dier el Bahri, found episode after episode in which the ancient Egyptians had rifled the graves of their own rulers. When the Twenty-First Dynasty (ca. 1090 B.C.) mummies of Hent-Towy and Nesit-Iset were discovered, for instance, Winlock and his associates thought they were perfectly intact. But closer examination revealed that the mummies had been unwrapped before interment and the valuable metal pectoral hawks and finger rings stolen. This deceit could only have been the work of the very undertakers commissioned to prepare the mummies for the hereafter. The pilfering of Egypt's royal tombs has continued for millennia, and in fact, much of

---

A.D./B.C./B.P. . . . Archaeology's Alphabet Soup

Throughout this book you will encounter a blizzard of stand-alone capital letters: A.D., A.C., B.C., B.P., and a bunch of others. Let me provide you with some concise definitions of the most commonly used abbreviations:

B.C. ("before Christ"): for instance 3200 B.C.

A.D. (literally *anno Domini,* meaning "in the year of the Lord"): indicating that a time division falls within the Christian era. Archaeologists generally place the "A.D." *prior to* the numerical age estimate; thus, you should say "A.D. 1560" rather than "1560 A.D." The earliest "A.D." date is "A.D. 1"; there is no "A.D. 0" because this year is already denoted by "0 B.C." and double-numbering is not allowed.

A.C. ("after Christ"): basically the same as "A.D.;" it's also written A.C. 1560 (with the abbreviation written *before* the number). This usage is confusing, and hardly anybody uses it anymore. We don't either.

B.P. ("before present"): Many archaeologists feel more comfortable avoiding the A.D./B.C. split altogether, substituting the single "before present" age estimate (with the calendar year A.D. 1950 arbitrarily selected as the zero point). By this convention, A.D. 1560 becomes 390 B.P.

the popular appeal of Egyptology is matching modern wits with those of the ancient architects of the tombs, who tried every trick imaginable to outfox looters, both ancient and modern.

Despite contributions in other fields, the classical Greeks did little to further the aims of modern archaeology. "The ancient Greeks for the most part held that the way to understand ourselves is to study ourselves, while what others do is irrelevant." Socrates, for instance, was concerned primarily with his own thoughts and those of his contemporaries; he showed marked disdain for the languages and customs of "barbarians" (by whom he meant all non-Greeks). The Romans, of course, traced their intellectual ancestry to the heroes of Greek legend; they imitated Greek protocol; and they shared in the pervasive Greek **ethnocentrism.** The ethnographies written by Greek historians Herodotus and Tacitus stand virtually alone in their concern with non-Greek and non-Roman customs and values.

Pre-Renaissance writings did little to foster the development of archaeological inquiry, but the Renaissance changed all this. It has been suggested that the major contribution of the Renaissance—particularly in Italy—was the distinction between the present and the past. Classical Greeks and Romans recognized only the most remote past, which they reified in myth and legend. Because the Europeans of the Middle Ages likewise failed to distinguish between themselves and the ancients, it fell to Renaissance scholars to point up the differences between classical and medieval times.

Petrarch, perhaps the most influential individual of the early Renaissance, defined an intellectual tradition that continues to be important in today's archaeology. Beyond his considerable talents as poet and linguist, Petrarch also provided strong impetus for archaeological research. To him, the remote past was an ideal of perfection, and he looked to antiquity for moral philosophy. But in order to imitate classical antiquity, one must first study it. In a real sense, Petrarch's approach led to a rediscovery of the past by those in the Western European intellectual tradition. Petrarch's influence can best be seen in the work of his close friend Boccaccio, who wrote extensive essays on classical mythology, and also in that of Giovanni Dondi, who is generally credited with the first systematic observations on archaeological monuments.

But it remained for the fifteenth-century Italian antiquarian Ciriaco de' Pizzicolli to establish the modern discipline of archaeology. After translating the Latin inscription on the triumphal arch of Trajan at Ancona, he was inspired to devote the remainder of his life to studying ancient monuments, copying inscriptions, and generally promoting the study of the past. His travels ranged from Syria to Egypt, throughout the islands of the Aegean, and finally to Athens. When asked his business, Ciriaco is said to have replied, "Restoring the dead to life"—which today remains a pretty fair definition of the everyday business of archaeology.

The antiquarian spirit was also alive and well in Great Britain. In fact, a group of eminent British historians and students of the classics formed an antiquarian society as early as 1572. The emphasis of this and later societies was to record and preserve the national treasures, rather than indiscriminately to acquire curios and *objets d'art*. Of course, many private collectors were still concerned only with filling their curio cabinets, but the goal of British antiquarianism was to map, record, and preserve archaeological ruins. By the late eighteenth century a healthy interest in classical antiquities was perceived as an important ingredient in the "cultivation of taste" among the European leisure classes, hence the term **antiquarian.**

Archaeological research to this point proceeded mostly within the tradition of Petrarch; it was concerned primarily with clarifying the picture of classical civilizations. This lore was readily digested by the eighteenth- and early nineteenth-century mind because it was in basic agreement with the religious teachings of the time. The Bible remained a natural access point into the understanding of classical cultures.

But a problem arose when very crude stone tools were discovered amid the ancient gravels of England and continental Europe. About 1836 or so, **Jacques Boucher de Perthes,** a controller of customs at Abbeville (France), began to find ancient axe heads in the river gravels of the Somme River. Along with those tools, he also found the bones of mammals long extinct. To Boucher de Perthes, the implication was obvious: "In spite of their imperfection, these rude stones prove the existence of [very ancient] man as surely as a whole Louvre would have done."

Few contemporaries believed him, in part because of prevailing religious beliefs. That is, in the early nineteenth century the orthodox opinion held that human beings had been on earth for roughly 6,000 years. Theological scholars, who had studied the problem of Creation in marvelous detail, simply refused to concede that there had been sufficient time for people to have coexisted with animals of extinct form. Paley's *Natural Theology* (1802) explained the matter something like this: The earth was created according to a splendid design, not unlike a fine watch; God was the ultimate watchmaker, and he had deliberately placed people on his earth about 4000 B.C.

Actually, this chronology had been suggested before. In 1642, Dr. John Lightfoot, master of St. Catharine's College and vice-chancellor of Cambridge University, published a treatise with the delightful title *A Few*

Boucher de Perthes found Paleolithic hand axes like this in the Somme River gravels.

and New Observations on the Book of Genesis, the most of them certain, the rest probable, all harmless, and rarely heard of before. Lightfoot's later, slightly refined chronology concluded that "heaven and earth, centre and circumference, were created all together in the same instant. . . . This took place and man was created by the Trinity on October 23, 4004 B.C. at nine o'clock in the morning." As archaeologist Glyn Daniel once dryly observed, "We may perhaps see in these dates and time a prejudice of a Vice-Chancellor for the beginning of an academic year and the beginning of an academic morning, but, at least, Lightfoot did provide an exact and absolute chronology which must have been very comforting."

By this reckoning, there was zero probability of an extensive human antiquity; there simply hadn't been enough time. Therefore, the thinking went, Boucher de Perthes must be mistaken—his rude implements must be something other than human handiwork. Some suggested that the "tools" were really meteorites, and others felt that the stones must have been produced by lightning, or elves, or fairies. One seventeenth-century scholar even suggested that the chipped flints were "generated in the sky by a fulgurous exhalation conglobed in a cloud by the circumposed humour."

Boucher de Perthes stuck to his guns. More finds were made in the French gravel pits at St. Acheul, and similar discoveries turned up across the Channel in southern England. The issue was finally resolved when the well respected British paleontologist Hugh Falconer visited Abbeville to examine the disputed evidence for himself. A procession of esteemed scholars followed Falconer's lead, until finally, in 1859 a paper was presented to the influential Royal Society of London supporting the claims of Boucher de Perthes. In no time, several eminent natural scientists declared their support.

The year 1859 turned out to be a banner year in the history of human thought: Not only was the remote antiquity of humankind accepted by many, but Charles Darwin published his influential *On the Origin of Species,* which suggested the process by which modern people had arisen from those ancient ancestors.

The floodgates now open, British archaeology took two rather divergent courses. One direction became involved with the problems of remote geological time and the demonstration of long-term human evolution. Other scholars, following the tradition of Petrarch, continued their course of classical studies, focusing particularly on the archaeology of ancient Greece and Rome. This philosophical split continues into modern times.

Sustained European contact with the Americas opened yet another option for **prehistoric** studies. Fairly early in the game, it became clear that in sheer antiquity, American archaeology would never rival the European finds: The New World was indeed new. Beginning with Columbus's triumphant return to Europe in 1493, several vexing issues cropped up. How could regions such as the Valley of Mexico and Peru boast fantastic riches, while many other places—such as the North American West—appear to be so impoverished, even primitive? When did people first arrive in the New World? Where had these migrants come from, and how did they get there?

Enormous confusion and speculation immediately arose. There was, for instance, the "Lost Tribe of Israel" scenario, which emphasized alleged Native American–Semitic similarities. And the fabled island of Atlantis was seriously proposed by some as the ancestral homeland of the Native Americans. Even voyaging Egyptians and Vikings were cited as hypothetical proto-Americans.

The mystery deepened with each new discovery of American ruins. How, for instance, does one account for the thousands of prehistoric earthen mounds that dot North America east of the Mississippi River? Once-prevalent racist theories generally assumed that Native Americans were simply incapable of constructing such monuments, and much debate during the eighteenth and nineteenth centuries centered on the mythic Mound Builders, who had mysteriously vanished before the arrival of Columbus.

Investigators gradually came to realize that considerable continuities existed between the unknown prehistoric past and the Native American population of the historic period. As such knowledge progressed, profound differences between European and American archaeology became more apparent. While the Europeans wrestled with their ancient flints—without apparent modern correlates—American scholars came to realize that the living Native Americans were indeed relevant to the interpretation of archaeological remains. In the crass terms of the time, to many Europeans, the Native Americans became "living fossils," accessible relics of times past.

So it was that New World archaeology became inextricably wed to the study of living Native American people. While Old World archaeologists began from a baseline of geological time or classical antiquity, their American counterparts began to develop an anthropological understanding of Native America. The **ethnology** of American Indian people not only became an important domain of Western scholarship in its own right, but the increased understanding of Native American lifeways quickly helped unravel questions such as the peopling of the New World.

Let me stress another important point here. As Europeans refined the archaeology of Europe, they were studying their own ancestors (Anglos, Celts, Balts, Slavs, Huns, etc.). But New World archaeology was basically a matter of Euroamericans often digging up somebody else's ancestors (mostly those of the Native Americans). This important difference explains several defining elements of New World archaeology:

1. Why racist, anti–American Indian theories dominated nineteenth-century Americanist archaeology
2. Why European governments enacted antiquity legislation decades before North American governments did so (because Europeans were taking care of their own ancestors' sites)
3. Why many contemporary Native American people still distrust conventional Western scholarship to interpret their past

We will return to each theme in the pages to follow.

Founders of Americanist Archaeology

> *People have a strong tendency to simply forget how much we've learned about the past. As new knowledge becomes part of the generally accepted mainstream of knowledge, we don't think about it anymore. It is knowledge for which most contemporary archaeologists can't take credit, and it is knowledge that apparently begins to fall into the category of always having been known.*
>
> JAMES N. HILL (1934–1997), ARCHAEOLOGIST

Now we are ready to begin looking more closely at how Americanist archaeology is currently practiced. Here, we draw upon Robert Dunnell's useful term *Americanist* to denote the kind of archaeology that has been developed in association with anthropology in North America. Although many other terms have been used—"scientific archaeology," "anthropological archaeology," and, too often, just "archaeology"—I prefer the phrase **Americanist archaeology** because it is the most descriptive, yet least pejorative. Let me also emphasize that archaeologists working in the Americanist tradition can (and do) practice their craft around the world.

The history of Americanist archaeology (all history, really) is a commingling of tradition and change. In this section, we meet a few of the more traditional figures, people who illustrate how archaeology was practiced during their lifetimes. You could say the subject matter is *evolutionary.* Then we shall discuss two people whose skepticism helped define contemporary archaeology; in a sense, that section is *revolutionary.* We'll also look at one of our better-known contemporary archaeologists, a person who has contributed to the theoretical diversity that characterizes Americanist archaeology on the eve of the twenty-first century.

Thomas Jefferson (1743–1826): America's First Prehistoric Archaeologist

The European Renaissance, which began in the fourteenth century and lasted well into the 1700s, produced a breed of scholars known for their prowess across a prodigious range of topics. Aptly known as *Renaissance men,* these cultivated gentlemen embodied the essence of intellectual and artistic excellence for their time. Although Thomas Jefferson postdates the Renaissance period in a chronological sense, his varied accomplishments place him well within the tradition of the Renaissance thinker.

Not only did the author of the Declaration of Independence later become the third president of the United States, he was also described by a contemporary as "an expert musician (the violin being his favorite instrument), a good dancer, a dashing rider, and proficient in all manly exercises." Jefferson was an avid player of chess (avoiding cards), an accomplished horticulturalist, a distinguished architect, and a connoisseur of fine French cooking.

These accomplishments aside, one of Jefferson's lesser-known achievements interests us here. Often labeled "the father of American archaeology," Thomas

Jefferson's curiosity about Native Americans' origins illustrates the initial stage of Americanist archaeology. Fascinated by Indian lore since boyhood and trained in classical linguistics, Jefferson believed that the Native American languages held valuable clues to the origins of the people. Jefferson personally collected linguistic data from more than 40 tribes and wrote a long treatise on the subject. Reasoning largely from his linguistic studies, Jefferson sensed an Asiatic origin for the Native Americans. But unlike his contemporaries, he was not content to restrict his speculation to armchair theorizing. Always a man of action, he tested his notions on some hard data.

Jefferson's contribution to Americanist archaeology was discussed in the only book he ever published, which appeared in a limited French edition in 1784 and in a widely distributed American edition in 1787. *Notes on the State of Virginia* dealt, in part, with the aborigines of Virginia. Jefferson listed the various Virginian tribes, relating their histories since the settlement of Jamestown in 1607 and incorporating a census of Virginia's current Native American population. As noted earlier, the origin of American Indians had been a compelling topic of speculation since the time of Columbus and probably even before. The Spanish explorer Hernando de Soto correctly surmised that many of the mounds served as foundations for priestly temples, but his astute observation was soon lost in a flood of fanciful interpretation. Racist attitudes prevalent in late eighteenth-century America had fostered the conception of the mythical Mound Builder People, who allegedly constructed the impressive monuments throughout the Americas before they either mysteriously vanished or underwent a profound degenerative process, rendering them smaller and less intelligent than modern Europeans.

Thomas Jefferson, archaeologist.

To Jefferson, solving the problem of the Native Americans' origins required a dual strategy: to learn as much as possible about contemporary Indian culture and also to examine their prehistoric remains. He argued emphatically that contemporary Native Americans were in no way mentally or physically inferior to the white races and rejected all current racist doctrines explaining their origins. He correctly reasoned that Native Americans were wholly capable of constructing the prehistoric monuments of the United States.

Then Jefferson took a critical step. Shovel firmly in hand, he proceeded to excavate a burial mound located on his property. Today, such a step seems obvious, but few of Jefferson's contemporaries would have thought of resorting to bones, stones, and dirt to answer intellectual issues. Contemporary eighteenth-century scholars preferred to rummage through libraries and archives rather than to dirty their hands with the hard facts from the past.

Written in the flowery style of the time, Jefferson's account provides quite an acceptable report of his investigation. First he describes the data—location, size, method of excavation, stratigraphy, condition of the bones, artifacts—and then he presents his conclusions: Why did prehistoric peoples bury their dead in mounds? He first noted the absence of traumatic wounds, such as those made by bullets or arrows, and also observed the interment of children, thereby rejecting the common notion that the bones were those of soldiers who had fallen in battle. Similarly, the scattered and disjointed nature of the bones militated against the notion of a "common sepulchre of a town," in which Jefferson would have expected to find skeletons arranged in more orderly fashion.

Jefferson surmised, quite correctly, that the bones had accumulated through successive burials and saw no reason to doubt that the mound had been constructed by the ancestors of the Native Americans encountered by the colonists. Today, nearly 200 years after Jefferson's excavations, archaeologists would modify few of his well reasoned conclusions.

Thomas Jefferson's primary legacy to archaeology is that he dug at all. By his simple excavation, Jefferson elevated the study of America's past from a speculative, armchair pastime to an inquiry built on empirical fieldwork. As a well educated colonial gentleman, Jefferson understood the importance of exposing speculation to a barrage of facts. The "facts" in this case lay buried beneath the ground, and that is precisely where he conducted his inquiry.

Unlike his contemporaries, Jefferson did not dig to obtain exotic curios for his mantel but initiated his excavations to answer specific, well formulated problems. He collected his data in as systematic a manner as possible and then drew carefully reasoned inferences from his fieldwork. Jefferson thereby pioneered the basics of archaeological reporting: recording his finds in meticulous detail, to be ultimately published for scrutiny by interested scholars.

C. B. Moore (1852–1936): A Genteel Digger

Clarence Bloomfield Moore was born into an affluent family of Philadelphia socialites. After receiving his B.A. degree from Harvard University in 1873, Moore followed the social circuit, rambling throughout Europe and joining

C. B. Moore.

safaris into exotic Africa. But by 1892, Moore found the well-to-do socialite lifestyle to be shallow, meaningless, and boring. Somewhere along the line, Moore was introduced to American archaeology and, at age 40, C. B. Moore was transformed from gentleman socialite into gentleman archaeologist.

Moore purchased a specially equipped flat-bottomed steamboat, which he christened the *Gopher,* and set off to explore the seemingly endless waterways of America's Southeast, excavating the major archaeological sites he encountered. Particularly drawn to the hundreds of burial and temple mounds, Moore enlisted the services of Dr. Milo G. Miller as secretary, physician, and colleague.

From the outset, Moore's annual archaeological campaigns were models of organization and efficiency. Aboard the *Gopher,* Moore and Miller conducted preliminary investigations so that likely sites could be located and arrangements could be contracted with landowners; actual excavations began in the spring. Moore hired and supervised the workmen and kept the field notes. As human skeletons were located, Dr. Miller conducted paleoautopsies on the spot, examining the bones in the field to determine sex, age, probable cause of death, and any unusual pathologies. The summers were spent cleaning and repairing the finds and then photographing and analyzing the collection. Moore prepared detailed excavation reports for publication and distributed the more unusual artifacts to major archaeological institutions.

Moore's first investigations concentrated on the shell middens and the sand burial mounds sprinkled along the Gulf Coast of Florida. Gradually, year after year, Moore worked his way around to Florida's eastern shore and eventually to the Sea Islands of coastal Georgia and South Carolina. In 1899, Moore returned to the Gulf Coast, traveled up the Alabama River, and examined the coast of northwest Florida. He excavated literally dozens of archaeological sites on each expedition.

Finally, in 1905, Moore paused on the Black Warrior River in Alabama to excavate intensively the ruins appropriately known as Moundville. With several trained assistants and a crew numbering 10 to 15, he explored the large temple mounds to examine the human burials and unearth spectacular pieces of pre-Columbian art. Moore concluded that Moundville had been a prominent regional center. He further surmised from the varied art forms that the ancient people of Moundville worshiped the sun, and that motifs such as the plumed serpent and eagle suggested strong ties with contemporaneous Mexican civilizations.

By 1916, Moore concluded that the *Gopher* had explored every southeastern river then navigable by steamer. Of course, archaeological techniques have improved markedly since Moore's times, and many a contemporary archaeologist wishes that Moore had been somewhat less thorough: He left so little for the rest of us.

Nels Nelson (1875–1964): America's First-Generation "Working" Archaeologist

Whereas Moore was born into a wealthy family, Nels Nelson grew up on a poor farm in Jutland, Denmark. Although first a farmhand, and a student only in his spare time, he did stumble onto the James Fenimore Cooper novels—*The Last of the Mohicans* and *The Deerslayer*—while still quite young and became fascinated with the lore of the Native Americans. Several of his relatives had already emigrated to America, and in 1892 Nelson's aunt in Minnesota sent him a steerage ticket to New York. On his way westward, he worked at a number of jobs (including driving a six-mule team and butchering hogs) and finally saved enough money to enroll in Stanford University, where he studied philosophy by day and took odd jobs at night to pay his expenses.

Quite by accident, someone invited Nelson to attend an archaeological excavation in Ukiah, north of San Francisco, and he was hooked. The dig apparently rekindled the same fascination with Indian lore he had experienced reading Cooper's novels. He immediately enrolled in all the archaeological courses available at the University of California.

Nelson's M.A. thesis was an archaeological survey of the shell middens surrounding San Francisco Bay. He later boasted that according to his pedometer, he had walked more than 3,000 miles during his reconnaissance and had recorded 425 prehistoric shell mounds. His report discussed the location of these sites relative to available natural resources, listed the animal bones found in the shell

Nels Nelson with an array of Dutch archaeological artifacts.

heaps, and pondered the ecological adaptation implied by such a bayside lifeway. Urban sprawl has today destroyed all but a handful of these once obvious sites, and Nelson's map, originally published in 1909, remains an irreplaceable resource to modern archaeologists interested in central California prehistory.

Then, in 1912, the American Museum of Natural History in New York launched an archaeological campaign in the American Southwest, and Nelson was hired to oversee this influential research program. Nelson's stratigraphic excavations in New Mexico proved to be a breakthrough in archaeological technique. In the next few years, he broadened his experience by excavating caves in Kentucky and Missouri, and additional shell mounds in Florida. In 1925, Nelson accompanied an American Museum expedition to Central Asia; his North American and European fieldwork continued until his eventual retirement in 1943.

Nels Nelson typifies the state of Americanist archaeology during the first quarter of the twentieth century. Although he had received infinitely better archaeological training than predecessors such as C. B. Moore, Nelson still learned largely by firsthand experience. Archaeology was still in a pioneering stage, and no matter where he turned, Nelson was the first archaeologist on the scene. In large measure, his prime responsibility was to record what he saw, then to conduct a preliminary excavation where warranted, and finally to proffer tentative inferences to be tested and embellished by subsequent investigators. Nelson also typified the new breed of early twentieth-century museum-based archaeologists. Nelson strongly believed that the message of archaeology should be brought to the public in the form of books, popular magazine articles, and, most of all, interpretive displays of archaeological materials.

Today, Nels Nelson is best remembered in archaeology for his contributions to stratigraphic technique. His 1912 excavations in the Galisteo Basin of New Mexico are generally acknowledged as the first significant stratigraphic archaeology in the Americas. At that time, the cultural chronology of the American Southwest was utterly unknown, and Nelson's painstaking excavations and analysis of the pottery recovered provided the first solid chronological framework.

A. V. "Ted" Kidder (1885–1963): Founder of Anthropological Archaeology

Although he was born in Michigan, the life and career of Alfred V. Kidder revolved about the academic community of Cambridge, Massachusetts. Kidder's father, a mining engineer, saw to it that young Alfred received the best education available. First Kidder attended a private school in Cambridge, then the prestigious La Villa in Ouchy, Switzerland, after that he registered at Harvard. Kidder soon joined an archaeological expedition to northeastern Arizona, exploring territory then largely unknown to the Anglo world. The southwestern adventure sealed his fate.

When Kidder returned to Harvard, he enrolled in the anthropology program and in 1914 was awarded the sixth American Ph.D. specializing in archaeology—

and the first with a focus on North America. In his dissertation he examined prehistoric Southwestern ceramics, assessing their value in reconstructing culture history. Kidder demonstrated how to decipher with the use of scientific procedures archaeology's most perplexing debris, the lowly potsherd. Urging accurate description of ceramic decoration, he explained how such apparent minutiae could be used to determine relationships among the various prehistoric groups. Kidder argued that only through controlled excavation and correlative analysis could inferences be drawn about such anthropological subjects as acculturation, social organizations, and prehistoric religious customs.

In 1915, the Department of Archaeology at the Phillips Academy in Andover, Massachusetts, embarked on a multiyear archaeological project. Largely because of his anthropological training, Kidder exemplified the new breed in archaeology, and he was selected to direct the excavations. After evaluating the possibilities, he decided on Pecos Pueblo, a massive prehistoric and historic period ruin located southeast of Santa Fe, New Mexico. Kidder was impressed by the great diversity of potsherds scattered about the ruins and felt certain that Pecos contained enough

A. V. Kidder supervising excavations at Pecos Pueblo (New Mexico).

stratified debris to span several centuries. In all, Kidder excavated at Pecos for 10 summers.

The excavations at Pecos were significant for several reasons. Kidder became the first archaeologist in America to test Nelson's stratigraphic method on a large scale, and he went beyond the pottery to make sense of the artifact and architectural styles preserved at Pecos. Working before the advent of radiocarbon dating or a tree-ring chronology, his intensive artifact analysis established the framework of southwestern prehistory, which remains intact today.

Kidder then joined the Carnegie Institution of Washington as director of the Division of Historical Research. Attracting several of his southwestern colleagues to work with him, he launched an aggressive archaeological program to probe the Mayan ruins of Central America. He directed the Carnegie's Mayan campaigns for the next two decades, arguing that a true understanding of Mayan culture would require a broad-based plan of action with many interrelated areas of research. Relegating himself to the role of administrator, Kidder amassed a staff of qualified scientists with the broadest possible scope of interests. His plan is a landmark in archaeological research, stressing an enlargement of traditional archaeological objectives to embrace the wider realms of anthropology and allied disciplines. Under Kidder's direction, the Carnegie program supported research by ethnographers, geographers, physical anthropologists, geologists, meteorologists, and, of course, archaeologists.

Kidder even proved the potential of aerial reconnaissance, by convincing Charles Lindbergh, already an international figure, to participate in the Carnegie's Mayan program. Early in 1929, Lindbergh flew Kidder throughout British Honduras, Yucatán, and the Petén jungle of Guatemala. Beyond discovering new ruins, the Lindbergh flights also generated a wealth of previously unavailable ecological data, such as the boundaries of various types of vegetation. Today, the interdisciplinary complexion of archaeology is a fact of life. But when Kidder proposed the concept in the 1920s, the prevailing attitude still reflected the "one person, one site" mentality.

In addition to his substantive Mayan and southwestern projects, Kidder helped shift Americanist archaeology toward more properly anthropological purposes. Unlike many of his contemporaries, Kidder maintained that archaeology should be viewed as "that branch of anthropology which deals with prehistoric peoples," a doctrine that has become firmly embedded and expanded in today's Americanist archaeology. To Kidder, the archaeologist was merely a "mouldier variety of anthropologist." Although archaeologists continue to immerse themselves in the nuances of potsherd detail and architectural specifics, the ultimate objective of archaeology remains the statement of anthropological universals about people.

James A. Ford (1911–1968): A Master of Time

James A. Ford is the last archaeological forefather to be considered here. Born in Water Valley, Mississippi, Ford's major research interest centered on the archaeology of the American Southeast. Ford was attending Columbia University when Nels Nelson retired from the Department of Anthropology at the American Museum of Natural History. Ford was chosen as the new assistant curator of North American archaeology.

James Ford came of age during the Great Depression, part of an archaeological generation literally trained on the job. As the Roosevelt administration realized that jobs must be created to alleviate the economic conditions, crews of workmen were assigned labor-intensive tasks, including building roads and bridges and general heavy construction. One obvious make-work project was archaeology, and literally thousands of the unemployed were set to work excavating major archaeological sites. This program was, of course, an important boost to Americanist archaeology, and data from government-sponsored Depression-era excavations poured in at a record rate. In fact, materials from the 1930s excavations are still being analyzed and published.

Ford worked at Poverty Point, the Louisiana site explored 40 years earlier by C. B. Moore. After completing his initial mapping and reconnaissance, Ford launched a series of stratigraphic excavations designed to define the prehistoric sequence. His overall objective was to read in human terms the meaning of the Poverty Point site, a goal considerably more ambitious than that of C. B. Moore, who dug primarily to unearth outstanding examples of artwork. Ford continually asked the question: What does archaeology tell us about the people? To Ford, Poverty Point represented more than a fossilized ceremonial center, and he attempted to recreate the social and political networks responsible for this colossal enterprise. In this regard, his approach typified the overarching anthropological objectives of mid-century Americanist archaeology.

The unprecedented accumulation of raw data during the 1930s created a crisis of sorts among Americanist archaeologists: What was to be done with all these facts? Ford and his contemporaries were beset by the need to synthesize and classify, to formulate regional sequences of culture chronology. Unlike Nelson, Kidder, and the others working in the American Southwest, Ford did not have access to deep, well preserved refuse heaps; southeastern sites were more commonly shallow, short-term occupations. To create a temporal order, Ford relied on an integrated scheme of surface collection and classification.

Ford had refined the techniques of ordering sequentially the various stages of pottery development. This technique is known as **seriation.** Later, we will explain the principles behind seriation, but the central idea is simple: By assuming that cultural styles (fads) tend to change gradually,

James A. Ford making a plane table map at Boca Escondida, north of Veracruz (Mexico).

archaeologists can chart the relative popularity of pottery decoration through time. Generally, a given pottery style is introduced at one specific locality. Its popularity gradually spreads throughout the region until the first type is successively replaced by another style. Thus, at any particular time, the available ceramic assemblage reflects the relative proportions of the available pottery styles. By fitting the various short-term assemblages into master curves, Ford developed a series of regional ceramic chronologies. Although sometimes overly simplistic, Ford's seriation technique was sufficient to establish the baseline prehistoric chronology that is still in use in the American Southeast.

Ford then synthesized his ceramic chronologies into patterns of regional history. When C. B. Moore was excavating the hundreds of prehistoric mounds throughout the Southeast, he lacked a system for adequately dating his finds. Ford, using seriation along with other methods, helped bring temporal order to his excavations, and he rapidly moved to synthesize these local sequences across the greater Southeast. He proposed the basic division between the earlier Burial Mound Period and the subsequent Temple Mound Period, a distinction that remains in use today.

Americanist Archaeology at Mid-Century

The biographies of these five forebears provide a sense of Americanist archaeology's past. Thomas Jefferson's archaeology was drastically different from that of, say, James Ford. Still, each person made a distinctive contribution to modern archaeology and each was clearly one of the very best among his contemporaries. These five careers define a colorful continuum, and some meaningful trends are evident.

Perhaps the most striking contrast is that brought out by comparing the scholars as individuals. Americanist archaeology began as a pastime of the genteel rich such as Thomas Jefferson and C. B. Moore. Not until the days of immigrant Nels Nelson could a "working-class" scholar hope to penetrate the archaeological establishment.

Through the years, archaeology developed into a professional scientific discipline. C. B. Moore was among the first generation of full-time professional archaeologists. As practicing specialists, some archaeologists from Moore's time and later have been affiliated with major museums and universities; others have joined the private sector, working to protect and understand America's long-term cultural heritage. This institutional support not only encouraged a sense of professionalism and fostered public funding, but such public repositories also were required to care for the archaeological artifacts recovered. The twentieth-century Americanist archaeologist is not a collector of personal treasure: All finds belong in the public domain, available for exhibit and study.

You will note, of course, that women are virtually invisible in most discussions of the early history of Americanist archaeology. Women were, in fact, contributing, but because they were excluded from traditional communication networks, their contribution is more difficult to find.

In Her Own Words

Archaeology's Unrecognized Working Women
by Mary Ann Levine

Although women are absent from much of the literature on the early history of Americanist archaeology, they have been contributing to the development of archaeology for over a century. In the 1880s, female anthropologists began to hold marginal positions in museums. Women participated in anthropology as loosely affiliated field workers who were generally unpaid but permitted to publish in museum proceedings, or as financial patrons for particular museums. For example, *Mary Hemenway* (1820–1894), a philanthropist, donated the substantial collection of materials unearthed by the Hemenway Southwestern Archaeological Expedition to Harvard's Peabody Museum. As possibly the first avowedly scientific research into that area's prehistory, Hemenway's Expedition helped establish the Southwest as a distinct culture area. Women such as Hemenway were active in Americanist archaeology prior to World War I and made notable contributions to the development of the discipline, but involvement was limited and circumscribed. Male organizations such as the Anthropological Society of Washington marginalized women from the

In the late nineteenth century, some female anthropologists started taking up marginal positions in museums, often as loosely affiliated (and generally unpaid) field workers or as financial patrons for particular expeditions. Although many women of this period made significant contributions prior to World War I, their involvement was fairly limited because male-dominated professional organizations marginalized them, keeping them from the mainstream professions in anthropology.

Then, beginning in the 1920s, women began to take advantage of increased educational opportunities. By the 1930s, they were earning doctorates for research in American archaeology and securing appropriate academic posts for the first time.

We can also see a distinct progression toward specialization in our five targeted archaeologists. So little was known about archaeology in the eighteenth century that a single scholar like Jefferson could control all the relevant data. But by the late nineteenth century, so much archaeological information had already accumulated that no single scholar could hope to know everything relevant to Americanist archaeology. Although C. B. Moore became the leading authority on Southeastern archaeology, he knew relatively little about the finds being made by his archaeological contemporaries in Peru, Central America, and even the American Southwest. By mid-twentieth century, archaeologists like Ford were forced to specialize in specific localities within limited cultural areas. Today, it is rare to find archaeologists with extensive experience in more than a couple of specialized fields.

mainstream of professional life in anthropology. The first generation of women in Americanist archaeology were excluded from both formal and informal networks of communication and were afforded few career opportunities.

The next generation of female archaeologists includes women born early in the twentieth century who launched their careers in the inter-war years, the 1920s and 1930s. Beginning in the 1920s, the range of professional pathways for women in archaeology widened while the education opportunities and socioeconomic backgrounds of women expanded. Although women in this second generation also faced sizeable obstacles to advancement and recognition, they achieved greater visibility in academic and museum settings.

Women were awarded Ph.D.'s for their research in cultural anthropology as early as 1914, but it was not until the 1930s that women earned doctorates in anthropology for their research in archaeology. The 1930s also witnessed female archaeologists securing academic posts for the first time.

MARY ANN LEVINE is assistant professor of anthropology at Franklin and Marshall College, Lancaster, Pennsylvania.

But possibly the greatest change has been in the quality of archaeologists' training. Although Jefferson was broadly educated in science, literature, and the arts, his archaeology was wholly self-taught and largely a matter of common sense. Moore, though Harvard-educated, was untrained in archaeology; his fieldwork was still based on personal trial-and-error methods. Nelson and Kidder, among the first professionally trained Americanist archaeologists, studied under America's most prominent archaeologists. From then on, Americanist archaeologists were, almost without exception, well versed in anthropology. As the chronological problems were solved, archaeologists like Ford used this anthropological training to transcend mere chronology to explicate cultural contexts and functions. Although Ford personally contributed to the refinement of local chronologies, he also participated in research programs designed to define settlement patterns and to reconstruct prehistoric social environments. Such was the state of Americanist archaeology at mid-century.

Revolution: Archaeology's Angry Young Men

The previous section chronicled the development of traditional Americanist archaeology. A succession of hardworking, intelligent archaeologists–the Moores,

Kidders, and Fords—symbolize the mainstream thinking of their day. The technology, assumptions, explanations, and speculation of Americanist archaeology evolved along an unbroken progression. But archaeology also grew by revolution. Beginning in the 1940s, a succession of scholars challenged such orthodox archaeological thinking, urging change and demanding instantaneous results. Two of these crusaders have been particularly influential in shaping modern archaeological thought.

W. W. Taylor (1913–1997): Moses in the Wilderness

Educated first at Yale and then at Harvard, Walter W. Taylor completed his doctoral dissertation late in 1942. After returning from overseas service in World War II, he published an expanded version of his dissertation as *A Study of Archeology* in 1948. It was a bombshell. Greeted with alarm and consternation by the archaeological community, the book was no less than a public call for revolution. Bourgeois archaeologists—the orthodox fat cats—were blasted, assailed, and berated by this wet-behind-the-ears newcomer. Few liked Taylor's book, but everybody read it.

Taylor launched a frontal attack on the elders of Americanist archaeology. This assault was particularly plucky, as Taylor was himself a rank beginner, having published little to establish his credentials as an archaeologist, much less a critic.

A Study of Archeology blasted A. V. Kidder, among others. What offended Taylor most was Kidder's alleged two-faced attitude, saying one thing yet doing another. Kidder repeatedly maintained that he was an anthropologist who had specialized in archaeology. Taylor then probed Kidder's end products to determine how well his deeds conformed to his stated anthropological objectives, and boldly concluded that there was no conformity. He could find in Kidder's research no cultural synthesis, no picture of life at any site, no consideration of cultural processes, no derivation of cultural laws—no anthropology at all.

These were serious charges, considered to be blasphemy by most archaeologists of the time. But Taylor supported his case with a vivid dissection of Kidder's published record. Kidder's research at Pecos, New Mexico, and elsewhere in the American Southwest was said to be full of "apparent contradictions," merely "description for its own sake." Taylor claimed

Walter W. Taylor during his archaeological survey of Coahuila (Mexico) in 1937.

that Kidder was incapable of preparing a proper site report, much less of writing the anthropology of the prehistoric Southwest.

Taylor then turned to Kidder's prestigious research into the archaeology of the Maya and, once again, accused him of failing to live up to his own goals. Granting that Kidder began his investigations with anthropology in mind, Taylor concluded that somewhere along the line Kidder went astray. Commenting that "the road to Hell and the field of Maya archeology are paved with good intentions," Taylor deduced that the Carnegie Institution, under Kidder's direction, "has sought and found the hierarchical, the grandiose. It has neglected the common, the everyday." Kidder had been blinded by the "pomp and circumstance" of Classic Maya archaeology, disregarding the pedestrian world of real people. To hear Taylor tell the story, Kidder not only botched his own research but also misdirected the explorations of literally dozens of archaeologists working under his aegis.

In 1948, Taylor was indeed archaeology's angriest young man, panning the "comparative" or "taxonomic" approach to archaeology. Although careful not to deny the initial usefulness of a comparative strategy, Taylor urged archaeologists to get on with the proper business of anthropology: finding out something about people. Chronology, to Taylor, was merely a stepping-stone, providing a foundation for more anthropologically relevant studies of human behavior and cultural dynamics.

Walter W. Taylor's prescription was his so-called **conjunctive approach** to archaeology. By conjunctive, Taylor emphasized the interconnection of archaeological objects with their cultural contexts. Whereas comparative scholarship emphasizes relationships among archaeological sites, the conjunctive perspective shifts the emphasis to a particular cultural entity. Taylor attacked Kidder's Mayan research on this basis: Kidder, you're preoccupied with comparing things—temples, glyphs, fancy potsherds—among sites; you've failed to decipher what goes on within any single Maya site.

A conjunctive approach would scrutinize the minutiae of a single Maya center, attempting to write a comprehensive ethnography of the Maya people who once lived there. In effect, Taylor urged archaeologists to forsake the temples for the garbage dumps. Messy business, this conjunctive archaeology, but Taylor contended that this was the only way for archaeologists to achieve their anthropological goals.

Going beyond the specifics of Maya archaeology, Taylor proposed reforms by arguing for a conjunctive approach in archaeology. Archaeologists must quantify their data (trait lists are rarely useful); they must test hypotheses and progressively refine their impressions (too often initial observations were taken as gospel); they must excavate less extensively and more intensively (too many sites were just "tested" then compared with other remote "tests" with no effort to detect patterning within sites); they must recover and decode the meaning of unremarkable food remains (the bones, seed hulls, and rubbish heaps were too often shoveled out); they must embrace more specialties in the analysis of finds (zoological, botanical, and petrographic identifications were too often made in the field and never verified); and they must write more effective site reports (too often only the glamorous finds were illustrated, with precise proveniences omitted).

In perusing Taylor's propositions nearly six decades after they were written, I am struck by how unremarkable they now seem. Where is the revolution? Today's archaeologists do quantify their results; they do test hypotheses; they do excavate intensively; they do save food remains; they do involve specialists in analysis; and they do write detailed site reports.

But archaeologists did not do these things routinely in 1940, and this is what Taylor was sputtering about. Taylor's suggestions of 1948 embody few surprises for today's student, testimony to just how far archaeological doctrine and execution have matured since Taylor wrote *A Study of Archeology*.

Lewis R. Binford (1930–   ): Visionary With a Message

American archaeology's second angry young man is Lewis R. Binford. After a period of military service, Binford enrolled in 1954 at the University of North Carolina, wanting to become an ethnographer. But by the time he moved on for graduate education at the University of Michigan, Binford was a confirmed archaeologist.

As a young professional, Binford was a man on the move—literally. He first taught a year at Michigan, then moved on to the University of Chicago, to the University of California at Santa Barbara, down the coast to UCLA, on to the University of New Mexico, and landed at Southern Methodist University in Dallas. During his travels, Binford came into contact with the brightest of an upcoming generation of archaeologists (and we shall meet many of them later in this book).

The mid-1960s was a hectic time for archaeology. Waves of social alienation and political confrontation were rolling across the nation, baby boom demographics inflated university enrollments, and archaeology was firmly embedded in the intellectual climate of the times. This revolutionary spirit derived in part from the general anxiety that permeated university campuses during the Vietnam War era. Things must change: not just war and poverty and racism and oppression, but also the academic edifice itself. Scholarship must become relevant; older concepts must give way to fresh perceptions. Such was the social environment in which Binford's ideas took hold. Without the revolutionary spirit and social upheaval of the mid-1960s, I believe that

Lewis R. Binford excavating at Mission Santa Catalina (Georgia).

Binford's archaeology would have taken on a rather different, perhaps less aggressive configuration.

An extraordinary lecturer, Binford rapidly assumed the role of archaeological messiah. His students became disciples, spreading the word throughout the land. Binfordians preached a gospel with great appeal in the 1960s: Archaeology does have relevance to modern problems; archaeology must transcend potsherds to grapple with issues of cultural evolution, cultural ecology, and social organization; archaeology must take full advantage of modern technology; archaeology must become more systematic, using uncompromising logic and more sophisticated, quantitative techniques; archaeology must be concerned with the few remaining preindustrial peoples in order to scrutinize firsthand the operation of disappearing cultural adaptations. As Binford's movement gained momentum, nothing was considered sacred in the traditionalist paradigm of archaeology. As Binford himself characterized these early years, he and his colleagues were "full of energy and going in all directions at once."

Binford and his students—and their students—became the primary agents of change in Americanist archaeology during the 1960s. The phrase **new archaeology** became associated with their way of interrogating the past. The battle plan for the new archaeology was set forth in a seminal series of articles published through the 1960s and early 1970s. Binford asked why archaeology had contributed so little to general anthropological theory. His answer was that in the past, material culture had been interpreted simplistically. Too much attention had been lavished on the artifacts of shared behavior, as passive traits that "blend," "influence," and "stimulate" one another. Echoing Taylor, Binford proposed that artifacts be examined in terms of their cultural contexts.

Binford underscored the importance of precise, unambiguous scientific methods. Archaeologists must stop acting like passive receptors, waiting for the artifacts to speak up. Archaeologists must formulate pointed questions (**hypotheses**); these hypotheses must then be tested on the remains of the past. Binford argued that because archaeologists always work from samples, they should acquire data that make the samples more representative of the populations from which they were drawn. He urged archaeologists to stretch their horizons beyond the individual site to the scale of the region; in this way, an entire cultural system could be assessed. Such regional samples must be generated from research designs based on the principles of probability sampling. Random sampling is commonplace in other social sciences, and Binford insisted that archaeologists apply these procedures to their own specific research problems.

Binford's strictly methodological contributions were gradually amplified by projects designed to demonstrate how the approach fosters the comprehension of cultural processes. Intricate statistical techniques were applied to a variety of subjects, from the nature of **Mousterian** campsites (some 50,000 years old) to the patterning of African **Acheulean** assemblages (hundreds of thousands of years old). These investigations were critical because they embroiled Binford in factual, substantive debate. Not only did he advocate different goals and new methods, but he also related to field archaeologists through these substantive controversies—

he argued about specifics, not just theory. Binford presented an extended consideration of post-Pleistocene human adaptations and conducted his own ethnoarchaeological fieldwork among the Nunamiut Eskimo, the Navajo, and the Australian aborigines.

In true Taylor-like fashion, Binford lambasted archaeology's principals, accusing them of retarding progress in the discipline. And yet his reception was quite different from Taylor's. Whereas *A Study of Archeology* had languished on the shelf, Binford was hailed as "the father of the new archaeology." Taylor was the harbinger of impending change, but Binford was the architect of that change.

Binford and his students set off a firestorm that quickly spread throughout the archaeological community. A 1970s generation of new graduate students and young professionals was greeted with the admonition: Are you a new archaeologist, an old archaeologist, or what? Make up your mind!

Today, the new archaeology of the 1960s has become the orthodoxy of the 1990s, transformed into what is termed the **processual agenda.** In several subsequent chapters, we explore the tenets of this position, and also examine how yet another wave of archaeological criticism—the so-called **postprocessual critique**—finds fault with Binford's approach and suggests some alternative directions.

Kathleen A. Deagan (1948–   ): Neither Angry nor a Young Man

Struggles between new and old make interesting history indeed, but this is not a history book. This book is about the methods, the techniques, the assumptions, and the goals of contemporary archaeology. But before grappling with these issues, let me introduce one more archaeologist, somebody who embodies the diversity and animation that is archaeology today.

No archaeologist represents contemporary Americanist archaeology better than does Kathleen Deagan, currently a curator and formerly chair at the Florida Museum of Natural History. An archaeologist specializing in Spanish colonial studies, Deagan received her doctorate in anthropology from the University of Florida in 1974. Like her mentor, Charles H. Fairbanks, Deagan is pushing the frontiers of traditional historical archaeology, pioneering the archaeological investigation of disenfranchised groups.

Kathleen Deagan is best known for her long-term excavations at St. Augustine (Florida), continuously occupied since its founding by Pedro Menéndez in 1565. As accentuated by splashy signs sprinkled throughout town, St. Augustine is the oldest European enclave in the United States (complete with the "oldest pharmacy," "oldest house," "oldest church," and so on). Deagan's research here dates back to her graduate student days, her doctoral dissertation neatly straddling the traditionally discrete studies of historical archaeology, ethnohistory, and anthropology.

Kathleen Deagan digging at Bas En Saline (Haiti), thought to be the site of La Navidad, established by Christopher Columbus on Christmas Eve, 1492.

Deagan addressed the processes and results of Spanish–Indian intermarriage and descent, a topic dear to the hearts of many anthropologists and ethnohistorians; the fact that people of such mixed descent *(mestizos)* constitute nearly the entire population of Latin America brought this issue to the forefront long ago. Similar processes took place in Spanish Florida, but the Hispanic occupation left no apparent *mestizo* population in La Florida, what Deagan calls "America's first melting pot." Accordingly, when she commenced her doctoral research, virtually nothing was known about such early race relations in North America.

Deagan hypothesized about how the *mestizo* population fit into this colonial setting. Given the nature of the unfortunate interactions that characterized eighteenth-century Florida, she expected the burdens of acculturation to have fallen most heavily on the Indian women living in Spanish or *mestizo* households. Because no *mestizo* people survive here, the tests for her hypothesis were necessarily archaeological. If her hypothesis was true, then acculturation should affect mostly the Native American women's activities visible in the archaeological record (food preparation techniques, equipment, household activities, basic food resources, child-related activities, and primarily female crafts such as pottery manufacture). Moreover, male-related activities (house construction technology and design, military and political affairs, and hunting weapons) should show less evidence of Indian infusion.

In 1973, to explore these processes, Deagan began a series of archaeological field schools at St. Augustine. This long-term, diversified enterprise excavated sites representing a broad range of income, occupation, and ethnic affiliation. Hundreds of students learned their first archaeology at St. Augustine, where a saloon still sports an aging placard celebrating the years of "Digging with Deagan."

It was not long before her explorations into Hispanic–Native American interactions led Deagan to the Caribbean, where between 1980 and 1985, she headed interdisciplinary excavations at Puerto Real, the fourth oldest European-style New World city (established in 1503). As she steadily moved back in time, Deagan's research eventually led her literally to the doorstep of Christopher Columbus.

In northern Haiti, Deagan apparently discovered La Navidad, the earliest well documented point of contact between the Spanish and Native Americans. On Christmas Eve, 1492–following two nights of partying with local Taino Arawak Indians–Columbus's flagship *Santa Maria* ran aground. He abandoned ship, moved to the *Niña,* and appealed to the local Native Americans for help. This disaster left the explorers one boat short. When Columbus sailed home with his world-shattering news, he left 39 compatriots behind, protected by a small stockade built from the timbers of the wrecked *Santa Maria*. Returning a year later, Columbus found the settlement burned, his men killed and mutilated.

Columbus soon established the more permanent settlements of La Isabela and Puerto Real–sites of the first sustained contact between Europeans and Native Americans–and Deagan is also conducting field excavations there. Having a population of nearly 1,500 people, La Isabela was home to soldiers, priests, stone-cutters, masons, carpenters, nobles, and warriors. Although this first Columbian town lasted only 4 years, an instant compared with the entire period of Hispanic–Native American contact, several critical events took place here: the first intentional introduction of European plants and animals; the first expedition into the interior; and the first Hispanic installation of urban necessities like canals, mills, streets, gardens, plazas, ports, ramparts, roads, and hospitals.

The biological effects of the Columbian exchange soon overtook La Isabela. European and Native American alike suffered from dietary deficiencies, an excessive workload, and contagious disease. Influenza struck during the first week, affecting one-third of the population. When Columbus ordered the settlement abandoned in 1496, fewer than 300 inhabitants were left. Deagan extended her research to investigate daily life in the initial colonial period, including the ways in which European colonists coped with their new and largely unfamiliar New World environment.

Beyond the new directions in historical archaeology, Deagan's research demonstrates the degree to which contemporary Americanist archaeology is played out in the public arena; she creates headlines wherever she works. Newspapers around the world chronicle her success, and her research was featured in consecutive years in *National Geographic* magazine. Deagan has shown extraordinary skill and patience with the onslaught of well meaning reporters.

Media types seem astonished that such a successful archaeologist can also be female. Here is how a reporter from the *Florida Times-Union* described her:

> Kathleen Deagan balanced on one foot in the parking lot: "You lose all pride in this profession, changing your clothes in a parking lot," she said with a wry grin. . . . Wind swirled through the parking lot and tousled her blond hair. . . . It would be Archaeology A-Go-Go.

Melodramatic coverage like this plagues archaeology these days, but Deagan overlooks the chatter because such reporting has a far more serious side. Archaeologists can no longer afford isolationist ivory-towerism. One way or another—whether through federal grants, state-supported projects, tax laws, or private benefaction—archaeology depends on public support for its livelihood.

Decades ago, Margaret Mead recognized the importance of taking the work of anthropologists to the public, and she spent considerable effort keeping anthropology alive in the print and electronic media. Today, archaeology enjoys unprecedented press coverage, and archaeologists like Deagan know that without such publicity, Americanist archaeology will have no future.

Beyond her appeal to the press, Deagan's research and publications have helped establish historical archaeology as a viable subdiscipline in the field of anthropology. Although awash in time-specific details and artifacts, she is ultimately addressing the general processes behind the particulars: the sexual and social consequences of Spanish–Indian intermarriage, the demographic collapse and biological imbalance resulting from Old World–New World interchange, and the processes behind the disintegration of traditional cultural patterns. Although her data are documentary and archaeological, Deagan is confronting issues of anthropological relevance.

Summary

The origins of archaeology can be traced to Nabonidus, a sixth-century B.C. Babylonian king who looked at the physical residues of antiquity to answer his questions about the past. Since then, archaeologists have continued "to restore the dead to life." New World archaeology has been inextricably wed to the study of Native Americans, who provided endless clues for those concerned with America's more remote past. Americanist archaeology evolved in the work of scholars such as Thomas Jefferson and C. B. Moore who, though lacking formal anthropological training, applied sound principles of scientific research to learn about the continent's early days. No longer the pastime of genteel rich males, twentieth-century Americanist archaeology has become a specialized discipline, requiring intensive training not only in techniques of excavation but also in ethnology, classification,

geology, and the philosophy of science. The gradual evolution of Americanist archaeological thought has been stimulated by a few revolutionary archaeologists,
most notably Walter W. Taylor in the 1940s and Lewis R. Binford in the 1960s.
Archaeology's "angry young men" urged their colleagues to stick by their anthropological guns, to attempt to define the processes operative behind the specifics
of the archaeological record.

> *If you want to make enemies, try to change something.*
>
> WOODROW WILSON (1856–1924), 28TH PRESIDENT
> OF THE UNITED STATES

Archaeology on the Internet

The Society for American Archaeology maintains an important Web site.
    http://www.saa.org

Society for Historical Archaeology Homepage includes a general statement about what historical archaeology is all about,
what the society does, some job listings, and an excellent guide
to graduate programs.
    http://www.azstarnet.com/~sha/

Archaeological Institute of America provides information
about meetings, publications, and issues.
    http://csaws.brynmawr.edu:web2/aia.html

Archaeology Magazine on the Internet is another good source
of information.
    http://www.he.net/~archaeol/index.html

World Archaeological Congress Home Page hosts an international forum dealing with ethics, protection, conservation, new
technologies, education, and archaeological impacts on indigenous peoples and their countries.
    http://wac.soton.ac.uk/wac

The World Wide Web Virtual Library: Archaeology provides
probably the most comprehensive links to archaeological stuff
throughout the world.
    http://www.lib.uconn.edu/ArchNet/

CHAPTER 2

Anthropology, Science, and the Humanities

❏ ❏ ❏

PREVIEW

This chapter situates archaeology within the dynamic worlds of anthropology, science, and the humanities. Each has its own distinctive approach and each is relevant to modern archaeology.

We begin with the basic anthropological *perspective—that the human condition is best understood from a holistic, all-encompassing view of humanity. You will also learn about culture and why it's important that culture be viewed in several different ways. Some anthropologists employ an* ideational *strategy, emphasizing the importance of ideas, symbols, and mental structures in shaping human behavior. Other anthropologists follow an* adaptive *strategy, isolating technology, ecology, demography, and economics as the key factors.*

We then take up the knotty question of just what archaeology is: A science? One of the humanities? Both? Neither? The question is more than semantic because it conditions the way archaeologists approach the past. If you're a scientist, you probably believe that there's a real world "out there" which can be known more or less objectively. But suppose you believe that archaeology is "pretty subjective" and that our knowledge of the past depends largely on who's doing the observing. If so, then you probably don't like conventional science very much; you're probably a humanist. Both viewpoints are relevant to modern archaeology.

We also set out the theoretical baseline for the rest of the book. Low-level *theory is required in order to make relevant observations about the archaeological record. This is how archaeologists get their "data," their facts. Theory at the* middle-level *is what links these archaeological data to human behavior. Sometimes archaeologists generate their data by conducting controlled experiments, sometimes by doing ethnoarchaeology, by making observations of ongoing, observable behavior to see how it's translated into the archaeological record. Finally, there is* high-level *(or "general") theory, which provides the overarching framework for understanding the human condition. General theory applies to all intellectual inquiry about human beings; it is not restricted to archaeology.*

I understand that many students are put off by obscure discussions of various "-ologies" and "-isms," but it's important that you understand these basic theoretical points. I promise to minimize the jargon, and hope that in the coming chapters, you will recognize the importance of understanding these basic theoretical concepts.

Science and humanism have been the two wings of the anthropological bird. With-out both of them, working together, the bird doesn't fly.

E. N. ANDERSON, ANTHROPOLOGIST (UNIVERSITY OF
CALIFORNIA, RIVERSIDE)

In the mid-1950s, Philip Phillips published a memorable article concluding that "archaeology is anthropology or it is nothing." More than any single statement, this mantra came to characterize mainstream Americanist archaeology for the next three decades.

The mantra's no longer true.

Americanist archaeology is many things, and some of them remain anthropological. But today's archaeology has a diverse toolkit. Many tools still come from anthropology's workshop, and we'll talk about those now. Some tools are borrowed from elsewhere.

What's an Anthropological Approach?

Everyone knows what anthropologists do, right? They study native people and fossils and chimpanzees. Anthropologists are Richard Leakey, Jane Goodall, and Don Johanson. Some people think that Stephen Jay Gould is also an anthropologist.

Anthropologists run in so many different directions at once that it's often difficult to find the common thread. In fact, anthropologists sometimes get so involved with the minutiae of their own deliberations that they themselves forget what they are.

So what makes an anthropologist an anthropologist?

The answer is deceptively simple: What all anthropologists share is a perspective, an outlook. Anthropologists believe that the best understanding of the human condition can arise only from a global and comparative approach. It is not enough to look at any single group—Americans, Chinese, Balinese, or **australopithecines**—to find the keys to human existence. Neither is it enough to look at just one part of the human condition, as do economists, historians, political scientists, and psychologists. Looking at part of the picture only gives you just that—part of the picture.

What holds **anthropology** together is its dogmatic insistence that every aspect of every human society—extant or extinct—counts. For a century, anthropologists have tried to arrive at the fullest possible understanding of human similarities and diversity. Because of this broad-brush approach, anthropology is uniquely qualified to understand what makes humankind distinct from the rest of the animal world.

This is not to say that all anthropologists study everything: Margaret Mead never excavated an archaeological site and Richard Leakey never interviewed a native Athabascan speaker. The Renaissance anthropologist—the individual who does everything—has long since passed into folklore. Today, nobody can hope to do everything well.

So anthropologists specialize, and archaeologists are clever enough to draw something useful from each of these branches of study. There are four basic fields within the overall umbrella of anthropology.

Modern **biological anthropologists** (also known as **physical anthropologists**) pursue a number of aspects of human biology. One major concern is the biological evolution of man. How did the modern species *Homo sapiens* come into being? An intricate family tree has been pieced together by physical anthropologists over the past century, working largely from fossil evidence and observation of living primates. Modern physical anthropologists also study human biological variability. No two human beings are identical, even though we all are members of a single species. The study of inherited differences has become a strategic domain of scientific investigation and also a matter of practical concern for educators, politicians, and community leaders.

The rest of anthropology, which deals with human beings as cultural animals, is conventionally divided into three parts: cultural anthropology (also sometimes called sociocultural anthropology), linguistic anthropology, and archaeology.

Cultural anthropologists describe and analyze the **culture** of human groups in the modern and relatively recent past. By questioning and observing people throughout the world, they try to evaluate how diverse cultural elements intermesh and change in contemporary human societies. Conventionally, cultural anthropologists who describe present-day cultures on a firsthand basis are termed **ethnographers.** The comparative study of multiple cultures is usually termed *ethnology.* Roughly half the Ph.D.'s in anthropology are awarded to cultural anthropologists.

Anthropological linguists concentrate on a more specialized cultural component—language—evaluating linguistic behavior in considerable detail: how sounds are made, how sounds create languages, the relationship between language and thought, how linguistic systems change through time, the basic structure of language, the role of language in the development of culture. The field of linguistic anthropology is shrinking.

This book is concerned with the fourth kind of anthropology—archaeology. Most archaeologists also attempt to understand human culture, but their technology and field methods differ radically from those of ethnologists and linguists. Because archaeologists commonly study extinct cultures, they work at somewhat of a disadvantage. Lacking living, breathing informants, archaeologists have formulated a powerful array of techniques for gleaning relevant information from the material remains of the past. As we will see, these methods sometimes let archaeologists figure out things that living, breathing informants probably would never have told them.

What Is Culture?

A dozen distinct academic disciplines purport to study culture (or at least cultural behavior): economics, sociology, linguistics, political science, history, cultural geography, psychology, and so forth. Classical historians, for instance, might investigate Greek culture, Roman culture, or Byzantine culture; their interest centers on the cultural characteristics of a particular society. But one does not expect to find classical historians discoursing on the general nature of culture, for if they did, they would cease to be classical historians; they would have become anthropologists. It is this generalized, overarching conception of culture that has traditionally formed the central theme melding the many diversified (and sometimes conflicting) concerns into a singular, collective anthropological perspective. As we will see later in this chapter, some of this solidarity within the anthropological community has weakened in recent years.

There is surprisingly little general agreement among anthropologists about just what culture is. Nearly 50 years ago, A. L. Kroeber and Clyde Kluckhohn compiled more than 200 distinct definitions of culture, proposed by as many anthropologists and social scientists. Since that time, the number of definitions of culture must have tripled.

Fortunately for us all, archaeologists need not be overly concerned with culture's ultimate definition. But we must recognize something about how human culture works and how anthropologists go about studying it. Suppose we begin with the classic definition offered by Sir Edward Burnett Tylor (the person considered by many to be the founder of modern anthropology). Tylor's (1871) definition of culture appeared on the first page of anthropology's first textbook:

> Culture . . . taken in its wide ethnographic sense is that complex whole which includes knowledge, belief, art, morals, law, custom, and any other capabilities and habits acquired by man as a member of society.

Culture in Tylor's sense is *learned,* embodied in a society's general body of tradition. Although this definition provides a proper baseline from which to investigate past cultural behavior, Tylor's formulation is too general. We must find a way of pinning down this broad definition by asking precisely how one goes about perceiving cultural behavior, both in the present and in the past.

The Emic Versus the Etic

The concept of culture provides the anthropological baseline. But culture is hardly a monolithic concept, and as you might expect, anthropologists who investigate culture tend to emphasize one aspect or another.

The dichotomy between *emic* and *etic* approaches is critical. The term **emic** is applied whenever anthropologists employ concepts and distinctions that are somehow meaningful, significant, accurate, or "appropriate" to the participants in a given culture. Most rituals and ceremonies, for instance, have a complex series of emic "rules" about how individuals should act. An emic research strategy might attempt to identify the categories and rules required to think and behave like a participant in a particular ritual. Emic statements—the "native's point of view"—can be approached from either a scientific or an empathetic perspective.

Anthropologist Marvin Harris has defined an opposite research strategy that relies on **etic** categories, based on concepts and distinctions that are meaningful and appropriate to the community of scientific observers. Etic observations of the same ceremony might enumerate participants, their relationship to one another, the quantities and values of material culture involved, and the prevailing ecological and economic conditions at each participating group. Such etic observations would not necessarily be familiar or understandable to the participants, and such statements could neither be verified nor negated by comparison with native categories. Successful etic statements, expressed in the vocabulary of science, can be verified only when independent observers using similar operations agree that a given event has transpired.

Both emic and etic approaches are useful, and the comparisons of emic and etic versions of culture provoke some of the most meaningful debates in anthropological inquiry.

Ideational Versus Adaptive Research Strategies

You must also understand a second basic dichotomy in anthropological thought. An **ideational strategy** focuses on ideas, symbols, and mental structures as driving forces in the shaping of human behavior. According to anthropologist Roger Keesing, the basic theme of the ideational approach to anthropology is simple: "The realm of ideas, the force of symbols is centrally important in shaping human behavior."

Culture in this ideational sense refers primarily to the complex sets of perceptions, conceptual designs, and shared understandings that underlie the way that people approach life. Culture, in this sense, is principally what humans learn, not what they do or make. This perspective on culture emphasizes cognition: ideas, thoughts, shared knowledge. Ideational culture does not encompass material belongings or performance.

Ideational views of culture suggest that one cannot comprehend human deportment without postulating a *cognitive code* for behavior. Much of what we perceive in the world, and hence endow with meaning, does not exist in the physical world at all. It exists only in the mind's eye. The ideational theorist insists on "getting inside the informant's head."

Alternatively, an **adaptive strategy** isolates technology, demography, economics, and **ecology** as the key factors defining human behavior. Cultures in this sense function in dynamic equilibrium with their ecosystems. So viewed, human beings maintain an adaptive relationship with surroundings in order to survive. Although this adaptation is mediated through the mechanism of culture, the process is guided by the same rules of natural selection that govern biological adaptation. Although there is a certain amount of disagreement as to how cultures actually adapt, all cultural adaptationists agree that economics (in its broadest sense) and its social correlates are in most cases primary. Ideational systems are secondary.

Neither viewpoint implies "always"; both seek only to discriminate causes that "tend to" produce observed effects. Both ideational and adaptive strategies allow for interplay and interaction between the mental and the material. The ideational approach maintains that sociocultural phenomena are best understood in terms of mental ingredients, while adaptivists feel that sociocultural differences are better understood by defining relevant materialistic parameters.

Current Theoretical Approaches in Archaeology

So you see that the anthropological toolkit contains a great variety of conceptual perspectives. Today, there is no general agreement—either within archaeology or in anthropology at large—about which tools are best. Within Americanist archaeology, epic struggles between materialism and idealism, and interpretive emics and explanatory etics have dominated the theoretical stage for the past couple of decades. This is basically a disagreement about which tools are best for the job at hand.

Many archaeologists in America believe that culture and the human past should be seen in systemic, scientific, materialistic, behavioral, relatively objective, explanatory, and etic perspective. So viewed, cultural behavior is a phenomenon basically driven by demographic, technological, economic, and ecological processes. Culture is largely independent of history and the ultimate job of archaeologists is to seek timeless and spaceless generalizations about the human condition. A couple of decades ago, this perspective dominated Americanist archaeology, and many continue to follow this view today.

But many other archaeologists express indifference to what people ate or how they earned a living. Taking the alternative perspective, they see culture from a basically symbolic, ideational, humanistic, mental, relatively subjective, interpretive, and emic viewpoint. Cultural behavior is driven by the realms of values, aesthetics, rules, beliefs, religions, and symbols. Culture is heavily dependent on an understanding of historical events; general laws of human behavior do not exist. This view looks beyond subsistence to seek the intrinsic meaning of artifacts and the roles they once played in the social environment.

Some contemporary archaeologists even believe that the concept of culture is itself irrelevant to understanding human behavior. They suggest that many cultural patterns can be more effectively explained in terms of broad biological principles, such as the drive to pass on one's genes to the next generation. Some feel that anthropology should be subsumed under biology if a real theory of human behavior is to be developed.

What's a Scientific Approach?

Science has evolved into an elegant and powerful way of allowing people to understand the workings of the visible world and the universe beyond. The goal of scientific theory building in archaeology is to develop theories that can be criticized and evaluated, to be eventually modified or even replaced by other theories that better explain the archaeological data.

Science (from the Latin "to know") refers, in its broadest sense, to a systematic body of knowledge about any field. The pursuit of such knowledge is commonly termed "pure science," to distinguish it from both so-called *applied science* (the practical application of scientific knowledge) and also from *technology* (through which such applications are achieved).

The world of pure science is generally divided into two classes: the physical sciences (including physics, chemistry and geology) and the biological sciences (such as botany and zoology). Some crossover takes place in the so-called interdisciplinary sciences, such as biochemistry (which attempts to understand life processes in terms of chemical substances and reactions). The social and behavioral sciences are also examples of interdisciplinary approaches to science. Anthropology is commonly considered to be a generalizing social science, along with economics, sociology, psychology, and political science.

Science as an Archaeological Method

The problem of creativity, of the source of fruitful theories and the questions that they generate, is not solved by scientific methods. Despite the high hopes of some fierce sciencemongers, there are no clear and certain methods of producing good ideas; scientific method is concerned with the process to follow once the question has been asked.

ALBERT SPAULDING (1914–1990), ARCHAEOLOGIST

The beginnings of a scientific approach to archaeology can be traced back to a time when people stopped viewing the past as myth. When they no longer thought of the past as merely another kind of story, but as something that left physical residues that could be retrieved and studied in order to find answers about antiquity.

The goal of scientific theory building is to develop theories that can be criticized and then evaluated, to be eventually modified or even replaced by other theories that better explain the archaeological—or any other kind of—data. When defining **scientific method,** most people employ two key concepts: **objectivity** and **testability.**

As scientists, archaeologists pride themselves on their ability to present analytically their aims, procedures, and results for full public inspection. Science is a public undertaking requiring that objectives be plainly and honestly stated, research procedures constantly reassessed, research methods explicitly described, and observer bias monitored.

Scientific methods in archaeology are often misunderstood because objectivity can never be complete. Objectivity is the scientific ideal, but the reality of science is what ethnographer A. L. Cerroni-Long has recently termed "a messy, bumbling, all-too-human affair."

Science is a human activity, conducted by culture-bound human beings. Because of this, conclusions can be swayed by prevailing worldview, emphasizing the importance of some observations over others. Scientists—in archaeology as elsewhere—employ judgment when selecting which theories to explore.

Then there is testability. From a scientific perspective, the more testable a theory is, the greater the chance that it will lead to new insights. The main characteristic of "testability" is, of course, *refutability* (often called "falsifiability")—the privilege of being wrong.

While observations are, of course, guided to some degree by an observer's theories, there is also the obstinate empirical quality of the real world. It determines that there will be agreement on observations by independent observers, in both daily life and in scientific research. This all occurs, of course, within a specific cultural context; it remains entirely possible that "independent observers" from a radically different culture might disagree about the supposed "empirical qualities of the real world."

Questions become "scientific" (1) if they are concerned with the publicly detectable properties of things, and (2) if the result of observations designed to answer the question cannot be predetermined by the biases of the observer.

Today, theoretical archaeology can be viewed along a continuum, with theories ranging from completely nontestable to highly testable. Most theories fall somewhere in between. In science, it does not matter where the questions come from. What matters is that they contain implications that can be examined by objective methods.

How Science Explains Things: The Maize Maze

It seems odd, but science in archaeology is better done than discussed. Archaeologists have been performing some pretty fair science, but only recently have they begun discussing their science in any detail. Consider, for example, how scientific methods were used to look for the origins of plant domestication in the Americas.

Enter Scotty MacNeish. Shortly after World War II, Herbert Dick (then a graduate student at Harvard) excavated a site in southwestern New Mexico named Bat Cave. The site yielded the typical prehistoric material culture from that area—projectile points, pottery vessels, shell beads, basketry, sandals, and so forth—and it also served up an unexpectedly primitive form of corn.

The archaeological contexts suggested that these stubby little corncobs were between 4,000 and 5,000 years old—the oldest and most primitive corn yet discovered. Later that same year, another archaeologist, Richard "Scotty" MacNeish, discovered similar specimens in the caves of Tamaulipas, not far below the Mexican border. Over the next few years, additional northern Mexican excavations recovered no corn older than about 5,000 years. Searching for more ancient evidence of plant domestication, MacNeish traveled far to the south, into Guatemala and Honduras. Although he found no ancient corncobs, he did stumble on fossil corn pollen in strata also dating about 3000 B.C.

Given these baseline data, MacNeish contemplated his next move. Corn was apparently no older than 3000 B.C. in either the United States or in Guatemala. MacNeish reasoned that if any older corn existed, it should be found somewhere

An early phase of MacNeish's excavation at Coxcatlán Cave in the Tehuacán Valley (Mexico).

between the two areas, probably in southern Mexico. This preliminary assumption was supported by intensive genetic studies conducted by MacNeish's colleague, Paul Mangelsdorf, indicating that corn had probably been domesticated from a highland grass. Putting these two pieces together, MacNeish decided that the best place to look for early domestication was in the uplands of southern Mexico.

To test his speculative theory, MacNeish made some specific predictions that could be tested in the field. Studying maps of southern Mexico, he narrowed his search to a couple of prime targets. He first explored Oaxaca, which was quickly rejected: No early corn to be found there. MacNeish then turned to his second choice, the Tehuacán Valley in the Mexican state of Puebla. Because corncobs generally survive best in deposits protected from moisture, he looked inside dry caves and overhangs. After personally delving into 38 such caves, MacNeish tested Coxcatlán Cave, which yielded six tiny corncobs more primitive than any previously discovered. Subsequent radiocarbon dating suggested that these cobs were about 5,600 years old, a full 500 years older than any other corn yet discovered.

These finds bolstered MacNeish's theory about the origins of corn in southern Mexico and also fostered an understanding of the processes that conditioned our early human relationships to domesticated plants and animals.

The scientific cycle in action. Beyond his contributions to our knowledge of maize domestication, MacNeish's investigation also clearly demonstrates the essential components of scientific methods as they apply to archaeology:

1. Define a relevant problem.
2. Establish one or more hypotheses.
3. Determine the empirical implications of the above.
4. Collect appropriate data through observation and/or experiment.
5. Compare these data with the expected implications.
6. Revise and/or retest hypotheses as necessary.

Like many archaeologists, MacNeish used other terminology to describe his procedures, but in actual practice he followed this scheme rather closely. In fact, procedures like these characterized much archaeological research throughout the twentieth century. Yet only during the last couple of decades have archaeologists begun to talk about these methods in any detail.

Let us review how these steps translate into actual scientific research. The first task is to define a relevant question and translate it into an appropriate hypothesis. The idea here is to get beyond the specifics of the known facts. To

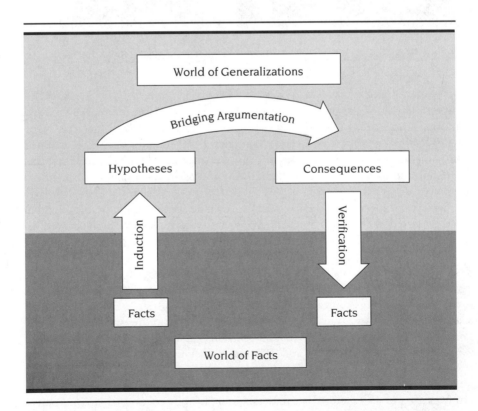

Major steps in the scientific cycle.

understand how hypotheses are derived, suppose that the "known facts" were a swarm of simple points drawn on a graph. Hypothesis formation is the process of drawing a single line to describe these points. There are, of course, an infinite number of hypotheses (lines) that can be drawn to account for the facts (the data points). The scientist must first examine the possible theories and select the most likely—that is, the most probable—for actual testing. On the graph, the most credible lines pass through every point, and plenty of such curves could be drawn. Most people feel that if the points tend to fall in linear fashion, then a straight line will form the simplest hypothesis to describe the known data.

Such hypotheses are generated through **inductive reasoning,** an inductive argument working from specific to the general; in this sense, the conclusions of an inductive statement contain more information than the premises do. The facts as known serve as premises in this case, as the resulting hypothesis not only accounts for these known facts but also predicts properties of unobserved phenomena.

Induction assumes that if something is true in a limited number of observed cases, it will also be true in similar, but unobserved, examples. The probability of being correct thus increases with the number of cases observed. Political opinion polls are an example of inductive reasoning.

There are no rules for induction (any more than there are rules for thinking up good ideas). Some hypotheses are derived by enumerating the data, isolating common features, and generalizing to unobserved data that share these common properties. At other times, archaeologists turn to analogies, relatively well understood circumstances that seem to have relevance to poorly understood cases. But equally common is the simple application of good sense. Judgment, imagination, past experience, and even guesswork all have their place in science. It does not matter where or how one derives the hypothesis. What matters is how well the hypothesis accounts for unobserved phenomena.

It is, of course, entirely possible that several hypotheses will apply to the same data, just as several lines can be drawn through the points on a graph. In practice, scientists generally work their way systematically through the various possibilities, testing them one at a time. This method of *multiple working hypotheses* has long been a feature of scientific methods. To distinguish among the various options, most scientists assume that the simplest hypothesis will tend to be correct. Thus they begin with the simplest hypothesis and see how well it holds up against some new data. If it fails the test, they then will try the next least complicated hypothesis, and so on.

Remember MacNeish's hypothesis about plant domestication? He began his research with a careful assessment of the known facts—the finds at Bat Cave and Tamaulipas, the reconnaissance in Guatemala and Honduras, and the available genetic information. These were, in a sense, his graph points to be accounted for. MacNeish could have come up with any number of hypotheses to explain these facts: Corn could have been domesticated simultaneously all over Mesoamerica in 3000 B.C.; corn could have been domesticated independently in both the north and the south at the same time (3000 B.C.); corn might not have been domesticated in Mesoamerica at all but, rather, traded from somewhere else, such as South

America or even Mesopotamia. These are just a few of the infinite number of possible hypotheses that could be cited to explain the archaeological facts. By choosing the hypothesis he did, MacNeish was selecting the simplest of the available possibilities. Regardless of which hypothesis is initially selected, none is accepted until it survives further, independent observations. Mere induction does not lead to scientific acceptance.

Once the hypotheses are defined, the scientific method requires their translation into testable form. Hypotheses can never be tested directly because they are general statements, and one can test only specifics. The key to verifying a hypothesis is simple: You don't. What you verify are the logical consequences of hypotheses.

Deductive reasoning is required to uncover the logical outcomes. A deductive argument is one for which the conclusions must be true, given that the premises are true. Such deductive arguments generally take the form of *"if . . . then"* statements: *If* the hypothesis is true, *then* we will expect to observe the following logical outcomes. Bridging the gap from *if* to *then* is a tricky step.

In the "harder" sciences, these bridging arguments derive directly from known mathematical or physical properties. In astronomy, for instance, the position of "unknown" stars can be predicted using a long chain of mathematical arguments grounded in Newtonian physics. The classic deductive method begins with an untested hypothesis and converts the generalities into specific predictions based on established mathematical and/or physical theory (the **bridging arguments**).

But how do archaeologists bridge this gap? Where is the "well established body of theory" that allows us to transform abstract hypotheses into observable predictions?

When MacNeish translated his general hypothesis into testable propositions, he was assuming that several bridging arguments existed (although like many archaeologists, he did not make these assumptions explicit). Experience told MacNeish that unburned corncobs can be preserved for millennia in an arid cave environment but rapidly decompose when exposed to moisture. So, MacNeish figured, we should concentrate the search on dry caves and skip the riverbottoms. Reasoning like this provided a "bridge" between the logical expectations and the archaeological record. Since the geneticists surmised that maize had been domesticated as a highland grass, MacNeish decided to confine his search to the highlands. Here is another bridge into the archaeological record, based this time on genetic theory.

In truth, modern archaeology is almost bereft of explicit theory. The bridging arguments necessary for determining the logical outcomes of hypotheses are generally seat-of-the-pants statements, and archaeological inference is hampered by this lack of precision. The development of *middle-level research* (also called *middle-range research*) is a significant direction in today's archaeology. We should add, somewhat parenthetically, that test implications can also be derived through induction, based on known prior probabilities of the various hypotheses. But for now, we shall keep things simple and consider only the deductive case.

The final operation in the scientific cycle is actually to test the implications. For MacNeish, this step required additional reconnaissance in archaeologically unknown regions of southern Mexico. These new data were then evaluated, and had his projections not been verified, his hypothesis would have been rejected. As it turned out, excavations in the Tehuacán Valley failed to reject MacNeish's particularistic hypotheses. Hence, MacNeish's preliminary notions on plant domestication survived an empirical test.

No such simple experiment can ever completely validate any hypothesis, and more intensive inquiry is generally required to increase credibility. Scientific methods are not really designed to prove anything; instead, the idea is more to eliminate the untenable hypotheses. MacNeish's work at Tehuacán generated new data ready for synthesis into new and more refined hypotheses (which in turn had to be tested as before). Scientific progress actually requires a pyramiding of verified hypotheses into a hierarchy of more generalized laws.

The process that we sketched is commonly called the *scientific method*. But I prefer the more accurate designation the *scientific cycle* because it emphasizes the reiterative, repetitive nature of the inquiry. A scientific cycle begins in the world of facts. Through the process of induction, these facts are probed, and hypotheses are invented to account for what is already known. But because hypotheses are general declarations, they cannot be tested against further facts until they are translated into their logical consequences, through the judicious use of bridging arguments. The final step reverts to the world of facts in the process of verification.

The scientific cycle thus begins and ends with facts. But these new facts themselves will suggest new hypotheses, and once again, the inductive reasoning will lead from the world of facts to the world of abstraction, thereby initiating a new cycle of investigation. As a method, science implies a continuing upward spiral in knowledge.

What's a Humanistic Approach?

No one is more convinced than I am that anthropology has profited by being born within the scientific tradition. . . . My conviction is simply that today the scientific and humanist traditions are not opposites nor mutually exclusive. They are supplementary, and modern anthropology handicaps itself in method and insight by neglecting the work of the great humanists.

RUTH BENEDICT (1887–1948), CULTURAL ANTHROPOLOGIST

Virtually all modern archaeologists, to one degree or another, subscribe to the basics of science. We all believe in careful scholarship, in generalizations backed by firm data, in honesty, in full consideration of negative evidence. Archaeologists do not follow a set of logical rules based on formal principles, but rather they are free to use creative imagination to solve problems of interest to archaeologists.

But archaeologists are not automatons and they are not emotionally neutral data-gathering machines. Archaeologists commonly have political opinions and sometimes these perspectives are reflected in their work. At times, archaeologists make moral or ethical judgments about the past (and particularly about its application to the present). This is because archaeologist are historically situated; they are products of their era. But many also bring a humanistic perspective to their understanding of the past. In this section, we will look at an example of how an archaeologist can be both a scientist and a humanist.

So what do we mean by **humanism?** In general, humanists tend to emphasize the dignity and worth of the individual. Humanistic-style inquiry begins with an important premise—that all people are rational beings, possessing a capacity for self-realization through reason. Unlike the purely scientific approach, which stresses objectivity and independent testing, humanists also believe that the value of their contributions lies in precisely the opposite direction—in the fact that their work is intuitive, synthetic, and idiosyncratic. By employing more *subjective* methods, humanists stress reality as perceived and experienced. The result of a humanistic study is heavily conditioned by a researcher's personal mental characteristics or attitude.

The humanist side of anthropology is most obvious in its concern with the languages, values, and artistic achievements of other cultures. Ethnographers spend long periods of time living with the people they study, and they share both joys and sorrows. They cannot, and should not, be dispassionate about the people whose trials and tribulations they share.

In practice, then, Americanist archaeology spans a broad philosophical spectrum. To understand the sweep of opinion that characterizes today's archaeology, we begin by defining the extremist positions, which far exceed ordinary practice. Once these questionable outer limits are defined, it will be possible to work our way inward, toward the more realistic middle ground.

It may be fair to say that the primary distinction between scientific and humanistic approaches revolves around the issue of objectivity. If you believe that archaeology is "pretty objective," then you probably lean more toward the scientific side. You probably think that there's a fairly clear separation between the observer and what is being observed—the "observed" being the "facts" of the archaeological record, which tend to have an inherent connectedness and regularity (which you might term "laws"). You probably believe that there's a world "out there" which can be known more or less objectively.

But if you say no, that archaeology is "pretty subjective," then you're probably more comfortable with the humanistic perspective, which maintains that the observer and the observed cannot really be separated—that our knowledge of the archaeological record pretty much depends on who's doing the observing. You probably don't like conventional science very much and are more comfortable with those who do literary criticism and philosophy. You probably believe that what we know about the archaeological record is itself a product of today's social forces—the product of how archaeologists relate to the archaeological record.

Today, fewer archaeologists than ever are interested in making people choose up sides, in name-calling one another into a frenzy. The watchword today is "pluralism"—accepting that archaeological reality may come in many shapes and sizes.

Today, we see both scientific and humanistic approaches to archaeology. In fact, it is impossible to classify most modern archaeologists as either scientist or humanist because, in truth, most are both. Although a few contemporary archaeologists continue to debate the tiresome "science versus humanities" issue, most believe that modern archaeology is—and must be—a mixture of both approaches.

Levels of Archaeological Theory

Theory is a term we have used very little so far, but it is important nevertheless. Social scientists use the word *theory* in a number of different ways. In one usage, theory is an untested explanation, which would probably be false if ever properly tested. We might speak of Erich Von Dähniken's goofy "Chariots of the Gods" theory, in which he argues that the major cultural advances on earth have resulted from visitations by extraterrestrial beings. Many archaeologists would call this "theory" an improbable and untested generalization. In this sense, theory is a putdown, almost a dirty word.

Theory also refers to a general set of untested principles or propositions—theory as opposed to practice. Thus a new invention to harness solar energy might work "in theory" (that is, on paper) but would require extensive field testing before one could decide whether it was a successful design. If the solar device functioned as expected, the theory would be valid; if the device failed, the theory would be held invalid.

Although both usages are common, neither one has much to do with archaeological theory. Instead, we will define theory at three fundamental levels: low-level, medium-level, and high-level theory. This is a critical distinction because the rest of this book will be organized in terms of these three sequential levels of archaeological theory.

Low-level theories are the observations that emerge from hands-on archaeological fieldwork. Although you may be accustomed to thinking of such observations as data or facts, we will see why even the baseline facts of archaeology are themselves really theories.

Middle-level theory links archaeological data with the relevant aspects of human behavior that produced them. This is a critical transition because it moves from the archaeologically observable (the "facts") to the archaeologically invisible (human behavior in the past). Middle-level theory building involves both methodological and substantive applications.

Finally, there is **high-level (or general) theory.** Theory building at this level provides the overarching framework for understanding the human condition. General theory is not specific to archaeology, but rather applies to intellectual inquiry in general. Some general theory is heavily scientific, some is not. Some general theory is adaptive, some is not. Some general theory involves strictly biological factors; some involves only cultural causality; some combines the two.

Low-Level Archaeological Theory

All too frequently, methodology-theory-practice discourses get lost in abstraction and become divorced from archaeological reality altogether. To avoid this problem, we will begin our discussion of low-level theory in archaeology by looking at some real archaeological data. The idea is to keep this discussion firmly grounded, basically down to earth.

We will introduce archaeological theory, beginning at the lowest level, in the context of real archaeological objects. To keep things simple, I will, from time to time, talk about some specific objects recovered in my own excavations. Two sites in particular—Gatecliff Shelter and Mission Santa Catalina—will crop up frequently.

Gatecliff Shelter (Nevada) is a prehistoric cave in the American Desert West, where people gathered beneath the shallow overhang for more than 7,000 years. I discovered Gatecliff in 1970, and throughout the 1970s, our interdisciplinary team excavated the stratigraphic deposits in the cave. Gatecliff provides a good example of how things work in archaeology.

The second archaeological case study, Mission Santa Catalina de Guale, is located in the fabled Sea Islands off the coast of Georgia. Here, a Franciscan mission was founded among the Guale Indians in the late 1500s, and for more than a century Santa Catalina defined the northern Spanish frontier along the eastern seaboard. It was overrun by British troops in 1680. I began searching for this lost mission site in 1978, the same year we finished digging at Gatecliff. Three years later, we discovered Santa Catalina and have been digging there ever since.

Gatecliff was discovered by old-fashioned, dogged fieldwork; we found Mission Santa Catalina using modern sampling theory and hi-tech remote sensing. The Gatecliff excavations were vertical—in some places nearly 40 feet deep—but nowhere at Santa Catalina have we dug deeper than 6 feet. The cultural deposits at Gatecliff were stacked up within a floor area of about 300 square feet, whereas Mission Santa Catalina sprawled across a dozen acres. Buried within Gatecliff Shelter were several thousand stone tools, weighing more than a ton; all the stone artifacts from Santa Catalina would easily fit in a single shoe box. Only three pieces of pottery turned up at Gatecliff, but 10,000 sherds so far have been cataloged from Santa Catalina.

The list of contrasts grows indefinitely, but my point is simple: Having spent two decades excavating at Gatecliff and Mission Santa Catalina, I have yet to excavate any important data from either. In fact, I dug up no data at all.

I found no data at Gatecliff or Mission Santa Catalina because archaeologists do not excavate data—anywhere. Rather, they excavate objects. Gatecliff Shelter and Mission Santa Catalina surrendered overwhelming artifact collections, thousands upon thousands of archaeological objects. But neither the physical sites nor the archaeological objects they contained are data.

Data arise only from observations made on such objects. Each observation is specifically designed to answer one or more relevant questions: How old is this part of the site? Who were the people? What language did they speak? Was the ancient climate similar to that of today? Why did they choose to live in this particular spot? What did they eat? What kinds of social groups were present? Where did they go? Each question may require a different set of observations, giving rise to several batches of dissimilar data. But remember that quite different observations can often be made on exactly the same objects.

The hallmark of today's archaeology is the precept that the objects of the past can (and must) be viewed from multiple perspectives. Gatecliff and Mission Santa Catalina provide recurring points of reference, and we use the objects from these two sites—plus many, many others—to illustrate differing perspectives on the past.

More than anything else, today's archaeology is flexible and broad based. Sometimes we ask questions about time; we also consider human adaptation; we may ask about religion and social organization; sometimes we might inquire about mind-set and cognitive structure; sometimes we operate as relatively objective scientists, while other times a more subjective, humanistic approach is more suitable. The theoretical perspective may vary widely, but the objects remain the same.

So Gatecliff Shelter is a collection of archaeological objects. The cultural objects—the **artifacts**—are made of chipped or ground stone, bone, plant fibers, tanned hides, shells, and turquoise. Archaeological sites contain other objects not made by humans, those relating to the natural environment, and archaeologists term such things **ecofacts.** Prehistoric pollen grains are ecofacts; so are food bones and piñon nut hulls.

Corncobs are borderline: To dirt archaeologists, cobs are ecofacts simply because they aren't artifacts; but to specialists in ethnobotany, corn is decidedly an artifact because it was produced by deliberate domestication.

But there's more to it than that. We see collections of archaeological objects in every small-town saloon in the West. Sometimes the assortment is no more than a bunch of arrowheads in a cigar box. More aesthetically minded collectors arrange their brightly colored arrowheads in decorative shadow boxes.

These frames are filled with prehistoric ancient artifacts, but the gin mills are not prehistoric archaeological sites. The reason for this is simple: The artifacts are merely isolates, objects displayed in a modern context. When we dug Gatecliff, we discovered prehistoric implements and ecofacts where they were discarded by their makers. The artifacts were **in situ**—in place. The artifacts had an ancient context.

Low-level theory begins with archaeological objects, then generates some relevant "facts" or "data" about these objects. Some data consist of physical observations. For example, *artifact 20.2/4683 is (a) made of obsidian, (b) 21.5 mm long, and (c) weighs 2.1 grams.* This statement contains three pieces of data—observations made on the same archaeological object. Other data might be contextual. For example: *artifact 20.2/4683 was found in unit B-5, 56 cm below the surface.* This observation places this artifact into a three-dimensional coordinate system.

An infinite number of observations can be made on any single archaeological object: distances, angles, weights, color readings, chemical compositions, manufacturing techniques, and so forth. But in practice, of course, archaeological data consist of a relatively standardized series of descriptive observations. At this level, archaeological data should be relatively objective and, if possible, reproducible by independent observers. Several subsequent chapters will show, in some detail, how archaeologists build their data into reliable cultural chronologies.

Low-level archaeological theory also addresses the data generated from ecofacts. Animal bones, for instance, are often recovered in archaeological contexts. Beyond the standard contextual data generated during excavation, these bones are commonly identified to taxa (Is it a deer bone or a rabbit bone?) and to body part (Is it a vertebra or a toe bone?). Data are also generated about the bone's condition (Is it broken or whole? Are butchering marks evident? Is it burnt?).

Overall, the important dimensions of low-level generalizations are the classical ones in archaeology: time, space, and form. Low-level theory does not refer to the archaeological record in terms of human behavior. Theory at this level merely demonstrates the existence of regularities to be explained; it does not attempt to explain those regularities.

Theory at the Middle Level

Middle-level archaeological theory (sometimes referred to as middle-range theory) addresses both substantive and methodological questions. But in both cases, middle-level theory links some specific archaeological data with the relevant aspects of human behavior that produced it. At this middle range, we make a critical transition because we move from the archaeologically observable (the low-level theoretical "facts") to the archaeologically invisible (relevant human behaviors in the past). How, you might wonder, does this transition actually take place?

The answer's pretty simple, if you remember what the archaeological record is: It is the contemporary evidence left by people of the past. Strictly speaking, the archaeological record comprises only static things—the artifacts and ecofacts that survive into today. The dynamic behavior that produced or interacted with these archaeological objects is long gone.

Archaeologists conducting such methodological research at the middle range spend time studying situations where archaeologically relevant behavior is still taking place, fashioning the theoretical tools by which past material culture can be translated. Methodological theory building at the middle range has proven to be an extremely productive research area, involving ethnoarchaeology, modern material culture studies, and experimental archaeology. Each topic is discussed in some detail in later chapters.

One methologically oriented field is **experimental archaeology.** Archaeologists sometimes conduct controlled experiments in which they manufacture their own stone tools. Here, they are studying specific stoneworking techniques to learn how human behavior is translated into specific archaeologically observable evidence (such as flaking scars, breakage patterns, and leftover flake by-products).

Experimental archaeologists also conduct intensive studies of pottery manufacture, house construction methods, hunting techniques and technology, to name but a few.

Middle-range research can also be conducted as **ethnoarchaeology,** in which archaeologists observe ongoing, present-day cultural contexts to see how behavior translates into the archaeological record. Several examples of such middle-range theory building are discussed in Chapter 6.

General Theory in Archaeology

High-level (or general) theory provides archaeologists with an overarching framework that structures the way we view the world. General theory is not specific to archaeology; it applies to all intellectual inquiry about the human condition. Some general theory is heavily scientific; some is not. Some general theory stresses environmental adaptation; some does not. Some general theory emphasizes strictly biological factors; some involves only cultural causality; some theory combines the two approaches.

General theory attempts to interrelate higher-level concepts, not to account for specific observations. It is not something that is open to direct empirical verification or rejection; people tend to believe in a particular body of general theory for highly personal reasons. This is why high-level theory is sometimes called one's "research strategy": Your general theoretical leanings influence how you view humanity, how you structure your questions about the present and the past, and how you interpret the answers you receive to these questions. General theories vary in the degree to which testable propositions can be derived from them. But general theory is never right or wrong: It is either an appropriate way to answer questions, or it is not—and everyone gets to judge what is meant by "appropriate." The next section examines the principles of high-level theory as they operate in archaeology.

Understanding Archaeology's Primary -isms and -ologies

Archaeologists subscribe to a broad range of research strategies, and an exhaustive discussion of such diverse views would take a long time. Since our purpose here is merely to tell you something about the role of high-level theory in archaeology, we will sketch only the two most prevalent strategies—cultural materialism and postmodern interpretivism.

But just doing this is not quite enough. Remember what I said earlier: "General theory is not specific to archaeology; it applies to all intellectual inquiry about the human condition." This means that we must also look at how these general research strategies translate into the practice of actual, down-to-earth, dirt archaeology.

High-Level Theory: Cultural Materialism

The most coherent adaptive approach in anthropology is termed **cultural materialism,** a movement with roots extending back at least a century. But today, cultural materialism is largely associated with Marvin Harris (now professor of anthropology at the University of Florida), who gave it its name. The cultural materialist strategy attempts to explain the evolution of differences and similarities in the global repertory of sociocultural systems.

Cultural materialists begin from the scientific premise that knowledge is acquired through public, replicable, empirical, objective methods. Such scientific research allows us to formulate theories to explain cultural differences and similarities. Rival theories are judged by the same criteria, based on their power to predict and to admit independent testing. By explicitly embracing a scientific framework, cultural materialists reject humanist and aesthetic theories that attempt to explain culture on nonscientific grounds. More than this, cultural materialism posits that environmental, technological, and economic factors—the material conditions of existence—are the most powerful and pervasive determinants of human behavior.

Cultural materialism focuses on behavioral events, which must be distinguished from mental events because they are observed in such different ways. They cannot be understood using the same set of criteria. Human behavior is available to the scientific community in a form that can be observed, measured, photographed, and objectively described. Human thought, the events of the mind, can be observed only indirectly. There are distinct relationships between behavior and thought, and these associations must be demonstrated and not assumed.

Although behavior has its emic component—the native's perception of what has transpired—cultural materialists prefer to concentrate on etic behavior, the observable outcome of human behavior. Within these guidelines, cultural materialistic research covers a rich array of topics: the origin and evolution of sex and gender roles, warfare, origins of dietary patterns and food avoidance, and settlement and demographic trends, to name just a few.

Marvin Harris.

Cultural materialists use the term **infrastructure** to denote those elements considered most important to satisfying basic human needs: the demographic, technological, economic, and ecological processes—the modes of production and reproduction—that are assumed to lie at the causal heart of every sociocultural system. Specifically, it is the *etic behavioral infrastructure* that mediates a culture's interactions with the natural and social environment.

At the next level, the sociocultural subsystem is made up of those interpersonal relationships that emerge as behavior: social

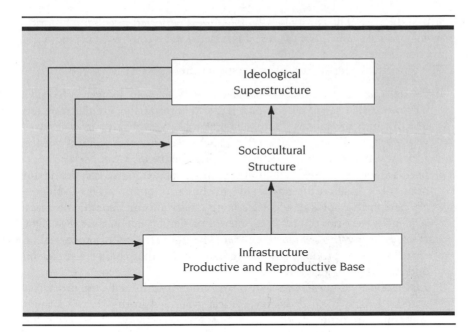

How the cultural materialist views causality.

organization, kinship, economics, ethics, and military and political organizations. This sociocultural subsystem is today subsumed by the term **structure.**

Finally, the term **superstructure** refers to values, aesthetics, rules, beliefs, religions, and symbols. Expressed in etic behavioral terms, superstructure is manifested as art, music, dance, literature, advertising, religious rituals, sports, games, hobbies, and even science.

What distinguishes cultural materialism from other approaches is the principle of **infrastructural determinism,** which has two basic premises: (1) that human society strives to optimize the costs and benefits for those genetically derived needs most important to the survival and well-being of human individuals (sex, sleep, nutrition, vulnerability to stress, and so forth), which occur primarily in the etic behavioral infrastructure; and (2) that such infrastructural changes determine changes in the rest of the sociocultural system.

The Processual Agenda: Cultural Materialism at Work in Archaeology

Processual archaeology applies the strategy of cultural materialism to evidence from the past. The processual agenda grew out of dissatisfaction with the increasingly sterile cultural-historical and largely descriptive archaeology of the 1950s. Processualists realized that they could not adequately explain how cultures operated in the past. The chronology-building tools perfected in cultural-historical archaeology were retained, but the rest was rejected in favor of what can be called the processual agenda.

The processual agenda has several key characteristics:

1. *Processual archaeology emphasizes evolutionary generalizations, not historical specifics.* The processual agenda is scientific rather than historical, emphasizing regularities and correlations. Processual archaeology explicitly associates itself with the generalizing social sciences, such as economics, political science, sociology, and ethnology. Just as Darwin's theory of natural selection defined the mechanism of biological evolution, archaeologists can define theories that condition the progressive evolution of culture. This evolutionary perspective holds that specific human decisions and specific historical sequences were not of particular interest or significance in their own right.

2. *Processual archaeology seeks universal laws.* The ultimate goal of processual archaeology is to produce law-like generalizations that could be useful for understanding modern society.

3. *Explanation in processual archaeology is explicitly scientific.* Initially, the processual agenda depended on deductive models grounded in the "hard" sciences and emphasized the importance of absolute objectivity. More recent formulations stress the interplay between induction and deduction and the relative objectivity of observations.

4. *Processual archaeology attempts to remain objective and ethically neutral.* Processual archaeology tries to provide positive evidence about the past. Politics of the present have nothing to do with the ancient past, and processual archaeologists avoid subjectivity. The processual agenda avoids passing moral judgments on people of the present or the past.

5. *Processual archaeology defines culture as humanity's extrasomatic means of adaptation.* In processual archaeology, the culture concept squarely focuses attention on the key elements of environment, technology, ecology, and economy. Religion and ideology are considered "epiphenomena"–cultural add-ons with little long-term explanatory value.

6. *The processual agenda views culture from a systemic perspective.* Viewing culture as a nonbiological adaptive system, processual archaeology could tap into a much larger body of established external theory (often called "general systems theory"). The general rules governing all systems–such as positive feedback, negative feedback, and equilibrium–could thus be applied to explain the behavior of the major parts of any particular system (regardless of the specifics of that system).

7. *Processual archaeology deals with etic phenomena.* While not denying that people have their own cultural views, processual archaeology defines culture strictly from the perspective of the outside observer.

I'd guess that well over half of today's practicing American archaeologists are pursuing the processual agenda, in one form or another (although many of these same archaeologists also agree with aspects of the *postprocessual critique,* introduced a little later in this chapter). Cultural materialism appeals to archaeologists for two obvious reasons. First, the cultural materialistic strategy emphasizes technology, economy, environment, and demography—all aspects of human existence that leave relatively clear-cut evidence in the archaeological record. Almost by default, Americanist archaeologists have for decades concentrated on precisely the same factors that cultural materialism holds as primary.

Equally important, cultural materialism needs archaeology. In several of his most important writings, Marvin Harris calls for archaeological support of his theories of human behavior. Harris urges archaeologists to throw off the constraints imposed by current ethnographic theory. Cultural materialism is important to archaeology in part because archaeology is important to cultural materialism.

High-Level Theory: Postmodern Interpretivism

Postmodern interpretivism is a world apart from cultural materialism. The differences between the two research strategies are profound, and each has produced its own archaeological offspring.

The postmodern movement arose in the 1960s as an intellectual antidote to the perceived excesses of scientific thought. Since its eighteenth-century beginnings, science was seen as a way to demystify and desanctify knowledge—a way to liberate human beings from the oppressive traditions of myth, religion, and superstition. Particularly in architecture, so-called "creative destruction" became an integral element of modernism—destroying the ancient, tradition-bound buildings that tied us unnecessarily to the past.

Modernism was about optimism and the pursuit of a better future. But twentieth-century reality—particularly the two world wars, the death camps, and the continued threats of nuclear annihilation—shattered many people's confidence in the modernist agenda. To many, the modernistic rationality of science became the logic of domination and tyranny.

Postmodernists want to strip away the prospect of such oppression by concentrating instead on social fragmentation and instability. The emphasis on decentralization and anarchy makes postmodernism itself a difficult concept to define, because of the way in which postmodern culture views the use of language. In simplest form, we can summarize these perspectives as follows:

Modernist thinking embodies a systematic, clinical, single-minded approach, emphasizing linear progress and goal-oriented behavior, ultimately seeking a carefully crafted finished product.

Postmodernist thinking embodies an empathetic, playful, dissociated series of approaches, emphasizing multiple and sometimes fragmented pathways toward indeterminate, decentralized, transitory performances.

While not entirely antiscientific, postmodernists put down deterministic, rigidly causal methods, praising instead new developments such as mathematical models that emphasize indeterminacy. In general, postmodern thinking shows an intense distrust of the universals and generalizations that provide the keystone to modern scientific reasoning.

Such views also castigate the imperialism of a modernity that presumed to speak for "the other" (colonized peoples, indigenous groups and minorities, religious groups, women, the working class) with a unified voice. The ideas of postmodernist thinkers held special appeal for the various social movements that sprang into existence in the 1960s, including feminists, homosexuals, ethnic and religious groups, and those seeking regional autonomy. The idea here is that each group has a right to speak for itself, in its own voice, and have that voice accepted as authentic and legitimate. This is an essential premise in the **pluralism** advocated by postmodernists.

With its distrust of the general, postmodernists have put down broad interpretive schemes like those of Karl Marx on modern communism or those of Sigmund Freud on psychoanalysis. Rejecting the idea of progress, postmodernism abandons all sense of historical continuity and memory, instead taking bits and pieces of the past quite eclectically and mixing them all together.

Deconstruction is a term borrowed from literary criticism to describe a primary research tool, if it may be called that, in postmodern thinking. Deconstruction minimizes the authority of the "cultural producer" and creates an opportunity for popular participation and democratic determination of cultural values.

Deconstructionists emphasize the notion of *textuality*—a view of language as it exists not only in books, but in speech, in history, and in culture. For the deconstructionist, language is much more than just words—either written or spoken. The world itself is "text" and meaning is nested in multiple ways, one of which is language.

Such texts exist within broader cultural backgrounds, which introduce countless conventions and codes. Given these hidden linkages, the content and meaning of texts become essentially indeterminate. Deconstructionists argue that our words cannot say what they mean because the perpetual interweaving of texts and meanings is beyond our control. This explains the deconstructionist impulse to look inside one text for another, to dissolve or build one text into another. To a deconstructionist, meaning also includes what is left out of a text, and what is silenced by it.

Deconstruction has been attacked by some as unintelligent, as philosophical restlessness, as the death of communication. Still it has become the leading school of literary criticism in the United States since the 1970s. Deconstruction has also extended far beyond philosophy and literary theory. The techniques and ideas of deconstruction are today employed by scholars in history, sociology, educational theory, linguistics, art, and—as we see below—anthropology.

Postmodern Interpretive Anthropology

As the seeds of postmodern thought blew through the intellectual establishment, they fell on particularly fertile ground in the world of cultural anthropology.

After all, the world had changed considerably since the beginning of anthropology. Colonial powers no longer dominate; the so-called "primitive" has disappeared; the geopolitical landscape has become violent and hostile to anthropologists; funding is more difficult; university and institutional priorities have shifted. For many, the post–Vietnam War era created a kind of "anthropological identity crisis."

There has been a postmodern call to action, and many social theorists have welcomed the chance to steer anthropology away from its roots in the "natural science of society." Sometimes calling themselves "interpretive" anthropologists, they embraced the postmodern critique, rejecting all causal viewpoints in favor of a quest for understanding different worldviews, symbol systems, values, religions, philosophies, and systems of meaning. Interpretive anthropology left behind all notion of overarching theories or systematic research on "the other." In its place was proposed a close consideration of such issues as contextuality and the meaning of social life to those who enact it. Instead of looking for regularities, postmodern anthropology seeks to explain the exceptions.

This meant that specific ethnographic situations could only be fully appreciated in their specific historical contexts. Ethnographic particulars had to be firmly situated into a broad framework of both time and space. There were no timeless and spaceless generalizations.

Many contemporary ethnographers believe their task is to analyze a culture in the way a literary critic would read a book or poem. The goal of discovering scientific truth about a culture is rejected in favor of composing interpretations about the "other" culture that are elegant and convincing. According to one postmodern critic, ethnography is not an empirical account—it is a species of fiction.

Anthropology in the postmodern world has found itself enmeshed in the cross-cultural attempt to strip away surface forms of knowledge in order to explore truths formerly buried and concealed. Deconstructionism was considered appropriate here because it got away from notions such as "what the culture was really like," to focus instead on hidden intentions and unexpressed biases of the ethnographer-author. Many cultural anthropologists have turned away from traditional "scientific" ethnography to embrace instead the tenets of postmodernism: All truth is relative; all perceptions are mediated by one's cultural and sexual identity.

If this is accepted, then science becomes merely one of many ways of telling a story about the world around us. Some have gone so far as to argue that scientific methods are merely tools used by the privileged to oppress the weak. Some anthropologists even oppose the term "evolution" because they feel it implies a hierarchy in which some cultures are considered "primitive." While some anthropologists have always believed this, the postmodern movement attracted a large following in cultural anthropology. At the extremes of anthropological theory, the pro- and antiscientific positions hardened. The gap has become so broad among some anthropologists, according to bioanthropologist Vince Sarich, that "you can dismiss someone's argument simply by calling them a 'scientist.'"

Archaeology's Postprocessual Critique: Postmodern Interpretivism at Work

We now turn to the *postprocessual critique,* a direct intellectual outgrowth of postmodern interpretivism. The postprocessual critique is the strategy of postmodern interpretivism applied to the past. This new way of viewing the archaeological past arose largely in Great Britain and Europe, a direct outgrowth of mainstream postmodernism. Under the leadership of Ian Hodder of Cambridge University, this distinctly postmodern brand of archaeology emerged during the 1980s. Although somewhat premature in calling themselves *postprocessual archaeologists,* this energetic and vocal band of scholars took up the banner of postmodernism and attacked the premises of processual archaeology full-force.

As we have just seen, postmodernism rejects the systematic, clinical, single-minded approach of modernism. With respect to the archaeological, the postprocessual critique similarly rejects the etic, evolutionary, antihistorical, objective, science-based, and ethical neutrality of the processual agenda. **Postmodernist interpretivism** emphasizes instead empathetic approaches, multiple pathways of belief, which produce sometimes indeterminate end products. The postprocessual critique seeks a similar approach to the archaeological record. Here are key characteristics:

1. *The postprocessual critique rejects cultural evolutionary generalizations.* The postprocessual critique has argued that cultural evolution's racist views of the past have developed because of reliance on the (western) notion of "progress."
2. *The postprocessual critique rejects the processual search for universal laws.* Consistent with postmodern interpretivism, the postprocessual critique holds that such universals of human behavior simply do not exist.

3. *The postprocessual critique rejects explicitly scientific methods.* Postprocessual critics point out, quite correctly, that much of the early processual literature rigidly adhered to rote rules of evidence and interpretation. Many involved in the postprocessual critique have shown a manifest distrust of science in any form (particularly during the earliest years of the critique).

4. *The postprocessual critique rejects the processual emphasis on objectivity and ethical neutrality.* To understand the past, many postprocessual archaeologists argue, one must develop an empathetic, particularistic approach to it. So called **empathetic explanations** of the past consider not only human thoughts and decisions, but also such highly subjective elements as affective states, spiritual orientations, and experiential meanings. Empathetic approaches assume that the inner experience of humanity is worthy of study both for its own sake and as a clue for interpreting the human past.

5. *The postprocessual critique rejects the systemic view of culture.* The "systems" approach, a central tenet of the processual agenda, has been ridiculed by postprocessual archaeologists as "the robotic view of the human past." The systemic view of human society suggests a coordinated, uniform "organism" responding only to environmental pressures. But to many postprocessualists, a society comprises conflicting individuals, groups, families, and classes, whose goals are not necessarily identical and whose interests and actions are commonly in conflict with the "adaptive" success and "functional" needs of the cultural system as a whole. This perspective allows for internal social dynamics as a significant engine of change, rather than merely a passive agent in systemic change instituted from the "outside."

6. *The postprocessual critique rejects the processual emphasis on etic phenomena.* Reversing the adaptive stance of processual archaeology, the postprocessual critique is based on a mentalist (emic) view of culture, emphasizing the role of artifacts as important symbols of social interaction.

This brief outline sets out some, but hardly all, of the basic premises of the postprocessual critique. Whereas the processual agenda saw itself as an integral part of anthropology, the postprocessual critique argues that because archaeology is uniquely qualified to study material culture, archaeology should be central to a new arena of social theory—quite apart from anthropology. Those involved in the postprocessual critique thereby proposed a rather different academic alignment: *Archaeology is archaeology and archaeology is history—but archaeology is not anthropology.*

The central topics of the postprocessual critique—gender, power, ideology, text, discourse, rhetoric, writing, structure, history, and the role of the individual—have come to dominate some areas of archaeology. But you should be aware that a large segment of Americanist archaeology continues to pursue the scientific, ecological, and evolutionary agenda of processual archaeology.

Contemporary Archaeology: Seeking a Middle Ground

Let me emphasize that the processual agenda and the postprocessual critique are really polar extremes of a highly complex dialogue about the way in which archaeologists encounter the human past. I have tried to show you how the processual agenda and postprocessual critique came to be. Both were historical events, each firmly grounded in specific places and particular times. But the issues raised by science, humanism, objectivity, and empathy have concerned thoughtful archaeologists for more than a century.

As an episode in the history of archaeological thought, the processual agenda had a demonstrably positive effect on theory and practice. But it was also characterized

In His Own Words

On Multiple Perspectives in Archaeology
by Robert W. Preucel

Current archaeological research resists being neatly dichotomized into a simple contrast between processual and postprocessual programs. There is a considerable diversity of approaches among practicing archaeologists today. It would seem that part of the postmodern condition is learning how to live with mutually irreconcilable views about the past. This does not imply that there was no real past, but rather that there are multiple perspectives that we can adopt to study the past in the present and that the perspectives that we favor depend upon our specific research interests. Our interests may be to explain change in prehistoric diet by measuring the ratios of different isotopes in bone, to understand the shifts in production and social organization in terms of structural transformations in material culture, or even to expose the cultural biases that we bring to our interpretation through a critique of ideology. Each of these approaches can and should have a place within a scientific archaeology for the simple reason that they make qualitatively different kinds of contributions to our knowledge base. To borrow a metaphor from the philosopher Charles Sanders Peirce, a strong archaeology is one that weaves different theoretical perspectives into a multistranded cable that can be used to join the past to the present in meaningful ways.

ROBERT PREUCEL is associate professor of anthropology at the University of Pennsylvania.

by "wretched excesses" as obvious as its accomplishments. Even some of the strongest advocates of processual archaeology recognized the problems of ignoring ideology and of pushing cultural materialism beyond its limits.

Today, it is no longer useful—nor even possible—to sort archaeology into such tidy subdivisions. Modern Americanist archaeology is neither processual nor post-processual: It embodies modified versions of both. The vast majority of individuals practicing Americanist archaeology fall somewhere toward the middle: There are very few hard-core processualists or die-hard postprocessualists around these days. Processual and postprocessual archaeologies are better understood as complementary and mutually reinforcing.

Modern archaeologists are wrestling with several questions: To what extent do we "discover" an objective past? Or are we "creating" alternative pasts from the same data? What is the proper mix of humanism and science in archaeology? What social responsibilities does the archaeologist have to properly use the past in the present? Each of these questions has been around for a century, and no clear-cut resolution appears on the horizon.

At present, most archaeologists share a dissatisfaction and discontent with the current state of archaeological theory and practice. No grand theoretical synthesis has emerged to replace the extremes of the processual agenda or the post-processual critique. Instead today's Americanist archaeology is best characterized by multiple paths toward understanding the past. There is simply too much theoretical diversity; too many approaches are being applied in the attempt to understand the human past. This isn't bad, just difficult to characterize.

Maybe this is simply the result of the postmodern condition—learning to live with mutually irreconcilable views about the past.

Summary

Anthropologists believe that a true understanding of humankind can arise only from a holistic, all-encompassing perspective. The biological anthropologist views people chiefly as biological organisms, whereas the cultural anthropologist analyzes people as creatures of their culture. Archaeology, as a branch of cultural anthropology, is deeply concerned with the concept of culture, the learned body of tradition that ties a society together.

Contemporary anthropological thinking can be characterized by two major strategies of research. The ideational strategy deals with mentalistic, symbolic, cognitive culture. Viewed in a reflexive sense, material culture is an instrument to create meaning and order in one's world. The contrasting adaptive strategy in anthropology emphasizes those aspects of culture that most closely articulate with the environment, technology, and economics. This infrastructure is seen as ultimately conditioning the character of both structure and superstructure. Archaeologists draw upon both ideational and adaptive perspectives and no single anthropological school dominates contemporary archaeology.

For more than a century, archaeology has been firmly grounded in a scientific perspective, which provides an elegant and powerful way of allowing people to understand the workings of the visible world and the universe beyond. The goal of scientific theory building is to develop theories that can be criticized and evaluated, to be eventually modified or even replaced by other theories that better explain the archaeological data. The scientific method relies heavily on the twin concepts of objectivity and testability. All archaeologists believe in certain scientific fundamentals: in honest and careful scholarship, in generalizations backed by firm data, and in full consideration of negative evidence.

But many archaeologists also believe in humanism, in the dignity and worth of the individual. Humanistically inclined archaeologists look for holistic syntheses of the cultural patterns of the past. For decades, archaeologists have prided themselves on their ability to straddle the fence between scientific and humanistic perspectives.

Archaeological theory is defined at three basic levels. *Low-level theory* involves the observations that emerge from archaeological fieldwork; this is how archaeologists get their "data," their "facts." *Middle-level theory* links archaeological data with the human behavior that produced them. Such theory is required to move from the archaeologically observable (the "facts") to the archaeologically invisible (human behavior in the past). *High-level (general) theory* provides the overarching framework for understanding the human condition. General theory applies to intellectual inquiry in general; it is not specific to archaeology. General theory attempts to interrelate concepts, not account for specific observations. In this sense, general theory is somewhat akin to a religious creed or dogma because it can never be directly confirmed or falsified. This is why theory at the general level is sometimes called a "research strategy."

This chapter also explored the two major research strategies in modern Americanist archaeology: the processual agenda and the postprocessual critique.

> *I went to the University of Chicago for a while after the Second World War. I was a student in the Department of Anthropology. At that time, they were teaching that there was absolutely no difference between anybody. They may be teaching that still. Another thing they taught was that nobody was ridiculous or bad or disgusting.*
>
> KURT VONNEGUT JR., AMERICAN AUTHOR

Anthropology on the Internet

The Internet contains a wealth of information about anthropologists. Here's a very small sampling:

AnthroNet, maintained by graduate students at the University of Virginia, provides a large set of Internet connections of interest to all brands of anthropologists.
    http://darwin.clas.virginia.edu/~dew7e/anthronet/

Anthropology Resources on the Internet provides a comprehensive listing of anthropological sources.
http://www.nitehawk.com/alleycat/anth-faq.html

The World Wide Web Virtual Library: Anthropology is another good source of information.
http://www.usc.edu:80/dept/v-lib/anthropology.html

The American Anthropological Association also has a Web site.
http://www.ameranthassn.org

CHAPTER 3

Chronology Building:
How to Get a Date

❑ ❑ ❑

PREVIEW

The next two chapters address a single problem—how archaeologists get a grasp on time. This chapter is all about dating archaeological sites—a topic of great interest to most archaeologists. Here, you will find a broad range of dating techniques: tree-ring dating, radiocarbon dating, thermoluminescence dating, and several others. When archaeologists get together, one of the first things mentioned is often the "neat new dates" just back from the lab. But what you don't hear so much—and you should—is exactly what these dates mean. The radiocarbon lab takes a chunk of an old, dead tree and figures out how long ago that tree died. By itself, this lab date tells you almost nothing of interest about your site. When a particular tree died becomes important only when its death is somehow related directly to some human event of interest—such as roofing over a pueblo room. But if you can establish that this particular tree was cut down to build the roof, then you have something of archaeological interest. Demonstrating the validity of such associations is really the key issue in archaeological dating.

It's important to keep the following point in mind while you read this chapter: The physics and chemistry behind dating technology is not unimportant, but it's the deep-down archaeological associations that make it all work.

What is time? If no one asks me, I know. If I try to explain it to someone asking me, I don't know.

SAINT AUGUSTINE (354–430), EARLY CHRISTIAN LEADER

The Fourth Egyptian Dynasty lasted from 2680 to 2565 B.C. The Roman Colosseum was constructed between A.D. 70 and 82. In the seventeenth century, Dr. John Lightfoot proclaimed that God created the entire earth in 4004 B.C., at precisely 9 A.M. on October 23. Each date represents the most familiar way of expressing chronological control—the **absolute date.** Such dates are expressed as specific units of scientific measurement: days, years, centuries, or millennia. But no matter what the measure (Lightfoot computed his estimate by projecting biblical life spans), all absolute determinations attempt to pinpoint a discrete interval in time.

Archaeologists also measure time in another, more imprecise manner by establishing the **relative date.** As the name implies, relative duration is monitored not through specific segments of absolute time but, rather, through relative relationships: earlier, later, more recent, after Noah's flood, prehistoric, and so forth. Although not as precise as absolute dating, relative estimates are sometimes the only dates available. Taken together, both forms of dating, absolute and relative, give archaeologists a way of controlling the critical dimension of time.

Tree-Ring Dating

Like many of archaeology's dating techniques, **tree-ring dating** (also called **dendrochronology**) was developed by a nonarchaeologist. The first systematic dendrochronologist was A. E. Douglass, an astronomer inquiring about the effect of sunspots on the earth's climate. Douglass began with the knowledge that trees growing in temperate and arctic areas remain dormant during the winter and then burst into activity in the spring. In many species, especially conifers, this cycle results in the formation of well defined concentric growth rings.

Because each ring represents a single year, it should be a simple matter to determine the age of a newly felled tree: Just count the rings. Douglass took this relatively common knowledge one step further, reasoning that because tree rings vary in size, they may preserve information about the environment in which individual trees grew. Because environmental patterning affects all the trees maturing in the environment, these regular patterns of tree growth (that is, ring width) should fit into a long-term chronological sequence.

Douglass began his tree-ring chronology with living specimens, mostly yellow pines near Flagstaff and Prescott, Arizona. He would examine a stump (or a core from a living tree), count the rings, then overlap this sequence with a somewhat older set of rings from another tree. But the dead trees and surface snags went back only 500 years or so. Beyond this point, dendrochronology had to rely on the prehistoric record.

Fortunately for him, Douglass worked in the American Southwest, where arid conditions enhance preservation. By turning to archaeological ruins, Douglass began mining a vast quarry of tree-ring data. Sampling ancient beams and supports, he slowly constructed a prehistoric "floating chronology," spanning several centuries but not tied into the modern samples. Douglass could use his floating sequence to date various ruins relative to one another, but the hiatus between prehistoric and modern sequences meant that his chronology could not be correlated with the modern calendar.

Douglass was therefore forced to work with two separate sequences. The absolute sequence permitted him to date with precision those ruins later than about the fourteenth century A.D. The second, relative sequence dated archaeological sites only in relation to one another, and this older sequence was expressed in purely arbitrary numbers followed by the designation R.D. (relative date). Thus arose "the gap," an unknown span of time separating the ancient, prehistoric

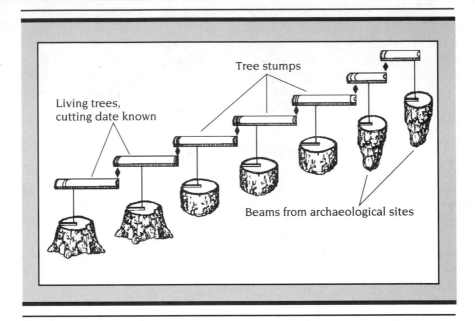

This schematic diagram shows how a tree-ring chronology is built up, working from known-age living trees (lower left) to older archaeological samples.

sequence from the known, historically grounded chronology. In the 1920s, a number of major institutions, including the National Geographic Society, the American Museum of Natural History in New York, and the Carnegie Institution of Washington, launched ambitious expeditions to locate logs from the pesky undated interval.

The "gap hunters," as they were known, experienced little initial success. Each sequence was occasionally extended a year or two, but the void persisted. The problem was that Pueblo peoples had built their substantial sites at Mesa Verde, Chaco Canyon, and elsewhere during the relative part of the sequence. After these sites were abandoned, the tree-ring trail evaporated. Some (unknown) time later, the "postgap" sites were occupied—after the Spanish arrived in the Southwest.

Attention shifted to contemporary Hopi towns, where people were known to have lived during the gap period. Striking a deal with the Hopi, the gap hunters started poking holes in the roof beams at Old Oraibi, with only limited success: Although the historic sequence was extended back to A.D. 1260, the gap lingered.

Finally, in 1929, the Third National Geographic Society Beam Expedition came across the ruins at Showlow, a modern village in east-central Arizona and an unappetizing place to dig, amid a disarray of pigpens and corrals. Morale sagged; the laborers were offered a bonus of $5 to anybody finding a specimen with 100 rings or more. At last, the excavators happened on a charred log fragment, which was routinely preserved in paraffin and labeled HH-39. With his intricate knowledge of tree-ring patterning, Douglass realized that sample HH-39 neatly bridged the gap. It was a breakthrough in American archaeology.

All that work, and here was the answer: The last year of the relative sequence was A.D. 1284. The sequences were united, creating impressive headlines in the pages of *National Geographic*. Almost overnight, Douglass was able to tell Southwestern archaeologists when their most important sites had been built: Mesa Verde was erected between A.D. 1073 and 1262, Pueblo Bonito in Chaco Canyon between A.D. 919 and 1130, the Aztec ruin between A.D. 1110 and 1121, plus dozens of others.

Ironically, when HH-39 was added to the picture, the gap hunters discovered that the former absolute and relative sequences actually overlapped by 49 years. Apparently a long period of drought during the thirteenth century had formed rings so minute that they had been previously overlooked. There had been no gap at all! The data had been there since the earlier expedition to the Hopi town of Oraibi, but it took a specimen like HH-39 to clarify the sequence.

Year-by-Year Chronology Becomes A Reality

Not only did tree-ring dating spread worldwide, but the methods have become increasingly sophisticated. In August 1927, Douglass traveled to Betatakin, an extensive cliff dwelling in northeastern Arizona. He collected two dozen samples that placed the construction of Betatakin within a decade of A.D. 1270. Accuracy to this degree was stunning back then—and still is, compared with every other technique.

But contemporary archaeology requires even more from its dating techniques. Jeffrey Dean of the University of Arizona's Laboratory of Tree-Ring Research spent 2 months collecting further samples from Betatakin in the 1960s. The important thing was to find samples with the bark still attached; in such "cutting" samples, you can be sure that the outer ring surviving in the sample was really the outer ring when the tree was alive; if not, then your "tree-ring" date does not actually date the felling of the tree. The total collection now represents 292 individual beams, and modern tree-ring technology documents the growth of Betatakin literally room by room.

Betatakin Cave was first occupied about 1250 by a small group that built a few structures that were soon destroyed. The occupation was probably transient, the cave serving as a seasonal camping spot for men traveling to plant fields at some distance from their home.

The actual village site at Betatakin was founded in 1267, when three room clusters were constructed; a fourth cluster was added in 1268. The next year, a group of 20 to 25 people felled several trees, cut them to standardized length, and stockpiled the lumber, presumably for future immigrants to the village. Additional beams were stockpiled in 1272, but none was used until 1275, which signaled the beginning of a 3-year immigration period during which more than 10 room clusters and a kiva (underground chamber used for ceremonial purposes) were added. Population growth at Betatakin slowed after 1277, reaching a peak of about 125 people in the mid-1280s. The village was abandoned sometime between 1286 and 1300 for unknown reasons.

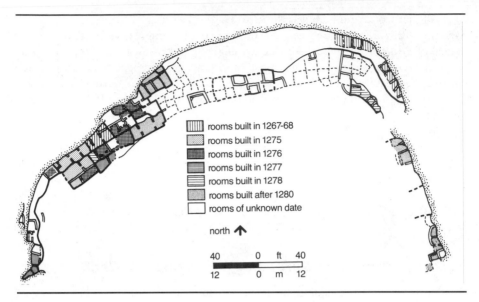

rooms built in 1267-68
rooms built in 1275
rooms built in 1276
rooms built in 1277
rooms built in 1278
rooms built after 1280
rooms of unknown date

north ↑

40   0   ft   40

12   0   m   12

Floor plan of Betatakin and the construction sequence inferred by Jeffrey Dean from the tree-ring evidence.

Tree-ring dating obviously has tremendous potential to provide absolute dates for archaeological sites, subject to one important limitation (shared with all other dating methods): There must always be a clear-cut association between the datable specimen and the definable cultural behavior. At Betatakin, Dean assumed that the wood was timbered during site occupation, as using dead trees or beams from abandoned structures provides erroneously ancient dates.

Tree-ring dating can be applied to many, but not all, species of trees. The most commonly dated species are piñon pine, ponderosa pine, Douglas fir, juniper, and white fir. Limber pine, bristlecone pine, and the giant sequoia have also been extensively studied. Even sagebrush is (sometimes) datable.

Matching unknown specimens to the regional master key can be a slow, laborious process requiring an expert with years of experience. Gradually, more automated means such as correlation graphs have been devised, and computer programs have been attempted (based on the statistical theory of errors). To date, no truly successful computer program is available because computers are unable to handle the problem of false and missing rings. Today's skilled dendrochronologist can still date samples much faster than any computer.

Dendrochronology also has potential for providing climatic data. Assuming that tree-ring width is controlled by environmental factors such as temperature and soil moisture, it is possible to reconstruct past environmental conditions by examining the band widths. Although tree metabolism is complex, great progress has been made in such ecological reconstructions. In the American Southwest, for instance, detailed models today exist telling us how much rain fell in the spring of the year A.D. 1088. Tree-ring data also demonstrate that catastrophic floods occurred in A.D. 1358. These very detailed climatic reconstructions have become extremely impressive, providing archaeologists with fine-grained paleoenvironmental chronologies—provided they work in an area with a workable dendrochronological sequence.

But even without such automated means, dendrochronological sequences have been developed in many areas, including the American Southwest, Alaska, the American Arctic, the Great Plains, Germany, Great Britain, Ireland, Turkey, Japan, and Russia. Next, we look at how tree-dating was productively applied to Viking Age archaeology in Scandinavia.

Dating a Viking Queen

The most dramatic discovery in Viking archaeology took place in 1904, when a large burial mound at Oseberg was excavated not far from Oslo, Norway. Buried inside was an incredibly well preserved Viking ship.

The Oseberg ship was an amazing piece of nautical design: lightly built, shallow of draught, and highly maneuverable. Riding like a swan on a wave, the

The original Oseberg ship, now on display at Oslo's Viking Ship Museum (Norway).

22-meter-long vessel could be either sailed or rowed with ease. In fact, a fairly similar "sister ship" (previously excavated from a burial mound at nearby Gokstad) had already been replicated and sailed across the Atlantic in 1892, to commemorate the 400th anniversary of the Columbian "discovery" of America. As the Scandinavian crew convincingly demonstrated, the Vikings were fully capable of sailing to America several centuries before Columbus's celebrated voyage.

Richly carved from stem to stern, the Oseberg ship served as the coffin of a Viking queen, who had been buried inside, surrounded by an astonishing array of personal furnishings—an unprecedented collection of Viking art, including several carved beds, sleighs (replete with mythical monster heads), oil lamps, kitchenware, tools, and equipment for weaving and spinning. The queen's grave goods revealed many aspects of the daily life of Viking royalty.

But when was the Oseberg ship buried? Until very recently, the find could be dated only by stylistic evaluations of the decorated wooden artifacts recovered in the excavations. In his initial analysis, Norwegian archaeologist Haakon Shetelig assigned them to the "Early Oseberg Style," thought to date around A.D. 800. Later, based on a reexamination of several Irish artifacts recovered at Oseberg, Shetelig changed his mind, moving the age of Early Oseberg Style to between A.D. 820 and A.D. 830; for him, this meant that the Oseberg burial must have taken place in about A.D. 850 or later (a revision which was, and still is, generally accepted).

But then as now, such stylistic dating remains pretty subjective. In attempting to refine these dates, the Radiological Dating Laboratory in Trondheim (Norway) processed a radiocarbon date on oak wood from the grave chamber in the Oseberg ship. The result was 1,190 ± 60 radiocarbon years B.P. (which, as discussed later in this chapter, converts to a calendar age of A.D. 880, with a range of A.D. 780–960). Although these radiocarbon results obviously bracket the stylistic dating of A.D. 850 or so, they also demonstrate that the error margin involved in radiocarbon dating is much too gross to help refine the already fine-grained Viking age stylistic sequence.

Recognizing this, archaeologists Niels Bonde and Arne Christensen recently proposed that tree-ring dating might pin down the true age of the Oseberg burial more precisely. This intriguing possibility arose because, over the past couple of decades, several master chronologies have been built up for oak trees growing in southern Scandinavia. This means that when local "floating chronologies" can be matched against the master sequence, it is possible to tree-ring-date specific archaeological sites and features.

It is instructive to see how these dates were obtained, because a series of assumptions and arguments of relevance are required to bridge the gap between the tree-ring dates and the past event of interest.

What, exactly, was being dated at Oseberg? Bonde and Christensen were specifically interested in establishing the age of the *queen's burial* inside the Oseberg ship; the date of the ship's construction could well be somewhat older than the funerary event.

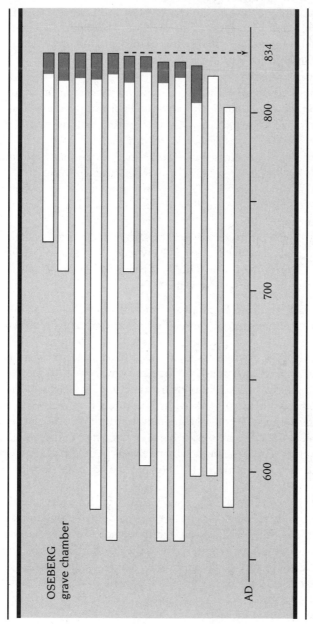

Bar diagram showing the position of the dated tree-ring samples from the Oseberg Viking ship burial, plotted against the A.D. time scale.

What samples were appropriate for tree-ring dating? Certain problems plague all attempts to use ship's timbers for tree-ring dating. For one thing, there is usually some doubt about just where the Viking shipbuilders obtained their supplies. Since ships are highly mobile, they could be built anywhere within their cruising range; in fact, evidence from one Viking ship recovered near Roskilde, Denmark, shows it was constructed from trees harvested in the vicinity of Dublin, Ireland. Obviously, the southern Scandinavian dendrochronological sequence would not be appropriate for dating Irish trees.

Dating a ship's construction is also complicated because of the distinct possibility that wood for shipbuilding was seasoned prior to being used in construction. If such seasoning lasted several years, then the "cutting dates" would provide a misleadingly early "construction date" for the ship itself.

Therefore, these investigators shifted their attention to the wood samples contained within the Oseberg ship. Plenty of wooden artifacts were buried here and many of these could, perhaps, be dated by tree-ring methods. But in nearly all cases, the assumptions required to date these artifacts were as difficult as those necessary for the ship itself.

This is why Bonde and Christensen decided to concentrate their investigation on the grave chamber itself, the small, wooden "tent" erected amidships to contain the Viking queen's corpse. This was the only construction that could be specifically tied to the mortuary event itself.

What assumptions were required? Even after deciding what should be sampled, several important assumptions were required before the tree-ring dating could be conducted.

Specifically, the investigators assumed that the oak trees used to build the funerary enclosure were felled shortly before construction of the grave chamber. This assumption was warranted, in part, by experiments showing that newly cut trees are considerably easier to work with hand tools than seasoned oak. It also seemed reasonable because the burial chamber was crudely constructed of roughly-hewn planks and posts. The masterful hand of the shipbuilder was nowhere to be seen here, suggesting that the burial chamber was built as part of overall mound construction and was never meant to be seen; it was built only to be quickly buried.

They also assumed that the felling site was not far from the intended location of the burial mound. If so, then transport of timber probably only took a matter of weeks, or maybe even days. This meant that the dendrochronological dates for the burial chamber should quite accurately reflect the age of the funeral itself.

This determined, the investigators took 12 dendrochronological samples from the gables, uprights, and planks of the Oseberg burial chamber. This was done by sawing off cross sections from each sample; these sections were replaced after the tree-ring analysis.

The 12 Oseberg samples yielded a floating chronology spanning 299 years. This relative sequence was then matched against master regional chronologies from southern Sweden and Denmark. The results showed that the Oseberg chronology spanned the interval from A.D. 536 to 834. The earlier date holds little archaeological interest (since it merely documents the oldest tree-ring available in the 12 samples); this interior ring was not "behaviorally relevant" to the mortuary event.

But, if the above assumptions were justified, then the late date–A.D. 834– should relate directly to the Oseberg queen's funeral. Then, by additional careful examination, Bonde and Christensen were able to push their results even further. They noted the following:

1. Ten of the dozen Oseberg samples contained intact *cambium* (or "sapwood"– the outer, growing part of the oak tree, directly beneath the bark).
2. Half of these had bark still attached, thus confirming, without doubt, that the A.D. 834 ring actually reflected a reliable "cutting date."
3. Moreover, since the bark rings comprised only "early wood," this meant that they must have been cut fairly early in the growing season of the year A.D. 834.
4. Because of the brief growing season at these northern latitudes, "early" could only mean "summer."

This chain of inference led Bonde and Christensen to their final conclusion: The Oseberg grave chamber was built during the summer of A.D. 834, probably in August.

As at Betatakin, this is phenomenal precision in archaeological dating. This example is important because it demonstrates both the amazing potential of tree-ring dating and also the necessary caution with which such investigations must proceed.

Once established, such precise dating not only pinpoints when the Oseberg burial mound was constructed, but it also enables archaeologists to refine stylistic chronologies for the artifacts contained inside. If we assume that these artifacts were not intrusive–that is, that they were not introduced into the mound *after it was built*–then it provides a firm date *before which* the artifacts must have been crafted.

As the Oseberg ship burial amply demonstrates, dendrochronology will always enjoy a precision unsurpassed in the arsenal of archaeological dating methods. But of course, tree-ring dating can still be applied only in certain limited contexts.

Radiocarbon Dating

Once you ask the question, where is the Carbon-14, and where does it go, it's like one, two, three, you have radiocarbon dating.
WILLARD F. LIBBY (1908–1980), AMERICAN CHEMIST

In 1949, a physical chemist named Willard F. Libby announced to the world that he had discovered a revolutionary new **radiocarbon (carbon-14) dating technique.** The world apparently agreed and handed Libby the Nobel Prize in chemistry for his breakthrough. The earliest radiocarbon dates worked on organic materials younger than about 30,000 years. But more recently, technical refinements have extended the effective range of the C-14 method to more than 75,000 years.

Kinds of Carbon

Like many great thoughts, the basic principle behind radiocarbon dating is deceptively straightforward. Cosmic radiation produces neutrons, which enter the earth's atmosphere and react with nitrogen to produce the "heavy" carbon isotope, carbon-14:

$$N^{14} + \text{neutron} = C^{14} + H$$

Carbon-14 is "heavy" because its nucleus contains 14 neutrons, rather than carbon's more common load of 12. The extra neutrons make the nucleus unstable and subject to gradual (radioactive) decay. Libby calculated that after 5,568 years, half of the C-14 available in a sample will have decayed; this is termed the **half-life** of C-14. Whenever a neutron leaves a C-14 nucleus, a radioactive (beta) particle is emitted, and the amount of radioactivity escaping can be measured by counting the number of beta emissions per gram of carbon.

$$C^{14} = \beta- + N^{14}+$$

These fundamentals established, Libby proceeded to convert the fact of radiocarbon decay into a chronometric tool. Once again, back to basics: Plants and animals are known to ingest atmospheric carbon in the form of carbon dioxide throughout their lives. When an organism dies, no more carbon enters its system, and that which is already present starts its radioactive decay. The rate of beta emissions from the dead organism indicates the C^{14}-to-C^{12} ratio, which is an indicator of the amount of time since the C^{14} started decaying. This is how you figure out roughly how long ago that organism died.

Radiocarbon decay is, strictly speaking, a random process, because nobody can ever predict exactly which C-14 molecule will decay. It is an actuarial matter, like a life insurance table (nobody knows who will die this year, but it's a dead certainty that a certain number will).

What the Radiocarbon Laboratory Can Tell You

In our excavations at Gatecliff Shelter, we ran 47 radiocarbon determinations on charcoal gathered there, and these samples illustrate how contemporary archaeologists actually use the radiocarbon method. The procedure is fairly simple: Collect appropriate samples in the field, correlate them with the known stratigraphy, and submit selected samples to a commercial radiocarbon laboratory. Radiocarbon dating is not cheap. Current rates run about $200 to $250 per sample for a "standard" sample (and perhaps twice that if specialized processing is required).

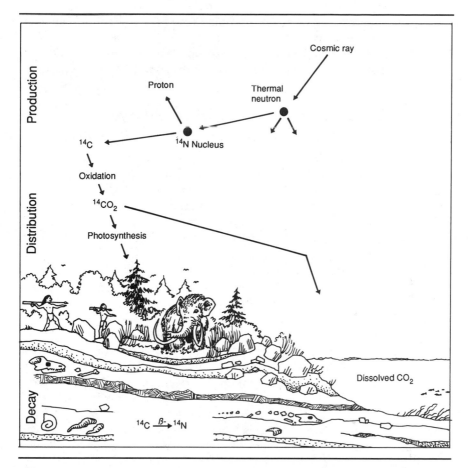

This reconstruction shows the theoretical basis of radiocarbon dating. The natural production of C-14 is a secondary effect of cosmic ray bombardment in the earth's upper atmosphere. Most of the C-14 is then absorbed into the oceans, but a small percentage becomes part of the terrestrial biosphere. Normal metabolic processes maintain an equilibrium of C-14 content in living organisms. But once the plant or animal dies, metabolism ceases, and the proportion of C-14 begins to decrease. Measuring the progress of such random decay provides the basis for modern radiocarbon dating.

The radiocarbon lab reports a date like this:

UCLA-1926A 5200 ± 120 radiocarbon years B.P.

This is an actual date, from charcoal found in Hearth A on Horizon 12 at Gatecliff Shelter. The first designation records the laboratory and sample number: University of California (Los Angeles) Radiocarbon Laboratory sample number 1926A. The second part—5200—estimates the age of the sample in radiocarbon years B.P., ("before present," arbitrarily defined as the year A.D. 1950). Keep in mind that the sample was measured in radiocarbon years, not calendar years. As we will see, radiocarbon dating has certain biases, and the laboratory date must be "corrected" to reflect actual calendar years. In short, the radiocarbon lab at UCLA told me this: A tree died 5,200 radiocarbon years before A.D. 1950, and charcoal from that tree turned up in Hearth A on Horizon 2 at Gatecliff Shelter.

Can You Handle the Uncertainty?

So far, so good. But remember that the lab report attached a " ± 120" to the age estimate. This **standard deviation** estimates the consistency (or lack of it) between the various "counting runs" performed at the laboratory. This statistical appendage, read as "plus or minus," is the standard deviation (or "sigma"), a projection of the error in the estimate. Because of their random, statistical nature, radiocarbon dates cannot be precise. Some samples, like this one, generate relatively minor inaccuracy (only 120 years, more or less). But sometimes C-14 determinations involve larger errors—up to several hundred years—and the plus-or-minus factor warns the archaeologist about this unusually high degree of uncertainty.

The standard deviation expresses the range within which the true date probably falls. In UCLA-1926A, the number "5200 (radiocarbon years)" estimates the actual age of the sample (which, of course, remains unknown); the standard deviation estimates the range of error. We know from statistical theory that there is a 2-in-3 (67 percent) chance that the true date falls within 1 "sigma." Specifically, by both adding and subtracting 120 from the age estimate, we will find the probability to be 67 percent that the true age of UCLA-1926A falls between 5,080 (5,200 *minus* 120) and 5,320 (5,200 *plus* 120) radiocarbon years B.P.

Because random probabilities are involved, we can never be absolutely certain that the true age falls in this interval, but the chances are good (2 in 3) that it does. If you want to be more certain, try doubling the standard deviation. In this case, there is a 95 percent chance that the actual date falls within ±2 sigmas. Thus, the chances are 95 in 100 that the true age of UCLA-1926A falls within 2 sigmas—or ±2(120) = ±240 years—that is, between 4,960 and 5,440 radiocarbon years B.P.

The standard deviation must never be omitted from the radiocarbon date, because without it one would have no idea how accurately the sample was actually measured. Statistical theory provides simple methods to test whether two radiocarbon determinations are the same or different.

Tree Rings Incite the Second Radiocarbon Revolution

Radiocarbon dating relies on a number of key assumptions, perhaps the most important being that the radiocarbon level—that is, the ratio between carbon-12 and carbon-14—has remained constant in the earth's atmosphere. Libby assumed this when developing the method, but we now know that this assumption is not valid. That is, levels of atmospheric carbon-14 have shifted somewhat over the past millennia. The first investigator to find fault with the atmospheric assumption was

H. L. De Vries of The Netherlands. De Vries cut several beams from historic buildings and determined the exact age of the wood by counting tree rings. When he later dated the known-age specimens by radiocarbon assay, he found the C-14 contrast to be 2 percent higher than expected for the known-age wood. Scientists at the time generally dismissed the work, as the errors De Vries discovered were relatively small, just barely outside the limits of expected error.

But the specter of larger errors finally inspired radiocarbon specialists to look more closely into the problem. This joint investigation was conducted by laboratories in Copenhagen, Heidelberg, Cambridge, New Haven, Philadelphia, Tucson, and La Jolla. In one landmark study, Hans Suess of the University of California at San Diego (La Jolla) analyzed wood from bristlecone pine trees. Native to the western United States, bristlecones are the world's oldest living organisms, some living up to 4,600 years. Working from live trees to ancient stumps, investigators had already extended the bristlecone tree-ring sequence back nearly 8,200 years. Suess radiocarbon-dated dozens of known-age samples and compared the results obtained by each method. It was clear that there were significant fluctuations in the atmospheric C-14 concentrations. The assumption of C-14 stability was false, rendering the hundreds of previous radiocarbon determinations in error. Although dates younger than about 1500 B.C. were not too far off, comparison with the tree-ring data showed that more ancient radiocarbon dates could be up to 700 years too young.

The fluctuations in carbon-14 appear to be worldwide because the earth's atmosphere is so well mixed. Once a gas is released into the atmosphere, it becomes evenly distributed throughout the entire global atmosphere within a few years. Hence the discrepancy between tree-ring and radiocarbon ages, first noted by De Vries, must be independent of geographic origin.

When radiocarbon dating was first introduced, Egyptologists told Libby that his dates did not square with the historically derived dynastic chronology. Libby attributed this disparity to experimental error, but now that we know that the effect is due to differential production of atmospheric C-14, it is possible to "correct" for these errors. A series of international conferences explored the problem, and several correction tables were constructed to enable archaeologists and others to "correct" their own dates. More recently, these tables have been incorporated into a series of readily available computer programs, each easily run on a desktop PC. The most popular such program, named CALIB, was written at the Quaternary Isotope Laboratory, University of Washington. Another calibration program, known as CAL15, was prepared by the Centre for Isotope Research, University of Groningen, The Netherlands. The third such program, OxCal, was devised at Oxford University. Considerable research continues on calibration issues, and these radiocarbon age calibrations are not likely to be the last.

Most regional sequences are unaffected by the correction factors. As long as all dating is by radiocarbon, the various subareas will remain in identical relationships, the only change being in the absolute dating. American cultural sequences, for example, remain intact, although all appear slightly older in absolute time. The Old World, however, is less fortunate because of disparities in dating techniques. In areas where writing was invented quite early, historic records provide firm chronology, over some 5,000 years. Radiocarbon dates for the Fertile Crescent and Egypt were corrected and supplemented by independent historical records. Western European chronologies, however, lacking historical evidence, were arranged strictly according to radiocarbon determinations. Over the years, Old World data were almost universally interpreted as indicating that the early traits of civilization, such as metallurgy and monumental funerary architecture, originally developed in the Near East, only later diffusing into the "culturally retarded" European area. The peoples of the Near East were considered the inventors and the barbaric Europeans the recipients.

The bristlecone correction changed much of that. Colin Renfrew has compared the process to a "temporal fault line." Most European chronologies are now placed several centuries earlier, but the classical Greek and Near Eastern chronologies remain unchanged. Stonehenge, formerly considered to be the work of Greek craftsmen who traveled to the British Isles in 1500 B.C., clearly predates even the Mycenaean civilization; Renfrew now refers to Stonehenge as the world's oldest astronomical observatory. These "corrected" radiocarbon dates suggest that

Is the Shroud of Turin the Burial Cloth of Christ?

Accelerator dating grabbed headlines around the world when AMS dating was applied to the famous **Shroud of Turin,** thought by many to be the actual cloth in which Christ's crucified body had been wrapped. Although the Roman Catholic Church never officially proclaimed the shroud to be Christ's burial cloth, neither did it discourage that belief. Three million of the faithful filed past the shroud when it was last displayed. Many believed they had looked into the face of Christ. What did they see?

The shroud itself is an unspectacular sheet of twill-woven linen cloth, slightly more than 14 feet long and a yard wide. On this cloth appears a pale sepia-tone image of the front and back of a naked man about 6 feet tall. Pale carmine stains of blood mark wounds to the head, side, hands, and feet. Believers took the shroud to be a true relic of Christ's Passion. But critics since the fourteenth century have been equally convinced that the shroud is a cruel, if clever hoax. Studying the Shroud of Turin became a scholarly and scientific discipline on its own.

For nearly 40 years, scientists argued that radiocarbon dating could definitively determine whether the Shroud of Turin dates to the time of Christ—but conventional radiocarbon methods would have destroyed a handkerchief-sized piece of the shroud, and Church authorities rejected all such requests. But because the new AMS method of radiocarbon dating requires only a minuscule sample of linen—easily removed from unobtrusive parts of the shroud—the Pontifical Academy of Sciences agreed to such dating.

Europe can no longer be viewed as a passive recipient of cultural advances from the Mediterranean heartland. Monumental temples were built on Malta before the pyramids of Egypt. The elaborate British megalithic tombs now appear to date a full millennium before those in the eastern Mediterranean. It is no longer possible to believe that agriculture moved from Asia into Europe. Although diffusion of cultural traits remains an important process, the recalibration in some cases reverses the direction of the arrow. In other instances the whole concept of a "cradle of civilization" seems irrelevant. The impact of the second radiocarbon revolution is clear in most recent discussions of European prehistory.

Accelerator Dating: The Third Radiocarbon Revolution

Radiocarbon dating has recently undergone a third revolution. But unlike the second one—which caused some to write off the technique entirely—this upheaval has no downside.

Three laboratories received a postage-stamp-size piece of the shroud, plus control specimens of various ages. Only British Museum officials, who coordinated the research, knew which specimen was which. When the owner of the shroud, Pope John Paul II, was informed of the outcome, his response was simple: "Publish it."

And publish it they did. A gathering of ecclesiastical and technological specialists hosted a news conference at which Anastasio Cardinal Ballestrero, Archbishop of Turin, solemnly announced that all three laboratories agreed that the flax plants from which the linen in the shroud was made had been grown in medieval times—between 1260 and 1390—long after the death of Jesus.

Although a certain degree of mystery still surrounds the shroud, particularly since nobody can explain how such an image was created using Middle Age technology, one thing is clear: Radiocarbon dating's "third revolution" seems to have resolved this controversy that spanned five centuries. The Shroud of Turin does not appear to be the authentic burial cloth of Jesus.

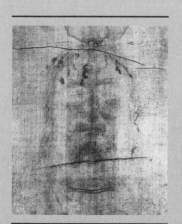

Shroud of Turin.

Archaeology tends to be viewed as an odd science by some because it progresses through unique and unrepeatable experiments. This is partially true. Digging remains our primary "experimental" method, and every excavation destroys the stratigraphic association of archaeological objects. For rare or unique finds, it is simply impossible to confirm the discovery by repeating. Maybe this is why archaeologists are always feuding with one another.

The recent development of the **accelerator mass spectrometric (AMS) technique** for radiocarbon dating drastically reduces the quantity of datable material required. When a Geiger counter is used to monitor the beta ray emissions, several grams of organics are required. But because the new accelerator technology counts the proportion of carbon isotopes directly, the sample required is only a few milligrams.

Armed with the new technology of radiocarbon dating, archaeologists have already begun to "redo the experiment." In some cases, this research has fundamentally changed our perception of the human past. AMS radiocarbon dating allows investigators to date the individual amino acid fractions extracted from partially fossilized bones and has already been used to date the earliest skeletal materials in the New World. For years, George F. Carter has argued from geomorphological evidence that humans have been in the New World for at least 50,000 years. His views sharply contradicted the conventional wisdom, which holds that humans crossed the Bering Strait no more than about 25,000 years ago. Carter was particularly vocal about some human skeletal remains found near San Diego, California. He identified five bones that he thought were especially ancient, and Jeffrey Bada (of the Scripps Institute of Oceanography) processed them using a problematical dating technique based on amino acids, with the following results: 26,000 years; 6,000 years; 28,000 years; 44,000 years; and 48,000 years. These dates strongly supported Carter's assertions of humans' long inhabitation of the New World. If accurate, Bada's amino acid determinations would become the oldest direct dates available for New World humans, at least doubling the time conventionally assigned to humans in the New World.

However, many archaeologists were skeptical, not only about the extreme age, but also about the accuracy of the amino acid technique. Until very recently, the skeletons in question could not be directly dated by radiocarbon because too much bone would have been destroyed in the process. But direct AMS radiocarbon dating has conclusively demonstrated that these skeletons are considerably later. Many range from 3,000 to 5,000 years in age, and the oldest is no more ancient than 11,000 years old. The technique of amino acid dating of bone is no longer used (although later in the chapter you will read about an adaptation of this technique on ostrich eggshells).

The dating revolution has affected everyday archaeology. One case in point is a cache of a dozen extraordinary duck decoys, long ago buried in the dusty depths of Lovelock Cave (Nevada) and excavated in 1924 by M. R. Harrington and L. L. Loud. Although they almost certainly were manufactured in prehistoric times, the desert aridity had preserved these singular artifacts in near-mint condition.

But nobody knew how old the decoys were. The excavators assigned the artifacts to an ill-defined "Late Period," and over the next five decades, various archaeologists studied the unique decoys and guess-dated their age. Although estimates ranged from 500 B.C. to the historic period, conventional wisdom among Great Basin archaeologists held the decoys to be about 2,000 years old.

The Lovelock Cave originals were curated at the Museum of the American Indian (Heye Foundation) in New York City. In 1969, L. Kyle Napton (California State University, Stanislaus) and Robert F. Heizer (University of California) secured a large-enough chunk from one of the decoys to submit for conventional radiocarbon dating. Incredibly, the irreplaceable sample was lost by the radiocarbon laboratory (giving new meaning to the term *laboratory error*). Although Napton tried to obtain additional samples, he realized that samples adequate for conventional radiocarbon dating would unacceptably damage the unique artifacts.

Then came radiocarbon's "third revolution" to the rescue. Knowing that extremely small samples could be dated, Don Fowler (University of Nevada) obtained permission to remove such samples from the Lovelock decoys. Under watchful curatorial eyes, he gingerly snipped off tule tidbits from inside two decoys. The priceless clippings, each the size of your little fingernail, were submitted for processing by the new University of Arizona accelerator mass spectrometer (AMS) facility.

The two statistically consistent AMS radiocarbon dates came out to be 2,080 ± 330 and 2,250 ± 230 radiocarbon years B.P. Taking into account the plus-or-minus factor, the dates overwhelmingly confirmed the previous conventional estimates: The Lovelock decoys are about 2,000 years old. But without the advent of AMS dating, we would still be wondering.

Obsidian Hydration

Obsidian—volcanic glass—has been fashioned into stone tools for millennia. As anyone who has ever fractured an obsidian nodule is well aware, the resultant razor-sharp flakes can be chipped into a host of handy artifacts: knives, scrapers, drills, projectile points, and so forth. Obsidian artifacts are found in archaeological sites on every continent except Australia and one day may rival ceramics as archaeology's most useful artifact for controlling time.

Two geologists working for the U.S. Geological Survey, Irving Friedman and Robert Smith, first started looking into the potential of obsidian as a time-marker in 1948. Friedman and Smith knew that obsidian is a fairly "dry" rock, containing only about 0.2 percent water. But when a piece of obsidian is fractured and the fresh surface is exposed to the environment, water is absorbed into the new surface. The absorption, or *hydration*, process continues until the obsidian reaches approximately 3.5 percent water, the saturation point. These zones, or rims, of hydration are denser than is the unhydrated inside, and the hydrated zone has different optical properties. Whenever obsidian is broken, the hydration process begins from scratch on the fresh surface. This much is simple geophysics, but Friedman and Smith propelled this knowledge into archaeological relevance by reasoning that the degree of hydration observed on an archaeological artifact could measure how long it has been since that surface was created by the flintknapper.

Some Rocks Are Wetter Than Others

The principle behind **obsidian hydration dating** is as clever as it is austere: The longer the artifact surface has been exposed, the thicker the hydration band will be. By making certain that the datable surfaces were only those exposed by deliberate flintknapping, obsidian hydration can be taken as a direct indicator of age.

To measure how much hydration is present, the artifact must be cut and a microscopic thin section prepared. To do this, a small wedge is removed from the edge of the artifact by making intersecting cuts with a diamond-impregnated saw. This section is then ground thin on a lapidary machine and affixed to a microscopic slide with Canada balsam. The obsidian wedge is ground once again, this time to less than 50 microns thick. The slide is finally ready for microscopic analysis using a polarizing light source.

Obsidian hydration dating is simple, rapid, and cheap: Ten obsidian hydration dates may be run for the cost of a single radiocarbon determination. Students can be readily trained to prepare obsidian hydration samples, and several laboratories are currently in operation for such dating. But obsidian dating is hardly without difficulty. After examining about 600 specimens, Friedman and Smith discovered that the rate of hydration is not uniform throughout the world. Of the several variables that seem to influence the hydration rate, atmospheric temperature seemed to be paramount. Once a sufficient number of global samples were analyzed, they constructed a world map describing the correlation between climate and hydration rates.

The origin (and hence chemical composition) of obsidian samples is another major factor in determining hydration rate. Donovan Clark, then a graduate student at Stanford University, analyzed hundreds of obsidian artifacts from five prehistoric California sites and compared the hydration rims with known radiocarbon determinations of the sites. Clark found that central California obsidian hydrates at slightly more than 1 micron per thousand years. Thus, by comparison with radiocarbon dating, Clark suggested a means of converting obsidian hydration from a simple rim thickness (measured in microns) to an actual age estimate (in years).

Photomicrograph, taken at 490×, with arrows indicating the obsidian hydration band (or "rim") that is 4.2 microns thick. This specimen is from Mono County, California.

Estimating Absolute Age With Obsidian Hydration Dating

A study by Frank Findlow and his colleagues illustrates how the obsidian hydration technique is used to date specific flows. The Government

Mountain–Sitgreaves Peak obsidian flow is one of the most heavily exploited in the American Southwest. Obsidian from this area ranges from gray to shiny black in color, and the matrix is free of inclusions. Its excellent fracturing qualities probably account for its wide distribution by trade throughout Arizona and southern Utah.

Obsidian from the Government Mountain–Sitgreaves source was recovered in 10 archaeological sites, ranging in age from about 1500 B.C. to historic times. After the samples were prepared for microscopic analysis and the hydration bands were read, the results were synthesized into the following rate of hydration:

$$Y = 43.58 + 158.16\ (x^2 - x)$$

where Y is the date (in years B.P.) and x is the hydration value in microns.

A few examples will illustrate how this hydration equation is used to date archaeological sites. Awatovi (Arizona) is a large Hopi city abandoned in A.D. 1630. Findlow and his associates dated 10 Government Mountain obsidian artifacts recovered from the latest occupation at Awatovi. The hydration rims averaged 1.8 microns thick, leading to an estimated age of

$$Y = 43.58 + 158.16\ (1.8^2 - 1.8) = 271 \text{ years B.P.}$$

This age converts to a calendar date of about A.D. 1680, in fairly close agreement with the historically dated abandonment of Awatovi.

This same procedure was used to date Stratum 3 at site CS-184, also in Arizona. The average rim thickness was 5.2 microns, which converts to an absolute age of 3,498 years B.P. In this case the obsidian hydration value agrees closely with the date estimated by the radiocarbon method.

Several factors conspire to render the future of obsidian hydration dating somewhat clouded: differential hydration rates for different obsidian sources, artifact reuse, short-term temperature fluctuations, and variable amounts of available moisture. It is known, for instance, that obsidians of different composition can hydrate at different rates. In studying obsidians from the central Mexican highlands, Joseph Michels found that green rhyolitic obsidian hydrated almost three times as fast as did the gray rhyolitic obsidian. That is, even under uniform temperature conditions, the green obsidian hydrates at a rate of 11.45 millimicrons per millennium, whereas the gray obsidian hydrates at a rate of only 4.5 millimicrons per thousand years. Fortunately, this differing composition was obvious by superficial inspection, but the problem of differing rates is compounded when seemingly identical obsidians are of different composition. A number of investigators are currently working on the physiochemical separation of various obsidian sources.

As long as the restrictions are kept in mind, obsidian hydration does provide a useful technique for dating archaeological sites. Even the best dating technique cannot be used without some restrictions and caution.

Radiometric Dating of Potassium

Many rocks, including volcanic minerals, contain traces of potassium—which, like carbon, occurs naturally in several isotopic forms. One of these, known as potassium-40, decays slowly and regularly into an inert, stable gas (argon-40). By comparing the relative proportions of these potassium and argon isotopes in an archaeologically relevant sample, it is possible to derive a radiometric clock for measuring the passage of time. Again, as with radiocarbon dating, the principle is simple: the more argon-40 in a sample relative to potassium-40, the older that sample must be.

So far so good, but how can one express such relative age estimates in more absolute terms? This initial datum for radiocarbon dating is the death of the absorbing organism, since C-14 acquisition ceases with death. Fortunately, volcanic rock provides a comparable method for "zeroing out" the potassium-argon clock. During all major volcanic eruptions, the temperature is so high that all gases—including argon-40—are driven out of the microscopic rock crystals. Such episodes in effect set the potassium-argon clock to zero because all argon-40 present must have accumulated since the last major volcanic eruption.

Potassium-argon dating involves assumptions similar to those of radiocarbon analysis. There must have been no argon trapped at the time of formation (that is, all argon must be the direct result of potassium decay), and all argon must be retained in the rock structure without absorption by the atmosphere. It is known that some rocks, such as mica, tend to leak argon, and so care must be taken in deciding which rock types to subject to potassium-argon dating.

This is why archaeologists love to find ancient sites in association with volcanic deposits. If fossils, for instance, are found just below a layer of volcanic ash, the potassium-argon (K-Ar) method will provide a minimum age estimate for the tools and fossils contained in the archaeological stratum.

The archaeological potential of potassium dating is more limited than that of radiocarbon because the K-Ar time range is so great (as much as several billion years). Rarely are archaeological deposits old enough. But some critically important early sites in Africa have been successfully dated by the K-Ar method. The late Glynn Isaac, for instance, discovered a mass of broken bones strewn across a 20-foot area in the badlands of Kenya. Scattered among the bones (mostly hippopotamus) were remains of stone tools, including flakes and a few pebble choppers. The so-called KBS site is embedded in volcanic tuff, and pumice cobbles within the tuff have been dated at 2.61 ± 0.26 million years by means of the potassium-argon technique.

Potassium-argon dating was also used to estimate the age of ***Homo erectus,*** one of our intermediate human ancestors. For decades, investigators generally believed that *Homo erectus* evolved exclusively in Africa. The earliest fossils are slightly less than 2 million years old; over the next 500,000 years or so, they developed an early Acheulean stone tool culture, characterized by large, tear-shaped hand axes. Then, sometime after 1.5 million years ago, these *Homo erectus* pioneers began moving out of Africa into other parts of the Old World.

Thus fossil hunters were shocked in 1971, when Garniss Curtis, then of the University of California (Berkeley), used potassium-argon methods to date the sediments associated with the *Homo erectus* fossil from Mojokerto, Java. Because Java is a long way from Africa, most investigators thought that the Mojokerto skull should be much younger than a million years. But Curtis estimated that the fossilized infant's skull from Mojokerto was nearly twice that age—1.9 million years old. This extraordinarily ancient age was rejected by most paleontologists, who were convinced that the only humans in the world prior to 1 million years ago lived in Africa.

Both these early dates and the dating technique itself came under criticism. Although potassium-argon dating had been around for decades, the laboratory methods were still somewhat cumbersome. In the laboratory, a given sample of crystals is first split into two subsamples. One of these is dissolved in acid, then passed through a flame; the wavelengths of light emitted allow estimation of the amount of potassium-40 in the sample. The other sample is heated directly, and the amount of argon-40 gas released is measured. This two-sample process increases the potential for error and contamination because there is twice the opportunity for things to go wrong.

Potassium-argon dating also requires several grams of volcanic crystals in order to process a single age estimate. While most of these crystals probably derive from the eruption that covered the fossil, the possibility always exists that other crystals, from volcanic eruptions millions of years older, may have become mixed in, thereby creating a date that vastly overestimates the age of the fossil in question.

Curtis has since teamed up with Carl Swisher of the Institute of Human Origins in Berkeley to develop a new method to date the age of key volcanic deposits. The so-called **argon-argon dating method** was specifically designed to avoid the contamination problems inherent in the earlier technique. The volcanic crystals to be dated are first irradiated. When a neutron penetrates the potassium nucleus, it displaces a proton, converting the potassium into argon-39, an "artificial" isotope not found in nature. The minute quantities of artificially-created argon and naturally occurring argon-40 can then be measured in a single experiment. Because there is no longer a need to split the sample, the argon-argon method produces superior results, even from tiny samples. This high-precision method also allows investigators to focus on single volcanic crystals, which can be dated one by one; thus any older contaminants can be discarded.

In 1992, Curtis and Swisher returned to Java to collect additional samples to be dated with the new argon-argon method. With some white volcanic pumice obtained from the matrix inside the braincase of the Mojokerto fossil, Swisher returned to Berkeley. Within a few weeks, he proclaimed that the new dates were equally ancient—1.8 million ± 40,000 years. They also tested additional sediment samples from another Java site where *Homo erectus* fossils had been found. The results, yielding an age of about 1.6 million years, confirmed the initial Mojokerto fossil date derived from the now "old-fashioned" potassium-argon dating method.

Although these dates remain controversial—many paleontologists continue to doubt that *Homo erectus* could have left Africa so early—it is clear that new high-precision dating techniques such as the argon-argon method will be increasingly important in evaluating the fossil evidence in the years to come.

Dating Ancient Ostrich Egg Shells

One of anthropology's Big Questions is this: When and how did anatomically modern people arise? Did modern *Homo sapiens* arise through gradual, global evolution? Or did modern humans evolve relatively recently and in one place (Africa), then expand throughout the world, displacing less successful forms? Currently, both positions are hotly defended.

But there is a problem. For years, archaeologists interested in dating the origins of anatomically modern humans have been confounded by a lack of relevant dating techniques. Specifically, there exists an irksome gap between the effective ranges of commonly used dating techniques, particularly the radiocarbon and potassium-argon techniques. As we have seen, the *maximum* reliable age for radiocarbon dating is about 40,000 years and the *minimum* reliable age of K-Ar dating is roughly 200,000 years B.P. The disparity between 40,000 and 200,000 years is hence a "gap" within which fall many of the important hominid fossils and their associated artifacts from Africa and the Near East. Until more precise dating was possible within this gap, little solid progress seemed likely in resolving the origins of anatomically modern people. Fortunately, a relatively new dating approach has bridged, or even closed, this gap between fossil dating methods.

This welcome resolution arose from a rather commonplace observation: African ostrich eggshell fragments litter archaeological sites throughout Africa, the Middle East, and as far as China and Mongolia. Sometimes, as in many northeastern African sites, eggshell fragments comprise the only identifiable faunal element (usually because all the bones have decayed away). Human use of ostrich eggs ranges from extremely ancient (1.8 million years at Olduvai Gorge) to the historic period. This extraordinarily broad range in time and space can be directly attributed to the importance of ostrich eggs to human populations: The contents were often used for food and the eggshells were ready-made water containers. And, for the last 30,000 years, people crafted eggshell fragments into ornamental beads.

Eggshells are organic by-products, of course, meaning that they contain carbon. For years, archaeologists dated archaeological eggshells using standard radiocarbon methods. But because the maximum age range of radiocarbon is about 40,000 years, the older ostrich eggshells—and in many cases, the archaeological sites with which they were associated—remained undated. This was unfortunate because many of the eggshell-bearing sites contained key hominid fossils which, accurately dated, could shed considerable light on the origin of anatomically modern humans.

Wouldn't it be nice to be able to date those older eggshells? In theory, at least, that should be possible because ostrich eggshells contain proteins (amino acids), which are known to decompose through time. Therefore if one could estimate the proportion of the eggshell protein that had decomposed, and relate that percentage to a calendrical scale, it should be possible to estimate the time elapsed since that eggshell was formed.

Archaeologist Allison Brooks and her colleagues at George Washington University and elsewhere devised a new way to date the amino acids contained in ostrich eggshells. Not only does this method expand the range of datable materials, but it promises to extend the range considerably beyond that of the current radiocarbon method.

Amino acids are protein compounds found in all living organisms. These compounds exist in two forms, which are mirror images of one another (and can be distinguished from one another only by their refractive properties). When placed under a polarized light, one molecule bends light to the left; the mirror-image compound bends the same light to the right. Such left-handed compounds are called L-isomers (*lepto* is Greek for "left"). The right-handed amino acids are called D-isomers, with "D" standing for dextrorotation (right-hand bending) of the polarizing light.

Most of the proteins in living organisms are left-handed. When the organism dies, the protein molecules begin to flip over, more and more of them converting to the right-handed form. Geophysicists have converted this reaction to a dating technique. Because living forms contain primarily L-isomers and fossil materials have mostly D-amino acids, the D-to-L amino acid ratio can be used as a measure of absolute age. The chemical reaction responsible for this change from L- to D-amino acids is called **amino acid racemization** (or simply **racemization**).

There is, of course, a catch. In order to use amino acid decomposition to estimate the age of an organic compound, it is first necessary to know the temperature history of that sample—both the temperature during which the sample was formed and also the temperature of the surrounding matrix (prior to archaeological excavation). Sometimes, the past temperature of an archaeological stratum can be derived from other materials buried in that stratum. Obsidian hydration, for instance, would provide one such cross-check. In other cases, on-site sensors can be employed to determine the modern sediment temperatures. And sometimes, it is necessary simply to estimate the ancient temperatures of the archaeological sediments in question.

This temperature estimate is critical in establishing the range of eggshell dating. Allison Brooks and her coworkers, for instance, figure that at normal sediment temperatures in the tropics and subtropics, the age range of eggshell amino acid should extend from modern times back to about 200,000 years. But in colder climates, the racemization rate slows down, meaning that in northern China and Mongolia, amino acid dating of eggshells could be accurate for up to 1 million years.

To be certain that their temperature estimates were reasonable, Brooks first explored a relatively recent archaeological site in the Kalahari Desert, in southern Africa. Various eggshell samples were easily datable using standard radiocarbon methods. Then she used the new amino acid dating method to date another eggshell fragment from the same strata. The dates obtained from the radiocarbon and amino acid methods corresponded so closely that the investigators decided that their dating experiment had potential.

So they moved to another site, this time at the other end of Africa, in the Sahara Desert of southern Egypt. They collected archaeological eggshell fragments from the site surface, using on-site sensors to estimate the effective temperatures. They then dated the fragments using both radiocarbon and racemization methods and found, as before, a satisfactory agreement between the two techniques. They moved to other archaeological sediments in the same area, comparing their new amino acid dates with stratigraphic ages obtained through other conventional techniques. Once again, the new method was able to mimic results obtained from established dating methods.

A Brief Warning About Arguments of Relevance

We have considered several current methods of obtaining chronometric dates for archaeological sites—and many more are currently available—but one important issue has yet to be addressed. In the section on dendrochronology, for instance, I said that tree-ring dating provides absolute dates for archaeological sites. Although this is true, it points to an important issue not yet discussed.

Archaeological sites can never be dated by simple equivalences. For example, a tree-ring cutting date provides the year, such as A.D. 1239, that a particular tree died. I also said that the UCLA radiocarbon laboratory dated 5,200-year-old tree charcoal in Horizon 2 at Gatecliff Shelter. By themselves, these dates tell us exactly nothing about archaeology. A dead tree assumes archaeological importance only when its death is somehow relevant to a human behavioral event of interest, such as the roofing of a pueblo room. The same argument applies to archaeology's other dating methods, which really only tell us when a clam died, or a piece of obsidian was broken, or a particular rock was heated.

In every case, the event dated must be demonstrated to be contemporaneous with a behavioral event of interest—building a boat, cooking a meal, or killing a deer. The demonstration of association is a key issue in archaeological dating.

Summary

Contemporary archaeologists are equipped with a powerful battery of techniques that can be used to date objects of the past. *Tree-ring dating* (dendrochronology) enables archaeologists to establish the precise year of death for many species of trees commonly found in archaeological sites. When properly correlated with known cultural events, these "cutting dates" can often pinpoint the exact occupation history of a site.

Radiocarbon dating is a physiochemical technique that monitors the degree of radioactive emission from organic specimens. During life, all plants and animals ingest atmospheric carbon (including C-14), and after they die, they cannot absorb any more C-14. Through the continuing process of radiocarbon decay, these C-14 molecules break down at a steadily decreasing rate. By determining the current rate of C-14 breakdown, one can estimate the length of elapsed time since the death of the plant or animal. Recently, physicists discovered that the atmospheric level of radiocarbon has changed somewhat over the last several millennia. Many archaeologists thus now "correct" their radiocarbon dates using an absolute chronology based on the radiocarbon dating of bristlecone pine samples of known age. New advances in accelerator-based radiocarbon methods permit archaeologists to use extremely small samples, vastly stretching the potential of the method.

Obsidian hydration is a microscopic technique that measures the amount of water absorbed into the freshly broken surface of an obsidian artifact or piece of waste chippage. The older the artifact is, the greater the degree of hydration.

Potassium-argon dating is an absolute technique that monitors the decay of potassium into argon gas. It involves assumptions similar to those of radiocarbon analysis. There must have been no argon trapped at the time of formation (that is, all argon must be the direct result of potassium decay), and all argon must be retained in the rock structure without absorption by the atmosphere. A variant of this technique, *argon-argon dating* is a high-precision method that dates single volcanic crystals, thereby eliminating important sources of potential contamination.

The maximum reliable age for radiocarbon dating is about 40,000 years and the minimum reliable age for K-Ar dating is roughly 200,000 years B.P. A relatively new dating technique, *amino acid racemization,* spans this critical gap by dating fragments of ostrich eggshells (which are commonly found in sites throughout Africa, the Middle East, and China).

Keep in mind that, by themselves, these various dating techniques tell us nothing about cultural activities. Dendrochronology, for example, can estimate only when a certain tree died; obsidian hydration tells us only when a certain piece of obsidian rock was fractured. In each case, the event being dated must be demonstrated to be coeval with a behavioral (cultural) event of interest.

It has taken the planet Earth 4.5 billion years to discover it is 4.5 billion years old.
GEORGE WALD, AMERICAN BIOCHEMIST AND NOBEL LAUREATE

Dating Techniques on the Internet

The Laboratory of Tree-Ring Research (University of Arizona) provides history and bibliography, plus software for the manipulation and analysis of tree-ring research.
http://www.ltrr.arizona.edu

Radiocarbon Homepage is provided by *Radiocarbon,* the main international journal for research articles.
http://packrat.aml.arizona.edu/

The CALIB Program for calibrating radiocarbon dates is available from the Quaternary Isotope lab.
http://weber.u.washington.edu/~qil/calib.html

The Oxford University Calibration Program (OxCal) can also be downloaded.
http://www.rlaha.ox.ac.uk/oxcal/oxcal_h.html

The Shroud of Turin Home Page has the latest on the shroud.
http://www.shroud.com/menu.htm

The Obsidian Hydration Analysis Service Home Page is another good resource.
http://www.pacific.net:80/~ohas/

CHAPTER 4

Chronology Building:
Low-Level Archaeological Theory in Action

❏ ❏ ❏

> ### PREVIEW
>
> *Archaeology commonly borrows methods, techniques, and theories from nonarchaeological colleagues. We saw this in the preceding chapter on dating techniques, which were heavily borrowed from chemistry, physics, geochemistry, and elsewhere. In later chapters, we shall also draw on the expertise of zoologists, botanists, and molecular biologists, to name just a few.*
>
> *Geology has been a particularly useful source of good ideas. It was geologists who first pulled together the major principles of the stratigraphic method. This chapter covers the concepts of superposition and index fossils—two extremely important stratigraphic principles that have been critical in our understanding of how the archaeological record has been put together.*
>
> *The index fossil concept has been directly incorporated into modern archaeological theory. For years, archaeology was almost totally artifact oriented—archaeological sites viewed as little more than mines in which to prospect for more artifacts. But gradually, archaeologists have shifted objectives, realizing that understanding the person behind the artifact is more compelling than the artifact itself. Today's archaeology has turned from simply filling up museum cabinets to discovering how people of the past actually lived.*
>
> *To do this, archaeologists have developed sometimes sophisticated methods linking artifacts with the human behavior that produced them. At the most fundamental level, artifacts must be accurately described; then they can be classified into meaningful categories. In this chapter, we look at how archaeologists classify artifacts into* temporal types, *using a specialized form of the* index fossil *concept.*
>
> *Here, we emphasize in particular the short-cut view of culture that archaeologists employ when building their chronologies. We use such time-markers to classify artifacts and also to build the larger, regional-level chronologies that tie together individual archaeological sites.*

> *Chronology is at the root of the matter, being the nerve electrifying the dead body of history.*
>
> BERTHOLD LAUFER (1874–1934), ARCHAEOLOGIST

Nicolaus Steno (1638–1687) initially formulated the **law of superposition.** Simply stated, Steno's law tells us that in any pile of **sedimentary** rocks undisturbed by folding or overturning, the strata on the bottom must have been deposited first. On a broader scale, this principle, almost preposterously simple, holds that–all else being equal–older deposits tend to be buried beneath younger ones. This canon facilitates the correlation of various geological exposures such as cliffs, stream valleys, and drill cores.

But geological correlation has its limits. It is impossible, for instance, to correlate geological exposures at the Grand Canyon directly with the white cliffs of Dover in England. Ever resourceful, our geological colleagues dreamed up a second principle, the **index fossil concept,** which assisted worldwide correlation.

This second concept is a bit more involved. In the early nineteenth century, a British surveyor named William Smith (1769–1839) began collecting data from geological strata throughout England. Smith gradually became enraptured by the fossils he found in various canals and vertical exposures. As he grew to understand the regional geology, he recognized that different exposures of the same **stratum** contained comparable fossils. Smith eventually became so knowledgeable that when somebody showed him a fossil, he could guess the stratum from which it had come.

Smith's French contemporaries were making similar discoveries. While mapping the fossil-rich strata surrounding Paris, Georges Cuvier (1769–1832) and Alexandre Brongniart (1770–1847) discovered that certain of their fossils were restricted to specific geological formations. After applying the law of superposition to arrange the strata in the proper chronological sequence, they then organized their fossil collection into the appropriate stratigraphic order. French fossil assemblages, it turned out, varied systematically according to the age of the parent strata. Cuvier and Brongniart then compared their fossils with modern species and discovered, as expected, that fossils characterizing later strata more closely resembled modern forms than did those of more ancient strata.

Fossils contained in a geological stratum thus became a clue to the relative age of the deposit. This is the *index fossil concept:* Rocks containing similar fossil assemblages must be of similar age. Obviously there are exceptions to both the index fossil concept and the law of superposition, but these two principles enabled geologists around the globe to correlate their stratigraphic sections into master chronologies. Both principles are likewise important as guideposts for interpreting the human record of the past.

Back in the first chapter, we examined Thomas Jefferson's eighteenth-century excavations in Virginia–generally acknowledged as the first application of stratigraphic principles to archaeology. Jefferson's firsthand stratigraphic observations enabled him to reconstruct the various stages of construction of the site he was exploring, suggesting its probable use as a burial feature. As it turns out, the stratigraphic techniques for analyzing archaeological sites have changed very little since Jefferson's time. The technology, of course, is vastly improved, but the bedrock philosophy is basically unchanged. Let me show you what I mean.

Fossil Footprints at Laetoli: The Law of Superposition in Action

Mary Leakey is one of the world's most famous fossil finders. Since the mid-1930s, she has scoured east Africa, seeking archaeological evidence of the earliest human ancestors who once lived there. With her esteemed husband, Louis Leakey, she electrified the world with finds that included the celebrated *Zinjanthropus* skull from Olduvai Gorge in northwestern Tanzania. To many, Mary Leakey's discovery of the "Zinj" cranium in 1959 heralded a new age, the beginning of modern paleoanthropological research in east Africa.

But, nearly two decades later, as she stood staring at the ground in a place called *Laetoli* (pronounced "lay-*toe*-lee"), it was Mary Leakey's turn to be shocked. As she dug down slowly, just below the surface of the Serengeti Plain, she found ancient footprints—hundreds of them—as clear as if they had been cast in fresh concrete. As always, she had been looking for fossils, any scrap of bone or tooth from which she might infer something about behavior in the remote human past. But here, at Laetoli, she found that early behavior was itself fossilized, right beneath her feet.

At some time in the remote past, a nearby volcano must have erupted, blanketing the landscape around Laetoli with a lens of very fine volcanic ash. Then

In Her Own Words

Finding the Famous Fossil Footprints
by Mary Leakey

They are the most remarkable find I have made in my entire career. As is often the case with important finds, the first of these animal tracks came to light in a rather unlikely way. Jonah Western, Kaye Behrensmayer and Andrew Hill were visiting us and one afternoon they were returning to camp after a long walk around the principal exposures.

For some reason they amused themselves by throwing lumps of dried elephant dung at each other and there was certainly plenty of it around in the flat open space where they were. Andrew fell down in the process and noted that he was lying on a hard surface which appeared to contain ancient animal footprints.

When we first came across the hominid prints I must admit that I was skeptical, but then it became clear that they could be nothing else. They are the earliest prints of man's ancestors, and they show us that hominids three-and-three quarters million years ago walked upright with a free-striding gait, just as we do today.

a light rain must have moistened the ash layer without eroding it, turning it into a thin slurry of concrete-like sediment. Various animals moved across this wet surface, apparently on the way to a nearby water hole: spring hares, birds, buffaloes, pigs, a saber-toothed tiger, and baboons—each leaving dozens of footprints in the gooey trackway. Before long, the ash layer dried, freezing the footprints in an enduring, rock-hard land surface.

But not only birds and 4-legged mammals had been there. At one point, a pair of very early hominids also strolled across the landscape. More than five dozen individual footprints clearly demonstrate a humanlike gait—fully bipedal with a stride and balance similar to our own. Across a distance of about 80 feet, two of our ancestors walked side by side, one larger than the other, close enough to touch each another. Were they mother and child? Male and female? One species or two? Almost everyone familiar with the evidence has one opinion or another, but the implications were clear.

If the evidence could be trusted—and if the presumed ancient age could be firmly established—these footprints would shatter one of paleoanthropology's most cherished concepts. For decades, specialists in human evolution had argued that upright posture—a preeminent human characteristic—must have arisen in response to tool use. After all, if you're going to make and use stone tools, it makes sense to have your hands free. But if Leakey was correct in her guess-dating of these, the world's oldest human footprints, they implied that our most ancient human ancestors were walking fully upright for more than a million years prior to the appearance of the oldest stone tools in the area. This was *big news!*

Let's Start With the Facts

The fossil footprints were contained in the upper portion of the so-called *Laetolil Beds,* within a geological subunit known as Tuff 7. The actual footprints were found near the bottom of the Tuff 7 formation in what Mary Leakey called, appropriately enough, the *Footprint Tuff.* But to determine the age of the footprints, it is necessary to place this key geological stratum within its appropriate stratigraphic context.

The geological investigation was spearheaded by Richard Hay from the University of Illinois (Urbana-Champaign). Over a period of 6 years, Hay worked out the complicated geological sequence at Laetoli, which can be summarized in the following generalized stratigraphic column:

Ngaloba Beds: sheetwash and mudflow deposits containing volcanic ash, pebbles, and cobbles

Olpiro Beds: volcanic tuff layers; maximum thickness about 20 feet (*Olpiro* is the name of a nearby village.)

Naibadad Beds: volcanic tuff layers; generally 35–50 feet thick

Ogol Lavas: a series of distinctive lava flows and ash deposits; in places, 750 feet deep (*Ogol* is the Masai word for "hard rock.")

Ndolanya Beds: sedimentary deposits; generally 60–75 feet thick; appear to be windblown

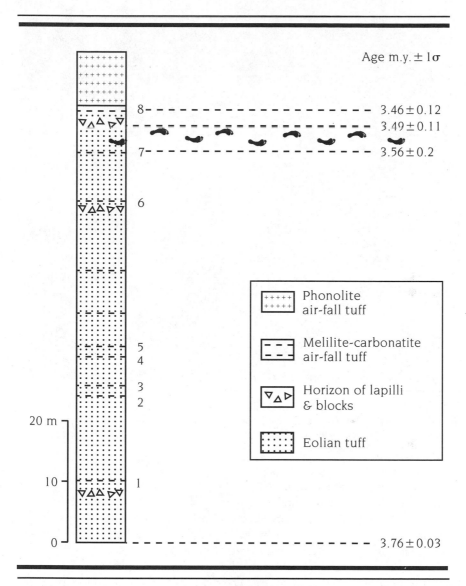

Detailed stratigraphic profile of dated tuff horizons within the upper unit of the Laetolil Beds.

Laetolil Beds: the basal stratigraphic unit, consisting of a complex series of compressed volcanic ash; in places more than 500 feet thick (*Note:* The name of the site is "Laetoli"; the basal formation is called the "Laetolil Beds.")

Hay clearly understood that the canons of good scientific fieldwork require that such primary data be published in detail to allow anybody to compare these field data with others recorded elsewhere. In the final report on Laetoli, these

Reconstruction of the early hominids (Australopithecus afarensis) *who made the 3.5-million-year-old footprints at Laetoli. Although the fossil-based proportions are accurate, many of the details (such as hair density and distribution, skin color, form of the nose and lips, and so forth) are entirely conjectural.*

descriptions run to more than 25 pages. Any qualified geologist would have generated comparable primary data.

But once these basic descriptive data are recorded, the objective shifts to interpretation. From evidence preserved on the surface of the Footprint Tuff, it was clear that the footprints had been buried rapidly, soon after they were formed. This accounts for their extraordinary state of preservation.

Geologists working at Laetoli could also infer something about the season in which the footprints were laid down. There was, for instance, no evidence of grasses at the base of the ash lens. This meant that the grass had probably been grazed off, leading the excavators to suggest that the eruptions took place during the dry season. But toward the middle of the Footprint Tuff, there is evidence that this surface was gently rained upon—actual raindrop impressions occur along with the footprints. Then, toward the upper part, widespread erosion occurs, which is attributed to full-blown rainy season downpours.

Therefore, the excavation team at Laetoli concluded, the Footprint Tuff must have been deposited over a short span of time, probably only a few weeks, beginning near the end of the dry season and lasting into the rainy season. This is an amazingly detailed reconstruction, based strictly on the available geological evidence.

Fine, but How Old Are the Footprints?

This is where the geological law of superposition comes to our immediate aid. Steno's law holds that, all else being equal, older deposits lie at the base of the stratigraphic profile.

So we work from the bottom up. The Laetolil Beds lie beneath the Ndolanya Beds: This is a geological fact. The law of superposition, applied to this stratigraphic fact, *suggests* that the Laetolil Beds *should be* older than the Ndolanya Beds: This is geological interpretation. Similarly, because the Ogol Lavas lie above both the Laetolil and Ndolanya Beds, these lavas should be younger still. And so forth. Because they lie uppermost in the stratigraphic column at Laetoli, the Ngaloba Beds should be the most recent of all. In each case, the law of superposition provides the interpretive key to unlock the *relative* stratigraphic sequence at Laetoli.

But to understand the age of the hominid footprints, we must move from relative to absolute dating methods. In the preceding chapter, we introduced the basics of *potassium-argon dating,* which was used to pin down the date of the famous footprints at Laetoli.

Beginning in 1975, Leakey and her research team began working with Robert Drake and Garness Curtis, geologists from the University of California (Berkeley), who processed a series of potassium-argon dates on samples from the major stratigraphic units recognized in the Laetoli area. The oldest date, from the base of the Laetolil Beds, is 4.32 ± 0.06 million years. The youngest date is 2.26 ± 0.06 million years, from near the top of the stratigraphic column (in the Naibadad Beds). The dates of intermediate age (between 3.76 and 2.41 million years) occur from strata sandwiched in the middle of the stratigraphic column. Note particularly how this suite of dates follows in precise stratigraphic order, from most ancient (at the bottom) to most recent (at the top). In this case, absolute dating technology confirms the stratigraphic sequence inferred from Steno's law.

The stratigraphic profile sets out results of additional potassium-argon dating conducted on specific tuff horizons within the Laetolil Beds. This sequence is important because, you will remember, the Footprint Tuff occurred near the bottom of Tuff 7 in the Laetolil Beds. In the more detailed stratigraphic section, the various numbered tuff horizons are dated by four K-Ar dates, ranging in age from 3.76 to 3.46 million years. As with the site as a whole, the dates within the Laetolil Beds fall into perfect stratigraphic order.

Finally, we can answer the single most important question at Laetoli: The fossil hominid footprints (located near the bottom of Tuff 7) must be somewhere between 3.76 ± 0.03 and 3.56 ± 0.2 million years old.

This depositional sequence, inferred entirely from the stratigraphic column, provides the basic chronological sequence at Laetoli; and the law of superposition was the key that unlocked the stratigraphic sequence. Nothing in the interpretation by Hay departs radically from that arrived at by Thomas Jefferson in 1784.

Although it is true that modern scientists have more precise and sophisticated technology, I am confident that had he been able to travel to Laetoli, Thomas Jefferson would have interpreted the **stratigraphy** in exactly the same way that Leakey and Hay did.

Unlocking the Stratigraphy at Gatecliff Shelter

Laetoli was, of course, an archaeological site—one of the world's most famous. Because of the peculiar circumstances of the Laetoli footprints—no artifacts, no household refuse, no construction debris—the basic contexts surrounding the Footprint Tuff were geological, so the principle of superposition could be applied directly.

But the human hand is applied more directly to most archaeological sites, creating stratigraphy that can be considerably more complicated to interpret. Gatecliff Shelter was one of these cases, and the stratigraphic profile encountered there illustrates some of quandaries involved in the workaday archaeological situation.

During our first three seasons at Gatecliff, I recorded and interpreted the Gatecliff stratigraphy myself. Drawing upon my somewhat limited classroom training in geology, soil science, and microstratigraphy, I drew and described the gross stratigraphy. This master profile served as the major descriptive device throughout the excavations.

As the field season wound down, it became clear that Gatecliff was too complex for me to continue the geological interpretation. This is not unusual in archaeology. On small-scale digs, archaeologists must often cover all the bases, from stratigrapher to photographer, from engineer to camp cook. But as the operation expands, specialists must be recruited to take over selected aspects. The trick is for an archaeologist to recognize the critical line separating flexibility from irresponsibility.

At Gatecliff, I was in danger of crossing over that fine line, so we soon arranged for some experienced Great Basin geologists to join the team. Although each had somewhat different ideas—and some rather heated debates took place—the diversity fostered a better overall interpretation of the stratigraphic column.

Over a decade, we had exposed a remarkably well stratified profile, more than 40 feet deep, spanning the last 7,000 years. Gatecliff Shelter has textbook stratigraphy, and that is why I discuss it here.

The Gatecliff profile resulted from a complex interplay of natural and cultural factors. The master stratigraphy demonstrates how two very different kinds of deposits resulted from each set of processes. The thin dark levels (such as those numbered 9, 11, and 13) are living surfaces, or cultural horizons. Each dark horizontal band represents a single campsite. The 16 cultural horizons occurred as the result of human habitation, and these surfaces contain the fire hearths, broken stone tools, grinding slabs, flakes, food remains, and occasional fragments of basketry and cordage.

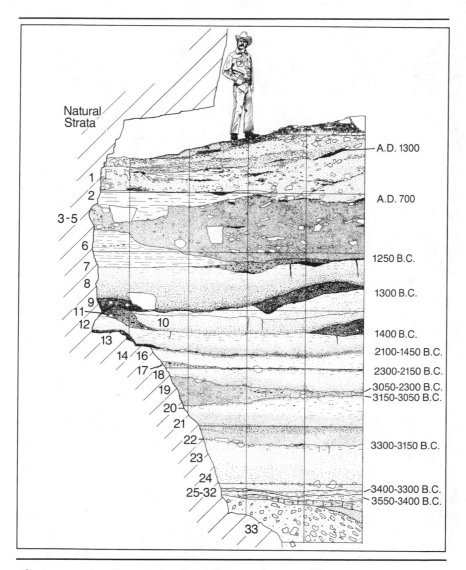

The master stratigraphic profile from Gatecliff Shelter. The standing figure is exactly 6 feet tall and the grid system shows 1-meter squares. Only the upper 33 of the 56 stratigraphic units are listed in this particular profile.

What makes Gatecliff so unusual is that living surfaces were capped by sterile, noncultural layers of purely geological origin. After the excavation was finished, we divided up the Gatecliff profile into a sequence of 56 geological strata: layers of more or less homogeneous or gradational sedimentary material, visually separated from adjacent layers by a distinct change in the character of the material deposited. Table 4.1 summarizes 36 of these strata.

Table 4.1
Part of the Physical Stratigraphy of Gatecliff Shelter

STRATUM	SOIL	NATURE OF DEPOSIT	FIELD DESIGNATION	CULTURAL ASSOCIATION	AGE (C-14 YR. B.P.)	DATE (C-14 YR. A.D./B.C.)
1	S-1	Rubble	GU 14	Horizons 1–3	0–1250 B.P.	A.D. 700–present
2		Sand and silt	Upper GU 13	—	1250 B.P.	A.D. 700
3	S-2	Rubble	Part of GU 12	Part of Horizon 4	1250–1350 B.P.	A.D. 600–700
4	S-3	Sand and silt	GU 13 & GU 12 Silt	—	1350 B.P.	A.D. 600
5		Rubble	Part of GU 12	Parts of Horizons 4, 5, 6	1350–3200 B.P.	1250 B.C.–A.D. 600
6		Sand and silt	GU 11	—	3200 B.P.	1250 B.C.
7		Rubble	GU 11 & GU 10R	Horizon 7	3250–3200 B.P.	1300 B.C.–1250 B.C.
8		Sand and silt	GU 10	—	3250 B.P.	1300 B.C.
9		Rubble	GU 9R	Horizon 8	3300–3250 B.P.	1350 B.C.–1300 B.C.
10		Sand and silt	GU 8 A&B	—	3300 B.P.	1350 B.C.
11		Rubble	GU 7R	Horizon 9	3400–3300 B.P.	1450 B.C.–1350 B.C.
12		Sand and silt	GU 7	—	3400 B.P.	1450 B.C.
13		Rubble	6 Living floor	Horizon 10	4050–3400 B.P.	2100 B.C.–1450 B.C.
14		Sand and silt	GU 5 Silt	—	4050 B.P.	2100 B.C.
15		Rubble	Part of GU 5	—	4100–4050 B.P.	2150 B.C.–2100 B.C.
16		Sand and silt	Part of GU 5	—	4100 B.P.	2150 B.C.
17		Rubble	GU 4	Horizon 11	4250–4100 B.P.	2300 B.C.–2150 B.C.
18		Silty sand	GU 3	—	4250 B.P.	2300 B.C.
19	S-4	Sand and rubble	GU 2	Horizon 12	5000–4250 B.P.	3050 B.C.–2300 B.C.
20		Silt and clay	GU 1A	Horizon 13	5100–5000 B.P.	3150 B.C.–3050 B.C.
21		Sand and silt	GU 1 & GU 7-74	—	5100 B.P.	3150 B.C.
22		Rubble	GU 6R-74	Horizon 14	5250–5100 B.P.	3300 B.C.–3150 B.C.
23		Gravel, sand, and silt	GU 6-74 & GU 5-74	—	5250 B.P.	3300 B.C.
24		Rubble	GU 4R-74	Horizon 15	5350–5250 B.P.	3400 B.C.–3300 B.C.
25		Silt	GU 4-74	—	5350 B.P.	3400 B.C.
26		Rubble	GU 3R-74	Horizon 16	5550–5350 B.P.	3550 B.C.–3400 B.C.
27–29		Silts	GU 3A-74	—	5500 B.P.	3550 B.C.
30		Sand	GU 3B-74	—	5500 B.P.	3550 B.C.
31		Rubble	GU 2R-74	—	5700–5500 B.P.	3750 B.C.–3550 B.C.
32		Fine sand and silt	GU 2-74	—		
33		Fine sand and silt	GU 12-76, GU 1-78 & GU 1-74	—		
34		Silt and very fine sand	GU 2-78	—		
35		Rubble	GU 3R-78	—		
36		Silty medium sand	GU 3-78	—		

SOURCE: From Thomas, (1983b), Table 3.

Some strata resulted from small ponds that occasionally formed at the rear of Gatecliff Shelter. The pond water acted as a sink for windblown dust particles, which settled out as finely laminated silts. Other strata consist of coarser sediments grading from gravels at the bottom to fine sand silts at the top. Apparently, the ephemeral stream flowing in front of Gatecliff Shelter occasionally flooded and surged through the shelter. The water of these flash floods would first deposit coarse sediments such as pea-sized gravels. As the water's velocity diminished, its carrying capacity decreased, and smaller particles would be deposited. Finally, when the water slowed, the tiniest silt particles would cap the stream deposits. Such floods occurred several times throughout the 7,000 years of deposition at Gatecliff, and each time the previous occupation surface was immediately buried. When the inhabitants returned to Gatecliff, they thus lived on a new campsite, separated from the previous one by as much as 2 feet of sterile alluvial sediments.

Fifty-six such depositional strata were stacked up inside Gatecliff Shelter. The accompanying box gives a detailed description of Stratum 22; it was written by our three project geologists (Jonathan Davis, Wilton Melhorn, and Dennis Trexler) and me. Note the detail of description. Exact depths are given relative to a central-site datum point, arbitrarily assigned a zero value of 0.0 meters. (Actually, the Gatecliff datum is 2,319 meters [7,606 feet] above sea level.) When paired with our horizontal grid system, these arbitrary elevations document the exact configuration of each geological stratum.

Each geological term is sufficiently well defined so that geologists who have never visited Gatecliff can still understand what Stratum 22 looked like. Note also how we separate such descriptions from our interpretation. This way, others can use our data to make their own assessments (disagreeing with us, if they wish). Geoarchaeologists sometimes use the term *stratification* to refer to the physical layers in a site, reserving *stratigraphy* for the geoarchaeological interpretation of the temporal and depositional evidence.

You can also see how we dated Stratum 22. Forty-seven radiocarbon dates were processed on materials from Gatecliff, and four dates were available from this particular stratum. This information, combined with the added radiocarbon evidence from adjacent strata, allowed us to estimate that Stratum 22 was laid down between about 5,250 and 5,100 years ago.

Other strata at Gatecliff provided different clues to help date the site. Stratum 55, near the very bottom of the site, contained an inch-thick lens of sand-sized volcanic ash (**tephra**)—fragments of crystal, glass, and rock once ejected into the air by a volcanic eruption. Not discovered until the last week of the last field season, the tephra was indistinct, mixed with the cobbles and rubble of Stratum 55. In the laboratory, however, geoarchaeologist Jonathan O. Davis—a leading expert on the volcanic ashes of the American West—confirmed that this ashy deposit was Mount Mazama ash. When this mountain in the Oregon Cascades blew up 6,900 years ago, it spewed out 11 cubic miles of pumice and related materials; the caldera formed by the Mazama explosion now contains Crater Lake. The Mount St. Helens eruption in 1980 was a cherry bomb in comparison. The

Physical Stratigraphy at Gatecliff Shelter

STRATUM 22, RUBBLE: Angular limestone clasts, charcoal firepit, and baked area at top, somewhat churned into the underlying silty top of Stratum 23. Maximum thickness 50 cm. on the southwest pile and formed continuous layer up to 15 cm. thick in eastern parts of excavation, but was discontinuous elsewhere. Almost as voluminous as Stratum 17, the top was about −4.85 m. on the southwestern pile and ranged from −5.50 to −5.30 m. elsewhere, and its bottom was about −5.30 m. in the southwest corner, −5.35 m. in the Master Profile, and −5.32 m. in the present excavation. Radiocarbon dates from Stratum 22, or from the surface on which it lay, are:

QC-290	4850 B.P. ± 95
UCLA-1926B	5370 B.P. ± 90
UCLA-1926F	5480 B.P. ± 80

The following radiocarbon date is also from this surface, but seems about 1,000 years too young if compared to the other dates:

QC-292	4140 B.P. ± 125

Stratum 22 was deposited by gradual accumulation of roof fall and talus tumbling over the shelter lip between 5,250 and 5,100 years ago. Stratum 22 was called GU 6R-74 in the field and contained cultural Horizon 14.

prevailing winds, coupled with the force of the explosion itself, carried Mazama ash across the western United States. Wherever the ash settled out, it created a "marker-bed." **Tephrochronology** has become a valuable tool for dating sites in volcanically active areas. When Davis found the Mazama ash at the bottom of Gatecliff, we had a critical, independent check on the largely radiocarbon-derived chronology at Gatecliff, and so we knew that Stratum 55 must be 6,900 years old.

In truth, I am not certain whether I would have recognized the volcanic ash at the bottom of Gatecliff. At Mummy Cave (Wyoming), near Yellowstone National Park, the excavators confused the thin layers of Mazama ash with wood ash; the important tephra lens was later recognized under the microscope. Fortunately, the Mazama tephra at Gatecliff was instantly recognized by Davis. Both cases highlight the importance of having specialists work on-site, during excavation.

Gatecliff is like a giant birthday cake. The sterile strata are the layers and the cultural horizons are the icing capping each layer. Both strata and horizons contained datable artifacts and ecofacts that could be used to reconstruct the human events and environmental background. Several of these studies will be introduced later. But the important point is that such objects would be relatively useless in archaeology had it not been for the stratigraphically controlled contexts in which they were recovered.

The Index Fossil Concept

Geologists proposed the law of superposition rather early in the game, in 1669! But fossils did not become a worthwhile tool for geological correlation until much later, during the early nineteenth century. So whereas an archaeologist like Thomas Jefferson could apply principles of superposition to his excavations, his successors had to wait nearly two centuries to learn—once again from geologists—how the index fossil concept might make human artifacts useful tools in dating archaeological sites.

Diagnostic Artifacts: Archaeology's Version of Index Fossils

Nels Nelson, one of archaeology's forefathers extolled in the first chapter, is generally credited with one of the very first uses of the index fossil concept in stratigraphic archaeology in the Americas. In 1912, the president of the American Museum of Natural History, Henry Fairfield Osborne, sent Nelson on a tour of European archaeological sites to bone up on the most recent methodological innovations (and also, not coincidentally, to round up collections of artifacts to be displayed in New York). While at Castillo Cave in Spain, Nelson participated for several weeks in excavating tightly stratified Paleolithic remains. Like Gatecliff Shelter, the Castillo grotto deposits, roughly 45 feet thick, comprised 13 archaeological strata ranging from Paleolithic times through the Bronze Age. Nelson was staggered by the fine-scale stratigraphic divisions possible at Castillo, and he eagerly looked for similar sites on his return to the American Southwest the next year.

But in his initial stratigraphic excavations in the Galisteo Basin (south of Santa Fe, New Mexico), Nelson was bitterly disappointed. It turned out that the trash heaps of the Southwest tend to be badly jumbled, not at all like the crisp strata found in European caves. Although he tested several sites, Nelson's **middens** contained either too short a time span or they had been riddled by prehistoric grave digging.

Nelson finally came across the stratigraphy he was seeking at Pueblo San Cristobal (ironically, the site where he had been working for the past three seasons). As he returned to San Cristobal in 1914, Nelson was determined to try out a new stratigraphic method.

Selecting an area with minimal disturbance, Nelson isolated a block of debris measuring 3 feet by 6 feet wide and nearly 10 feet deep. Clearly the midden had accumulated over a long interval, and several discrete kinds of pottery were buried here. But there was still a problem because the greasy black midden lacked the sharp stratigraphic divisions Nelson had seen in the Paleolithic caves of Europe. How do you dig stratigraphically without perceptible strata?

Not one to be easily deterred, Nelson did the next best thing: He created his own stratigraphy. First dividing his test block into 1-foot vertical sections, Nelson dug each level in the way he had learned to dig the strata in Europe, accurately cataloging the sherds recovered by level. To Nelson, the only difference was that the Castillo Cave strata were readily discernible, whereas the "stratigraphy" at San Cristobal was arbitrarily imposed as 12-inch levels. Apparently mistrusting his workmen to maintain proper controls, Nelson later noted, "I performed this work with my own hands, devoting fully three days to the task." Imposing arbitrary levels on nonvisual stratigraphy seems almost pedestrian today, but in 1914, Nelson's stratigraphic method was a dazzling and revolutionary innovation, immediately seized by New World archaeologists as a fundamental of excavation.

Given these arbitrarily imposed divisions, Nelson could apply the principles of superposition to look for culture change within a midden column. All else being equal, the oldest trash should lie at the bottom, capped by more recent accumulations. Even though the dense midden lacked tangible stratigraphy, Nelson began to search for time-markers in the form of diagnostic pottery **types.** The concept is precisely that of the index fossil, developed a century before by geologists Cuvier and Brongniart. Just as geologists had learned to distinguish certain extinct life-forms as characteristic of various rock strata, so too could archaeologists use diagnostic artifact forms to characterize (and hence date) strata across archaeological sites.

So it was that Nels Nelson applied the index fossil concept to the prehistoric ceramics of San Cristobal. Pottery was a natural choice, as sherds were the most common cultural debris and Nelson knew that ceramic styles varied considerably across the American Southwest. More than 2,000 sherds turned up in the 10-foot test section at San Cristobal. First grouping the sherds into obvious stylistic categories, Nelson then plotted their distribution according to depth below the surface (see Table 4.2). Column 1 contains the frequency of corrugated pottery, the most common everyday cooking ware. Because the relative frequency of corrugated sherds remained fairly constant throughout the occupation of San Cristobal, Nelson rejected Column 1 as a potential index fossil. Column 2 tabulated the frequencies of "biscuit ware," a dull whitish yellow pottery that Nelson felt was traded into San Cristobal from someplace else. But these frequencies did not change markedly throughout the stratigraphic column either, and so biscuit ware also was rejected as a potential time-marker.

Nelson then turned to the three remaining kinds of pottery—which he termed Types I, II, and III—and discovered, just as Cuvier and Brongniart had with their French fossils, that certain forms were associated with specific stratigraphic levels. The most ancient levels at San Cristobal contained a predominance of black-on-white painted pottery (Nelson's Type I). Type I sherds were most numerous below the 8-foot mark and only rarely recovered above 7 feet. Type II pottery—red, yellow, and gray sherds ornamented with a dark glaze—occurred most commonly above the 7-foot mark.

Table 4.2					
Potsherd Frequencies From Pueblo San Cristobal, New Mexico					
DEPTH BELOW SURFACE	CORRUGATED WARE (1)	BISCUIT WARE (2)	TYPE I (BLACK-ON-WHITE) (3)	TYPE II (2-COLOR GLAZE) (4)	TYPE III (3-COLOR GLAZE) (5)
1st foot	57	10	2	81	5
2nd foot	116	17	2	230	6
3rd foot	27	2	10	134	3
4th foot	28	4	6	93	0
5th foot	60	15	2	268	0
6th foot	75	21	8	297	1?
7th foot	53	10	40	126	0
8th foot	56	2	118	51	0
9th foot	93	1?	107	3	0
10th foot	84	1?	69	0	0
Total	649	83	364	1,283	15

SOURCE: From Nelson (1916), p. 166.

This evidence meant that Type I sherds were "diagnostic" of the 8-foot and below strata and the Type II sherds characterized the upper deposits. The Type III pottery (three-color glazed ware), though rather rare at San Cristobal, appeared only in the uppermost levels of Nelson's column. This made sense, as three-colored wares were still being made when the Spaniards arrived in New Mexico in the sixteenth century.

Creating simulated stratigraphy was a brilliant stroke, and remains today the preferred method of excavation whenever visible stratigraphic units are absent. Nelson's arbitrary levels made possible the definition of three important time-markers (archaeology's equivalent to index fossils). Not only did he document the specific ceramic changes at San Cristobal, but the presence of these pottery types elsewhere provided clues to the age of undated archaeological deposits.

Kidder Does Nelson One Better

Nels Nelson thus blazed the trail, but it remained for A. V. Kidder to put Nelson's stratigraphic method on the map. Kidder visited with Nelson at the San Cristobal dig and shortly thereafter adapted Nelson's technique for use at his own large-scale excavations at Pecos Pueblo, less than 25 miles to the southeast. From his earlier research, Kidder surmised that, like San Cristobal, the early Pecos sequence was characterized by black-on-white pottery, followed by a later phase in which glazed ceramics predominated. The last of these, the Glaze 5 period, arose sometime before the Spanish conquest and survived until nearly 1680.

By 1915, Kidder had located several rich deposits laid down during the later phases, but the early black-on-white period was poorly represented. Kidder resolved the next year to uncover the earliest Pecos occupation. Unlike modern searchers—who can call on nondestructive, noninvasive remote sensing techniques—Kidder dug a series of long exploratory trenches, cut at intervals of 100 feet or so. Finding almost no refuse on the barren west slope of Pecos—probably owing to the fierce prevailing west winds that still buffet the Pecos valley—Kidder shifted his trenching to the leeward side of the ruin. Just inside the defensive perimeter, Kidder located a series of chambers with razed walls rising less than 18 inches. When only black-on-white rubbish was found stacked against these walls, Kidder knew he had found the earliest dwelling at Pecos. Here indeed lay the founding settlement, the nucleus of Pecos Pueblo. Burials interred in the black-on-white rubbish comprised the first Pecos cemetery. The succeeding Glaze 1, 3, and 4 walls were built south of this early occupation, and they in turn were swamped by tons of Glaze 5 and 6 trash.

Kidder's Pecos investigations verified Nelson's techniques again and again. By carefully following the course of the various trash heaps, characterized by the time-marker sherds, Kidder reconstructed the several centuries of habitation at Pecos Pueblo. And when walls or burials were encountered, they could be dated by applying the index fossil concept to the associated midden.

Types of Types

We need more rather than fewer classifications, different classifications, always new classifications, to meet new needs.

J. O. Brew (1906–1988), archaeologist

Archaeology's basic unit of classification is termed a type. Be careful here because *type,* like *culture* and *personality,* is an everyday word appropriated by anthropology and reassigned a specific, nonintuitive meaning. Artifact types are abstract, ideal constructs artificially created by the archaeologist to make sense of past material culture.

Although archaeologists excavate specimens, they analyze types. Rather than poring over each of the thousands of individual items recovered on a dig, archaeologists usually abstract them into a few (dozen) carefully selected typological categories. Artifact types come in all shapes and varieties, and the naked word *type* must never be applied without an appropriate modifier. One must always describe precisely which type of type one is discussing.

The same objects can, of course, be classified in many ways. Think about a familiar set of modern artifacts, say, a workshop of woodworking tools. Carpenters classify their tools by function—hammers, saws, planes, files, drills, and spokeshaves. But when insuring a carpenter's workshop, the insurance agent uses another set of classifications, sorting these same tools into new categories such as

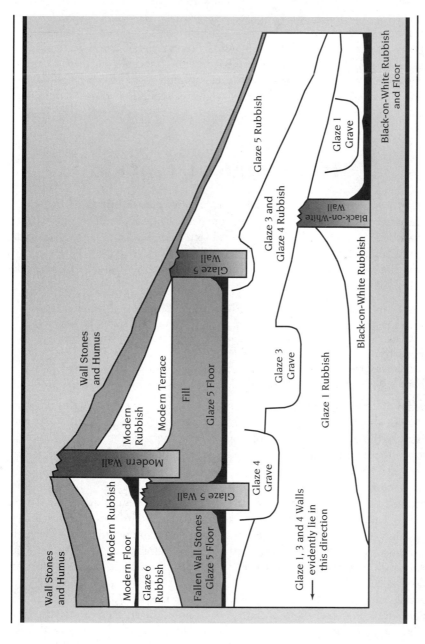

Kidder's cross section of Pecos Pueblo, showing walls, burials, and ceramics.

Wall Stones and Humus

Modern Rubbish

Modern Floor

Glaze 6 Rubbish

Fallen Wall Stones
Glaze 5 Floor

Glaze 1, 3 and 4 Walls
evidently lie in
this direction

Wall Stones
and Humus

Modern
Rubbish

Modern Terrace

Fill

Glaze 5 Floor

Modern Wall

Glaze 5 Wall

Glaze 4
Grave

Glaze 5
Wall

Glaze 5 Rubbish

Glaze 3 and
Glaze 4 Rubbish

Glaze 3
Grave

Glaze 1 Rubbish

Black-on-White
Wall

Glaze 1
Grave

Black-on-White Rubbish

Black-on-White Rubbish
and Floor

"flammable" and "nonflammable" or perhaps according to replacement value: "under $10," "between $10 and $25," and so on. Should the carpenter relocate, the furniture movers will group these same tools into another set of divisions such as "heavy" or "light," "bulky" or "compact," or perhaps (if you're lucky) "fragile" and "nonbreakable."

The point here—and the crux of archaeological classification in general—is this: Each classification must be formulated with a specific purpose in mind. Archaeology has no general, all-purpose classification; the more classifications the better. Archaeologist Irving Rouse urged archaeologists to ask continually, "Classification—for what?"

Morphological Types

Modern observers exploring the range of material remains left by an extinct group will encounter many unfamiliar, even meaningless, artifacts. To make sense of the past using these remains, the first analytical step is to describe the artifacts carefully and accurately by grouping them into *morphological types*.

Emil Haury, an eminent Southwestern archaeologist, drafted one such description in his report on Ventana Cave, Arizona:

> *Discs*—Of the twenty-four stone discs, twenty-two are centrally perforated. They were all made of schist, from 36 to 75 mm. in diameter and averaging 8 mm. in thickness. The customary way of producing them was by breaking and then smoothing the rough corners by abrasion. . . . Only one was well made. . . . Drill holes are bi-conical and not always centrally placed. Two were painted red. Next to nothing is known about these discs.

Haury did not even speculate what the disks were used for. But he did illustrate and describe them in enough detail so that contemporary and future colleagues can visualize the artifacts without having to view them firsthand. Such bald description is the primary function of a morphological type (often termed a *class* in archaeological literature).

Morphological types have a second basic property: They are abstract. Types are not artifacts but are composite descriptions of many similar artifacts. Accordingly, every morphological type must encompass a certain range of variability: Several colors may have been applied; the quality of manufacture might vary; absolute size usually fluctuates; and so forth. W. W. Taylor called this abstract quality an *archetype* to emphasize the elusive "ideal form" implicit in every morphological type.

Establishing types at this level merely groups like with like. Nelson simply concentrated on the most flagrant differences among the stacked-up potsherds on the table. Forget for now the complex issues of why pottery changes, how the pottery was made, or what different kinds of pottery were used for. Interesting issues perhaps, but they can be resolved only during a later stage of analysis.

Temporal Types in Prehistoric Archaeology

To reiterate our earlier caution: The naked word *type* must never be applied without an appropriate modifier. Archaeologists use the term in so many ways that it is essential to distinguish which type of type is meant. So far, we have dealt strictly with morphological types, defined for baseline descriptive purposes. We now turn to a second, more important type, the **temporal type** (or **time-marker**). As the name implies, temporal types help archaeologists monitor change through time.

Perhaps without knowing it, you already took the first step toward defining a workable set of time-markers, by grouping the individual artifacts into morphological types. The next step is to see which of the morphological categories has significant temporal associations. If morphological type B occurs only in strata dating between A.D. 500 and 1000, then this descriptive type can be elevated to the status of a temporal type. This promotion is useful because when artifacts belonging to temporal type B turn up in undated contexts, the dates A.D. 500 to 1000 become the most plausible hypothesis.

Southwestern Ceramic Time-Markers

Nels Nelson's San Cristobal ceramic **typology** illustrates the process. Step 1 was to sort the 2,300 sherds into five piles. After naming each category, he published concise descriptions so that other archaeologists could see how the classification was defined. Nelson then turned to the stratigraphic distribution of each morphological type. Two such types—corrugated and biscuit ware—were distributed throughout the 10-foot section. Nelson concluded that these categories were useless for chronological purposes, and so he put them aside. But the frequencies of three other types changed markedly through the stratigraphic profile at San Cristobal, and he devoted considerable time to discussing the temporal significance of his Types I, II, and III.

Procedures haven't changed much since 1914, but the terminology has. In the modern idiom, the five piles of potsherds were morphological types, basically descriptive hypotheses to be tested against the stratigraphic record. Only three morphological types (Types I, II, and III) passed the test. Because of their demonstrated stratigraphic significance, Nelson elevated them to the status of temporal types. When sherds of these three types were found in new, undated contexts, the San Cristobal stratigraphic associations suggested further temporal hypotheses for testing.

And these hypotheses have indeed been tested. Nelson's Type I, the early black-on-white pottery, is now known as Santa Fe Black-on-White (note the convention for naming ceramic types: place name first, followed by key description). Tree-ring dating suggests that Santa Fe Black-on-White was first made about A.D. 1200, remaining popular until about A.D. 1350. Nelson's Types II and III (the two-color and three-color glazed pottery) are now placed in a ceramic series called Rio Grande Glaze (a *series* is a higher-level category, grouping together several

Nelson's Type I pottery (Santa Fe Black-on-White: A.D. 1200–1350).

Nelson's Type II pottery (Rio Grande Glaze, two-color: A.D. 1300).

Nelson's Type III pottery (Rio Grande Glaze, three-color: A.D. 1300).

Nelson's Type IV pottery.

similar temporal types). Rio Grande Glaze ceramics show up in sites dating about A.D. 1300, the later types running into the historic period. In short, Nelson's temporal hypotheses have been wholly confirmed and refined by techniques not yet invented in 1914.

Temporal types are important stepping-stones. But once the time-markers are suitably in hand, it is necessary to go beyond the specifics of stratigraphy and dating techniques to view culture in its full systemic context.

Seriation

One powerful upshot of the typological concept is *seriation,* a technique that permits archaeologists to place stylistic periods into a relative chronological sequence. Unlike absolute dating procedures such as radiocarbon and dendrochronology, seriation works strictly with qualitative, relativistic ordering.

Seriation implicitly assumes that people are fickle: Sometimes styles change; sometimes new technologies arise. Most such new ideas are slow to catch on, with only a few pioneers participating in the fad. But fashions have a way of becoming chic in one group, eventually replacing earlier vogues, and then gradually falling into disuse.

Curves like this often assume a characteristic form. As illustrated in the accompanying diagram, new lighting technologies are gradually introduced, flourish for a while, and then slowly disappear. In the mid-nineteenth century, most houses in Pennsylvania were illuminated by candles and oil lamps; only a few households had gas lamps. But over the next 50 years, more and more families switched to gas lights. Those who could not afford such installations started using kerosene lamps (made possible by the growing petroleum industry in Pennsylvania and elsewhere). By the turn of the century, gas lights had virtually disappeared. Then along came another invention, electricity, and incandescent light bulbs started lighting the houses of Pennsylvania in increasing numbers. By 1940, "everybody" had electric lights, the gas and kerosene lamps fading into nostalgia.

The shape of such popularity curves, which struck James Ford as somehow "battleship shaped," established the basis for seriation. By arranging the proportions of temporal types into lozenge-shaped curves, one can determine a relative chronological sequence. The classic late nineteenth-century example of such ordering was made by Sir Flinders Petrie, who examined the contents of hundreds of Egyptian graves. After studying the ceramics, Petrie "seriated" the pottery styles in time simply by looking at the characteristics of the handles.

This same phenomenon is evident in Nelson's sherd counts from San Cristobal Pueblo (refer again to Table 4.2). When San Cristobal was first built, ceramics

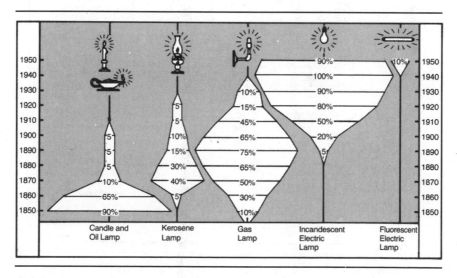

Seriation diagram showing how methods of artificial illumination changed in Pennsylvania between 1850 and 1950.

were most commonly decorated with black-on-white painting. Moving up Nelson's stratigraphic column, two-color glaze rapidly takes over in popularity, with black-on-white embellishment fading out. Near the top of the column, three-color pottery comes into use. The town dump at San Cristobal faithfully preserved these ceramic fads, helping archaeologists date the prehistoric sites of the American Southwest.

Artifacts tend to "seriate" in stratified deposits. This principle of seriation has been adapted by archaeologists to create a relative dating technique that works in the absence of stratified deposits.

All seriation diagrams implicitly assume that the observed variability is due to temporal change; that is, only the shared aspects of culture (styles) are reflected

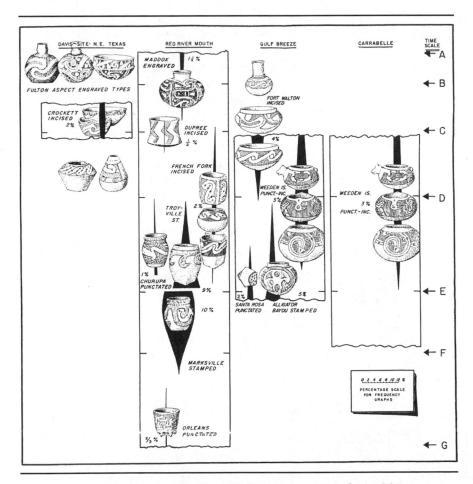

Cultural-historical archaeology in action. James Ford's 1952 presentation of unimodal curves representing pottery type frequencies, with illustrations of vessels of each type also on the chart. Here, Ford attempted to correlate the ceramic sequences from northeast Texas, Louisiana, and Florida.

in frequency change through time. Of course this assumption will be incorrect in many cases, because artifact frequencies often reflect functional, technological, and societal variability as well. When too much nontemporal variability is reflected, the collections simply do not seriate very well.

Time-Markers in Historical Archaeology

Over the years, historical archaeologists have developed an impressive array of dating techniques suitable for historic-period artifacts. The same basic principles of classification apply to prehistoric and historic-period archaeological sites, but the specific procedures vary somewhat.

Pipe Stem Dating

Changing technology has created a vast array of time-marker artifact types in historical archaeology: Before 1830, the fiber of the metal ran crosswise to the axis of a nail; after that, the fibers ran lengthwise. Nineteenth-century glass often had a purplish cast (caused by sunlight reacting with magnesium oxide, but magnesium was no longer added after World War I). Examples proliferate endlessly.

Historical archaeologists have been particularly clever in finding increasingly fine-grained ways to partition time on their sites. One classic way to date colonial-period American sites was developed at mid-century by J. C. "Pinky" Harrington. Clay tobacco pipes changed form markedly in the seventeenth and eighteenth centuries, and broken fragments turn up by the hundreds on many archaeological sites of this period. Everybody recognized that clay pipes held great potential as time-markers: They were manufactured, imported, smoked, and thrown away, all within a year or so. Some people studied changes in pipe bowl shape. Others observed that stem thickness also changed through time. Stem length bore a direct relationship to period of manufacture, starting with 6-inch to 8-inch pipes in the early seventeenth century and extending to the long "church warden" pipes of the early eighteenth century. The trend then reversed itself, ending in the short-stem pipes made during the nineteenth century.

Each method has merit, but the same problem plagued each one because the fragile clay pipes rarely survived in a condition sufficiently complete to allow fruitful analysis. While working with the pipe collection from Jamestown, including some 50,000 small chunks of broken stems, Harrington observed that the early pipe stems seemed to have relatively large bores which became smaller in the later specimens. Following up on this, Harrington measured the stem hole diameters for a series of 330 known-age pipes from Jamestown and Colonial Williamsburg (Virginia) and Fort Frederica (St. Simons Island, Georgia).

It turned out that inside diameter did indeed change through time, and systematically at that. The resulting pipe stem chronology began in 1620 and lasted

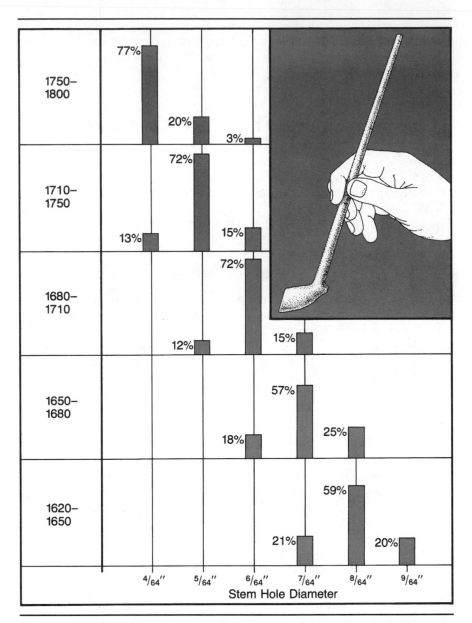

J. C. Harrington's diagram showing how he used pipe stem hole diameters to date archaeological sites.

through 1800. Harrington divided this period into five cultural periods. Best of all, the technique was simple and cheap. As Harrington put it, "in making use of this dating device, the first requirement is a 39-cent set of drills; the second is common sense."

Fifteen years later, Lewis Binford decided Harrington's method was "clumsy" and reworked the original data to derive a statistical regression formula for estimating age from the size of pipe stem holes:

$$Y = 1931.85 - 38.26X$$

where X is the mean stem bore for a sample of pipe fragments and Y is the projected mean date. In effect, Binford moved the technique from a series of ordinal categories to the more precise (but not more accurate) metric estimates. Archaeologists have debated the pros and cons of pipe stem dating ever since, many investigators ignoring Harrington's original cautions and "commonsense" strictures.

Documentary Evidence to Define Time-Markers

Nothing about the pipe stem example differs from procedures used in prehistoric archaeology. Harrington began with empirical observation, tested his notions against known-age controls, and then formulated his time-markers; Binford simply streamlined the estimates. But in many cases, those working on historic sites have a decided advantage over those studying prehistoric remains because historical archaeologists also have access to documentary evidence that can help create even finer-grained temporal divisions.

One particularly handy method has been the study of period paintings to learn more about ancient artifact forms. When Kathleen Deagan was researching the shapes of Hispanic bottles used in the New World, for instance, she was dismayed to find that although green and clear glass littered sixteenth-century sites, not a single complete bottle from this period survived anywhere in Florida and the Caribbean. But rather than simply give up, she temporarily turned art historian because bottles, it turns out, are frequently depicted in sixteenth-century Spanish art, such as *The Last Supper* by Juan de Juanes. Such paintings provided rare clues to unknown forms of Hispanic bottles, and Deagan was able to construct a chronological sequence of bottle forms abstracted largely from such paintings.

Noël Hume considered the role that paintings can play in reconstructing British colonial artifact forms. One particularly illuminating source is William Hogarth, an eighteenth-century English artist whose paintings, drawings, and engravings depict a vast spectrum of everyday, domestic artifacts of the time. For instance, in the well known tavern orgy scene from Hogarth's series *The Rake's Progress,* done in 1735, a roving rake sprawls in Rose Tavern, charmed and robbed by an obliging cadre of trollops, awash in artifacts of their day: chairs, clothes, caps, a watch, drinking glasses, plates, a sword, candlesticks, and so forth. Working from an enlargement of this print, the observant historical archaeologist should be able to learn plenty about artifact styles typical of the first third of the eighteenth century, right?

Perhaps, but historical archaeologists have learned to be cautious in evaluating the historical accuracy of surviving documents and commentary. Some paintings are as good as photographs. Historical archaeologists have concluded, for instance, that most artists in the Dutch and Flemish traditions can be trusted to render faithfully both people and objects. These artists sat directly across from the subjects they painted.

But Hogarth is a problem because his own writings suggest that most of his creations came from memory, often assembled from sketches squirreled away in his files. Sure enough, when specialists study the orgy scene, they find his rendering of everyday items is suspect: The brickwork is unrealistic; the scimitar-shaped knife wielded by the young lady is all wrong; and the bottles are about 30 years too early for the period of the print. Hogarth had learned how to draw

Circa 1550   Circa 1550   Circa 1630

CA 1640   CA 1700   CA 1750   CA 1760

Some of the sixteenth-century bottle forms found in archaeological sites throughout the Caribbean.

The Last Supper *by Juan de Juanes (ca. 1550). The bottle forms evident in paintings like this assist historical archaeologists in building temporal types.*

The orgy scene from An Evening at the Rose Tavern: The Rake's Progress, Scene III, *engraved in 1735 by William Hogarth.*

a bottle during his early life, and kept on drawing that type, ignoring the changes that had taken place in the intervening years. Noël Hume concluded that "in all probability, therefore, having drawn, say, a rat trap two or three times, Hogarth knew what a rat trap looked like and thenceforth extracted it from his memory 'prop room' whenever he needed it. Consequently, every trap he drew looked more or less the same, no matter whether it had been outmoded by new and better rat traps developed later on in his life." This case underscores the general point that historical archaeologists must be discriminating when dealing with documentary evidence.

Basic Units of Regional Archaeology

This chapter has set out the methods by which archaeologists construct their cultural chronologies. But before moving on to more advanced archaeological objectives, we must still consider how these temporal types are synthesized into chronologies extending beyond the individual site. In effect, time-markers are the first building blocks laid down to create the foundations of regional chronology.

Americanist archaeology has adopted a relatively standardized framework for integrating chronological information on a large scale. This regional infrastructure was initially set out by Harvard archaeologists Gordon Willey and Philip Phillips in their influential book, *Method and Theory in American Archaeology,* published in 1958. Although nomenclature still varies somewhat from region to region, the framework proposed by Willey and Phillips remains the most generally accepted system in the Americas.

Remember how temporal types are defined: You group individual artifacts into relatively homogeneous categories (morphological types), and then test them against independent data (such as site stratigraphy, correlation with other known sites, and direct artifact dating). Morphological types found to change systematically are elevated to the status of time-markers.

The next analytical step is to determine how temporal types themselves cluster to reflect site chronology. The first critical unit in the synthesis is called a **component,** a culturally homogeneous stratigraphic unit within a single site. "Culturally homogeneous" is the buzzword here, the line separating homogeneous and heterogeneous often existing only in the excavator's mind. Many archaeological sites contain only a single component; that is, the artifact assemblage is essentially homogeneous (with respect to time) throughout the entire site. Most archaeological sites contain more than one component.

Because defining archaeological components rests on the intangible factor of cultural homogeneity, there can be no firm rules. At sites like Gatecliff Shelter, the strata are strikingly obvious from the stratigraphic profile. Throughout most of the site, distinct lenses of sterile, noncultural silts separate the deposits into discrete living floors. These various surfaces can then be kept distinct (as individual components) or grouped together on the basis of shared time-markers or absolute dates. Gatecliff contained five distinct cultural components, each incorporating one to six living surfaces. Elsewhere, at places like Pueblo San Cristobal, the trash heaps had been churned and mixed. Although components still existed, they bled stratigraphically one into another without visible breaks. In such cases, components must be isolated analytically, without the assistance of obvious physical stratigraphy.

Components are thus site specific. But the components from several sites must usually be analytically combined to define the master regional chronology. The next analytical step is the **phase**: similar components as manifested at more than one site. The phase has become the practicable and intelligible unit of archaeological study, defined by Gordon Willey and Philip Phillips as "an archaeological unit possessing traits sufficiently characteristic to distinguish it from all other units similarly conceived . . . [and] spatially limited to the order of magnitude of a locality or region and chronologically limited to a relatively brief interval of time."

Like the component, the phase concept is encumbered by weasel words like "sufficiently characteristic," "similarly conceived," and "relatively brief interval." No matter how hard archaeologists try, some degree of wishy-washy subjectivity lingers, and decisions still rely heavily on simple familiarity with the archaeological data at hand.

At Gatecliff Shelter, we recognized five components, each defined by shared time-markers and radiocarbon dates. The uppermost component was characterized by such time-markers as Desert Side-Notched and Cottonwood Triangular projectile points, and Shoshone Brownware ceramics. It began in about A.D. 1300 and lasted until Anglo-American contact, about 1850 in central Nevada. The other components were similarly defined, each composed of different temporal types and spanning other episodes of time.

When talking only about Gatecliff, the analytical unit remains the component. But actually we excavated nearly a dozen sites in Monitor Valley, and several of these sites contained a late assemblage similar to that recognized at Gatecliff. At the site level, these assemblages comprise a component. At a regional level, similar components are synthesized into a phase, which we named Yankee Blade after a nineteenth-century silver mine in nearby Austin.

Look at the following figure that diagrams the relationship between component and phase. Three archaeological sites have been tested within a region, and as is often the case, no single site contains the complete cultural sequence: The first site has components A and B; the second site contains a new component called C; and the third site has components A and C but lacks component B. By analyzing the temporal types shared among the components and comparing the absolute dates, a regional sequence of phases can be constructed from evidence at these three sites.

The component is site specific, whereas the phase spans an entire region. So defined, the phase becomes archaeology's basic unit of areal synthesis. To ensure that the phase concept remains viable in practice, the definition is left purposely vague. Phases can be as short as a few generations, especially in areas where the chronology is based on dendrochronologically controlled painted ceramics. The length of the phase depends in part on the kind of archaeological remains involved

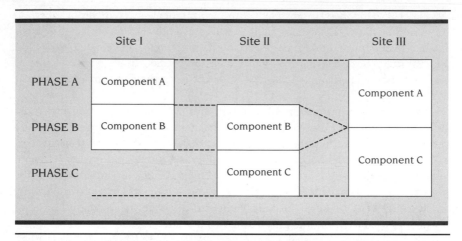

Relationship of archaeological sites to the analytical concepts of "component" and "phase."

and also on our contemporary knowledge of these remains. Well studied areas tend to have shorter phases.

The phase concept allows archaeologists to treat time, actually a continuous variable, as if it were a set of discrete points. The overall Gatecliff Shelter sequence lasted for about 7,000 years, and "years" are a perfectly viable way to think of time. But "years" can create difficulties in archaeological sites. We found it better to view Gatecliff in terms of five components, one stacked on another.

Each component has an associated array of dates and a set of characteristic artifacts. Gatecliff components can be compared with components at other nearby sites, and a regional chronology can be constructed. Using the phase as our smallest unit, we can establish regional contemporaneity. Strictly speaking, two events can never be truly "contemporary," even if we measure time in millimicroseconds. Time has no intrinsic units, and the smallest subdivision can always (at least in theory) be subdivided.

The job of archaeology's phase concept is to impose a set of minimal units on time, and the phase is that minimal unit. When we discuss the Yankee Blade phase, we are treating the time span from A.D. 1300 to A.D. 1850 as if it were an instant. By definition, two components of the Yankee Blade phase are simultaneous, provided that "simultaneous" is understood to last 550 years. As knowledge of the Yankee Blade phase expands, we may be able to distinguish divisions within the phase. It might be possible, for instance, to distinguish an early Yankee Blade component from a late Yankee Blade component. When this happens, the initial phase is segmented into *subphases.* This increasing subdivision reflects the amount of research accomplished on each phase and underscores the degree to which our knowledge of the archaeological record is a contemporary phenomenon.

Culture Chronology Versus Culture History

Archaeology's *chronological* aim makes two assumptions:

1. Variability not attributable to time (and/or space) is irrelevant.
2. Temporal variability is best isolated by monitoring only shared cultural behavior.

In *chronological* analysis, the archaeologist addresses only the isolated segments of the archaeological record that differ across time and/or space. This assumption is simplistic, to be sure, for the archaeological record contains plenty of nontemporal, nonspatial variability. But it is precisely this complexity that leads us to simplify. For chronological purposes, any source of variability other than temporal or spatial is random noise and temporarily irrelevant.

Let us look at the case of Shoshone pottery to make one final point. Such ceramics appear suddenly in many parts of the Desert West about A.D. 1300, and the Shoshone people are known to have made similar pottery until about 1860. Shoshone brownware pottery thus implies certain limits involving time (A.D. 1300–1860) and space (the Desert West). Note that the early boundary (A.D. 1300) is only an estimate derived from radiocarbon dating, whereas the late date (1860) is based on historical documentation. The initial 1300 date is thus subject to considerably more error than is the termination date. Such is often the case with time-markers, but this disproportionate error will cause no particular difficulties so long as we recognize it.

Its temporal parameters suitably estimated, Shoshone pottery becomes a useful time-marker in the chronology of the Desert West. Sites containing lots of these potsherds can be tentatively assigned to the A.D. 1300–1860 interval (subject, of course, to independent verification by suitable dating techniques).

But Shoshone pottery, taken as a time-marker, leaves many more questions unanswered. What about the origins of the Desert West ceramic complex? Was this post-1300 pottery introduced as the result of a migration of Shoshone-speaking peoples? Did the idea of pottery simply spread across the Desert West? Or did the peoples of the Desert West independently invent the idea of pottery?

These are not easy questions, and answering them requires a deep, thorough understanding of the local cultural history. Is it possible to document a population movement across the Desert West at A.D. 1300? If so, where did these newcomers come from? And what happened to the pre-1300 inhabitants of the Desert West? What conditions would allow the replacement of one group of hunter-gatherers by another group? Are there signs of warfare in A.D. 1300? Did the climate change to render the pre-1300 adaptation untenable, thereby enabling the Shoshone to invade the Desert West? Could it be that a ceramic-using population moved into the Desert West and intermarried with the previous inhabitants? Did the ecological adaptation somehow change to make ceramic vessels more efficient after A.D. 1300? Were the vessels actually manufactured in the Desert West, or were they traded in from neighboring ceramic-manufacturing areas? If so, what did Desert West peoples trade for the ceramics, and why did this exchange begin only after A.D. 1300?

Data-free questions like these can pile up without apparent end. The point here—and a compelling point indeed—is that the mechanics of cultural change cannot be understood strictly by looking at time-markers. By definition, we base our time-markers on selected aspects of shared culture; time-markers deliberately ignore most of what is cultural. Obviously, questions such as diffusion, migration, and independent invention are complex, reflecting changes in the overall cultural matrix. Time-markers are patently inadequate for unraveling the mechanics of cultural systems.

Thus it is that we distinguish between **cultural chronology** and cultural history:

- A *cultural chronology* documents a temporal and spatial change in selected artifacts.
- A *cultural history* documents what people actually did.

Cultural chronology does not equal cultural history.

The time-marker Shoshone pottery tells us that distinctive potsherds occur in archaeological deposits dating from A.D. 1300 to 1860 across the Desert West. But viewed as a time-marker, Shoshone pottery tells us nothing about why pottery was introduced in 1300. For some reason, one segment of the Desert West cultural system changed, and people began using (if not manufacturing) pottery. This complex issue can be studied only by pursuing related shifts in the lifeway, drawing evidence from the settlement pattern and demography, cultural ecology, social organization, and religion. If one posits that the pottery was introduced through the people's physical migration, then a second cultural system must be examined: the system operative in the area from which the newcomers migrated.

Cultural history cannot be understood merely by using time-markers; a broader perspective is required. Time-markers document only changes in material culture (as reflected by selected kinds of artifacts); they do not tell us why such changes have occurred.

This warning is repeated several times throughout the text. It is a critical point that speaks to the very objectives of archaeology. You cannot study the more sophisticated aspects of the human past until you have a chronology, and your chronology must be based on reliable time-markers. Once your chronology has been thoroughly refined and repeatedly tested, then you are free to explore the rest of culture—provided you redefine the basic units of analysis. Do not confuse the initial, chronological objectives of archaeology with the more sophisticated aims to be considered later in this book.

Summary

Archaeologists love to pirate useful techniques and concepts from other disciplines. When dealing with stratigraphy, they have relied on two essential geological principles. The *law of superposition* holds that (all else being equal) older geological strata tend to be buried beneath younger strata, and the *index fossil concept* states that strata containing similar fossil assemblages must be of similar age. Exceptions exist, but these principles have enabled geologists around the world to correlate individual stratigraphic sections into master chronologies. Archaeologists commonly use the law of superposition to unravel complex sequences of stratification within archaeological sites. They have also modified the index fossil concept for use in archaeological contexts. Changing ceramic patterns, for example, become clues for stratigraphic interpretation and correlation.

We also discussed ways in which archaeologists establish and monitor such cultural change. Artifacts are the material cultural remains of human activity, and the *type* is the basic unit of artifact analysis, an idealized construct that allows archaeologists to transcend individual artifacts to consider more generalized categories. The *morphological type* reflects the overall appearance of a set of artifacts, emphasizing broad similarities rather than focusing on specific traits. Morphological types are descriptive, enabling the archaeologist to summarize large sets of individual artifacts into a few ideal categories. The *temporal type* serves a more specific function, to monitor how artifacts change through time. Temporal types are best defined through stratigraphic analysis, by using the index fossil concept.

Seriation is a relative chronological method that also enables archaeologists to follow systematic artifact change through time. Seriation operates on the implicit assumption that stylistic change tends to begin gradually and then to pick up speed as the style catches on. After this peak of popularity, the frequency of the style tapers off gradually, until it disappears entirely. Thus relative popularity takes on a characteristic "battleship-shaped" curve when plotted on a seriation diagram.

Historical archaeologists have been particularly clever in finding increasingly detailed ways to partition time on their sites: dating small fragments of tobacco pipe stems, evaluating evidence for time-markers in period paintings, and extracting a mean occupation date by averaging ceramic dates of manufacture across entire assemblages. But despite such differences—and the fine-grained results they produce—the basic procedures and assumptions behind artifact classification differ little between historical archaeology and archaeology in general.

The next analytical step is to see how the time-markers themselves cluster to reflect site chronology. The first critical unit in the synthesis is called a *component,* a culturally homogeneous unit within a single site. Components are site specific, but similar components at different sites can be synthesized into *phases* that are archaeological units of internal homogeneity, limited in both time and space. In general, phases comprise the basic archaeological building blocks for regional synthesis.

Archaeologists derive scant comfort from fact that over and above the certainties of death and taxes, they are blessed with the additional constant of a seemingly limitless quantity of sherds to classify.

PRUDENCE M. RICE, ARCHAEOLOGIST
(SOUTHERN ILLINOIS UNIVERSITY)

Chronology Building on the Internet

The U. S. Geological Survey maintains an excellent home page.
   http://www.usgs.gov

The National Park Service provides general visitor information on Pecos National Historical Park.
   http://www.nps.gov

Analytical Software/BASP provides plenty of statistical aids–including seriation–for archaeologists.
   http://www.lib.uconn.edu/ArchNet/Software

Jamestown Rediscovery includes emphasis on recent archaeology and fieldwork opportunities.
   http://www.apva.org

Williamsburg has a Web site with information on guided tours.
   http://www.williamsburg.com/wol/tour/tour.html

Ft. Frederica National Monument also has a Web site with useful information.
   http://www.nps.gov/fofr

CHAPTER 5

Fieldwork:
Why Archaeologists Walk Straight Lines and Dig Square Holes

❑ ❑ ❑

PREVIEW

Now the fun begins. In this chapter, you will see what it's like actually to do archaeology. For many of us—myself certainly included—fieldwork is why we became archaeologists in the first place. This said, there are two important warnings that every introduction to archaeological field technique should begin with:

- *There is no "right" way to look for and excavate sites (but there are plenty of wrong ones).*
- *Nobody ever learned how to do proper archaeological fieldwork from a book (even this one).*

Despite recent advances, archaeological fieldwork remains as much craft as science. All we can do here is look at some common techniques, some archaeological standards and conventions, and, perhaps most important of all, what it feels like to participate in an archaeological exploration.

> X *never, ever marks the spot.*
>
> INDIANA JONES (IN *INDIANA JONES AND THE LAST CRUSADE*)

Every archaeologist addressing a general audience will, sooner or later, be asked the same question: How do you find your sites? *How do you know where to dig?*

There are as many answers as archaeologists. Some **archaeological sites** have been known for centuries—they were never lost. The mythical locations of other sites have been handed down through the generations, preserved in oral and written traditions. For example, the site of Tula in northern Mexico was finally identified as the prehistoric Toltec capital by tracing and testing Aztec traditions. Sites are sometimes deliberately discovered in large-scale systematic surveys, during which entire valleys or islands are scanned for the remains of previous habitation. But some of the best archaeological sites in the world were found by accident. Hard work and luck help, too.

Let's begin by exploring some of the ways to find sites. Many archaeologists—and, once again, I include myself here—feel that it's much more fun to find the sites than it is to dig them.

Good Old Gumshoe Survey

Let me begin with a brief recap of my own experiences in finding Gatecliff Shelter, Nevada. In several places throughout this text, we will return to excavations at Gatecliff as an example of how Americanist archaeology actually works in practice. But before we could excavate Gatecliff, we had to find it.

My experiences at Gatecliff Shelter are probably typical. While working in the Reese River Valley of central Nevada one summer, we assembled our field crew for steak dinners in the nearby town of Austin. In the high desert, "nearby" meant taking a dusty ride for an hour or more, but the push seemed worth it. We relaxed, gnawed T-bones, and spun rattlesnake and stuck-truck stories into the morning hours.

Austin is small-town America, and when two dozen grubby archaeologists come to town for steaks and beverages, word soon gets around. When our waitress politely inquired who was in charge and somebody pointed to me, she told me about her husband, a mining geologist who had prospected the western mountains for 40 years. There are few places Gale Peer had not been. So when we met, I asked him about any archaeological sites he might have seen. We were hoping to find a local cave or rock shelter with some stratified cultural deposits, in order to check our Reese River findings.

Mr. Peer indeed knew of such a cave—over in Monitor Valley, a dozen miles east of Austin. "There are pictures of people and animals," he told us, "plus a lot of writing I don't understand. Top of the shelter's caved in. Maybe in an earthquake. There's not much of the cave left. Drive out there when you get a chance. I'd like to know what's in that cave." He sketched a map on his business card. He remembered exactly where the cave was relative to the canyon, but he was not sure exactly which canyon. I stashed the card in my shirt, and thanked him for the tip.

This is the essence of gumshoe survey—hanging out in saloons and gas stations, listening to those who know more about the landscape than you do. I hoped that Mr. Peer's advice was as good as his memory seemed to be. Maybe this was the deep cave site I'd been looking for. But of course I had heard of a dozen similar caves, all of which proved uninteresting when investigated.

It took us nearly a year to find Mr. Peer's rock shelter. Beginning at the southern end of Monitor Valley, we drove up and down each side canyon, slowly working our way north. We would see something, stop the truck, and skitter up the hillside. But each time, it turned out to be a shadow, an abandoned mine shaft, or just a jumble of boulders. Finally, as we started up Mill Canyon, a brooding black cliff loomed ahead. The scarp was riddled with small caves and rock shelters. We became more and more discouraged as we moved upcanyon, scanning each small alcove for pictographs.

The deepest stratigraphic sounding at Gatecliff Shelter. The archaeologists are making detailed maps of strata evident in the vertical sidewalls. Standing about 40 feet below the modern ground surface, they are pointing to strata deposited about 7,000 years ago.

Only one section remained to be inspected, where the black cherty formation was swallowed up beneath the alluvial Mill Canyon bottomland. The paintings were not visible until we crawled into the mouth of the cave. There they were, just as Mr. Peer had said a year before: small human figures, painted in red and yellow pigments. On the other wall were cryptic motifs in white and black. And, yes, the roof had caved in years before. Half the floor was buried beneath tons of chert. One boulder would have dwarfed the truck we had left in the canyon.

So we decided to excavate a small **test pit** in the floor of the cave. Old World archaeologists sometimes call these exploratory excavations **sondages.** I always like the ring of that word—what class. In Nevada, we just call them test pits.

The first day's finds were not impressive: several pieces of broken bone, a few of them charred, and a dozen stone flakes, probably debris from resharpening stone knives or projectile points. Not exactly treasure, but we knew that at least one prehistoric flintknapper had paused here to ply his craft. Still, we were

---

In His Own Words

What Archaeological Survey Was Like in 1907
by A. V. Kidder

In the first chapter, we mentioned Ted Kidder's baptism into Southwestern archaeology. Here is Kidder's own account of the way in which he and two fellow Harvard undergraduates were instructed to conduct their archaeological survey through the mesas and canyons of the Colorado Plateau:

Thursday, July 4th [1907]: Up, as usual in this country at four, to take advantage of the delicious hours of the early morning and forenoon. At ten or eleven the heat of the day comes on and lasts till after four. We pitched our tent, as this is to be our headquarters for some time, unpacked our duffle-bags and with Mr. Hewett started up the mesa that separates the canyons of the McElmo and the Yellow Jacket. It is usual, he told us, to find sites on mesas that overlook the junctions of important drainages, so we walked out along its flat sage-brush covered top. Near the tip we found a partly fallen zig-zag wall set with a tower. It extended clear across the mesa, defending the end. Mr. Hewett predicted a pueblo on the protected tip and, sure enough, this lay a bit further out. It was entirely gone except for the butts of a few walls.

My diary says very little of what we look out upon. I think I was dazed by that view, my first of such a vast desolation; naked red rock below and all about, mesas, pinnacles, ragged canyon walls, sheer cliffs. I must, too, have been a bit overcome by what Mr. Hewett so casually told us we were to do. He waved an arm, taking in it seemed, about half the world, "I want you boys to make an archaeological survey of this country. I'll be back in three weeks."

So much for explicit research designs (but they sure did find plenty of neat new sites).

disappointed. The rock art already spoke of the occasional prehistoric visitor. We were looking for something more.

Across the sagebrush campfire that night our small crew assayed the finds. The rock art was neat; only two similar sites were known in the central Great Basin. The stones and bones were suggestive enough, but the shelter seemed hardly the deep site we had hoped for all year. It probably had stratigraphy like most desert caves, so jumbled that they look as though they had been rototilled. At best, our test pit results were borderline.

As it turned out, we were wrong about this site, which we eventually called Gatecliff Shelter, after a local geological formation. The site came to dominate my archaeological life for more than a decade. The prehistoric deposits were not a few feet deep, as I had initially thought. Gatecliff turned out to be 40 feet deep, maybe the deepest rock shelter in the Americas. The strata were also not mixed as I first feared. Over the millennia, the shelter had been inundated every so

Twenty-one-year-old A. V. Kidder (right) and Jesse L. Nusbaum conducting an archaeological survey at Mesa Verde (Colorado) in 1907.

often by flash floods. The surging waters laid down thick layers of mud, forming an impenetrable cap of rock-hard silt. This flooding occurred at least a dozen times, stratifying the deposits into horizontal "floors."

Gatecliff had what textbooks—including this one—describe as "layer-cake stratigraphy." The shelter had been occupied for much longer than just the last few centuries, as I had thought at first. Gatecliff was old, at least 7,000 years old, as radiocarbon dating would later establish. The sediments also contained ample evidence about the past environments of Monitor Valley.

Once I came to the American Museum of Natural History in New York, I ultimately convinced the museum to dispatch five major field expeditions to Gatecliff Shelter. More than 200 people helped excavate the site over the years. In addition to supporting part of the fieldwork, the National Geographic Society prepared an educational film about the site. They also wrote a book about our excavations at Gatecliff. The *New York Times* and *The New Yorker* magazine published stories about Gatecliff. Then there was television and radio. Even a United States congressman became involved in the struggle to preserve the site. Gatecliff Shelter was decidedly on the map.

And that is how we found Gatecliff—through a fortunate combination of happenstance, hard work, and trial-and-error. James O'Connell calls the process *gumshoe survey* because such rudimentary archaeological reconnaissance closely resembles detective work: Set out a problem, get some leads, track them down, and if you're fortunate, you crack the case. In archaeology, "cracking the case" can mean turning up just the right site to answer a question that's bothering you.

How to Find a Lost Spanish Mission

Let me also tell you something about Mission Santa Catalina, a site lost somewhere in Georgia's Sea Islands for more than 300 years. I had the good fortune of leading the team that rediscovered this lost Franciscan mission. The story of how we did it shows yet some other ways that archaeologists are learning about the archaeological record, this time drawing on space-age technology.

But first, a word of background about this little-known chapter of American colonial history. At its seventeenth-century zenith, Spanish Florida had three dozen Franciscan missions, each a satellite settlement heavily dependent on the colonial capital at St. Augustine. To the west lived the Timucuan, Apalachee, and Apalachicola Indians; to the north, toward St. Catherines Island, lay the province of Guale. Although a dozen sixteenth- and seventeenth-century missions once existed in the present state of Georgia, not one such mission site could be identified archaeologically when we began our search for Santa Catalina.

Like many historians and archaeologists before us, we felt that the lost mission of Santa Catalina lay along the western margin of St. Catherines Island, a 14,000-acre tract 50 miles south of Savannah. Unique among the so-called Golden

Isles, St. Catherines Island has not been subdivided and suburbanized. The Georgia-based, not-for-profit St. Catherines Island Foundation owns the island and strictly regulates a comprehensive program of research and conservation. This enlightened and progressive land management policy ensured that Mission Santa Catalina was not destroyed beneath the crush of condos and fast-food joints that typify too many of the southern barrier islands.

In 1974, when I first visited St. Catherines Island, the combined French, English, and Spanish historic documentation supplied only vague geographic clues; and although several first-rate archaeologists had previously worked on the island, none had successfully located this important mission site.

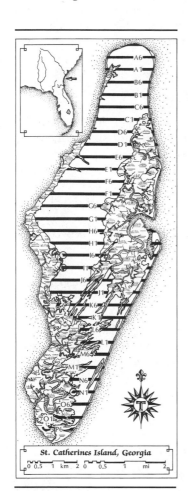

Systematic transect research design used to derive a 20 percent regional randomized sample on St. Catherines Island (Georgia). Occurrences of sixteenth- and seventeenth-century Spanish ceramics have been circled.

Virtually uninhabited, St. Catherines Island is today blanketed with dense forest, briar patches, and almost impenetrable palmetto thicket. When we began our search for Santa Catalina, I was overwhelmed by the huge area involved. We knew so little that I could not overlook any portion of St. Catherines Island.

A Randomized Transect Approach

By its nature, archaeological fieldwork is slow and tedious—and nobody could (or should) excavate an entire island—so we began by random sampling. We worked out a method requiring that the archaeological team walk a series of 31 east-west transects, each 100 meters wide. Our crews attempted to follow a specific compass heading without deviating from the survey transect. This randomized approach forced us to look into the most unlikely, inaccessible places (even when we didn't expect to find anything).

Using a **transect sampling strategy,** we took a 20 percent randomized sample of the archaeology of St. Catherines Island, looking for, among other things, the lost mission of Santa Catalina de Guale.

Our survey turned up 135 mostly unrecorded archaeological sites, ranging from massive shell middens to isolated shell scatters. We investigated each site with two or more 1-meter-square test units, in all excavating more than 400 such test pits. Viewed from the air, the island began to look like Swiss cheese, except that the holes were square.

Controlled survey sampling told us that sixteenth- and seventeenth-century Spanish ceramics occurred at only 5 of the 135 archaeological sites, all but one along the western perimeter of the island. The ruins of Mission Santa Catalina almost certainly lay buried in a target area the size of 30 football fields along the southwestern margin of the island.

But 30 football fields is still a huge area to dig with dental pick and camel hair brush. Moreover, although our confidence was growing, we were forced to admit almost complete ignorance of what we were looking for. Did Santa Catalina survive merely as heaps of sixteenth- and seventeenth-century garbage? Or could we realistically hope to find evidence of buried buildings as well? Clearly it was time to scratch the surface.

A Power Auger Approach

Looking around for better ways to find the needle hidden in this haystack, we learned from Kathleen Deagan about her successful search for sixteenth-century St. Augustine. She and her students had used a gasoline-powered posthole digger and excavated hundreds of round holes. Following her lead, we did the same on St. Catherines Island. With this noisy, nasty machine, two people can dig a 3-foot-deep hole in less than a minute. The power auger throws up a neat doughnut of dirt, to be hand-sifted for artifacts.

Once the field testing was complete, we identified all materials recovered and plotted the distribution in a series of simple dot-density maps. Since then, a number of readily available computer programs have greatly assisted the data conversion process. But even using the hand-plotted maps, the power auger data allowed us to focus further field evaluation on a single 100-by-100-meter square in the overall sampling grid for St. Catherines Island.

In effect, then, the simple and expedient auger testing narrowed our search area from 30 football fields to a target zone smaller than 3 acres. Although we found broken Guale Indian pottery almost everywhere we dug in that area, diagnostic mission-period artifacts were largely restricted to a single, well circumscribed area. By 1981, we had defined this 100-meter-square area as the most probable location for the central mission complex.

A Proton Magnetometer Approach

So-called Quad IV was a totally undistinguished piece of real estate, covered by typical scrub palmetto and live oak forest. The only evidence of human occupation was a little-used field road for island research vehicles. Although aboriginal shell scatters could be seen here and there, Quad IV betrayed absolutely no surface clues of what lay below.

At this point, we shifted our field strategy once again, switching from preliminary subsurface testing to noninvasive, nondestructive **remote sensing.** Choosing the right method depends on what you expect to find. What, exactly, were we looking for? For more than a century, Santa Catalina had been the northernmost Spanish outpost on the eastern seaboard, and this historical fact implied considerable size and permanence. The seventeenth-century mission must have had a fortified church, some buildings to house the soldiers and priests, plus enough granaries, storehouses, and dwellings for hundreds of Guale Indian neophytes.

We reasoned that the mission buildings had been built by a **wattle-and-daub** technique. Freshly cut timbers were probably set vertically along the walls and reinforced with cane woven horizontally between the uprights. This sturdy wattle-work was then plastered ("daubed") with a mixture of marsh mud, sand, and plant fibers (probably Spanish moss). Roofs were thatched with palmetto.

So constructed, wattle-and-daub buildings are biodegradable. Left to nature, the roof will go first; if it does not burn off, the thatch will either blow away or simply rot. And once directly exposed to the weather, mud and twig walls will simply wash away. Archaeologists seeking such a dissolved mission would soon be out of business.

But if we were lucky—and many archaeologists would secretly rather be lucky than good—the mission buildings would have burned, firing and hardening the daub walls, like a pot baking in a kiln. Fired daub, nearly as indestructible as the ubiquitous potsherd, thus became a key in our search for Santa Catalina.

But how do you find chunks of fired daub buried beneath a foot of sand? It turns out that the marsh mud used in daub plaster contains microscopic iron particles. When intensely heated, the particles orient toward magnetic north—like a million tiny compass needles. To pinpoint these magnetically anomalous orientations, we relied upon a **proton precession magnetometer.** The theory behind this device is a bit complicated, but the principle is simple: Magnetometers measure the strength of magnetism between the earth's magnetic core and a sensor controlled by the archaeologist. If hundreds of these readings are taken across a systematic grid, a computer plotter can generate a magnetic contour map reflecting both the shape and the intensity of magnetic anomalies beneath the ground surface.

Many subsurface anomalies are archaeologically irrelevant magnetic "noise"—interference from underlying rocks, AC power lines, or hidden iron debris. The earth's magnetic field fluctuates so wildly on some days that the readings are meaningless, and electrical storms can hopelessly scramble magnetometer readings. Even minor interference such as the operator's wristwatch or eyeglasses can drive a magnetometer crazy.

But when everything works just right, the magnetometer provides the equivalent of an areal CAT scan, telling archaeologists what is going on beneath the earth's surface. Many archaeological features have characteristic magnetic signatures—telltale clues that hint at the size, shape, depth, and composition of the archaeological objects hidden far below. Shallow graves, for instance, have a magnetic profile different from, say, a buried fire pit or a wattle-and-daub wall.

We worked with Ervan Garrison (now of the University of Georgia) and a magnetometer team from Texas A&M University. As they were packing up their field equipment, to work up the data in their lab, they shared a couple of hunches,

How Kathleen Deagan Found Old St. Augustine

Working with historians and town planners in 1976, Kathleen Deagan set out to find the exact boundaries of sixteenth-century St. Augustine, founded in 1565. The problem was that St. Augustine had been continuously inhabited since prehistoric times, and the presumed sixteenth-century settlement lay sandwiched between prehistoric occupational debris and four centuries of later debris.

By comparing modern street plans with existing sixteenth-century maps, project historians nominated a nine-block area to the south of the town's central plaza as reflecting the original settlement's layout. Some 600 power auger holes were drilled along a systematic grid throughout downtown St. Augustine to test this hypothesis.

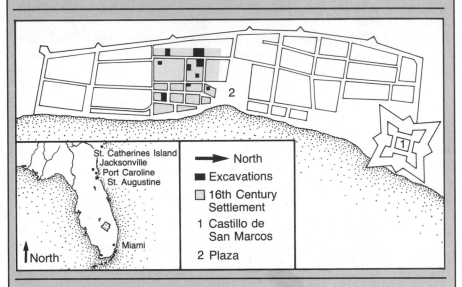

St. Catherines Island
Jacksonville
Port Caroline
St. Augustine

→ North

■ Excavations

□ 16th Century Settlement

1 Castillo de San Marcos

2 Plaza

Miami

↑ North

Historical continuity in St. Augustine (Florida). The shaded area shows the extent of the sixteenth-century occupation, superimposed on the street plan of the walled eighteenth-century St. Augustine (which remains virtually identical as that in the city today).

based strictly on their raw magnetometer readings: "If we were y'all, we'd dig in three places: here, over yonder, and especially right here." We took their advice, exploring each of the three magnetic anomalies in the few days remaining in our May field season. One anomaly—"especially right here"—turned out to be an iron ring. Excavating further, we came upon another ring and more below that. At about 9 feet down, we hit the water table. Digging underwater, we finally encountered a well-preserved oak well casing.

To do this, Deagan used a "modified systematic sampling strategy," in which auger tests were drilled along a 5- and 10-meter grid system, tied into existing street corners. The auger proved a particularly efficient tool for digging through driveways, parking lots, and shell middens. The survey technique was a relatively fast, inexpensive, reliable, and fairly nondestructive method of gathering information needed for the long-term inventory of St. Augustine's cultural and historical resources.

One potential problem was that the presumed sixteenth-century town lay in a highly developed downtown section. Fortunately, St. Augustine is acutely aware of its unique history, and residents were intensely interested in helping to learn more about the "oldest city." The power auger technique was pivotal here, for it caused minimal disturbance to both the archaeological record and the modern citizenry. Nonetheless, gardens and lawns were temporarily uprooted; sections of St. Augustine's streets were occasionally removed; and the local schoolchildren had to give up their playground for a season, giving Deagan and her crew time to test their property.

Two archaeologists muscle a gasoline-powered soil auger into the ground, looking for subsurface evidence of sixteenth-century St. Augustine.

As it turned out, the sixteenth-century artifacts clustered exactly where the historians had predicted. Deagan then initiated a program of excavation to refine these preliminary town boundaries and to probe the households of the early Spanish settlers as they adapted to life in their New World.

Archaeologists love wells because, like privies, they can be magnificent artifact traps. After removing the bones of an unfortunate fawn (which had long ago drowned), we found an array of distinctive Hispanic and Guale Indian potsherds and a metal dinner plate dropped (or tossed) into the construction pit. All artifacts were typical of the sixteenth and seventeenth centuries. We had indeed found Mission Santa Catalina, and we pressed on to see what else the magnetometer might have turned up.

Our second magnetic anomaly—the one "here"—was a small mound. We thought at first it might be a grave or tomb. But after removing the overburden, we came across a burned daub wall that, as it fell, had crushed dozens of Spanish and Guale domestic artifacts: imported tin-enameled glazed cups, painted ceramic dishes, a kitchen knife, and at least two enormous pots for cooking or storage. Charred deer and chicken bones littered the floor, and dozens of tiny corncobs were scattered about. This time, the magnetometer had led us to the kitchen (or *cocina*) used by seventeenth-century Franciscan friars at Santa Catalina.

Finally, we began digging the "over yonder" anomaly, which proved to be a linear daub concentration more than 40 feet long, obviously the downed wall of yet another, much larger mission building. Here excavations turned up none of the everyday implements and debris so common in the scorched kitchen. Instead we found human graves, the first of more than 400 Christianized Guale Indians buried here.

The search was over. We had discovered the church, the paramount house of worship at Santa Catalina de Guale. Our magnetometer survey had given us

Deborah Mayer O'Brien and Ervan Garrison looking for Mission Santa Catalina (on St. Catherines Island, Georgia) using a proton magnetometer. She is holding the "sensor" and he is recording magnetometer readings.

Full-scale excavations at the convento *(friar's housing) at Mission Santa Catalina (Georgia). Archaeologists in the foreground are mapping finds within the horizontal grid system and those in the midground are excavating using the "shovel-skimming" technique. All excavated dirt is screened in the gasoline-powered sifters evident in the background.*

trustworthy directions to the buried daub walls and iron barrel hoops. Even without computer enhancement, the magnetometer had taken us to the very heart and soul of Mission Santa Catalina.

After the discovery of Santa Catalina, we spent a dozen years excavating the church ruins. The lateral church walls were constructed of wattle and daub that, when encountered archaeologically, consisted of a densely packed linear rubble scatter; this is what the magnetometer "saw" in Quad IV. Beneath the nave and sanctuary of the church we discovered the cemetery, where approximately 400 to 450 Christianized Guale Indians had been interred.

The search for Santa Catalina illustrates the maturation in Americanist archaeology. Rather than rip into the site with trowels and shovels—much less backhoes and front loaders—we, like many archaeologists, first drew on today's technological arsenal, which includes dozens of noninvasive, nondestructive techniques to assess the archaeological record. Remote sensing—to be discussed in greater detail in the following sections of this chapter—allowed us to gather archaeological data even before we excavated any objects, features, and buildings.

Data at a Distance

It's kind of fun to do the impossible.
WALT DISNEY (1901–1966), AMERICAN FILM PRODUCER

Modern archaeology has much in common with modern medicine. It was not long ago that a slipped disk or blown-out knee—both common archaeological ailments—meant immediate and sometimes radical surgery. And surgery was often more painful than the injury itself. Although your knee joint bounced back pretty quickly after the cartilage was removed, it took months for the muscle tissues and nerves to recover from the 10-inch incision required to get at the injured area. Here was a classic case of the cure almost being worse than the disease.

Modern medical technology has changed all that. CAT scans and MRI technology today allows the physician to map in detail afflicted areas without any nasty "exploratory" surgery or damage to the patient. And when surgery is warranted, techniques like arthroscopy and laser microsurgery permit physicians to trim, cut, excise, and repair even gross damage with only the slightest incision. Today's *noninvasive* medicine minimizes tissue damage and surgical intervention.

Americanist archaeology is undergoing a parallel revolution. In the good old days, archaeologists simply blasted away at their sites, leaving ruined ruins in their wake. For example, the earliest excavations at Colonial Williamsburg were conducted by architectural historians who used an extraordinarily destructive method known as *cross trenching*, digging parallel trenches a shovel blade in width and throwing up the dirt on the unexcavated space between. The strategy was designed to disclose foundations for restoration, but the workmen paid little attention to the artifacts and none whatsoever to the stratigraphy encountered. To archaeologists at mid-century, the greatest technological revolution was the advent of the backhoe as a tool of excavation.

Americanist archaeology today views its sites differently. There is a new conservation ethic that suggests we dig less, and save more of our archaeological remains for the future. Equally important has been the development of noninvasive technology for doing relatively nondestructive archaeology. Using the archaeological equivalents of CAT scans and ultrasound, archaeologists can now map subsurface features in detail—without ever excavating them. And when it does become necessary to recover samples, we can execute pinpoint excavations, minimizing damage to the rest of the site. The idea is to leave large parts of our sites unexcavated, as a legacy for our archaeological grandchildren, who doubtless will possess methods, theories, and technology we cannot even imagine.

Some purists would restrict the term *remote sensing* only to applications of *photogrammetry*–to those devices not in direct contact with the ground. However, when archaeologists speak of "remote sensing," they generally mean the total array of techniques used in geophysical observation. In this broad sense, remote sensing technology includes not only the various forms of aerial photography, but also such land-based techniques as proton magnetometry, soil resistivity, ground-penetrating radar, and so forth. Each of these methods relies on some form of electromagnetic energy–it might be raw electricity, light, heat, or radio waves–to detect and measure some characteristics of an archaeological target. Most of these techniques were initially designed to measure geophysical features on the scale of several yards or even miles. Yet to be most effective in archaeology, such operations must be scaled down to the order of inches and feet.

Today, many archaeologists have come to rely on remote sensing technology as a "space-age" way to learn about the past. In 1982, radar aboard the space shuttle penetrated the Saharan sands, revealing the presence of previously undiscovered ancient watercourses. A generation of archaeologists has since been mapping out these so-called radar-rivers and the desert towns they once served.

The promise of remote sensing is awesome. You saw one application in the preceding section describing our work at Mission Santa Catalina. In the sections that follow, we explore other ways in which archaeologists are gathering their data at a distance. We begin with a firsthand example of how this technology tells us things we just can't know in any other way.

High Altitude Imagery

The first well documented application of remote sensing methods in archaeology took place in 1891, when a British archaeologist tied a camera to a crewless balloon to get better pictures of the site he was digging in India. Since then, archaeologists have used an array of aerial techniques–at first balloons and airplanes, more recently the space shuttle and satellites–to sense their sites "remotely."

Perhaps the most famous early application of remote sensing methods was by none other than Charles Lindbergh, the famous American aviator-explorer. Working closely with Ted Kidder, Lindbergh photographed important archaeological ruins at Chichen Itza (Mexico) and Tikal (Guatemala). He also did extensive photographic reconnaissance at Chaco Canyon, New Mexico. As it turned out, these innovative photographic records have proved invaluable to archaeologists working in these areas today. Archaeologists–armed with new knowledge and more advanced technologies–can find in these 1920s photographs traces of the past that would have surprised even Lindbergh, who took the pictures. Here's an example of how it works.

The Ancient Roads of Chaco Canyon

Many archaeologists were slow to recognize the potential of photogrammetry as a systemic research tool. They felt that the things they were studying were too small to be observed aloft. That misconception changed dramatically with the discovery of the ancient Anasazi road system connecting Chaco Canyon with its hinterlands. Although proto- and early Anasazi people lived in pit houses, between A.D. 700 and 1000 the Anasazi began constructing their distinctive multiroom apartment complexes that would give their descendants, the Pueblo Indians of New Mexico, their name.

The Anasazi of northwestern New Mexico generated a sustained burst of cultural energy in Chaco Canyon, a place that still amazes: hundreds of contiguous rooms made of beautifully shaped and coursed stonework, three or four stories high, forming huge sweeping arcs. Within its 30-odd square miles, the canyon contains more than 2,400 archaeological sites: nine full-blown towns (the "Great Houses"), each with hundreds of rooms.

Then, between A.D. 1050 and 1300, something happened. During these so-called "classical" times, two distinct kinds of sites appeared. Throughout the Anasazi area, numerous smaller pueblo sites dotted the landscape. But in Chaco Canyon and a few other places on the Colorado Plateau, huge sites were built. Pueblo Bonito (the Spanish name for "Beautiful Town"), in Chaco Canyon, reached five stories into the sky and housed a thousand people. America would not witness a larger apartment building until the Industrial Revolution of the nineteenth century. Pueblo Bonito was centrally located amid a cluster of smaller sites, defining a "community." By A.D. 1100, the large, formal Chaco towns had sprung up.

In 1970 and 1971, archaeologist R. Gwinn Vivian was mapping what he thought was a series of ancient Anasazi canals in Chaco Canyon. As he began excavating, Vivian realized that this linear feature was like no canal he'd ever seen. Instead of being U-shaped, the Chaco "canal" was obviously a deliberately flattened and carefully engineered roadway. Although some archaeologists working earlier in Chaco had speculated about possible roads, they lacked the technology to trace these for more than a mile or two, and their ruminations were buried deep inside voluminous field notes, unavailable to Vivian.

Gwinn described his curious find to Thomas Lyons, a geologist just hired to experiment with remote sensing possibilities in Chaco Canyon. Together, Gwinn and Lyons started looking at the available aerial photographs from the area. One set, taken in the 1960s, was compared with a 1930s series, taken before grazing was permitted at Chaco National Monument.

The more they looked, the more they saw—unmistakable traces of a prehistoric road network. New flights were commissioned and road segments were field-checked against the aerial photographs. By early 1973, more than 80 miles of prehistoric roads had been confidently identified in the Chaco area. By the end of the same year, identification had been extended to more than 200 miles of the network. Amazingly, the Lindbergh photographs of Chaco Canyon, taken in the

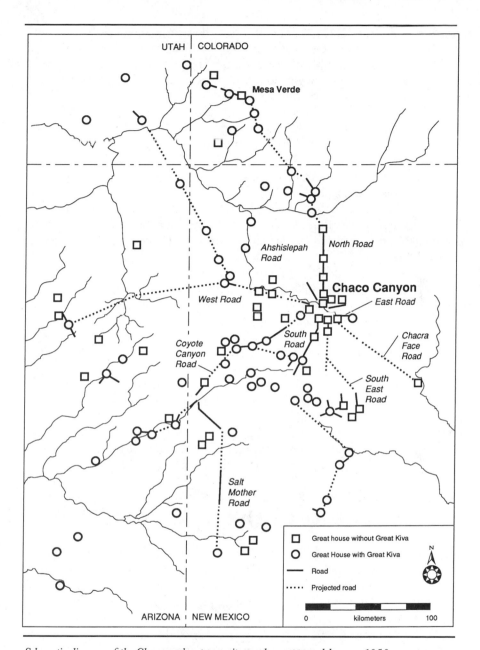

UTAH | COLORADO

Mesa Verde

Ahshislepah Road

North Road

Chaco Canyon

East Road

West Road

Coyote Canyon Road

South Road

Chacra Face Road

South East Road

Salt Mother Road

	Great house without Great Kiva
○	Great House with Great Kiva
—	Road
·····	Projected road

N

0   kilometers   100

ARIZONA | NEW MEXICO

Schematic diagram of the Chaco road system as it may have appeared by A.D. 1050.

1920s, actually show the famous Chacoan roads. But nobody recognized them as such in the photos until 1971, when archaeologists had a clue of what to look for.

Today, analysis of aerial photographs has revealed more than 400 miles of ancient roadways radiating out from Chaco Canyon. On the photos, the roads appear as narrow, dark lines running through the surrounding landscape. Sometimes they are completely invisible at ground level because they are merely shallow depressions only a couple of inches deep and 25 to 35 feet wide. They often turn with sudden, angular, dogleg jogs and are occasionally edged by low rock berms. The roads are littered with potsherds.

The longest and best-defined roads, probably constructed between A.D. 1075 and 1140, extend more than 50 miles outward from Chaco Canyon. In places the Chacoans constructed causeways, and elsewhere they cut stairways into sheer cliffs. The generally straight bearings suggest that the roads were laid out—"engineered"—prior to construction, although archaeologists still argue about exactly how this was done.

Why would the Chaco people build arrow-straight roads running hundreds of miles into the surrounding desert? This elaborate road system covered more than 100,000 square miles. Why are the roads so wide, so straight? What were they used for?

Maybe the well built Chaco roads operated like a lowercase version of the amazing Inka road system. Like the Inka roads, the Chacoan roads could have served for communication as well as transport. Several related mesa-top signal stations have been found near Chaco that provided for line-of-sight communication—presumably by smoke, fire, or reflected light.

In both cases, the Inka and the Chaco roads tied far-flung regions together, moving the goods and people required to build and maintain extensive public works. The roads themselves may also have become symbols of authority, linear banners proclaiming affinity and cooperation, signifying participation in a system whose importance exceeded the mere sum of its parts.

Whatever the answer, it is clear that archaeologists had walked over the remains of the Chaco road system for decades without recognizing them for what they were. It was just a matter of getting a new perspective, of starting to sense data "remotely."

A Soil Resistivity Approach

Not all remote sensing technology flies over the ground. **Soil resistivity** survey monitors the electrical resistance of soils in a restricted volume near the surface of an archaeological site. Perhaps partially because of its relatively low cost, soil resistivity survey has become a popular technique of geophysical prospection over the past three decades.

The degree of soil resistivity depends on several factors, the most important of which is usually the amount of water retained in the soil—the less water, the greater the resistance to electrical currents. Compaction such as occurs in house floors, paths, and roads tends to reduce pore sizes and hence potential to retain water; this registers as high resistance. In effect, when electricity is sent through the soil, buried features can often be detected and defined by their differential retention of groundwater (and hence their differential resistance to electrical charge).

The aggregation of fill in pits, ditches, and middens will also alter resistivity. Foundations or walls, particularly those in historic-period sites, generally have greater resistivity than surrounding soil, while the generation of humus by occupation activity increases the ion content of the soil, reducing resistivity.

To illustrate how soil resistivity survey actually works in archaeology, we return to our search for Mission Santa Catalina. After the initial discovery and pilot resistivity survey, Mark Williams and Gary Shapiro returned to St. Catherines Island to conduct a more comprehensive resistivity study.

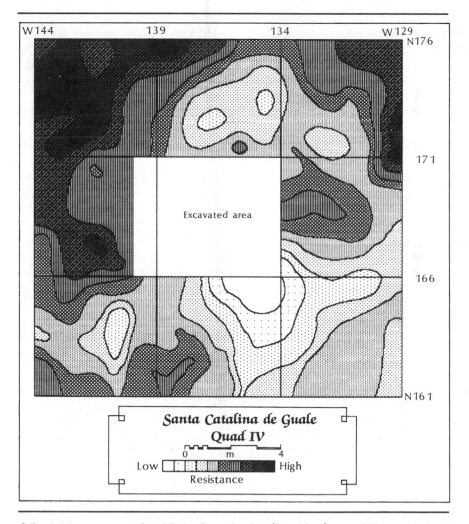

Soil resistivity contour map from Mission Santa Catalina (Georgia). The top of this map is oriented toward magnetic north; the buried kitchen building appears as a large squarish outline, oriented at 45° off north.

Soil resistance was measured by setting four probes in line at 1-meter intervals, each probe inserted to a depth of 20 centimeters. When an electrical current was passed between the probes, the electrical conductivity (the opposite of resistivity) was recorded between the two center probes. In this way, readings were consistently taken on east-west grid lines at 1-meter intervals (each 20-meter line resulting in 21 readings). The line was then advanced 1 meter north or south, and another 21 readings were taken. This procedure resulted in a gridded array of resistance values, recorded in the field on graph paper and eventually transferred to computer disks. Locations of trees, backdirt piles, roads, and other features that might influence earth resistance were also charted.

One of the preliminary resistivity surveys was conducted in a test square straddling a 5-by-5-meter area of Structure 2 at Santa Catalina, initially located by the proton magnetometer survey. From our test excavations, we knew that this building was the *cocina* (kitchen), but we had no idea of the building's configuration. The resistivity diagram of this area clearly shows the margins of the unexcavated building. Later excavations have conclusively confirmed the accuracy of the soil resistivity diagram.

A Ground-Penetrating Radar Approach

Another remote sensing approach uses **ground-penetrating radar.** The technique was first developed in 1910, but a significant peak in relevant articles appeared in the early 1970s, coinciding with the Apollo 17 lunar sounding experiment. Today, ground-penetrating radar techniques are commonly employed by environmental engineering firms to aid in selecting routes for proposed rights-of-way; to find buried rock or deep swamp deposits; to investigate foundations; in mineral studies; to search for peat, lignite, and coal; in siltation studies; to locate and identify caverns in limestone; in groundwater studies; and to investigate ground pollutants.

Ground-penetrating radar (GPR) operates as an echo-sounding device, transmitting energy over a frequency band. Radar pulses directed into the ground reflect back to the surface when they strike targets or interfaces within the ground (such as a change of stratum, interface between soil and rock, presence of groundwater or buried objects, and void areas). As these pulses are reflected, their speed to the target and the nature of their return are measured. The reflection time of the signal can provide useful information about the depth and three-dimensional shape of buried objects.

By using transducers of various dimensions, it is possible to direct the greatest degree of resolution to the depth of specific interest. A pulsating electric current is passed through a bow-tie shaped antenna, inducing electromagnetic waves that radiate toward the target and return in a fraction of a microsecond to be recorded. The dimensions of this transducer influence the depth and detail that are desired in any specific archaeological application.

As the antenna is dragged across the ground surface, a continuous profile of subsurface electromagnetic conditions is printed on a graphic recorder. The location and depth of subsurface targets can be inferred from, and tested against, this graphic record.

Radar seems to work best when the soil resistivity is high, as in well drained soils and those with a low clay content. Subsurface wells, foundations, cellars, voids, cavities, and well defined compacted zones, such as house floors, are known to provide clear radar echoes. Ground-penetrating radar equipment is relatively portable. It may be transported on a handcart as the transmitter-receiver is dragged across the earth's surface.

Cerén: The New World Pompeii?

Remote sensing studies work best when instrumentation and imagery are calibrated to local conditions and when extensive field verification studies can be conducted. Such a situation exists at the site of Cerén, located in the Zapotitlan Valley of El Salvador (just northwest of the capital city of San Salvador). The Zapotitlan Valley is surrounded by large volcanoes and cinder cones, all of which are either currently active, or soon will be.

The Cerén site was discovered in 1976 by a bulldozer operator as he was attempting to level a platform on which to build some grain storage silos. When he noted that his bulldozer blade had uncovered the corner of a deeply buried building, this workman did a remarkable thing: Instead of just plowing ahead, he stepped down, looked around, and when he found some old-looking pottery buried in the building, he stopped work and notified the National Museum in San Salvador. Unfortunately, when a representative of the museum arrived 3 days later, he dismissed the find as very recent construction and gave the heavy equipment operator his blessing to continue working. As an unfortunate result, several other ancient buildings were bulldozed.

Two years later, when Payson Sheets and his students from the University of Colorado arrived to conduct a survey of the Zapotitlan Valley, townspeople told them of the unusual find, and showed them where some of it remained. Sheets saw some adobe columns protruding from the disturbed area and expected to find bits of plastic and newspaper eroding out of the ruined building. Even when he found some Classic Maya polychrome pottery (thought to date A.D. 500–800), he still assumed that the building was modern—the thatch roof was almost perfectly preserved, even though it was buried beneath 16 feet of volcanic ash.

But after a few hours of careful excavation, Sheets found lots of ancient Maya artifacts—without any historic-period material turning up at all. Writing later about his experience, Payson Sheets noted that he "began to perceive two very different possibilities: (1) I was on the brink of a massive professional embarrassment if I prematurely announced the find of these structures as prehistoric, and they turned out to be recent, or (2) they were in fact prehistoric, and therefore the site is of extreme importance." The whole issue turned, of course, on dating. Sheets carefully collected some of the buried roof thatch for radiocarbon analysis. When the results of the tests came back, he no longer worried about embarrassing

Adobe columns and flooring of Structure 1 at the Cerén site (El Salvador). This Maya house was buried instantaneously in about A.D. 590 by nearly 20 feet of volcanic ash from the nearby Loma Caldera eruption. When archaeologist Payson Sheets and his crew excavated this house, they found all artifacts left in place. Even the thatched roof had been preserved.

himself professionally—all of the thatch samples (and therefore the buried houses as well) were 1,400 years old.

Today, the Zapotitlan Valley find, known as the Cerén site, clearly dates to the Classic Maya period. The entire village had been instantaneously buried in about A.D. 590 by up to 20 feet of volcanic ash from the nearby Loma Caldera eruption. Because the ash had cooled off considerably by the time it hit, nearly all of the ancient agricultural features and cultural artifacts were miraculously preserved—crops still in the field, orchards, a central public plaza surrounded by Classic period adobe houses with artifacts left exactly as buried, and even the ancient Maya farmers' footprints. Although others sites have been proposed as the "Pompeii of the Americas," Cerén certainly remains one of the leading contenders.

So completely did the volcanic ash cover the area that nothing of Cerén remained visible on the ground surface. How could Sheets map something that was buried beneath 20 feet of volcanic debris?

Payson Sheets and his colleagues turned to ground-penetrating radar as a way to see what lay below the surface. The depositional conditions at Cerén were almost ideal for remote sensing. The overlying volcanic ash contained relatively little clay and there was only minimal soil formation. One of the radar antennas, using 80 MHz frequency radar energy, could penetrate more than 7 meters deep; but this long wavelength would only resolve buried features greater than 1 or 2 meters in diameter. However, when a 300 MHz antenna was employed, and the maximum depth was reduced to 5 meters, then features as small as 45 to 50 centimeters could be delineated.

But these radar antennas are unwieldy and difficult to pull over rocky terrain. And to make matters worse, much of the ground surface at Cerén was a functioning maize field. Sheets decided to load their ground-penetrating radar system into the back of an oxcart, the most common mode of transport in rural El Salvador, first introduced by the sixteenth-century Spanish colonists. This imaginative solution worked quite well, although it was an incongruous sight—a wooden cart laden with hundreds of pounds of hi-tech radar equipment being pulled by slowly plodding oxen through a Salvadoran cornfield.

The entire ancient landscape at Cerén was mapped and reconstructed from the GPR results (and verified with numerous test pit and block excavations). The population density of the buried zone was surprisingly high. On the day it was buried, Cerén was a prosperous farming village with closely packed domestic, civic, and religious buildings constructed on elevated platforms, with all intervening space between them taken up by agricultural crops.

Ground-penetrating radar unit collecting data on subsurface stratigraphy at the Cerén site (El Salvador). The sending-receiving antenna is attached to the rear of the oxcart. Inside the oxcart are the oscilloscope, instrumentation tape recorder, graphic recorder, and gas-powered generator.

Because of its extraordinary preservation, the Cerén site is one of the most important places in Central America for studying ancient land-use practices. GPR mapping had proved to be a cost-effective method for discovering buried houses—some of which were excavated, the rest preserved for the future. By carefully working out the various radar signatures from the excavated houses, remote sensing and associated computer-modeling techniques allowed these pre-Columbian houses to be precisely mapped even though unexcavated.

The Emperor's Secrets Are Buried: No Digging Allowed

Ground-penetrating radar is being applied around the world today. In Japan, this technology, together with more conventional archaeological discoveries, is threatening to upset the political applecart.

The interpretive sign at the Nishitonozuka mound, placed there by the Imperial Household Agency of the Japanese government, officially declares that it is the tomb of a sixth-century empress. This designation is meaningful because this site is today revered as an important religious shrine.

But archaeologists working outside the fenced-off area, in the moat surrounding this huge keyhole-shaped mound, have found sherds of a distinctive funerary-style pottery suggesting that it may actually have been built 1,600 years ago—making it a century older than the sign says. Now in many places, a disparity of a century in dating would not be a big deal. But in Japan, where the ceramic chronology is highly refined, a single century can make quite a difference.

But are the sherds actually associated with the mound, or are they later fill that accumulated in the moat? Any competent archaeologist could resolve the problem with a few carefully placed test pits. Numerous contemporary mounds—but not those of the royal family—have been excavated, and they are known to contain grave goods such as weaponry, household items, and jewelry—all items that can be dated fairly accurately. The problem is that archaeologists are not allowed to dig here. A specific directive from the Imperial Household Agency states that this mound and the 455 other royal tombs it seeks to protect contain the remains of emperors, empresses, and other royal relatives—no digging allowed.

The official governmental position follows the tradition that Japan's imperial family line stretches back unbroken for more than 2,500 years—making it the world's oldest continuously reigning monarchy—descended directly from the Sun Goddess. The first emperor, Jimmu, was recorded to have taken the throne on February 11, 660 B.C.

But the historical records allegedly documenting this unprecedented line of succession are kept in secret governmental files. Fifty years ago, a historian named Sokichi Tsuda was convicted of insulting the dignity of the royal family when he questioned whether the first nine emperors were actual historical figures.

Today, most Japanese historians view the first 10 to 15 emperors as purely mythical, and they believe that the royal line actually began in the fifth or sixth century A.D. Some even suggest that the earliest emperors may have had Korean blood coursing through their royal veins—a heresy to many modern Japanese nationalists. The Imperial Household Agency continues to refuse any archaeological exploration of the mounds because, they claim, it would desecrate the graves of the emperor's ancestors—who remain the objects of worship and veneration.

But critics charge that political motivations lie behind the ban on excavation. Those who oppose archaeological investigations have a vested interest in perpetuating the myth of the unbroken line and the mystique of the imperial throne.

Each year, a delegation of archaeologists petitions the Imperial Household Agency for permission to explore the mounds of questionable age. And each year, according to Masayoshi Mizuno of Nara University, the answer is always the same: There is no answer.

So how can scholars conduct valid historical research on these off-limit mounds? Dean Goodman (Geophysical Archaeometry Laboratory, University of Miami Japan Division) and Yasushi Nishimura (Archaeological Operations, Nara National Cultural Properties Research Institute) believe that remote sensing technology may be the answer. Goodman and Nishimura have recently been conducting ground-penetrating radar studies to determine the internal configuration of such "official" royal tombs.

The Kanmachi Mandara keyhole burial mound in Ishikawa Prefecture is one of the protected mounds. It is believed to date to the early Kofun period, roughly A.D. 30–350 (toward the early end of the "official" claim to the throne). It has a square rear mound with burial remains and a triangular shaped frontal extension. Because of its relatively small size, the ancient mound was not initially recognized as such by road engineers, and the triangular part was partly destroyed by a road.

The intact part of this mound is protected by Japanese cultural property law—no digging allowed. But nondestructive remote sensing is permitted, and this was done to determine the location and shape of the burial area contained within and also to learn something about the structural design.

A series of parallel radar profiles—called "time slices"—were run through the Kanmachi Mandara burial mound. A **time slice** is an analytical method for synthesizing the various radar passes at a specific vertical level. Time slices can be made at various radar-scan depths, creating remotely sensed site plans for various depths below the ground surface—and all based strictly on nondestructive data.

Using the time-slice technique, at a projected depth of about 0.5 meter below the ground surface of the Kanmachi Mandara burial mound, a remarkable pattern appeared. By looking at the internal structural data, one sees the general orientation and location of the coffin remains clearly evident as the large central anomaly.

To determine even more detail, a second radar survey was run across the coffin area, this time at a 90-degree angle. From this second radar perspective, it seems clear that a large burial pit was first excavated, into which a clay foundation was set to anchor the wooden coffin containing the deceased and various

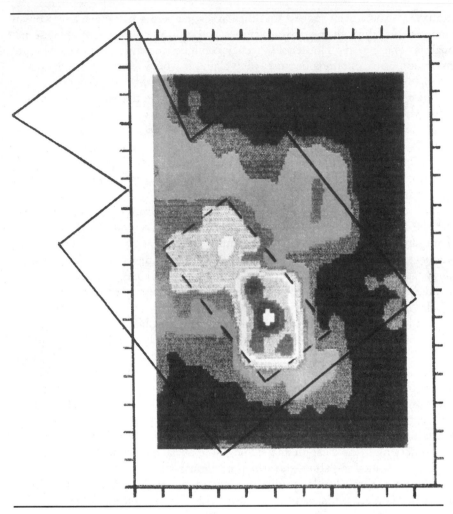

A "time slice" of the Kanmachi Mandara burial mound, generated by ground-penetrating radar. The large central anomaly (the whitish area) is believed to be the central tomb; the dark area in-side that is probably the coffin remains.

grave goods. This foundation originally sloped upwards to encase the lateral sides of the coffin, which has today probably deteriorated.

    These ground-penetrating radar results tell us a great deal about the internal structure of the unexcavated Kanmachi Mandara keyhole burial mound and, if excavation were permitted, the various radar-generated site plans could be used to pinpoint relatively small test excavations to obtain samples for radiometric dating. But since such excavations are not permitted, archaeologists are limited to the relatively general internal site plans—intriguing in their own right, but not of sufficient resolution to shed any significant light on the highly controversial longevity of Japan's Imperial family.

The Potential of Noninvasive Archaeology

Remote sensing can lead us to new ways of defining traditional concepts in archaeology, provided that we work out unambiguous relationships between the things still buried and the reasons we know they are there. Doing this requires that we construct the requisite linkages between the more traditional archaeological concepts—walls, structures, and features—and the way they are perceived ("remotely") by the sensors of geophysical machinery.

Remote sensing technology can give archaeologists a cost-effective means of making a noninvasive, nondestructive assessment of the archaeological record. In the early developmental stage, the emphasis has necessarily been on technology—but for such technology to pay off in archaeology, the hardware must be thoroughly integrated into the mainstream theoretical fabric of working archaeology. Newer developments in geophysical technology and field technique cannot be viewed merely as refined ways of generating traditional archaeological data.

Remote sensing can act as a bridge between the empirical record of geophysical technology and theory building in archaeology. Archaeologists are now building a baseline library of geophysical signatures for key archaeological sites. They are not only comparing the results between geophysical survey and actual excavation, but they are also examining the efficiency of the various geophysical media. Although preliminary, such exercises should ensure that in the future, at places like Mission Santa Catalina, destructive exploratory groping can be avoided. Subsurface research designs can be guided instead by a sequence of unambiguous, nondestructive geophysical signatures.

The use of remote sensing technology also makes archaeologists look once more at the nature of their data. "Empirical observation" in yesterday's archaeology was conducted by "tactile sensing"—you-know-what-something-is-after-you've-dug-it-up-and-can-hold-it-in-your-hand. Although archaeologists working in this framework soon fill up empty museum cases and storerooms, they are often confused about what archaeological data really are. As discussed earlier, archaeological data are not the objects or things that archaeologists retrieve. Rather, archaeological data are the counts, measurements, and observations made on these recovered objects. There can be no archaeological data in this sense until an archaeologist observes them. Data cannot exist passively. Archaeological data are deliberately generated (sometimes decades after objects are recovered from their contexts). Remote sensing is simply one more way of generating archaeological data. But in this case, archaeologists are making their counts, measurements, and observations on objects and features that have not yet been excavated.

Some Basic Excavation Strategies

When I excavate sites and touch things that have lain untouched for centuries, I know why I am an archaeologist.

JANET D. SPECTOR, ARCHAEOLOGIST (UNIVERSITY OF MINNESOTA)

In the beginning of this chapter, I wrote about the discovery of Gatecliff Shelter. Although sometimes electrifying, finding sites like Gatecliff is only the beginning. Our excavation strategy and tactics evolved dramatically as we learned more about the site and its potential.

We began with two simple test pits dug the same year we found the site. From day one, we wanted to learn two things: how long people had used Gatecliff Shelter and what the buried deposits could tell us about the human chronology of the region. These two questions were clear-cut, and so was our fieldwork. Our earliest excavation strategy was vertical, designed to supply, as expediently as possible, a stratified sequence of artifacts and ecofacts associated with other potentially datable materials.

Like most archaeologists, I dig "metrically" in test pits typically 1 meter square. There is, of course, a minimum size in such exploratory soundings: Squares much smaller would squeeze out the archaeologists, and larger units are overly destructive (and too time-consuming).

Test pits tend to be quick and dirty, particularly because they must be excavated "blind," without knowing what stratigraphy lies below. Nevertheless, even in test pits, archaeologists must maintain three-dimensional control of the finds: the X axis (front to back), the Y axis (side to side), and the Z axis (top to bottom). This is why archaeologists dig square holes. Provided the sidewalls are kept sufficiently straight and perpendicular, excavators can use the dirt itself to maintain horizontal control on the X and Y axes by measuring directly from the sidewalls. As test pits deepen, however, the sidewalls may start sloping inward, cramping the digger and biasing the measurements. Field archaeologists call these sloppy pits "bathtubs"—decidedly bad form.

What about vertical control? At Gatecliff, we dug test pits in arbitrarily imposed 10-centimeter levels. Everything of interest—artifacts, ecofacts, soil samples, and so forth—was kept in separate level bags, one for each 10-centimeter level. The Z dimension for each level was usually designated according to distance below the ground surface: Level 1 (surface to 10 centimeters below), Level 2 (10 to 20 centimeters below), and so forth.

Excavation procedures vary widely, depending on the stage of excavation, the nature of the deposit, and the impulse of the archaeologist in charge (remember, digging is perhaps still as much craft as science). Because they are so small, test pits are often dug by trowel (rather than by shovel), maintaining a horizontal working surface. Deposit is scooped into a dust pan, dumped into a bucket, then carried off-site for a closer look.

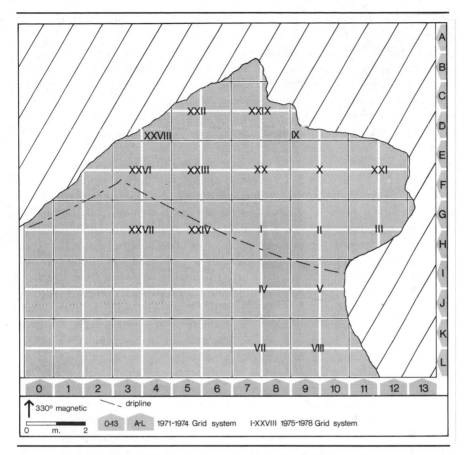

Plan view of the two grid systems used at Gatecliff Shelter. The alphanumeric (numbers and letters) system defined 1-meter excavation squares used in the first four seasons. Roman numerals designate the 2-meter squares used later, when large horizontal exposures were excavated.

The test pits told us that Gatecliff Shelter warranted a closer look, and we returned the next year to do just that. The site was divided into a 1-meter **grid system,** oriented along the long axis of the shelter. We assigned consecutive letters to each north-south division and numbered the east-west division. By this method, each excavation square could be designated by a unique alphanumeric name (just as in Bingo—A-7, B-5, and the ever-popular K-9). The east wall of the "7-trench"—so named because it contained units B-7 through I-7—defined a major stratigraphic profile, a vertical section against which all artifacts, features, soil and pollen samples, and radiocarbon dates were correlated.

A vertical **datum point** was established at the rear of the shelter. For all on-site operations, this single point was arbitrarily designated as zero. All site elevations from this point on were plotted as "*x* centimeters below datum." Using an altimeter and a U.S. Geological Survey topographic map, we determined the elevation of this datum point to be 2,319 meters (7,607 feet) above sea level; to-day, we might use some high-tech, satellite-driven technology.

All archaeological **features**—fire hearths, artifact concentrations, sleeping ar-eas, and the like—were plotted on a master site map, and individual artifacts found in situ were plotted in three dimensions. All fill was first carefully troweled, then taken outside the cave for screening (as discussed in the next section); artifacts and ecofacts found in the screen were bagged by stratigraphic or **arbitrary level.** Field notes at this stage were kept by individual excavators in bound graph pa-per notebooks. Good field notes record everything, whether or not it seems im-portant at the time. Depending on the nature of the site (and the stage of exca-vation), field notes can either be taken "formless" or recorded on specific unit-level forms, with precise categories defined for each kind of necessary infor-mation.

At this stage, we were looking primarily for change through time. At Gate-cliff, this meant looking for key time-sensitive artifacts to be grouped into tem-poral types, which enabled us to place previously undated archaeological contexts into a meaningful sequence as we excavated. Laboratory work subsequently tested these preliminary field hypotheses, what geologists call their "horseback correla-tions."

The vertical excavation strategy is a deliberately simplified scheme designed to clarify chronology. By the end of our fourth field season, our major strata-trench had reached a depth of 9 meters below the ground surface. By then we knew a good deal about Gatecliff. In the preceding chapter, we discussed how the master stratigraphic sequence was worked out and how the dozens of radiocar-bon dates provided us with absolute dates for each stratum. We had successfully defined the cultural sequence of Gatecliff Shelter, but our vertical excavation strat-egy had also left us with a series of extremely steep and hazardous sidewalls. Even though the excavation was stairstepped downward to minimize these sidewalls, the sheer verticality of the site made it dangerous. Change was clearly in order, both conceptually and logistically.

Gatecliff Shelter held potential far beyond mere chronology. Several strati-graphic units contained short-term, intact occupational surfaces, and the remain-ing excavations at Gatecliff concentrated on the spatial distributions within these key stratigraphic units.

As we shifted away from chronological objectives, we also shifted our digging strategy. As the focus moved from the *when* and *where* to the more elusive *what,* digging mine shafts became inappropriate. With the stratigraphy suitably defined, we concentrated on opening entire living surfaces simultaneously. The cultural lenses at Gatecliff were slowly excavated by hand, with thicker stratigraphic units removed in arbitrary 10-centimeter levels. Exposing living floors proceeded more slowly than had the previous vertical excavations, and excavators were instructed to recover and map all artifacts in situ. Features were screened separately, and flotation samples were retained for laboratory processing. Significant debitage scat-ters were plotted, as were concentrations of bone and other artifacts. The exca-vated deposits were then placed in buckets and carried to the screening area where they were passed through ⅛-inch screens, and as before, artifacts missed by the excavators were saved along with all fragments of chippage and bone.

The horizontal strategy required significantly more control within contemporary stratigraphic units. A single crew chief took excavation notes for the entire site at this point (rather than having individual excavators do it, as before). Three-dimensional data were transferred to site notebooks, and living floor maps were plotted for each surface at the time of the excavation. A single excavator was assigned to each 2-square-meter unit, and all artifacts, features, and large ecofacts were plotted onto the large-scale living floor maps. Since then, sophisticated computer-driven systems have been developed to assist in piece-plotting objects on living surfaces.

Some Rules and Principles Guiding Archaeological Excavation

Our Gatecliff Shelter excavations covered the basics of archaeological excavation: stratigraphy, recovery, **provenience.** Although the strategies are universal to archaeology, the tactics are site specific. For example, ancestral Pueblo sites in New Mexico, containing well defined room clusters, must be excavated very differently from a high-altitude cave in Nevada. Peeling off sequential levels in a Maya temple in Guatemala differs radically from excavating through seemingly homogeneous shell midden deposits in Georgia. Underwater archaeology uses a host of techniques and equipment totally alien to terrestrial contexts.

Still, certain considerations transcend the site-specific context, and the rest of this chapter addresses the more universal characteristics of archaeological fieldwork.

Sifting the Evidence

No matter how carefully you excavate, it is impossible to see, map, and recover everything of archaeological interest. This is why archaeologists today use fine-screen sifters to find things that hand excavation misses.

Archaeologists generally agree that Marshalltown makes the only trowel worth owning—but when it comes to sifters, all agreement evaporates. Because most archaeologists manufacture their own sifters, the design and workmanship vary from dig to dig. Some screens are suspended from tripods; others have two legs. Some are mounted on rollers and others are driven by gas engines. When we dug Alta Toquima Village (Nevada), at 12,000 feet, we invented a "backpacker" design for our screens.

Modern archaeologists spend plenty of time thinking about sifters and how they facilitate archaeological excavation. There is near-universal agreement that sifters of some sort are necessary on all terrestrial sites. As recently as the 1970s, the occasional archaeologist in America could still be caught simply troweling or shoveling the deposit, sorting through the loosened matrix for artifacts and then tossing the dirt on a spoil pile; but today we recognize that simply too much archaeological material is lost when the deposit is not screened; in fact, some deposits contain such minute remains that even sifting is inadequate, in which case, a more precise recovery technique (such as flotation, discussed in a moment) should be used.

Screen size affects what is recovered. For my M.A. thesis project, I built a three-decker screen with superimposed layers of ¼-inch over ⅛-inch over 1/16-inch mesh screens. The idea was to find out how screen size affects the recovery of animal bones in archaeological sites. We found that the then-standard ¼-inch mesh is entirely adequate when the midden contains only bones of large animals such as bighorn or bison, but significant numbers of medium-sized animals, such as rabbits and rodents, are lost through the ¼-inch gauge. A ⅛-inch mesh screen is recommended whenever the faunal assemblage includes these smaller mammals. In fact, significant amounts of small mammal bones are even lost through ⅛-inch screens! When one is concerned with recovering animals the size of, say, pack rats or small birds, a flotation method of recovery is strongly recommended. The nature of the archaeological debris must be carefully considered before selecting a method of excavation.

Flotation

In some archaeological sites, like the upper parts of Gatecliff Shelter, the deposits are sufficiently protected from moisture so that plant remains simply dry up and can be recovered by screening. But in more humid climates, plant remains generally are preserved only when they have been burned and carbonized. The most common method of recovering such plant remains is **flotation,** a technique that has become standard at most (if not all) digs during the last few decades.

There are several procedures for "floating" archaeological samples, but all of them do basically the same thing. Dirt does not float; but burned seeds, bones, and charcoal do. By using water (or chemical) flotation, archaeologists can float most ecofacts (and even some artifacts) out of samples of archaeologically recovered dirt.

In one of the earliest applications, Stuart Struever floated soil samples from 200 features attributable to the Middle Woodland component at the Apple Creek site (Illinois). The samples were hauled to nearby Apple Creek, where they were placed in mesh-bottomed buckets and then water-separated by students who worked midstream. More than 40,000 charred nutshell fragments, 2,000 carbonized seeds, and some 15,000 identifiable fish bones were collected in this manner. Standard dryland excavation techniques would have missed most.

While excavating at Salts Cave in Kentucky, Patty Jo Watson and her associates were not blessed with a nearby stream, so they improvised. The sediments to be floated were placed in double plastic bags and carried outside the cave. The samples (weighing a total of 1,500 pounds) were spread in the shade to dry. Two 50-gallon drums were filled with water, and the dry samples were placed in metal buckets whose bottoms had been replaced with window screen. The buckets were submerged in the 50-gallon oil drums, which had been filled with water. After a few seconds, the investigator skimmed off the charcoal and carbonized plant remains that had floated to the surface, using a small scoop made from a brass carburetor screen. Both the debris that floated to the top (the "light fraction") and the stuff that sank (the "heavy fraction") were placed on labeled newspaper to dry once again. The sediments at Salts Cave yielded carbonized remains of hickory nuts and acorns, seeds from berries, grains, sumpweed, chenopods, maygrass, and amaranth.

Today, flotation is not an expensive or even a particularly time-consuming process. Flotation techniques can (and should) be fitted to the local requirements. At Mission Santa Catalina, we used a converted 55-gallon drum, and one person

---

Archaeology's Conservation Ethic: Dig Only What You Must

Archaeologists have always protected their excavations against vandals and pothunters. At Gatecliff, we tediously backfilled the site by hand every year, to protect the archaeology from the curious public, and the public from the dangers of open-pit archaeology.

On St. Catherines Island, a different problem arose. Because the island is difficult to reach and access is controlled, there is no real threat from pothunters. It was thus possible to open a few test units on several sites, return to the laboratory to process the finds, and then come back to the more promising sites for more intensive excavation. St. Catherines Island is a great place for an archaeologist to dig.

But these circumstances highlight today's responsibility for site conservation. Archaeology is a destructive science, ruining its sites in the very process of excavation. Sites can be excavated only once, and so it is imperative to do things right. On strictly research projects—like our work at Mission Santa Catalina—the sites are not threatened by outside incursions, and one must adopt an enlightened and conservative strategy of excavation. Many archaeologists vow never to excavate more than half of a site not threatened by development or erosion.

Whatever the rule, responsible investigators start with a suite of questions that are generally asked by all, plus additional questions specific to each excavation. The trick is to excavate no more than necessary to answer such questions, leaving as much intact as possible for further investigators, who undoubtedly will have more enlightened questions to ask and superior techniques with which to find the answers. And, as we have seen, remote sensing technology and archaeological survey techniques sometimes provide archaeologists with low-impact ways of learning without digging at all.

could process dozens of samples each day. Some elaborate power-driven machines are available for separating specimens chemically.

But technology is not the issue. What is important is that for decades archaeologists meticulously saved, cataloged, and identified all scraps of bone but ignored plant remains. The resulting skew led archaeologists to overemphasize hunting aspects and ignore the gathering component altogether. Now that flotation techniques have come into their own, archaeologists are placing proper emphasis on the gathering of wild and domesticated plant foods.

How Do People Learn How to Dig?

From the outset, I emphasize the importance of hands-on experience in archaeology. There is no substitute for personal field experience, and no textbook or classroom exercise satisfactorily simulates the field situation. Learning to excavate means getting your hands dirty. It all boils down to going on a dig, and there are three ways to do this.

Most archaeologists get their first taste of fieldwork by enrolling in an organized archaeological field school. Major universities and colleges offer such opportunities, sometimes on weekends but more often during the summer session. Field schools are conducted on virtually every kind of archaeological site, and living conditions vary from pup tents to relatively plush dormitories. Some instructors require only a passing classroom familiarity with archaeology, whereas others accept only relatively advanced graduate students.

It is increasingly possible to join a dig as a volunteer or intern. Several branches of the federal government and many large research projects rely on nonpaid participants to supplement the paid staff. A number of overseas excavations rely almost exclusively on volunteers who pay for their own transportation and exchange their on-site labor for room and board. Over the years, I have directed nearly a dozen such sessions at both Gatecliff Shelter and Mission Santa Catalina.

Avocational ("amateur") archaeological societies also offer numerous opportunities to excavate. In many cases, these nonprofessional groups are well trained and adequately supervised. The best ones coordinate their own excavations with ongoing professional-level research. But some caution is advised here. Current ethical standards discourage private collectors from digging up artifacts. In many instances, "pothunting" is illegal, and recent legislation has made it easier for the courts to crack down on looters. Although most archaeological societies discourage illegal and unethical destruction of archaeological sites, a few outlaw groups still sponsor "digs" for the sole purpose of obtaining artifacts. If you have any question about the integrity of an archaeological society, I suggest that you contact a local university, government agency, or museum to clarify the situation. As a rule of thumb, you might ask a couple of key questions: What professionally trained archaeologists are involved in the excavations, and what happens to the artifacts once they have been dug up? If no responsible archaeologist is involved, and/or if the artifacts end up in private hands, steer clear of the dig.

Fieldwork opportunities vary from year to year, and you should obtain the most current information before making plans. And having supervised a dozen such digs, let me enter a personal plea: Before signing on with any expedition or field school, be certain you know what you are getting into. Archaeological excavation is physically taxing, and field camps can be socially intense. Neither you nor the dig will benefit if you are unable or unwilling to participate fully. If you have specific questions, by all means talk to the archaeologist in charge before making a commitment. Do not get in over your head.

Summary

Archaeological sites are found in several different ways and there is no single formula. Many of the archaeological sites discussed here were found by a combination of luck and hard work. Others were discovered as part of a systematic regional reconnaissance. But many archaeologists are not actually seeking a place to excavate. Sometimes the reconnaissance itself produces sufficient information for understanding the archaeological record. Sometimes, these areas are sampled using one or more probability-based sampling designs to minimize bias in recovering settlement pattern data.

Americanist archaeology is undergoing a revolution. A century ago, archaeologists simply blasted away at their sites, leaving ruined ruins in their wake. To archaeologists at mid-century, the greatest technological revolution was the advent of the backhoe as a tool of excavation.

Today, we view archaeologial sites in a radically different manner. Part of this new conservation ethic reflects the definition of archaeological remains as nonrenewable resources. But equally important has been the development of noninvasive technology for doing relatively nondestructive archaeology. Using the archaeological equivalents of the CAT scan, archaeologists can now map subsurface features in detail without ever excavating them. And when it does become necessary to recover samples, we can, like the orthopedic surgeon, execute pinpoint excavations, minimizing damage to the rest of the site.

This chapter presented several examples of remote sensing technology: proton magnetometry, high altitude imagery, soil resistivity, and ground-penetrating radar. These are just a few weapons in today's high-tech arsenal, which includes a dozen noninvasive, nondestructive techniques to assess the archaeological record.

Despite such recent advances, archaeological excavation remains as much craft as science. Here, we looked at some common techniques, some archaeological standards and conventions, and, perhaps most important of all, what it feels like to be on a dig. Diverse excavation strategies represent different assumptions and different objectives. In a vertical strategy, designed largely for chronological control, artifact provenience generally means little more than stratigraphic placement; the exact location within a given stratum is analytically irrelevant.

But in a horizontal strategy, designed to explore the conditions of past lifeways, the context of artifacts and ecofacts within excavation strata becomes critical; artifacts found in situ are commonly plotted relative to one another on living floor maps. When an excavator misses an artifact—and it turns up in the screen—a significant piece of information has been lost because it can then be located only within the excavation square.

Modern archaeologists spend plenty of time thinking about recovery techniques, and both mechanical sifters and flotation devices are commonplace. From test pit through full-scale excavation, archaeologists maintain exact records of the three-dimensional provenience of the objects being recovered, and computer-assisted equipment is now available for this purpose.

It's hard to overemphasize the importance of hands-on experience in archaeology. There is no substitute for personal field experience, and no textbook, computer simulation, or classroom exercise satisfactorily simulates the field situation. Learning to excavate means getting your hands dirty. It all boils down to going on a dig.

> *My fieldwork was a picnic with a purpose.*
> DOROTHY KEUR (1904–1989), ARCHAEOLOGIST

Archaeological Fieldwork on the Internet: How Can I Get on a Dig?

There are dozens of opportunities each year for the inexperienced to join up with a dig, but people are often puzzled about where to begin. Here are some useful contacts:

Archaeological Fieldwork Server is a first-rate way to find current information.
　　http://www.cincpac.com/afs/testpit.html

Preserv/Net is a national listing of internships.
　　http://www.preservenet.cornell.edu/pnetopp.htm

Internship and Fieldwork Listings Nationwide is another good resource.
　　http://minerva.acc.virginia.edu/~career/intern.html

Participate in Archaeology is the National Park Service's link, which tells you how to do it, where to do it, what to do it with, and what to read.
　　http://www.cr.nps.gov/aad/particip.htm

ArchNet provides access to the University of Connecticut Anthropology Department World Wide Web Virtual Library: Archaeology.
　　http://www.lib.uconn.edu/ArchNet

Frequently Asked Questions About a Career in Archaeology in the U.S. is an excellent Internet service provided by David L. Carlson, associate professor of anthropology, Texas A & M University. It includes an up-to-date section on archaeological fieldwork opportunities.
　　http://www.skidmore.edu/academics/classics/archfaq2.htm

CHAPTER 6

Middle-Range Research:
Ethnoarchaeology and Experimental Archaeology

◻ ◻ ◻

PREVIEW

To this point, we have explored how archaeologists locate and excavate their sites, and some of the ways they construct cultural chronologies. All these activities fall into what we call low-level archaeological theory.

Now it is time to move up the theoretical scale a notch, to see how middle-range research is conducted in modern archaeology. We begin with a look at the various natural and cultural processes that combine to create the archaeological record. Low-level theory enabled us to generate data from this record. Then, using theory developed in middle-range research, we can begin to relate these data to past human behaviors. Here, we see how ethnoarchaeologists *study the way modern behavior is translated into the archaeological record— among the Nunamiut people in Alaska, for instance—and also how the garbage that each of us discards daily is being incorporated into the archaeological record of industrial North America. Each study contributes, in its own way, to our theoretical knowledge at the middle range.*

There is another way to do this: by experimentally recreating the necessary conditions and looking for the linkage between systemic and archaeological context. Known as experimental archaeology, *this research has the same middle-range objectives as ethnoarchaeology. But ethnoarchaeologists work within a functioning behavioral system, whereas experimental archaeologists do their middle-range research through controlled and directed replication. Although sometimes involving newer, high-tech methods, experimental archaeology is not itself new; many of these questions have been around a long time, and so have experimental archaeologists.*

Behavior is the first thing to go when you're dead.

LARRY MARTIN, PALEONTOLOGIST

Simply stated, the archaeological record is the contemporary evidence left from prehistoric or historic cultures. These are the static remains of past dynamic behavior. Both natural and cultural factors have impinged on these remains to such a degree that the archaeological record is rarely a direct reflection of past behavior. There are three key components to the archaeological record.

First, as we have already seen, *the archaeological record is a contemporary phenomenon.* Although the objects and their contexts might have existed for centuries or millennia, observations and knowledge about those objects and contexts remain as contemporary as the archaeologists who do the observing.

The second significant point is that although created through dynamic behavior, *the archaeological record itself is static, dead, lifeless, and noninformative.* Michael Schiffer of the University of Arizona has brilliantly clarified this critical realization. Schiffer began with the key distinction between *archaeological* and *systemic* contexts. The artifacts, features, and residues with which archaeologists deal once were part of an ongoing, dynamic behavioral system. Arrowheads were manufactured, used for specific tasks, often broken, sometimes repaired, and then lost or deliberately discarded. Potsherds were once part of whole pots, which were manufactured and decorated according to prescribed cultural criteria, used for utilitarian or ceremonial functions, and then either broken or deliberately discarded, perhaps as part of a rite or ritual. Food bones are the organic residues resulting from a succession of activities—hunting, butchering, cooking, and consumption. While these materials are being manufactured and used, they exist in their **systemic context**. These items are part of the actual behavioral system.

By the time such materials reach the archaeologist's hands, they have long ceased to participate in this behavioral system. The artifacts, features, and residues encountered by archaeologists are recovered from their **archaeological context**, where they interact only with the natural environment. Although these natural conditions still remain dynamic and interactive, the cultural milieu has become static and noninteractive. It is common, of course, for items to move back and forth between contexts. During the archaeological excavation at Gatecliff Shelter, for instance, artifacts were removed from their archaeological contexts and placed into the systemic contexts of the 1970s. In effect, doing archaeology is part of today's systemic context.

Formation Processes That Create the Archaeological Record

To this point, we have perceived the archaeological record as contemporary, yet static and distinct from the behavioral processes that produced it. Our definition of the archaeological record contains a third key attribute: *Because of a variety of intervening factors, both natural and cultural, this record is not usually a direct reflection of past behavior.*

These "intervening factors" are what condition the archaeological record as we know it today. Before archaeologists can meaningfully encounter the archaeological record, they must grasp the important transformations that wrenched the objects, features, and residues from their behavioral interactions and deposited them into the static record we encounter today. Once again, we are indebted to

Michael Schiffer for defining an appropriate framework for understanding the transformational processes, both cultural and noncultural, that create the archaeological record.

Schiffer has defined **cultural processes** as the "processes of human behavior that affect or transform artifacts after their initial period of use in a given activity." For our purposes, it is sufficient to distinguish among four distinctive cultural transformations that directly influence the creation of archaeological sites: deposition, reclamation, disturbance, and reuse.

Depositional Processes

Cultural deposition transforms materials from a systemic to an archaeological context. In contrast, **depositional processes** are the operations directly responsible for the accumulation of archaeological sites.

Cultural deposition processes are relatively easy to study, and they constitute the dominant factor in forming the archaeological record. For example, when a pottery vessel is broken and discarded on the trash heap, it has ceased to function in the behavioral system and becomes incorporated in its new archaeological context: This is cultural deposition. Similarly, when an individual dies and is buried, the physical being has been transformed from a systemic to an archaeological context.

Depositional processes need not involve deliberate discard or ritual; one major depositional process is the simple loss of still-useful artifacts. In this case, the transformation from systemic to archaeological context is accidental, involving artifacts that are still capable of performing tasks in the behavioral system. Archaeologists are generally quite familiar with cultural deposition processes because they are directly relevant to conventional archaeological interpretation.

In Chapter 4, we discussed the *law of superposition,* the most general statement governing depositional processes in archaeology. Other principles governing cultural deposition are more complex. Size, for instance, has been found to have a major influence on the way that items are deposited in the archaeological record. One study of discard behavior, conducted on the campus of the University of Arizona, showed that small items (those less than 4 inches in overall dimensions) were discarded almost independently of the location of trash cans, although larger items almost always found their way into trash cans when they were available. A number of specific transformations ("transforms") condition the way in which artifacts and ecofacts enter the archaeological record.

Reclamation Processes

Somewhat more elusive is the **reclamation process.** As the name indicates, this is the transition of cultural materials from the archaeological back into the systemic context. It is not uncommon to find evidence that archaeological artifacts have been scavenged for reuse by both nonindustrial and industrial peoples. Whenever a discarded projectile point is resharpened, a potsherd picked up and used to scrape hides, or an old brick reused in a new fireplace, reclamation has occurred. The act of archaeological excavation is itself reclamation: Artifacts are removed from their archaeological contexts and integrated into the functioning behavioral system of the archaeological profession. A common and recurring problem when dealing with surface sites is to recognize and account for previous collecting on that site.

We know, for instance, that when people collect artifacts from the surface of a site, the larger, more complete artifacts generally are the first to be picked up. If either scientific collection or unethical "pothunting" continue, the remaining complete artifacts will be removed, along with the smaller, harder-to-find ones. After years of artifact collecting, all that is left is a scatter of barely recognizable bits and pieces. Archaeologists oblivious to the ongoing reclamation processes would probably produce differing (systemic) interpretations for the same site, depending on the stage of prior collecting at which they encounter the site. Unlike cultural deposition, reclamation has received relatively little attention from archaeologists until very recently.

Disturbance Processes

The first two cultural formation processes pertain to the transference of materials between archaeological and systemic contexts. But the archaeological record is also heavily conditioned by transformations within the archaeological and systemic contexts. **Disturbance processes** change the contexts of materials within the archaeological site itself. Examples include such diverse cultural mechanisms as dam building, farming, and heavy construction. Although the disturbance process has few direct implications for systemic contexts, the modification (and, indeed, preservation) of archaeological sites is a major and pressing problem facing modern archaeology.

Reuse Processes

The final relevant cultural mechanism is reuse, or the transformation of materials through successive states in the behavioral system. The **reuse process** moves a single object through a series of different behavioral settings. Potsherds, for example, are sometimes ground up to be used as temper in manufacturing new vessels, and broken arrowheads are rechipped into drills and scrapers.

A host of noncultural formation processes also influences the archaeological record. The natural environment affects cultural materials, in both systemic and archaeological contexts: microscopic and mechanical decay; churning by rodents and earthworms; geological events such as volcanic eruptions, earthquakes, and flash floods.

A complex suite of natural and cultural transformations interact to create each unique archaeological site, and they must be recognized in order to project contemporary meaning onto our observations of the past. So viewed, the archaeological record is a "distorted" reflection of the structure of past cultural systems. These distortions occur as the result of both cultural and noncultural processes, and the regularities in such processes are of major concern to contemporary scholars studying the archaeological record.

Throughout the rest of this chapter, we shall see how (and why) archaeologists are conducting "actualistic" studies to learn more about the systemic contexts in which the archaeological record is initially formed. From conducting fieldwork among native people to digging up their own garbage, these archaeologists are trying to define the dynamics that link behavior to the static archaeological record.

Middle-Range Research: What Is It?

Remember from Chapter 2 that archaeogists employ theory at three basic levels. *Low-level theories,* at one end of the spectrum, are the observations that emerge from basic archaeological fieldwork, the actual "data" or "facts" of archaeology. In earlier chapters, we saw how these data are generated.

At the opposite end of the theoretical spectrum is *high-level (or general) theory,* the broad, overarching research strategies that condition archaeological theory. The research strategy of cultural materialism, for instance, informs what became the *processual agenda* for doing Americanist archaeology. An alternative viewpoint, the *postprocessual critique,* arose from the general postmodern interpretivist reserarch strategy. We introduced these concepts in Chapter 2, and their influence on the interpretation of the archaeological record is a recurring theme.

In this chapter, we see how the high- and low-level theoretical extremes are brought together. By conducting so-called *middle-range research,* archaeologists are generating the knowledge necessary to relate the world of archaeological facts to the world of general behavioral theory. We shall consider several ways to do this, using ethnoarchaeology, experimental archaeology, and the heralded "Garbage Project" as examples of how archaeologists study the processes of site formation.

But before doing this, we will look more closely at why theory at the middle range is necessary. Why, after all, is it so difficult to link the archaeological facts with the behaviors that produced them? This is archaeology's so-called *linkage problem.*

The Linkage Problem

Facts never speak for themselves; facts are known, particular observations; the mission of science is to use these facts to generate universal statements called *theories.* In reality, the facts of archaeology are contemporary observations made on the material remains of the past. Archaeology requires external input from today's behavioral world in order to bridge the gap between these contemporary observations and past behavior.

Geologists face a similar problem. The geological record, like that of archaeology, consists of only two things: the objects and the relationships among them. A "geological fact" is an observation made by a contemporary geologist on objects from the geological record. Since rocks do not speak, how do geologists advance from their contemporary observations to meaningful pronouncements about the remote geological past? This obstacle was addressed long ago by pioneering geologists. The modern science of geology is said to have begun largely through the efforts of James Hutton. An eighteenth-century medical doctor and gentleman farmer, Hutton formulated a simple principle that provided the very cornerstone of modern geology. Hutton's principle, called the **doctrine of uniformitarianism,** asserts that the processes now operating to modify the earth's surface are the same ones that operated long ago in the geological past. It is that simple: *The geological processes of the past and the present are assumed to be identical.*

Here's an example. We know from modern experiments that as today's glaciers move, they deposit distinctive glacial debris, often in distinctive formations (called **moraines**). Thorough study of modern glaciers has convinced geologists that moraines and striations are formed only through glacial action. Now, suppose a geologist finds moraines and striated rocks in Ohio, California, or New Mexico, where no glaciers exist today. Armed with a knowledge of contemporary glacial processes, the geologist can readily frame and test hypotheses explaining ancient glacial action. This is an important point: *Observation of contemporary, ongoing processes provides the bridging arguments (or linkages) necessary to assign meaning to the geological objects of the past.*

Precisely the same logical stricture applies to archaeology. Archaeologists recover the material remains of past cultural processes. Like geologists, archaeologists can frame hypotheses that account for the formation and deposition of these physical remains. Input from contemporary anthropological observation supplies the **bridging arguments** necessary to translate general hypotheses into specific, observable outcomes that can be expected to appear in the archaeological record. Anthropology allows archaeologists to bridge this important gap between contemporary observation and relevant statements about past behavior. This is what **ethnoarchaeology** is all about.

Some Bones of Contention

Let me illustrate this relationship more fully with an example. As we shall discuss in Chapter 7, archaeologists often study the abundance and distribution of animal bones to learn about past diets, hunting practices, how animals were domesticated, how animals were butchered, the season in which the hunt or harvest was conducted, and a host of other related questions. This is called **faunal analysis.**

Most of these faunal studies begin with a consideration of the relative frequencies of various animal bones in archaeological sites. When analyzing the bones from Suberde, a seventh-millennium B.C. Neolithic village in Turkey, Dexter Perkins and Patricia Daly observed that the upper limb bones of wild oxen were usually missing. These static facts—contemporary observations—were then interpreted in terms of past human behavior. In this case, the investigators suggested that the relative frequencies of the bones resulted from the way in which the oxen had been butchered: The animals must first have been skinned; then the meat was stripped from the forequarters and hindquarters, and the upper limb bones thrown away. The investigators presumed that the meat was piled on the skin and the lower limb bones were used to drag the hide bearing the meat back home. Calling this the **schlepp effect** (from the Yiddish word meaning "drag" or "haul"), they figured their interpretation explained why the upper limb bones were left at the kill site and the lower limb bones were discarded at the habitation site.

R. E. Chaplin analyzed the bones recovered from a late ninth-century A.D. Saxon farm in the Whitehall area of London. The facts in this case also indicated a shortage of limb bones, and Chaplin suggested that the limb bones of sheep and cattle disappeared because the carcasses were dressed and exported to market. Chaplin then hypothesized about the marketing and animal husbandry strategies implied by such trade.

Investigators working on American Plains Indian sites also discovered that the upper limb bones of food animals were often missing. When Theodore White analyzed these facts, he decided that the bones must have been destroyed during the manufacture of bone grease from the marrow.

I could cite other examples, but the point is clear. Exactly the same archaeological fact—that habitation sites contain more lower limb bones than upper limb bones—has been construed in three different ways:

1. *Perkins and Daly:* Upper limbs were discarded at the *kill site,* and lower limbs were hauled with the meat back to the campsite.
2. *Chaplin:* Upper limb bones were selectively butchered and traded to market.
3. *White:* Upper limbs were pulverized into bone grease and hence destroyed at the campsite.

The relative frequencies of animal bones comprise some real data—these observations are the "facts" of archaeology. But they have been read differently by three teams of archaeologists, each interpretation suggesting dissimilar behaviors that allegedly created these same facts. Which (if any) interpretation is correct?

This is a problem archaeologists face daily: several competing hypotheses to account for the same body of facts (namely, that lower limb bones were more common than upper limb bones). One hypothesis holds that the animals had been butchered away from the habitation area and that some bones were discarded at the butchering locale while others were carried to camp with the meat. Let us term this perfectly reasonable first suggestion H^1. A second hypothesis, H^2, postulates that after butchering, the choice cuts were traded away, which is why the upper limb bones were rarely found at the habitation site. A third proposal, H^3, hypothesizes that the larger bones had been ground into bone grease, thereby increasing the relative frequency of the smaller elements in the archaeological record.

Dozens of additional hypotheses could be framed to explain why upper limb bones were less common than the lower limbs and feet. Perhaps some bones were venerated in a shrine away from the habitation area. Or maybe the larger bones were made into awls and bone pins. Or possibly the largest bones were used as clubs. At this point in the scientific process, one is perfectly justified in using imagination (and genius, if available) to generate worthwhile hypotheses. There are no rules governing how to get a good idea.

But scientific protocol does stipulate how to select among the competing hypotheses. Let us restrict our attention to the three numbered hypotheses (H^1, H^2, and H^3). Each one is a generalized statement about human behavior. A contemporary archaeologist can never hope to observe somebody butchering a Neolithic wild ox. None of us will ever observe firsthand the making of bone grease by a nineteenth-century American Plains Indian. Those opportunities are gone. Instead, archaeologists must concentrate on finding the material consequences of activities like butchering Neolithic oxen or making bison bone grease.

We do this by constructing a series of logical *if . . . then* statements: If bone grease was manufactured from bison bones, then we should find artifacts X, Y, and Z and physical residues M, N, and O; bones should be distributed in patterns C, D, and E; and specific bone elements (J, K, and L) should be missing. Similarly, to test H^2, we must generate some *if . . . then* statements regarding the trading of meat and bones. Which are the best cuts to trade? How far can meat be transported to be traded before it spoils? Is meat marketed only in the winter months? Are carcasses butchered in special ways so that certain cuts can be traded? These *if . . . then* statements are bridging arguments that translate general, untestable hypotheses into specific expectations that can be tested using archaeological evidence.

But—I hope you are wondering—how do we know these things? Why do archaeologists surmise that making bone grease requires artifacts X, Y, and Z? And how do we know which bone elements are destroyed in the process? *Hypothesis testing is only as robust as these if . . . then bridging arguments.* If we generate incorrect implications, then our hypothesis testing will be worse than useless, because it will lead us to specious conclusions.

Here is where the notion of *middle-range research* comes into play. Because the facts are incapable of speaking for themselves, it is necessary for archaeologists to provide firm bridging arguments to breathe behavioral life into the objects of the past. In the earlier analogy between archaeology and geology, I cited the doctrine of uniformitarianism: The processes that now operate to modify the earth's surface are the same processes that operated in the geological past. Precisely the same issues face contemporary archaeologists when they attempt to interpret the material remains of past cultural processes. Archaeologists also must frame hypotheses to account for the formation and deposition of these physical remains, and so they require bridging arguments to translate the general hypotheses into specific outcomes that can actually be observed in the archaeological record.

Properly formulated, middle-range research links our ideas about the world to the world itself and attributes meaning to our empirical observations. Middle-range research dictates the way we perceive the past and is quite different from the research used to explain that past. In this case, defining middle-range relationships requires that we also develop the precise relationships between concepts and an appropriate class of empirically observable phenomena. Such a linkage has been extremely important to both past and contemporary Americanist archaeology.

Lewis Binford inspecting an abandoned aborigine camp near MacDonald Downs Homestead (Australia). James O'Connell took this picture as part of his long-term ethnoarchaeological research among Alyawara-speaking aborigines. The melons scattered about are the kind formerly cultivated here when the site was occupied.

Middle-range linkage has been an important aspect of archaeological inquiry for more than a century. Lewis Binford's call for middle-range studies served largely to focus this research, and even critics of the new archaeology recognized the importance of middle-range research.

Archaeologists interested in learning about middle-range theory cannot restrict their attention to the past. In order to develop relevant bridging arguments, archaeologists must observe firsthand the workings of a culture in its systemic contexts, much as geologists defined their processes through contemporary observation. This is why they are turning to living peoples for clues to the interpretation of prehistoric remains. Although people are never considered as data, the insights gained by participation in a functioning society have opened the eyes of modern archaeologists.

In all such research, it is necessary to look around and select the closest available analogies for study. Geologists interested in glacial processes cannot today study firsthand the massive continental glaciers that once draped the North American continent, but they can examine the numerous mountain glaciers that occur at the highest altitudes and the higher latitudes.

Archaeologists are now doing similar things, studying possible analogies in order to understand the processes that condition the archaeological record. Sometimes, it is possible to reconstruct such conditions experimentally (and we shall discuss several such experiments). In other cases, contemporary human societies can be found that continue to function under conditions that—in a limited way—are analogous to specific circumstances of the past.

What Is Ethnoarchaeology?

Before the mid-1960s, archaeologists only rarely worked directly with informants (although plenty of them relied on data from ethnographers). Since that time, ethnoarchaeology has become fairly common. Archaeologists have come to realize the importance of establishing a relevant middle-range theory, and the study of living peoples is perhaps the best single way to do so. Then, as archaeologists reach beyond mere chronology, they can make assumptions about the behavior behind the static archaeological record. Increasingly such critical assumptions are tested through firsthand ethnoarchaeological research.

Ethnoarchaeology had a fairly modest beginning. Richard Gould, for instance, was trained as an archaeologist at the University of California and spent months living with the aborigines of Australia and the Tolowa people of northwestern California. Gould was observing the behavior behind the processes that form the archaeological record. Why, he would quiz his informants, are arrowheads made in a particular manner? How does one go about surviving in a harsh environment without benefit of agriculture or industry? Exactly who lives with whom, and what would these houses look like 100 (or 1,000) years from now?

Gould once asked some Tolowa to look at his ongoing archaeological excavations, hoping they could solve some of the puzzles he had encountered. Gould had started digging under the then-standard assumption that habitation areas are best located by looking for surface concentrations of artifacts and midden deposit. But despite repeated digging, he was unable to locate any prehistoric house remains on an otherwise promising site. Seeing his dilemma, the Tolowa informants were quite amused: "Them old-timers never put their houses in the garbage dump. . . . They don't like to live in their garbage any more than you would." His informants pointed, instead, to a steep slope on the edge of the site. Although this hillside had seemed to Gould an unlikely spot on which to construct a house, he followed their suggestion. After only 20 minutes of digging, he came upon a well preserved redwood plank house buried only 18 inches below the surface. Gould's Tolowa informants grinned knowingly.

Such are the lessons of ethnoarchaeology.

Lewis Binford Takes Off for Points North

Ethnoarchaeological inquiry such as this provides the arguments necessary to bridge the gap between observable archaeological contexts and nonobservable systemic contexts. These propositions, by their nature, will apply to systemic contexts both present and past. Ethnoarchaeology is based on the premise that if generalizations cannot cover the contemporary contexts, they cannot be viewed as adequate. Lewis Binford conducted significant ethnoarchaeological research in the 1970s among the Nunamiut people of Alaska. These people were particularly appropriate to Binford's interest because he had studied reindeer bones on Mousterian sites in France and wanted a chance to work with people still hunting reindeer. The Arctic environment was also somewhat similar to that of the Middle Paleolithic French occupation sites he had studied. But Binford emphasized that "the focus on fauna and my study of the Nunamiut were not research choices made because of an abiding interest in either fauna or Eskimos. My primary interest was in evaluating the utility of certain concepts commonly employed by the archaeologist."

He accompanied the Nunamiut hunters on practically all the various kinds of hunting they practice today. He was concerned with recording what the hunters

> ## In His Own Words
>
> ### *Why I Began Doing Ethnoarchaeology*
> ### *by Lewis R. Binford*
>
> In 1967 I received funds to go to Europe for a year to work more closely with François Bordes in Bordeaux. My program for research was the following. If we could not study the chipped stone directly, perhaps we could study faunal remains and the horizontal distributions, on excavated archaeological floors, of both fauna and chipped stone. Then it might be possible to relate variability in the lithics to these other properties of the archaeological sites in question. I worked for a year in France, identifying and plotting all the stone tools and animal bones by anatomical part and by breakage pattern.
>
> Then began the first of a whole series of disillusionments. I performed one correlation study after another—so many, in fact, that I needed a great steel trunk in order to carry all the papers back to the United States. I could tell you cross-correlations between any pair of Mousterian tool-types, between tools and bones, between bones and the drip-lines in cave sites, between almost any type of data you care to name. What I found, of course, was many new facts that nobody had seen before. But none of these new facts spoke for themselves.
>
> My metal trunk was so big and heavy that I decided to return home by boat and that five-day trip from Le Havre to New York gave me an opportunity for some disconsolate self-reflection. The whole project was obviously a total failure. What had I done wrong? What had I not done that I should have done? Could it really be that archaeologists simply cannot learn anything about the past? Where was I missing the real problem?
>
> By the time we steamed into New York City, just before the New Year of 1969, some of the answers to these problems were suggested, at least in my thoughts. I prepared a research proposal to go to the Arctic in the spring of 1969 to live with a group of Eskimo hunters. My reasons for going there were little more specific at that stage than that it could hardly fail to be a good educational experience. If I was ever to be able to make accurate inferences from archaeological facts, I was convinced that I had to understand the dynamics of living systems and study their static consequences.

did at each locality and what debris would be left for the archaeologist. Binford was struck by the general lack of correlation between observed activities and the artifacts that were deposited in the archaeological record. He characterized the Nunamiut technology as "almost exclusively curated," meaning that artifacts are reused and transported so much that they are rarely deposited (lost) in contexts that reflect their actual manufacture and use. One problem for archaeologists is that localities that are demonstrably different in behavioral (systemic) terms may produce archaeological sites that are almost identical. Differentiation among activities is possible only by means of artifacts, which are very rare and nearly always broken and heavily modified through use. The more that artifacts are curated, preserved, and transported, the less correspondence there will be between the systemic and archaeological contexts of given sites.

Since then, Binford has expanded his ethnoarchaeological fieldwork across three continents. In Australia, he joined James O'Connell to study site structure and butchering patterns among the Alyawara aborigines. He traveled to South Africa to observe firsthand the effect of hyenas and other scavengers on bone assemblages. Binford also returned several times to the Nunamiut, mapping, collecting, and observing the linkages between modern behavior and the archaeological record it creates.

The Garbage Project: The Archaeology of Yesterday's Lunch

Wait a thousand years and even the garbage left behind by a vanished civilization becomes precious to us.
ISAAC ASIMOV (1920–1992), AMERICAN WRITER

Why wait a thousand years?
WILLIAM L. RATHJE, ARCHAEOLOGIST (UNIVERSITY OF ARIZONA)

Another example of ethnoarchaeological research is the self-declared Garbage Project. Emil Haury was the senior archaeologist at the University of Arizona for decades. A specialist in southwestern prehistory, Haury continually taught his students that "if you want to know what is really going on in a community, look at its garbage."

Haury's earthy advice was not lost on his students and colleagues. In 1971 the University of Arizona launched a long-term, in-depth study of just that—garbage. But it must have surprised Haury when he found out which community the Garbage Project decided to study; they were after the garbage of contemporary Tucson, Arizona.

The Garbage Project was started by William Rathje, a Harvard-trained archaeologist who had previously specialized in the Classic Maya. Through the Garbage Project, Rathje (now a professor at the University of Arizona) was attempting to apply archaeological methods to the analysis and description of modern societies.

The Garbage Project has several practical applications, each of which we now examine in some detail.

Quantifying Today's Material Reality

The archaeology of contemporary society began as a rather bizarre concept, but a considerable amount of such ethnoarchaeological research has been conducted over the past 25 years. Rathje was dissatisfied with available research techniques for dealing with contemporary society, particularly the dependence on interviews and questionnaires. He saw the very act of conducting an interview or administering a questionnaire as a foreign element intruding into the social setting under study. Respondents are continually aware of their status as subjects, and the questions themselves can act as agents of change and bias. Sociology and psychology have become largely the science of administering questionnaires and interviewing informants. Nothing in the training of sociologists or psychologists equips them to deal with actual physical evidence. This is sometimes a problem in traditional ethnography as well.

Archaeologists, of course, have been dealing with mute material evidence for over a century. But why restrict ourselves to behaviors that have become extinct? For more than two decades, Rathje has searched for ways to apply established archaeological methods and theory to the analysis of contemporary behavior.

The key term here is *nonreactive*. Whereas conventional questionnaires condition the nature of the response, material culture is static and relatively easy to quantify. Garbage is garbage, discarded without the knowledge that some archaeologist is going to be sorting through it—this is what is meant by *nonreactive*.

Operating continually since 1973, Rathje's Garbage Project began in Tucson, an urban community with a population of slightly more than 360,000. A strict sampling design ensures the proper correlation with relevant socioeconomic variables, and garbage is picked up from randomly selected households. Student

Garbage Project archaeologists at the sorting table.

volunteers from the University of Arizona sort the garbage on special sorting tables provided by the sanitation department's maintenance yard in Tucson. (As with all archaeological fieldwork, the student workers are required to take the appropriate inoculations and are given appropriate field equipment—in this case, laboratory coats, surgical masks, and gloves.) Students sort garbage items into about 150 categories under the larger headings of food, drugs, sanitation products, amusement and educational items, communication, and pet-related products. The data are then recorded on forms for computer processing. The standard principles of archaeological classification provide objective, repeatable categories of data retrieval. Satellite projects have been launched throughout North America, and over the years the Garbage Project has involved some 1,000 students and 60 organizations, recording more than 2 million items from 15,000 household refuse samples.

University of Arizona archaeologists, however, are hardly the first to snoop in somebody else's garbage can. The most sensational garbage probe occurred some years ago, when A. J. Weberman—a self-proclaimed "garbage guerrilla"—investigated the private lives of celebrities as reflected in their garbage. In one sense, Weberman was following up the same discrepancy that bothered the sociologists—people say one thing yet often do another. Pop singer Bob Dylan, for instance, proclaimed benign disinterest in popular fan magazines, boasting that he never read what they wrote about him. But when Weberman ransacked Dylan's New York garbage pail, he reported that "the many rock magazines wasted Bob's claim that he didn't follow the rock scene."

Dylan, of course, was outraged and reportedly directed his housekeeper henceforth to deliver his trash directly to the sanitation workers. Weberman conducted similar garbage exposés on other celebrities such as boxer Muhammad Ali, playwright Neil Simon, and yippie Abbie Hoffman. Rathje terms such tactics "a rip-off, a threat to the conduct of garbage research as a means of quantifying the resource management strategies of population segments."

To combat the adverse publicity that resulted from the Bob Dylan and Muhammad Ali cases, the Garbage Project instituted elaborate safeguards in their collection procedure so as to ensure the complete anonymity of all individuals and households. The sample garbage is collected by sanitation department foremen, who are not present when the bags are opened and who are denied access to the Garbage Project data. Personal data such as names, addresses, photographs, or financial statements are never recorded and are not analyzed. The Garbage Project field director and/or one senior Garbage Project field supervisor are always present during analysis to ensure that no personal items are examined or saved. Participating students are required to sign pledges against even looking at such personal items. No garbage of any kind is saved; all aluminum is recycled, and the rest of the garbage is sent to sanitary landfills.

Examining Social Issues

The Garbage Project has used its accumulated data to study a number of contemporary social issues, one of them being alcohol consumption. Years ago, the

Pima County Health Department conducted interviews with 1 percent of the households in the city of Tucson. Questions had been phrased like this: "On the average, how many cans or bottles of beer does _____ have in a usual week?" The sample had been carefully chosen using conventional sociological procedures, and informant anonymity had been assured. The health department then published its findings, which were taken by many as an accurate indication of the rate of alcohol consumption in Tucson.

How do the questionnaires stack up against the material evidence? Rathje's garbage volunteers record the presence of beer bottles and cans as part of their routine sorting. They also note the kind and volume of the containers discarded and have even tried to monitor the amount of recycling of aluminum cans.

Rathje points out a discrepancy between front-door answers given to interviewers and back-door behavior as reflected by the actual contents of the trash. Garbage cans don't lie, and the differences from the health department questionnaire were striking. In one tract, only 15 percent of the respondent households admitted to consuming beer, and no household reported drinking more than eight cans in a week. But the Garbage Project data from that same area showed that more than 80 percent of the households had beer containers in their garbage pails and that fully 54 percent discarded more than eight cans each week. In fact, these households averaged about two and a half six-packs each week. Although the details varied among the sampling tracts, the patterning was always the same: significantly heavier beer consumption—in the form of more drinkers and higher rates of drinking—than was reported to the interviewers.

That the interview data are distorted should astound nobody. People simply drink more beer than they own up to. But the degree of distortion is noteworthy, and the analysis of the material remains even provides future interviewers with a means for correcting this inevitable bias. The skewing, it turns out, is also correlated with socioeconomic factors. The low-income Mexican American households typically distorted their interviews by reporting no beer consumption at all. By contrast, middle-income Anglo respondents, although they admitted to limited beer consumption, significantly underreported the amount of beer they actually consumed. These preliminary findings point up future directions not only for garbage research but also for the administration of health questionnaires.

Linking Past to Present

The Garbage Project also attempts to compare modern food discard behavior with past trends. They give American householders mixed reviews. On the one hand, the actual waste of food has declined through time. During World War I, the War Food Administration collected large-scale food discard data for U.S. households (one of the few known precursors to Rathje's Garbage Project). In 1918, households discarded between 25 percent and 30 percent of the total amount of solid food acquired. This compares with only 10 percent to 15 percent food waste in Tucson during the period since the Garbage Project began (which may, or may not, represent trends for the entire United States). The decrease in waste is probably linked to increasingly available technology for processing, packaging, storing, and transporting food. But although this represents a significant improvement, Rathje points out that it was achieved in a typically American way: by turning to technology to solve our problems.

The Garbage Project data also disclose some surprises about the effectiveness of modern recycling campaigns. The advertising media have given great coverage to campaigns by beverage companies and aluminum factories to recycle aluminum cans; Boy Scouts sponsor newspaper drives to raise money and to save trees; and more Christmas cards are printed on recycled paper each year.

Rathje's research found that the households of Tucson recycled only 19 percent of all wood fiber; this figure stands in marked contrast to the 35 percent national average that was recycled during World War II. Similarly, studies of a mid-1800s trash deposit in Magdelena, Mexico, show that only broken bottles were discarded, and these had apparently been reused extensively before breakage. In the 1970s, the average Tucson household discarded about 500 whole bottles each year; of these, more than 10 percent were made of returnable glass and could have—ideally—been used up to 40 times had they been returned.

Want some more examples of waste?

■ Health-conscious America is eating less fat from red meat and slimming down to minimize the risk of colon and breast cancer. To do this, people are buying fewer steaks, roasts, and chops (because you can *see* all the fat they contain!). What do they buy instead? Mostly sausage, bologna, hot dogs, and luncheon meat—products that contain even more fat. But because it's "invisible," it's OK, right?

■ Because of a botulism scare, people throw away even slightly dented cans of food. The problem? Only an *expanded* can indicates danger from botulism.

■ Garbage Project figures suggest that the citizens of Tucson, Arizona, daily discard $3,000 in coins. But before you quit your day job and head for the landfill, remember that your daily haul in coins is embedded in 600 tons of garbage.

Looking at America's Landfills

Shortly after World War II, the "landfill" became the most popular way to dispose of refuse in the United States. Five decades later, more than 70 percent of our garbage—180 million tons annually—is tossed into the 5,500 active landfills across the country. Every man, woman, and child in the United States generates 4 pounds of trash a day—a staggering thought. For most of us, once this trash is dumped in a garbage can, it's gone, off to a landfill someplace. But our landfills are filling up and the cost of dumping trash is skyrocketing. Little thought has been given to the long-term environmental and societal consequences. Our landfills are nearing full capacity, and few new ones are being approved.

America has precious little idea what's going on in her landfills and how to plan for the future. Our annual trash bill is about 15 billion dollars and rising.

No wonder Rathje speaks of a "serious garbage problem." But all is not lost—archaeology to the rescue!

The Garbage Project devised a plan to employ systematic archaeological methods to explore a series of landfills across the United States. To date, the Garbage Project has completed excavations in 15 landfills from California to New York, from Toronto to Florida, recovering and analyzing about 12 metric tons of debris initially deposited between 1952 and 1989.

Perhaps the most impressive excavation took place at the Fresh Kills landfill on Staten Island, New York City. First opened in 1948, it receives 17,000 tons of refuse daily. Today, the landfill occupies 2.4 billion cubic feet, covering 3,000 acres—25 times the size of the Great Pyramid at Giza. It is one of the largest human-made monuments in the world.

Rathje argues that "if we are making such a large contribution to future generations, we should know exactly what we are bequeathing them. The only way to unlock these entombed secrets is to excavate—with hands-on digging, sorting, analyzing, and even smelling."

How do you dig a landfill? Basically, the Garbage Project employs well established archaeological methods. For one thing, the various "strata" can be chronologically ordered using newspapers and magazines. Season of deposition can be monitored, for instance, by the presence of pine needles and Santa Claus logos on packaging in "Christmastime" deposits. Telephone books are particularly good stratigraphic markers because everybody receives new ones at the same time and most toss out the old with the next day's garbage. The new findings suggest that decomposition proceeds more slowly than anticipated in recent landfills, suggesting that a revamping of our garbage priorities may be in order.

Landfill exposures were made by backhoe trenches (up to 25 feet deep) and bucket-auger wells, reaching down 100 feet. With their hands-on, archaeological perspective, the Garbage Project personnel can calculate exactly what's going into America's landfills. When most people think of trash heaps, they think of plastic bags, plastic cups, and disposable plastic diapers. Plastic is what Rathje calls "everybody's favorite villain. . . . We will believe anything bad about plastic." In fact, the Garbage Project excavations show that plastic might not be so bad after all. Surprisingly, our landfills contain relatively little plastic, only about 15 percent by volume.

The big culprit, it turns out, is *paper*—packaging, newspapers, telephone books, glossy magazines, and mail order catalogs. Paper takes up fully 40 to 50 percent of American landfills. Despite the growing commitment to local recyling programs, the amount of paper is steadily rising—up from only 35 percent in 1970. And, here's the really bad news: Contrary to popular opinion, paper doesn't biodegrade very well. The Garbage Project has found 40-year-old newspapers, still fully readable.

In fact, **biodegradation** is one of the biggest myths in the trash business. Our landfills are constructed, literally, in the belief that the nasty stuff inside will—sooner rather than later—simply decompose on its own, like some kind of monumental compost heap.

Wrong. Very little in our landfills is actually biodegrading. Backyard compost heaps work well, but only when we chop up the organics, add lots of fluids, and regularly churn the whole batch. This process does not happen in landfills: Nothing is chopped up, fluids are often prohibited, and landfill debris is compacted, not churned. The end result is that our landfills are incredibly inefficient in terms of biodegradation. Organics will, to be sure, eventually break down, but this is a very, very slow process.

Want to know one of the most common foods preserved in landfills? Hot dogs–those preservatives really work! If you want a 20-year-old hot dog, Rathje's got one.

Most of our knowledge about solid waste disposal and landfill design comes from laboratory experiments, but the inside workings of landfills–what actually happens–has remained almost entirely unknown. The U.S. government governs, and there are plenty of federal policies regulating landfills. But usually, these government planners plan by making "logical assumptions" about what landfills "should" contain.

Rathje doesn't assume; he digs. If we are interested in finding sensible ways to dispose of our trash, doesn't it make sense for us to know *exactly* what is being thrown away? And he has learned that many of the long-held assumptions about America's garbage are just that–rubbish.

So there you have it. The Garbage Project is an important component of middle-range theory building in contemporary archaeology, highlighting the importance of applying archaeological methods to discern modern, ongoing trends. It is so radical that comparable data are almost nonexistent.

Like much of the middle-range research, the Garbage Project has two basic goals. On the one hand, Rathje and his team are finding out how material

---

In His Own Words

Garbage and Our Future
by William L. Rathje

I wonder sometimes how future generations will see us when they look at our garbage. I interpret the Classic period of the Maya civilization as one of profligate waste, followed by a period of decline. The Maya woke up and discovered resources were in short supply, and they became very efficient very fast–they recycled, they reused. But it was too late.

If we compare our garbage to theirs, I think we can see we're still in a classic phase; that is, we're still discarding tremendous amounts of valuable resources on a daily basis. We have an important opportunity today. We can go into a period of efficiency and pragmatism, and in that way sustain our society in the style to which we've become accustomed for a much longer time.

remains relate to the behavior that produced them: This is a *methodological* objective. They are also attempting to find workable explanations of specific and recurrent patterns they observe in the archaeological record: This is a *substantive* objective.

Taken together, this is what middle-range research is all about: linking archaeological data with the relevant aspects of human behavior that produced it. Because ethnoarchaeologists like Rathje work in contemporary society, they can observe this behavior, providing important analytical tools for use on more ancient trash deposits, where the human behavior vanished long ago.

Experimental Archaeology as Middle-Range Research

Another way to explore middle-range theory is through *experimental archaeology,* studying the archaeological process through experimental reconstruction of earlier conditions. The origins of this approach can be traced back to Saxton Pope, a surgeon at the University of California Medical Center (San Francisco). The poignant story began in 1911, when a beaten and defeated Indian, later named Ishi, was found crouching in a slaughterhouse corral near Oroville, California. His family either had been murdered or had starved, and Ishi himself had lost his will to live. The local sheriff locked him in the jail, as "wild" Indians were not allowed to roam about freely in those days. Through good fortune, Alfred Kroeber, a young anthropologist at the University of California, learned of Ishi's plight and arranged for his release. Kroeber brought Ishi to San Francisco and secured quarters for him in the university museum. From that time until Ishi's death in 1916, Kroeber and his staff taught Ishi the ways of "civilization," and the Indian revealed his secrets of survival in back-land California; clearly Ishi had more to offer.

Ishi (ca. 1860–1916), a Yana-Yahi man.

Ishi soon developed a tubercular cough —which later cost him his life—and was treated daily by Dr. Pope. Over their short association, Pope and Ishi found common ground in their interest in archery. An odd combination: Pope, the urbane physician-scholar, paired with the Yahi Indian, hair singed in tribal custom, together shooting arrows through the parks of downtown San Francisco. Pope was a good student, and after Ishi's death, Pope continued his research into the almost lost art of archery, studying bows and arrows preserved in museum collections and often test-shooting the ancient specimens.

Pope wrote *Hunting With the Bow and Arrow* in 1923, describing his experiments in archery. The book not only provided baseline information for interpreting ancient finds but also quickly became the bible of the bow-hunting fraternity. Apparently, as many sportsmen as archaeologists were intrigued by the fine points of this nearly extinct art. Now, of course, archery is big business. This is but a single example of how the techniques of a nearly lost survival art were salvaged by timely observation and experimentation.

Stone Tools: How Were They Made?

Unlike archery, many other prehistoric techniques died with their practitioners, and experimental archaeologists have been forced to rediscover the lost technology.

Making a stone tool is not easy. Appropriate raw materials—rocks such as flint, obsidian, and basalt—must be located, tested, and collected. Sometimes, it is necessary to heat-treat them to improve "flakability." Then a series of stone flakes is knocked off the "core" to create a shaped tool; sometimes, you use the already-sharp flakes as tools. Anyway, anybody who thinks it's easy to make a stone tool should give it a try—it is not as easy as it might seem. Unfortunately, over the millennia, plenty has been forgotten about the technology required to make good stone tools from a pile of rocks.

Fortunately, a school of dedicated experimentalists has spent years rediscovering some of the virtually extinct technology used to make stone tools. Don Crabtree (affiliated with the Idaho State University Museum) began this research by undertaking a series of carefully documented studies to uncover the nature of prehistoric stoneworking. One of Crabtree's many projects was to rediscover the techniques once used during the years of the **Folsom culture** to fabricate spear points like those discovered at the Lindenmeier site in Colorado. Folsom points, some of the world's most exquisite stone artifacts, were originally made between 10,000 and 11,000 years ago. Mounted on spear shafts, these artifacts were used for hunting larger, now-extinct forms of American bison. Although each spear point is only about 2 inches long, Crabtree counted more than 150 minute sharpening flakes removed from the surface.

The distinctive property of Folsom artifacts is the **flute** (or channel flake) removed from both sides of the base. Nobody is really sure why these artifacts were thinned in this distinctive fashion, but everybody agrees that fluting is an extraordinary feat of **flintknapping**—almost impossible to achieve. The technical quality and intrinsic beauty of the Folsom point intrigued Crabtree. Most projectile points can be fashioned in a few minutes (by somebody who has spent years studying the techniques). But making the Folsoms must have required hours, assuming that one understood how to do it in the first place. And in the twentieth century, nobody did.

Archaeologists speculated for years how the flutes were removed. Frank H. H. Roberts, the archaeologist who excavated the Lindenmeier Folsom points, concluded that the channel flakes must have been driven off with a bone or antler punch serving as an intermediary to transfer the blow to the artifact. Interested in flintknapping for most of his life, Crabtree thought about this, tried it out himself, and concluded that Roberts's technique would not work.

So began an experimental period that lasted more than 40 years. Crabtree tried every way he could think of to manufacture Folsom replicas. In his published account, he described the 11 different methods he had tried to remove fluting flakes. Most techniques simply did not work: Either the method was impossible with primitive tools or the resulting flute was different from those on the Folsoms. One method succeeded only in driving a copper punch through his left hand.

Crabtree eventually concluded that fluting flakes could be removed in only two ways. In one experiment, he placed an antler shaft on the bottom of the unfinished artifact and then struck the punch with a sharp upward blow. But because placement of the antler punch was critical, this technique requires two workers—not a very satisfactory solution. At one point, Crabtree came across a documentary source describing some long-lost flintknapping techniques once practiced by Native Americans. Particularly interesting were the observations of a Spanish Franciscan friar, Juan de Torquemada, who had traveled through the Central American jungles in 1615:

> They take a stick with both hands, and set well home against the edge of the front of the stone, which also is cut smooth in that part; and they press it against their brest [*sic*], and with the force of the pressure there flies off a knife. . . . Then they sharpen it [the tip of the crutch] on a stone using a hone to give it a very fine edge; and in a very short time these workmen will make more than twenty knives in the aforesaid manner.

Torquemada was describing how flakes could be driven off a polyhedral core, but Crabtree wondered whether the method might work to produce meaningful results on his Folsom replicas. Crabtree manufactured a chest crutch following Torquemada's descriptions, padding one end and equipping the other with a sharp antler flaker. He tied an unfinished, unfluted Folsom point into a wood-and-thong vise, which he gripped between his feet. Bracing the crutch against his chest, he successfully detached perfect fluting flakes, time after time. The resulting artifacts were almost identical to the prehistoric Lindenmeier Folsom points.

Crabtree's pioneering research unleashed an avalanche of interest in the fluting problem. Henry Irwin was able to detach fluting flakes with **direct percussion,** using wood or stone as a "backstop." J. Jeffrey Flenniken did it with a modified version of Crabtree's method of indirect percussion. C. Tunnell used **indirect percussion** with a grooved anvil-and-backstop arrangement. Eugene Gryba reported several experiments in which he detached channel flakes with a simple, hand-generated pressure technique. George Frison and Bruce Bradley once dug up a portion of elk antler amid Folsom point-manufacturing debris at the Agate Basin site in Wyoming; after extensive experimentation, they concluded that channel flakes could be successfully removed with a wood-and-antler lever/fulcrum device. Somebody else used indirect percussion with a grooved anvil-and-backstop

Accomplished flintknapper Bruce Bradley uses a bone flaker to remove pressure flakes from a large corner-notched projectile point. Although he attempts to protect himself with a leather shield, flintknapping is a bloody business and Bradley sports numerous scars from his years of experimental flintknapping.

arrangement, and yet another experimenter was able to detach channel flakes with a simple, hand-generated pressure technique.

Which method was actually used in Folsom times? Who knows? I find it fascinating that all these grown scientists are spending so much time knocking rocks and bloodying their fingers to figure out what was common knowledge 10,500 years ago.

Bruce Bradley has recently injected a spiritual tone into the fluting question. Speaking as one of the world's experts on prehistoric lithic technology, Bradley wonders why anybody would bother to do something so tricky in the first place. He thinks that the complex fluting process probably started out as an expedient way to thin the point's base, to make it easier to tie onto the shaft. But as in many human endeavors, once risk of failure increases, so does desire for supernatural assistance.

Bradley thinks that flintknapping became ritualized during Folsom times. After all, many contemporary Native American cultures include projectile points in sacred bundles, believing that stone points have their own spirit, that they can be used to secure supernatural power.

Life was risky in Folsom times. Not only was fluting a tricky business, but so was putting meat on the table day after day. Could fluting one's Folsom points have become an integral part of some prehunt ritual, a way of making a lithic sign of the cross? Bradley thinks so.

How Does George Frison Hunt Extinct Mammoths?

The people who made Folsom points are classified by archaeologists as **Paleo-Indians**—among the very first people to set foot in America. But the first human footprint in America was not left by the Folsom folks, but probably by their predecessors, those of the **Clovis culture.** The name *Clovis* comes from an important site near Clovis, New Mexico, where Clovis period artifacts were found lying stratigraphically beneath diagnostic Folsom artifacts.

Not only does it predate Folsom, but Clovis is the oldest well documented occupation of the Americas (consistently dating 9500–8500 B.C.). Although claims for pre-Clovis Americans abound, none of these claims has been satisfactorily substantiated. For now at least, the Clovis culture can lay claim to the title "first Americans."

So far, about 20 Clovis sites are known with solid stratigraphic associations. The most common bones associated with Clovis points are mammoth, with bison running a distant second. Camel and indigenous American horse may also have been hunted. Even bear and rabbit have turned up in Clovis contexts.

So it seems unlikely that the Clovis people were totally dependent on mammoth hunting for their survival. Few nonagricultural people focus exclusively on a single food source—particularly one so difficult to hunt as an elephant. Perhaps, as one archaeological wag put, the average Clovis hunter probably saw a mammoth once in his life, and never stopped talking about it—like some archaeologists.

Be that as it may, the fact is that mammoth kills remain the most visible evidence we have of the first Americans. Because they are all we have, archaeologists are always going to dig Paleo-Indian sites and study ancient hunting implements. But these same archaeologists are increasingly hoisting themselves out of the trenches and pushing back from the lab tables, looking for suitable analogies to "see" such ancient behavior patterns firsthand.

Looking at analogies is nothing new in science. We saw, for instance, the elaborate experimentation that has taken place in the attempt to replicate the distinctive Folsom spear points.

But what about studying Clovis hunting practices? Mammoths can no longer be hunted; they have been extinct since Clovis times. So how can science stage a confrontation between a modern hunter and a mammoth? And besides, who would want to?

One archaeologist seems to have found the way. Although a professor and practicing archaeologist at the University of Wyoming, George Frison is also an experienced hunter, and a lifelong student of preindustrial hunting practices. Figuring that the best analogy to a mammoth must be the modern African elephant, Frison took off for Zimbabwe, where he conducted extensive experiments on endangered African elephant populations.

Such "experimentation" was possible only because these elephants have multiplied far beyond the carrying capacity of the national parks, forcing game officials to cull the herds. The Zimbabwe Division of Wildlife agreed to carefully supervised experimentation with Paleo-Indian weaponry—provided only dead or dying animals were targeted.

So there was Frison, Clovis-style replicas in hand, trying to learn what Clovis hunters knew 12,000 years ago. He came away from the experience understanding several things not evident from simply studying archaeological remains.

For one thing, Frison was impressed with the physical strength required to down an elephant with a spear. Hunting elephants is not only dangerous, it's hard work! He knew from looking at frozen Siberian mammoth hides that Ice Age elephants were protected across the vital rib cage area by a half-inch-thick hide. African elephants are built about the same, and it takes an extraordinarily well designed weapon to penetrate such natural protection.

Two huge and carefully crafted Clovis points recovered from the Richie-Roberts site, near Wenatchee (Washington).

It turns out that Clovis points are not only gorgeous, but that they were deliberately made to maximize penetration and minimize breakage. The lateral indentations—the distinctive "flutes"—allowed them to be smoothly and efficiently tied to foreshafts. The point bases were ground smooth, probably to keep them from cutting the shaft bindings.

The Clovis point was the business end of a thrusting spear or dart. Paleo-Indian weaponry probably included a throwing stick (**atlatl**), which Frison found gave him a good combination of leverage and distance. The Clovis point was tied with sinew to a bone or wooden foreshaft which, in turn, fit into a long, heavy mainshaft, probably with a carefully designed hole so the foreshaft would fit snugly.

This composite shaft-foreshaft-point construction provided Clovis hunters with a detachable lance head—a sophisticated piece of hunting equipment well suited for killing at close range. When ambushing, tracking, or holding quarry at bay, hunters could make numerous accurate shots at vital nerve centers. Retrieving the lance and inserting another foreshaft with a stone point could be done in seconds—a much safer and more effective technology than trying to carry and manipulate several lances in such a dangerous situation.

Weapons, Frison discovered, become a subtle extension of the hunter's own body. He thinks that Clovis hunters must have spent considerable time making and maintaining the weapons. If the shaft is not perfectly straight, the spear may not transmit the necessary force to the stone point. And even invisible flaws in the stone point can cause a Clovis point to fail at the critical moment—perhaps allowing a prey to escape or exposing the now-unarmed hunter to sudden danger. Clovis hunters must have continually tested and retested their equipment before setting off on a large-scale kill.

Frison's Zimbabwe experience had made him skeptical of earlier reconstructions of Clovis hunting. Traditionally, artists have drawn Clovis hunters armed with spears, darts, and rocks incapacitating a mammoth trapped in a bog or pit. Barking dogs, women, and children are often pictured in the background, creating a general picture of mayhem and commotion.

Frison thinks this scenario goes against smart hunting know-how. If a healthy mammoth was mired in mud and unable to escape, no band of human hunters would be able to drag it out after the kill. The mammoth would be unbutcherable. The smarter hunter would remain on solid ground, away from crowds, relying on individual prowess and a carefully prepared set of weapons.

What Does Replicative Experimentation Prove?

But what do all these experiments mean? If Crabtree was right, was Irwin wrong? Or maybe Crabtree was wrong and Flenniken was right? But if Gryba is right, does this mean that Crabtree, Irwin, and Flenniken all were wrong? Considerable confusion exists on this point. A widely distributed review article on anthropological flintknapping suggests a series of "formal procedures" by which such replicative experiments are to be judged: The first step is to identify correctly the techniques involved, which are then controlled for several variables, ultimately producing a "statistically valid sample." Experimental results have even been compared technologically with prehistoric controls as a measure of assessing validity. One overenthusiastic proponent wrote: "If valid, the replicator has reproduced a tangible aspect of prehistoric human behavior and demonstrated the reality of that behavior."

The results of experimental archaeology cannot be judged in this way. Adventurer and author Thor Heyerdahl once argued that Easter Island had been populated from the east, by Peruvians, rather than by Polynesians from the west. When skeptics told him that the ocean currents made a westward voyage impossible, Heyerdahl took up the challenge and launched his famous (and successful) raft trip aboard the *Kon-Tiki* westward from South America into Polynesia. But what did Heyerdahl prove? Did he "reproduce tangible aspects of prehistoric human behavior" by his raft trip? Did he "demonstrate the reality" of the past? Hardly. The voyage of the *Kon-Tiki* merely demonstrated to the world that such a westward raft trip was *not impossible*.

While this is a relevant finding, no amount of trans-Pacific bravado will ever *prove* that prehistoric Peruvians had floated to Easter Island. This is an empirical matter, requiring archaeological validation.

So too with lithic experimentation. Crabtree demonstrated that it was *not impossible* to use a chest crutch to replicate the Lindenmeier Folsom points. Gryba showed that hand-held percussion tools could be used to recreate channel flaking. But none of the experimental flintknappers demonstrated conclusively how the Lindenmeier Folsom points were *actually made*. Once again, this is an empirical question, requiring considerable archaeological verification. Like any other scientists, experimental archaeologists should not attempt to think in terms of "right" and "wrong." Replicative experiments do not "demonstrate the reality" of anything; experiments demonstrate only that a given technique could have been used in the past—that it was *not impossible*. So long as these objectives are kept in mind, experimental flintknappers can make significant contributions to the growing body of middle-range research in Americanist archaeology.

Summary

Because the "facts" of archaeology are incapable of speaking for themselves, it is necessary for archaeologists to develop middle-range theoretical arguments to breathe behavioral life into them. Archaeological objects have actually existed in two discrete contexts. When these artifacts, features, and residues were created and used, they existed in *systemic contexts*. But by the time they reach the hands of the archaeologist, the objects have long ceased participating in their behavioral system and have passed into *archaeological contexts*.

Archaeological sites are formed by four basic processes: cultural deposition, reclamation, disturbance, and reuse. Each process has certain regularities, but archaeologists are only beginning to understand the complex mechanisms involved.

Middle-range research links our ideas about the world to the world itself and gives meaning to our empirical observations. Middle-range research dictates the way we perceive the past. In this case, defining middle-range relationships requires that we also define the precise relationships between concepts and an appropriate class of empirically observable phenomena. Such a linkage has been extremely important to both past and contemporary Americanist archaeology.

One way to supply these *bridging arguments* between archaeological and systemic contexts is to study firsthand the workings of ongoing societies. *Ethnoarchaeologists* study living societies, observing artifacts, features, and residues while they still exist in their systemic contexts. To date, ethnoarchaeological studies have examined, among other things, the mechanisms of artifact curation and reuse, and the social correlates of stone tool manufacture and use. Ethnoarchaeologists are also examining the relationship of material culture to modern industrial society, as illustrated by the Garbage Project at the University of Arizona.

Archaeological formation processes are currently being defined by experimental archaeologists. Whereas ethnoarchaeologists work within a functioning behavior system, the experimental archaeologist attempts to derive relevant processes by means of experimental replication; both share a primary interest in middle-range research. Much of this initial experimental work has concentrated on the manufacture and use of stone tools, although archaeologists are currently experimenting on a wide range of problems. Thor Heyerdahl's epic trans-Atlantic and trans-Pacific voyages can even be considered to be a variety of experimental archaeology.

> *Perhaps how it comes to be is really more distinctive than what it is.*
> ALFRED L. KROEBER (1876–1960), AMERICAN ANTHROPOLOGIST

Middle-Range Research on the Internet

Ethnoarchaeology Bibliography has been compiled by Nicholas David of the University of Calgary.
http://www.ucalgary.ca/UofC/faculties/SS/ARKY/nicintro.html

ArchNet-Ethnoarchaeology is a Web site with much useful information.
http://www.lib.uconn.edu/ArchNet

Lithic Resources on ArchNet provides catalogs, overviews, and references.
http://spirit.lib.uconn.edu/ArchNet/Topical/Lithic/Lithic.html

CHAPTER 7

How People Get Their Groceries:
Reconstructing Human Subsistence and Ecology

❏ ❏ ❏

PREVIEW

Archaeologists have a well-stocked arsenal of methods and techniques available for reconstructing how people made a living in the past. In this chapter, we shall discuss many of these.

We begin with bones, one of the most common archaeological finds. Such bones not only enable the archaeologist to study ancient hunting methods and dietary practices, but they can often assist in reconstructing the environments in which people have done their shopping. Getting at the meaning behind the bones is neither easy nor straightforward. This chapter provides you with the basics for understanding what can—and cannot—be done with a bunch of archaeological bones.

Tree-ring analysis is just one way—a very important one—to study how people and plants interacted in the past. Archaeological plant remains also tell us about ancient diets: what wild plants people collected, the domesticated crops people grew, and even the roles played by plants in past rituals (as, for example, in funerary offerings). We have already seen how the study of tree-rings provides archaeologists with a trustworthy way of dating specific events of the past—when a certain Pueblo dwelling was built, or when a Viking queen was buried. Tree-ring analysis also indicates something about past climates, the local history of forest fires, and the previous distributions of certain trees.

Plant remains recovered from sites can provide first-rate information about what people ate, what they used for fuel, how wild plants were domesticated, what past environments looked like. These examples reflect both of contemporary archaeology's major research strategies—the processual agenda and the postprocessual critique.

Bones are documents as are potsherds and demand the same scrupulous attention both on the site and in the laboratory.

SIR MORTIMER WHEELER (1910–1970), ARCHAEOLOGIST

In 1957, Jerry Chubbuck, an amateur archaeologist, was driving through a ranch near Cheyenne Wells, Colorado, when he noticed an eroded area with a discontinuous outcropping of large bones protruding from the surface. Upon investigation, he found a Paleo-Indian projectile point and an endscraper. Chubbuck wrote to Joe Ben Wheat (at the University of Colorado Museum) about his find, but Wheat was momentarily occupied on another dig and unable to inspect the site. Meanwhile, Chubbuck also told Sigurd Olsen about the site and by an odd co-incidence, Olsen had, in 1937, found the tip of an ancient spear point near the same spot.

At the suggestion of curators at the Denver Museum of Natural History, Olsen and Chubbuck began to dig test pits into the site. On the basis of their test find-ings, Olsen and Chubbuck became convinced of the importance of their site. Once again they contacted Wheat, who first visited the site in April 1958. Olsen and Chubbuck refrained from further excavation so that Wheat could field a crew from the University of Colorado Museum. The summers of 1958 and 1960 were spent excavating at the site—which was named Olsen-Chubbuck, after a coin-toss established the sequence of names.

When Wheat first visited the Olsen-Chubbuck site, he found a deep fur-row plowed lengthwise through the outcropping of bones. This furrow, coupled with the pits excavated by Olsen and Chubbuck, revealed a "river of bones" ly-ing in an arroyo, or filled-in gully. Wheat established a baseline to the south side of the bones and divided it into 2-meter sections, establishing the basic units of excavation. Wheat's crew began dig-ging the odd-numbered sections, starting from the western end of the site. They worked slowly using trowels, various small knives, dental tools, and brushes. Shovels were used only to move backdirt and to trim the sides of the trenches. Each bone and carcass was wholly exposed in place and recorded.

The "river of bones" excavated by Joe Ben Wheat at the Olsen-Chubbuck site (Colorado). The bones were originally buried in a narrow arroyo where the bison were driven and killed. The stairsteps and vertical sidewalls result from Wheat's care-ful archaeological excavation.

This procedure both defined the site margins and created a series of vertical profiles of the arroyo and bone bed. Once the profiles had been drawn and photographed, the even-numbered sec-tions were excavated, exposing the entire bone bed.

The major problem at Olsen-Chub-buck was how to analyze the roughly 190 bison that had been killed there. Wheat devised a series of terms to assist in the task. Completely articulated individuals (those so deep in the arroyo as to preclude butchering) were cataloged as "animal units." Partially butchered skeletons were treated similarly: pelvic-girdle units, rear-leg units, front-leg units, and so on.

More than 4,000 unarticulated, disassociated bones were present at Olsen-Chubbuck.

Modern bison are characterized by short, curving horns and are known as *Bison bison*. The Olsen-Chubbuck bones were identified as *Bison antiquus,* an extinct species roughly 25 percent larger than *Bison bison,* with nearly straight horns. The adult males at Olsen-Chubbuck probably weighed about 2,250 pounds (as compared with 1,800 pounds for a modern bison bull). The females probably weighed up to 1,000 pounds.

Because the bones were meticulously plotted and cataloged, Wheat could make certain inferences regarding the herd composition at Olsen-Chubbuck. Both sexes and all ages were represented in the single bison kill. About 6 percent were

In His Own Words

Ancient Bison Hunting at Olsen-Chubbuck
by Joe Ben Wheat

Down in the valley the little stream flowed gently southward. Pleasant groves of trees were heavy with their new burden of early summer leaves. To the north, a small herd of 200 to 300 long-horned bison—cows, bulls, yearlings, and young calves—were grazing in the small valley. A gentle breeze was blowing from the south.

As the bison grazed, a party of hunters approached from the north. Quietly, under cover of the low divide to the west and the steep slope to the east, the hunters began to surround the grazing herd. Moving slowly and cautiously, keeping the breeze in their faces so as not to disturb the keen-nosed animals, they closed in on the herd from the east, north and west. Escape to the south was blocked by the arroyo. Now the trap was set.

Suddenly the pastoral scene was shattered. At a signal, the hunters rose from their concealment, shouting and yelling, and waving robes to frighten the herd. Spears began to fall among the animals, and at once the bison began a wild stampede toward the south. Too late, the old cows leading the herd saw the arroyo and tried to turn back, but it was impossible. Animal after animal pressed from behind, spurred on by the shower of spears and the shouts of the Indians now in full pursuit. The bison, impeded by the calves, tried to jump the gully, but many fell short and landed in the bottom of it. Others fell kicking, twisting and turning on top of them, pressing them below even tighter into the confines of the arroyo. In a matter of seconds, the arroyo was filled to overflowing with a writhing, bellowing mass of bison, forming a living bridge over which a few animals escaped. Now the hunters moved in and began to give the

juveniles. Most of the young bison appeared to be a month or two old, although a couple of animals could not have been more than a few days old. Reasoning from figures for modern American bison, Wheat estimated that the kill could have occurred as early as April or as late as August, but the evidence points to a time fairly late in the calving season, probably late May or early June. Although he could not count the ones that got away, Wheat estimated that nearly all of the herd had been ambushed, as 200 is near the optimal modern herd size.

Careful analysis revealed even more details about that late spring day some 10,000 years ago. The lower half of the arroyo contained skeletons of 40 whole or nearly whole animals who were virtually inaccessible. Of these, 15 had been violently twisted on or around the axis of the vertebral column. Many bison had

coup de grace to those animals on top, while underneath, the first trapped animals kept up the bellows and groans and their struggle to free themselves, until finally the heavy burden of slain bison above crushed out their lives. In minutes the struggle was over.

One hundred ninety bison lay dead in and around the arroyo. Tons of meat awaited the knives of the hunters—meat enough for feasting, and plenty to dry for the months ahead—more meat, in fact, than they could use. Immediately, the hunters began to butcher their kill. As it was cut off, some of the flesh was eaten raw, but most of the meat was laid on the skin to keep it clean. Some carcasses were wedged well down in the arroyo, and these were too heavy for the hunters to move. The beautifully flaked spear points which had killed these animals went unretrieved. Wherever a leg jutted up, it was cut off, and other accessible parts were butchered; but much remained which could not be cut up.

For many days, the butchering, feasting, preparation of hides, and meat drying went on. In time, however, the meat remaining on the carcasses became too "high" for use, and the hunters had dried as much meat as they could carry; so finally they moved on, leaving the gully filled with bones and rotting flesh.

Several thousand years passed before this last remnant of the arroyo was filled. By 1880, there were no bison left, and the last Indians began to be replaced by White cattlemen. In 1957, the sod was broken for planting; shortly thereafter, the combination of drought and fierce winds that marked the early 1950s began to erode away the upper deposits that had covered the gully. By 1957, the bones that filled the one-time arroyo were once again exposed on the surface.

Joe Ben Wheat (1916–1997) was curator of anthropology at the University Museum, University of Colorado.

backs broken just behind the rib cage, and the forepart of the animal had rotated up to 45 degrees. Three animals had been completely doubled up into a U-shape, wedged against the sides of the arroyo. The herd had obviously been stampeded from north to south, based on orientations of the unbutchered carcasses.

Only a handful of cultural items were associated with the Olsen-Chubbuck bones, mostly artifacts discarded in the ambush and subsequent butchering of the bison: projectile points, scrapers, knives. Most striking were the two dozen beautifully flaked spear points found lodged in the bodies of the lowermost animals in the arroyo. Wheat concluded that the very first animals to the arroyo had been ambushed. These animals were inaccessible to later butchers and could only have been speared as they were charged by the waiting hunters. Spears were probably heaved at the flanks of the moving herd, striking the lead animals and coercing the herd toward the arroyo. These animals would have tumbled into the arroyo first, precisely where Wheat found them.

Olsen-Chubbuck illustrates what a clever archaeologist can figure out from a carefully excavated, well preserved collection of ancient bones.

What's an Archaeofauna?

When archaeologists refer to "archaeofauna," they are referring to an assemblage of animal remains recovered from an archaeological context. Faunal materials are found in two contexts. Sometimes archaeologists discover bones and shells resting precisely where the animals were butchered or eaten. Called **primary refuse,** these deposits offer archaeologists an opportunity to reconstruct the sequence of events preceding the abandonment of the site. A **kill site,** such as Olsen-Chubbuck, is an example of bones being discovered in their primary contexts. In many cases, the butchered carcasses can be carefully exposed and mapped in situ. Analysis is facilitated in such cases because the animal units are often intact and the archaeologists can readily infer the activities that occurred.

Bones also occur as **secondary refuse,** discarded away from their immediate area of use. For example, although Nelson saved only the ceramics from the San Cristobal trash heap, literally hundreds of bone scraps were also present. Today's more ecologically aware archaeologist would attempt to recover and analyze these faunal materials, in addition to the ubiquitous potsherds. At Gatecliff Shelter, we recovered more than 60,000 animal bones (mostly bighorn sheep, rabbits, and rodents). But the depositional contexts were complex. In some places, we found bones exactly where they had been dropped after butchery; but most of the bones had been tossed into secondary discard areas near the drip line of the site, away from where people actually lived.

The contexts of the faunal materials condition, in large measure, the recovery techniques used in excavating archaeological sites. Primary refuse is commonly mapped in place and then removed to the laboratory for further study. The isolation of living floors enables analysts to determine rather accurately the nature and composition of archaeological faunal assemblages. Secondary refuse creates more difficulties because it consists of reworked trash heaps, whose primary contexts have been destroyed.

Once the faunal materials have been removed from the ground, the archaeologist is faced with the task of identification and analysis. A number of field archaeologists are highly qualified in the identification of mammal, bird, mollusk, and even fish bones. In addition, there are specialists who are experts in the analysis of archaeofauna. Many graduate programs in archaeology offer courses in the identification of faunal remains.

Identifying archaeological fauna can be a complex procedure. One must first assign the specimen to a particular part of the body. Is it a rib splinter, part of the pelvis, or a skull fragment? Doing this requires a working knowledge of comparative anatomy. Next the specimens must be identified as accurately as permitted by the condition of the specimen (and the expertise of the analyst). In many cases, the elements are so fragmentary that they cannot be identified as to species, but only to higher-order groups like family or even class. When possible, the bones are then identified by sex and age of the animal; sometimes the individual specimens are also measured and/or weighed (depending on the objective of the analysis). Many departments of anthropology have assembled their own comparative faunal collections, so that archaeological specimens can be readily and routinely identified. Often, archaeologists must do a "first sort" before consulting a faunal expert to deal with the more problematical and fragmentary specimens.

Analysis to this point is fairly routine and really concerned only with the zoological nuances of the material recovered. But analysis beyond the mere identification stage requires serious archaeological input. Were these bones found in primary or secondary context? Have the specimens been butchered? Or worked into tools? Has the deposit been disturbed by erosion, or predators, or by later scavenging? Questions such as these can be answered only by a careful, step-by-step consideration of the archaeological contexts.

The Basic Problem: What to Count?

Jumping from bones to lifeways requires a large leap. How do we proceed beyond mere identification of archaeological bones? Olsen-Chubbuck was a special case. The bones themselves were distributed stratigraphically in still-articulated skeletal portions (Wheat's "animal units"), such as forelimbs, hindlimbs, and vertebral columns. Animal units can often be recognized during excavation, assigned to taxon and even sex and age. At sites such as Olsen-Chubbuck, one can readily determine the number of animals involved (about 190), the sex distribution (about 57 percent were female), and even the season of the kill (late May or early June). The stacks of butchering units at Olsen-Chubbuck eventually allowed Joe Ben Wheat to reconstruct the order of the steps in the butchery process by invoking the law of superposition.

But sites like Olsen-Chubbuck are extremely rare, and in most cases, the task facing the faunal analyst is considerably more difficult. Bones found articulated in situ are relatively unusual; most sites require archaeologists to draw inferences directly from hundreds, often thousands, of isolated bone fragments strewn throughout habitation sites.

To illustrate some of the problems posed by such sites, let me serve up a piece of my own research, done a long time ago. Early in my archaeological career, I was given the chance to analyze the food bones recovered from Smoky Creek Cave, a small site located in northern Nevada.

In looking over this diverse collection of burnt and broken bones, it was immediately obvious that several species were represented, ranging in size from mice to bighorn sheep. No two bones had been found articulated with one another. After identifying the excavated bones to genus and species, I wanted to see what, if anything, we could say about the overall food intake represented by the bones from Smoky Creek Cave.

But how do you move from bone counts to statements about human diet? Obviously, you can't simply count up the number of bones per species and then work out a simple percentage—clearly a mouse bone should count for less edible meat than, say, a bighorn sheep bone.

To take the vast size difference in these various prey species into account, I multiplied the total raw fragment counts by the meat potentially available from each species. After butchering several experimental animals and working my way through the available literature, I estimated that the average deer provided about 100 pounds of usable flesh per animal. Because jackrabbits contribute only about 3 pounds per individual, one must kill more than 30 rabbits to obtain as much meat as is available from a single deer carcass. These elementary cost–benefit relationships would seem to have some implications for prehistoric hunting practices, and I combined the size-adjusted bone frequencies into a chart that provided a rough idea of the relative importance of food animals hunted in the Smoky Creek Cave vicinity.

The accompanying diagram shows that bighorn sheep *(Ovis)* declined in overall dietary importance during the occupation of Smoky Creek Cave but that the cottontail rabbit *(Sylvilagus)* increased markedly in significance. The bottom of the site, about 150 centimeters, dates to about 1000 B.C.; the site was abandoned about A.D. 600; and the figure suggests that mountain sheep decreased in importance after about A.D. 1. Whether this change is due primarily to environmental shifts or different hunting patterns, I did not speculate.

My diagram differs from Wheat's estimates in an important way. At Olsen-Chubbuck, Wheat dealt with actual individuals (the 190 *Bison antiquus*), whereas the Smoky Creek Cave data are only relative. When dealing with isolated bones, one has no way to tell how many individuals were involved. A single bone could represent an entire animal or only one small part, which was perhaps scavenged and brought into the cave. The Olsen-Chubbuck estimates provided data about the probable number of calories consumed, whereas the Smoky Creek Cave estimates were viewed only relative to one another and were not translated into an absolute figure.

My approach seemed perfectly reasonable (even inventive) at the time. But virtually everything I concluded about the Smoky Creek fauna turned out to be

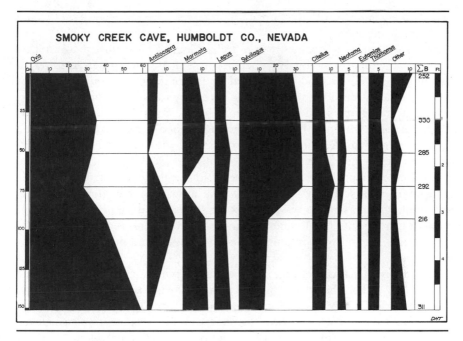

SMOKY CREEK CAVE, HUMBOLDT CO., NEVADA

Estimates of the percentage meat intake through time at Smoky Creek Cave (Nevada). The text explains the assumptions that such diagrams require (and why the results are probably wrong).

incorrect. Inadvertently I had made a number of hidden assumptions, which we now know are untenable. I bring up the Smoky Creek Cave research only to highlight how far the analysis of bones from archaeological sites has come in the last three decades.

Note first what I was counting: Lacking obvious analytical units such as those at Olsen-Chubbuck, the most tempting way to proceed was simply to use raw bone counts as an indicator of relative frequency: If you dig up 100 bighorn bones and only 5 antelope bones, then bighorn must have been 20 times more important than antelope, right? The **number of identified specimens (NISP)** formed the standard measure of archaeological fauna 30 years ago, but we now realize that many problems arise with such simple counts.

First of all, one can never be certain whether all the various bone fragments are independent of one another. What if the 100 bighorn *(Ovis)* bones from the bottom of Smoky Creek Cave came from a single animal, whereas each antelope *(Antilocapra)* bone belonged to a different individual? In that case, antelope would be five times more abundant than the bighorn. The animals may also have been butchered differently, so that some bones were highly fragmented (and hence have disappeared from the archaeological record) or else identifiable elements, such as teeth, became dispersed and inflated the overall count. I had assumed that each bone recovered from Smoky Creek Cave could be considered as independent.

Today, nobody familiar with the formation processes at archaeological sites would accept that assumption.

Because of such difficulties, some archaeologists have turned to another technique of comparing animal frequencies, called the **minimum number of individuals (MNI)** method. Long used in paleontology, this method determines the smallest number of individuals necessary to account for all the skeletal elements of a given species from a site. That is, if you dig up 100 fragments of bighorn bone, what will be the minimum number of individual bighorn required to account for the bones? To figure this out, you tabulate bone frequency by element (left femur, right tibia, hyoid, and so on), looking for the most common skeletal element. If the proximal end of four right femurs shows up in the 100 bone fragments, then you will know that at least four bighorn "stand behind" the fragments. In this way, archaeologists have reduced large collections of bone fragments into the minimum number of individuals required to account for the bones and also to minimize the problem of interdependence among bones.

Several problems have arisen, however, in the minimum number of individuals approach. When the bones are highly fragmented, it is entirely possible that the four right femurs are really all fragments of the same whole bone. Thus, it is necessary to determine whether two fragments could have come from a single animal. If so, then only a minimum of three individuals are represented.

The results also depend on what one takes as a sampling universe. At a place like Smoky Creek Cave, that had poorly stratified deposits and was occupied over a long period of time, it would certainly be possible to have computed a minimum number of individuals over the entire occupation. But this approach has the unfortunate consequence of reducing hundreds of bone fragments to a minimum of one or two individuals, obviously a poor choice. Sometimes investigators choose to calculate their minimum numbers based on stratigraphic breaks observed during excavation. But once again, the minimum number per species depends on how fine one wishes to draw the stratigraphic boundaries.

There is also the hidden assumption that all bones recovered in our archaeological excavations must have resulted from human activities. Today, few archaeologists would be willing to so assume. If you spent tonight in Smoky Creek Cave, you would probably hear the scurrying of pack rats that still live there. You probably would not see them, but coyotes, bobcats, and owls also occasionally stop by. By dragging in food bones, by leaving scats or owl pellets, or simply by dying there, each species may have contributed to the faunal remains we encountered in Smoky Creek Cave.

We realized at the time some difficulties in separating "natural" from "cultural" bone, and I even tried to figure out a way to correct for the problem. But the truth is that the depositional contexts are so complex in such caves and rock shelters that the natural and cultural assemblages may be hopelessly intermixed. Given our knowledge of the processes involved in the formation of the archaeological record in places like Smoky Creek Cave, no simple chart relying on *number of identified specimens* can hope to reflect anything close to behavioral reality. The newer taphonomic approaches and the advent of stable isotope analysis point to more fruitful lines of inquiry.

Taphonomy

Only a small part of what once existed was buried in the ground; only a part of what was buried has escaped the destroying hand of time; of this part all has not yet come to light again, and we know only too well how little of what has come to light has been of service for our science.

OSCAR MONTELIUS (1843–1921), ARCHAEOLOGIST

Taphonomy is a synthetic term coined by a Russian paleontologist, I. A. Efremov, combining the Greek word for "tomb" or "burial" *(taphos)* with that for "law" *(nomos)*. Generally considered a subdiscipline of paleontology, taphonomy is the study of the processes that operate on organic remains after death to form fossil deposits. As archaeologist Diane Gifford-Gonzalez has pointed out, taphonomy embraces two distinct but necessarily related lines of investigation.

The first focus is basic middle-range, "actualistic" research: documenting the observable, contemporary processes involved in the transition from behavioral to systemic contexts (observing so-called "fossils-in-the-making"). The second analyzes the archaeological evidence in light of what is learned through the middle-range studies.

When an archaeologist encounters bones in a site, the first question is usually: Was this animal eaten by people? The answer is sometimes obvious. Joe Ben Wheat knew immediately that Olsen-Chubbuck's "river of bones" resulted from a prehistoric bison drive. But sometimes, both natural and cultural agents are doubtless responsible for depositing bones in the archaeological record. The picture becomes considerably more complex when dealing with late Pliocene and early Pleistocene sites. In many cases, documenting the presence of hominids depends on faunal evidence, and considerable research has been conducted in the attempt to find whether distinctly human patterns of bone butchery exist.

Butchering patterns at Olsen-Chubbuck were distinct. Not only were cut marks evident on individual bones, but still-articulated butchering units such as forelimbs, hindlimbs, and vertebral columns could be identified in the field. These stacks of anatomically articulated butchering units allowed Joe Ben Wheat to reconstruct the order of the steps in the butchery process by invoking the law of superposition. Although "signature" bone piles have some chance of preservation at such kill sites, it is rare that they survive in camps or village sites. Archaeologists cannot simply assume that bone distribution is indicative of butchering techniques or that it is necessarily reflective of social organization.

Taphonomic studies by Andrew Hill and Anna Behrensmeyer suggest that there may be a pattern in the sequence of natural skeletal disarticulation. They studied sequences of skeletal disarticulation across a broad range of African mammals in a tropical savanna environment. The first joint to disarticulate is the forelimb-to-body, followed by caudal vertebrae-to-sacrum and scapula-to-proximal humerus. The last joints to disarticulate tend to be various vertebrae from one another. Basically, these findings confirm the commonsense perception that more work is required to cut apart tighter joints than looser ones.

Such documented sequences of "natural" disarticulation provide a baseline against which to judge the distinctiveness of human butchering practices. By comparing "natural" sequences of disarticulation with the clear-cut cases of butchery by humans at Olsen-Chubbuck, Hill and Behrensmeyer found profound similarities between the two, regardless of the agent of disarticulation. In other words, they found that simple frequencies of disarticulation and articulation of joints in a bone assemblage did not permit archaeologists to infer that hominids had butchered the carcasses.

Reconstructing Human Diet From Animal Bones

So far, we've highlighted some of the major procedures involved in the analysis of archaeological bone assemblages. With these basics, we can look at some of the primary questions archaeologists ask of the bones.

At Olsen-Chubbuck, Joe Ben Wheat wanted to know how much meat was available to this Paleo-Indian hunting party. Taking into account the sex and age distribution of the herd, the degree of butchering, and the amount of usable meat per individual, Wheat estimated that the hunters at Olsen-Chubbuck obtained almost 30 tons of usable meat from this single kill, plus 4,400 pounds of tallow and nearly 1,000 pounds of marrow grease. But of the 190 bison killed, roughly 10 percent were not butchered in any way (wasting more than 6,000 pounds of usable meat).

How long did this butchering take? Working from a number of ethnographic accounts describing similar communal bison hunts on the Great Plains, Wheat estimated that about 210 person-hours were required for the heavy butchering, and another 15 or so person-hours for the partly butchered animals. Thus, 100 people could have completed the butchering in about 2.5 hours. Alternatively, a party of 10 could have butchered the entire herd in less than 3 days.

Wheat also plotted the spatial distribution of elements within the Olsen-Chubbuck bone bed. The grouping of hyoid bones (from near the throat) suggests that many tongues were removed—and presumably eaten on the spot—before or during the early stages of the butchering. Similarly, the distribution of shoulder blades suggests that some animals were butchered early on, to get at the internal organs, the hump, and the ribs. Ribs were choice pieces, probably cooked immediately and consumed while the remainder of the herd was being butchered. Feasting was a common occurrence among historic Plains tribes, and the evidence suggests that a victory feast was indeed held at Olsen-Chubbuck.

Wheat also notes that even the heftiest bull was wholly butchered. Because the neck meat from these massive animals was generally so tough it defied chewing even when dried, he suggests that the people working at Olsen-Chubbuck must have been making pemmican, which was the only really effective way of using neck meat from bulls.

Joe Ben Wheat thus learned a great deal from his meticulous excavations and equally detailed analysis of the Olsen-Chubbuck archaeofauna. But that knowledge did not come easily. If his estimates are correct—that something like 250 person-hours of labor were invested 10,000 years ago to butcher these 190 bison—then there's no question that Wheat himself spent more than twice this time figuring out what all those bones meant. This may not be a very cost-effective procedure, but that's the way archaeologists learn things.

Reconstructing Early Californian Cuisine

Archaeologists also study food bones from historic-period sites. Such sites often have independent documentation which, though often biased, opens up the possibility of building middle-range bridges between the bones themselves and the behaviors they represent.

Let's focus on an important study that examined food bones from Gold Rush frontier sites in California. The decades following the Civil War saw unprecedented differentiation in lifestyles between the rich and poor. In the remote outpost of Sacramento, established in 1848, considerable economic wealth was channeled into the hands of the already well-to-do. Although the historical archaeologist has numerous techniques for studying this process of sociocultural differentiation, faunal remains are particularly useful because they are abundant, little subject to "curation" before being discarded, relatively unaffected by looting, and potentially informative about the daily life across a broad social spectrum.

Peter Schulz and Sherri Gust demonstrated the usefulness of combining historical documentation with faunal data derived from archaeological excavation in their analysis of four late nineteenth-century sites in Sacramento:

The City Jail: Minutes of the City Council indicated that meals were brought to the prisoners already prepared; an 1866 food contract allowed 30 cents per chain gang worker and 18 cents for other prisoners. Since nearly half of this went for bread, Schulz and Gust suspected that only the cheaper cuts of meat were purchased.

Hannan's Saloon: Judging from the complete lack of newspaper advertising for this saloon, and the fact that owner Owen Hannan lived in his bar and was never mentioned in the numerous county histories, Schulz and Gust suspected this to have been a low-level establishment.

Klebitz and Green's Saloon: The prosperous owners advertised daily in local papers and later expanded their interests to include real estate holdings and a sheep ranch. They paid to have biographies appear in local county histories; moreover, their saloon served as the Sacramento depot for the Bavarian Lager Beer Brewery.

Golden Eagle Hotel: This hotel and oyster bar was one of the most highly regarded in the state, advertising in commercial, literary, and travel periodicals throughout the Pacific Coast area and announcing well-to-do guests in the local papers. This establishment occasionally hosted dinners honoring millionaire railroad barons and touring American presidents.

From cheap, assembly-line meals dished out to city prisoners to the sumptuous repasts served to California's powerful at the Golden Eagle, these four sites span the range of status in post–Gold Rush Sacramento. Hannan's saloon was a cut above the jail, but well below Klebitz and Green's saloon.

These inferences derive strictly from historical documentation available for each site: local newspaper accounts, city directories, tax assessment rolls, census schedules, and business license registers. But remember that Rathje and his Garbage Project colleagues found huge discrepancies between such self-reports and actual out-the-back-door evidence. How do we know that such documents accurately portray nineteenth-century reality?

These four sites were excavated as part of urban renewal of the original mercantile district of Sacramento. More than 1,500 beef bones were recovered during these excavations. Contemporary accounts indicate that shortly after California's famous Gold Rush, Anglo-American settlers in Sacramento found beef to be more abundant than any other meat. But throughout this period, beef prices varied from extremely expensive for the choicest steaks to relatively cheap for the less desirable shanks and neck.

Using contemporary advertising from the late nineteenth century, Schulz and Gust established retail prices for the various cuts of beef. Although prices were expressed at the time in dollars and cents, the available nineteenth-century documentation is not sufficiently precise to allow an exact price to be assigned to each cut. Instead, Schulz and Gust rank-ordered their data, reflecting a price scale from cheap (shanks and necks) through expensive (steaks cut from the short loin).

In effect, they determined the nineteenth-century "relative cost" of each cut, and these results can be displayed as cumulative curves for each site, as in the accompanying figure. The cumulative curve technique is becoming an increasingly popular way of statistically demonstrating trends in nonmetric data. If a faunal assemblage contained an "equal mix" of all beef bones, then a straight line would result. Expensive cuts cause the curve to bow outward; cheap cuts make the curves sag.

The figure also shows some interesting relationships among the four target sites. The faunal assemblage from the Golden Eagle Hotel contains a disproportionate number of expensive cuts; more than 50 percent of the sample consists of T-bone cuts (derived from the short loin, the most costly portion of the beef carcass). By contrast, the bones from the Sacramento jail are mostly soup bones. Saloons of the day served free lunches to draw customers into the bar. Judging from the bone distributions, the saloon owners used mostly roasts—easy to cook, available in quantity, and ready throughout the day to be sliced by the bartender.

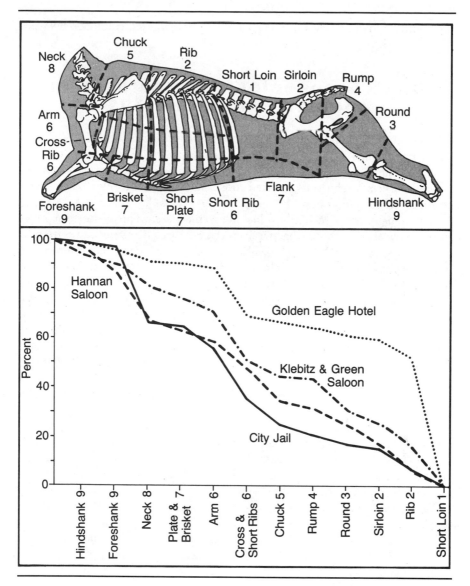

Diagrams showing faunal remains from Gold Rush–era Sacramento (California). The upper drawing shows how cows were butchered, ranked according to late nineteenth-century retail prices. The bottom graph shows beef cut frequencies from four archaeological deposits in Sacramento (plotted as cumulative percentages), with cuts ranked in ascending economic value (expensive cuts to the right).

This innovative study demonstrates how food bones can be used to examine dietary differences by social status, at a time before any dietary surveys were taken in the United States. Whereas most archaeological data from the historical period relate to individual households, this study suggests a potential for understanding more about the nature of Victorian urban life by providing quantitative measures not available through documentary evidence alone.

What Archaeologists Learn From Ancient Plant Remains

Bones, of course, are not the only objects of archaeological study. Information about ancient plants is available from several sources. Sometimes, archaeological sites contain large concentrations of easily recognizable plant remains: caches of corncobs, baskets of pine nuts, charred roof beams, and acorn mush adhering to the inside wall of a food bowl.

Plant remains are particularly vulnerable to the biases of archaeological preservation. For years, much of what we knew about ancient plants came from archaeological sites in arid climates, which provided a far better environment for preserving **plant macrofossils.** The archaeological deposits inside Danger and Hogup caves (in Utah), for instance, consisted almost entirely of plant seeds, hulls, and chaff. In places, virtually no soil was present, even though the deposits were deeper than 10 feet. From column samples of the fill, investigators were able to reconstruct a picture of the vegetational history and climatic change in the vicinity of both sites. Studies like this sometimes show how modern plant distributions can mislead the archaeologist studying the cultural ecology of even the fairly recent past.

Unfortunately for the archaeologist, plant macrofossils are hard to come by; the Utah samples were preserved only because of the general aridity of the environment. In more humid climates, plant remains usually survive only when they have been carbonized. The most common method of recovering plant remains is water flotation, a technique (discussed in Chapter 5) that has become standard archaeological procedure only within the last couple of decades. Plant remains are also sometimes preserved in unlikely places, such as waterlogged contexts (shipwrecks, mudslides, and wells), sun-dried adobe bricks, wattle-and-daub walls, and ceramics.

Plant remains turn up in some very curious places, such as inside ancient human stomachs (preserved through mummification, for instance) and in **coprolites** (dessicated human feces); this evidence of past diets is about as "direct" as one could hope for.

Many sites also contain microscopic plant parts, such as pollen grains and **phytoliths** (microscropic silica bodies contained inside many plants). Evidence of past plant consumption is even preserved inside human bones; by measuring various stable isotope ratios, for instance, it is possible to learn a great deal about past diets.

An **archaeobotanist** is basically one interested in recovering and identifying plant remains from ancient contexts; interpretations may be cultural or noncultural. But if you're specifically curious about past plant–people interactions, you'll probably call yourself a **paleoethnobotanist.** But regardless of the terminology, pcople who study ancient plant remains make an important contribution to our understanding of the archaeological record. Throughout the rest of this chapter, we will examine some of these insights.

Applying Palynology to Archaeology

Palynology, the analysis of ancient plant pollen and spores, has long been one of archaeology's most informative methods for examining prehistoric ecological adaptations. The basics of palynology are not difficult to understand.

Most plants shed their pollen into the atmosphere, where it is rapidly dispersed by both insects and wind action. Pollen grains—microscopic single-celled organisms produced during plant reproduction—are present in most of the earth's atmosphere; a single pine branch can produce as many as 350 million individual pollen grains. Small wonder that pollen grains are so common in archaeological sites.

Determining what these pollen concentrations mean can be quite challenging, but the initial steps in extracting and identifying pollen are rather simple. Sometimes, pollen is recovered by core sampling, from a circular tube forced downward into a sediment column. Pollen samples are also taken from the sidewall of test pits or trenches, special care being taken to prevent contaminating the sample with foreign pollen. Such samples, taken at 5- or 10-centimeter intervals, provide a continuous record of the pollen rain throughout the period of deposition.

Ancient pollen can sometimes be found in sealed deposits (such as buried floors), and "pollen washes" are taken from the surfaces of plant-related, archaeologically sealed artifacts (such as grinding stones). Pollen is occasionally found associated with human burials, on the inside of ceramic vessels, trapped inside the weave of ancient baskets, or even adhering to the working surface of a stone tool.

But in each case, the excavator must be certain that the artifact has been collected from a very recently exposed surface. Good pollen samples are still difficult to come by. Most contexts are problematical, and considerable caution is required in making palynological interpretations.

Pollen grains are isolated from the sample soil matrix with repeated acid baths and centrifuging. Palynologists then scan microscope slides containing the fossil pollen grains at magnifications between 400× and 1,000×. The individual grains are then identified and tabulated until a statistically significant number have been recorded. Although sample sizes vary, most palynologists feel that 400 to 500 pollen grains are required for statistically significant samples from each slide. It takes a skilled analyst about an hour to obtain a 200- to 300-grain count from a single archaeological sample. These figures are converted to percentages and integrated into a pollen spectrum, indicating the proportional shift between stratigraphic levels within the site. The pollen profiles are then correlated with the known absolute and relative dates for each stratum.

Pollen diagrams provide several different kinds of data. Some help to reconstruct past environments, on the assumption that fluctuating pollen percentages through time reflect changes in ancient habitats. The postglacial climatic sequence in Europe, well known from hundreds of pollen samples, contains notable fluctuations in the forest cover, as indicated by the frequencies of hazel, oak, birch, and grass pollen. Once a regional sequence has been developed (often from noncultural deposits), archaeological samples can be statistically compared with the pollen rain from known extant plant communities. The ratio of tree *(arboreal)* to nontree pollen, for example, generally indicates the degree of forestation.

Star Carr: Assessing Human Impact on Postglacial Forests

Palynology has been applied to Star Carr, a **Mesolithic** site in northern England, occupied about 7500 B.C. The accompanying figure is the primary pollen diagram from Star Carr, which reflects pollen frequencies determined from small

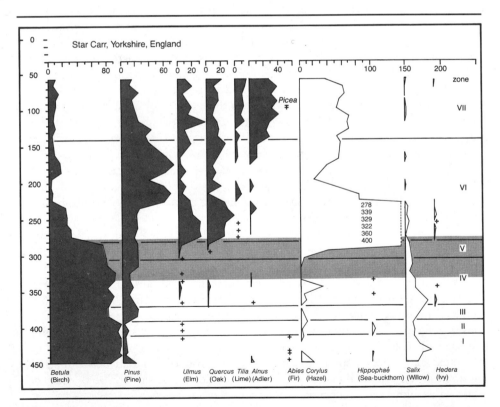

Pollen diagram from geological deposits near the site of Star Carr (England). The human occupation of the site is denoted by the shaded horizontal band.

uncontaminated samples of peats or lake muds. These samples were arranged in stratigraphic order, with the oldest at the bottom. The stratigraphic profile is divided into seven zones, with the human occupation of Star Carr spanning the transition from zone IV to zone V. The figure expresses pollen frequencies as percentages of the total tree pollen. Tree pollen frequencies are black, and the herbaceous vegetation is represented by white polygons.

This is only one of several pollen profiles available from the Star Carr vicinity. These profiles, coupled with the identification of preserved plant macrofossils, enabled J. G. D. Clark and his collaborators to reconstruct the ecological development of the Star Carr area. Zones I, II, and III represent the late glacial period. The vegetation was apparently a park tundra dominated by herbaceous communities, with dense stands of birch or pine trees. This vegetation lasted until the human occupation of Star Carr, roughly 7500 B.C. About this time the vegetation shifted to birch and pine forest, the park tundra disappearing altogether. Note how the increasing abundance of hazel pollen suggests a shift to woodland conditions. Pollen diagrams from nearby localities also reflect the presence of species that attest to a warming climate during this time. In zone VI, after the human abandonment of Star Carr, hazel achieved dominance in the forest, and elm and oak also became more abundant. This shift reflects the transition from birch woodland to mixed oak forest. Later pollen profiles from this area document the extension of herbaceous plant communities, which resulted from human deforestation.

The pollen evidence suggests what the Star Carr landscape must have looked like during Mesolithic times. The pollen diagrams show absolutely no indication of any large-scale deforestation during the early occupation of Star Carr. The abundant faunal remains also suggest that although the Mesolithic people took advantage of the rich forest fauna, they left the forest itself virtually untouched.

Shanidar Cave: Pointing Up the Need for Controls

Shanidar Cave (Iraq) provides another classic application of palynology to archaeological deposits. This important site was occupied sporadically over the last 100,000 years, with cultural remains spanning from **Middle Paleolithic** into fairly recent times. During his fourth season at Shanidar, archaeologist Ralph Solecki discovered a Neanderthal skeleton that appeared to have been intentionally buried roughly 60,000 years ago. The fragile bones were encased in a plaster jacket, earth and all. The box containing the Shanidar IV burial was stored in the Iraq Museum, where it remained unopened for 2 years. Later, investigators discovered that the Shanidar IV grave actually contained four individuals—three adults and an infant.

Following routine field procedures, Solecki took soil samples from around and within the area of Shanidar IV. Although he had no specific purpose in mind, Solecki knew from previous excavations of Native American burial mounds in Ohio that soil samples can provide unexpected dividends. Some 8 years later, the soil samples from Shanidar would provide "significant, if not startling results."

Project palynologist Arlette Leroi-Gourhan eventually processed the Shanidar IV samples and—to everyone's surprise—pollen was found in great quantities at the Neanderthal grave site. Microscopic examination of the pollen spores indicated that the matrix around Shanidar IV contained dense concentrations of at least eight species of brightly colored wildflowers, including grape hyacinth, bachelor's button, and hollyhock.

Leroi-Gourhan suggested that the flowers had been woven into the branches of a pinelike shrub, which apparently grew nearby on the Ice Age hillside. She also concluded that the individuals found in the Shanidar IV grave were laid to rest sometime between late May and early July. At the time, these suggestions had a profound effect on our understanding of Neanderthal ritual and belief.

But let's look a little more closely at the formation processes involved. Clear, the pollen grains were extracted as an afterthought, without an adequate set of

Neanderthal skull as it was being exposed at Shanidar Cave (Iraq). This person was probably killed by roof fall inside the cave.

noncultural control samples. Later investigators have suggested that the flower pollen grains had nothing to do with the skeletons—they were simply contained in the cave sediments, introduced by either natural or other cultural agencies. That is, maybe these pollen grains were inside Shanidar Cave before the grave pit was dug. If so, then the flower pollen inside the burial pits has little relationship to the bones (and actually predates them). Because the samples were analyzed without adequate controls from elsewhere in the surrounding deposits and without consideration of the formation processes involved, it is today impossible for us to understand what the Shanidar Cave pollen really means.

Analysis of Plant Phytoliths

Another good way of learning about both wild and domesticated plants is to analyze microscopic plant opal *phytoliths* (literally, "plant stones"). Phytoliths are formed when the silica ordinarily dissolved in groundwater is carried through plant roots and deposited in mineral form inside the plant, in places where water is used or lost through transpiration. When dead plant material decays, the almost indestructible opal phytoliths are deposited in the ground. Phytoliths have been found in sediments older than 60 million years. Distinctive phytoliths occur in members of the grass family and are also found in groups such as rushes, sedges, palm, conifers, and deciduous trees.

Phytolith analysis is superficially similar to pollen analysis. Both deal with plant remains at a microscopic level; samples for each are collected in the same way; and the same laboratory can be used for both analyses (in fact, the same sample can be used for both).

But there are differences. Some plants produce pollen but not phytoliths, and vice versa. Different taxa are commonly analyzed by each technique. Although pollen is produced in a single form, phytoliths vary considerably within a single species. Phytoliths are preserved under a wider range of soil conditions than pollen. These critical differences render the methods complementary, and when taken together, they provide independent sources of data for the ethnobiologist.

Although phytoliths have been recognized in archaeological sites for decades, before 1970 only occasionally were archaeological deposits analyzed for phytoliths. Since then, interest in this unusual technique has exploded, and today, the identification and analysis of phytoliths recovered from archaeological sites hold great promise for reconstructing paleoenvironments and for tracking the process of plant domestication. But difficulties of taxonomy still plague phytolith analysis and hamper its widespread utilization in archaeological research.

Considerable progress has been made recently on these taxonomic issues, particularly in the grasses. Phytoliths are being used to study rice, millet, barley, and wheat. Particularly important to Americanist archaeology has been Deborah Pearsall's identification of corn *(Zea mays)* phytoliths, which allowed the introduction date of maize to be pushed back in Ecuador by several millennia. But to truly make a contribution to our understanding of how maize was domesticated, criteria for identifying the phytoliths of *teosinte*—the probable wild ancestor of maize—must be developed. Recent work using computer-assisted image analysis may help distinguish wild varieties of teosinte from cultivated primitive maize; similar diagnostics have now been defined for beans and squash.

High Altitude Archaeology

Phytolith analysis was successfully employed on samples we recovered in the high altitude excavations at Alta Toquima Village (Nevada). Less than 5 miles south of Gatecliff Shelter, Alta Toquima is located in what is today a cold, windswept tabletop, at an elevation of 11,000 feet. About A.D. 1000, a seasonally used base camp was established there, and the large number of grinding stones suggest that people were gathering summer-ripening seeds. But the area today supports no grassland; perhaps it never has, or maybe the serious overgrazing by sheep during the historic period eradicated this biotic community.

Flotation analysis did not produce sufficient carbonized plant remains, so we submitted to Irwin Rovner a series of 48 soil samples from the features, interior house floors, cultural middens, and exterior sterile zones at Alta Toquima. We were hoping that the phytoliths, if present, could tell us whether suitable grasslands existed during prehistoric times in the Alta Toquima area.

Rovner found pine phytoliths in every sample (no great surprise, since Alta Toquima is perched on the upper margin of the limber pine treeline). The exterior samples contained the most abundant amount of pine phytoliths, with considerably less on the interior floors, and very little in the feature samples. High altitude festucoid grass phytoliths did occur at Alta Toquima, but in inverse relationship to the pine distribution.

Most of the grass phytoliths occurred in the archaeological features, with little grass outside or inside the prehistoric houses. Rovner concluded that during the late prehistoric period, Alta Toquima was inside a pine grove, and the grasses were introduced to the site through human transport. This grass had not been used for flooring, bedding, or roofing. Rovner thinks that the Alta Toquima residents harvested now-extinct grasses, and phytoliths from these foodstuffs ended up in the refuse deposits.

Thomas Jefferson's Elusive Garden

Phytolith analysis has also assisted historical archaeologists in reconstructing Thomas Jefferson's once-elaborate plantings. Among his other achievements, Jefferson was an avid and astute gardener, employing part of his Monticello (Virginia) plantation as a natural laboratory. One of Jefferson's objectives was to experiment with different kinds of livestock fodder—grasses, clover, alfalfa, and so forth. But whereas Jefferson left numerous drawings, plans, and accounts of the decorative portions of his garden, only a single sketch survives showing these more practical aspects of his garden. The Monticello Foundation has been reconstructing this garden, but will only restore those features whose existence can be confirmed independent of the surviving documentation.

Determining whether Jefferson really planted fodder fields at Monticello seemed a suitable test for phytolith analysis. Irwin Rovner knew that the site was predominantly woodland before Jefferson established his plantation there. If fodder fields actually existed, they should produce phytolith assemblages distinct from the woodland and natural grasses surrounding the plantation.

Archaeologist Scott Shumate collected a series of 19 "blind" samples from various locations in and around Jefferson's garden, some from the designated fodder plots. Rovner processed these samples without any knowledge of their provenience. With the exception of only four individual particles found in scattered samples, all diagnostic grass phytoliths belonged to the projected fodder species and were found in samples coming from the fodder plots. Almost no native grasses turned up in the samples. If this initial sampling proves representative of the rest of Monticello, the procedure can provide significant clues to the landscape architects reconstructing Thomas Jefferson's eighteenth-century home.

Estimating Seasonality

Many foraging groups can be characterized by their *seasonal round*—how they move between various locations, following key resources season by season. **Seasonality** studies are particularly important in archaeology because they enable investigators to deduce what time of year various sites and resource areas were utilized. Put enough such contemporary seasonally specific sites together and you can reconstruct an ancient seasonal round.

Excavating and Interpreting Seasonal Diagnostics

Sometimes it's easy to tell the season during which a site was used. We have already seen, for instance, how Joe Ben Wheat figured out the season in which the Olsen-Chubbuck bison kill took place. But Olsen-Chubbuck is something of an ideal case, since archaeologists can only rarely assume that their sites accumulated from a single event (such as a bison herd ambush). More commonly, sites accumulated over hundreds, even thousands, of years. In fact, archaeological sites are often compared to a **palimpsest**—a parchment or tablet that has been erased and subsequently reused (sometimes multiple times). Like the palimpsest manuscript page, archaeological sites are commonly used and reused, making the assignment of "season of use" difficult.

Sometimes, plant remains can be used to estimate seasonality. The accompanying chart shows Kent Flannery's listing of the seasonal availability of important plant foods in the environment of the eastern valley of Oaxaca (Mexico). Considerable seasonal variability is evident in this ecosystem, with some plants becoming available at the start of the rainy season (beginning in June), others

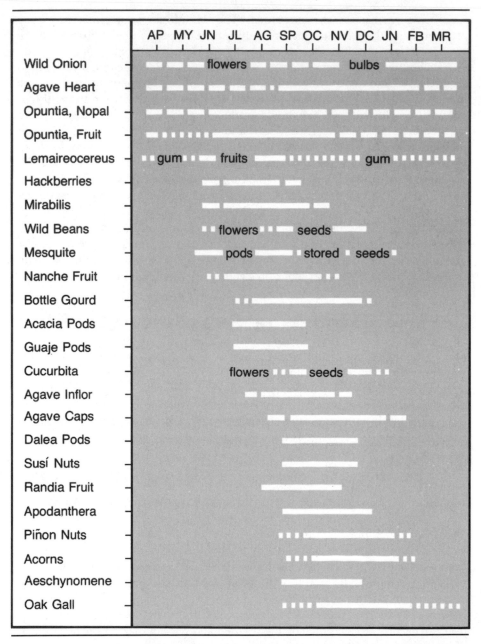

	AP	MY	JN	JL	AG	SP	OC	NV	DC	JN	FB	MR
Wild Onion		flowers						bulbs				
Agave Heart												
Opuntia, Nopal												
Opuntia, Fruit												
Lemaireocereus	gum		fruits					gum				
Hackberries												
Mirabilis												
Wild Beans			flowers		seeds							
Mesquite			pods			stored	seeds					
Nanche Fruit												
Bottle Gourd												
Acacia Pods												
Guaje Pods												
Cucurbita			flowers		seeds							
Agave Inflor												
Agave Caps												
Dalea Pods												
Susí Nuts												
Randia Fruit												
Apodanthera												
Piñon Nuts												
Acorns												
Aeschynomene												
Oak Gall												

*Seasonal availability of various plants in the Guilá Naquitz area near Oaxaca (Mexico). Solid lines in-
dicate periods of peak availability; dashed or dotted lines indicate periods of occasional availability.*

toward the end of this period (around November), and still others during the dry
season (in about April). By looking at deliberate caches of these wild plant foods,
Flannery and his colleagues could tell something about the human utilization of
Guilá Naquitz Cave.

Estimating site seasonality is hardly new in archaeology. In a classic study from the 1920s, Hildegarde Howard demonstrated the potential of noncultural remains for reconstructing lifeways by identifying the avifauna (birds) from the Emeryville Shellmound on San Francisco Bay. Howard identified several of the bones as those of cormorants, birds that bred on offshore islands in the early summer. After about a month, the nestlings moved onshore, where they were killed by prehistoric hunters. Because the bones found in the mound were those of relatively immature birds, Howard reasoned that the prehistoric hunts must have taken place between the middle of June and the end of July. Cormorant bones were found throughout the midden, leading Howard to infer that the site was occupied at least during the summer months. Howard also noted the presence of a foot bone from a young great blue heron and took it as evidence of a May occupation.

This single bone was used to extend the summer occupation of the site backward to include part of the spring, an example of what is now termed the *presence-absence* method of inferring seasonality. Though certainly not in conflict with the cormorant data, Howard's adding a spring component on the basis of a single bone is nevertheless a risky inference. Even if one could be certain that this bone had been introduced by humans, it seems more reasonable to require the presence of several different indicators for a given season as a basis for advancing a seasonality estimate.

Defining Seasonality at Star Carr

Several other techniques have been used to estimate the season of use in archaeological sites, but caution is required here. J. G. D. Clark, for instance, used antlers to derive seasonal information at Star Carr, the Mesolithic site in northern England discussed earlier in the chapter. Large samples of food bones were recoverd at Star Carr, with red deer the most abundant. Virtually every red deer stag skull still had antlers attached, and Clark knew that modern red deer carry their antlers from mid-October until late April. Assuming similar timing for red deer of 9,500 years ago, Clark postulated a wintertime occupation for the site.

Star Carr also contained a large number of shed red deer antlers. Clark suggested that these must have been retrieved almost immediately after they had been shed; otherwise the deer themselves would have devoured them. This assumption suggested that Star Carr must have been occupied until at least early April, when modern red deer normally discard their antlers. Determining exactly when the occupation at Star Carr began was problematical. Nearly half of the elk stags had antlers, indicating that they were killed sometime before December and perhaps as early as October.

In Clark's view, then, the Star Carr settlement dated from midwinter through springtime. Like Howard's study of the Emeryville Shellmound, Clark's excavation and interpretation of Star Carr is classic, a pioneering achievement in the application of ecological approaches to archaeology.

But some archaeologists have their doubts. Clark had assumed that his excavations at Star Carr recovered evidence from a complete Mesolithic settlement.

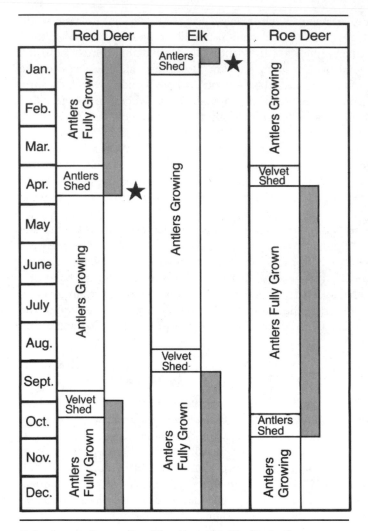

Inferred seasonal occupation of Star Carr, Yorkshire (England).

Archaeologist Mike Pitts has suggested instead that the excavated area was really a specialized activity zone, where deer antlers were fashioned into tools and animal hides were processed. Pitts believes that all the deer antlers recovered at Star Carr were not food items, but rather were collected as raw materials, to be made into barbed spear points. Thus, if red deer antlers were being collected throughout the year for tool manufacture, then they cannot be used for seasonal estimates. If Pitts is right, then Clark's interpretation must be incorrect.

Clark's reconstruction of seasonality at Star Carr has also been questioned by John Andresen and his colleagues. Relying on experimental and ethnoarchaeological studies, they believe that Star Carr was probably not a long-term settlement (as Clark suggested). They think the site was probably a hunting and butchering site, visited for very short periods at various times in the year.

They also question the use of red deer antlers as a seasonal indicator: Fewer than 40 percent of the antlers recovered had actually been shed, and even these could easily have been stored. The unshed antlers could have been acquired any time between late summer and April. Clark had argued that in order for antlers to be worked into tools, they must have been collected shortly after they dropped; otherwise, they would have been too deteriorated to serve as raw materials for tool manufacture. Andresen and his colleagues question this technological assumption, noting that shed antlers were not worked with any greater frequency than were their unshed counterparts. They also emphasized that two elk skulls lacked antlers, indicating they were collected in January or later.

Several other seasonality studies rely on growth lines in marine shells. Season of death can be estimated from thin sections of these shells. Fish remains are also highly sensitive seasonal indicators. But a note of caution is required. Each technique can tell the archaeologist only when one or more animals died. The fact that some cormorants died at Emeryville in June or July is, by itself, archaeologically irrelevant. Archaeologists must be continually concerned with demonstrating that the death of a clam or a bighorn is somehow contemporaneous with (and relevant to) a specific behavioral event of interest. Without the demonstration of such relevance, the seasonal dates might tell us something about red deer or cormorant archaeology, but nothing about people.

"Reading the Fuel" in the Ancient Andes

We have emphasized several times that Americanist archaeology has recently broadened its interpretive framework. For two decades, processual archaeologists emphasized the analysis of "natural" resources—such as plant remains—as a key to understanding how people coped with the ecological and environmental issues of the past. More recently, postprocessual critics have suggested that archaeologists must set aside their compulsive fixation with the purely physical environment in order to explore how humans in the past constructed the worlds in which they lived.

As is true for the rest of Americanist archaeology, paleoethnobotanists have registered the postprocessual shock waves. Rather than simply looking at what plant remains can tell us about past economies and ecologies, some archaeologists are exploring how to investigate the social, symbolic, and political dimensions of the interface between plants and people.

To explore how such research might proceed, we turn to a pioneering study in which Christine Hastorf and Sissel Johannessen analyzed the changing patterns of fuel use in the Upper Mantaro region in the central Andes of Peru. This high, intermontane valley begins at 3,500 meters in elevation. The intensively settled and cultivated valley floors are surrounded by rocky hillsides, supporting a few rocky fields, but mostly grasses, a few shrubs, and small trees.

Thousands of years of intensive cultivation and herding have undoubtedly changed the character of these upland valleys, but nobody is certain just how. Although some investigators believe that the landscape was originally forested, pollen analysis suggests that this area has been relatively treeless since humans first moved in several thousand years ago.

The Upper Mantaro Archaeological Project excavated numerous house compounds from six archaeological sites spanning the period A.D. 500–1500. During what was designated the Wanka II period, the population of the Upper Mantaro area aggregated into large walled towns located on protected knolls just above the rolling upland zone. The archaeological evidence suggests that this was a time of considerable intersite tension, with land use probably restricted to areas close to the walled settlements. After the Inka conquest during Wanka III times, the population was relocated into small villages on the valley floor.

Six-liter soil samples were collected and processed from the floors, middens, pits, and hearths encountered in each excavation unit. The more than 900 samples contained thousands of pieces of charcoal and plant fragments, recovered by both dry screening and flotation of the archaeological sediments. The recovered plant remains were classified into three readily observable categories: "grass," "stem" (small-diameter twig fragments), and "wood" (pieces of mature wood). The "wood" category was further subdivided if the tree source could be identified.

The accompanying bar chart sets out the results of the paleoethnobotanical investigation, plotted according to the thousand-year-long sequence of the Upper

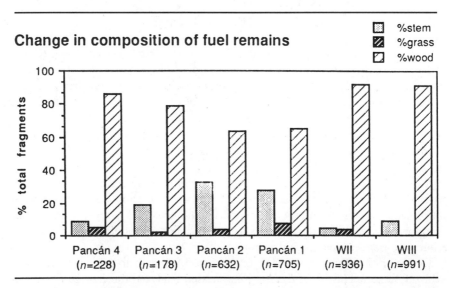

Bar graph showing the changing composition of fuel remains in the Upper Mantaro region (Peru).

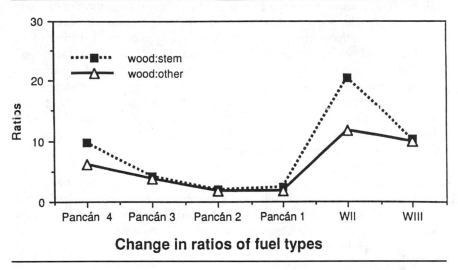

Graph of the changing ratios of wood to other fuel types through time in the Upper Mantaro region (Peru).

Mantaro Valley. Everyone can recognize the trends evident here. First, it is obviously that mature wood is the dominant category throughout the sequence. This trend coincides with the expressed preferences of people living in this area.

Another pattern is also evident: Prior to A.D. 1300 (that is, during the Pancán phases), the relative proportion of mature wood fragments dropped, with a corresponding increase in stem and grass fragments. Then, during Wanka II and Wanka III times, this trend reversed, with stem and grass remains decreasing again, as shown in the accompanying graph.

Finally, these investigators noted that the species composition of the mature wood shifted somewhat through time. Up to 40 different kinds of wood are present in the Upper Mantaro Valley samples, with no particular taxa being especially dominant. But the most common taxa did change in relative frequency through time. The five most popular wood types during the early Pancán phases (from as yet unidentified trees) dropped out entirely by Wanka II times. And beginning in A.D. 1300 or so, new wood types appeared. One notable example is *Buddleia* (locally called *quishuar*), a high-elevation tree that becomes the most popular fuel source during Inka (Wanka III) times.

How Can These Patterns Be Explained?

Can the charcoal distributions shown on our graph be attributed to factors other than fuel use? Is it possible that we are looking at changing patterns in the use of house construction materials, changing subsistence practices, or perhaps differential plant preservation through time?

Hastorf and Johannessen reject such possibilities, noting that most of the charcoal in these samples seems to have come from fire refuse accumulated over a span of several months or years. Although there is the possibility that some of the charcoal resulted from inadvertent fires (such as accidental burning of thatch roofs and roof beams), the investigators assume that the vast majority of the charcoal recovered reflects intentional fuel use for heating and cooking. They also note that the construction materials of the house compounds (mud and stone), the general subsistence remains, and the depositional contents are basically constant throughout the 1,000-year sequence. There is also little reason to believe that rates of preservation changed significantly through time.

From this baseline, Hastorf and Johannessen moved to interpret the charcoal distributions strictly in terms of changing fuel use patterns. Beginning their paleo-ethnobotanical analysis in fairly standard processual fashion, they looked to see whether the archaeological patterning of fuel use revealed long-term shifts in the relationship between these highland people and their environment.

From this strictly economic perspective, the increased reliance on twigs and grasses during the Pancán sequence is just what one might expect in a relatively treeless landscape. Through time, the increasing human population and more intensive agricultural land use patterns should be expected to create conditions of fuel scarcity. It makes sense that, as people denuded their landscape of trees (the best locally available fuelwood source), they were forced to use less desirable, yet more costly sources of fuel (in this case, the small shrubby plants, twigs, and grasses).

But if so, it is difficult to see why this trend should reverse during later Wanka times. Contrary to strictly ecological expectations, the archaeologically recovered plant remains show that the use of high-quality fuels actually *increased* after A.D. 1300.

Perhaps the evidence from settlement pattern archaeology provides a clue. Beginning in Wanka II times, an elite class began social and political consolidation of the area. If so, then maybe this elite mandated some sort of fuel management program, perhaps in the form of tree cultivating, resulting in more available mature wood sources. This scenario is certainly possible, since we know that tree cultivation was practiced during Inka times.

Although tree farming is certainly a rational response to increasing wood shortage, this explanation raises some other difficult questions:

- Why does the change take place in Wanka II times? Why not earlier (when the population also increased) or later (when the Inka took over and restructured the location of the production system)?
- Why would cultivation be chosen to alleviate the fuel shortage? Why not simply go farther afield to gather fuel? Or why not just shift to lower-quality fuels?
- And why do certain tree taxa show up during Inka times, when they were absent before?

Fuel, of course, has an important economic role in Andean life; it is a basic requirement of life. And the increased fuel management/possible tree cultivation hypothesis provides a workable explanation in economic terms, but leaves several questions unanswered.

Moving Beyond Econo-Think

At this point, the investigators decided that it was necessary to consider explanations that moved beyond conventional economic and ecological factors. They delved into the modern and ethnohistoric records available to document the relationships between Andean people, the upland forest, and traditional fuel sources. Hastorf and Johannessen discovered that this relationship is considerably more complex than a strictly economic perspective might indicate: "Wood and trees in the Andes are much more than fuel; they also have social, symbolic, and political dimensions."

Collecting fuel was an important aspect of Andean life during the ethnohistoric period, consuming up to 4 hours each day for some segments of the Inka population. We know from documentary accounts that logs, kindling, and straw were also important tribute items in the Inka state. And even within households, fuel sometimes had a ritual function like food, being exchanged to cement social relations. Wood and straw, for instance, were sometimes provided by brothers-in-law to relatives at a wake.

Trees had important, symbolic connotations in Andean cosmology. Certain sacred trees were planted at administrative sites. Others were symbolically linked with deities. Wood from *quishuar,* mentioned earlier, was burned in large quantities at festivals, and human figures carved of *quishuar* were ritually burned as sacrifices to the divine ancestor of the Inka dynasty. Trees were also symbolically associated with water (the source of life), as well as with women, clouds, winter, and the moon.

From such ethnohistoric and ethnographic examples, Hastorf and Johannessen defined "several dimensions of meaning given to planted trees, linking the people to their land and to their ancestors, providing a reason to nurture and plant trees. This provides a fuller understanding of why an Andean people might plant trees, not just as their fuel source, but as a symbol of the linking reciprocal relationship of a kin group with their land."

Relating Ideology to the Past

As they expanded their focus to include the cultural world of the Andean past, Hastorf and Johannessen supplemented their strictly ecological perspective with a new appreciation of the overarching "cultural" relationship between ancient Andean people and their environment. Initially, the researchers had viewed such "natural" fuel supplies as basically "passive" entities in the environment, "out there" to be exploited, extracted, and used up by the humans living in this environment. But as they broadened their perspective, Hastorf and Johannessen came to recognize a dynamic cultural interaction between these ancient Andean people and their resources. They came to redefine their paleoethnobotanical approach as "reading the fuel," reflecting the postprocessual fascination with the archaeological record as a surrogate text, available for "reading."

The postprocessual critique has suggested some new ways of approaching some old questions about the changes evident in the paleobotanical record. Why, for instance, did the major change take place in Wanka II times?

Hastorf and Johannessen believe that the ideology associated with the planting of certain trees could have been a factor in establishing the local political consolidation occurring at that time: The tree symbolized family continuity on the land, with the roots symbolizing ancestors, the fruits the children. A ritual step in contemporary marriage ceremonies is termed "to bring the branch" and involves the bringing forth of ritual offspring. The dramatic increase in the use of *Buddleia* or *quishuar* might thus be attributed to its ritual significance of bringing social groups together into larger entities, rather than simply its mundane use as firewood.

These investigators believe that the act of planting trees—which readily could be interpreted as a purely economic response to a fuel shortage—was chosen from the other available alternatives due to cultural values concerning the ways in which cultivation and trees functioned as symbols of life and lineage, socially and politically.

They are careful not to imply that economic factors were irrelevant in this case, but they argue that a purely economic explanation is insufficient to an understanding of the patterning evident in the archaeological record of the Andean highlands.

Summary

For the archaeologist, the study of subsistence generally focuses on the way in which people go about feeding themselves. A variety of techniques are now available to assist the archaeologist in such subsistence reconstructions. *Faunal analysis*—the study of animal remains in archaeological sites—can be directed toward a number of relevant objectives. In some cases, the faunal remains provide direct evidence of which species were hunted (or collected) for food, how these animals were captured, and the butchering methods employed. Some sites can provide clues as to exactly how many animals were killed at a time and how much meat was subsequently consumed (or wasted). Sometimes the reconstruction of hunting practices implies the presence of correlated patterns of social organization, as, for instance, the coordinated bison hunts that occurred on the American Plains.

Plant remains are also a powerful source of data regarding ancient life. *Macrofossils* (intact plant parts) have been important not only to paleoclimatic reconstruction but also as direct evidence of which plant species were exploited, the season during which these plants were collected, and exactly how the various plant parts were cooked. Flotation is the most commonly used method for recovering plant macrofossils from archaeological sites. Plant *microfossils*—pollen grains, phytoliths, and spores—are also of interest to archaeologists. Fossil pollen grains can be systematically recovered from archaeological deposits and used to construct a pollen diagram, which plots the changing frequency of pollen throughout the occupational history of the site. Coupled with relevant data on modern plant biogeography, the pollen diagram enables the archaeologist to reconstruct the distribution of prehistoric plant communities and to document how these floral associations have changed through time. A regional pollen analysis can be used as a relative dating technique. The frequencies of pollen types can also serve as clues to the economic functions of specific intrasite areas, such as storage rooms and ceremonial areas.

For decades, archaeological plant remains were used mostly to reconstruct past subsistence practices. But some paleoethnobotanists are moving beyond relatively straightforward ecological interpretations to explore the overarching "cultural" relationships between ancient people and their environment. Particularly when solidly tied to independent ethnohistorical and ethnoarchaeological documentation, this relatively new direction in analyzing ancient plant remains stands to make a considerable contribution to the ideational objectives of the postprocessual critique.

Ancient Subsistence and Paleoecology on the Internet

Zooarchaeology Home Page provides extensive links including on-line libraries, appropriate field schools, and discussion groups.
http://home.sprynet.com/sprynet/fdirrigl

Old Sacramento on the Internet is a resource with a lot of information about California's early days.
http://www.oldsacramento.com

ArchNet: Botanical Resources/Archives and Catalogues includes a wealth of searchable databases from the U.S. Department of Agriculture that are of special interest to anthropologists.
http://spirit.lib.uconn.edu/ArchNet/Topical/Botan/Botan.html

Native Americans and the Environment contains a huge bibliography on traditional environmental knowledge.
http://www.indians.org/library/subt.html

Geosciences, University of Arizona provides a lengthy listing of palynology resources.
http://www.geo.Arizona.edu/palynology

CHAPTER 8

Some Bioarchaeological Perspectives on the Past

❏ ❏ ❏

PREVIEW

Here, you'll meet the bioarchaeologist, *someone who feels at home in both biological anthropology and Americanist archaeology. Bioarchaeology is an important new field that specifically examines the human biological component in the archaeological record. Bioarchaeologists study the origin and distribution of ancient diseases, they reconstruct human diets, they analyze the evidence for biological stress in archaeological populations, and they reconstruct past demographic patterns—all by looking directly at the evidence preserved in human tissues. We pay special attention to the very new and flourishing field of molecular archaeology—itself a subdivision of bioarchaeology—which is taking advantage of new DNA-related technologies to learn about both the very recent and the ancient human past. Although this chapter is a bit heavy on chemistry and biology, I hope you will agree that the archaeological payoff is well worth the effort.*

> *Every man is the builder of a temple, called his body, to the god he worships, after a style purely his own, nor can he get off by hammering marble instead. We are all sculptors and painters, and our material is our own flesh and blood and bones. Any nobleness begins at once to refine a man's features, any meaness or sensuality to imbrute them.*
>
> HENRY DAVID THOREAU (1817–1862), AMERICAN WRITER

In Chapter 2, I distinguished between biological and cultural approaches to anthropology, clearly placing the field of archaeology in the "cultural" camp. Like most black-and-white criteria, this distinction is not really as clear-cut as I have led you to believe. But in books like this, one must draw lines somewhere, and so I excluded biological anthropology from our immediate domain of interest. Now it is time to redress the balance.

For years, archaeologists excavating mortuary sites would call in a biological anthropologist to help out with the human bones after they were recovered. For a long time, however, it was rare for archaeologists to invite a biological anthropologist to the site itself, and even rarer for them to solicit advice about the best way to go about testing the site and removing the human burials. We used to call these specialists *osteologists* (*oste* = "bones," and *ologists* = "people who study"). This made some sense, since **osteology** is that branch of anatomy dealing with bones, and that is what these osteologists did.

But over the years, the biological anthropologists who helped out on digs came to do more than just study human bones. For one thing, they insisted (correctly) that they should be full-scale members of the archaeological team. In many cases, they often became skilled archaeological excavators themselves, who preferred to excavate personally the bones they would study. So these so-called "osteologists" not only studied ancient bones, but they also knew how to excavate and record such remains. And very often, their "osteological" studies went far beyond the bones, as when mummified human tissue or human hair turned up. They found that, while it is possible to learn quite a bit about human diet from studying bones, they must also factor in the plant and animal remains recovered from sites, because this was another important source of information that could be used to cross-check results obtained from human bones.

Over the years, as the field of "archaeological osteology" became more specialized, various names have been proposed for those who do it: osteoarchaeologist, human zooarchaeologist, biological archaeologist, and so forth. Here, we will follow Clark Spencer Larsen's self-description of **bioarchaeologist** to describe those who study the human biological component of the archaeological record.

Paleopathology and Skeletal Analysis

We begin with **paleopathology,** the study of ancient disease (which comprises one of the most challenging branches of bioarchaeology). Although paleopathologists must often be satisfied with identifying a "disease cluster" rather than naming a specific pathogen, the fact that research is limited to dry bony tissues has not precluded the development of alternative stategies of inquiry.

The past two decades have seen significant advances in several directions. First has been the progress toward identifying specific diseases (and disease complexes), through both the diagnosis of skeletal materials and the development models for disease patterns in specific regions. Another important research direction has been the investigation of "nonspecific" indicators of stress, particularly as caused by nutritional deficiencies and/or infectious disease. Paleopathological researchers have succeeded relatively recently in developing chemical techniques for reconstructing ancient nutritional patterns. The search for diseases of the past is hardly a new enterprise, but some disorders can now be placed in a more reliable biocultural matrix—for instance, the impact of malaria and hyperostosis in the eastern Mediterranean, the problem of iron deficiency anemia in early-historic New World populations, and the relationship between malnutrition and infectious disease.

One particularly important application has been the study of how increased population density is reflected in the proliferation of specific diseases. Jane Buikstra and Della Cook reported on a pattern of disease in western Illinois fully

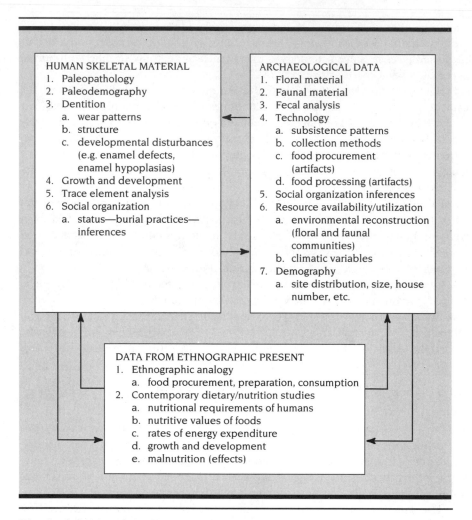

HUMAN SKELETAL MATERIAL
1. Paleopathology
2. Paleodemography
3. Dentition
   a. wear patterns
   b. structure
   c. developmental disturbances
      (e.g. enamel defects,
      enamel hypoplasias)
4. Growth and development
5. Trace element analysis
6. Social organization
   a. status—burial practices—
      inferences

ARCHAEOLOGICAL DATA
1. Floral material
2. Faunal material
3. Fecal analysis
4. Technology
   a. subsistence patterns
   b. collection methods
   c. food procurement
      (artifacts)
   d. food processing (artifacts)
5. Social organization inferences
6. Resource availability/utilization
   a. environmental reconstruction
      (floral and faunal
      communities)
   b. climatic variables
7. Demography
   a. site distribution, size, house
      number, etc.

DATA FROM ETHNOGRAPHIC PRESENT
1. Ethnographic analogy
   a. food procurement, preparation, consumption
2. Contemporary dietary/nutrition studies
   a. nutritional requirements of humans
   b. nutritive values of foods
   c. rates of energy expenditure
   d. growth and development
   e. malnutrition (effects)

Bioarchaeological interrelationships among human skeletal, archaeological, and ethnographic data.

consistent with a diagnosis of tuberculosis. However, although the presence of tubercular-like skeletal lesions is well documented in these mortuary samples, Buikstra suggests that the responsible pathogen may no longer exist. That is, we are seeing archaeological evidence of a disease that has become extinct.

Reconstructing Diet by Analyzing Stable Isotopes in Human Bones

We already encountered the concept of isotopes in talking about radiocarbon dating. Carbon, you will remember, has both stable and unstable isotopes—essentially the same molecule but with differing numbers of neutrons in the nucleus. One stable form, C-12, makes up about 99 percent of the world's carbon; C-13 is also stable but accounts for only about 1 percent. The unstable isotope, C-14, most familiar to archaeologists because of its important implications for dating technology, is extremely rare.

Over the past decades, researchers have determined that some kinds of plants differentially absorb these carbon isotopes. The first such "pathway," discovered in experiments with algae, spinach, and barley, converts atmospheric carbon dioxide into a compound with three carbon atoms. This so-called *C₃ pathway* is characteristic of sugar beet, radish, pea, and wheat. A second pathway converts carbon dioxide from the air into a complex compound with four carbon atoms. This *C₄ pathway* includes many plants from arid and semiarid regions, such as maize, sorghum, and millet—the cereal staples of the Americas and Africa. A third *CAM pathway* (an acronym for "crassulacean acid metabolism") is found in succulents such as cactus.

These findings proved to be critical to reconstructing past diets because we now know that human bone reflects the isotopic ratios of the various plants ingested. Thus, by determining the ratios of carbon (and sometimes nitrogen) isotopes contained in bone collagen, bioarchaeologists can reconstruct the dietary importance of various kinds of plants and animals. Although stable carbon isotope analysis is just emerging from its developmental stage, it has already revolutionized the way in which archaeologists reconstruct prehistoric diets.

Maize in the Tehuacán Valley of Mexico

The use and implications of the stable isotope method can be illustrated by returning to the Tehuacán Valley of Mexico. In Chapter 2 we outlined how Richard MacNeish used direct archaeological methods to reconstruct dietary change throughout the 7,000-year occupation of this highland Mexican valley. Now, with the help of stable isotope analysis, archaeologists have an unusual opportunity to double-check MacNeish's innovative and pioneering work.

The accompanying diagram synthesizes MacNeish's theory about the changing subsistence patterns reconstructed from the Tehuacán Valley excavations. Michael DeNiro and Samuel Epstein analyzed the stable isotopes in samples of human bone from the Tehuacán Valley, to provide an independent test of MacNeish's conclusions. They began by converting MacNeish's theory—expressed as changing dietary proportions of plants and animals—into a series of expectations in terms of stable carbon and nitrogen isotope ratios. Basically, this meant that DeNiro and Epstein were required to derive isotope ratios for the various foods that MacNeish recovered archaeologically; this is middle-range research.

They began with the plants, classifying each according to the appropriate photosynthetic pathway. Several of the Tehuacán Valley species used a C₃ pathway; maize is a C₄ plant; and cacti belong to the CAM category. Similar assignments were made for the nitrogen isotopes. Because living plants displayed a range of isotopic ratios, average values were used as estimates.

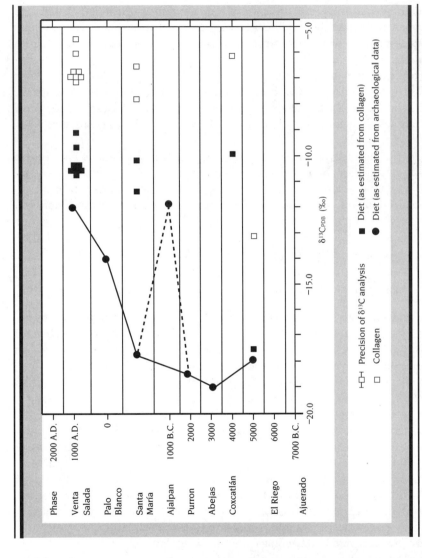

C-13 values of the diets of people living in the Tehuacán Valley, as derived from analyzing stable isotopes in bone collagen. The solid line shows the major trend—an increased reliance on a maize-based diet. The dashed line shows periods for which the data are unreliable.

But the prehistoric Tehuacános also ate meat, and so isotope ratios were required for the various meat sources as well. These results were less satisfactory because DeNiro and Epstein did not know the percentage of C_3 and C_4 plants that these long-dead animals had consumed. It would, presumably, be possible to derive these values precisely using mass spectrometry on the actual animal bones recovered archaeologically; but instead, they used a complex, and less satisfactory, "mass balance equation" to derive the animal bone estimates and then combined the plant and animal ratios mathematically by phase.

Our diagram also illustrates the stable isotope conversion of MacNeish's dietary reconstruction (represented by the solid line). This curve, in effect, summarizes the logical implications of MacNeish's initial theory, but expressed in stable isotope terms. Actually, because of the relatively primitive state of middle-range research on isotopic correlates, three different conversions were attempted, but only the simplest is discussed here.

DeNiro and Epstein then sampled some of the human bones recovered by MacNeish and his team at Tehuacán. The sample from only 12 burials was relatively small because several potential samples no longer contained enough bone collagen to allow computation of carbon and nitrogen isotope ratios. The bone isotopic ratios were then obtained using mass spectrometry analysis.

Refer again to the diagram. As you see, it compares the new carbon isotope data with expectations from MacNeish's reconstructions. The isotopic findings for the El Riego phase closely match MacNeish's interpretation. At this early phase, the Tehuacános subsisted strictly by hunting and by gathering wild plants—mostly C_3 food—with meat making up slightly more than half of the diet.

MacNeish's reconstruction suggested that later, between the El Riego and Santa María phases, hunting and wild plant gathering slowly declined in importance as domesticated plant foods assumed greater importance. This process accelerated rapidly during the Palo Blanco and Venta Salada phases as maize became the staple. Specifically, MacNeish thought that during the Coxcatlán and Abejas phases, wild plants comprised about half the diet, domesticated plant materials being of minor but increasing importance (about 20 percent); meat sources remained significant but were proportionately declining (to about 30 percent). MacNeish believed that wild plant consumption continued through the Palo Blanco phase, ending only with the advent of maize farming during the Venta Salada phase.

But the isotopic evidence suggests otherwise. Rather than a gradual introduction of maize agriculture, the isotope ratios in the human bone suggest a dramatic dietary shift toward maize much earlier, between the El Riego and Coxcatlán phases. The isotope ranges suggest that most of the diet during Coxcatlán times and later consisted of C_4 plants, probably maize.

Although this discrepancy has important ramifications for our understanding of plant domestication in the New World, both dietary reconstructions are plagued with problems. The difficulty in translating MacNeish's proportional diagram into its isotopic correlates is a shortcoming of middle-range research that can be overcome only by a better understanding of isotopic fractionation in living plant populations.

Another biasing factor is that MacNeish's reconstruction is based entirely on data from five cave excavations (because these are the best places to find preserved animal bones and plant remains). But the Tehuacán caves were occupied only seasonally, and one wonders how representative these data are of the overall picture of Tehuacán subsistence. After all, sedentary villages were established elsewhere in the valley during the later phases, the cave sites being used in only marginal and specialized ways.

The stable isotope analysis results are thus equivocal. MacNeish's view on Tehuacán Valley subsistence held up only for the earliest part of the sequence (the El Riego phase). For the last 6,000 years, there remains a discrepancy between MacNeish's archaeological reconstruction and the one suggested by isotopic analysis of human bone. Current evidence does not permit an informed choice between the two alternatives. Perhaps MacNeish underestimated the importance of early agriculture in the Tehuacán Valley. Or perhaps the small sample size and premature assumptions involved in the bone isotope technique make these results suspect. Nevertheless, it is clear that stable isotope determinations will provide an important tool for archaeologists attempting to reconstruct prehistoric diet.

Maize in the Chavín Civilization of Peru

Although the town of Chavín de Huántar is today just one of a multitude of small district capitals in highland Peru, the archaeological site next to it has taken on an importance analogous to Rome or Jerusalem for specialists in Peruvian archaeology.

GEORGE R. MILLER, ARCHAEOLOGIST (CALIFORNIA STATE UNIVERSITY, HAYWARD), AND RICHARD L. BURGER, ARCHAEOLOGIST (YALE UNIVERSITY)

The site of Chavín de Huántar (pronounced "cha-*veen*-day-*whan*-tar") is one of the most celebrated ceremonial centers in the Andes. It flourished from about 850 to 200 B.C., making it one of the earliest civilizations in South America.

Chavín de Huántar is located at an elevation of 10,000 feet above sea level, ringed by snow-covered mountains (with peaks rising over 18,000 feet). Some scholars believe that the establishment of places like Chavín de Huántar may be related to an early form of mountain worship. The initial settlement was a small ceremonial center surrounded by numerous domestic structures, homes to a vigorous highland community. Its location on a key trade route midway between the Peruvian coast and the lowland tropic forest to the east made Chavín de Huántar a natural trade center.

The site has given its name to the world-famous Chavín art style, which some believe represents the pinnacle of Andean artistry. Chavín art is characterized by a range of fantastical and representational figures, usually combining the features of humans, snakes, jaguars, caymans (alligators), and birds with intricate geometrical and curvilinear motifs.

The most elegant expression of the Chavín style is found in the exquisite stonework of the huge Chavín de Huántar temple complex. These ceremonial buildings are honeycombed with rooms, passageways, stairways, vents, and drains. The main object of worship, perhaps the earliest oracle at Chavín de Huántar, is a knife-shaped monolith 15 feet tall, set into an interior gallery. The top of the elaborately carved sculpture reached through the ceiling, into a gallery above, where the priests of Chavín de Huántar, acting as the voice of the oracle, spoke to the worshipers below.

Understandably, the mysterious Chavín art style and associated temple architecture has attracted the attention of Andean archaeologists, causing them to slight the study of the mundane aspects of the Chavín lifeway.

Archaeologists have long attempted to explain the subsistence base of the remarkable Chavín culture, Peru's first highland civilization. At Chavín de Huántar, archaeologists have found evidence of clearly stratified social organization and accomplishments in metallurgy, textile manufacture, monumental architecture, irrigation technology, and stone sculpture.

Such achievements require a stable and highly productive subsistence base, both to support the legions of specialized artisans and elite, and also to sustain the thousands of people who supplied the labor necessary to build such temple complexes.

So what did the Chavín people eat? Until very recently, one could only guess at their subsistence by exploring the iconography of the roughly 150 stone sculptures that once ornamented the temple buildings. But studying religious inscriptions is not a very fruitful way to understand everyday diet.

George Miller and Richard Burger advocate a more direct approach to the problem. After all, Chavín de Huántar was not just a ceremonial center. Thousands of people lived around there and, like people everywhere, they ate things (and threw away the garbage). Why not find the garbage and see what it contained?

When Burger first went to Chavín de Huántar, there was no reliable chronological sequence (except for sculptural style), so he conducted a number of basic excavations to bring temporal order to the sites. Subsistence remains were, of course, also encountered in the domestic structures and in the refuse heaps around the ceremonial center. There, they recovered more than 12,000 fragments of discarded food bone, from which they were able to reconstruct, in great detail, how subsistence patterns shifted from hunting of wild animals to dependence on domesticates (mostly llama).

But what about the role of plants in the ancient Chavín cuisine? In particular, what about maize, known to have played a critical role in the formation of complex societies elsewhere in the Americas?

Earlier in this chapter, we looked at the importance of maize cultivation in early Mesoamerican civilization, where it became an important dietary component in a surprisingly short time. We also know that at the time of Spanish contact, maize enjoyed both ceremonial and economic importance in the Inka empire in Peru.

Many archaeologists believe that maize must have been a major factor in stimulating the development of early, pre-Inka Peruvian civilization as well. Some have argued that the remarkable spread of the Chavín art style was made possible because of its association with a new, improved variety of maize. Others have noted the depiction of maize on early Chavín-style ceramics. Maize kernels have also been recovered in recent excavations at Chavín de Huántar (where maize continues to be one of the most popular local crops today).

But on balance, the quality of the evidence supporting this position is rather poor. Because of its overtly religious overtones, iconography is not itself a particularly reliable indicator of subsistence base, and cultivated plants of any kind are rarely depicted in Chavín art. Direct archaeological evidence, in the form of macrobotanical remains, is also unsatisfactory in this case. Undoubtedly many types of plant crops were consumed at Chavín de Huántar—certainly maize, squash, beans, and potatoes—but poor conditions of preservation have destroyed most of the evidence. And while it is true that maize macrofossils were recovered at Chavín de Huántar, the total recovered sample consisted of merely two maize kernels—hardly the stuff on which robust theories are based.

Recognizing the limitations of the archaeological data, Richard Burger and Nikolaas van der Merwe turned to stable carbon isotope analysis as a means of assessing the importance of maize as a staple for the Chavín civilization. The basics of this technique have already been discussed, but the application of stable isotope analysis to Chavín differs in some important ways from the Mesoamerican example.

The high-altitude environment surrounding Chavín de Huántar precludes the growth of indigenous C_4 pathway grasses. With a very few exceptions, all plants involved in the human food chain in the high Andes photosynthesize along the C_3 pathway. But the exceptions are important because maize (a C_4 plant) and prickly pear cactus (a CAM plant) were probably both introduced from Mesoamerica.

This botanical baseline suggests that prior to the introduction of maize into the high Andes, the diet of people like those living at Chavín de Huántar should have been based exclusively on C_3 pathway plants. Because diet composition directly conditions the stable carbon isotope character of human bone, it should be possible to test for a significant presence of maize in past diets. All you need is a decent sample of human bone from the Chavín civilization.

As it turns out, obtaining such bone samples was not an easy matter. Despite the decades of digging at Chavín de Huántar, no tombs had been found from the appropriate time period. Burger and van der Merwe were able, however, to sample four skulls that had been left as votive offerings, along with complete vessels and wild fruit in the fill of an Urabarriu-phase platform (constructed ca. 850–460 B.C.) located about a mile from the main temple at Chavín de Huántar. Another sample was taken from a young child who had been interred in a niche in a house wall. They also conducted isotope analysis on a control sample of camelid bones (presumably llama) from refuse deposits excavated at Chavín de Huántar.

Despite the variability in the samples, the stable isotope values were remarkably similar: Each bone sample suggests that only about 18 percent of the carbon came from C_4 sources (presumably maize). One of the camelid samples, however, was aberrant, with more than 50 percent of the carbon attributable to C_4 sources. This intriguing result suggests that the llama herds may have been fed on maize fodder. Although the results were obtained on very small sample sizes, the findings were supported by additional stable isotope analysis on human bone from a neighboring valley.

The two primary conclusions from this carbon isotope analysis are (1) that maize seems not to have been an important factor in the genesis of highland Peruvian civilization, and (2) that maize was not the staple even in the fully developed Chavín lifeway. Despite the lack of direct archaeological evidence, it seems certain that C_3 crops, such as potatoes, contributed the bulk of the dietary intake.

This pattern contrasts vividly with the result of isotope analysis from elsewhere in the Americas (including the study from the Tehuacán Valley, discussed a little earlier). It would seem that the central Andes already enjoyed a rich array of indigenous domesticated plants and animals prior to the importation of maize from Mesoamerica. Because their plant foods were locally adapted, they were frost resistant, capable of sustained production even with limited rainfall, and could be stored for long periods. As a newcomer, maize simply could not prosper in the extreme Andean environments until extensive terracing and irrigation systems had been constructed (as they were during Inka times).

Looking for Indicators of Stress

Another way to look at human diets is through the documentation of generalized stress responses in human hard tissue. Both the causes and the effects of malnutrition are complex and can rarely be traced precisely. So instead, paleopathologists prefer to study the effects of **stress,** defined as any environmental factor that forces the individual or population out of equilibrium.

Stress is a behavioral impact that cannot be observed directly in archaeological skeletal populations. To overcome this problem, Alan Goodman modeled the effects of generalized stress. Past nutritional deficiencies can be inferred from the pattern and severity of the effects of stress on individuals, as well as the distribution of that stress on the contemporary population. This model views the degree of physiological disruption as dependent on both the severity of environmental stressors and the adequacy of host response.

A range of cultural factors—technological, social, and even ideological—can dampen the effect of stress on human populations. A particular nutritional constraint can, for instance, be overcome by (1) changes in technology that broaden (or intensify) the subsistence base, (2) social modifications that effectively distribute food to those in need, or (3) an ideology rewarding and reifying a sharing ethic. Culture likewise can increase stress: Intensifying agricultural production is known to increase the potential for nutritional deficiencies and infectious disease, and relying on monocropping makes populations vulnerable to drought-induced crop failure and protein inadequacies. When insufficiently buffered, stress creates

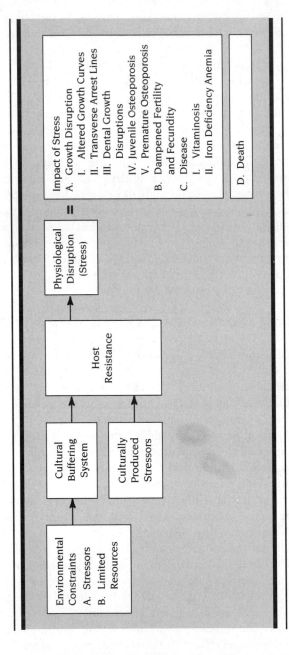

The interaction of environmental, cultural, and biological factors that can enhance or inhibit human nutrition.

physiological havoc by disrupting growth, decreasing fertility and fecundity, triggering (or intensifying) disease, and, in some cases, causing death.

The human skeleton retains evidence of stress in several ways: As some investigators have put it, "bone provides a 'memory' of past events and the behavior of its cells up to the point of the individual's death." Numerous methods exist for evaluating the way in which environmental stress affects the growth, maintenance, and repair of the long bones.

Harris lines, for instance, are bands of increased bone density—observable on X rays of human long bones. They are often caused by a variety of nutritional stressors, especially severe and short-run dietary deprivation. Harris lines, which generally show up between birth and 18 years, have been observed on dozens of archaeological samples and are consistently associated with decreased longevity.

Another common technique for monitoring physiological stress is the analysis of **dental hypoplasias,** growth arrest lines formed from birth through 6 years. Hypoplasias are often evident from gross examination, although some investigators also look at enamel cross sections. Not only does the presence of hypoplasias betray the presence of environmental stress, but their size also can be measured, allowing estimates of the duration of metabolic stress. Dale Hutchinson and Clark Larsen examined dental defects on a large sample of human skeletal materials from St. Catherines Island (Georgia), ranging from prehistoric burial mound populations through the seventeenth-century Christianized Guale Indians buried in the cemetery at Mission Santa Catalina. They found that the historic-period hypoplasias were wider than those during the precontact period. This pattern strongly suggests that the duration of stress was longer after the European contact, probably reflecting the long-term metabolic stresses associated with the arrival of the Europeans, through the introduction of Old World epidemic diseases and increased health risks overall.

These techniques, when applied to skeletal remains from meaningful archaeological contexts, can be extraordinarily helpful for understanding the effects of nutritional stress among human populations of the past.

Paleodemography

As with all other archaeological samples, the corpus of human skeletal materials available in the archaeological record contains great potential for understanding the past. But by the same token, such skeletal populations can carry with them several sources of biases. Thus, extreme caution is required when skeletal populations are taken as representative of the behavioral populations from which they derive. One problem is the differential preservation of human skeletal samples. For example, older bones tend to be more badly decomposed, and earlier burials in cemeteries are often disturbed by later interments. Despite such distortions, important conclusions can be drawn about prehistoric population profiles, provided there are sufficient controls.

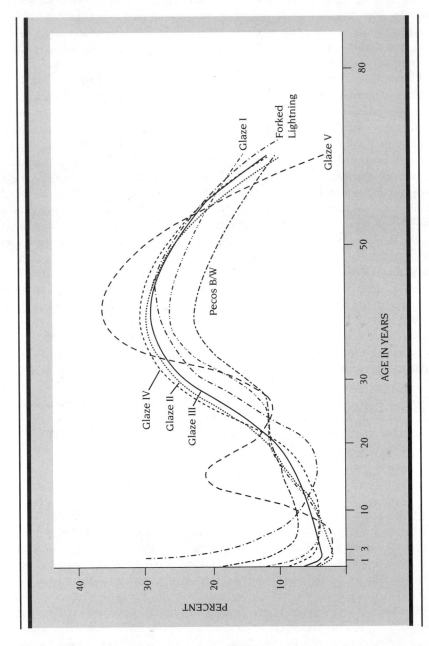

Mortality curves for various human skeletal samples, plotted by phase, from Pecos Pueblo (New Mexico).

A particularly significant skeletal series was recovered by Ted Kidder when he dug at Pecos Pueblo (New Mexico). More than 2,000 human burials were recovered, dating from A.D. 1300 to the historic period. When initially analyzed in the 1920s, T. W. Todd crowed that "no other collection surpasses this one for completeness of skeletons, precision of data, and thoroughness of care." The skeletal material from Pecos has been reanalyzed several times, and the changing nature of these analyses reflect the maturation of biocultural analysis.

Charles Mobley attempted to reconstruct the human demography at Pecos by using the raw age data initially published in 1930 and adding earlier prehistoric material from nearby Forked Lightning Ruin. Mortality, survivorship, and life expectancy curves for the Native American samples from Pecos were grouped across the seven chronological periods, as shown in the accompanying figure. Using the mortality curve as an example, we find that the earliest samples—Forked Lightning (A.D. 1150–1300), Pecos Black-on-White (1300–1375) and Glaze I (1375–1425)—exhibit the highest young-child mortality in the Pecos area and the lowest percentage of deaths in the 30- to 50-year age interval. By contrast, the Glaze II, III, and IV (A.D. 1425–1600) samples show relatively fewer child deaths and a higher percentage of deaths in the 30- to 50-year interval (the aberrance of the Glaze V sample was attributed to the small sample size). When compared with other available North American Indian population profiles, this demographic structure suggested to Mobley that the Pecos populations probably enjoyed better-than-average nutrition and superior hygiene, or perhaps both.

Mobley's study—like all those involving the archaeological record—was grounded in middle-range assumptions. When reanalyzing the same skeletal series from Pecos, Christopher Ruff found that in his earlier analysis, Earnest Hooton had consistently overestimated the ages of the adult sample because of the limited criteria available in the 1920s to estimate age of death from skeletal material. Hooton's criteria also apparently contained systematic biases in the sexing of the Pecos skeletons, resulting in a suggested male-to-female adult sex ratio of 60:40. Ruff thinks that Hooton and Todd were unprepared for the striking robustness encountered at Pecos, and hence they classified some females as males (a worry also voiced by Hooton in 1930). Using modern criteria, Ruff reconstructed a sex ratio much closer to 50:50.

Ann Palkovich has pointed up an additional problem with Mobley's analysis. Only about 30 percent of the Pecos skeletal sample could be assigned to the temporal periods. Palkovich's statistical analysis shows that this one-third sample does not represent an unbiased sample of the entire archaeological population.

It turns out that infant remains are underrepresented in the ceramically dated samples—perhaps because of cultural preferences at Pecos or a bias in excavation. But in any case, this unrepresentative sample strongly suggests that the demographic profiles may be seriously biased.

We dissect this example not to pick on Mobley but, rather, to underscore a general problem: Even relatively advanced archaeological interpretations—though potentially informative for reconstructing past lifeways and population dynamics—still depend heavily on the fundamentals of sampling and reliable chronology.

Exploring the Frontiers of Molecular Archaeology

DNA was the first three-dimensional Xerox machine.
KENNETH BOULDING (1910–1993), ECONOMIST

Today's technology now permits bioarchaeologists to analyze the past on an entirely different level. Calling on the most recent developments in the field of genetic experimentation, so-called **molecular archaeologists** can now actually study the past at the level of the individual molecule. Like its counterpart, molecular biology, this newly emergent field addresses the ultimate physiochemical organization of life, focusing particularly on the molecular basis of human inheritance. Although just over a decade old, molecular archaeology has already racked up some spectacular successes, providing unexpectedly precise answers to questions long explored through more conventional approaches.

Our first topic in this discussion presents a recent application of molecular archaeology—the use of DNA fingerprinting to track down the long-missing remains of the last Russian czar and his family. With these basics in hand, we then back

Hair as Data?

Archaeologists are often accused of splitting hairs, but now they really are doing it—literally. Archaeology has just found a neat new source of data: hair.

Until a few years ago, nobody even thought about looking for hairs while excavating. But today, Robson Bonnichsen (now affiliated with Oregon State University) and his team routinely attempt to recover hair whenever they dig. And they find it, sometimes in great quantities. In dry caves, in wet caves, in permafrost, and in open-air sites, hair seems to be everywhere, once you actually look for it.

Hair is surprisingly durable, and it can enter the archaeological record in several ways. Not just from haircuts or simple shedding, but also in human feces and even regurgitated stomach contents.

But identifying ancient hair is not easy. After cleaning in the laboratory, the recovered hair must first be mounted on microscope slides. Then, at high magnification, characteristics such as color, scale pattern, size, and shape allow investigators to determine the species of animal from which the hair came. Some hair is hollow, and the pattern of air pockets (which look like a string of grapes) can tell the skilled investigator whether the hair came from a moose, a caribou, or a white-tailed deer.

Detailed examination can also show whether the animal (human or otherwise) suffered from scalp diseases or parasites. It also seems likely

up a bit to examine something of the biological fundamentals behind DNA analysis. Then we look at some of the more recent applications of DNA fingerprinting to the question of our remote human ancestry.

The Case of the Missing Russian Czar

A Russian geologist and a Moscow filmmaker working in 1979 on the outskirts of Ekaterinburg (Siberia) made a bizarre find—a shallow mass grave containing what appeared to be human bone. They reported their discovery to Russian authorities, and in 1992, their find was finally investigated. To everyone's surprise, nine virtually complete skeletons were found, along with 14 spent bullets, some rope fragments, and a shattered jar that had once contained sulfuric acid.

The news was immediately splashed across the headlines. Ekaterinburg was, after all, where deposed Czar Nicholas II had been imprisoned during the Russian Revolution. At midnight, July 16–17, 1918, Czar Nicholas II and his family—the last of the Romanovs—along with their servants, were ordered into the basement, where they were gunned down by a Bolshevik death squad. One reporter called it "one of the most fateful mass executions in this century."

that trace elements can eventually be extracted from hair, then evaluated (as in stable isotope studies of human bone). If so, these ancient hair samples should provide valuable insights into ancient diet and disease patterns. Hair can also be directly dated (using AMS radiocarbon methods). Hair sometimes contains ancient DNA, which has been recovered from hair shafts less than an inch long. Because this DNA is the same as that recovered from bones and soft tissue, it is possible to use the entire toolkit of molecular archaeology on even tiny samples of ancient hair.

Particularly intriguing is the hair recovered from the Mammoth Meadow site in southwestern Montana, where preliminary identifications have turned up hair from 18 species, including extinct mammoths, caribou, and horses. Human hair was also found beneath a lens of volcanic ash dated to about 11,200 years ago. This is human hair that was shed more than 550 generations ago (perhaps in pre-Clovis times).

Bonnichsen and his team hope that the analysis of these hair fragments may eventually answer some stimulating questions: When did the first Americans initially arrive? In how many waves? What did they eat? What diseases did they have? What animal species did they hunt?

Right now, the potential for ancient hair recovery and analysis seem virtually unlimited.

Great care was taken to dispose of the bodies. According to one account, they were piled on a funeral pyre, then doused with gasoline and set afire: "I stood by to see that not one fingernail or fragment of bone remained unconsumed. Anything of that sort the Whites [pro-Czarists] found I knew they would use as a holy relic." When all was reduced to powder, the ashes were allegedly scattered to the Siberian wind.

At first, the executions were officially defended as an act of revolutionary justice, but because of the outrage from the rest of the world, the massacre soon became an embarrassment to the Russian government. Even the house where Nicholas II and his family had been imprisoned and murdered became a destination for pilgrims from throughout the Soviet Union, attempting to pay homage to the memory of the last czar. The house was eventually bulldozed, reportedly on direct orders from Boris Yeltsin. Details surrounding the massacre at Ekaterinburg remained a tightly guarded Soviet secret, and the remains of the czar and his family were never found.

For years, rumors circulated that some, perhaps all, of the czar's family had somehow escaped. Each of the royal children has had multiple claimants. Even Nicholas II himself was rumored to be living comfortably somewhere in Poland.

So in 1992, royalty-watchers around the world were all wondering the same thing: *Could these bones be those of the murdered Czar Nicholas II and his family?*

Today, thanks to the modern techniques of DNA fingerprinting, we know the answer. Let us examine the Ekaterinburg case in some detail; it illustrates the same DNA-related methods being currently applied by molecular archaeologists to considerably more ancient archaeological remains.

Czar Nicholas II (in 1916).

Where's the Last Romanov Ruler?

Suspecting that the bodies might be those of the royal family, Russian officials invited both national and foreign forensic experts to examine the skeletal remains. Age, gender, stature, and ethnicity were assigned to each skeleton. Additional detailed measurements were taken, the bullets were studied, and dental work was examined. One big problem was that the facial bones appeared to have been deliberately disfigured at death (perhaps, the team wondered, to keep pro-Czarist forces from recognizing the remains, should they be found). While the

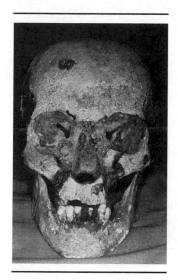

Czar Nicholas II (in 1992).

skeletons were certainly consistent with those of the czar and his family, the skeletal identifications remained inconclusive.

Then, in 1993, a British research team, examining some of the Ekaterinburg finds, found traces of DNA still present in the bones. **DNA (deoxyribonucleic acid)** is the characteristic double-stranded molecule in all living cells that encodes specific genetic information. At the time, some courts were beginning to admit DNA evidence as a way of determining a suspect's guilt or innocence. Although still controversial, DNA fingerprinting did seem to offer a way of establishing whether or not these were the remains of the Romanovs.

British Royalty Clinches the Case

Because the Romanovs were royalty, the family bloodlines were well documented. Queen Victoria of England—called by some "the grandmother of Europe's royal families"—was the murdered Czarina Alexandra's grandmother. Another of Victoria's granddaughters, Princess Victoria, was the grandmother of Prince Philip, Duke of Edinburgh. Therefore, investigators reasoned, because certain kinds of diagnostic DNA are inherited through the female line, Prince Philip's blood should match that of Queen Victoria, Czarina Alexandra, and all her five children.

In July 1993, Prince Philip agreed to donate a sample of his royal blood, from which DNA was extracted for comparison. But there was still a problem because the degraded 75-year-old DNA from the Ekaterinburg bones was available only in minute quantities. Fortunately, a new laboratory technique—known as **PCR (polymerase chain reaction)**—had just been developed, enabling investigators to create trillions of copies of the degraded DNA (we will explain this process later in the chapter). Enough of the Ekaterinburg DNA was then available to match against DNA segments from a living relative, in this case, Prince Philip of Britain.

Then, through computer-assisted means, selected small segments of complicated DNA sequence—the so-called "hyper-variable regions"—were matched up. Whenever the two sets of DNA match up at these critical checkpoints, investigators can be virtually certain that the DNA is the same.

This is exactly what happened: Prince Philip's DNA proved to be a virtually perfect match with that extracted from the bones. Both samples reflected, within a very small statistical error, the distinctive blood of the Romanovs. Just to double-check, the skeleton of Nicholas's younger brother George, who died at age 28 of tuberculosis in 1899, were exhumed from the royal crypt. Similar DNA testing showed another conclusive match on the other side of the family.

Russian officials accepted the unavoidable conclusion that the bones from the mass grave at Ekaterinburg must indeed be those of the murdered czar and his family. On February 25, 1996, the Russian Orthodox Feast of Absolution, the royal remains were reburied in the imperial family vault–final resting place of Romanov czars for three centuries, inside the cathedral of St. Peter and Paul Fortress in St. Petersburg.

A Little Background on DNA

Now, in order to understand how forensic techniques are being applied in molecular archaeology, we must explore a couple of these basics in a bit more detail. Bear with me while I run through a quick overview of how DNA operates as the so-called "Code of Life," and how molecular biologists are learning to decipher the code.

How Is DNA Inherited?

Most of our genetic information exists inside the nucleus of our cells; this stuff (called **nuclear DNA**) makes each human being unique, and it's inherited from both parents. But nuclear DNA degrades fairly quickly, and by the time the human body decomposes, the nuclear DNA has virtually disappeared. You can see why nuclear DNA was not very important in the early studies of molecular biology.

Instead, researchers concentrated on another, more specialized source of DNA–**mitochondrial DNA (mtDNA)**–which is also found inside the cell, but outside the nucleus. Unlike nuclear DNA, mtDNA survives longer, making it much easier to find in ancient sources.

In life, mtDNA exists in two places: in the female ovum and in the tail of the male sperm. But after the sperm fertilizes the egg, the sperm tail breaks off. This means that mtDNA is inherited only through the maternal line. If you are female, you will pass along the mtDNA to your children. If you are male, none of the mtDNA will be passed on.

From the mitochondrial point of view, the father's genetics are irrelevant. This means that human lineages (through the female line) remain distinct generation after generation, making it possible to define molecular phylogenies (family trees). This was, in effect, what was being traced in the Romanov case: Queen Victoria passed along her mtDNA to her daughter (without any input from her husband Prince Albert), who in turn passed along her mtDNA to the murdered Czarina Alexandra. Alexandra's five children, also present at the massacre, received their mother's mtDNA, without any input from the Czar. The forensic analysis of the Ekaterinburg bones was based on the royal family tree, *traced strictly through the female line*.

Mitochondrial DNA has another important characteristic for molecular archaeologists. When compared to nuclear DNA, mtDNA evolves fairly rapidly.

But even so, the actual changes in the mtDNA code take place only about once every 3,000 or 4,000 years. If one is willing to assume that this rate of change has been constant through time, then the degree of divergence between related mtDNA samples can be used to estimate the time elapsed since the various branches of the tree diverged. Obviously, insufficient time has elapsed in the Romanov case to allow for such divergence. But projected on an archaeological time scale, mtDNA has assumed considerable importance as a clock for monitoring the movements of human populations in the remote past.

What Is PCR?

So far, so good. Nuclear DNA degrades rapidly and is of little use to the archaeologist. Mitochondrial DNA is more robust, and can actually survive in many archaeological samples. But mtDNA is still a pretty fragile molecule and ancient DNA survival depends on some fairly special conditions of preservation. And even then, ancient DNA generally survives only in extremely small quantities. Initial research on archaeological samples was continually hampered by a lack of suitable surviving mtDNA.

All that changed with an important recent breakthrough in molecular biology, which has partially offset the preservation problem. As mentioned earlier in the chapter, the *polymerase chain reaction* (usually just known as *PCR*) is a laboratory technique for rapidly synthesizing large quantities of a given DNA segment. PCR methodology enables researchers to make millions (or even billions) of copies of a very small sample mtDNA, so that this genetic material can be more readily studied.

Basically, PCR works in two steps. First, it melts down the double-strand DNA helix into two single complementary strands, then it builds up a new second strand from a bath of free-floating nucleic acid bases. This way, a single DNA molecule becomes two; then these two become four, and so on geometrically, until a bucketload of DNA results. The significance for molecular archaeology is that even a single surviving molecule of DNA can be studied—an incredibly important consideration when studying ancient DNA.

The problem is that PCR cannot distinguish the ancient DNA under consideration from later contaminants. Modern DNA is all around us, and the problem here is to keep out the skin cells constantly being shed by archaeologists or museum curators as they handle archaeological samples. Dust particles are a big problem, as are minute amounts of DNA from earlier experiments conducted in the same room. But regardless of where it comes from, if the tiniest piece of modern DNA is introduced during the processing of an ancient DNA sample, the PCR method will multiply both the ancient and the modern DNA over and over again. This means that if you slough off a single DNA cell into the laboratory sample, PCR will blindly reproduce your DNA along with the ancient stuff.

This actually happened when one molecular laboratory reported that it had successfully extracted dinosaur DNA from fossil bones. But once it was compared against control samples, it was discovered to be modern DNA, somehow inadvertently introduced and multiplied by the PCR technique.

This is why molecular biologists are fanatical about laboratory "protocols"—specific rules and procedures designed to minimize the possibility of modern contamination, such as conducting different experiments in separate rooms, not allowing ventilation systems to connect one PCR laboratory to another, and so forth. This is also why control samples are so important. Sometimes, independent PCR tests are run in different parts of the same lab, as another safeguard against contamination.

In truth, most archaeologists don't care about the details of mtDNA, PCR, or laboratory protocols. It's like radiocarbon dating: Few archaeologists care much about the intricacies of carbon isotopes, but they love getting all those neat dates on their sites. In both cases, what's important is what the technology has allowed investigators to learn from the archaeological record. This is what we look at next.

Prospecting for Ancient DNA

The Romanov case, solved in the early 1990s, relied heavily on the techniques of DNA analysis pioneered by Allan Wilson and his research team at the University of California at Berkeley. In 1984, Wilson and his team became the first to identify genetic materials from old tissue. When they cloned DNA from the 140-year-old skin of **quagga**—a recently extinct zebra-like African beast—the Berkeley team showed the world that DNA could indeed survive after the death of the organism.

The next year, a Swedish researcher, Svante Pääbo cloned DNA from a 4,400-year-old Egyptian mummy. This was the first time that PCR techniques had been applied to ancient humans. Not long after, Pääbo pushed the barrier back another 2,600 years into the past by extracting ancient DNA from human brains miraculously preserved at the Windover site in Florida.

Some 7,000 to 8,000 years ago, ancient Native Americans at Windover buried their dead in a spring that flowed through an ancient limestone sinkhole. Water levels fluctuated seasonally, with a maximum depth of less than 4 feet. In the soft bottom deposits were preserved several distinct strata of peat—compact, dark brown organic material built up from the partial decay and carbonization of vegetation. The team of archaeologists, headed by Glen Doran of Florida State University, dug into these peat levels, while pumps bailed out the encroaching water. The skeletons were extremely well preserved, some even still held in place by large stakes, probably placed there at the time of burial to keep the bodies from floating to the surface.

The low oxygen level and neutral Ph of such boggy conditions were also perfect for preserving soft tissue. More than 60 well preserved human brains turned up at Windover, including the one used by Pääbo in his pioneering extraction of ancient DNA. Geneticists were particularly excited about the large numbers involved, since it provided the first chance to examine gene frequencies across an entire prehistoric population. Microbiologists at the University of Florida were surprised to find how little the genetic makeup of the Windover population had changed during the thousand years that the burial ground was used, possibly a sign of ancient inbreeding. If this trend would hold for other early Native American populations, it would suggest that early Indian groups tended to stay put, perhaps explaining the remarkable linguistic diversity in the New World.

The Story of African Eve

The work at Windover signaled the birth of molecular archaeology as a viable way of exploring the human past. But as spectacular as the 8,000-year-old brains from Windover might be, Wilson's research team at Berkeley had only begun to examine the possibilities in studying ancient DNA.

Wilson and his team collected mtDNA samples from around the world, compared the human specimens with those of chimpanzees (as a control). The most striking thing about mtDNA is how much of it we all share. At the molecular level, all living human groups share all but about 0.6 percent mtDNA. As you might expect, human and, say, chimpanzees share somewhat less; humans and horses share even less, and so forth. The 0.6 percent figure is important because it suggests a way to determine the "relatedness" between all living individuals and groups.

By examining the mtDNA from various modern human populations, Wilson could see what a close-knit species we really are. This was a surprise because mtDNA evolves fairly rapidly. Components of the modern global sample turned out to be remarkably alike—both within geographical populations, and also between continental groups. The result was a family tree for all of (surviving) humanity. Africa provided the longest branch on the tree, suggesting this is where human mtDNA began to differentiate. Those of African descent showed the most variability among themselves, and also were the most distinct from other populations of the world. Wilson argued that this pattern is precisely what one would expect, if modern humans had descended from a single population in Africa.

These investigators went a step further, suggesting that all the genetic composition evident in living human populations could be traced to a single ancient African ancestor. Because mtDNA is passed down strictly through the maternal line, this fictive ancestor must have been female. She was quickly nicknamed—what else—Eve, after the biblical first woman and wife of Adam.

Even more controversial than Eve's African origin was the "molecular clock" that Wilson and his group also derived. Because geneticists are willing to assume that mtDNA changes at a constant rate, the 0.6 percent figure is important for another reason: It provides a relatively-fine grained way to gauge the first appearance and development of human beings. Although this so-called molecular clock does not keep perfect time, it does suggest some genetic limits within which human evolution may have taken place.

Wilson's molecular clock suggests that Eve must have lived about 200,000 years ago. If so, then the first descendants of Eve (early modern humans) must have fanned out of Africa to supplant other hominids about this time. This theory, which has come to be known as the "out of Africa" hypothesis, had, it turned out, also been framed independently strictly on the basis of the fossil evidence (although other paleoanthropologists also read the same fossils as contradicting the "out of Africa" hypothesis).

To call the Eve hypothesis "controversial" is an understatement. Shortly after Wilson published his results, critics from around the world weighed in. Some found fault with Wilson's family tree for humanity, suggesting that equally plausible alternative reconstructions could point to an Asian origin for humanity. Others charged that the Eve hypothesis was based strictly on modern genetic distributions. It could be tested by using paleo-DNA, extracted from ancient bone; but such research has only begun. And when using ancient DNA, it will be difficult to employ the molecular clock, since it is hard to tell whether an old specimen is truly the direct ancestor of a present-day species; could it be that modern and ancient DNA sequences merely share an ancestor further back in time? Some paleoanthropologists reject the genetic-based approach in its entirety, suggesting that debates about human ancestry will be settled by studying fossils rather than molecules.

Regardless of whether the Eve hypothesis survives or itself goes extinct, it is clear that the molecular approach is providing an entirely new perspective from which to view the human past.

Tracking the First American

The most consequential, if least dramatic event in the history of the Americas came when that first human footprint appeared in the New World. Nobody knows exactly when this happened, or where. We do not know what these Paleo-Indians wore, spoke, looked like, or thought. We do not know when they left their Asian homeland or what conditions they experienced along the way.

And yet there remains no reasonable doubt that the first Americans did indeed travel across a land bridge from Asia during the late Pleistocene. As we will see, biology, language, and archaeology all point to an Asian homeland; it is the timing and conditions surrounding their arrival that remain unknown.

Clovis is the earliest cultural complex in the New World, appearing sometime between 11,000 and 12,000 years ago (see Chapter 6). This relatively conservative estimate remains reasonable because despite decades of concerted research, no undisputed evidence of a pre-Clovis presence has been uncovered anywhere in the Western Hemisphere.

But were Clovis people the very first Americans? Numerous sites throughout North and South America offer tantalizing suggestions, but none provides iron-clad proof acceptable to all archaeologists. Many archaeologists believe that it's just a matter of time before solid pre-Clovis evidence turns up. In fact, many modern archaeologists have begun to acknowledge, if sometimes only privately, that Native Americans could easily have arrived as long as 40,000 years ago.

But if that is true, how can we tell?

One answer, of course, is simply to dig more. But other archaeologists, frustrated with the difficulties of finding such early remains, have tried to resolve the issues by resorting to bioarchaeological evidence. Christy Turner, a physical anthropologist from Arizona State University, has conducted extensive studies of variability in human teeth. Focusing on the crown and root areas, Turner discovered that modern and precontact American Indian teeth are most similar to those of northern Asians. Turner postulates an initial migration out of northeast Asia at the end of the Ice Age, followed by two later migrations. A very similar story emerges from recent research on Native American languages.

Today, it is possible to contrast the strictly archaeological, linguistic, and dental evidence with an important new source of information—the testimony from mtDNA, which is a sensitive marker for those curious about the number, timing, and age of migrations into the Americas.

As explained in the following box, Greenberg's language families remain controversial, but geneticists are still fond of using these simple groupings as baseline configurations against which to compare the genetic results. Some molecular archaeologists believe that the initial population moving out of northeastern Asia ran into a severe "bottleneck" as they passed across the Bering Strait into the New World, limiting the molecular diversity in the newly-arrived population. This is why the molecular biologists argue that the genetic differences between Asian and Native American populations must generally postdate their separation. Thus the measurement of the genetic distance becomes a valid estimator of the time elapsed since they separated. An initial estimate placed this separation between 21,000 and 42,000 years B.P.

In one recent study conducted at Emory University, investigators examined the mtDNA from 18 tribes throughout the Americas. Employing a mutation rate of 2.2 percent per million (derived from some of their earlier work), they computed how long ago these people had diverged from a common ancestor. The answer turned out to be 22,000 to 29,000 years ago, suggesting a pre-Clovis presence in the Americas.

Critics, however, have pointed out that the Emory study depends on a critical, and unconfirmed assumption: that all of the observed genetic diversity began after these tribes crossed the Bering land bridge into the New World. But suppose the tribes had split up someplace in Asia, prior to arriving in America. If that happened, then the molecular clock would have begun ticking prematurely.

Comparisons of genetic similarities and differences in widely separated contemporary American Indian groups strongly suggest that these people share a common genetic ancestor, with an estimated divergence varying between about 15,000 and 30,000 years. Some molecular archaeologists even argued that more than 95 percent of all Native Americans are descended from a single pioneering founder population—perhaps a few families that crossed the Bering Strait together in the late Ice Age. The same genetic evidence suggests that the Eskimo-Aleut and

Tracking the First Americans Through Historical Linguistics

One controversial line of evidence regarding the first Americans comes from linguist Joseph Greenberg of Stanford University, who has reanalyzed the available data from every known American Indian language—a gargantuan task. Like many archaeologists, Greenberg believes that Native Americans arrived in the New World in three distinct groups—Amerind, Na-Dene, and Eskimo-Aleut—each descendants of separate migratory pulses, with the Eskimo-Aleut and Na-Dene populations arriving in relatively recent times.

This reconstruction suggests that the earliest wave of immigrants—the large "Amerind" language family—must have arrived about 12,000 years ago; they were the people of the Clovis complex. These ancestral American Indians spread throughout most of North, Central, and South America. According to Greenberg, virtually all the indigenous languages spoken throughout the Americas derived from this single ancestral language.

But Greenberg's reconstruction has come under heavy fire from his linguistic colleagues. One linguist called this classification "distressing. . . . 'Amerind' is discounted by nearly all specialists." Others worry about the lack of specifics: How, specifically, were the individual languages compared? What kinds of statistics were employed? What steps were taken to screen out linguistic similarities due to language contact? And what about the possibility of multilingualism among these groups? Why do linguistic differences necessarily reflect just migration histories?

Na-Dene people—today confined mostly to the northern rim of North America—may derive from later migrations out of Asia, perhaps 7,500 years ago.

As was the case with African Eve, we presently lack any kind of final, definitive word about the peopling of the New World. But the preliminary results are sufficiently teasing to suggest that whatever the solution may be, molecular archaeology provides a major new source of data regarding the first Americans.

Summary

Bioarchaeology is the study of the human biological component evident in the archaeological record. This specialty requires expertise in the method and theory of both biological anthropology and field archaeology. Many of the bioarchaeologists discussed here have years of experience with hands-on excavation of the remains they study.

One branch of bioarchaeology is called *paleopathology,* the study of ancient disease. The search for diseases of the past is hardly a new enterprise, but some disorders can now be placed in a more reliable biocultural matrix: for instance, the impact of malaria and hyperostosis in the eastern Mediterranean, the problem of iron deficiency anemia in early-historic New World populations, and the relationship between malnutrition and infectious disease.

Bioarchaeologists also study past human diets by determining the ratios of carbon (and sometimes nitrogen) isotopes contained in bone collagen; thereby they can reconstruct the dietary importance of various kinds of plants and animals. Although stable carbon isotope analysis is just emerging from its developmental stage, it has already revolutionized the way in which archaeologists reconstruct prehistoric diets.

Another way to look at human diets is through the documentation of generalized stress responses in human hard tissue. Since the causes and the effects of malnutrition are complex and can rarely be traced precisely, paleopathologists prefer to study the effects of *stress,* defined as any environmental factor that forces the individual or population out of equilibrium.

Harris lines, for instance, are bands of increased bone density—observable on X rays of human long bones. They are often caused by a variety of nutritional stressors, especially severe and short-run dietary deprivation. Harris lines, which generally show up between birth and 18 years, have been observed on dozens of archaeological samples and are consistently associated with a shortened life span.

Another common technique for monitoring physiological stress is the analysis of *dental hypoplasias,* growth arrest lines formed from birth through 6 years. Hypoplasias are often evident from gross examination, although some investigators also look at enamel cross sections. Not only does the presence of hypoplasias indicate the presence of environmental stress, but their size also can be measured, allowing estimates of the duration of metabolic stress.

Today's technology also permits bioarchaeologists to analyze the past on an entirely different level. Calling on the most recent developments in the field of genetic experimentation, so-called *molecular archaeologists* can now actually study the past at the level of the individual molecule. Molecular archaeology, like its counterpart, molecular biology, addresses the ultimate physiochemical organization of life, focusing particularly on the molecular basis of human inheritance. Although just over a decade old, molecular archaeology has already racked up some spectacular successes, providing unexpectedly precise answers to questions long explored through more conventional approaches.

> *We can now dream of catching molecular evolution red-handed.*
> ALLAN C. WILSON, BIOCHEMIST

Bioarchaeology on the Internet

Paleopathology Resources facilitates exchange of information, including a database.
> http://www.usd.edu/~archlab/paleo.html

Human Origins includes recent finds, an evolutionary/geological time line, a skull study module, and plenty of background.
http://euler.ntu.ac.uk/lsteach/origins.html

Human Origins and Evolution in Africa provides links to prehistoric diet, African prehistory, paleoecology, plus on-line research tools from the journals *Nature* and *Science*.
http://www.indiana.edu/~origins/

CHAPTER 9

Understanding the Social Systems of the Past

□ □ □

PREVIEW

Here, we approach the study of past social systems in several ways. Beginning with a fairly conventional "anthropological" perspective, we emphasize the way in which the concepts of social status and role serve to integrate community and nonresidential groups.

We then examine how such social statuses are assigned to members, through achieved and/or ascribed means. Archaeologists have found this approach to be a fruitful way to chart the origins of social inequity. To illustrate this approach, we turn to a classic study by Christopher Peebles and Susan Kus, who examined community-level inequities in the burials at Moundville (Alabama).

Then we shift the emphasis from social roles to social practice. Employing a postprocessual perspective, Randall McGuire relied on the allied concepts of human agency and social power to examine the ancient Hohokam (of Arizona). The contrasts between these approaches employed in the Moundville and Hohokam studies illustrate the broad interpretive range in today's Americanist archaeology.

Finally, we will look at the broader issues of human agency and power as they are reflected in the postprocessual context.

A consideration of ideology and power means that we are no longer able simply to "read off" the nature of past societies from material evidence. Instead the archaeological record must be understood as actively mediated and manipulated as part of the social strategies of the individuals and groups that constituted a past society.

DANIEL MILLER, ARCHAEOLOGIST (UNIVERSITY COLLEGE, LONDON),
AND CHRISTOPHER TILLEY, ARCHAEOLOGIST
(UNIVERSITY OF CAMBRIDGE)

This chapter is about social systems of the past: what they were and how archaeologists find out about them. We begin with ethnologist Walter Goldschmidt's classic definition of **social organization**: "The structure of a society involves two things: first, there is a division into smaller social units, which we call groups; and second, there are recognized social positions (statuses) and behavior patterns

243

appropriate to such positions (roles)." This will be our primary distinction: The *group* is a social subdivision, distinct from the network of *statuses* that define and influence the conduct of interpersonal relations.

The Nature of Social Groups

Social groups are either residential or nonresidential in character. **Residential groups** consist of domestic families or households, territorial bands, or community-level villages. The residential group is spatial, local, and territorial—consisting of relatively permanent aggregations of people. By contrast, the **nonresidential group** consists of associations formed to regulate some specific aspect of society.

Residential and nonresidential groups have quite different origins and courses of development. Residential groups are physical agglomerations of people; they are truly face-to-face associations. But nonresidential groups are groups only in the abstract sense, and as such, they do not necessarily ever convene. The solidarity of nonresidential groups is usually maintained through the use of symbols such as names, ceremonies, mythologies, or insignias of membership. Their boundaries can be fixed and sometimes can be recognized in the archaeological record (as, for instance, ceramic motifs, rock art patterns, and burial style). In a sense, the residential group functions to regulate discrete spatial matters, whereas the nonresidential group binds these territorial units together.

The Nature of Social Status

Status consists of the rights, duties, privileges, powers, liabilities, and immunities that accrue to a recognized and named social position. A single social status is a collection of rights and duties. In our own society, the status of "mother" is determined both by the duties she owes to her son or daughter and the reciprocal responsibilities she can legitimately demand of her children. Similarly, a child owes certain obligations to a parent, and can expect certain privileges in return.

Social status is apportioned according to a number of culturally determined criteria. Nearly all societies categorize their members in terms of their age and their consequent position in the life cycle. Ethnographer Paul Bohannan notes that for African societies the list of male age categories generally runs like this: newly born infant, child on the lap, uninitiated boy, initiated bachelor, married man, elder, and retired elder. The specifics vary from culture to culture, of course, but the underlying principle of age almost always influences one's social standing in the society at large.

Sex is another ubiquitous way in which societies allot status, and it is important here to remember the difference between **sex** and **gender.** The term *sex* refers to inherited, biological differences between males and females. *Gender,* a culturally constructed concept, emphasizes such biological differences to varying degrees.

To emphasize the multifacctcd meaning of gender, we will follow Margaret Conkey and Janet Spector in distinguishing gender role from gender ideology. **Gender role** refers to the differential participation of males and females in the various social, economic, political, and religious institutions of a given cultural group; such roles describe appropriate behavior for gender categories. **Gender ideology** refers to the culturally specific meaning assigned to terms such as "male," "female," "sex," and "reproduction." Both role and ideology vary considerably from culture to culture and cannot be merely assumed (as in biological determinism).

Another conditioner of status is **kinship.** As with sex and age, kinship in a sociocultural sense depends on a biological counterpart but is rarely identical to it. Kinship terms provide cultural labels for the social positions that determine how interpersonal relations are conducted. Ethnographers commonly study social organization through the kinship network. The *kinship group* (or *descent group*) is an association of people who are somehow related to one another. Kinship statuses are really just special cases within a society's overall status framework.

An obvious yet important point to be made here is that all individuals in a society simultaneously possess several different *social statuses* (sometimes called social identities). For example, for a given adult male, "father" is only one of several statuses that are operative. That individual may also be a colonel in the air force, a captain of the bowling team, and a Harvard graduate. Each social position has its own collection of rights and duties. Which identity is currently operating depends on those with whom the individual is interacting. The composite of the several identities maintained by a single individual is termed the **social persona.** It is this encompassing social persona that is reflected in the archaeological record, along with individual status categories such as sex and age.

Role and status are the basic social parameters that define social structure and influence individual behavior and worldview. Sex, ethnicity, age, wealth, power, and religion add up to define individuals and social personae.

Joining a social group requires that one meet a series of culturally prescribed guidelines for "appropriate behavior." For example, such "rules" will generally govern where a couple lives after they are married and how they are to behave toward particular categories of people. Social organization thus embraces the structure and functions of the groups within a society, including how individual statuses relate to one another. Kinship, marital residence, and descent reckoning all are part of a society's internal organization.

Many human societies are also integrated along status lines. Sometimes these statuses correspond closely to residential or nonresidential groups, but more commonly the status divisions crosscut conventional social groups. The statuses *male* and *female* might, for instance, comprise two separate residential groups, but usually they do not. Similarly, membership in a specific nonresidential group might confer some degree of high status, or it might not.

With this general orientation, let us see how archaeology goes about reconstructing social organizations that functioned in the past.

Engendering the Human Past

We have often mentioned how ethnographic and ethnohistoric evidence can be used to model what the archaeological record might be expected to look like. But what we haven't said—yet—is how heavily such expectations rely on methodological and theoretical assumptions.

To emphasize this point, let me take up an example very close to home—my own doctoral dissertation. About the time we were searching for Gatecliff Shelter, I was also attempting to tap the rich ethnographic and ethnohistorical record from the Great Basin to project a series of behavioral activities into the regional archaeological record. The idea was to design a computer simulation that would emulate behavior from a known group of people (the nineteenth-century Western Shoshone) in a known spot (the Reese River Valley, central Nevada) for a known period of time (immediately prior to European contact in the area, roughly A.D. 1840).

We made a number of gender-based inferences. For one thing, we inferred that women and children harvested piñon pine nuts during the fall months because (1) several Western Shoshone women said they did this in the nineteenth-century, and (2) numerous eyewitnesses reported seeing Shoshone women and children doing this a few decades later. Similarly, we thought that hunting parties comprised of all-male adults stalked bighorn sheep for the same reason. We further believed that entire family groups participated in communal jackrabbit drives, once again because this is what Western Shoshone informants and ethnohistoric accounts told us. We tried to determine the gender composition of various camp and task groups for the entire seasonal round of the mid-nineteenth century Western Shoshone people.

But archaeologists do not encounter camp and task groups; archaeologists recover artifacts and ecofacts. Thus it was then necessary for us to assign material culture implications for each activity—once again based on appropriate ethnographic analogs. The distribution of these various artifacts and ecofacts was then projected across the target area in the central Nevada landscape. The regional randomized archaeological survey (somewhat like that discussed for St. Catherines Island in Chapter 5) was designed specifically to see how well these ethnographically grounded projections anticipated the archaeological record of the Reese River Valley.

At the time, it seemed to make perfect sense to employ the available ethnographic information to project human behavior into the recent past. Today, 30 years later, such inferences still make sense—provided there is direct historical continuity between the ethnographic and archaeological records.

Clear-cut linkages between the documentary and archaeological record existed for the Western Shoshone research—so long as we were discussing the mid-nineteenth century. But how far back in the past could we legitimately project the gender-specific ethnohistoric information? Another century (to the mid-eighteenth century)? A millennium? A million years?

The Man-the-Hunter Myth

I raise this point to highlight an increasingly important issue, that of gender bias in reconstructing the past. More than a decade ago, Margaret Conkey and Janet Spector explored this matter in some detail; their now-classic research stands as the first call for an explicit, gender-based approach to the archaeological record.

Conkey and Spector found that conventional archaeological interpretation was permeated with unrecognized (and presumably unintentional) gender bias and *androcentrism.* They uncovered case after case of archaeologists—both male and female—projecting their own ill-defined stereotypes into the past: They criticized the then-dominant processual agenda for creating a false sense of objectivity about how gender roles are encoded in the archaeological record.

The focus of the Conkey and Spector critique was the so-called *Man-the-Hunter* model of human evolution. In effect, this widespread view projected modern gender stereotypes back into the remote past: Males were typically portrayed as "stronger, more aggressive, more active, and in general more important than females . . . [who were] presented as weak, passive, and dependent."

The Man-the-Hunter model assumed a long-term continuity in gender arrangements and ideology, extending from the present back to the earliest humans. This model implied a relatively rigid division of labor along gender lines, a sort of inevitability about gender roles. Specific artifact forms were also viewed as sex-linked—weaponry for hunting was always male, plant collecting apparatus was always female. Men always made the projectile points. Women always made the pottery. Women who are found buried with a grinding stone were assumed to have used this artifact in life. If a man was buried with the same grinding stone, it was because he manufactured it.

Conkey and Spector found that most archaeologists failed to identify the sources for their assumptions and rarely tried to confirm or validate them. Archaeologists were "gendering" the past on the basis of their intrinsic, stereotypical notions about male and female roles.

This is the myth of Man-the-Hunter—drawing upon androcentric assumptions about human nature and society, with the unintended consequence of either ignoring women's activities altogether or characterizing them in secondary, subservient terms. This model overemphasizes the importance of male activities and results in "gender-exclusive" reconstructions of past human behavior.

Anybody doubting that such androcentric gender-bias exists need look no further than the neighborhood museum diorama or a popular publication on archaeology. Age and gender stereotypes about our human past are everywhere—once you actually begin to recognize them.

Seeking Archaeology's Amazingly Invisible Woman

> *The entire village left the next day in about 30 canoes, leaving us alone with the women and children in the abandoned houses.*
>
> CLAUDE LEVI-STRAUSS, FRENCH ANTHROPOLOGIST

In Her Own Words

The Real Flintstones?
by Diane Gifford-Gonzalez

THE DRUDGE:

You have probably seen her, frequenting the diorama scene at your local museum or in that coffee table book on human evolution. It's likely you've not given her a second glance, she is so much a part of the scenery. She is the "Drudge-on-the-Hide"; the woman on her hands and knees scraping away at the skin of a large animal, on the margins of the home camp scene. The men are usually center stage foreground, doing something interesting, while she's over there, hiding out. You usually can not see her face; she is looking down, and the artist may not have bothered to sketch in her brows or mouth. She is not talking to anyone; no one is talking to her.

Conventionalized representations such as the drudge repeat themselves through the works of various artists, their postures and actions suggesting that artists have drawn from their own fine arts traditions, rather than from ethnographically informed suggestions from their scientist collaborators. The "Drudge-on-a-Hide," for example, mimics the scullery maid scrubbing the floor in the background of the 18th century evocations of bourgeois success.

THE GUY-WITH-A-ROCK:

Another common motif, the "Guy-With-a-Rock" about to hurl a huge rock into a pit containing a large and unhappy beast (mammoth, mastodon, woolly rhino, or cave bear), suggests Herculean figures in portrayals of classical myths. Though his hunting mates sport the latest ballistic weapons, this stone-age conservative has a hefty rock as his weapon of choice from 2 million B.C. to Holocene bison hunts in Dakota. . . .

Archaeologists can readily testify to the difficulties of assigning gender or maturational stage to most of the activities portrayed, in view of humanity's global diversity in cultural practices. Yet the graphic story reaching out from the museum halls and coffee table pages treats men's and women's—and youngsters' and oldsters'—estate as foregone conclusions. When viewed cumulatively, as we would see them in our lifetimes of museum-going and reading, the vast majority of existing portrayals give us a narrow and repetitious view of prehistoric human life.

Conkey and Spector established the archaeology of gender as a focus of intense study. In several places throughout this text, we discuss how feminist archaeology is changing our perception of gender in the past. Here, we focus on one immediate response to Conkey and Spector's critique: the attempt to

As an archaeologist trained in an anthropological view of the past and a citizen of an ethnically and racially diverse nation, I believe we can serve the greater public by expanding the range of possible pasts represented in depictions of prehistoric people. I am not arguing for revising past worlds as they have conventionally been represented using a representational quota system, by which various ages, genders, and races get their fair share of prestige as defined in these works—where women hunt, men scrape hides, old folks run and dance—though all probably did a good deal of these activities. Rather, why not combine scientific rigor and creativity to offer viewers social arrangements different from any known today, or hominid species with truly different adaptations and behaviors? By picturing unexpected past worlds—inhabited not by mimics or parodies of ourselves but by those who may have been strong, successful, yet very unlike us— we might succeed in actually drawing more viewers into the real problems, possibilities, and pleasures of research on the past.

DIANE GIFFORD-GONZALEZ is professor of anthropology at the University of California, Santa Cruz.

Life-size reconstruction of a Neanderthal family group roughly 50,000 years ago at the site of Le Moustier (France).

develop methods and concepts to attribute gender to specific sets of material culture.

The processual agenda generally assumed the existence of "knowable" correlations between the world of material remains and particular activities, behaviors, and beliefs. It was just a matter of operationally defining the linkages between the archaeological record and the behavior that produced it. There seemed to be every reason to assume that gender is variously encoded in material remains and their spatial arrangements.

Some archaeologists have specifically addressed the counterpoint to the Man-the-Hunter model: the apparent invisibility of women in the archaeological record. Glynn Isaac, for instance, noted that, "As long as we do not correct for the imbalance created by the durability of bone as compared with that of plant residues, studies of human evolution will always have a male bias." Embedded in Isaac's statement is, of course, the assumption that men always hunt and women always collect plant foods.

When I analyzed the artifacts from Gatecliff Shelter, I took up the same issue, speaking specifically of "The Amazingly Invisible Woman":

> There is also an important correlation between the sexual division of labor and the productive modes in hunter-gatherer society. Males tend to be highly visible in the archaeological record because many male fabrication activities involve subtractive technology [particularly stone tool manufacture]. Conversely, females make few artifacts subtractively, and their archaeological visibility suffers accordingly.
>
> Although both males and females employ additive technology, female fabrication is dominated by this self-corrective, centripetal mode of production, particularly basket making, fiber clothing manufacture, weaving, sewing, and, in some cases, pottery making. . . .
>
> Neither technology is sex specific, but there is an obvious association between the mode of technology and the sexual division of labor. Male tool kits are simply more archaeologically visible than female tool kits. This bias must be kept in mind when reconstructing the activity structure of the various Gatecliff occupational surfaces.

When this was written, Isaac and I both felt that the archaeological record of hunter-gatherers was intrinsically biased against recognizing female activities. But if we just tried hard enough, we thought, we could perhaps recover enough solid evidence to "find women in the past" after all.

Conkey and Spector addressed the same subject—the so-called invisibility of women in the archaeological record—but they attributed the problem to a pervasive androcentric bias and a host of unquestioned assumptions made by archaeologists such as myself. To them, the problem was "more the result of a false notion of objectivity and of the gender paradigms archaeologists employ than an inherent invisibility of such data. One can claim that female-related data in the archaeological record is invisible only if one makes some clearly questionable assumptions, such as the existence of an exclusive sexual division of labor."

This was an important point, which drew considerable attention as feminist archaeology matured. Nearly 15 years after writing her critique with Janet Spector, Margaret Conkey joined with Joan Gero to edit an important book, *Engendering Archaeology: Women and Prehistory,* published in 1991. The remaining topics in this section recap some of the key points made in that influential volume.

The Difference Between Sex and Gender

It is critical here to clarify once again the difference between *sex* and *gender*. To some extent, this is merely a semantic distinction, but it also has some important attendant conditions.

As explained earlier in the chapter, the term *sex* refers strictly to the biological differences between males and females; these are the facts of biology. But *gender* is a culturally constructed concept, which may or may not emphasize biological differences. Some cultural traditions claim that male–female differences are almost completely biological, while others pay very little attention to biology.

Bioarchaeology: The "Smoking Gun" of Gender Studies?

Some have suggested that attempts to engender the past should begin with the biological basics. Sex, after all, has a genetic basis. It has been argued, for instance, that the "smoking gun" of gender studies might be the actual human skeletal remains. The bones should establish, once and for all, the presence of human beings in the past, in indisputably sex-specific terms.

This is not so. It is important to note that the bones, by themselves, provide only information about sex, not gender: Gender involves the expected roles, norms, values, and relative statuses of biological males and females (at least as they were treated at the time of death). These culturally based practices can, perhaps, be understood by studying the materials accompanying human burials.

There have even been problems with deriving biological, sex-specific information from human bones. In Chapter 8, for instance, we discussed how human remains are used to reconstruct ancient demography. We mentioned the particularly significant skeletal series recovered by A. V. Kidder at Pecos Pueblo. More than 2,000 human burials were excavated, dating from A.D. 1300 to the historic period. Surely a sex-based study of grave goods, disease, and nutrition would reveal a great deal about the respective roles of men and women at Pecos. After all, determining sex and age of human skeletons is a straightforward, "objective" technique of bioarchaeology, right?

Again, things were not so self-evident. When physical anthropologists "sexed" the skeletons from Pecos, they did so by observing certain universal characteristics of the bones, and then attributing biological femaleness and maleness. As we have seen, the operational definitions of biologically "male" and "female" skeletons have not remained static through time: What to Hooton were "females" are today considered to be "males." This is because of the evolving nature of the middle-range biological research linking skeletal remains of the past with their biological correlates.

Recently, the search for sex attribution has gone high-tech. It is now possible, at least on a limited basis, to ascribe sex on the basis of DNA (using techniques discussed in the preceding chapter). In one pilot study by Mark Sutton and his colleagues, human DNA was extracted from human coprolites (desiccated feces) found in archaeological sites in California and Nevada. Two of the samples are from women, one from a man (the fourth was indeterminate). When these results are expanded to much larger samples, it may eventually be possible to detect gender differences in cuisine, pharmacology, and access to certain foods in the past.

So it would seem that, despite early difficulties with linkages, bioarchaeologists will indeed provide some useful tools for projecting sex into the past. But what about the difficulties in reading the material culture record? After all, there are fundamental differences between biological and cultural correlates. When physical anthropologists "sex" skeletons, they are working from biology. But in examining the material dimensions of gender, archaeologists are approaching culturally conditioned and culturally variable behavior. When archaeologists explore the relative locations of male and female remains in a burial mound, when they observe gender-specific "status" differences in grave goods, and when they infer male and female activity-areas in archaeological sites, they are looking at culturally and historically specific expressions of what it meant to be "male" and "female" at a particular point in time and space. These are not biological givens to be assumed; they are cultural variables to be explored.

Gender Attribution: Do We Really Need It?

Such are the difficulties that attend attempts to link specific aspects of the archaeological record with male and/or female behaviors. But Conkey and Gero caution that such gender-attribution studies are really questions of *method* and may not be central to the thrust of feminist archaeology. Calling such methodological breakthroughs mere "band-aids" masking a large problem, Conkey and Gero argue for a much broader research program.

Many of those engaged in feminist archaeology—including Conkey and Gero—heartily endorse the major propositions of the postprocessual critique. By adopting gender as an analytical concept, they argue for a radically redefined view of prehistory and archaeological reasoning. Many of the postmodern principles we have already considered have today been incorporated as mainstays in a feminist approach to archaeology.

Viewed this way, the process of gender attribution—the linking of material culture with males and/or females—becomes another form of middle-range theory building. The postprocessual critique, which is highly critical of theory at the middle range, argues that human behavior observed in the present cannot readily be transferred back into the past by referring to any single system of laws. The relevance of one observation to another must be established by a network of local understandings.

In short, many of emerging approaches aimed at engendering the human past fit quite comfortably within the overall thrust of postmodernism in Americanist archaeology. Conkey and Gero, for instance, insist that an archaeology employing gender as a central concept must emphasize the individual as an active social agent—an important point that is central to the postprocessual critique. Like other participants in the postprocessual critique, many pursuing gender-based research reject the systematic, clinical, single-minded approaches of the past. Many also reject the etic, evolutionary, antihistorical, objective, rigidly science-based, and ethically neutral approach of the processual agenda.

The primary topics of the postprocessual critique—gender, power, ideology, text, discourse, rhetoric, writing, structure, history, and the role of the individual— are also central to many aspects of feminist approaches to the past.

But it is important to note that gender-related studies can take on many different forms and follow several different theoretical frameworks. While some gender studies fit quite comfortably within the postprocessual critique, that relationship is neither exclusive nor required.

The Origins of Social Inequality

Societies have developed two rather different ways of assigning statuses—through ascription and through achievement. An **ascribed status** is assigned to individuals at the moment of birth, without regard to innate differences or abilities. Alternatively, a society can provide for statuses to be achieved, requiring that an individual possess certain admirable qualities (which are, of course, culturally defined). Rather than being assigned at birth, **achieved statuses** are left open until filled through competition and individual effort.

Egalitarian Societies

The concept of status allows us to leap from the level of the individual to that of the entire society. A society is termed *egalitarian* when the number of valued statuses is roughly equivalent to the number of persons with the ability to fill them. Such societies lack the means to fix or limit the number of persons capable of exerting power; **egalitarian societies** are therefore characterized by generally equal access to important resources.

The social system of the nineteenth-century Great Basin Shoshone people was generally egalitarian, with leadership taken over by those believed to be most capable of supervising others. Authority was restricted to a particular, short-term circumstance. A good hunter might, for instance, assume a position of leadership when a group of men joined to hunt bighorn. Or an accomplished dancer might take charge of the communal gatherings *(fandangos)*. A gifted talker might keep the villagers informed about the ripening of plant foods in different areas and urge the people to cooperate for the good of the group. The key to leadership here is experience and overall social standing; such social position is *not* inherited in an egalitarian society.

Ranked Societies

A **ranked society** is one in which the positions of valued status are limited, so that not everyone of sufficient talent to occupy such statuses can actually achieve them. Such a social structure embodies an intrinsic hierarchy in which relatively permanent social stations are maintained, with people having unequal access to basic life-sustaining resources. Although the distribution of labor is determined by sex and age in both egalitarian and ranked societies, ranked societies tend to have economies that redistribute goods and services throughout the community. Many tribes of the American Northwest coast are ranked societies. Localized kin groups— not individuals—control the resources, and major economic goods flow in and out of a finite center.

The categories *egalitarian* and *ranked* define a social spectrum that archaeologists believe can be traced through analysis of material culture. Mortuary remains, for instance, are commonly analyzed in order to examine the workings of extinct social systems. For the past three decades or so, many archaeologists have made an important assumption when dealing with burial assemblages: *Persons who are treated differentially in life will be treated differentially in death.*

Death, in a sense, is a period of separation and reintegration for both the deceased and those left behind. The dead are separated from the living and must be properly integrated into the world of the dead. Social ties existed between the living and the once-living, and the ceremonial connections at death reflect in large measure these social relations. Archaeologist Christopher Peebles has emphasized the importance of studying human burials as the *fossilized terminal statuses* of individuals. Although these terminal statuses commonly differ from those studied by ethnographers, models defined archaeologically are thought to be every bit as real as those observable among ethnographic cultures.

Community-Level Inequity: Rank and Status Markers at Moundville

Let us examine the ranking of social status evident at Moundville, one of the best-known and most intensively investigated ceremonial centers in the United States. Sprawling across about 300 acres, Moundville overlooks Alabama's Black Warrior River. Three thousand people once lived here—an astonishing number. For the next five centuries, no city in the American Southeast would again reach that size.

Moundville was a major participant in the **Mississippian** tradition, a term referring to the hundreds of late precontact societies that thrived between about A.D. 800 and 1500 (or later) throughout the Tennessee, Cumberland, and Mississippi river valleys. In their heyday, the Mississippian elite presided over breathtaking ceremonial centers (as at Moundville). The Mississippian aristocracy was invested with power by the thousands of farming people who lived in smaller palisaded hamlets and farmsteads.

The Moundville complex of two dozen earthen mounds was a bustling ritual center between about A.D. 1000 and 1500. Like most Mississippian polities, this maize-based society engaged in extensive trade, and their skilled artists worked in stone, ceramics, bone, and copper. Moundville contains 20 major ceremonial mounds, large flat-topped earthen structures designed both to function as artificial hills elevating temples above the landscape and also as mortuary areas. Moundville had a large central plaza and was protected by a stout palisade.

Initial archaeological investigations at Moundville were conducted in 1905 and 1906 by the ubiquitous C. B. Moore (see Chapter 1). Moore excavated both platform mounds and village areas, and although his work was not up to contemporary standards, his basic data are still quite usable. The Alabama Museum of Natural History then excavated at Moundville from 1929 through 1941. Over half a million square feet of the village areas at Moundville were uncovered during this 12-year period, in part by workers in the Civilian Conservation Corps.

More than 3,000 burials have been excavated at Moundville, and they have provided an excellent database for studying Mississippian social structure. This task is complicated by the different methods of excavation employed, but work by Christopher Peebles and Susan Kus clearly indicates that a special kind of "salvage archaeology"—studying museum collections excavated decades ago—can be fruitful indeed.

Local and Supralocal Symbolism

Peebles and Kus began their analysis by studying the abundant Moundville grave goods, many of which display the distinctive symbolism characteristic of the so-called **Southern Cult**. Also called the **Southeastern Ceremonial Complex,** this huge ritual network was concentrated in three regional centers: Moundville (Alabama), Etowah (Georgia), and Spiro (Oklahoma).

The striking similarities in Southern Cult themes, motifs, and media imply more than simple trade networks; there was a higher degree of social interaction at work. The conch shell gorgets and cups, the copper plates, the ceremonial axes and batons, the effigy pipes and flint knives found at Spiro and elsewhere contain a distinctive set of Southern Cult symbols. The forked eye, the cross, the sun circle, the hand and eye, the bi-lobed arrow, among others, suggest a shared symbol system that extended beyond the limits of any single Mississippian polity, spreading from Mississippi to Minnesota, from the Great Plains to the Atlantic Coast. In addition to small, "expensive" items, Southern Cult exchange may have involved critical subsistence resources such as food and salt.

Many of the representations of crosses, hand and eye, sun symbols, serpent, woodpecker, falcon, raccoon, and others, plus

An image in the Southern Cult style, pounded in copper. Note particularly the forked eye motif around the eye, which probably represents a symbolic association with the duck hawk (or peregrine falcon), both known for their keen vision and skill as hunters (from Spiro, Oklahoma).

ceramics modeled on animal and human forms, continued (in the various forms) into the belief systems of postcontact Native Americans of the Southeast—in their folk tales, myths, and religious observances.

Whatever the Southern Cult really was—and archaeologists still debate the point—it crosscut the boundaries of many distinctive local cultures. Peebles and Kus termed the Southern Cult artifacts *supralocal* because of their widespread distribution, far beyond the boundaries of Moundville.

They also recognized a second distinctive kind of grave goods, the *local symbols*. These artifacts are specially constructed animal effigy vessels, or parts of animals such as canine teeth, claws, and shells. The local symbols seem to have functioned as status items within a single site (that is, presumably within a single community), while the supralocal symbols designated the rank of individuals in the overall region.

Each mound at Moundville appeared to have contained a few high-status adults. Grave goods include copper axes, copper gorgets, stone discs, various paints, and assorted exotic minerals such as *galena* (cubes of natural lead) and *mica* (paper-thin sheets of translucent silicate minerals). Each mound also contained some less well accompanied (presumably lower-status) individuals, furnished with only a few ceramic vessels.

Because each of the Moundville mounds once supported temples, it seems that the high-status burials in the mounds may be specifically associated with those ceremonial structures. The lower-status burials—particularly the infant and isolated skull burials—were probably ritual accompaniments to the high-status individuals.

Only the most elite were accompanied by the supralocal symbols—including ceremonial axes and sheet copper plumes that depict the "eagle being" and the "dancing priest." Presumably these individuals had statuses and reputations recognized throughout the entire Moundville cultural system. By correlating the presence of higher-status and lower-status symbols, Peebles and Kus inferred that social position at Moundville seems to have been inherited automatically by all family members. This inference is reinforced by the fact that sometimes even infants and children—clearly too young to have accomplished anything very noteworthy in life—were buried with lavish grave goods. And because the most valuable grave goods were buried only with truly high-status individuals, status at Moundville must have been assigned at birth, not because of what an individual had done in life.

Two Axes of Social Patterning

On the basis of comparable ethnographic evidence, Peebles and Kus predicted that the Moundville population may have been subdivided along two major social axes, which they termed the superordinate and subordinate.

Unlike the elite discussed above, a *subordinate* division in a ranked society consists of a "commoner" class, within which social rank—manifested in certain symbols and the energy expended on mortuary ritual—is based exclusively on age and sex. With respect to age, the older the individual, the greater the opportunity for

CLUSTER

N= Number of individuals

Increasing complexity of mortuary ritual →

Segment				
A	IA N=7	IB N=43	II N=67	
B	III N=211	IV N=50		
B	VII N=55	VIII N=70	IX N=46	
C	V N=55	VI N=45	X N=70	
C	No grave goods N=1,256			

Segment	Cluster	Characteristic	Artifacts	Burial context	Age Infant-Child-Adult %
A	IA	Copper axes		Central mound	
A	IB	Copper earspools, Stone disks	Bear teeth, Red or white paint	Mounds and cemeteries rear mounds	
A	II	Shell beads, Oblong copper gorgets	Galena	Mounds and cemeteries rear mounds	
B	III	Effigy vessels, Animal bone	Shell gorgets, Fresh water shells	Cemeteries near mounds	
B	IV	Discoidals, Bone awls	Projectile points	Cemeteries near mounds	
C	V VIII	Bowls and/or jars		Cemeteries near mounds and in village areas	
C	VI VII IX	Water bottles		Cemeteries near mounds and in village areas	
C	X	Sherds		Village areas	
	No grave goods			"Retainers in mounds" Isolated skulls with public buildings Cemeteries near mounds and in village areas	

Graphic representation of the hierarchial social clusters represented in burials at Moundville.

lifetime achievement, and hence the higher the deathbed rank can be. This means that at Moundville (along the subordinate axis, at least), adult burials should be more lavish than those of children, and children should be accompanied by more grave goods than infants. And because subordinate ranking is also graded by gender, men and women should not be expected to have equivalent grave goods.

The *superordinate* division at Moundville is a partially hereditary ordering based on criteria other than age and sex. Among the elite (superordinate) division—people whose status was assigned at birth—some individuals will be infants, some children, and the rest adults.

In sum, Peebles and Kus predicted that the statuses should form a pyramid-shaped distribution. At the base of the pyramid are the commoners, whose statuses are determined strictly by sex and age. The next step up the social ladder consists of those few individuals with ascribed—inherited—status. Finally, at the top will be the paramount individuals, those who enjoy all the emblems of status and rank available in the society.

Quantitative Distribution of Moundville Grave Goods

The model proposed by Peebles and Kus was tested by performing an in-depth statistical analysis on 2,053 of the best-documented burials from Moundville. Cluster IA—the supreme division—were presumably chiefs, those individuals enjoying the highest of statuses and the ultimate political authority. All males, these supreme elite were buried in large truncated mounds, accompanied by a lavish array of material culture, including numerous Southern Cult–adorned artifacts. Infants and human skulls (of individuals presumably sacrificed for the occasion) were buried as part of the Cluster IA ritual. Large copper axes found in these graves seem to symbolize the high offices held by these rulers.

Cluster IB burials, both children and adult males, were interred nearby. They also had a number of Southern Cult artifacts, plus mineral-based paints, included in their grave goods. Apparently, these second-order ritual or political officers seem to have been those charged with the ceremonial application of body paint or tattoos to others. Cluster II, the final cluster of the superordinate segment, included adults and children buried in cemeteries near the mounds and in **charnel houses** near the main plaza; their grave goods included chest beads, copper gorgets, and galena cubes.

Hierarchically below the superordinate elite of Segment A are those of subordinate Segments B and C (who enjoyed status strictly on the basis of sex and age differences). In Cluster III, for instance, stone ceremonial axes are found only with adult males, whereas infants and children have "toy" vessels, clay "playthings," and unworked freshwater shells. Unworked bird claws, and deer and turtle bones were found only with adults. The individuals in the lowest segment, C, were buried away from the mounds and major ceremonial areas at Moundville.

Burial context appears to clarify the nature of ranking in the Moundville society. The most elite were buried in a sacred area and accompanied by symbols of their exalted status. The Moundville elite apparently lived in larger, more complex dwellings than did the commoners. Elite membership was conditioned by genealogy, and because social position was inherited within the elite, even children occupied such social positions.

Farther down the ladder, the villagers' graves also reflected their social stations in life, positions conditioned largely by sex and age distinctions rather than by inheritance. Their less glamorous grave goods were distributed in a different way. Graves contained pottery vessels, bone awls, flint projectile points, and stone pipes, all of which were distributed mostly among older adults. Peebles and Kus infer that these individuals were required to *achieve*–rather than inherit–their social status. The prize artifacts for villagers went to the "self-made," those who had achieved status on their own. More than half of the Moundville graves contained commoners buried with no grave goods at all.

Peeble and Kus tried to place Moundville into a regional framework consisting of the 20-plus sites that seemed to be part of a single system, held together by a common social organization and common ritual. Part of the production of this society as a whole was used to support a number of specialized politico-religious offices, mostly associated with Moundville itself, as well as some minor ceremonial centers and villages in the hinterlands. Recruitment to these high offices was probably limited to members at the apex of the social organization. Nevertheless, bonds of kinship and genealogical relationship probably integrated the whole society.

Peebles and Kus suggest that Moundville conformed to a *chiefdom* model, characterized by a status framework with fewer valued positions than there were individuals capable of handling them. The economy was probably redistributive, with Moundville serving as a center for the regional distribution of key goods. Subsequent to the Peebles and Kus research at Moundville, ranked forms of social organization have been recognized at other Mississippian sites in Tennessee, Georgia, Oklahoma, and the lower Illinois Valley. In all cases, burial populations served as the source of inference. We will have more to say about chiefdoms later, when we consider the evolution of various social forms in some detail.

Alternative Interpretations of Mortuary Patterning

Situated as it was, firmly within the processual agenda, the Peebles and Kus study of Moundville makes a number of implicit assumptions about the nature of social systems–how they operate and how they change. Taken together, these assumptions dictate how the social organization of an ancient society can be reconstructed from its mortuary record.

There are many strengths to this approach. For one thing, the generalizing, systemic approach advocated by Peebles and Kus holds that evidence from a particular target society can be grouped with data from similar societies into a larger, evolutionary framework according to the degree of organizational complexity. In addition, the available ethnographic evidence confirms that mortuary patterning alone often predicts the rest of the social pattern—such as egalitarian and ranked organization.

Nevertheless, several postprocessualists, including Michael Parker Pearson and Randall McGuire, have found fault with this approach to past mortuary behavior. The systemic perspective has been heavily criticized because it implies that scientists can readily divide the "whole" of the past into distinct, yet interrelated subsystems. Employing a systemic premise, the Moundville study approaches mortuary data as a subsystem that reflects the overall social system.

Postprocessual critics have suggested that such reflections may not be so clear-cut after all. In the next section, we will briefly examine an example—trying to understand the social organization of the ancient Hohokam of the American Southwest—the kind of explanation that flows from a postprocessual perspective. After that, we will return to a couple of the key concepts—agency and power—that inform this alternative perspective.

Life and Death Among the Hohokam

The Hohokam people once lived in the blistering deserts of southern Arizona and northern Sonora, Mexico. **Hohokam** is an **O'odham** (also known as Pima) Indian word meaning literally "all-used-up," but usually it is given the more generic translation of "ancient" or "old ones."

Shortly after A.D. 1, groups of part-time farmers moved into the sizzling Lower Sonoran Desert. Before long, relatively large settlements sprouted, reflecting their successful experimentation with diversion dams, ditches, and levees that dramatically increased farming productivity. By A.D. 700, farming communities were prospering along the major river systems of the Phoenix Basin, and the Hohokam heartland had grown to encompass roughly 4,000 square miles. Communities at this point ranged in size from a few extended families to more than several hundred people.

Soon these expanded into still larger villages, with intensive canal irrigation, increased population size, and amplified ceremonialism. Trade networks stretched far beyond previous frontiers, funneling scarce and expensive resources to talented Hohokam artisans. Hohokam communities straddled major continental trade routes, from the California coast to the Great Plains, from the complex civilizations in Mexico to the resource-rich Rocky Mountains. Intrepid Hohokam middlemen eventually bartered and transported merchandise as diverse as deer skins, sea shells, turquoise, obsidian, rare minerals, finished textiles, salt, exotic feathers, and ceramics. Artistic excellence was expressed in increasingly diverse media including stone, bone, shell, and ceramics.

The Hohokam: Egalitarian or Socially Complex?

For more than a century, archaeologists have been trying to make sense of Hohokam social organization. Dozens of archaeologists have looked at architectural

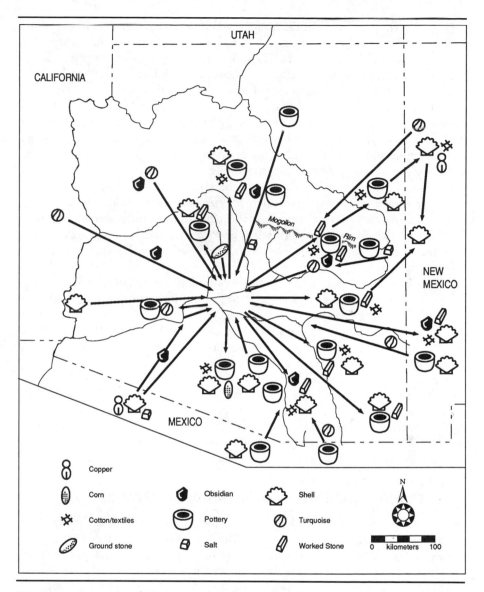

Hohokam trade networks. This network reached its peak between A.D. *800 and 1100.*

data, settlement pattern evidence, artifacts, and mortuary patterning. In the 1890s, Frank Hamilton Cushing interpreted Classic period Hohokam social organization as nonegalitarian (that is, ranked). Then, during the 1930s, archaeologists Harold Gladwin and Emil Haury developed a model of Hohokam society as basically egalitarian, much like ethnohistoric Tohono O'odham, living in dispersed autonomous communities along major river margins. Within the last couple of decades, the tempo of Hohokam archaeology has accelerated dramatically and today several explanations of Hohokam social organization exist. Although some archaeologists still view the Hohokam in largely egalitarian terms, many others argue for greater social complexity, suggesting that Hohokam society must have been ranked, perhaps even operating at the chiefdom level. Some have argued that a privileged elite must have emerged, enjoying their wealth, living in large house clusters, and burying their dead in richly accompanied cremation burials. The Tohono O'odham people themselves have oral traditions suggesting that their ancestors were once ruled by powerful political leaders, who organized warfare on a massive scale.

Implicit in most such models is the assumption that ancient Hohokam society should be viewed as a coherent, functioning, integrated system. This perspective derives from the basic processual agenda, which maintains that any given part of an interconnected system necessarily carries with it important implications for the rest of the system. Accordingly, any aspect of the material culture record should provide a direct, if not straightforward, reflection of the overall cultural system. Consider, for instance, mortuary patterning. Properly analyzed, these data should tell us about correlative organizations, practices, and relations within the rest of the social and economic system. In practice, this means that archaeological research has commonly attempted to isolate these various subsystems—architecture, mortuary patterning, and other material categories—and studied them independently, without regard to the context *within the society under study*.

Conflicting Evidence in Hohokam Archaeology

With specific reference to the Hohokam at the site of La Ciudad (not far from downtown Phoenix, Arizona), Randall McGuire has rejected this systemic approach in favor of a nontypological, nonsystem approach. He employs a *contextual* view that seeks understanding through an examination of power relations and internal contradictions within Hohokam society.

McGuire looked first at Hohokam architecture (to simplify matters, we will concentrate strictly on evidence from the Colonial period, A.D. 725–1000, and the Sedentary period, A.D. 1000–1100). There is extensive archaeological evidence to suggest that Hohokam houses were simple structures with sidewalls and roofs of reeds, supported by a framework of posts and covered with an external earthen veneer. Sometimes, covered sheltering extensions *(ramadas)* were attached to the exterior walls. Although there is little direct evidence of what these structures looked like, archaeologists commonly assume that these Hohokam houses were all built of the same materials, were roughly the same shape, were relatively impermanent, and varied in size only.

What do these houses tell us about Hohokam social organization?

To McGuire, the important point is the lack of any clear-cut examples of elite structures during the Colonial and Sedentary periods (although there *is* such evidence for later phases). Had such high-status residences been present, one might reasonably infer some degree of social inequality between commoners and elite. But lacking evidence for elite dwellings, one would conclude—from an overarching *systemic* perspective—that the social organization must have been relatively egalitarian, lacking social ranking.

But the mortuary evidence tells a different story, one that contradicts the notion of everyday equality in Hohokam life. The Hohokam cremated their dead, then buried the ashes with appropriate grave goods. Some burials contain huge amounts of mortuary items, others contain none. The grave goods, when present, include items that seem to have been worn by the deceased at the time of cremation (such as finely made shell bracelets, beads, and hair ornaments). Also included were utilitarian artifacts such as stone tools and pottery vessels; some may have been personal possessions and others were perhaps offerings for use in the afterworld. There were also inclusions of shell wastage, suggesting, perhaps, craft specialization on the part of the deceased. Several Hohokam cremations contained what archaeologists have called "esoterica"—exotic goods such as stone palettes, clay figurines, and incense burners; the consensus is that such finely worked and specialized artifacts held special meaning for the Hohokam, both in life and after death.

McGuire's Contextual Approach

Taken by itself, the presence of a few very richly accompanied individuals certainly would seem to suggest the existence of real-life inequities in Hohokam life, with the elite enjoying more formalized status and differential access to economic and political power. But McGuire believes that Hohokam social organization cannot be understood from this either-or perspective. He rejects the idea that "complexity" or "stratification" can be encapsulated into a single dimension.

Instead, McGuire argues for a more contextual approach, in which mortuary ritual, as a manifestation of Hohokam ideology, played a role in "negotiation of power relations in Hohokam society." He views burial ritual, first of all, as embedded within the active negotiation, reproduction, and legitimization of the social order. Following a **dialectical approach** derived from Marxist theory, he emphasizes the need to identify and analyze "contradictions" between various artifact classes (such as burials and architecture) and between different social categories (such as mundane and ritual).

McGuire takes exception to the view that architectural and mortuary data must have the same meaning, or even necessarily agree. Emphasizing the overall cultural landscape, McGuire believes that, for the Hohokam, houses were largely

In His Own Words

Marxist Approaches in Anglo-American Archaeology
by Randall H. McGuire

The labels *processual* and *postprocessual* archaeology often lack a precise definition within archaeology, despite their frequent use as an opposition. I do not like to characterize my work as postprocessual. This label includes far too much. I would call my work Marxist.

Marxism is not a single, coherent theory of society that can be hitched to our purposes or dismissed in a few terse sentences. It is, instead, a philosophy, a tradition of thought, a mode of theoretical production, which has produced, and will produce, many theories. The theory of archaeology that I use springs from a tradition of Marxist thought that is dialectical and historical.

Within the great variety of theories that characterize Marxism in Anglo-American archaeology, there is a set of general principles that all, or most, of these views share:

1. Each claims Marx as an important intellectual ancestor and as a source of inspiration. In all of these archaeologies, his work is a starting point, not an end point.
2. All seek to account for sociocultural change in terms of a similar theoretical and philosophical framework that puts social relations at the core of our research and seeks to break down the oppositions that bedevil our research; oppositions between mentalism and materialism, humanism and science, history and evolution, relativism and determinism.
3. Each treats society as a whole, a totality, that should be ultimately understood as such. They reject the idea that scholars can come to a

taken for granted. The built environment "forms the stage for all human action." Dwellings were simply a part of mundane, everyday reality.

But nothing about the mortuary ritual, he argues, is mundane. Death can produce immense emotional impact—the shock of losing a loved one, apprehension over one's own eventual death, resentment toward the supernaturals who control life and death, wariness regarding the corpse, and so forth. McGuire points out that death will always be the final rite of passage, creating stress for the individuals involved and for their personal social linkages. Although the ethnographic record contains a broad range of attitudes and beliefs regarding burial rites and mortuary rituals, the event of death is rarely considered to be routine.

So, returning to the question posed earlier: Were the Colonial and Sedentary people an egalitarian or a ranked society? McGuire argues that the

better understanding of social process by reducing social phenomena to their parts and examining those parts.

4. All emphasize contradiction and conflict as vital features of human society and internal sources of change in those societies. As such, they reject functionalism, the notion that social phenomena can be adequately understood in terms of how they function to maintain society or allow it to adapt to an environment.

5. Each takes a human-centered view of history that gives human action or *praxis* some significant role in the process of history. They therefore reject any form of determinism (environmental, material, or technological) and the idea of abstract knowledge divorced from the action of people.

6. All recognize that our knowledge of the past is created in a social and political context, that people make knowledge. And, that this knowledge can never be merely a reflection of the reality of that past, nor should scholars simply make it up to fit our own political and social agendas.

7. Each shares a commitment that the power relations and structure of the modern, capitalist-dominated world is unjust and destructive to people. All advocate some form of socialism as the alternative to this system.

These principles can be used to contrast Marxism as a way of knowing the world, as a critique of the world, and as a means for action in the world, with the other theoretical approaches current in Anglo-American archaeology.

RANDALL H. MCGUIRE is professor of anthropology at the State University of New York, Binghamton.

Hohokam were both. Whereas the everyday architecture suggests a sense of sameness and equality, the inequalities of the Hohokam social order were revealed ritually in the assemblage of mortuary items. After the cremation ceremony, the bone fragments and broken artifacts were gathered up and placed in the ground—disappearing from the everyday world. McGuire believes that Hohokam mortuary ritual brought the living and the dead together in a purposeful way; it revealed and mediated the tensions between an egalitarian ideal and the real-world inequities of everyday Hohokam life.

McGuire's analysis emphasizes the *social negotiation* within and between social groups, with grave goods establishing a complex of cultural debts and debits. McGuire concludes that Hohokam social organization "was too intricate to yield characterizations of evolutionary stage, level of complexity, or simple oppositions between egalitarian and ranked or achieved and ascribed status."

A Larger Postprocessual Context

The Hohokam and Moundville studies were selected because they approach past social organization from rather different angles. Operating largely from a processual perspective, Peebles and Kus made some important assumptions:

- Material culture associated with the deceased—grave goods, monuments, place of burial, and so forth—should directly reflect the amalgamated social statuses (the *social persona*) in life. In effect, the grave is viewed as carrying on these various social forms after death.
- The material expressions of these composite statuses are comparable from individual to individual, from site to site, and from culture to culture.
- The differential patterning evident in these mortuary contexts is reflective of ranked hierarchical relations that once existed in the society under study.

From this baseline, Peebles and Kus employed the inferred system of social ranking (as reflected by mortuary patterning at Moundville) to explore the nature of Mississippian social relations in general. They argued that Moundville likely operated as a **chiefdom,** with numerous local groups organized under authority of a regional elite. The mortuary record—reflecting as it does the "fossilized terminal statuses" of the individuals at Moundville—permits archaeologists to reconstruct the nature of past social systems.

McGuire's consideration of Hohokam social organization questions these theoretical assumptions and substitutes a rather different viewpoint:

- What if the archaeological record results *not* from social roles and status? What if that record is shaped instead by recurrent social practices?
- What if *social power* is central to the operation of such social systems?
- What if burial practices have been *manipulated* by the powerful to rationalize, reify, or mask existing social inequality?
- What if culture is not so *systemic* after all?

Viewed from this vantage point, burial practices may actually *contradict* other important aspects of social structure, revealing some tensions and covering up others. McGuire argues that looking for and exploring such contradictions may be the most fruitful avenue for approaching past social structure and understanding how these structures changed through time.

McGuire's research reflects the larger postprocessual critique, which has shifted the debate on ancient social organization. Postprocessual critics suggest that archaeologists should look more closely at the role of power and human agency in an attempt to understand the larger meaning of the human past. We will now look at these concepts in more detail.

The Issue of Human Agency

A key operative assumption behind the processual agenda is that human beliefs, desires, and choices are not a factor—at least not a significant factor—in structuring the archaeological record or in establishing important trajectories of cultural change. Relying on a *systemic view of culture,* the processual agenda assumes the existence of superhuman, "extra-somatic" forces that condition everyday life—forces over which individuals have little or no control.

But a number of contemporary archaeologists have come to believe that this perspective is wrong, as it not only overemphasizes the role of adaptation, but also undervalues the power of the human mind—both today and in the past. As archaeologist Ruth Tringham once put it, the processual agenda demeans people of the past, in effect reducing them to "a lot of faceless blobs."

Today, there is a heightened interest in what is termed *human agency*—the role of thoughts and decisions in shaping the evolution and structure of human society. As card-carrying humans, each of us knows—from very personal experience—that many of us do indeed think, and that we often jump into action *in the real world* directly because of our thoughts. The postprocessual critique decries the way in which the processual agenda has removed the individual from archaeological analysis.

The Importance of Power

Political power grows out of the barrel of a gun.
MAO TSE-TUNG (1893–1976), PRINCIPAL FOUNDER OF
THE PEOPLE'S REPUBLIC OF CHINA

Postprocessual critics argue that processual approaches define problems and construct explanations in ways that marginalize or ignore the role of social power. The highly conservative process of socialization is thought to ensure that cultural traditions are maintained, in all societies at all social levels. Cultural change, when it occurs, is generally a response to *exterior change*—particularly environmental and/or technological—rather than change from within.

When addressed at all, the issue of social power is largely *epiphenomenal,* less important than the larger issues of adaptation, complexity, or energy capture. According to German social historian Max Weber, power is "the probability that one actor within a social relationship will be in a position to carry out his own will despite resistance." So viewed, *social power* is considered largely in negative terms. Social science has traditionally equated power with force—the ability of a person or a social group to act in a desired manner.

By this view, power accrues mostly in formal, sociopolitical institutions. By looking, for instance, at the way societies employ sanctions, power is conceived as being set apart from society as a whole—something found in some institutions and not in others (and hence something possessed by some individuals but not by others). Members of the social elite have more power than the commoners. Egalitarian social groups, by their very nature, are assumed to have little power; the distribution of power becomes a social issue only with the advent of ranking.

Social power at Moundville is viewed as having been menacing and coercive—the compelling force that motivated commoners to construct the massive mortuary mounds and pay for the expensive symbolic riches that accompanied their elite to the afterlife. The funerary remains at Moundville are taken as directly reflecting the strength of centralized, formal leadership—the chiefs, priests, elite, and lords. Power is something embodied in a social institution. This is the processual perspective on power.

Postprocessual critics generally distance themselves from the notion that power is strictly negative or menacing. Daniel Miller and Christopher Tilley have elaborated this point, making the useful distinction between "power to" and "power over." Max Weber's power-as-domination was basically about *power over,* a negative, coercive form of social control. But this traditional view overlooks a second, more inclusive form of power—the *power to* that attends all human actions.

Power to is an integral and recursive element in all social life. Power in this sense is not a simple commodity, something to be hoarded and parceled out in enlightened self-interest. Everyone enjoys the *power to* interact with his or her own world on a daily basis. *Power to* permeates all social life, with both positive and negative consequences. This approach recognizes human agency, the human capacity to modify or transform—which does not necessarily require or even involve *power over.*

Looking at power as a broad-based concept opens up a large arena of inquiry, including (but not restricted to) the temples, residences, and luxurious graves of the elite. The inventory of power-laden social relations expands extraordinarily and becomes embedded in everyday life: husband–wife, parent–child, doctor–patient, owner–worker, and so forth.

But when the elite exert their "power to," members of the nonelite can likewise marshall a "power *not to.*" *Power not to* includes an ability to resist domination, to fight back, and to circumvent authority. Open defiance—as in revolution and strikes—is the most commonly recognized form of resistance. But the so-called "powerless" also have at their disposal a number of more subtle weapons—foot dragging, false compliance, embezzling, feigned ignorance, slander, arson, sabotage, and so forth.

Social science has traditionally looked mostly at power in the hands of the dominators, less often at the use of power (resistance) by those dominated. But archaeologists have the ability to look beyond the temples and tombs of the powerful; an archaeological record of resistance by the "powerless" presumably exists in the sanctuaries of the weak—barrios, exploited villages, lower-status households, and so forth.

This broader view of social power crops up several times in the remaining chapters of this book, and we will examine both ends of the power spectrum—both the "powerful" and the "powerless." For instance, we will see how the Chavín elite derived power from control over both sacred ritual knowledge and also the tribute offered to regional ceremonial centers by travelers and pilgrims. In this way, religious ideology seems to have played a critical role in promoting and legitimizing profound social changes. I'll also show you how the archaeological record reflects the numerous strategies of both overt and covert resistance evident among African Americans.

Summary

This chapter deals with social systems of the human past, defining what they were and how archaeologists study them. The basic social unit is the *group* (both residential and nonresidential), which is quite different from the network of *statuses,* the rights, duties and privileges that define the nature of interpersonal relations. Social statuses are apportioned according to culturally determined criteria. The term *kinship* refers to the socially recognized network of relationships through which individuals are related to one another by ties of descent (real or imagined) and marriage.

We also distinguished between *sex* (which refers to inherited, biological differences between males and females) and *gender* (which is a culturally constructed concept and varies considerably from culture to culture).

We also delved into the way in which societies assign social statuses. *Ascribed statuses* are parceled out to individuals at birth, without regard to the characteristics of those receiving status. But societies can also allow members to *achieve* their statuses. Achieved statuses remain unfilled until the necessary competition and individual effort defines who gets them.

The concept of status allows us to leap from the level of the individual to that of the entire society. A society is termed *egalitarian* when the number of valued statuses is roughly equivalent to the number of persons with the ability to fill them. Such societies lack the means to fix or limit the number of persons capable of exerting power; egalitarian societies are therefore characterized by generally equal access to important resources. But even in egalitarian societies—when the number of valued statuses is roughly equivalent to the number of persons with the ability to fill them—there is an intrinsic hierarchy. Egalitarian and ranked societies are often studied through the patterning of their mortuary remains, but considerable difference of opinion exists about how directly such burial associations reflect social organization.

This chapter also considers the role of sex and gender in studies of our foraging past. For years, archaeologists employed a *Man-the-Hunter* approach and assumed long-term continuity in gender arrangements and ideology, extending from the present back to the earliest humans. This model implied a relatively rigid division of labor and a sort of inevitability about gender roles: Hunting was always male, plant collecting was always female, and so forth. This model overemphasizes the importance of male activities and results in "gender-exclusive" reconstructions of past human behavior.

Many of those engaged in "engendering" the human past heartily endorse the major propositions of the postprocessual critique. By adopting gender as an analytical concept, they argue for a radically redefined view of prehistory and archaeological reasoning. Many of the postmodern principles we have been considering have already been incorporated as mainstays in a feminist approach to archaeology.

> *Individuals are not simple instruments in some orchestrated game and it is difficult to see how subsystems and roles can have "goals" of their own. Adequate explanations of social systems and social change must involve the individual's assessments and aims.*
>
> IAN HODDER, ARCHAEOLOGIST (CAMBRIDGE UNIVERSITY)

Ancient Social Systems on the Internet

The National Park Service lists where Mississippian archaeology can be seen firsthand and provides an overview of Mississippian culture.
   http://www.cr.nps.gov/seac/misslate.htm

The Moundville Archaeological Park Home Page offers access to information about the Moundville burials.
   http://www.olcg.com/al/atc/central/map.html

Hohokam Farming Systems is another Web site with valuable information.
   http://fadr.msu.ru/rodale/agsieve/txt/vol5/3/art1.html

A Tohono O'odham Creation Story is available on the Internet.
http://hanksville.phast.umass.edu/poems/Papagocreation.html

CHAPTER 10

General Theory in Archaeology:
Some Neo-Evolutionary Approaches

◻ ◻ ◻

PREVIEW

This chapter sketches some of the milestones in the long-term evolution of culture. For more than a million years, our ancestors pursued a hunting, gathering, and scavenging existence. Then, within the last 10,000 years, people began domesticating plants and animals. The farming lifeway had profound implications for human beliefs and social practices. Without an agricultural baseline, the development of large communities, urban centers, and state-level organization would never have taken place.

Here, we examine the various conceptual tools used by archaeologists to understand the evolution of human social organization. As you might anticipate, considerable diversity of opinion surrounds such large-scale questions. We will explore how these various evolutionary and neo-evolutionary perspectives came to be and how they are being modified in light of archaeology's current emphasis on understanding the role of the individual in cultural evolution.

> *[Evolution is] a change from an indefinite, incoherent homogeneity to a definite, coherent, heterogeneity, through continuous differentiations and integrations.*
>
> HERBERT SPENCER (1820–1903), ENGLISH SOCIAL PHILOSOPHER

> *Evolution is a change from a no-howish, untalkaboutable all-alikeness to a somehowish and in-general-talkaboutable not-all-alikeness, by continuous somethingelse-ifications and sticktogetherations.*
>
> REV. THOMAS KIRKMAN, BRITISH MATHEMATICIAN
> (AND SPENCER CRITIC)

With the publication of *On the Origin of Species* in 1859, Charles Darwin provided Euroamericans with new ways to view their world. Sometimes called "the book that shook the world," *On the Origin of Species* sold out on its first day of publication (and it is still in print and even available on the Internet).

Darwin argued that because the world's food supply is inherently inadequate, the young of any species must struggle to survive (and most of them don't). The survivors who live to foster the next generation do so because of certain naturally favored characteristics; this is the process of **natural selection.** These physical variations will be passed along to the next generation. The evolutionary process, being gradual and continuous, eventually gives rise to new species. Darwin's theory not only introduced the notion that all organisms are descended from a common ancestor, he also provided evidence that the earth with its various life-forms was dynamic and ever-changing.

Although Darwin did not actually use the term "evolution," the very last word in the first edition of *The Origin* is "evolved," and the term "evolutionary theory" will forever be associated with his name. Darwin supplied the world of science with a coherent rationale for the rich diversity of life. Although many religions of the world came to accept Darwin's view, others loathed the concept of descent with modification.

The Rise and Fall of Unilinear Evolution

Darwin did more than just theorize about the diversity of life on the planet. He also provided his Euroamerican audience—unintentionally—with a scientific rationale for the then-prevalent belief in racial inequality. The so-called **social Darwinists** believed that people, like all other organisms, compete for survival and hence for success in life. Those becoming rich and powerful, in this view, are the "fittest." Lower socioeconomic classes are thus "the least fit," as are the "primitive" people of the world. Social Darwinism suggested that human progress depends on competition, and in the nineteenth century this theory was used to justify global imperialism, racism, and the excesses of capitalism.

Social Darwinists argued that human societies varied in their evolutionary status from "highly evolved" groups (such as Europeans) to those who were seen as differing only slightly from the advanced apes. In this view, less civilized people were also regarded as less capable intellectually and emotionally.

Early anthropology grew up in this intellectual climate. Anatomical parallels were drawn between Neanderthal crania and contemporary Australian aborigines, and some suggested cultural parallels as well. In the nineteenth-century perspective of social Darwinism, cultural evolution became a logical extension of biological evolution.

Morgan's Unilinear Evolution

Social Darwinism played well on both sides of the Atlantic. To many, the United States was all about progress and natural destiny. Nineteenth-century Euroamerican society was held to be the culmination of human achievement. The move westward toward the Pacific was both inevitable and laudable. According to the social Darwinian perspective, Native Americans were culturally and biologically ill-equipped to resist; long-term selective pressure had doomed the Indians to extinction.

One of the most influential nineteenth-century anthropologists was Lewis Henry Morgan, a Rochester lawyer-turned-ethnologist. Morgan argued that contemporary institutions can be understood only by reference to how they had evolved; the present could not be understood wholly in terms of the present.

Morgan's *Ancient Society* (1877) divided the progress of human achievement into three major "ethnical periods"—savagery, barbarism, and civilization—which were subscaled into seven major categories:

1. *Lower status of savagery:* Commenced with the infancy of the human race in restricted habitats, subsisting on fruits and nuts; no such tribes surviving into the historical period
2. *Middle status of savagery:* Commenced with catching of fish and the use of fire; humanity spreading over a greater portion of the earth's surface; exemplified by Australian aborigines and Polynesians
3. *Upper status of savagery:* Commenced with the invention of the bow and arrow; exemplified by the Athapascan tribes of Hudson's Bay Territory
4. *Lower status of barbarism:* Commenced with the invention and manufacture of pottery; exemplified by the Native American tribes of the United States east of the Missouri River
5. *Middle status of barbarism:* Commenced in the Eastern Hemisphere with the domestication of animals, and in the Western Hemisphere with cultivation by irrigation and the use of adobe brick and stone in architecture; exemplified by villages in New Mexico and Mexico
6. *Upper status of barbarism:* Commenced with the manufacture of iron; exemplified by Grecian tribes of the Homeric Age and Germanic tribes of the time of Caesar
7. *Status of civilization:* Commenced with the use of a phonetic alphabet and the production of literary records; divided into ancient and modern

Morgan's was only one of several schemes of **unilinear cultural evolution** to be devised during the late nineteenth century. Each defined a sort of "evolutionary ladder," with both contemporary and ancient societies arrayed along it vertically. Although differing in detail, the bottom rung exemplified "savagery"—the primeval, rudimentary, and primitive. The top of evolution's ladder was reserved for various "advanced" societies, with the uppermost rung occupied by modern Western civilization, particularly that of western Europe.

How "Evolution" Became a Dirty Word

In the early twentieth century, the anthropological world turned against this ethnocentric notion of progress (and its distinct racial overtones). Franz Boas—often called the "father of American anthropology"—and several of his students soundly rejected cultural evolution as a worthwhile way to study the human condition.

The Boasian program called for anthropologists to study a culture in all its aspects; each culture is unique, Boas argued, and should be valued as such. Cultures change in ways unique to themselves and no generalizations are possible from culture to culture. This doctrine, known as **cultural relativism,** questions the existence of any universal standard by which to judge either the degree of development or intrinsic worth of different cultures.

For Boas and the others arguing for **historical particularism,** use of the comparative method was the cardinal error of the evolutionist school. Boas argued that sociocultural evolution was so complex and had taken so many diverse paths that there could have been no progressive evolution in the human past. The simplest kinds of technology (as among Australian aborigines), they argued, are today accompanied by the world's most complex forms of social organization. Boas also argued that human institutions such as slavery, private property, and the state level of government are today associated with an amazing array of concomitant sociocultural features.

Boas took a stand against evolutionary schemes that embraced all humankind in a single developmental formula. Although he did admit to some degree of regularity in history, Boas believed that the amount of regularity had been grossly exaggerated, at the expense of culturally specific, ethnographic detail. Boas believed that the patient accumulation of historical data would eventually lead to improvement of anthropological theory.

Neo-Evolutionism: What Is It?

So it was that unilinear cultural evolution fell into disfavor under the withering assault from Boas and his students. But the cultural particularism that characterized the first half of the twentieth century was in turn discredited by mounting evidence from archaeology and ethnography showing that, in one form or another, cultural evolution had indeed occurred. So-called *neo-evolutionary* thought began in the 1950s and 1960s and continues to exert a significant influence in Americanist archaeology.

Neo-evolutionism differs in some important ways from the earlier unilinear evolutionism. Nineteenth-century evolutionary models emphasized the role of the individual in culture change, with gifted individuals often thought to be responsible for bettering the quality of human life (by inventing, for instance, plant and animal domestication, ceramics, metallurgy, writing, calendrics, etc.). By contrast, neo-evolutionism accentuates the role of ecological, demographic, and/or technological determinism by stressing dynamic relationships between human cultures and the rest of the ecosystem.

Marshall Sahlins and Elman Service have argued that cultural evolution is most profitably viewed at two levels: "Any given system—a species, a culture or an individual—improves its chances for survival, progresses in the efficiency of energy capture, by increasing its adaptive specialization. This is **specific evolution.**

The obverse is directional advance or progress stage by stage, measured in absolute terms rather than by criteria relative to the degree of adaptation to particular environments. . . . A man is higher than an armadillo. . . . This is **general evolution.**"

Neo-Evolution and the Processual Agenda

Bruce Trigger has written of a "present mindedness" in American culture, which grows out of the mistaken impression that America has somehow freed itself from the legacy of a European past. As a result, history—both as an academic discipline and as a way of knowing the past—has long been viewed with a sense of distrust in America. Henry Ford seems to have reflected a national contempt when he said simply, "History is bunk."

Archaeology's processual agenda equated history with chronology, description, and a preoccupation with irrelevant occurrences. According to the processual view, explaining solitary events would doom archaeology to remain a particularistic, nongeneralizing field. Cultural-historical objectives were considered inferior to formulating general rules of cultural behavior.

Processual archaeology embraced instead a form of cultural ecology, downgrading history to a merely descriptive rather than explanatory role. The neo-evolutionary perspective likewise plays down the importance of individual human decisions in cultural change (viewing the human capacity to reason and plan as being powerfully directed by cultural forces). Specific human decisions and specific historical sequences are not of particular interest or significance in their own right, according to neo-evolutionists.

The processual agenda viewed human beings as the *locus of interaction* for a variety of cultural elements. Although individual humans might effect a new synthesis of these forces, human inventiveness and innovation were not seen as independent forces capable of bring about major changes. As a neo-evolutionist, Lewis Binford believes that there has been great regularity in human behavior and that ethnographic study would reveal much about aspects of past cultures not directly observable from the archaeological record.

Processual archaeology attempted to employ scientific methods for testing generalizations about human behavior across long spans of time. As Bruce Trigger has pointed out, these evolutionary leanings "encouraged a major devaluation of an already weak historical perspective in favor of an evolutionary one." Neo-evolutionists, of course, would argue that they had already taken history into account in the distinction between specific and general evolution.

A Sample Evolutionary Sequence

The first human being who hurled an insult instead of a stone was the founder of civilization.

ATTRIBUTED TO SIGMUND FREUD (1856–1939),
FOUNDER OF PSYCHOANALYSIS

To explore how this neo-evolutionary perspective operates, we must first introduce some key terms and concepts commonly used in the discussion of social and political evolution.

Hunting and gathering bands are the least complex of human societies. Virtually all our ancestors lived this way 15,000 years ago. Although few true hunter-gatherer bands survive today, they were still common in many parts of the world during the nineteenth century. They survive on wild plants and animals, and often change location several times a year. Most settlements number less than three dozen people, although larger aggregations occur when resources are particularly abundant.

Hunting and gathering bands are *egalitarian,* meaning they lack hereditary differences in social rank or authority. Such societies are integrated on the basis of age and gender. Leadership is informal and temporary, based mostly on age, competence, and personal magnetism. The Great Basin Shoshone are frequently cited as an example of band structure, as are the Inuit (Eskimo), South African Bushmen, and Australian aborigines.

Were it not for the domestication of plants and animals, the entire world would still be living a hunting and gathering lifestyle. But agriculture seems to have come into being in the Near East by about 7000 B.C. New World agriculture began between 5000 and 3000 B.C. in both Mexico and Peru.

With the advent of agriculture came *autonomous village societies,* characterized by larger and more sedentary settlements. Such communities occur throughout the world and vary considerably in appearance. Although community size is generally larger than in those of hunters and gatherers, autonomous village societies still lack hereditary differences in rank, and larger villages maintain no authority over smaller neighboring communities. Although everyone in such societies is equal at birth, considerable disparities in prestige can accrue during one's lifetime, and ritual privileges are often differentially distributed along gender lines. Several early twentieth-century autonomous village societies have been well studied by ethnographers, including Pueblo Indian groups of the American Southwest, communities in highland New Guinea, and many villages in the Amazon Basin.

A third social form, *ranked society,* at times evolves from autonomous villages. Here, the egalitarian ethic (downplaying success and prestige) gives way to the belief that individuals are inherently unequal at birth. Commonly, certain family groups are considered to have descended from esteemed ancestors. The closer this relationship, the greater one's hereditary rank and power. Marrying wisely becomes a way to enhance the rank of your children.

Ethnologist Robert Carneiro has pointed out that two kinds of ranked societies populated the nineteenth-century world. Some, like the nineteenth-century communities along the American Northwest coast, had hereditary ranked differences, but each community was autonomous from the others.

But in some societies, such as the Natchez (who lived along the lower Mississippi River), the smaller villages were subject to the powerful, hereditary leadership of the larger, stronger communities. These societies—large-scale ranked societies with loss of village autonomy—are called *chiefdoms.*

Powerful chiefs could bring thousands of people under their control. Chiefly leaders and their kin differentiated themselves with a variety of symbols, including precious trade items, lavish dwellings, and prominent temples for worship by the elite. Smaller villages were vulnerable to raiding, and the vanquished were frequently converted to slaves. Warfare between rival chiefdoms was distinctly unpleasant, typically involving torture, mutilation, human sacrifice, and the taking of human trophy skulls.

Under certain conditions, **archaic states** evolved from competing chiefdoms. The term "archaic" is employed here to distinguish this ancient social form from modern industrial states, which are commonly governed by presidents or prime ministers.

Most archaic states operated as kingdoms, characterized by a strong and centralized government with a professional bureaucratic ruling class. These societies devalued the kinship bonds evident in less complex political forms, and the social structure was highly stratified by social class. States maintain their authority through an established legal system and the power to wage war, levy taxes, and draft soldiers. States generally have populations numbering (at least) in the hundreds of thousands, and urban centers generally exhibit a high level of artistic and architectural achievement. A state religion is generally practiced, even in areas of linguistic and ethnic diversity. The Classic Maya and the Aztecs are examples of state-level organization.

One final term needs some attention: **civilization.** In neo-evolution, the notion of "civilization" is closely associated with the development of the archaic state. The development of writing and keeping of bureaucratic records is commonly considered to be a characteristic of "civilized" society (but since the Inka did not have writing, this criterion is hardly ironclad). Please be sure to note: When anthropologists use the term "civilization," *no value judgment is implied (in the sense of refinement or good manners).*

Evolving Frameworks for Understanding Hunter-Gatherers

The first humans on earth were hunter-gatherers, and some vestige of this lifeway persisted for 99 percent of the human past. Anthropologists—many of them archaeologists—have conducted in-depth projects aimed at defining the processes that underlie this hunting-gathering existence.

Robert Bettinger suggests that before the mid-1960s, such studies were generally conducted within a "Hunter-Gatherer as Primitive" framework, emphasizing largely the negatives of hunter-gatherer existence. Working within the tradition of Lewis Henry Morgan, hunter-gatherers were viewed as occupying the bottom rung of the evolutionary ladder. Although many other evolutionary schemes have been proffered, they all shared—with Morgan's stages—the perception of the hunter-gatherer as exemplifying "savagery" in one way or another—basically primeval, rudimentary, and primitive.

A flurry of ethnographic studies, mostly conducted in Australia and Africa during the 1960s, suggested that hunter-gatherers may not have been so primitive after all. Contrary to widespread belief, hunter-gatherers were not huddled on the brink of extinction. And surprisingly, their lives were not nasty, not brutish, not short. Bettinger calls this the "Hunter-Gatherer as Lay Ecologist" framework.

Anthropologist Richard Lee, for instance, found that water was the single most important resource in determining the settlement pattern and human demography of the !Kung people he studied. Because flowing water is practically unknown on the Kalahari Desert, the !Kung anchor their camps to a few well-known springs. Throughout the 2,500 square miles of the Dobe and Nye Nye regions, only five water holes are "permanent," and of these, three are known to have failed. According to Lee, the seasonal movements of the !Kung "must be continually revised in light of the unfolding rainfall situation throughout the growing season and beyond." In years of relatively abundant rainfall, camp location was dictated by availability of food and known locations of neighboring groups. In moderately dry winters, the !Kung established themselves near the five best water sources. But in drought years, Lee found as many as seven normally autonomous groups coexisting at a single water hole. This is how the availability of water structured the !Kung settlement pattern.

Such studies show how ethnographers and ethnoarchaeologists looked at the ecological adaptation of hunter-gatherers, always with an eye to the past. In part because of the rich ethnographic descriptions and films available on the !Kung, they came to be viewed as somehow prototypical hunter-gatherers: well nourished, working short hours, relying on plant foods collected by women, and maintaining low birthrates—thereby keeping their population within sufficiently low limits to minimize threats to local resources. Exhilarated in large measure by such descriptions of the !Kung, anthropologist Marshall Sahlins once crowed that hunter-gatherers were the "original affluent society."

But over the past few decades, archaeologists and ethnoarchaeologists have begun approaching hunter-gatherers from another perspective. Some researchers took a second look at the !Kung, concluding that these foragers may not have been "affluent" after all. Other researchers branched out and studied other foraging groups and found that the !Kung are not very "typical."

Several investigators believe that a processual understanding of hunter-gatherers can be obtained from the larger body of developing theory in evolutionary biology. One increasingly popular method of inquiry involves the use of the **optimal foraging theory,** a broad-based theoretical perspective that attempts to develop a set of models general enough to apply to a wide range of animal species used for food, yet rigorous and precise enough to explain the details of behavior exhibited by a particular forager.

James O'Connell proposes that the underlying logic behind the application of optimal foraging theory to archaeology may go something like this: Because archaeologists embrace such a huge empirical domain, a general theory of behavior may be required. Much of the relatively recent archaeological record was created under conditions similar to those observed ethnographically. Provided that one exercises the cautions implicit in good archaeological practice, there is every likelihood of success in accounting for the general structure of the archaeological record in behavioral terms. Middle-range research is critical to this endeavor; mature general theory may not be.

The temporally more remote segments of the archaeological record lack adequate analogies. The patterns of behavior in the remote past are simply too dissimilar from those of the present to allow any acceptable linkage between the two. Optimal foraging theory may offer a partial solution to this problem. Although past behavior may have been vastly different from the present, a *uniformitarian* assumption holds that the principles that shape the behavior of modern *Homo sapiens*—and in fact, all organisms—are constant and unchanging in time and space. Evolutionary ecologists have embodied theory at a general level, anchored in assumptions derived from basic postulates of natural selection theory. This approach uses mathematical and graphic representations for the rigorous deduction of testable hypotheses.

The stock of evolutionary ecology is clearly rising, with both generality and testability capable of drawing adherents who are seeking a way to understand and explain human variability (in both the present and the past). Although neither whole nor unified, optimal foraging models are general and offer some degree of explanatory power. Specific applications so far remain provisional and directed at limited aspects of cultural systems, but because optimal foraging models are grounded in the general theory of natural selection, such models do indeed hold the promise of moving toward a general, more unified interpretation of human behavior—provided that the assumptions hold for the archaeological record, and provided that the applications hold up under empirical scrutiny.

Perhaps the greatest appeal of optimal foraging models is their ability to bring specific testable projections of human behavior to bear on real data. Although most such "testing" has been conducted by biologists, applications to human populations have appeared in the past decade. The potential of foraging theory for archaeology was somewhat overstated by early proponents, but more recent studies present balanced views of both costs and benefits. Today, applications of optimal foraging theory to modern human populations command the serious attention of the anthropological community.

Numerous applications of optimal foraging models to strictly archaeological data have been attempted. Shifting empirical referents from the ethnographic present to the archaeological past means that neither behavior nor environment can be directly observed. But before optimal foraging theory—or any other general theory—can be brought to bear on archaeological data, it is necessary to infer past behavior from the archaeological record and also to infer past environmental states from the paleoenvironmental record. Both records are static, and all dynamics must be inferred through middle-range linkages.

We might also point out that the process of reconstructing (or inferring) past behavior is itself often a theory-dependent endeavor. If, for instance, one reconstructs the behavior of *Homo erectus* (an extinct species), a theoretical framework is necessary to define the possible alternative behavioral models that could be tested archaeologically. Theory is implicated at every stage because it sets the direction of research and anticipates the range of plausible results. We cannot simply dig a number of sites, reconstruct behavior, and then seek an explanation in general theoretical terms.

Why Were Plants and Animals Domesticated?

Countless theories have been constructed to account for the initial efforts at domesticating plants and animals. Anthropologists of the eighteenth and nineteenth centuries were concerned largely with devising worldwide evolutionary schemes, yet lacked the relevant archaeological data. Cultural evolutionists relied instead on analogies with contemporary "primitive societies" and linguistic evidence. As we saw, Lewis Henry Morgan in *Ancient Society* (1877) suggested that animal domestication (pastoralism) must have preceded agricultural villages throughout the Eastern Hemisphere.

According to Morgan's study of "Aryan" (Indo-European) languages, plant domestication provided the most expedient way to feed the already domesticated herds: "[That] the discovery and cultivation of cereals by the Aryan family was subsequent to the domestication of animals is shown by the fact that there are common terms for these animals in the several dialects of the Aryan language, and no common terms for the cereals or cultivated plants."

Childe's Oasis Theory: Symbiosis

Through the years, a number of other theories appeared, and their evolution is instructive, indicating major avenues of thought. One of the most compelling explanations—the *oasis theory*—was devised in the 1940s by Australian-British archaeologist V. Gordon Childe. Briefly, Childe's theory held that as the Pleistocene glaciers melted (at the end of the Ice Age), the world's climate became warmer and drier. In desert areas, especially those of the Near East, finding water became the single major problem for survival. Both people and animals flocked to oases and rare desert streams in search of water, and this forced association eventually produced a **symbiosis,** that through time developed from mutual benefit to mutual dependence.

Childe explained the mechanisms (processes) for the beginnings of animal domestication in fairly simple terms:

> The huntsman and his prey thus find themselves united in an effort to circumvent the dreadful power of drought. But if the hunter is also a cultivator, he will have something to offer the famished beasts: the stubble of his freshly reaped fields will afford the best grazing in the oasis. Once the grains are garnered, the cultivator can tolerate half-starved mouflons or wild oxen trespassing upon his garden plots. Such will be too weak to run away, too thin to be worth killing for food. Instead, man can study their habits, drive off the lions and wolves that would prey upon

them, and perhaps offer them some surplus grains from his stores. The beasts, for their part, will grow tame and accustomed to man's proximity.

Clearly, in Childe's scheme, the domestication of animals was possible only after people had become successful cultivators of plants.

Childe was less clear about how and where plants were initially domesticated. Childe believed, based on then-available evidence, that plants had been domesticated before animals, probably in places such as the nearby Nile Valley. The "nobler grasses"–ancient ancestors of modern wheat and barley–apparently grew in abundance on the banks of the Nile, where they were subjected to annual flooding and enrichment by the fertile alluvial soil. Childe felt that the plants of the Nile Valley were sustained by nature's perfect irrigation cycle and that it remained only for "some genius" to produce similar artificial irrigation conditions elsewhere.

Braidwood's "Hilly Flanks" Theory: Culture Was Ready for It

Although Childe's explanation seemed plausible at the time, supportive data were fairly weak. The chronology for the Near East–Nile Valley region was sketchy, and no archaeological evidence for early food production was available for the area.

Shortly after World War II, Robert Braidwood of the University of Chicago decided to search for some relevant data. Traveling to the foothills of Iraq, he spearheaded a series of excavations to test–in the field–various explanations regarding the origins of domestication. Braidwood obtained some of the first archaeologically relevant C-14 dates.

His empirical results questioned the existence of significant post-Pleistocene climatic shifts in the Near East. Braidwood and his team found that the climate had been essentially stable during the period of animal and plant domestication. These data suggested that Childe's oasis theory had to be rejected.

Braidwood proposed a new explanation, which came to be known as the "hilly flanks" theory. Rather than calling on environmental change to explain the origins of agriculture in the Near East, Braidwood and his colleagues concluded instead that agriculture arose as a "logical outcome" of culture elaboration and specialization. The hunters and gatherers simply "settled in" after the end of the Pleistocene, becoming intimately familiar with their plant and animal neighbors. As culture evolved further, so did people's means of exploiting the environment. Agriculture, in this view, was merely another natural link in the long evolutionary chain.

Southwestern Asia was a logical place for this to occur because the wild plants suitable for domestication (especially wild wheat, barley, and legumes) were already growing there naturally. Wild cattle, sheep, and goats also occurred there– becoming the natural targets for animal domestication.

Although Childe and Braidwood used different data and reached conflicting conclusions, they agreed on the fundamental processes that triggered the initial domestication of Old World plants and animals. Both theories implicitly assumed that humanity continually seeks to improve its technology and subsistence. Whenever the proper conditions came along, it is "logical" that plants and animals would be domesticated, because domestication provided a more technologically advanced economic base.

Why were plants and animals domesticated? The Childe and Braidwood theories suggest that domestication occurred simply as a natural consequence of people's continual struggle to improve technology, driven by population pressure—the root cause of domestication. Because growing crops and keeping flocks are more advanced means of subsistence, people quite naturally stopped foraging to become full-time farmers and herdsmen. Once agriculture was adopted, the human population was free to increase dramatically. The wholesale shift to domestication came to be known as the **Neolithic** revolution.

Stress Models: Domestication for Survival

Childe and Braidwood assumed that people will continuously attempt to increase their food supply. Yet the archaeological record clearly shows long periods of technological and economic stability. How can such stability be explained in the face of such progress?

In the past few decades, many anthropologists have found it particularly difficult to accept the implied economic and ecological determinism. Childe argued that when the climate changed, people would readily turn to domestication. Braidwood rejected Childe's notion, arguing instead that domestication arose as an evolutionary elaboration of the "settling-in" process. In both cases, cultural change was determined by environmental conditions.

Several archaeologists have suggested a different way of looking at population growth. Lewis Binford, for instance, argued that people adopt new energy sources (such as domesticated plants) only when forced to do so. In his so-called *density-equilibrium model,* Binford rejected Braidwood's notion that agriculture developed because "culture was ready for it." On this point, Binford agreed with Childe's earlier argument that domestication constitutes a new **ecological niche,** one imposed by changing conditions. But whereas Childe named climatic and environmental changes as the initiating factors, Binford proposed that the true stress on these groups was pressure from other human populations.

Specifically, population pressure was exerted by groups of people with an extremely successful **Mesolithic** adaptation who were occupying the same habitat, such as the Fertile Crescent. The post-Pleistocene emphasis on river and lakeside food sources (fish, shellfish, sea mammals) permitted a more sedentary and comparatively lavish existence than that of the more traditional hunter-gatherer modes of subsistence. The competitive pressure on nonsedentary peoples must have been severe, and it is in these marginal areas, Binford suggests, that people first turned to domestication for survival.

Binford's hypothesis attempted not only to explain most of the known facts but also to provide directly testable implications for further archaeological fieldwork. Specifically, Binford proposed the following:

1. In the optimal zones, there must have been a population increase owing to a new and efficient Mesolithic lifeway before the first domestication.
2. The earliest evidence of domestication should come not from these optimal zones where the Mesolithic lifeway functioned well but, rather, in the marginal, less favored areas (as the law of evolutionary potential would suggest).
3. The material culture of the earliest Neolithic populations should be essentially similar to that of their Mesolithic neighbors.
4. There should be no circumscribed center of domestication; the process should have occurred simultaneously in several areas under population pressure.

Kent Flannery then applied Binford's "density-equilibrium" model to the archaeology of the Near East. Following Binford's arguments to their logical conclusion, Flannery suggested that the "optimal" habitats would have been the centers for population growth, with the marginal areas receiving the emigrant overflow. Flannery postulated a "broad-spectrum" revolution that began about 20,000 B.C. and amounted to a major broadening of the subsistence base from mostly hunting terrestrial game to include larger amounts of fish, crabs, water turtles, mollusks, and migratory waterfowl. To Flannery, this change in subsistence was due less to post-Pleistocene climatic change than to a simple overuse of prime land. The demand for the previously ignored invertebrates, fish, waterfowl, and plant resources would have increased in precisely those "marginal" areas in which Binford believed that the initial domestication of plants occurred. Domestication occurred in these areas because the demand for other food types could not be satisfied. Flannery, like Binford, contended that the population increase could have functioned as a major factor, encouraging hunting-gathering groups to begin cultivating plant crops.

The Flannery–Binford model was roundly criticized, and both have heavily revised their earlier arguments. Some pointed out that this model lacked empirical support, as the archaeological record shows no evidence of inland migration near the early agricultural centers. Critics also noted that the "broad-spectrum" adaptation was not restricted to seacoasts and that agriculture actually arose earlier and in areas other than those recognized by Flannery and Binford. Even though no longer a viable theory, Binford's discussion proved to be a turning point because it tried to identify the stimuli that changed hunter-gatherer adaptations into agriculture-based lifeways.

Mark Cohen took matters one step further by suggesting that population growth was *even more pervasive* than many believe. Cohen posed two important questions:

1. Why would successful hunter-gatherers decide to become agricultural in the first place?
2. Why did people all around the world acquire agriculture at about the same time?

Cohen's answer was that by about 15,000 B.P. in the Old World, and 8,000–10,000 B.P. in the New World, human populations had spread out across most of the inhabitable landscape, exhausting available strategies for garnering a living through hunter-gatherer lifestyles. The quality of life began to deteriorate as people were forced away from the desirable (but scarce) large fauna toward more plentiful, if less desirable, "secondary" resources (such as grains and tubers). In light of a continually growing human population, no options remained except agriculture—and that's what people did, by intensifying their exploitation of the more productive plant species, some of which changed genetically in the process.

Cohen's heavy reliance on population pressure has been variously challenged. Some assert that population pressure could not have been such an important causal factor because many people—both "advanced" and "primitive"—knew how to control population levels before they reached carrying capacity. Others see population pressure as a problem restricted to relatively recent times, the result of health advances made during the Industrial Revolution.

A Selectionist Perspective

So far, we have considered various relationships among (1) human sedentism, (2) population growth, and (3) resource-choice strategies. There is a good deal of debate as to which of these variables should be assigned causal priority over

---

In His Own Words

Why Did People Domesticate Plants?
by Kent V. Flannery

I have always been struck by the fact that while paleontologists most frequently ask *how*, anthropologists most frequently ask *why*. Paleontologists are concerned with evolutionary mechanisms, and they try to answer the *how* question by studying the intervening fossil forms from an evolutionary transition. Anthropologists are concerned with human aspirations, with what [David] Rindos has called "intentionality," and they try to answer the *why* question by studying culturally patterned behavior. Paleontologists do not picture reptiles saying, "let's turn into birds," but many anthropologists do picture hunter-gatherers saying, "Let's plant those seeds on the talus slope below our cave."

We can ignore human intentionality and concentrate on the underlying biological aspects of domestication, producing a universal model as Rindos has recently done. The trouble is that while such a model may satisfy biologists, it often does not satisfy anthropologists: Anthropologists want cultural explanations for cultural behavior and are not usually satisfied when culture is reduced to biology. Anthropologists know that human hunter-gatherers are mammals, primates, and

the other two. Childe and Braidwood argued that sedentism must have come first, followed by domestication and population growth. Others contend that population growth was primary, with the other two variables falling into a secondary role.

There is, however, another way to view things—by focusing instead on the underlying process of natural selection. Like the optimal foraging models discussed earlier, this approach relies heavily on Darwinian principles developed by evolutionary ecologists working in the fields of genetics, plant ecology, and, most recently, molecular plant biology.

Employing his **selectionist explanation,** David Rindos has argued that the origins of agriculture are best understood through a consideration of the evolutionary forces at work. So viewed, plant domestication is not an evolutionary stage of cultural development, but rather a process—the result of *coevolutionary* interactions between humans and plants. The key word here, **coevolution,** suggests that agricultural origins can be explained in terms of a mutual selection among components, rather than a linear cause-and-effect sequence.

Rindos asserts that the relationships between plants and people must be appreciated without recourse to either cultural adaptations or human intent. *Incidental domestication* occurs as the product of the dispersal and protection of wild plants

predators, but that is not what anthropologists find most interesting about them.

My main worry about Rindos's model is that, in the process of finding some analogies for agriculture elsewhere in the animal kingdom, he has concluded that human domestication of plants can be filed away as just one more case of a well-known biological process. In 1957, when I was a zoology student at the University of Chicago, that might have seemed like a great idea, but now that I am an anthropologist, I have some reservations.

I suggest that what we have here is a classic case of scholars from two different disciplines talking past each other. Rindos, trained as a biologist, is content with reducing domestication to a biological model that is admirably general but (by his own admission) lacks the resolution to explain the origins of agriculture in any area. He apparently does not realize that anthropologists, trained to seek explanations in terms of cultural, social, political, and economic decisions, are most interested precisely in the testable, high-resolution explanations that his model fails to provide. The fact that there are biological analogies for human behavior is as big a bore for anthropologists as human intentionality is for Rindos.

KENT FLANNERY is the James B. Griffin Distinguished University Professor and curator of the Museum of Anthropology, University of Michigan.

by members of nonagricultural human societies, the direct result of human feeding behavior. Eventually, this relationship selects for certain changes in the plants involved, "preadapting" them for further domestication. Initial domestication promotes a "conservative" interaction between people and plants. The size of human populations carried by the plant communities is limited, and in return the rate of change in the incidental domesticate is low (compared with what will develop later).

Specialized domestication occurs as new types of plant–people interactions develop. As humans become the dispersal agents for various species of plants, these plants spread into the specific areas where humans live. In effect, a new brand of ecological succession takes place—as plants become more important as human food, they also become more common in places where people are living. This change is largely demographic, the effect of people changing their environment so as to indirectly benefit the domesticated plant. That is, people become so dependent on the plant communities that the survival of both is interdependent. People also begin selectively destroying various unwanted plant species around their communities, in effect setting the stage for the development of complex agricultural systems. Full-blown *agricultural domestication* takes place when practices like weeding, irrigation, and plowing create new opportunities for plant evolution, thereby increasing the rate at which domesticated plants evolve.

Rindos's model of coevolution has been used to explain plant domestication in many parts of the world. The coevolutionary explanatory framework has the advantage of moving beyond single-factor, "prime mover" arguments. Cohen's argument, for instance, assigns strict causal priority to population growth. Under the coevolutionary approach, however, the question of which came first—population growth, plant domestication, or sedentism—becomes irrelevant.

So does the question of why humans would enter into such a coevolutionary relationship with plants. To Rindos, this is "a question without real meaning. We might as well ask why certain ants established coevolutionary relationships with fungi or certain birds with specific fruits." The coevolutionary approach holds that changes occur as a result of maximizing adaptive fitness at a particular time, in a particular place: "They were neither inevitable nor desirable, but merely happened."

Rindos completely sidesteps issues such as human intent, conscious selection, the "cultural factors" that give rise to domestication, and even the when and where of agricultural invention—focusing instead on the coevolutionary relationships that developed between and among plant and animal species. To those pursuing a processual agenda, this adaptive perspective is a welcome change.

But many contemporary archaeologists and neo-evolutionists take exception to this view. They are uncomfortable with what they see as Rindos's "slavish" adherence to a Darwinian model for cultural evolution; so viewed, human inventiveness—like genetic mutation—becomes simply another random process.

The big issue here is *human intent*. Robert Carneiro cannot believe that developing agriculturalists were oblivious to the changes happening in what they ate. Didn't those ancient Mesoamerican farmers deliberately decide that they wanted their corncobs to be larger? Carneiro views intent as an "intermediate element" between ecological pressures and cultural outcome. Intent is always a factor, but is not likely to be the most persuasive determinant.

There is no need to explore other theories attempting to account for plant and animal domestication (and believe me, plenty of additional explanations exist). The point is not to define the exact moment that somebody first planted a seed or monkeyed around with the genetics of penned animals but, rather, to illustrate how the search for the process proceeds.

How Did the Archaic State Arise?

There are two basic contemporary approaches to the study of societal and political dynamics of cultural institutions. The *synchronic* procedure emphasizes the in situ analysis of functioning cultural systems. This is the basic concern of ethnographers, sociologists, economists, psychologists, and ethnoarchaeologists. Synchronic studies provide a picture of the dynamics of a system that operates at a single point in time: now. Archaeologists also conduct synchronic studies of another time period: then. In effect, the general objective of reconstructing past lifeways is to unravel the specifics and dynamics of single societies.

Anthropology's second fundamental approach is *diachronic,* emphasizing the development of societies over a span of time. Although the ethnographer can justly point to the richness of the detail available in contemporary society, such studies invariably fall short in an evolutionary sense because the time factor is lacking. Of course, archaeological data lack great ethnographic detail, but archaeology can provide a chronicle of in situ cultural developments without which diachronic studies cannot proceed.

The previous section considered some theories of plant and animal domestication, one of the most important technoecological developments in the history of human evolution. We shall now turn to the evolution of sociopolitical institutions as another example of how archaeologists are working to construct general theories to account for stability and change.

What Is the Archaic State?

The *archaic state* has been defined in a number of ways over the years, and to simplify this discussion, we will follow Kent Flannery's definition:

> The state is a type of very strong, usually highly centralized government, with a professional ruling class, largely divorced from the bonds of kinship which characterize simpler societies. It is highly stratified and extremely diversified internally, with residential patterns often based on occupational specialization rather than blood or affinal relationships. The state attempts to maintain a monopoly of force, and is characterized by true law.

Archaic states generally have powerful economic structures and often a market system. The state economy is controlled by an elite, which maintains its authority by means of a combination of law and differential access to key goods and services. Archaic states generally have populations numbering at least in the hundreds of thousands, and this population is often concentrated in large cities. Much of the population consists of economic specialists, dependent on the labor of others for subsistence. Archaic states are also known for a high level of artistic achievement, monumental architecture, and an overall state religion.

The archaic state is thus a complex form of sociopolitical organization. Ethnographers and other social scientists have studied the modern state for decades, and its dynamics are relatively well understood. But it is clear that these contemporary states are the products of a long chain of sociopolitical evolution, and how they came to be remains an unanswered question. "Archaic" archaeological states are evident throughout the world. Although contemporary ethnographic studies can satisfactorily unravel the synchronic dynamics of functioning state-level organization, no amount of study of modern states can explain their evolution. The state as we know it today is a worldwide phenomenon, with a long history preserved in the archaeological record. Only through a consideration of the archaeological evidence can an accurate diachronic study be made of societies as they developed to the state level.

Theories about the origin of the archaic state go back to the nineteenth-century cultural evolutionists, introduced briefly in the first part of this chapter. A number of causal factors have been suggested to account for the development of the archaic state: irrigation, warfare, population growth, circumscription, trade, cooperation and competition, and the integrative power of great religions.

Next, we will sample a few such explanations.

Wittfogel's "Irrigation Hypothesis"

To see how archaeologists, as social scientists, attempt to unravel the evolution of the archaic state, we begin by looking at one of the historically important theories, Karl A. Wittfogel's *irrigation hypothesis*. As before, we are more concerned with the nature of the search than with providing the ultimate truth.

In his influential book *Oriental Despotism* (1957), Karl A. Wittfogel asserted that the mechanisms of large-scale irrigation were directly responsible for creating the archaic state. He argued that the great oriental societies (China, India, Mesopotamia) followed a radically different evolutionary course than did the societies of Western Europe and elsewhere. The archaic state evolved because of special conditions required by large-scale irrigation: the imposition of inordinately strong political controls to maintain the hydraulic works, the tendency for the ruling class to merge with the ruling bureaucracy, the close identification of the dominant religion with governmental offices, and the diminution of private property and economic initiative. Wittfogel contended that after a creative period in which the bureaucracy developed, stagnation set in, corrupting power and leading to a despotic and feudal system. Wittfogel saw the hydraulic society as an initial step

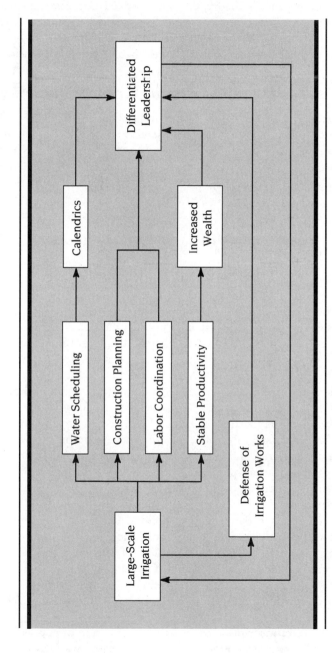

Schematic diagram of Wittfogel's irrigation hypothesis for the origin of the state.

to totalitarianism, and his theory of the state was clearly framed with twentieth-century Cold War perspectives in mind.

According to Wittfogel's theory, the state evolved in direct response to the demands of large-scale irrigation. The need for coordinated labor, massive construction, and so forth, led to increased wealth, military strength, and eventually to the powerful ruling bureaucracy that characterized state development.

Carneiro's "Warfare and Circumscription Hypothesis"

A second explanation for the origin of the archaic state, offered by ethnologist Robert Carneiro, rests on a different initial premise, namely that autonomous political units never willingly surrender their sovereignty. Carneiro terms Wittfogel's irrigation hypothesis a "voluntaristic" theory, one requiring that "at some point in their history, certain peoples spontaneously, rationally, and voluntarily gave up their individual sovereignties and united with other communities to form a larger political unit deserving to be called a state." This is why he objects to the irrigation hypothesis.

Carneiro argues, instead, that egalitarian settlements will be transformed into chiefdoms, and chiefdoms into kingdoms, only when coercive force is involved, and that warfare is especially pertinent to this transformation. Of course, some tribes might agree to cooperate in times of stress, but such federations are temporary and voluntarily dissolve once the crisis has passed. Carneiro's initial premise stipulates that political change of lasting significance will come about only as the result of coercive pressure. Warfare is the only mechanism powerful enough to impose bureaucratic authority on a large scale. Thus warfare—the world's main coercive device—plays an important role in the origin of the state.

But it is clear from the archaeological record that warfare is considerably older and more widespread than the state is. Because warfare does not invariably lead to archaic state formation, Carneiro is quick to add that, although necessary, warfare is not sufficient in itself to account for the state. According to Carneiro, it is in areas where agricultural land is at a premium—areas that are environmentally "circumscribed"—that warfare predictably leads to state formation. Competition over land arose first where arable land was restricted by natural barriers such as mountains, deserts, or seas. The vanquished peoples had no place to flee and thus were required to submit to the expanding political units of the victors. Carneiro points out that the early archaic states near the Nile, the Tigris-Euphrates (Mesopotamia), the Indus Valley, and the valleys of Mexico and Peru all evolved in areas of circumscribed agricultural land. Conversely, in areas where agricultural land was plentiful—such as in northern Europe, central Africa, and the eastern woodlands of North America—states were quite late in developing, if they did at all.

In Carneiro's **circumscription theory,** the combination of population growth and circumscribed agricultural resources leads to increased warfare, which in turn leads to the centralized political organization characteristic of state-level complexity.

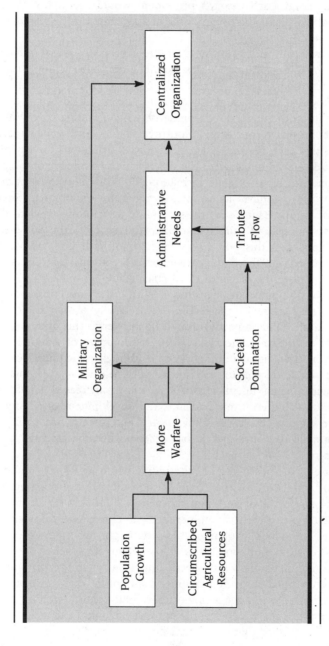

Schematic diagram of Carneiro's circumscription and warfare hypothesis for the origin of the state.

Multicausal Theories of State Formation

Both the irrigation and circumscription hypotheses are examples of general theory in anthropology. Each theory's proponent would claim that all else being equal, his theory explains the origin of the archaic state throughout the world, at any time.

But more recently, in his review of the tremendous quantity of data now relating to state-level organization in Mesopotamia, the Indus Valley, Mesoamerica, and the central Andes, Henry Wright has suggested that the regularities postulated by Wittfogel, Carneiro, and others cannot be sustained by the archaeological record, as it is now understood. Similarly, while granting that Wittfogel and Carneiro have stimulated considerable controversy and worthwhile research, Mark Cohen asserts that their theories "have 'failed' as explanations to varying degrees because localized research has failed (1) to confirm the existence of the postulated common element in areas of state formation; (2) to demonstrate its absence in other areas; or (3) to confirm its postulated role in the evolutionary process."

In the discussion dealing with the origins of agriculture, we considered Cohen's views on the role of human population pressure in the domestication of plants and animals. At this point, you might think that perhaps Mark Cohen would have jumped into the particularistic breach with his own population pressure theory to explain the origin of the archaic state.

Cohen asked a compelling question: "Why did many independent human populations begin to organize themselves hierarchically at the same time after so many millennia of egalitarian structure?" The answer to this question, according to Cohen, lies in the consequences of the abandonment of a hunting-gathering lifeway in favor of an agricultural strategy. Although agriculture potentially increased the available calories to feed human society, it also left people more vulnerable to environmental fluctuations. As such stress increased, so did the development of cultural buffering mechanisms: the development of storage systems, increased interregional trade (in both luxury and subsistence items), and the greater importance of centralized authorities who became essential to ensuring economic security.

Well aware of the possibility of "alternative pathways" to civilization, Cohen proposed two hypotheses for the origin of the state: (1) as occurring in "special environments" and/or (2) as an "epiphenomenon." The first explanation suggests that if population pressure-driven vulnerability to environmental fluctuations is a major stimulus to political evolution, then one might expect the process of centralization to be most pronounced under conditions in which vulnerability was high. Such large populations would need "buffering" against environmental variability, in which populations were "circumscribed," or in which environments were sufficiently varied to encourage a single centralized political system.

But, admitting that such environmental and ecological explanations are problematical, Cohen decided that they might not explain the specific evolution of archaic states, since "there appears to be ample justification for recognizing a common set of adaptive problems as underlying the more *general* emergence of centralized governments."

Alternatively, suppose that the earliest state developed as just an *epiphenomenon*—something explainable only by historical factors. If so, then the process may reflect "random creative processes" rather than more systematic selective processes. In short, although Carneiro's integrated theory relies on the potential territorial expansion of a social unit as the key factor in state formation, Cohen suggests that no single "prime mover" may ever be found.

Let me mention one final theory regarding the evolution of the archaic state. Drawing on three case studies—France and Japan (both during the Middle Ages) and the Inka of the Andes—ethnologist Allen Johnson and archaeologist Timothy Earle concluded that state formation can indeed be explained on the basis of a few universal factors.

They find subsistence intensification to be a necessary, if not sufficient, cause of archaic state formation. Without capital improvements, carefully regulated agricultural cycles, competition for prime lands, and populations sufficiently large to support a market economy, a society would not be economically integrated enough to lead toward this level of social complexity. Rather, state-level organization can develop only when two conditions are present: "high population density, with explicit needs for an overarching system of integration; and opportunities for sufficient economic control to permit the stable financing of regional institutions and to support a ruling class. Where these two sets of conditions occur together, we find the rapid expansion of the political economy and the beginning of the state."

Ideational Explanations of Cultural Evolution

So far, we have explored several theories stressing the importance of technology and material forces in cultural evolution. The processual agenda emphasizes that significant cultural change takes place when the technoeconomic base is somehow altered. This subsistence-level change produces changes in social interaction, which in turn cause shifts in social organization. Ideological changes develop as a means to validate the new social organization. A more Darwinian view (such as Rindos developed to explain the origins of agriculture) might suggest that selective pressures operate to promote the survival of technologically more efficient social systems.

This materialistic position has the advantage that it emphasizes those aspects of cultural behavior that are most obviously subject to a few fundamental, ecological principles. We saw, for example, how archaeologists have employed *optimal foraging theory* to explain human foraging practices in terms of the general principles developed in evolutionary ecology.

As discussed in Chapter 2, the processual agenda in archaeology relies heavily on the principles of cultural materialism, a special case or subclass of

Darwinian evolutionary processes. The explicit linkage of human population growth to biological evolution confers on this position a certain epistemological strength; such principles are, at least in theory, quantifiable and testable. Ideational views of causality are not so easily quantified or tested.

Archaeologists also have commonly turned to materialist explanations because of the availability of large-scale data on subsistence remains and settlement patterns, which can readily be interpreted in terms of ecology, hydraulic systems, population dynamics, and systems of exchange. Drawing on the cultural materialistic explanatory framework, these archaeologists have explicitly denied a causal role for ideology, which was dismissed as being *epiphenomenal*—merely legitimation of existing economic and political realities.

But as such ecologically oriented archaeology proceeded, many came to believe that population growth and irrigation alone could not be the overriding factors in explaining cultural change. In some studies there were indications that the archaeological research focus on single valleys, drainages, or other ecologically defined universes might be obscuring major interregional, interethnic patterns that were important in the rise of complex society. Furthermore, increased chronological control demonstrated that Wittfogel's irrigation (hydraulic) hypothesis did not hold up in either the New or the Old World.

Kent Flannery and Joyce Marcus have criticized the ecological approach, mainly for assuming that changes in resource exploitation and population growth are the most significant factors in cultural evolution. Flannery argues for a more systemic approach, with mutual causal interactions among a wide range of variables, including not only those often considered as prime movers in the ecological approach, but also such variables as ideology and political organization (features which, from a strictly materialistic view, derive from the tehnoeconomic).

Within the past decade or so, archaeologists have increasingly turned to the ideas that lie behind the materials of prehistory. Some are now reversing the causal arrow to suggest that *ideology* may have provided the major stimulus driving cultural change. In the next chapter, we will look in some detail at how archaeologists examine the role of ideology in the past. For now, we focus strictly on ideologically based theories that have been proposed to account for the development of state-level organization.

By **ideology**, we mean the ritual, religion, and explicit cosmology that, taken together, provide group members with a rationale for their existence. Leslie White has characterized the extreme ideological position as follows: "Ideas come first; they are the real things; they endure forever; material objects and sensory experiences are merely imperfect and ephemeral manifestations of the ideas . . . [which] are the original seeds, the prime movers." The ideologist's basic argument is that whenever a new form of behavior is encountered, it has been immediately preceded by an idea. The best way to explain cultural change is to begin with ideas and determine how they came to modify behavior.

Many critics shifted the focus toward ideology, stressing the role of political legitimization in early state formation. Some approaches invoke ideology as a powerful driving force in cultural change. Others moderate this view, stressing that the role of ideology is simply to reinforce and justify existing arrangements of political power and exploitive economic order.

Most contemporary ideological approaches do not explicitly reject cultural ecology or the emphasis on technoeconomic factors. Rather, they insist that somehow, explanations of cultural change must integrate ideology into the standard mix of ecological, economic, and political factors. Kent Flannery has argued that ideology is a dynamic element in cultural change, operating as an information-regulating mechanism and thereby influencing a group's possible adaptive responses to the natural and social environment. For many archaeologists, this approach provides a workable common ground between idealist and materialist positions. Others disagree.

Including ideology is, of course, much easier when dealing with ethnohistoric and historically known empires; such cases rely heavily on a **direct historical approach.** The ideological arguments, however, become more tenuous and less convincing when applied to prehistoric cases.

Here, we have dealt almost exclusively with materialistic views in neo-evolution. In the next chapter, we will explore in detail the role of ideology in the formation of Andean civilization.

Neo-Evolutionism: Pros and Cons

Neo-evolutionary theory is today in flux. Some see its stock on the rise, others declare it bankrupt. In this section, we will first briefly review some of the most common criticisms of neo-evolutionism, and then we will look at how neo-evolutionists are modifying their approach in response to their critics.

Criticisms of the Neo-Evolutionary Program

Criticisms of neo-evolutionism abound. Some critics hark back to earlier arguments advanced by Boas, who mistrusted generalizations and advocated a position of extreme cultural particularism. Others, such as Rindos and the rest of the selectionists, believe that neo-evolutionism does not go far enough. Still others, while generally sympathetic with neo-evolutionary objectives, feel that specific research methods need to be modified before the nature of cultural evolution can be understood.

Here are some of the most common criticisms of the neo-evolutionary agenda:

Neo-evolutionism relies too heavily on ecological determinism. Critics argue that neo-evolutionary theory relies on biological approaches—bodies of theory incapable of explaining human symbol systems and cultural motivation. Human behavior, they believe, is too complex to be understood as simply the product of orderly evolutionary processes. Nobody will ever be able to explain the workings of culture change in general because it is impossible to predict (to *retrodict*) how specific ways of life changed in the remote past. That can be known only by studying specific sequences of development in their particularistic complexity.

Neo-evolutionism relies on simplistic typologies of evolutionary stages. Neo-evolution requires that a particular kind of economy gives rise to a particular social matrix: Egalitarian bands and tribes have reciprocal forms of exchange, chiefdoms are characterized by redistribution, and so forth. Critics charge that such stages address culture in piecemeal fashion, failing to consider cultural diversity, sociocultural detail, and relevant historical particulars. Some also feel that the use of evolutionary stages implies a set of stable social formations which, when beset by external problems (such as population growth or environmental change), simply move to the next higher stage or break down (depending on the circumstances). Archaeologist Norman Yoffee has termed this view "the stepladder" perception: Bands become tribes, which become chiefdoms, which finally become states. Such critics argue that instead of defining static, ideal-type stages, archaeologists should explore how political actors in the past constructed and maintained polities and other sociocultural institutions.

Neo-evolutionism ignores internal social differentiation. Some reject neo-evolutionism as an adequate model of overarching, societywide change. Norman Yoffee, for instance, criticizes models of "holistic change" because they tie all social institutions—politics, economics, and social organization—into a single, tidy bundle. In this view, when cultural change takes place, it must occur in all institutions at the same time, in the same place, and in the same direction. What is lacking in neo-evolutionary theory, such critics charge, is any sense of *internal* social division. Intra-social conflicts such as inequality, stratification, and incomplete social integration should perhaps form the heart of social evolutionary theory.

Neo-evolutionism demeans the role of the individual. Another objection to processual-style neo-evolutionism is that individual human beings become devalued and irrelevant. Postprocessual critics, on the other hand, have championed a human-centered perspective, with an emphasis on meaning, symbolism, and social context.

Neo-evolutionism artificially separates history from evolution. Neo-evolutionists carefully distinguish the culturally specific (the "historical") from the cross-culturally general (the "scientific" or "evolutionary"). Postprocessual critics reject this distinction, arguing instead that cultural change is largely dependent on culturally specific cosmologies, astronomical beliefs, art styles, religious beliefs, and other topics deliberately marginalized in the processual agenda. Many argue that the two approaches must merge into a new kind of history, regarded as somehow scientific in nature.

An Emergent Middle Ground?

Today, there seems to be an emerging middle ground on neo-evolutionism. Many believe that isolating and explaining cross-cultural generalities remains a central mission of Americanist archaeology. But today, many also reject the old processual assertion that *only* cross-cultural regularities are worthy of study. There is much to understand in specific historical cultural sequences; to ignore this contextual richness is to degrade and disparage major areas of human experience.

Archaeologist Charles Spencer has recently argued for a dual approach to neo-evolutionism. At one level, neo-evolutionism continues to seek common principles in the evolution of all civilizations. This *transformational* approach suggests that—regardless of specific historical contexts—the evolution of social forms involves profound and relatively rapid restructuring of administrative organization. State emergence, when it occurs, involves certain transformations that can be studied cross-culturally. Suppose that you wish, for instance, to compare the rise of the ancient Zapotec state (valley of Oaxaca, Mexico) with, say, the lowland Classic Maya (centered at Tikal, Guatemala). If you focus strictly on contextual details—the iconography, calendrical systems, political developments, warfare histories, and so forth—then the two civilizations are not directly comparable, for each took place in a very different environment and was shaped by its own unique cultural and historical systems and by a different series of human decisions.

To define a cross-cultural common ground, it becomes necessary to reduce the Zapotec and Classic Maya cases to their conceptual basics. This is where the stagewise progression comes into play: the band, the chiefdom, the archaic state. These neo-evolutionist abstractions provide workable, if incomplete, characterizations of stepwise, qualitative change. To be sure, the stagewise evolutionary sequence from bands to the archaic state factors out the role of individual actors. It is the *system*—variously comprising population pressure, environmental change, and internal class struggle—that drove human societies into new evolutionary stages. Like all broadly generalizing approaches, this second approach has, and will continue to spark, intense debate, particularly when it seems to take the humanity of the past and "reduce the actors to pawns."

The second part of Spencer's approach, which he terms the *gradualist* position, clearly recognizes the historical, contextual dimension. Systemic pressures, while not discounted, are balanced against the realization that all cultural events take place as a result of a particular individual's decisions. That is, although humans have always themselves interacted with a natural environment, this interaction has been heavily conditioned by the culture they brought with them: their beliefs, cosmologies, ideologies, customs, and traditions. This relationship had a prior history, shaped partly by human decisions and partly by factors entirely out of the control of the human actors.

Human decisions, more than likely, did not attempt to overthrow the system (in revolutionary fashion). Instead, most actors operated on the basis of enlightened, if short-term, self-interest; the consequences of their decisions were not always fully realized until much later.

Sometimes, significant changes originated within the system, producing problems that the actors had to resolve. But sometimes, change was initiated by the actors operating in their own self-interest. This middle ground approach emphasizes the diachronic interplay of system and actor.

This "dual" neo-evolutionary approach attempts to combine the *historical* with the *comparative,* to define a common ground between history and evolution. Only time will show whether or not this modification to neo-evolutionism is going to bear theoretical fruit.

Summary

In his revolutionary *The Origin of Species,* Charles Darwin not only came up with a coherent rationale for the rich diversity of life, but he also inadvertently provided his Euroamerican audience with a scientific rationale for the then-prevalent belief in racial inequality. So-called *social Darwinists* argued that human progress depends on competition, and evolutionary theory was used to justify global imperialism, racism, and the excesses of capitalism.

This is the climate in which early anthropology matured. Lewis Henry Morgan devised a *unilinear* scheme of cultural evolution that created a sort of "evolutionary ladder," with both contemporary and ancient societies arrayed along it vertically. Morgan's bottom rung exemplified "savagery"—the primeval, rudimentary, and primitive. The top of evolution's ladder was reserved for various "advanced" societies, with the uppermost rung occupied by modern Western civilization, particularly that of western Europe.

The early twentieth-century anthropological world turned against this *ethnocentric* notion of progress (and its distinct racial overtones). Franz Boas and his students rejected cultural evolution, calling instead for a *cultural relativism* which questioned the existence of universal standards for judging the degree of development or intrinsic worth of different cultures.

Archaeology's processual agenda of the 1960s brought back an interest in evolutionary processes by focusing on the degree of regularity in human behavior. Neo-evolutionism attempts to explain the processes behind the development of these successive sociocultural levels, from band through archaic state.

Critics of neo-evolutionism raise numerous objections, including too heavy a reliance on ecological determinism and simplistic typologies of evolutionary stages, ignoring internal social differentiation and denying the role of the individual. Postprocessual critics argue that neo-evolutionism artificially separates history from evolution.

A middle ground seems to be emerging through explicit recognition of two distinct pathways of cultural change, one toward the general (and hence the comparative) and the other toward the specific analysis of context (and hence ultimately to the unique). This "dual" neo-evolutionary approach attempts to combine the *historical* with the *comparative,* to define a common ground between history and evolution. Only time will show whether or not this neo-evolutionism is going to bear theoretical fruit.

It must simply be recognized that there are two different paths here—one toward the general and hence the comparative; the other toward the specific analysis of context and hence ultimately to the unique.

COLIN RENFREW, ARCHAEOLOGIST (CAMBRIDGE UNIVERSITY)

Neo-Evolution on the Internet

The Origin of Species (complete hypertext version) is available on the Internet.
http://darwin.emergentmedia.com/~madsen/origin/intro.html

Biography of Charles Darwin is another valuable source of information.
http://oz.plymouth.edu/~biology/history/darwin.html

Natural Selection and Evolution are two more topics that you can research on the Web.
http://www.ed.uiuc.edu/EdPsy-387/Bonnie-Sklar/evolution.html
http://www.biohaven.com/biology/evol.htm

Social Darwinism on the Internet provides good discussion of this topic.
http://www.webleyweb.com/lneil/forge.html
http://www.stile.lut.ac.uk/~gycnr/STILE/t0000015.html

CHAPTER 11

An Archaeology of the Human Mind

□ □ □

PREVIEW

In recent years, a cognitive revolution of sorts has swept Americanist archaeology. Concerned with defining an "archaeology of the human mind," cognitive archaeologists have pursued a broad agenda, ranging from relatively scientific to relatively humanistic. But regardless of their methodological approach, cognitive archaeologists all seek to find out about concepts and perceptions in the past through the archaeological record. Although a huge range of human behavior falls under this category, current directions in cognitive archaeology stress the importance of ritual and religion, symbolism and iconography, and the development of human consciousness.

In this chapter, we explore the sweep of modern cognitive approaches to the archaeological record and provide several examples of the ongoing inquiry.

The processual agenda maintains that while the questions being asked by archaeologists may to some degree reflect contemporary social conditions, sufficient data and sound analytical procedures will ultimately produce scientifically valid statements uncontaminated by ideology or personal prejudice.

The postprocessual critique emphasizes that we live today in a postmodern world. As explained in Chapter 2, postmodernism is a dramatic shift in perception that resonates through the world's cultural, political, economic, and artistic outlook. The postmodern view emphasizes social fragmentation and instability, decentralization and anarchy—and this includes the way archaeologists view the past. Here, we explore some empathetic ways to view the human past, attempts to get at the intentions and thoughts of long-gone actors.

> *Humanists must cease thinking that ecology dehumanizes history, and ecologists must cease to regard art, religion, and ideology as mere "epiphenomena" without causal significance. In an ecosystem approach to the analysis of human societies, everything which transmits information is within the province of ecology.*
>
> KENT FLANNERY, ARCHAEOLOGIST (UNIVERSITY OF MICHIGAN)

When processual archaeology took off in the 1960s, it fostered numerous important studies of prehistoric demography and changing settlement patterns, the origins of agricultural and irrigation technologies, and the human use of soils, plants, and animals. These approaches relied heavily on scientific methods and rigor. The focus was materialistic, with processual archaeologists believing that subsistence behavior provided the infrastructure for the rest of the cultural system.

At the outset, archaeologists framing the processual agenda were fairly optimistic that *all aspects* of the human condition were available for archaeological investigation. This upbeat assessment differed markedly from previous attitudes that stressed the limitations of archaeology and focused mostly on writing culture history.

Throughout the 1970s and 1980s, processual archaeology remained distinctly lukewarm, if not outright hostile, toward "cognitive" approaches to the past. To many, the realm of "ideas" was too shaky and the archaeological record of these things too ambiguous to be approached in an explicitly scientific, objective manner. Others put down the cognitive aspects of culture—such as religion and ideology—as "epiphenomena" (mere dependent variables deriving from the technological and economic basics). Cognitive elements were considered to be nonessential, second-rate avenues of study.

Lewis Binford, primary architect of the processual agenda, decisively distanced himself from any form of ideological or symbolic inquiry. If processual archaeologists were to attempt a cognitive approach, Binford quipped, "We would be *paleopsychologists,* and our training equips us poorly for this role."

The early appeal of cultural materialism to Americanist archaeology is fairly easy to understand. This is a research strategy that places theoretical priority on just those things that archaeologists are most confident in recovering from their sites—evidence about past environments, technologies, ecosystems, and economies.

Not all archaeologists bought into these notions at the time. Some felt that such heavy-handed materialism dehumanized the past. They argued that archaeologists should try to include more of the values, ideas, beliefs, and cognitive processes that make us all human. A growing cadre of archaeologists turned to an ideational emphasis in their research, examining the active role of ideology in shaping the ultimate social, and even technological, structure of societies.

This point of view was well expressed by Kent Flannery, who felt that the processual agenda was too narrow. Human ecosystems, he said, are characterized by exchanges of matter, energy, and information.

The extreme paleoecological position emphasizes strictly the matter–energy exchange and altogether ignores the informational aspects (art, religion, ritual, writing systems, and so on). Flannery accused the cultural ecologists and cultural materialists of focusing too heavily on technological and subsistence matters: "To read what the 'ecologists' write, one would often think that civilized people only ate, excreted and reproduced."

Arguing for a more inclusive "ecosystem approach," Flannery suggested that *all* information-processing mechanisms be included in the ecological whole. The problem here, of course, is that ritual, religion, cosmology, and iconography were traditionally considered almost the exclusive province of the ethnographer. Processual archaeology lacked any established, scientifically valid procedures for dealing with such intangible phenomena.

So-called ecological, materialist attitudes certainly slowed the growth of cognitive archaeology, but some scholars remained interested in the role of cognition. By the early 1980s, several archaeologists (some of them former members of the processual camp) began developing cognitive approaches as antidotes to the heavy-handed materialism of the time.

This group began working to develop a way to discover an interpretive system that would (1) not rigidly preassign chronological or causal priority to economy, demography, technology, and ecology, and (2) incorporate internal societal diversity, human initiative and enterprise, and ideology in theories of cultural change.

Contemporary Approaches in Cognitive Archaeology

The term *cognition* refers to the act or process of knowing. Taken in its widest sense, cognition includes sensation, perception, conception, memory, reasoning, judgment, and imagination. **Cognitive archaeology**–what many would call "the archaeology of the mind"–involves the study of material remains in order to learn about religion and belief systems, symbolism and iconography, and the origins and development of human consciousness. Following the lead of Kent Flannery and Joyce Marcus, we will divide the subject matter of cognitive archaeology into four primary areas, each a product of the human mind: cosmology, religion, ideology, and iconography. Let us briefly explore each arena.

Cosmology

Every society wants to understand how its universe–its *cosmos*–works. **Cosmology** is the study of the universe as a whole–how it originated and developed, how the various parts fit together and what laws they obey, plus a glimpse at what the future of the universe holds in store.

We in the Western world have an ample paper trail to help us trace our evolving cosmological beliefs. Six thousand years ago, the ancients in Mesopotamia believed that the earth was at the center of the universe, with the heavenly bodies moving around it. The Greek philosopher Aristotle endorsed this notion, suggesting that the stars moved about the earth on rotating crystalline spheres.

Then, in the sixteenth century A.D., the Western world came to accept a cosmological system in which planets (including the earth) revolve in circular orbits around the sun. Today, our shared cosmology, in the form of the so-called Big Bang theory, suggests that the universe was created in a gigantic explosion, sometime between 7 billion and 20 billion years ago.

Cognitive archaeology attempts to combine traditional analysis of past subsistence and settlement patterns with an understanding of cosmologies that operated in extinct, nonliterate societies. As we will see here and elsewhere, such cognitive approaches are generally most fruitful when the strictly archaeological evidence can be heavily augmented by relevant ethnographic and/or ethnohistoric information.

Ritual and Religion

Using words to describe magic is like using a screwdriver to cut roast beef.

TOM ROBBINS, AUTHOR

Broadly speaking, *religion* is a specific set of beliefs based on one's ultimate relation to the supernatural. *Religion* is a society's mechanism for relating supernatural phenomena to the everyday world—a set of rituals, rationalized by cosmology, that enlists supernatural powers for the purpose of achieving or preventing transformations of state in humans and nature.

Religion is universal because of the ubiquitous cultural desire to influence change in people and nature. Sometimes the objective is to effect the quickest possible transformation; sometimes the goal is to prevent an undesired change from occurring. The primary objective of religious behavior is to influence the course of this change by appeal to a supernatural power, a power quite separate from that of the muscles, the brain, or the elements of nature.

Religious beliefs are manifested in everyday life in a "program of ritual," a succession of discrete events such as prayer, music, feasting, sacrifice, and taboos. These stereotyped sequences are the cultural mechanisms by which individuals attempt to intercede with the supernatural. It is fair to say that ritual is the fundamental religious act.

This particular definition of religion is especially relevant to archaeology because of its emphasis on ritual and its de-emphasis on the overall cosmology. Most rituals, after all, are closely related to material culture and, as such, are often represented in the archaeological record. Cosmology is quite difficult to define without recourse to documentary evidence. The analysis of past ritual behavior is thus archaeology's major contribution to the study of religion.

Ideology

Ideology is defined as a systematic body of concepts and beliefs—often political in nature—about human life or culture. Communism is an ideology, as are democracy and fascism. Ideology differs from religion because it addresses society and politics (although they certainly can overlap).

The term *ideology* is used here in two distinct senses. In Chapter 2, we discussed "ideology" in terms of the research strategy of cultural materialism. In this sense, religion and ideology can be viewed as epiphenomena—cultural add-ons with little long-term explanatory value.

But another, rather different use of "ideology" derives from the writings of Karl Marx, who believed that ideologies were counterfeit systems of political, social, and moral concepts both invented and perpetuated by ruling classes out of self-interest. As employed in modern usage, the term *ideology* has come to carry with it this pejorative meaning. Thus, adherents to any particular sociopolitical system are free to dismiss competing arguments as "ideologically based" (that is, false because they reflect only the ideological biases of the opponent, rather than a true state of affairs). Because this tactic can be used to argue against *any and every* ideology, the clash of modern ideologies has become strident and hot-blooded, more closely resembling propaganda than rational argument.

Iconography

The term **iconography** refers to the study of how people use art forms to represent their religious, political, ideological, or cosmological beliefs. Iconographic analysis covers a broad range from well known complex systems—such as Egyptian hieroglyphs and Mayan inscriptions—to cryptic incisions on ancient stone and bone artifacts.

In the next two sections of this chapter, we will see how iconographic studies explore two very different kinds of symbolic data. We begin with iconographic research on the La Marche antler, a 14,000- to 15,000-year-old engraved artifact from the European Upper Paleolithic period, which may (or may not) contain evidence relevant to the origins of later formal systems, such as writing, arithmetic, and true calendrics. Then we turn to the complex iconography of the Chavín horizon, earliest of the distinctive Andean civilizations of South America. In the preceding chapter, we explored some of the major theories about the evolution of state-level sociopolitical organization. In this chapter, we will examine the critical importance of Chavín iconography and cosmology in the evolution of the Andean state.

Seeking the Origins of Iconography

Since about 1865, a steady flood of carved and incised fragments of bone and antler have been recovered from various Old World sites. Such so-called *mobiliary* artifacts seem to be a portable adjunct to the spectacular Ice Age art images and signs that adorn the walls of the ancient "sanctuary" caves in France and Spain.

For more than a century, archaeologists have attempted to ascribe meaning to the mysterious ancient engravings, variously considering them to be counts of prey animals killed, systems of symbolic notation, mathematical conceptions of the cosmos, implied numbering system, and mnemonic support for recitations.

For the past quarter-century, Alexander Marshack has examined thousands of these objects—through the lens of a binocular microscope. In his influential book *The Roots of Civilization,* Marshack discusses how his research began as a relatively straightforward search for the origins of scientific thought. To his surprise, Marshack found that near-scientific thinking could be traced back only to early agricultural societies, and then the trail disappeared. Largely because he felt that "something was missing," Marshack began his attempt to trace the origins of rational "processual" observations and thought back to an earlier time. Eventually, this quest led Marshack to personally study nearly the entire body of engraved, symbolic materials from the **Upper Paleolithic,** including the "signs" and images of animals and humans. In so doing, he pioneered a method for studying and seeking meaning in the ancient inscribed artifacts.

The La Marche Antler Under the 'Scope

Marshack's approach can be demonstrated by his analysis of an incised antler from the Upper Paleolithic site of La Marche in central France. Several hundred stone and bone artifacts were excavated here in 1937 and 1938. Most of the incised materials came from the **Magdalenian** levels, dating approximately 13,000–12,000 B.C. One of the visually less exciting pieces was a discolored, deteriorated antler fragment that was engraved with a series of faint marks and lines.

Early in his research, Marshack used low-power microscopy to analyze the La Marche antler. His study turned up an unsuspected complexity. The antler had apparently initially been fashioned as a kind of tool for straightening spear

Three views of the La Marche antler. Note the faint, yet distinctive engravings on all sides.

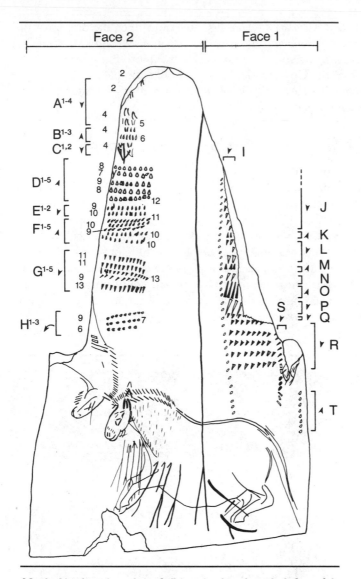

Marshack's schematic analysis of all intentional marks on both faces of the La Marche antler. Note that the engravings are broken down into sets, that several different engraving points were used, and that the totals of marks for each set have been included. Also shown are the two horses, with later engraved additions.

shafts. At some point, it broke and was reshaped into a flaker for finishing or re-sharpening stone tools.

But the functional uses for this antler tool were less interesting than the intricate engravings, barely visible on its surface. Look at the accompanying schematic rendition of the La Marche antler, particularly the two horses carved near the bottom. The unbroken horse seems to represent a pregnant mare with a rounded belly. Marshack's microscopic study suggested that this mare had three eyes, three ears, a second mane, and two backs. What's going on here?

Marshack's microscopic technique is similar to the ballistic analysis used in law enforcement. Each minute scratch is examined to determine the nature of the tool that performed the carving, and the sequence in which the marks were made. Some tools were relatively flat and blunt, and others made a deeper, more V-shaped groove. The analysis suggested that each of the mare's three ears was carved by a different stone point, presumably at different times.

The series of tiny marks covering the rest of the La Marche antler comprise a sequence of engravings that Marshack thinks is neither random nor decorative but, rather, a complex form of notation. Row H, for instance, has been inscribed by a cutting edge that flares near the top, creating an irregular angle in cross section. The marks were incised by a turning or twisting stroke, with the set angled about 15 degrees from the baseline of the antler. By contrast, the engravings immediately above row H are perpendicular to the axis of the antler and were made by a single downward stroke.

Marshack's microscopic analysis suggested that numerous distinctive tool tips were used to engrave the various sets and that sometimes in marking neighboring

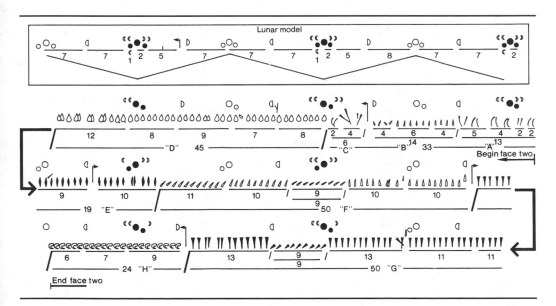

Marshack's lunar "test" of the La Marche engravings. This chart begins at the upper right and proceeds sequentially in alternative directions along each line, ending at the bottom left. One space in each 2 months (the right-angle arrow) represents zero, providing the proper total of 59 marks for 2 months in a model scaled to 60. The lettered sets, subsets, and cue marks are indicated, along with the astronomically correct observation point. The differences in the engraved points are schematically rendered.

sets the antler was turned 180 degrees. The internal complexity of the marking suggests that the sets were accumulated through time. The two surfaces were probably carved at different times yet almost certainly within the same cultural context.

An Ancient Lunar Calendar?

But what do such ordered accumulations of marks mean? A number of hypotheses have been considered to explain the engravings on the La Marche antler. For instance, one investigator suggested that the marks are hunting tallies; another saw a recurrent use of the number 7, a suggested early ritual number.

Marshack proposes that the marks could be recording the passage of time by observations of the moon, and he tested the La Marche marks against a lunar model. Beginning with block A in the upper right corner of the accompanying diagram, the counts are arranged sequentially, as indicated by microscopic analysis, with an overlay of modern astronomic observations placed atop the counts. The darkened circles represent invisibility, and the white circles represent the full moon.

The fit with the lunar model was surprisingly close. Of 23 subsets of marks observable on the single face of the La Marche antler, only four (E^2, F^2, G^1, G^2) fail to begin or end around normal observational phases of the moon. Of these, three subsets correspond to the period of the crescents and new moon, when precise observation is difficult. According to this interpretation, the marks cover a span of $7\frac{1}{2}$ months.

But why, some 14,000 years ago, would Magdalenian hunter-gatherers care about observing and recording the periodicities of the moon? Looking at ethnographic data from a range of Native American and Siberian cultures, Marshack notes that in many cases, **shamans** maintained lunar (or "month" records) of one form or another. Months were named according to their seasonal and regional significance, triggering appropriate ritual or economic responses. Marshack believes that the Upper Paleolithic notations, such as those on the La Marche antler, were also maintained by ritual specialists. If the La Marche notations began with the thaw in late March, then the notation would have ended in mid-November, at approximately the time of the first freeze or snow. Such a sequence of marking can be maintained without complex arithmetic. Marshack suggests that both the accumulation of sets and the reuse of animals on the La Marche antler argue for a "scheduled," "time-factored" cultural year, even in Upper Paleolithic times. He has supported this argument by studies of the seasonal character of many Magdalenian animal depictions.

Marshack contends that the La Marche antler could have been used as a notational device for keeping track of the sequences of moons. As we will see, this "lunar hypothesis" has received a great deal of critical attention from archaeologists. But in one sense this is unfortunate, as it represents but a single aspect of Marshack's innovative research.

At a different level of abstraction, Marshack is also concerned with understanding the cognitive processes and strategies involved in the making and use of all forms of Upper Paleolithic imagery. The lunar notations—if, in fact, that is what they are—represent a prewriting, prearithmetic symbol system that was related to other modes of symbolizing in these cultures. The same cultures created an elaborate iconography in the French and Spanish caves, yet these paintings involved very different symbol systems. Doubtless, there were also other forms of symboling and ritual that have not been preserved archaeologically.

Marshack thinks that the cognitive strategies utilized on the La Marche (and on other early nonarithmetical) notations differ from the records found in later settled farming villages. He maintains that the Upper Paleolithic engravings were made and used by the engraver alone as an early scheduling device. As later cultures became increasingly complex, more formal systems of record keeping developed, leading finally to the development of true writing for agricultural, temple, and commercial uses.

Thus, at one level, Marshack is examining symbolic artifacts to determine their function within a specific cultural setting. But simultaneously, Marshack raises profound questions concerning the evolution of human cognitive and intellectual capacity. Surely an evolving notational system that spans some 25,000 years implies something about the developing cognitive powers of the people who used it. Marshack has also examined artifacts made by Neanderthals to determine whether the symbolic behaviors of those populations implies that they had language. Marshack's research has explored the extremely variable and complex capacity of *Homo sapiens* for art and symbol, with special emphasis on the evolution of intelligence and language.

A Call for Middle-Range Controls

When first published, nobody knew what to do with Marshack's research. He was asking new questions, generating new data, and offering new interpretations. Reactions were characteristically mixed. Many archaeologists were skeptical, suggesting that Marshack had "gone beyond the data," ignored "all likely alternative explanations," and failed to present the data necessary to support his hypotheses. But others lauded Marshack's analytical approach, using terms such as "significant breakthrough" and "breaking new ground." One investigator raved that Marshack "has come as close as any archaeologist ever to reading the mind of ancient man." Today, many would credit Marshack with an innovative effort in establishing the field of cognitive archaeology.

But regardless of personal opinions, many recognized the potential of this new analytical technique, and it was clear that Marshack had opened up an entirely new direction in cognitive archaeology. Several follow-up studies soon appeared.

As it turned out, the first of these occurred by accident. Randall White, an archaeologist at New York University, was conducting experiments with *burins,* chisel-ended stone tools common in both European and North American assemblages. White manufactured a sample of 25 burins, then conducted use-wear experimentation on fresh bone and sandstone cobbles. After examining the edge damage incurred on the burins—the main reason for the experiment—White made a curious discovery. Quite by accident, when preparing some of the worked bone surfaces for photography, he discovered that the various burin experiments had produced some characteristic incisions on the bone. When used for scraping, the burins produced a flat, shallow, U-shaped groove; when the corner of the burin was offset and used for graving, a characteristic V-shaped groove resulted.

Thinking that this three-part subdivision of incisions "was too good to be true," White compared his results with photomicrographs published by Marshack, to see how closely the experimental incisions compared with examples from Paleolithic portable art (like the La Marche antler). The fit was precise. White's experiments seemed to contradict Marshack's hypothesis that different observable cross sections must have been produced by different tools: White produced three characteristic cross sections with the same burin—simply held three different ways. White's burin study raised a major question about the validity of Marshack's method of analysis.

As we know from the preceding chapter, modern archaeologists are increasingly concerned with assessing the degree to which their own biases impact the archaeological data they collect. White has suggested that Marshack's analytical method is essentially "internal," dependent on unexplicit, nonreplicable criteria. How, for example, does Marshack distinguish actual, intended notation from mere decoration? Does the distinction between notation and decoration have any validity outside our own Western tradition? Marshack has argued that such discriminations are analytically apparent. White, however, has raised the now-familiar point that construction of meaning is very much a cultural matter.

That is, what if Marshack's "objective" method of microscopic analysis isn't so objective after all? Marshack expresses great confidence in his ability to identify human-made markings—defining the direction of tool movement, possible changes in tool tips, shifts in orientation of the worked object, superposition of one incision over another, and the direction and sequence of engraving—all by relying on the microscopic observation of archaeological marks. He also believes he can identify and discount the simple random, careless, and meaningless markings from intentional incisions.

White decries Marshack's "purity of observation. For him the processes by which the marks were created are self-evident. . . . We are led to believe that Marshack's photos are indisputable depictions of reality when in fact they are *visual arguments* which can be countered by other visual arguments." White believes that different results can be produced by varying lighting conditions, magnification, and scale.

When questioned about his criteria for ascertaining notation and problems that others have had in reproducing his results, Marshack has responded that White's own microscopy and "visual arguments" are often seriously flawed even when he is making "cross-sectional" comparisons, and that White's symboling arguments have been made largely *a priori*—before he had adequately studied the variability and complexity of the Upper Paleolithic engraving traditions.

This is basically a problem of *middle-range theory*—of linking observable archaeological data with the relevant human behavior that produced them. In earlier chapters, we discussed several experimental approaches involved in middle-level theory building. Archaeologists sometimes experimentally manufacture their own stone tools, studying how specific stoneworking techniques are translated into specific archaeologically observable evidence (such as flaking scars, breakage patterns, and leftover flake by-products). Experimental archaeologists experiment with techniques of pottery manufacture, house construction, hunting, fishing, and plant collection, to name just a few. Remember that some of the better middle-level research involves "blind" experiments to test both the accuracy and the repeatability of archaeological technique.

White suggests that similar rigor is necessary to lend credibility to Marshack's results. When he distinguishes human-produced marks from "natural" scratches (such as carnivore or rodent gnawing), or identifies marks made by different tool points, Marshack's inferences should be supported by a body of middle-range theory—an external understanding of how differing tools, techniques, raw material, tool breakage patterns, and artifact surfaces affect the outcome. As we will see next, White and others have recently designed a series of experiments to create bridging theory between observations and interpretation.

The La Marche Antler, Revisited

Francesco d'Errico, a researcher now at the University of Bordeaux (France), has expressed similar reservations about Marshack's results, particularly his failure to describe diagnostic criteria for the microscopic analysis and the absence of replication experiments.

Attempting to provide such experimental controls and to replicate Marshack's earlier results, d'Errico recently returned to the La Marche antler. To establish a systematic protocol, d'Errico made rubber molds of critical areas of the artifact and also conducted several new experiments. Numerous experimental marks were made on various species of antler, each series with a different tool. Some marks were made on dry antler, others on water-soaked antler. Fracturing of the tool tips was noted.

The various experimental tool tips and replicated incisions were cast in rubber molds, which were then used to produce positive resin replicas that could be examined microscopically. The resulting images were computerized into density profile plots for both tools and incised lines. In this way, the experimental results could be compared with the original La Marche engravings by means of image-analysis equipment. Computerization permitted overlaying and enhancement to define continuities and changes in tool tips. Changes of tool tip and direction of working were recalculated on the basis of the experimental evidence. The idea was to use sophisticated imaging technology to eliminate investigator bias and inconsistency.

This experimentally based, painstaking analysis produced a second, independent "reading" of the various incisions on the La Marche antler. Significantly, a number of differences emerged between the analyses by Marshack and d'Errico. Sometimes, d'Errico discounted Marshack's marks as natural depressions.

Other marks, previously noted as separate, were combined into a single mark. Still others were excluded as postdepositional marking or as counting errors in the earlier analysis. D'Errico concluded that the marks on the La Marche antler could have been produced by no more than seven or eight tool points (a number considerably lower than Marshack's estimate).

As in White's experiments, d'Errico's analysis questions Marshack's key assumption that such fine incising causes no appreciable wear or damage to the engraving tool. Experiments show that, particularly on dry antler, the tool breaks rather frequently. Ancillary experimental evidence further suggests that the La Marche antler may have been soaked to minimize tool breakage.

To summarize, Marshack's interpretation of the La Marche antler as a lunar record hinges on two important steps: (1) recognizing numerous tool changes between the various sets of marks (interpreted as the result of accumulations over different time spans), and (2) testing the accumulation of sets against a lunar model. D'Errico's new analysis challenges both assumptions, suggesting that an accumulation of marks over a period of time did not play a major role on the La Marche antler. Still, this conclusion does not directly preclude the possibility that the engraving represents a lunar notation. But if it did, then it must have been planned beforehand because d'Errico's analysis indicates that the antler was probably engraved in a single session.

Marshack's measured response to this criticism is instructive. On the one hand, Marshack credits d'Errico with a major technological breakthrough in the study of ancient incised materials. There is every reason to believe that d'Errico's experimental mode of engraved cross-section analysis will be widely applied (and improved upon) in future research. It is an important step in minimizing the variability between observers in such purportedly "objective" analysis.

Marshack admits that "at the level of technology and the development of technical 'criteria' for the study of cross sections, d'Errico's research and his recent article represent major contributions. But technology is not science." Marshack is far less generous in his appraisal of d'Errico's reinterpretation of what the La Marche antler really means. He points out that the La Marche antler falls within a highly variable, yet continuously developing tradition of Upper Paleolithic notation. And he faults d'Errico for his failure to take this variability and development into account.

When d'Errico's recounting of the La Marche accumulations failed to turn up the number 28, he rejected the notion that lunar months (of supposedly 28 days each) were being counted. But Marshack responds: "I have never argued that an observational lunar notation required groups of 28, or precision in the recording of periods." Rather than focusing on an arithmetical 28-day lunar month, Marshack argues that an observational lunar notation is not arithmetical. Instead, he suggests that only through the analysis of long sequential accumulations of sets can one test for observational correlations: The number 28 might *never* occur, but in long sequences a pattern of lunar observation would be made apparent.

To show this is true, Marshack uses d'Errico's revised counts (those obtained using engraved cross-section analysis) to show that just such a long-term sequence is evident on the La Marche antler. In his original analysis, Marshack had concluded that his counts indicated a notation for 7½ lunar months; d'Errico's new counts of 212 marks show the period to be almost precisely 7 lunar months (212/29.5 = 7.18 months). Thus, Marshack argues, d'Errico's method provides even stronger support for a long-term lunar record than did his own original analysis.

Without question, d'Errico's method improves upon and "corrects" counts obtained by Marshack a quarter-century earlier. But the meaning of the marking and the viability of the lunar hypothesis (even though the La Marche markings appear to be a notation) remain very much an open question—dependent on additional testing and verification on other Upper Paleolithic examples. As Marshack puts it, it is clear that "study of the La Marche antler is not finished. It will have again to be 'revisited.'"

Exploring Ancient Chavín Cosmology

We discussed the Chavín horizon of the central Andes earlier. In Chapter 8, we saw how carbon isotope analysis could determine the degree of maize dependence of both human and animal populations living at this same site. This study employed a fairly conventional, materialistic perspective to flesh out ancient patterns of Andean settlement and subsistence, sometimes in great detail.

But to most archaeologists, the term *Chavín* conjures up more than llama bones and maize kernels. Chavín is commonly considered to be Peru's first highland civilization due to its stratified socioeconomic organization and achievements in metallurgy, weaving, monumental architecture, irrigation systems, and stone sculpture. For the first time, ancient Peru was united by a shared religion and technology. Chavín was the first great Andean civilization.

Chavín also left a lasting legacy in Andean ideology. Somehow the iconography evident at Chavín de Huántar established the tone of subsequent central Andean cosmology. All deities of the succeeding generations in the central Andes looked more or less like the god in the temple at Chavín de Huántar.

This decidedly ideational view differs sharply from the materialistic approaches employed earlier in discussing the bones from Chavín de Huántar. In this section, we will explore the nature of Chavín cosmology, looking in particular at the distinctive Chavín iconography that seems to have played a key role in the spread of civilization throughout the central Andes.

Seeking the Catalyst of Chavín Civilization

In the preceding chapter, we considered several theories designed to explain the origins of the archaic state. Our attempt was to illustrate the diversity of opinion about this controversial subject. No single set of prior conditions or prime movers seems to explain the origin of the state in all its manifestations.

Archaeologist Richard Burger has explored many of the same models in an attempt to understand why Chavín civilization arose where and when it did, and why it was so monumentally successful in spreading across the central Andes in a relatively short period of time. Here, we recap his findings.

First, we look at Burger's view of Wittfogel's "irrigation hypothesis." Karl Wittfogel, you will recall from Chapter 10, argued that state-level bureaucracies commonly arose as an integral part of agricultural irrigation management. Extensive supervision was required to coordinate and direct the operation of local canal systems. This in turn led to a concentration of administrative power to control and exploit the farming peasantry. In this view, the administration of irrigation systems paved the way for social stratification and centralized agriculture in arid lands.

Burger rejects this hypothesis for the Chavín. Irrigation systems in the central Andes, he says, were small-scale affairs, even after large, centralized states had arisen. Irrigation was a matter controlled at the community level, without the need for the irrigation bureaucracy required by the Wittfogel hypothesis.

Burger also evaluated Carneiro's "warfare and circumscription hypothesis." Briefly stated (see Chapter 10), Robert Carneiro suggested that the state arose in areas of circumscribed population growth; after conflict occurred, the resulting class stratification and administrative needs led to state formation.

Although Carneiro used the Andean case to support his initial argument, Burger feels that sufficient archaeological evidence for warfare is lacking at major Chavín settlements. While granting that the processes described by Carneiro are important in other periods of Andean prehistory, Burger rejects the "warfare and circumscription hypothesis" as an explanation for state level organization at Chavín de Huántar.

In fact, Burger rejects all of the available materialistic, processual explanations for formation of the Chavín state. He argues instead that it was the power of cosmology and religion that accounted for the origins of Chavín civilization.

Animal Symbolism in Chavín Iconography

The site of Chavín de Huántar has given its name to one of the Americas' most famous art styles—Chavín—generally thought to be the religious iconography of an expansive cult, once widespread throughout the central Andes. Symbols of the Chavín cult—derived from stone sculptures at Chavín de Huántar—were reproduced on locally made ceramics, textiles, goldwork, and stone. Some believe that Chavín art represents the pinnacle of Andean artistry.

Since its inception, the community of Chavín de Huántar depended on a range of highland animals, including wild deer and vicuña, plus llamas and guinea pigs. These were local beasts, probably encountered by local residents on a daily basis. Processual, materialist perspectives emphasize just these aspects of subsistence and settlement pattern at Chavín de Huántar.

The elaborate Chavín iconography, however, does not feature these commonplace local animals; rather, the Chavín style drew symbolic inspiration for its stylized fangs and talons, feathers and scales, from the jaguar, harpy eagle, monkey, serpent, and cayman (alligator). These are all creatures native to the tropical north coast and rainforest, located several hundred miles to the east.

As Miller and Burger put it:

> The paradox of Chavín existence can . . . be seen as dividing itself along the classic lines of cultural materialistic vs. ideational views of culture. The cultural materialist examining only the fecal residue of Chavín behavior finds an emergent Andean agropastoral economy and a community filling its belly from the typical menu of highland food animals. The ideationalist, reading only the iconographic data, perceives an entirely different world at Chavín de Huántar, a cosmos inhabited by fearsome creatures entirely foreign to the daily lives of the Chavín farmer or artisan.

At first glance, all of this seems pretty obvious. After all, if you're going to myth-make about animals, do you pick something exotic and rarely seen, or do you worship something in the everyday stew pot?

But Miller and Burger emphasize that the distinction between sacred and profane is not merely a matter of emphasis; it is absolute. The highland animals upon which the citizens of Chavín de Huántar depended for food and transport were *never* depicted in Chavín iconography. The locally available llama, vicuña, white-tailed deer, and the rest are entirely and conspicuously absent from the thousands of known temple sculptures, ceramics, and textiles that displayed the widespread Chavín style.

Instead, the supernaturals were imported from afar, from the distant tropical rainforest:

> The ideology of Chavín de Huántar, with its heavy emphasis on carnivorous and tropical forest fauna, can be seen as mystifying the society's source of wealth and power, rather than mapping it in metaphorical terms. . . . It seems . . . probable that the priests of Chavín de Huántar intentionally chose alien metaphors of profound mystery to fuel their spirits. . . . Caymans and jaguars were good to think, llamas were good to eat.

The entire cast of sacred characters appears to have been derived from the cloud forests and rainforest of the eastern Andean slope, if not the floodplains of Amazonia itself. These same animals—jaguar, snake, crested-eagle, and cayman—still play a prominent role in the mythology and religious symbolism of modern people of Amazonia.

Yet today in the Andean highlands, both colonial and modern Quechuan myths feature local Andean fauna such as llama, deer, condor, fox, and hummingbird. Note the parallel pattern: Amazonian animals in modern Amazonian mythology; Andean animals in modern Andean mythology.

Not so with Chavín religious imagery—an ancient Andean mythology based on Amazonian characters. What Burger terms the "intrusive" character of Chavín symbolism extends even to agricultural crops: manioc, bottle gourd, hot peppers, and possibly peanuts—all eastern lowland crops impossible to grow in Andean environments such as that around Chavín de Huántar.

This is the single question that has plagued all archaeologists attempting to explain the extraordinarily rapid and widespread distribution of the Chavín cult: *Why are the major animals of Chavín religious art drawn from outside the local highland environment?*

Explaining Where Chavín Cosmology Came From

Richard Burger has noted that three possibilities exist to explain this puzzling aspect of ancient Chavín cosmology. The first possibility is that the climate was radically warmer and more humid during Chavín times. If so, then maybe the lowland complex of animals—the jaguar, the cayman, the crested-eagle, and so forth—could have once lived in the highlands around Chavín de Huántar. Thanks to recent paleoenvironmental studies, it is possible to reject this climate-change model out of hand.

Several lines of independent evidence demonstrate that the climate was very similar to the modern pattern during the Chavín time period (900–200 B.C.); remember that the animal bones recovered from Chavín de Huántar belong to the same species as modern highland animals—camelids, deer, and so forth. Clearly, significant paleoenvironmental change will not explain the nature of Chavín iconography.

Perhaps, then, the lowland plant and animal complex was introduced to Chavín de Huántar by immigrants from the tropical forest. This second possibility—the migration hypothesis—was championed by Peruvian archaeologist Julio Tello, discoverer of Chavín civilization and first excavator at Chavín de Huántar (in the 1930s). More recently, this thesis was advocated by Donald Lathrap, an archaeologist at the University of Illinois, who argued that population pressure in the lowland Amazonian or Orinoco basins must have forced the early Chavín folk into the Andean highlands. According to Lathrap, the heavy Amazonian component of Chavín religious art displayed homage and deference to the ancient homeland and subsistence regime that was responsible for the initial success of the Chavín elite.

Burger questions this reconstruction. For one thing, the earliest ceramics at Chavín de Huántar—the pots made by the first occupants—show a conspicuous lack of Amazonian characteristics. If a tropical forest people had moved wholesale into the Andes, their ceramic traditions should show a direct relationship to the Amazonian homeland. But the pottery looks local rather than imported. It also seems clear that the basic high-altitude mixed agricultural subsistence pattern practiced by the pioneer population at Chavín de Huántar was not Amazonian at all; it had developed in place—in the highlands—at least 1,000 years earlier. The ceramic and subsistence evidence makes it highly unlikely that a tropical forest group was responsible for the lowland iconography evident on the earliest buildings at Chavín de Huántar.

For these reasons, Burger advocates a third hypothesis to explain the obvious Amazonian elements of Chavín cosmology. Emphasizing the importance of Chavín de Huántar's strategic gateway position, Burger argues that Amazonian symbolism was deliberately imported by Chavín's religious leaders, perhaps in the belief that these exotic lowland people curated especially powerful esoteric knowledge. This interpretation, supported by ethnographic and ethnohistoric documentation, suggests that shamans and healers may have made pilgrimages to the distant lowlands—viewed as the source of powerful sacred knowledge, medicinal plants, and other ritual necessities. In this view, the Chavín cult imported to the Andean highlands religious knowledge from the remote exotic tropics.

Analysis of Chavín iconography provides some of the details, explaining the cult's remarkable success. Early sculptural evidence suggests that Chavín ideology held that priests had the ability to turn themselves into mythical beasts, in order to intervene with supernatural forces. Temple sculptures clearly demonstrate that, by employing hallucinogenic snuff and beverages, Chavín shamans could transform themselves into jaguar or crested-eagles. Specially designed drug paraphernalia—stone mortars, bone trays, spatulas, miniature spoons, and tubes—all seem to be part of the Chavín ritual toolkit. Use of similar artifacts can be documented among modern South American people.

Burger believes that this model—based on sixteenth-century ethnohistoric sources—may explain the singular success of the Chavín cult in uniting previously unrelated cultures throughout the Andean highlands and along the Peruvian coast.

The sixteenth-century example shows how a religious network could have operated 2,000 years earlier. At the center of this regional cult was a large ceremonial complex featuring an **oracle,** access to whom was restricted to certain cult specialists. Based on the oracle's secret projections, cult members were able to provide "insider information," offering favorable intervention with the natural elements, protection against disease, and specialized knowledge concerning auspicious times for planting and harvesting.

Under this broad, regional system, local communities could establish "branch shrines" by petitioning cult headquarters and pledging support for cult ideology. If accepted, a local priest was assigned, but in return, local communities allotted agricultural lands to produce tribute and promised public labor for farming and herding. In effect, these local branches supported cult headquarters with large quantities of cotton, corn, dried fish, llamas, guinea pigs, raw materials (such as gold and obsidian), and manufactured goods (such as fine cloth).

Burger suggests that this ethnohistoric cult provides a workable model of the distinctive regional organization that characterized Chavín civilization. He believes that the oracle cult center was located at the archaeological site of Karwa, which unfortunately was looted during the 1970s. Iconographic elements—particularly stylized felines and raptorial birds—woven into textile fragments recovered from tombs at Karwa show unmistakable ties to the sculptures at Chavín de Huántar. Despite the nearly 400 miles separating the two sites, the complex elements of Chavín cosmology seem to have been transported intact, without simplification or misrepresentation.

Head of a mythical Chavín priest, almost completely transformed into a feline state. The long strands of mucus running out of the nostrils suggest usage of hallucinogenic snuff.

The Role of Cosmology in Andean Civilization

This model suggests that the overall regional cult known as Chavín was subdivided into a number of localized branches, each sharing in the major elements of Chavín iconography—probably reflecting major deities—but complemented by distinctive localized elements. According to this view, the Chavín cult maintained its characteristic regional flavor, but also demonstrated a willingness to incorporate motifs and symbols significant to local constituencies.

Burger emphasizes that the long-standing interest of archaeologists in Chavín iconography has led to a deep understanding of how this distinctive civilization came to be. Had this research taken place within a strictly materialistic framework, Burger suggests, the direction would have been much different, and considerably more restricted. He stresses that interregional exchange and tribute in the form of gifts to the religious center contributed to sociocultural complexity. He also argues that the wealth that fueled the emergence of social differentiation came from selective expropriation of nonlocal resources rather than from local agricultural products.

The spread of Chavín elements (500–250 B.C.) across the central Andes happened at a turbulent time, following the collapse of many early coastal polities. An unprecedented amount of contact occurred between distant and previously unrelated groups, producing an unprecedented degree of sharing of ideology and technology, reinforced by the actual movement of goods and people. "Thus, the Chavín horizon," says Burger, "can be viewed as a forerunner of later attempts to forge a single Andean civilization out of the staggering diversity of local cultures."

So why did Chavín succeed where earlier attempts failed?

Relying on historical evidence from the sixteenth-century regional ceremonial complex, Burger argues that Chavín was a large-scale religious cult, transcending political and ethnic boundaries. Chavín ideology and rituals were sufficiently powerful to support a hierarchical organization, with officials overseeing local cult activities and monitoring deviation among local congregations. Although considerable regional diversity was evident throughout the reach of the Chavín cult, a degree of central authority was exerted, with tribute directed toward the center of the system. Thus, as in the model, the Chavín cult spread not because of political expansion, but as a result of a powerful shared cosmology, rendered visible in ritual objects and manifest through the growth of complex interregional exchange networks.

Civilization had appeared in the central Andes by about 400 B.C. According to Burger, the centers of the Chavín horizon rivaled the classic Greek cities in size and beauty: These were massive public structures with finely cut-and-polished masonry, and these settlements were home to a complex society, differentiated by both social status and economic activities.

Burger argues that this power came from the original priestly occupants of Chavín de Huántar, who focused the growing Chavín mythology on the mysterious rather than the mundane. It was these mysterious animals of the lowlands that ultimately determined the long-term success of Chavín society and economy:

One message of Chavín art may have been that the prosperity and well-being of the community depended on maintaining the favor of forces alien to the local habitat and daily experience, forces redolent of the powers of the distant and mysterious tropical forest. The mediation of this relationship required the services of ritual specialists.

This explanation suggests that Chavín ideology—heavily emphasizing the exotic tropical forest fauna—ritually reinforced the wealth and power of Chavín de Huántar society.

Current evidence suggests that social stratification may have first appeared in the highlands, in association with long-distance exchange—offering local leaders an unparalleled opportunity to control and manipulate the existing socioeconomic system. Burger believes that tribute supplied to regional ceremonial centers by travelers and pilgrims could have been a major source of wealth and power for newly emerging elites.

Religious ideology seems to have played a central role in promoting and legitimizing these profound sociopolitical transformations, suggesting that many of the key ingredients for social complexity existed in the central Andes prior to the Chavín horizon.

Blueprints for the Archaeology of the Mind

Progress is marked less by a perfection of consensus than by a refinement of debate. What gets better is the precision with which we vex each other.

CLIFFORD GEERTZ, INTERPRETIVE ANTHROPOLOGIST
(PRINCETON UNIVERSITY)

To sum up what's been said about cognitive approaches in archaeology, we must be clear about two important points:

- Cognitive archaeology is a hot topic.
- Considerable debate exists about how best to proceed.

As we've seen throughout these pages, the extremes are defined by processual and postmodern perspectives, with plenty of room for defining an expanding middle ground.

Previously, we discussed how cognitive approaches were stifled under archaeology's processual agenda. But today, few modern anthropologists believe in absolute value neutrality and complete objectivity. Most philosophers of science clearly recognize that science exists as part of culture, not outside it. Values, properly factored in, can be productive, not contaminating.

Although some persist in pursuing their version of ultimate truth—the way it *absolutely, really* was—most Americanist archaeologists are assessing the degree to which their interpretations express their own cultural biases. Few archaeologists adhere to strict empiricism—the view that data are so self-evident that the analyst can passively experience data.

With the advent of postmodernism, the debate shifted away from rigid objectivity and oppressive scientific methodologies. Postmodernism by its very nature encourages cognitive, ideational approaches to the past. In the words of one postmodern thinker, Jean-Francois Lyotard, consensus has become "an outmoded and suspect value."

Postmodern views of the past replace scientific unanimity with a sense of theoretical *pluralism*. No grand synthesis is expected to emerge. According to the postprocessual critique, archaeology will come to be characterized by multiple paths toward understanding the past. A primary plank in the postmodern agenda is to learn how to live with mutually irreconcilable views about the past.

The recognition of multiple pasts is one of the undeniably positive aspects to be derived from the postprocessual critique. It has produced a new openness, an insistence on theoretical multiplicity. This perspective stands to benefit archaeology in several ways.

Often, the shortcomings of a given theory can only be appreciated from the vantage point of a competing theory. Because such competition tends to raise the level of theoretical inquiry, it is essential to have competition. Adequate quality control demands a deluge of diverse and conflicting theories. Theories do not just disappear on their own—they generally hang around until something "better" replaces them. So it becomes important to generate a host of diverse and contrasting theories, which can be qualified and enlarged, or rejected and replaced—all as part of the everyday archaeological process.

But good theories are hard to come by. So, to generate more theories, some researchers have suggested relaxing the methodological constraints that hinder the free-flowing generation of theories. Some archaeologists do not think this is a good idea.

Without doubt, such postmodern perspectives have opened many avenues of inquiry into the "archaeology of the human mind." But some self-described cognitive archaeologists—luminaries like Kent Flannery, Joyce Marcus, and Colin Renfrew—continue to advocate fairly stringent scientific controls.

Renfrew warns of the dangers inherent in "new-age archaeology," adamantly insisting that cognitive archaeology proceed only within the framework of acceptable scientific method. First, one must recognize that archaeology (re)captures only certain, limited aspects of ancient ideas. Renfrew expresses contempt for attempts to reconstruct "worldviews" or "totalities of thought"—emphasizing the notable lack of success ethnographers have had trying to do this (and they are working with living people whose "totality of thought" is very much intact).

Projecting ideas into the past within a framework of rigid, testable, fully objective science is not feasible. But even lacking such uncompromising testability, Renfrew insists that at least one's cognitive inferences must be induced "carefully" from the data and limited to statements that can be inferred directly from those data. In this way, statements open to empirical assessment can be "distanced" from the investigator.

Flannery and Marcus deride those who employ cognitive archaeology as "a shortcut to the kind of 'armchair archaeology' that requires no fieldwork or rigorous analysis of any kind. As a result of this shortcut, many of the worst fears of the materialists have been realized—namely that *any* fanciful mentalist speculation is allowed, so long as it is called 'cognitive archaeology.'" Flannery and Marcus worry about the numerous "idiosyncratic fantasies," which tell us more about the archaeologist in charge than the ancient culture under study. Be skeptical, they argue, when authors ask that we trust their "highly-developed intuition" rather than addressing any acceptable evidence for their interpretation.

They insist that iconography is not merely some esoteric skill. Such procedures can work in concert with established subsistence and settlement perspectives, integrating the findings drawn from the natural and social sciences. Marcus and Flannery believe that cognitive archaeology can indeed follow relatively rigorous methods, provided ample ethnohistorical and ethnographic documentation is available.

Putting the "I" Back in the Archaeological Past: Defining an Empathetic Approach

The increase in gender-based studies and increasing involvement of ethnic minorities are just two examples illustrating the changing directions within Americanist archaeology. Just as some have attacked the antihistorical, generalizing, and materialist biases of processual archaeology, others have taken issue with the way in which processual approaches dismiss the role of the individual.

We have already taken up the issue of human agency and the role it plays in the postprocessual critique. The debate of how best to bring individuals into theories about the past has crystalized archaeology's so-called "cognitive revolution," addressed in this and the preceding chapter.

Human Agency, Revisited

Some archaeologists believe that in order to reintroduce human agency into the past, we must develop a more *empathetic* approach, involving not only human thoughts and decisions but also such highly subjective elements as affective states, spiritual orientations, and deep-down meanings. This approach assumes that the inner experiences of individuals are worthy of study, both for their own sake and as a clue for finding meaning in the human past.

To do this, empathetic methods assume the existence of a common, shared structure behind all human experience, a structure that allows an investigator to "bridge" into the feelings, hopes, and meanings of the past. It is assumed that modern investigators and ancient target groups share similar cognitive configurations, more or less.

An empathetic approach to the past requires two key assumptions. First, it is necessary to assume that thoughts and decisions really do have agency—that is,

In Her Own Words

On Archaeology and Empathy
by Janet Spector

Until now, when I wrote about [archaeological] sites and objects, I felt no connection with the past, my own or that of the people whose cultural landscapes I unearthed. Writing "What This Awl Means," a story about a Dakota girl who lost a carved awl handle a century and a half ago, brought back thoughts and feelings I had experienced as a young girl drawn to archaeology. As I learned about the discipline—and, especially how to write about archaeology for academic readers—I found myself increasingly distanced from the question that had fascinated me since childhood: What was life like for people in the past? While composing the awl story in place of the standard archaeological report or scholarly article, I was reminded of my original reasons for wanting to be an archaeologist. The motives are empathetic—a longing to discover essences, images, and feelings of the past—not detached, distanced, objective.

It took me a long time to reconnect with the past.

I began studying archaeology in 1962 as a freshman at the University of Wisconsin at Madison, but I found the subject much less interesting than I had expected. This disappointed me, since I had decided in the ninth grade to become an archaeologist, despite having been told that girls could not be archaeologists and not knowing what it took to become one. With a few exceptions the readings in undergraduate courses bored me. I learned from these courses that archaeologists

that they are truly individual, not just reflections of some "superstructure" that derives directly from underlying material "forces" (as is assumed in the processual agenda). Second, empathetic approaches also assume that collective actions and shared institutions can be interpreted as the direct products of decisions and actions of past individuals.

Clearly, this is a sharp break from the processual agenda, which focuses on the cultural system that, to one degree or another, conditions all human actions. Taken together, these two assumptions provide the basis for "the cognitive revolution" in archaeology.

Reflexive Ethnography

But how do we actually introduce *agency* into our understanding of the human condition? One way, postmodernists argue, is to modify the narrative style in which anthropological findings are expressed. Not unlike Jefferson's perspective apparently considered artifact classification more important than the people who had made the tools, about whom very little was said. The archaeology I was taught was objective, object oriented, and objectifying.

For almost a decade of summers I excavated at Indian sites in Wisconsin, [but] neither professors of archaeology nor authors of archaeology texts suggested that we might get closer to these people by studying contemporary Indian languages, religions, or philosophies. They implied that too much time had elapsed, too much change had occurred, too much history separated people from their pasts. People occupied these "prehistoric" sites long before traditional Indian culture had "disintegrated" through contact with Europeans. Contemporary Indians were disconnected from their ancestors. But no one I knew ever bothered to ask Indian people about these notions.

["What This Awl Means"] incorporate[s] voices and viewpoints other than my own–those of the Dakota people, as well as the fur traders, officials, explorers, and missionaries that the Indians encountered, sometimes in harmony but more often in conflict. Throughout I have tried to convey the turmoil of the times and avoid the rhetoric of archaeology that frequently obscures the people being studied.

Shaping my work are the ongoing tensions between archaeologists and Indian people. These conflicts exemplify the archaeological premise that the past shapes the present. A viewpoint archaeologists less often acknowledge is that the present shapes our rendering of the past.

JANET SPECTOR is affiliated with the University of Minnesota.

discussed earlier in the book, modern interpretive anthropology stresses the importance of *context*–not just the context in which the subject exists, but also the context within which the observer, the ethnographer, operates. Such ethnographic inquiry is "interpretive" in that the explanatory framework is extended from the observed to the observer, from the described to the describer.

Such interpretive approaches–both in ethnography and archaeology–result directly from a postmodern perspective that challenges many current forms of representation, transcending history, political science, economics, sociology, psychology, law, art, and even architecture. Postmodern methods attempt to "deconstruct" various means of communication by critically analyzing–by *contextualizing*–how they were constructed and how they attempt to convey credibility.

Today, cultural anthropologists worry about the issue of *authenticity*. For decades, ethnographic credibility has derived from a sense of "having been there," emphasizing the believability of a trained observer who has directly experienced another culture and a different language. Traditionally, such experiences were considered adequate to empower the ethnographer as a competent translator of other cultures.

Interpretive anthropologists have heavily criticized the traditional role of such "ethnographic authority," questioning in particular the anthropologist's ability to separate the observed from the observer. Modern cultural anthropology is increasingly critical of time-honored forms of ethnographic writing because they fail to relate what is being described (the people under study) to the describer (the ethnographer conducting the study). Great concern has been expressed about how various identities—one's subjects, the ethnographer, the ethnographic project itself—are negotiated in the various places that anthropologists conduct their fieldwork.

A new form of ethnographic writing has sprung up in response to this concern, emphasizing the importance of reflexivity by defining the role of the anthropologist in the ethnographic inquiry. **Reflexive** accounts are *self-conscious* in that they emphasize the conditions under which anthropological knowledge is produced, discarding the "naive" assumptions of objectivity and realism. Postmodern, interpretive ethnographic writing increasingly reflects a sense of reflexive collaboration, in which informant and ethnographer collectively construct a text.

In Her Own Words

People in the Past—More Than Faceless Blobs
by Ruth E. Tringham

[In April 1988] I was taken kicking and screaming to the conference "Women and Production in Prehistory" in the marshes of South Carolina, convinced that gender differences were not visible in the archaeological record, least of all in the architectural remains of deep prehistory, with which I was most concerned. I was moreover at a loss as to how I should rework my current research strategy to face the question of what women were doing in the houses that I was so busy studying.

I had an "Aha" experience.

I presented a summarized version of my paper about investigating household organization and architectural remains in prehistoric southeast Europe to the 20 or so participants round the table. They listened politely—the archaeologists did—and worried about the validity of the data I presented for my conclusions.

And then someone said, "Yes, but how do you envisage these households?" It was Henrietta Moore, I think.

"You mean how do I imagine their composition?" thinking: Oh, heavens, she wants me to imagine their kinship structure, but I am interested in what households *did* not what they comprised. . . .

As George Marcus has put it, the reflexive perspective requires us to replace the objective eye with the more personal "I."

Reflexive Archaeology

Similar trends can be found in modern archaeological thought. Many archaeologists have backed away from the notions of absolute objectivity and glacial impartiality. Following the lead of interpretive ethnography, archaeologists are once again putting the "I" back into their own writings.

This trend, of course, flies in the face of traditional views of scientific discourse. Although many undergraduates are still advised to remove first-person references from their technical writings, some archaeologists feel that removing the "I" effectively denies the self and the author—in effect replacing the authority of the actual archaeologist involved with an unwarranted faceless, impersonal objectivity.

More and more, archaeologists are including in their site reports the sense of revelation and unfolding that characterizes most excavations, imposing a feeling of sequence, discovery, and surprise. As every participant of an archaeological excavation realizes, the hands-on process of archaeological inquiry is neither simple

Henrietta said "No, how do you envisage them going about their daily actions?"

You can imagine, I felt quite defensive. "Archaeologists don't do that. We don't go around envisaging people leading cows to pasture and gossiping around the household chores."

"Yes, but what *if* you were allowed to do it; just relax; no one will tell. Now, just tell us how you see them. What do they look like?"

"Well," I said, "there's a house, and cows, and pigs, and garbage . . ."

"Yes, but the people, tell us about the people."

"Well . . . ," I said. And then I realized what I saw. "I see," I said, ". . . a lot of faceless blobs."

And then it dawned on me what she wanted me to see. That until, as an archaeologist, you can learn to give your imagined societies faces, you cannot envisage gender. Or, in somebody else's term (Conkey's?) you cannot engender prehistory.

And until you can engender prehistory, you cannot *think* of your prehistoric constructions as really human entities with a social, political, ideological, and economic life.

Ahaaaa!

RUTH E. TRINGHAM is professor of anthropology, University of California, Berkeley.

nor clear-cut. Every day on a dig poses new questions to the diggers, specialists, supervisors, and site directors: Why was this wall destroyed? Is this really a house floor? Should we dig through this fire hearth to see what's below? Why was this A.D. 1200 potsherd found in a posthole that apparently dates to A.D. 600?

Some blame the disembodied, colorless character of archaeological writing for obscuring the dynamics of the archaeological process. Archaeology isn't dull. It isn't boring. And it certainly isn't self-evident. So why must modern archaeologists still present their findings in a mind-numbing, prepackaged, matter-of-fact style?

Nobody is suggesting a return to eighteenth-century rhetoric. Thomas Jefferson's account of his Virginia excavations is *not* a model for modern site reportage. But many archaeologists are drawing on some qualities evident in Jefferson's seminal text: a return to first-person narrative, an openness to diversity of opinion rather than consensus, an emphasis on the role of the archaeologist in conditioning the outcome. Such archaeological texts not only come alive, but also more clearly reflect how down-and-dirty archaeology is really done. Many would also claim that this shift in narrative style reveals deeper changes in the underlying structure of archaeological thought.

Thinking Yourself Into the Past

Current empathetic approaches in archaeology draw their inspiration in part from the writings of English historian and philosopher Robin George Collingwood. In his influential writings, Collingwood argued that in order to understand events in the human past, it is necessary to distinguish between the "outsider" and "insider" views of the past. The "outsider" (or etic) view, to Collingwood, could be described in terms of bodies and their movements—people participating in the observable events of the past. But the "insider" (what today we would term emic) view can be described only in terms of the thoughts once held by those people. This is the goal of an empathetic approach to the past—to transcend the past event and actually insinuate oneself into the role the actor played in that event.

Collingwood's "from the inside" approach—attempting to get at the intentions and thoughts of actors in the past—found ready acceptance in the postprocessual critique, most notably in Ian Hodder's influential *Reading the Past,* published in 1986. Following Collingwood, Hodder argued that knowing the past is not merely the passive reception of facts; it is, rather, the discerning of the thought that took place inside the event. According to Hodder's reading of Collingwood, archaeologists must "think themselves into the past."

Summary

Americanist archaeologists are increasingly concerned with defining an "archaeology of the mind." Although processual archaeology was initially optimistic that *all aspects* of the human condition were available for archaeological investigation, the processual approaches during the 1970s and 1980s were distinctly lukewarm, if not outright hostile, toward "cognitive" archaeology.

Modern cognitive archaeology is developing methods for studying all those aspects of ancient culture that are the product of the human mind: the perception, description, and classification of the universe; the nature of the supernatural; the principles, philosophies, ethics, and values by which human societies are governed; the ways in which aspects of the world, the supernatural, or human values are conveyed in art.

For one thing, archaeologists attempt to understand *cosmology,* how various past cultures have explained their universe–how it originated and developed, how the various parts fit together and what laws they obey, plus a concern with what the future of the universe holds in store.

Archaeologists are also attempting to understand past *religions*–the specific set of beliefs based on one's ultimate relation to the supernatural. Such religious beliefs are manifested in everyday life in a "program of ritual," a succession of discrete events such as prayer, music, feasting, sacrifice, and taboos.

Ideology is defined as a systematic body of concepts and beliefs–often political in nature–about human life or culture. Communism is an ideology, as are democracy and fascism. Ideology differs from religion (although they certainly can overlap) because it addresses society and politics.

To illustrate some current cognitive approaches in archaeology, we draw on recent studies of *iconography*–the way in which people have employed art forms to represent their religious, political, ideological, or cosmological beliefs. Iconographic analysis covers a broad range, from well-known complex systems–such as Egyptian hieroglyphs and Mayan inscriptions–to cryptic incisions on ancient stone and bone artifacts.

The stated goal of processual archaeology is to create universally valid generalizations that should ultimately prove to be of practical value for the improvement and management of contemporary societies. Contrasting postprocessual approaches have affirmed the right of each special interest group–colonized peoples, indigenous groups and minorities, religious groups, women, and the working class–to speak for themselves, in their own voice, with that voice accepted as authentic and legitimate. The current spirit of theoretical *pluralism* characterizes contemporary archaeology and has curated a more diverse set of research objectives, expressed in a less authoritarian manner. The increase in gender- and ethnic-based studies underscores the changing directions within Americanist archaeology.

Some archaeologists believe that in order to reintroduce human agency into the past, more *empathetic* approaches should be employed, involving not only human thoughts and decisions but also such highly subjective elements as affective states, spiritual orientations, and deep-down meanings. This approach assumes that the inner experiences of individuals are worthy of study, both for their own sake and as a clue for finding meaning in the human past.

> *Archaeology shows more clearly, perhaps, than any other activity that we go out and "get" the past. The past isn't just there. The relationship between present and past is not a "given." We go and dig it up.*
>
> IAN HODDER, ARCHAEOLOGIST (CAMBRIDGE UNIVERSITY)

CHAPTER 12

Archaeology in the Twenty-First Century

□ □ □

PREVIEW

Throughout the first 11 chapters, I've told you lots of stories, trying to give you a graphic, yet realistic picture of what Americanist archaeology is all about. Here, in this concluding chapter, I want to leave you with just a few more stories, but these are more serious.

Although this chapter addresses our knowledge of the past—the stuff that archaeology's made of—it's a little different from earlier chapters because it's mainly concerned with the uses of archaeological knowledge—today and tomorrow, next year and the next millennium. These are stories whose endings are still being written.

Archaeology was once widely regarded as some sort of backward extension of recorded history, offered as some kind of shadowy reconstruction of the past. To-day, rather suddenly, archaeology seems relevant and relevant in a very international way.

COLIN RENFREW, ARCHAEOLOGIST (CAMBRIDGE UNIVERSITY)

Americanist archaeology is struggling to escape the myths promulgated by movies and television. As everybody knows, Hollywood archaeologists are pistol-packing, hard-drinking professors who circle the globe seeking ancient treasure, braving the occult and political intrigue, muttering "To hell with the mummy's curse."

These mythical macho men are accompanied by buxom yet plucky research assistants—always young, female, and foxy. Together, they are academic but death-defying as they oversee their crew of a thousand sweating, cursing, rebellious natives. They usually have a treasure map.

The history of our field does reveal a glimmer of truth in the stereotype. Archaeologists do, from time to time, carry guns. Fieldwork has sometimes been hazardous. Some archaeologists drink too much. And one or two even have worked as CIA spies.

Although today's reality is quite different, many myths persist. Here, we will try to explode several of the most common fictions:

- *Myth No. 1: Most Americanist archaeologists are university professors and museum curators.* In this chapter, we see that the vast majority of archaeologists in this country make their living protecting America's cultural heritage, not by teaching or working in museums.
- *Myth No. 2: Americanist archaeology is just for macho men.* Although archaeology has traditionally been a male-dominated venture, men and women pursuing advanced training in archaeology today are nearly equal in numbers, and perhaps one-quarter of all fully employed archaeologists in America are female.
- *Myth No. 3: Archaeologists spend a lot of their time bossing and/or bullying native people.* In truth, most modern archaeologists are actively seeking the hands-on collaboration of indigenous and minority people—not just as laborers and/or informants, but as active participants in research and applied archaeological projects. Native people and minorities are increasingly receiving high-level professional training and several are today employed as full-time archaeologists.

In this final chapter, we will show you some specifics illustrating what real-life archaeologists actually do.

Indiana Jones in Raiders of the Lost Ark—*portrayed by actor Harrison Ford—artfully personified a world of stereotypes regarding archaeologists.*

Conservation Archaeology: Caring for America's Cultural Heritage

Many countries, including the United States, are attempting to resolve the conflicting goals of economic development and heritage preservation by creating laws and regulations to protect the past. The sum total of these statutes and the methods for their execution have come to be known as **conservation archaeology** or **cultural resource management** (CRM).

What Is Cultural Resource Management (CRM)?

Cultural resource management exists today at two levels. In

one sense, looking out for the global heritage is just one more way of protecting an endangered worldwide environment. CRM in this larger context meshes readily with other efforts designed to comply with current environmental requirements, including legislation protecting endangered species, wetlands, water and air quality, timber and mineral management.

The roots of environmentalism in America extend back to nineteenth-century writers such as Henry David Thoreau, John Muir, and Ernest Thompson Seton. They and many others inspired readers to take an interest in the natural world around them and to heed the increasing human impact on that landscape.

Some, appalled at the needless slaughter of the Great Plains bison in the late nineteenth century, started the movement to save the continent's wildlife. Others, called to action by the publication of George Perkins Marsh's widely read *Man and Nature* in 1864, became concerned with wholesale environmental degradation around the world.

President Theodore Roosevelt was particularly concerned about Marsh's plea that disturbed environments be allowed to heal naturally, or be restored by specific conservation management plans. Roosevelt insisted that large areas of forest and grazing land in the United States be set aside to protect timber supplies *for future use and development*. At the same time, John Muir, founder of the Sierra Club, argued for leaving large tracts of western lands untouched *for their long-term aesthetic values*. These two often-conflicting philosophies remain with us today.

In the 1960s and 1970s, a large portion of the American public—many aroused by Rachel Carson's *Silent Spring* (1962)—recognized that wilderness and wildlife refuges alone could not stem the tide of pollution. In the mid-1960s there were demonstrations such as Earth Day, and thousands of people chanted non sequiturs like "Save the Ecology" or displayed bumper stickers like "I'm for Ecology." The voter appeal of these popular movements was not lost on the legislators, and many of them became "conservationists" too. In fact, sufficient power came down on the side of the ecologists for laws to be drafted protecting the *nonrenewable resources* of the nation.

Largely as a result of such efforts, in 1970 the U.S. Congress established the Environmental Protection Agency (EPA) to protect and maintain the environment for future generations. The initial charge was to control and lessen air and water pollution, noise pollution, and pollution by radiation, pesticides, and other toxic agents. In the late 1980s, the mission of the EPA was expanded to include problems of global warming and environmental change.

But what are these so-called nonrenewable resources? Most people think of redwoods and whooping cranes and baby seals. Others think of energy-related assets like oil, coal, and uranium. But most legislators have a legal background, and in the course of legally defining national resources, they realized that properties of historic value must be included as well. After all, they reasoned, how many Monticellos do we have? Shouldn't archaeological sites be considered national resources too?

As a result of this reasoning, archaeological sites were included in the ecological legislation of the late 1960s and the 1970s and are now legally protected resources, just like the redwoods, whooping cranes, and shale-oil fields.

Obviously, "cultural resource management" is only a small part of today's concern with saving the planet. And, it must be stressed, archaeology is only part of CRM efforts (although, in terms of dollars spent, archaeology is a *major* part of the program). Archaeology, in this context, is part of a multidisciplinary, applied effort that draws on the expertise of cultural anthropologists, historians, architectural historians, historical architects, landscape architects, engineers, archivists, and many others. Cultural resource management is concerned with all kinds of historic buildings and structures (such as bridges), artifacts, documents, and, of course, archaeological sites. For decades, cultural resource managers shared in the responsibilities of identifying, evaluating, preserving, managing, and treating these resources.

CRM legislation has defined a new philosophy of governmental decision making, requiring that environmental and cultural variables be considered side by side with technological and economic benefits when planning future construction. These new requirements have created thousands of archaeological contracts, which produce reports detailing the nature of the archaeological resources endangered and how a project's impact should be mitigated.

The immediate result has been to spotlight the need for accurate information regarding archaeological sites. Sometimes the federal agencies have the resources to undertake such studies, but more commonly the agencies contract with academic institutions, museums, archaeological contracting firms, and qualified private individuals to prepare the required reports. Although hard numbers are difficult to find, it has been estimated that at least 90 percent of all archaeological research in the United States is today contract related.

The nature of conservation archaeology has changed in recent years. Environmental impact mitigation no longer means merely finding a few sites that might be nice to dig. Federal agencies are now taking steps to locate at least the major archaeological sites in areas that are under the agency's control. These sites are then evaluated against a recent set of federal standards known as the Criteria of Eligibility for the National Register of Historic Places.

The Structure of CRM in America

Many governments around the world claim outright ownership of all archaeological resources in their territory. But the situation is different in the United States, where archaeological sites on private land generally are the legal and exclusive property of the landowner (and hence are subject to no external control). There are exceptions, of course, such as federally assisted projects involving private property, or in some states, abandoned cemeteries and unmarked burials. But in most cases, archaeological resources on private property are privately owned, and hence unprotected.

In contrast, archaeological sites located on federal land are legally protected by an elaborate network of federal legislation, policies, and regulations. Protection for sites on state-owned jurisdictions varies considerably, ranging somewhere between the firm control exercised over federal lands and the negligible safeguards offered sites on private lands.

Federal authority for protection of archaeological resources tends to be fragmented and decentralized. Most federal agencies employ their own CRM personnel. Some of the largest—such as the Forest Service, Army Corps of Engineers, and the Bureau of Land Management (BLM)—maintain multimillion-dollar annual budgets devoted to CRM planning, compliance, and public education. Both the National Park Service and the Advisory Council on Historic Preservation have overarching preservation responsibilities, but no single agency oversees the entire archaeological operation.

This decentralized approach to federal CRM offers some advantages, since it requires little coordination between agencies (often a stumbling block both in the United States and in other countries). But the truth is that some agencies take on their preservation responsibilities with a real sense of stewardship, while others seem content merely to carry out the letter of the law. Moreover, federal agencies often find themselves seriously underfunded. A fairly recent survey indicated, for instance, that less than 10 percent of all federal lands had even been inventoried for archaeological resources.

In a recent overview, Ricardo Elia found contemporary CRM archaeology in the United States to be "highly idiosyncratic and beset with many problems." He highlights, for instance, the difficulties in conducting adequate archaeological surveys and creating workable site inventories. The results are disappointing and difficult to compare from area to area. Although millions are being spent annually, still more millions are required to build an adequate regional base. Despite the avowed interest in conserving sites, too many are still being excavated (when they could readily have been kept intact). Furthermore, he found that during such excavations, sampling percentages are still distressingly low. It is not uncommon in some areas to have sites completely destroyed after less than a 10 percent sampling. Not only the overall lack of CRM funding, but also competitive bidding for contracts seems to guide many such decisions.

Despite its problems and growing pains, CRM is today the most influential force in Americanist archaeology. Increasing numbers of young archaeologists are being hired in the private and government sectors, while the number of more traditional teaching and museum-based jobs has stabilized or even begun to shrink. This means that the raw bulk of archaeological work being done has shifted from the academic to the private and government sectors.

Conservation Archaeology as a Career

Within a period of two decades or so, CRM has radically transformed the practice of Americanist archaeology, particularly with respect to career opportunities, funding sources, and guiding philosophy. In 1981, the annual funding for CRM was estimated to be about $300 million, involving 2,000 full-time CRM staff in federal and state agencies, with another 250 academic and nonprofit institutions and 500 private firms, employing perhaps 4,000 full-time staff, providing CRM services on a contract basis.

Although nobody seems certain just how much money is being spent on CRM today, it far exceeds the early 1980s level and outstrips funding available for more traditional academic and institutional research archaeology. By way of comparison, two of the largest sponsors of archaeological research, the National Science Foundation and the Wenner-Gren Foundation, spent only $3.4 million for archaeological research in 1991.

In this context, the conservation archaeologist acts as the point of contact between the government (required by statute to protect archaeological sites) and various developers and other interested parties wishing to modify the environment. So positioned, it is the responsibility of the CRM archaeologist to ensure compliance with the broad and sometimes confusing range of federal, state, local, and other national laws, regulations, standards, guidelines and procedures, as well as international conventions and recommendations and standards of professional practice.

People participate in CRM archaeology in a variety of ways. Some work strictly in the field, others only in the lab, some in museums, some in offices with a phone glued to their ear and a computer fused to their lap. A few focus their efforts on teaching conservation values to the general public and to children, in hopes that CRM will not have such an uphill struggle in the future.

Today's CRM archaeologists are tackling, on a daily basis, the future of the past: What does America's archaeological record really consist of? What must we study and protect for future benefit? What can we live without?

All archaeologists are aware that sites are vanishing at an unprecedented rate. But it is the archaeologist specializing in CRM who must wrestle with the implications of this fact on a day-to-day basis.

The Current Status of Women in Archaeology

Like all social scientists, American archaeologists will always remain creatures of their own culture. Throughout this text, we have explored how contemporary attitudes toward race, politics, religion, and gender color our specific interpretations of the past. In this chapter, as we focus on the "business of archaeology," it makes sense to examine how Western cultural biases have influenced the degree to which women participate in this profession.

A History of Excluding Women From Professional Archaeology

Traditional Americanist archaeology has, without question, been a male-dominated venture. Chapter 1 sketched the history in terms of eight "forebears"; not until we reached the 1970s, could a woman, Kathleen Deagan, be selected to represent the field. Choosing America's premier archaeologists reflects somewhat my own view of the profession and also the fact that for decades women were excluded from Americanist archaeology. And the written histories of the field necessarily reflect this bias.

Without question, although women have been participating archaeologists for more than a century, their contributions have largely been overlooked. The first generation of women working in archaeology comprised a small group, including several women who were sufficiently affluent to afford a career in archaeology, where they served mostly as unpaid and loosely affiliated field workers. During the nineteenth century, access to formal training in archaeology for women was severely limited, fieldwork opportunities almost nonexistent, and publication outlets nil. These women are not well represented in the written histories of the field. A second generation of female archaeologists appeared in the 1920s. Several women even broke into the formal ranks of university-level teaching.

But women interested in archaeology continued to face substantial obstacles in the 1930s and 1940s, and their career advancement was still seriously hampered by gender-based status discrimination. Most archaeologists get their first taste of fieldwork in academic-based field schools, and although some archaeological field schools admitted women in the 1920s, it was not until the early 1970s that "mixed" digs became commonplace. Documented cases exist in which a male archaeologist attempted to undermine publications by his female colleague, and a senior male professor insisted that a female junior faculty member fetch his lunch daily. Also on the record is a statement by a senior male archaeologist suggesting that women were better suited to laboratory work because it closely resembled housework. One prominent male archaeologist felt that women were an "unreliable element" in archaeological field crews because they were likely to get married (and hence disappear); apparently unmarried men were not a problem, since if they did get married, their wives could always serve as unpaid lab assistants.

H. Marie Wormington, a pioneer in the field of Paleo-Indian archaeology, attributed much of the earlier bias against women in archaeology to the mistaken beliefs that "women could not withstand the rigors of the field" and that marriage and childbearing would preclude devotion to an archaeological career. As she noted dryly, "Activities by many archaeologists, who are women, have amply demonstrated that this is not the case."

> *I always published under my initials, H. M. Wormington. The director of the museum felt nobody would read a book written by a woman.*
> HANNAH MARIE WORMINGTON (1914–1994), ARCHAEOLOGIST

A History of Excluding Gender-Based Inquiry

Over the past three decades, processual archaeology has been firmly grounded in an adaptive, systemic approach to the past. The stated goal of processual archaeology is to create universally valid generalizations that should ultimately prove to be of practical value for the improvement and management of contemporary societies. Informed by the strategy of cultural materialism, processualists focused on large-scale structures and long-term dynamics, deliberately looking beyond archaeological detail and historical specifics.

In sharp contrast, the postprocessual critique puts down attempts by "authority" to speak for "the other"—women, colonized peoples, indigenous groups and minorities, religious groups, and the working class—with a unified voice. Each group has a right to speak for itself, in its own voice, and have that voice accepted as authentic and legitimate. This postmodern spirit of *pluralism* has penetrated contemporary archaeology, creating a more diverse set of research objectives—expressed in a less authoritarian manner. The postprocessual critique calls for and welcomes multiple perspectives on the past.

Advocates of a pluralistic view of archaeology argue that the processual agenda exerted a stultifying effect on gender-based research. Explanation in processual archaeology, they say, operated at the level of the cultural system, defining a focus on systemwide mechanisms—specifically those mediating adaptive responses to the environment.

This system-based approach contrasts sharply with the needs of gender-based inquiry. During the 1970s and 1980s, emerging feminist theory began to define major arenas of interest—gender identities, gender roles, and gender ideology—which were highly variable, involving ideational and symbolic components. Small wonder, then, that gender-based inquiry fell largely outside the purview of processual approaches, which, by definition, specifically focus on adaptation, demography, and technology. Gender systems were largely ignored in materialistic, processual archaeology.

Alison Wylie has argued that processual approaches made key assumptions about gender that denied (or overlooked) the relevance of women in understanding the past through the archaeological record. In its search for a single, coherent, and comprehensive ("true") understanding of the past, processual archaeology downplayed the possibility of seeking alternative perspectives that direct attention toward the activities of men and women. The postprocessual critique demonstrated (to the satisfaction of many) that the so-called value-neutral scientific approach was full of androcentric biases and assumptions.

In addition, processual archaeology—operating within a highly structured, "objective" framework—generally viewed gender-based variables as "too soft," "too subjective" to be reconstructed on the basis of archaeological data. Gender-based inquiry seemed unsuitable for properly scientific methods of hypothesis testing (an integral part of the processual agenda). Those who argued for study of the symbolic, ideational bases of gender relations were commonly put down as nonscientific and irrelevant.

Today, we find considerable variability within the emerging field of gender archaeology, and it is easy to see why feminist scholars welcomed archaeology's postprocessual critique. Although not all feminist archaeology is postprocessual in nature, many of the themes developed in feminist writing are consistent with those of the postprocessual critique: a concern with meaning and human agency, a willingness to listen to other voices, a concern with power and self-reflexive views of the past.

Modern Equity Issues for Women in Archaeology

Recent estimates have suggested that women comprise about 25 percent of all fully employed archaeologists in America. Today, the proportion may be even higher, and many female archaeologists are quite successful and making significant contributions to the field.

Compared with a decade or two ago, a much higher proportion of the graduate and undergraduate students specializing in archaeology are women. The numbers of men and women pursuing advanced training in archaeology today are nearly equal; women are apparently enjoying equivalent levels of success in school, as measured by research performance, funding, and publication. Many believe that "times have changed."

Maybe so, but there remain some disturbing trends. For one thing, it seems that women drop out of graduate school at a higher rate than men. A larger proportion of women also disappear from the job pool after they complete their degrees. This may suggest, at least in part, that more women tend to make nonacademic career choices than men. But such "choices" may reflect not only decisions in favor of spouse and family, but also lowered career expectations in academic or other archaeological careers.

Even after completion of graduate training, women assume proportionately fewer leadership positions, publish fewer books, receive fewer research grants, and generally receive less recognition for their work. Women are still underrepresented in senior positions in archaeology. One result of this is that young women deciding on career directions have few female role models.

Anthropologists Nancy Parezo and Susan Bender describe the "chilly climate" in which female professional archaeologists sometimes work: male-dominated, male-controlled, and male-oriented. Recent research suggests that in some cases, the contribution of female archaeologists has been marginalized, their voices not heard, their work considered trivial. Analysis of these data suggest that the differentials between men and women are societal, not individual. Women are still sometimes discouraged, given the cold shoulder, through various subtle attitudes and behaviors such as stereotyping, devaluation, exclusion, isolation, tokenism, and outright sexual harassment. In the academic world, chilly climates result in slower rates of promotion, lower pay scales, and in the more subtle practice of ignoring the work of women whenever similar ideas originate with a male author.

In sum, it is clear that women today still enjoy a lower status than men in archaeology, reflected in lower income and lower prestige. Sarah M. Nelson and Margaret C. Nelson suggest the following strategies could change this picture in the future:

- Encourage women to pursue archeology as a career.
- Increase the number and percentage of women in managerial and administrative roles.

- Encourage women to become more visible through publication and original research.
- Work to change the dysfunctional stereotypes still operating in the professional culture of archaeology.

As Nelson and Nelson put it, "giving women their due improves working conditions for everyone."

This leads us to one more point. As several archaeologists (including Joan Gero, Mary Whelan, and Margaret Conkey) have emphasized, the inclusion of female archaeologists in the Americanist mainstream involves more than "just add women and stir." We simply are not seeing women coming in and doing the same things as the men.

The field of Americanist archaeology is necessarily changing as a result of integrating a distinctive group of people (women) because all of us reflect—to one degree or another—our own cultural experience when we interpret the past. Women's experiences are different from men's because women occupy a different place in American society than men do. The theoretical diversity in Americanist archaeology is closely linked with our ability to encourage diversity among the participants in the field—be they women, Native Americans, African Americans, or other previously disenfranchised ethnic groups.

Some Other Unintended Consequences: An Exclusion of Minority-Based History

Minority groups in America—particularly American Indians, but also African Americans, Asian Americans and many others—are sometimes puzzled and dissatisfied with processual archaeology's strident insistence on evolutionary, antihistorical generalizing about human behavior. The almost clinical hypothesis-testing agenda of processualism largely precluded exploration of the specific historical events of interest to many Indian groups. The unrelenting focus on ecology and adaptation effectively ignored and belittled the importance of cultural and religious tradition. Processual archaeology sent an unspoken message to minorities in America: We will be using the archaeology of your ancestors for ends that have no special relevance to your living people. Bruce Trigger has suggested that the heavy-handed pursuit of law-like generalizations created an unintended, chilling effect, "spiritually alienating" the Euroamerican archaeologist from Native American and other minority communities.

For the rest of this chapter, then, we focus on two such groups—African Americans and Native Americans—emphasizing in particular their changing relationship to the field of Americanist archaeology. First, however, we examine the impact of historical archaeology on these cultural issues.

The Rise of Historical Archaeology in America

Historical archaeology has proved to be extremely fertile ground for post-processual interests in culture-specific historical contexts. Postprocessual approaches require a more "situated" archaeology—a view of the past more closely attuned to contextual specifics. So-called text-aided archaeology became a logical focus for postprocessual studies because of the wealth of documentary evidence available with which to *contextualize* the archaeological record. This was a call to project oneself into the particular contexts of the past, to discover the significance and meaning of particular past actions. The study of the symbolic meaning of material remains also proceeds much more comfortably in the text-aided context, where independent confirmation or disconfirmation can be found in the documentary record.

Bruce Trigger has pointed out that most successful symbolic studies lie in the field of historical archaeology, concluding that "the cultural specific (emic) meaning of artefacts that cannot be embraced by the direct historical approach may forever lie beyond the realm of scientific study." Viewing material culture as a "text" is difficult because multiple readings are always possible and because no informant can be consulted to clarify meaning. But in the world of historical archaeology, at least there is written documentation (and sometimes oral tradition) that can be called on to determine which interpretations are more appropriate than others, which explanation best fits the data.

Postprocessual critics have also argued that mainstream archaeology should be more politically aware and involved. After all, their argument goes, the internal political structure of archaeology itself mediates the larger political effect of the discipline, determining what kind of research is pursued, who is empowered to pursue these objectives, what standard of adequacy constrains this investigation, and, therefore, what conception of the past will be acceptable as archaeological knowledge.

Some have argued that processual archaeology itself has played a rationalizing role for Western technological society. In this view, processualism is not an objective, scientific approach to the past, but rather a cleverly disguised use of special interpretations of the past to rationalize the present. The criticism here is that processualists have failed to acknowledge that their scientific program serves a political role within today's society.

The often-stated political aims of the postprocessual critique usually emphasize the goal of emancipating the individual. One way to accomplish this is to expose those ideologies that systematically mask the contradictions within society, and manipulate them to effect change.

These diverse threads, taken together, comprise archaeology's postprocessual critique—the call for increased political awareness, multiple views of the past, an explicit concern with power relations, more humanistic approaches, and the symbolic meaning of the past—and all fit quite comfortably with the text-aided and culturally connected complexion of historical archaeology. This diversity in approach makes historical archaeology one of the most exciting and rapidly growing subfields in all of Americanist archaeology.

The Evolution of African American Archaeology

The archaeology of African American people, particularly the study of slavery, has grown rapidly over the past couple of decades and today has become a major new horizon for Americanist archaeology. Numerous social, political, and intellectual forces spurred the origin and growth of African American archaeology: black activism, passage of historic preservation legislation, emergence of an archaeological interest in the immigrant ethnic groups of America, and the increased use of archaeology in the public interpretation of historic sites (such as plantations).

The field of African American archaeology is in its infancy, still developing theoretical frameworks to advance the inquiry beyond the previous, mostly descriptive approach. According to Theresa Singleton, a leader in the field, four major elements hold particular promise for understanding the archaeological record of slavery:

1. Living conditions under slavery
2. Status differences within the plantation community
3. Interplay of planter dominance and slave resistance
4. Formation of African American cultural identity

But in Singleton's view, no amount of theory building will correct the major drawback in this growing field: the lack of attention to African American perspectives. To illustrate how African Americans are becoming actively involved in the archaeology of their communities, let us briefly examine a project that will shape the future of archaeology in this country for years to come.

The Archaeology of New York's African Burial Ground

The bones of 427 enslaved Africans, interred by their own community and forgotten for centuries, were discovered beneath a parking lot in downtown New York City in 1991.

The island of Manhattan is a long way from the land of cotton, and few today remember that colonial New York was former slave territory. Too often recalled as an exclusively southern institution, slavery was deeply ingrained in the economy of the colonial North as well. That story is being told in excavations at New York's African Burial Ground.

In Her Own Words

Why Are So Few African-Americans Doing African-American Archaeology?
by Theresa A. Singleton

By concentrating on ethnic minorities that are both culturally and physically distinct from the white majority in the United States, archaeologists inadvertently created an ethnic archaeology of the Other. The result, combined with the fact that the archaeological profession in this country is almost totally white, has produced a study of ethnicity that more often reflects the perspectives of its investigators than the perspectives of those being investigated—an outcome that is the exact opposite of what this research was intended to do. Such realities are difficult to face and when raised are highly controversial, but archaeologists are beginning to address these concerns. . . .

The fact that too few of the archaeologists engaged in this research are African-Americans is only part of the problem. A far more serious problem is that African-Americans are rarely involved in this research in any substantive way. Most discussions concerning the involvement

---

Slavery in Old New York?

The narrative begins in 1626, when the Dutch West India Company unloaded its first shipment of enslaved Africans in New Amsterdam (today's New York City): 11 young men captured from what today is the Congo-Angola region of southwestern Africa. Two years later, the Dutch imported three African women "for the comfort of the company's Negro men." The Dutch at the time were experiencing a labor shortage in their colonies, and they found slave labor to be the answer to building and maintaining the colony. In 1664, the Dutch ceded Manhattan to the British. At that time, the population of enslaved Africans made up about 40 percent of New Amsterdam's total population.

The British colonists continued to import slaves during the first half of the eighteenth century. Everywhere one looked in colonial New York, there were toiling slaves—loading and unloading ships on the waterfront, building the streets, and erecting the buildings to house the people of this bustling port city crowded onto the southern end of Manhattan.

On the eve of the American Revolution, New York City had the largest number of enslaved Africans of any English colonial city except for Charleston, South Carolina. In fact, New York City had the highest proportion of slaves to Europeans of any northern settlement. Despite the lily-white perspectives found in most American history books, it is clear that the African population had a significant hand in the building of colonial New York.

of blacks in African-American archaeology consider blacks only as consumers of this research, rather than as part of the research process. Input from African-Americans should also be considered in generating questions to be investigated and in the interpretation of the results. . . .

Only when archaeologists begin to realize that the inclusion of African-Americans is an asset to this research will African-American archaeology cease to be just another anthropological discourse of an Other.

THERESA A. SINGLETON is associate professor of anthropology, Syracuse University.

Theresa Singleton.

Eighteenth-century New York followed a policy of "mortuary apartheid," meaning that the burial of Africans in Manhattan's churchyards was strictly pro-

Nineteenth-century engraving depicting an African being auctioned into slavery in Dutch New Amsterdam.

hibited. Left without a place to bury their dead, New York's African population eventually established a cemetery on a deserted tract of land lying just outside the city's protective wooden palisade (the "wall" giving modern Wall Street its name). There, between 1712 and 1790, somewhere between 10,000 and 20,000 people, mostly black but also a few lower-class whites, were buried. A 1755 map of downtown New York clearly shows a "Negro Burial Ground" covering perhaps five city blocks.

Some scholars question 1712 as the appropriate beginning date for the cemetery. Since Africans had lived in the area since at least 1624, some burials could easily have taken place earlier. To African American historian Christopher Moore, the date 1712 is significant only because that is when "the first European noticed that blacks were burying their dead."

It was not until 1827 that New York finally abolished slavery altogether. In the meantime, African American populations had abandoned the downtown area, moving northward in New York City. Over the subsequent centuries, the Negro Burial Ground was slowly swallowed up by urban expansion. By the late twentieth century, Manhattan's forgotten African cemetery lay buried beneath 20 feet of fill, a scant two blocks north of New York's City Hall.

Archaeology Becomes Contentious

But the Negro Burial Ground was not destined to lie undisturbed. In 1990, the city of New York sold the property to the General Services Administration (GSA), the arm of the U.S. Government responsible for constructing and maintaining federal buildings. The GSA had grand plans to build a 34-story office tower at 290 Broadway—complete with an adjacent four-story pavilion on the parking lot area—to house the U.S. attorney's office, the regional office of the Environmental Protection Agency, and a district office of the Internal Revenue Service. Although administrators knew at the time that the GSA pavilion was slated to rise directly above a colonial cemetery, they seriously underestimated its extent or the extraordinary degree of burial preservation.

The United States has an elaborate legal framework to protect its archaeological resources—particularly those lying on federal land. Part of this legislation requires that an environmental impact statement be filed before any construction can begin. Archaeologists and historians routinely participate in preparing such impact statements. The archaeological firm retained for the 290 Broadway historical inventory correctly noted that the "Negro Burial Ground" appeared on historical maps of the area, and probably lay nearby. But, recognizing the longstanding construction history of the site, the impact statement concluded that the digging of nineteenth- and twentieth-century basements had probably obliterated any human remains within the historical boundaries of the cemetery. Although the environmental impact statement did note that a portion of the old cemetery might perhaps have survived intact beneath an old alleyway, nobody expected much in the way of human remains to surface when construction began.

Still, because there remained a possibility of finding significant archaeological deposits in the construction zone, federal law required that exploratory archaeological excavation be undertaken. Suspecting that only a handful of human bones might turn up, a team of archaeologists began the small-scale excavations in September 1991. Right away, they found human bone—not just a few scattered remains, but dozens (then hundreds) of intact human burials.

The unexpectedly productive excavations at 290 Broadway began interfering with construction schedules. Worried that the archaeology might delay the $276 million project, the GSA insisted that the archaeologists work faster, excavating skeletons 10 and 12 hours a day, 7 days a week. Laboratory crew members were reassigned to field excavation duty—anything to speed things up.

At this point, word of the new finds got out to New York's African American community. Here, lying 16 to 28 feet below the modern street level, some 427 skeletons had been found from the long-forgotten Negro Burial Ground (soon

A 35- to 40-year-old woman with her child, interred at the African Burial Ground. Both probably died during childbirth, or shortly thereafter.

termed the "African Burial Ground" by community representatives). African American leaders were concerned that there was no community involvement in the 290 Broadway project. As one citizen put it, "If it was an African find, we wanted to make sure that it was interpreted from an African point of view." But the GSA countered that appropriate notification had been made as mandated by law: "We didn't include the Harlem community board because the project isn't in Harlem, it's in lower Manhattan."

The situation reached a flash point when a backhoe operator, excavating for the tower's foundation, destroyed several of the burials. Once word of the destruction leaked out, large-scale protests ensued, culminating in a 1-day blockade of the site that shut down all construction on the GSA tower project.

The excavations and the subsequent laboratory analysis drew nationwide attention. To some, the debate surrounding the African Burial Ground excavations became a "microcosm of the issues of racism and economic exploitation confronting New York City."

The GSA eventually commissioned an advisory committee—comprised of historians, anthropologists, museum professionals, architects, attorneys, clergy, government officials, and concerned community members—to represent the interests of the African descendant community at large.

There were, naturally, differences of opinion about how the remains should be treated. Some in the African American community felt that archaeological investigations were disrespectful, adding the insult of grave robbing to the injury of slavery. Others believed that a thorough yet respectful scientific study of the skeletons was not only a way of honoring the dead, but also of restoring them to their rightful place in American history.

But eventually, a working consensus was forged. A research team, headed by Michael L. Blakey, was chosen to carry out a 5-year research program on the remains, at Howard University's Cobb Biological Anthropology Laboratory. Bringing in Blakey was a popular decision. Having received his Ph.D. in biological anthropology at the University of Massachusetts, Amherst, he had an established track record in bioarchaeology, including important work at the First African Baptist Cemetery in Philadelphia. Not insignificantly, Blakey is an African American employed by the nation's premier black research university. Blakey's active participation became an overt symbol to the African descendant community that their wishes were indeed being considered.

Supported by then-Mayor David N. Dinkins (New York's first African American mayor), New York City's African descendant community became actively involved in the preservation, dedication, and management of the cemetery site. It soon became clear that the GSA plans for the proposed federal building would have to be modified.

The African Burial Ground Today

Eventually, so that the site could be appropriately memorialized, all plans to erect the four-story pavilion were scrubbed. On February 25, 1993, the New York City Landmarks Commission designated the site the African Burial Ground and the Commons Historical District. Later that year, the African Burial Ground achieved National Historic Landmark status.

Visitors are flocking to the African Burial Ground from around the world; at last count, more than 30,000 people have watched historical slide presentations and gone on laboratory and site tours. Some visitors have come all the way from Africa. Mme. Albertina Sisilu, at the time the only elected black member of parliament in South Africa, visited the African Burial Ground in late 1994. In a separate, private ceremony, a Yoruba priestess and a Kemet priest reenacted a West African ceremony while the excavations were still in progress, passing a newborn back and forth across the open excavation pits to symbolize the continuation of life.

Today, visitors to 290 Broadway are confronted by a striking memorial mosaic created by artist Roger Brown. Across the bottom are row after row of human skulls, a graphic reminder of those buried in the African Burial Ground. Above the skulls are honeycombed portraits of the multiple races that today populate New York City. Along the top of the mosaic are stylized depictions of New York landmarks such as the Brooklyn Bridge and the Empire State Building. Nearby, on the facade of the Federal Office Building stands the Clyde Lynds relief sculpture "America Song," which combines reinforced concrete and stainless steel with fiber optic light in a tribute to those still buried below.

Guided tours and videotapes of the African Burial Ground project are now available through the Office of Public Education and Interpretation of the African Burial Ground, which is actively engaged in bringing the findings to a broader public. Public educators deliver slide presentations both on- and off-site. Symposia and workshops are held to discuss the significance of the African Burial Ground, and a quarterly newsletter keeps the community apprised of the ongoing research

A Yoruba priestess, and Hru Ankh Ra Semahj Se Ptah, a Kemet priest, pass a newborn child back and forth over a recently excavated grave at the African Burial Ground. This West African custom symbolizes the continuation of life.

programs. The African Burial Ground Archival Center screens related films and sponsors internships and volunteer programs. Sherrill D. Wilson, an anthropologist of African American descent who directs this program, notes that the sudden involvement of black scholars was "very revolutionary. . . . [Such scholarship] is going to set a precedent for what happens to African burial grounds in the future and how African heritage will be viewed by the public."

This episode, which began with straightforward archaeological excavations at an eighteenth-century cemetery, evolved into a story about African American empowerment—a watershed occurrence in the larger struggle of descendant communities attempting to reclaim their heritage. Furthermore, the archaeological record remains a chilling reminder that New York City has been free soil for less than half of its history.

Archaeology in Indian Country

Although there is a long history of archaeologists working with (and sometimes for) Indian tribes, the last decade has seen a dramatic increase in such

---

In Their Own Words

Contrasting Views of "Significance" at Zuni Pueblo by Roger Anyon and T. J. Ferguson

Cultural resources management (CRM) in the USA is conducted under a patchwork of legal and regulatory mandates promulgated by people educated, working, and living in a Euroamerican cultural milieu—rather than being informed by Zuni values. The differing cultural views of archaeological sites and of human burials are instructive.

As viewed by archaeologists, and enshrined in federal regulatory language, archaeological sites are valued for their potential to inform about the past: sites are abandoned inanimate things from which information can be extracted.

As viewed by Zunis, archaeological sites are an essential link to the land, their ancestors, their culture and traditions: sites embody life forces. Religious offerings made when sites were established and lived in, and when they were left during the tribe's migrations, still have power and significance in present day Zuni religion. Zunis have no concept of sites having been abandoned. Ancestral spirits continue to reside in these places, the stewards of the land that provide a temporal link to present day Zuni. . . .

In general, the Euroamerican view of cultural resources is restrictive, limiting them to archaeological remains and to those places actively used today in a cultural tradition. These small "cultural islands" within the larger landscape have a fixed significance. For Zunis cultural resources are any tangible or intangible aspect of the world that has meaning, regardless of when it was last active in any ceremony. Cessation of ritual activities at a shrine or disused trail for hundreds of years does not diminish its present cultural significance. Nor are cultural resources bounded for Zunis. How can one bound and separate a spring at which a deer drinks from the ancestral archaeological sites this deer visits to pay its respect to the spirits inhabiting that site?

interactions—archaeologists helping Native American communities establish their own archaeology programs and pursuing tribally defined archaeological objectives. Some Native American groups use archaeology to provide evidence relevant to land claims cases. Other Indian tribes are conducting archaeology to encourage tourism, to inform educational programs, and to preserve sacred sites on their own land. Some are sponsoring archaeological excavations in tandem with oral history programs, retrieving a past directly relevant to tribal members. Some Indian groups welcome the postprocessual interest in Native American religion, power, authority, and gender roles; others question whether these are appropriate areas of study.

Faron Nastacio, a Zuni tribal member, takes a tree-ring sample from a historic structure at Ojo Caliente, as part of a large-scale dendrochronology on the Zuni Indian Reservation.

In the Zuni view the entire landscape is a cultural resource, with no fixed boundaries and no fixed significance. Temporal and spatial contexts de-fine meaning and significance, and these may change— for example, by time of year, by virtue of the conduct of a particu-lar ceremony, or depending upon the landscape scale within which it is viewed.

ROGER ANYON and T. J. FERGUSON work for Heritage Resources Management Consultants, a private company in Tucson, Arizona, dedicated to assisting Indian tribes and governmental agencies manage cultural resources.

Indigenous groups throughout the world are defining their own connections with the past through archaeology. They want to contribute their perspectives and knowledge about their own cultures and histories, drawing on a variety of sources including oral tradition, and the knowledge of religious leaders and elders. Such inclusion and self-expression did not commonly occur under archaeology's processual agenda.

This is not to say, of course, that processualism per se made Indian participation impossible or that postprocessualism automatically ensures Native American participation. Indigenous people began participating in archaeology for multiple reasons, only one of which was the theoretical configuration of the field. The social, political, and civil right movements of the 1960s had a significant impact on scholarship and participation in it. Issues about the treatment of women and minorities—as subjects of study and as participants in various fields—emerged in tandem with the processual/postmodern dialogue.

And yet there are problems. Earlier in the chapter, we mentioned that the body of legislation related to cultural resource management is what fuels most of the archaeology currently conducted in this country. This legislation was framed by a consortium of professional archaeologists, historians, architects, and lawmakers, who hammered out the current definition of "significance" in the archaeological record.

But critics believe that the current approach to "significance," while perhaps adequately serving the archaeological community, falls flat in the real world. What if *significance* lies instead in the eye of the beholder? The legal framework of archaeolgoy in this country simply assumes that significance is *inherent* in historic properties. But many archaeologists today see major problems when CRM-style concepts of "significance" are applied to sites in Indian Country.

Conceptual difficulties such as this bring us to the final major topic of this volume. Archaeology—the study of the past through the systematic recovery and analysis of material remains—is a destructive process. We destroy parts of our past in order to learn about it. Western law holds that when you destroy something, you must first ask permission from the rightful owner.

Who is the rightful owner of America's archaeological record? Does archaeology belong to the American people at large, or only to those whose direct ancestors created that archaeology? This larger question—*who owns the American past?*—deserves a detailed examination because the answers will determine the nature of Americanist archaeology during the twenty-first century.

Who Owns America's Remote Past?

> *If you desecrate a white grave, you wind up sitting in prison. But desecrate an Indian grave, you get a Ph.D. The time has come for people to decide: Are we Indians part of this country's living culture or are we just here to supply museums with dead bodies?*
>
> WALTER ECHO-HAWK (PAWNEE), CIVIL RIGHTS ATTORNEY

In 1988, the Senate Select Committee on Indian Affairs was told by the American Association of Museums that 43,306 individual Native American skeletons were held in 163 United States museums. Native American representatives pointed out that although Indian people represent less than 1 percent of the U.S. population, their bones comprise more than 54 percent of the skeletal collection in the Smithsonian Institution. Many senators were shocked.

This testimony spurred the U.S. Senate into action and brought an end to decades of wrangling that pitted museums, universities, and federal agencies against Native American tribes. In 1990, Congress passed and President George Bush signed into law a piece of landmark legislation called the *Native American Graves Protection and Repatriation Act*–**NAGPRA** for short.

NAGPRA resonated throughout Indian Country. A significant triumph for Indian people, NAGPRA is important human rights legislation that permits the living to exercise traditional responsibilities toward the dead. NAGPRA also rocked the world of Americanist archaeology, forever changing the business of the past.

NAGPRA covers five basic areas of concern:

1. Protecting Indian graves on federal and tribal lands
2. Recognizing tribal authority over treatment of unmarked graves
3. Prohibiting the commercial selling of Native American dead bodies
4. Requiring an inventory and **repatriation** of human remains held by the federal government and institutions that receive federal funding
5. Requiring these same institutions to return inappropriately acquired sacred objects and other important communally owned property to Native American owners

NAGPRA requires all universities and museums receiving federal money to summarize and inventory objects of material culture. Then, once the items have been identified, the museum community is required to consult with appropriate Native American representatives regarding the "expeditious return" of funerary objects, sacred materials, and items of *cultural patrimony* (once owned communally by the entire tribe).

This legislation has mandated an intensive and continuing interaction between archaeologists and tribal representatives. At first, these interactions were colored with mutual mistrust and apprehension. For decades, many Native American people had felt uncomfortable visiting public museums where their cultural heritage was on display. Some Indian people saw NAGPRA as placing them on equal footing with museum and university officials. Other Native American representatives believed that NAGPRA unfairly favored the museum community, hindering native people in gaining control over materials that rightfully belong to them (and which never, in their view, should have left Indian land in the first place).

> *How would you feel if your grandmother's grave were opened and the contents were shipped back east to be boxed and warehoused with 31,000 others . . . and itinerant pothunters were allowed to ransack her house in search of "artifacts" with the blessing of the U.S. government? It is sick behavior. It is un-Christian. It is punishable by law.*
>
> WILLIAM TALLBULL (NORTHERN CHEYENNE ELDER)

The archaeologists, for their part, are wary of dissolving collections long held in the public trust; such procedure is contrary to every museum charter. Many museum collections contain pieces specifically commissioned for exhibit and for study purposes. Museums would argue that, far from robbing Native American people of their heritage, ethnographers and archaeologists attempted to preserve this heritage for the future and the common good.

But after an initial period of discomfort, some members of both archaeological and tribal communities are beginning to take a more positive view, looking on NAGPRA as a way to foster new collaboration and cooperation in the preservation of Native American traditions and scholarship. A number of repatriations have already taken place, with both sides working toward the common goal of "doing the right thing." A number of tribal museums have already opened, sometimes with the help and cooperation of the museum establishment.

NAGPRA, of course, covers not only artifacts, but also human remains. Not unexpectedly, this issue has touched off considerable controversy and ill feeling. The Native American community has become deeply involved in deciding what to do about the thousands of remains that resulted from the nineteenth-century practice of collecting Indian bones and skulls.

A century ago, a basic issue—esteem for the dead— underlay much of the resistance shown by Native people to their forcible removal from their traditional lands. For instance, when federal troops forced Cherokee and Choctaw people to move from their southeastern U.S. homeland to Oklahoma, some families dug up and took the bones of their relatives along on the bitter "Trail of Tears." The ancestral bones were reburied after arrival in Oklahoma.

At the very basic level, there is complete agreement: All archaeologists, no matter how concerned with preservation of scientific evidence, agree that the bones of known relatives should be returned to demonstrable descendants. The disagreement comes over what is "demonstrable," and the specifics of the NAGPRA legislation are still being hammered out.

At issue here, of course, is our perception of human remains. Many archaeologists call upon the long-standing social policy in America that emphasizes the common heritage of the citizenry. So viewed, the scientific community is responsible for understanding the human condition of all, including Indian people, ancient and living. By removing cultural materials from museums and reburying skeletal remains, selected elements of the common heritage are being removed from the public domain. A vocal minority views NAGPRA and the repatriation effort as the blatant destruction of archaeological collections. They urge archaeologists to stand up for their rights and duties as scientists.

> *It is most unpleasant work to steal bones from a grave, but what is the use, some-one has to do it.*
>
> FRANZ BOAS (1858–1942), "FATHER" OF AMERICAN ANTHROPOLOGY

This argument holds that as scientists, archaeologists are bound to an ethical system requiring honest reporting and preservation of the evidence. Repatriation and reburial efforts are viewed as "censorship," undermining the ability of scientists to inspect the work of others for errors and misinterpretations–a procedure basic to all modern science. This view holds that human remains contain vital scientific data and should be kept in the public domain. Other archaeologists–and most Indian people–feel otherwise.

Today, many seek to define a workable middle ground in the reburial and repatriation dispute. Passing judgment on anybody's values or beliefs is tricky business. But so long as people with very different religious beliefs and cultural backgrounds must coexist, some such assessment cannot be avoided. One of the key challenges for those charged with managing America's cultural resources is to find accommodation between the scientific and ethnic concerns.

Most modern archaeologists still resist the demand for universal repatriation; taken to their illogical extreme, these arguments would insist that every Picasso hang in Spain, that all da Vincis be repatriated to Italy, and that every archaeological artifact be returned to its country of origin.

Suppose, as many paleoanthropologists believe, that we are all descended from a single, very early African population. If all the world's population is actually descended from one African "Eve," do we all "own" any artifact of the human past that is more than 200,000 years old? And what would such ownership mean? Certainly not the right to go to Africa and, on our own, dig up million-year-old skulls: The African countries where such remains are found are too conscious of their importance to the history of humanity to allow most of us anywhere near them. For this reason, African nations closely control access to their ancient archaeological record. But perhaps we all have the right to make an interpretation of its meaning.

What about the archaeological site of L'Anse au Meadows, the important Viking settlement in Newfoundland, radiocarbon dated to about A.D. 900? Does L'Anse au Meadows "belong" to the Canadian people because the site is on Canadian soil? Or does the site "belong" to modern Scandinavians, whose ancestors lived there?

And what about actress Shirley MacLaine, who claims (quite sincerely from all accounts) that she's a reincarnated Inka princess. Should we seriously consider negotiating with Ms. MacLaine if she were to launch a "repatriation" claim for Inka gold held by museums?

The issue revolves around ownership of the past–not just the objects of the past, but also the broader perceptions of that past. Some would argue that all "scientific," "objective" archaeology is really just the imposition of Western ideals and dominant ideology upon minority people.

But, scientifically oriented archaeologists respond: Suppose that we accept American Indian, Black African, or Maori views of their own past as legitimate. How then can we deny those who believe in "crackpot archaeology" or the role of ancient astronauts in creating the great monuments of the past?

In truth, the answers to such difficult questions are fundamentally political. In most countries, science is still associated with a position of moral authority. Traditionally at least, scientists have been our teachers, with most people accepting most of their statements most of the time. For the greater part of this century, the world has believed in its scientists because they can make concrete predictions and demonstrate the consequences of their conclusions.

If one rejects the basic premises on which scientific reasoning is founded, then none of the rest is acceptable. This is the position of some Christians for whom the Bible is literally true: They believe the world was created 6,000 years ago—not millions— so human evolution is quite unacceptable. Many Native American people firmly believe in their own traditions that document their eternal presence in America. They reject scientific claims that Indian people are descended from the migrants who traveled across the Bering Strait from Asia.

Ownership of the past is thus impossible to divorce from our beliefs about it and who should write about it. There can be no single answer to such questions.

Looking Ahead at the Past

Today, I suspect that many (perhaps even most) archaeologists are sympathetic to the multiple voices being heard in modern archaeology. Most would agree that it's a good thing to have increased Native American participation in national archaeology meetings (even if some don't like the specific messages being delivered). Most archaeologists are glad that female voices are being increasingly included in the profession, their contributions openly recognized and rewarded (although some are uncomfortable with specific views being expressed by some feminists). And I also think that the upsurge of interest in fields such as African American and Hispanic American archaeology is a vital new direction in the field. These are all important new voices in Americanist archaeology at the millennium.

But there is a real question about the degree to which postmodern thought has penetrated the American psyche. To be sure, there is an increased level of tolerance for other opinions within the academic world of professional archaeology, the rest of social science, and the humanities. But how much of this is strictly academic fad and fancy?

As archaeology becomes increasingly inclusive, as previously disenfranchised groups are empowered and their voices heard, as power is more broadly and more democratically distributed, what is the message for the American public?

Will we continue to hear about the "death of authority"—or only the "death of *your* authority"? Will the new openness remain open, or will we experience the same old intolerance to different ideas, this time with power shifted from the traditional "haves" to the "have-nots"? The widespread call for multiple voices and diverse perspectives does not necessarily ensure tolerance for opinions that differ from one's own. Will the new inclusiveness turn out to be just a warmed-over version of the old exclusionism—dressed up in a different mix of racial, sexual, economic, and ideological dogma?

Archaeologists have special responsibilities here—not only to recover and interpret evidence of the human past, but also to ensure that the past is not used for malevolent purposes in the present. This is not an easy task because it requires that individual archaeologists balance and sort out the sometimes conflicting realities.

This, it seems, is perhaps the greatest challenge facing the archaeologists of the twenty-first century.

Summary

America is losing major parts of her cultural heritage, and archaeologists are today helping decide which part of the past we can save, and which parts we can do without.

Cultural resource management (CRM) is concerned with all kinds of historic buildings and structures (such as bridges), artifacts, documents, and, of course, archaeological sites. CRM is today the most influential force in Americanist archaeology. The raw bulk of archaeological work being done has shifted from the academic side to the private and government sectors. Currently, perhaps 90 percent of all archaeological research in the United States is related to providing such information about sites.

Today's applied archaeologists are tackling, on a daily basis, the future of the past: What does America's archaeological record really consist of? What must we study and protect for future benefit? What can we live without?

Compared with a decade or two ago, a much higher proportion of the graduate and undergraduate students specializing in archaeology are women. The numbers of men and women pursuing advanced training in archaeology today are nearly equal; women are apparently enjoying equivalent levels of success in school. Today, women comprise perhaps one-quarter of the fully employed archaeological workforce in America. Some experience a "chilly climate" in which female professional archaeologists find the field to be male-dominated, male-controlled, and male-oriented. Others believe that "times have changed."

Another important current trend is the emergent field of *African American archaeology*. Several contemporary forces have contributed to the emergence of this exciting new field: the emergence of black activism, the legislative emphasis on historic preservation (particularly in urban America), the stepped-up emphasis on ethnicity, and the realization that archaeologists need to be more involved in the public interpretation of historic-period artifacts.

Related to the issue of African American archaeology is the recent archaeological exploration of New York City's African Burial Ground, long-forgotten burial place for thousands. Perhaps more than any other site discussed in this book, the African Burial Ground illustrates the interplay of science, community involvement, ethnic pride, and sociopolitical reality.

Finally, there is the overall issue of "Who Owns the American Past?"—a thread that runs through this entire book. After considering a number of international repatriation claims, we examine in some detail the impact of recent U.S. legislation that addresses the relationship between archaeological research and Native American communities.

As archaeologists face the millennium, they have increasingly important and sensitive responsibilities—not only to recover and interpret evidence of the human past, but also to ensure that the past is not used for inappropriate purposes in the present.

More Archaeology on the Internet

Preserve/Net is a resource for preservationists, planners and architects.

> http://www.preservenet.cornell.edu/preserv1.htm

Preserve/Net Index lists information on preservation education, conferences, employment, and organizations. The PNLS aids lawyers, activists, and owners in understanding the laws relating to preservation.

> http://www.preservenet.cornell.edu/

African Burial Ground news is available on the Internet.

> http://www.afrinet.net/~hallh/abg.html

African-American Archaeology is the newsletter of the African-American Archaeology Network.

> http://www.newsouthassoc.com

Bibliography: Slavery and African-American History is another Web site with useful information.
http://www.monticello.org
http://earth.library.pitt.edu/%7Ehilmlib/afro/afamerican.html

Repatriation and Reburial Issues are monitored at this Web site, including a legal summary, consideration of case studies, ethics codes, state laws, organizations, bibliographies, and articles.

> http://www.uiowa.edu/~anthro/reburial/repat.htm

Glossary

❏ ❏ ❏

absolute date: See *dating, absolute.*

A.C.: Literally "after Christ"; basically means the same as "A.D."

accelerator mass spectrometric (AMS) technique: A relatively new method of radio-carbon dating that counts the proportion of carbon isotopes directly (rather than using the indirect Geiger counter method), thereby dramatically reducing the quantity of datable material required.

Acheulean: Named for the site of St. Acheul in northern France, a cultural tradition dating from more than 1 million years ago to about 100,000 B.P. Acheulean artifacts are known throughout Africa, across Europe, and into India.

achieved status: See *status, achieved.*

A.D.: Stands for *anno Domini,* literally meaning "in the year of the Lord," indicating that a time division falls within the Christian era. Written with the abbreviation before the year (e.g., A.D. 1560).

adaptive strategy: A research perspective that emphasizes technology, ecology, demography, and economics in the definition of human behavior.

Americanist archaeology: The brand of archaeology that evolved in close association with anthropology in the Americas; it is practiced throughout the world.

amino acid racemization: A dating technique that utilizes postmortem changes in proteins to estimate age at death; it has commonly been applied to bones and eggshells from archaeological sites.

anthropological linguistics: A subdiscipline of anthropology that emphasizes the relationships between cultural behavior and language.

anthropology: The study of all aspects of humankind, extant and extinct, employing an all-encompassing holistic approach.

antiquarian: An eighteenth- and nineteenth-century term for someone who collects antiquities.

arbitrary level: The basic vertical subdivision of an excavation square; used only when easily recognizable "natural" stratification is lacking.

archaeobotany: The recovery and identification of plant remains in archaeological contexts; the term *archaeobotanist* refers to all such specialists, regardless of their discipline.

archaeological context: See *context, archaeological.*

archaeological site: Any concentration of artifacts, features, or ecofacts manufactured or modified by humans.

archaeology: The study of the human past through the systematic recovery and analysis of material culture.

archaic state: A centralized political system found in complex societies, characterized by having a virtual monopoly on the power to coerce.

argon-argon dating method: A new method to date the age of key volcanic deposits. This high-precision method also allows investigators to focus on single volcanic crystals, which can be dated one by one; thus any older contaminants can be discarded.

artifact: Any movable object that has been used, modified, or manufactured by humans.

ascribed status: See *status, ascribed.*

atlatl: A throwing stick used as an extension of the arm to propel a dart shaft through the air.

australopithecine: A genus of small-brained, bipedal fossil hominid that lived between 2 million and 3.75 million years ago.

B.C.:   Literally "before Christ," indicating that a time division falls before the Christian era. Written with the abbreviation after the year (e.g., 3200 B.C.).

bioarchaeology: The study of the human biological component evident in the archaeological record.

biodegradation: Decomposition of trash through the action of microorganisms.

biological anthropology: A subdiscipline of anthropology that views humans as biological organisms; also known as *physical anthropology.*

Boucher de Perthes, Jacques: A nineteenth-century controller of customs at Abbeville (France), who discovered ancient axeheads in the river gravels of the Somme River, in association with the bones of mammals long extinct.

B.P.:   Literally "before present." Many archaeologists feel more comfortable avoiding the A.D./B.C. split altogether, substituting the single "before present" age estimate (with the calendar year A.D. 1950 arbitrarily selected as the zero point). By this convention, A.D. 1560 becomes 390 B.P.

bridging argument: Logical statements linking observations on the static archaeological record to the dynamic behavior that produced it.

charnel house: A ritual house or chamber in which human corpses and/or isolated bones are deposited.

chiefdom: A regional polity in which one or more local groups are organized under a single leader (chief) who heads a ranked hierarchy of people.

circumscription theory: A hypothesis associated with Robert Carneiro that suggests that warfare, as a result of increasing population density and environmental (and social) circumscription, led to the development of the state.

civilization: A complex urban society, with a high level of survival and reproductive success of individuals or groups best adjusted to their environment, leading to a perpetuation of genetic qualities best suited for a particular environment.

Clovis culture: The oldest well documented occupation of the Americas (consistently dating 9500–8500 B.C.). The name comes from an important site near Clovis, New Mexico, where Paleo-Indian artifacts were first found in stratigraphic association (beneath diagnostic Folsom artifacts).

coevolution: A theory of cultural evolution that suggests that changes in social systems are best understood as mutual selection among components rather than a linear cause-and-effect sequence. See also *natural selection* and *selectionist explanation.*

cognitive archaeology: The study of all those aspects of ancient culture that are the product of the human mind: the perception, description, and classification of the universe; the nature of the supernatural; the principles, philosophies, ethics, and values by which human societies are governed; the ways in which aspects of the world, the supernatural, or human values are conveyed in art.

component: A culturally homogeneous stratigraphic unit within an archaeological site.

conjunctive approach: As defined by Walter W. Taylor, an approach that emphasizes defining the explicit connection of archaeological objects with their cultural contexts.

conservation archaeology: A movement in contemporary archaeology that explicitly recognizes archaeological sites as nonrenewable resources.

context, archaeological: Artifacts, features, and residues as found in the archaeological record.

context, systemic: Artifacts, features, and residues as they functioned in the behavioral system that produced or used them.

coprolites: Dessicated feces.

cosmology: A cosmological explanation that demonstrates how the universe developed—both in totality and its constituent parts—and also what principles keep it together.

cultural anthropology: A subdiscipline of anthropology, emphasizing nonbiological aspects—the learned social, linguistic, technological, and familial behaviors of humans.

cultural chronology: An archaeological approach that documents temporal and spatial change through the analysis of selected artifacts.

cultural deposition: The transformation of materials from a systemic to an archaeological context. Cultural deposition processes constitute the dominant factor in forming the archaeological record. For example, when a pottery vessel is broken and discarded on the trash heap, it has ceased to function in the behavioral system and becomes incorporated in its new archaeological context: This is cultural deposition.

cultural materialism: A research strategy that assumes that technological, economic, and ecological processes—the modes of production and reproduction—lie at the causal heart of every sociocultural system; largely associated with the research of Marvin Harris.

cultural process: The cause-and-effect cultural relationships not bound by time and space; the "why" of culture and the ultimate aim of Americanist archaeology.

cultural relativism: The view that cultures are different, with no one cultural perspective better or worse than another.

cultural resource management (CRM):   The conservation and carefully planned investigation of archaeological materials; generally refers to efforts to safeguard remains of the past through legislation and applied archaeology.

cultural system: The nonbiological mechanism that relates the human organism to its physical and social environments; one shares cultural traits but participates in the overall cultural system.

culture: The nonbiological mechanism of human adaptation. E. B. Tylor's (1871) definition of culture appeared on the first page of anthropology's first textbook: "Culture . . . taken in its wide ethnographic sense is that complex whole which includes knowledge, belief, art, morals, law, custom, and any other capabilities and habits acquired by man as a member of society."

data: Relevant observations made on objects, which then serve as the basis for study and discussion.

dating, absolute: Dates expressed as specific units of scientific measurement, such as days, years, centuries, or millennia; absolute determinations attempt to pinpoint a discrete, known interval in time.

dating, relative: Dates expressed through relativistic relationships, such as "earlier," "later," "more recent," "after Noah's flood," "prehistoric," and so on.

datum point: The zero point, a fixed reference used to keep vertical control on a dig. Combining this with the grid system, an archaeologist can plot any find in three dimensions.

deconstruction: A philosophy of trying to understand how meaning is constructed by writers, texts, and readers.

deductive reasoning: Reasoning from theory to account for specific observational or experimental results.

dendrochronology: Tree-ring dating.

dental hypoplasias: Growth arrest lines in teeth, usually formed from birth to 6 years of age.

depositional process: The transformation of materials from a systemic to an archaeological context. Such processes are directly responsible for the accumulation of archaeological sites, and they constitute the dominant factor in forming the archaeological record.

dialectical approach: A perspective emphasizing the tension or opposition between two interacting social forces or elements.

direct historical approach: A general technique for extending knowledge of the historical period into the past. Carefully done, this procedure allows documentary evidence to be cautiously applied to archaeological data from the more ancient past, *provided* a linkage can be established between the historical and ancient cultures.

direct percussion: A flintknapping technique that involves hitting a core (or flake) with a stone (or antler) hammer.

disturbance process: Changing the contexts of materials within the archaeological site itself. Examples include such diverse mechanisms as dam building, farming, and heavy construction, as well as noncultural activities such as freeze–thaw cycles, landslides, and simple erosion.

DNA (deoxyribonucleic acid):   The characteristic double-stranded molecule found in all living cells that encodes specific genetic information.

doctrine of uniformitarianism: An assertion that the proceses now operating to modify the earth's surface are the same processes that operated long ago in the geological past. This simple premise provides the cornerstone of modern geology.

ecofact: The nonartifactual remains found in archaeological sites, such as seeds, bones, and plant pollen.

ecological niche: The functional role of a species within a community; not only where that organism lives, but also what it does and eats and how it responds to the environment.

ecology: The study of entire assemblages of living organisms and their physical milieus, which together constitute an integrated system.

egalitarian society: A society in which the number of valued statuses is roughly equivalent to the number of persons with the ability to fill them.

emic: A term referring to anthropological concepts and distinctions that are somehow meaningful, significant, accurate, or "appropriate" to the participants in a given culture.

empathetic explanation: A view that reconstructs not only thoughts and decisions, but also elements such as affective states, spiritual orientations, and experiential meanings.

ethnoarchaeology: The study of contemporary peoples to determine how their behavior is translated into the archaeological record.

ethnocentrism: The belief that one's own ethnic group is superior to all others.

ethnographer: One who performs a primarily descriptive study of living people.

ethnology: That branch of anthropology dealing chiefly with the comparative and analytical study of cultures.

etic: Concepts and distinctions that are meaningful and appropriate to the community of scientific observers.

experimental archaeology: A means of studying archaeological process through experimental reconstructions of necessary conditions.

faunal analysis: The study of animal remains from archaeological sites to illustrate past hunting and dietary practices.

feature: The nonportable evidence of technology. Usually refers to fire hearths, architectural elements, artifact clusters, garbage pits, and soil stains.

flintknapping: The art of manufacturing stone tools.

flotation: The use of fluid suspension to recover tiny plant and bone fragments from archaeological sites.

flute: Distinctive thinning flake or flakes evident on Folsom and Clovis projectile points.

Folsom culture: A Paleo-Indian manifestation, dating about 9000–7000 B.C., distributed throughout much of North America.

gender: The culturally specific elaborations and meanings attached to sexual (biological) differences.

gender ideology: The culturally specific meaning assigned to terms such as "male," "female," "sex," and "reproduction."

gender role: The differential participation of males and females in the various social, economic, political, and religious institutions of a given cultural group; such roles describe appropriate behavior for gender categories.

general evolution: The overall advance or progression, stage by stage, as measured in absolute terms; the evolution from heterogeneity toward homogeneity.

grid system: The two-dimensional intersecting network defining the squares in which archaeologists dig; usually laid in with strings, stakes, and a transit.

ground-penetrating radar: Remote sensing device that transmits a radar pulse into the soil. When a discontinuity is encountered, an echo returns to the radar receiving unit, where it can be interpreted.

half-life: The time required for half of the C-14 available in an organic sample to decay.

Harris lines: Bands of increased bone density, often caused by nutritional stressors, especially severe and short-run dietary deprivation. Observable on X rays, Harris lines generally show up between birth and 18 years.

high-level (or general) theory: The overarching framework for understanding the human condition. General theory applies to all intellectual inquiry about human beings; it is not restricted to archaeology.

historical archaeology: As defined by Kathleen Deagan, "the study of human behavior through material remains, for which written history in some way affects its interpretation." (See Deagan 1982, p. 153.)

historical particularism: The view that each culture is the product of a unique sequence of developments in which chance plays a major role to bring about cultural change.

Hohokam: A long-lived cultural tradition centered in the deserts of southern Arizona and northern Sonora, Mexico. Four cultural periods subdivide the Hohokam tradition: Pioneer (A.D. 1–725), Colonial (A.D. 725–1000), Sedentary (A.D. 1000–1100), and Classic (A.D. 1100–1450).

Homo erectus: Human ancestor that lived between 0.5 million and 1.6 million years ago.

humanism: A doctrine, attitude, or way of life featuring human interests or values. In general, the humanistic approach tends to reject supernaturalism and stress the individual's value, dignity, and capacity for self-realization through reason.

hypothesis: A statement that goes beyond bare description; a suggestion that must be tested on independent evidence.

iconography: The study of how people use art forms to represent their religious, political, ideological, or cosmological beliefs.

ideational strategy: The research perspective that defines ideas, symbols, and mental structures as driving forces in shaping human behavior.

ideology: A systematic body of concepts and beliefs.

index fossil concept: A theory that proposes that strata containing similar fossil assemblages will tend to be of similar age. In archaeology, this concept enables archaeologists to characterize and date strata within archaeological sites using diagnostic artifact forms.

indirect percussion: A flintknapping term, referring to the use of a punch, placed between the object being flaked (core or flake) and the hammer.

inductive reasoning: Working from specific observations to more general hypotheses.

infrastructural determinism, principle of: A research strategy used by cultural materialists, in which causal priority is assigned to the modes of production and reproduction. Technological, demographic, ecological, and economic processes become the independent variable, and the social system is the dependent variable. Domestic and political subsystems (the "structure") are considered to be secondary; values, aesthetics, rituals, religion, philosophy, rules, and symbols (the "superstructure") all are tertiary.

infrastructure: Those elements considered by cultural materialists to be the most important to satisfying basic human needs; the demographic, technological, economic, and ecological processes (the modes of production and reproduction) assumed to lie at the causal heart of every sociocultural system.

in situ: A term referring to the position in which an item is initially encountered during excavation or survey.

kill site: The place where animals are dispatched and where primary disarticulation takes place.

kinship: Socially recognized relationships based on real or imagined descent and marriage patterns.

law of superposition: The principle that states that in any pile of sedimentary rocks that have not been disturbed by folding or overturning, the strata on the bottom will have been deposited first.

low-level archaeological theory: Baseline observations (data) that emerge from hands-on archaeological fieldwork.

Magdalenian: The last major culture of the European Upper Paleolithic period (ca. 16,000–10,000 B.C.); named after the rock shelter La Madeleine, in southwestern France. Magdalenian artisans crafted intricately carved tools of reindeer bone and antler; this was also the period during which Upper Paleolithic cave art in France and Spain reached its zenith.

Mesolithic: The Middle Stone Age; a period of transition from hunting and gathering to agriculture, featuring settlements based on broad-spectrum wild resource exploitation.

mestizo: A person of mixed blood (particularly used to denote mixed European and Native American ancestry); the female form is *mestiza.*

midden: Refuse deposit resulting from human activities, generally consisting of soil, food remains such as animal bone and shell, and discarded artifacts.

middle-level theory: Investigation aimed at linking the static data from the archaeological record with the dynamic processes that formed it.

Middle Paleolithic: Generic grouping for those cultures that flourished between about 35,000 and 100,000 B.P.; the best-known such tradition is termed *Mousterian,* the culture carried by Neanderthals.

minimum number of individuals (MNI): The fewest number of individual animals necessary to account for all the skeletal elements of a particular species found in a faunal assemblage.

Mississippian: A widespread cultural tradition across much of the eastern United States from A.D. 800–1500. Mississippian societies engaged in intensive village-based maize horticulture and constructed large, earthen platform mounds that served as substructures for temples, residences, and council buildings.

mitochondrial DNA (mtDNA): Genetic material found outside the cell nucleus. More robust than nuclear DNA, mtDNA is easier to find in ancient sources; inherited only through the maternal line.

modernist thinking: A philosophy that embodies a systematic, clinical, single-minded approach, emphasizing linear progress and goal-oriented behavior, ultimately seeking a carefully crafted finished product.

molecular archaeology: Study of the human past, conducted at the level of the individual molecule. This newly emergent field addresses the ultimate physiochemical organization of life, focusing particularly on the molecular basis of human inheritance.

Although less than a decade old, molecular archaeology has already racked up some spectacular successes, providing unexpectedly precise answers to questions long explored through more conventional approaches.

moraine: Distinctive deposits of glacial debris.

Mousterian: A culture from the Middle Paleolithic period (Middle Old Stone Age) that appeared throughout Europe between about 180,000 and 30,000 years ago (named after the Le Moustier rock shelter in southwestern France). Mousterian artifacts are frequently associated with Neanderthal human remains.

NAGPRA: The Native American Graves Protection and Repatriation Act (NAGPRA) of 1990, devised to protect Native American burial sites and to return certain kinds of religious materials removed from Indian land. Most Indian people view this statute as an important initial step in reversing the transgression against Native Americans over the last 500 years.

natural selection: A natural process resulting in changes in a social system that is best understood as mutual selection among components rather than a linear cause-and-effect sequence. See also *coevolution* and *selectionist explanation*.

Neolithic: The New Stone Age, during which self-sufficient agriculture developed; commonly characterized by use of polishing and grinding stones, and the use of ceramics.

new archaeology: A label commonly associated with Lewis R. Binford and his students, emphasizing the importance of understanding underlying cultural processes; today's version of the new archaeology is sometimes called the *processual agenda*.

nonresidential group: An abstract, often symbolic, association of individuals formed to regulate some specific aspect of society. Such "groups" do not necessarily ever convene.

nuclear DNA: Genetic information stored in the cell nucleus and inherited from both parents. Because it degrades fairly quickly, nuclear DNA is not useful for studying ancient genetic patterning.

number of identified specimens (NISP):   A largely outdated measure of sample size in archaeological fauna.

objectivity: The attempt to observe things as they actually are, without prejudging or falsifying observations in light of some preconceived view of the world—reducing subjective factors to a minimum.

obsidian: Volcanic glass often used as raw material for the manufacture of stone tools.

obsidian hydration dating: The technique of dating obsidian artifacts by measuring the microscopic amount of water absorbed on fresh surfaces.

O'odham: Native American group living in the Sonoran Desert in the Gila and Salt River valleys, near modern Phoenix, Arizona. The O'odham speak a Piman language; the names *Pima* and *Papago* are commonly used to designate the O'odham people.

optimal foraging theory: A broad-based theoretical perspective used in evolutionary biology that attempts to develop a set of models general enough to apply to a broad range of animal species, yet rigorous and precise enough to explain the details of behavior exhibited by a particular forager.

oracle: A shrine in which a deity reveals hidden knowledge or divine purpose.

osteology: The branch of anatomy dealing with bones.

paleoethnobotany: Analysis and interpretation of interrelationships between people and plants from evidence in the archaeological record.

Paleo-Indian: A term applied to late Pleistocene and early Holocene (ca. 13,000–8,000 B.P.) cultural tradition found throughout much of North America.

paleopathology: Analysis of the cause, nature, and distribution of disease using evidence recovered from archaeological sites.

palimpsest: A parchment or tablet that has been erased and subsequently reused (sometimes multiple times).

palynology: The techniques through which the fossil pollen grains and spores from archaeological sites are studied.

phase: An archaeological construct possessing traits sufficiently characteristic to distinguish it from other units similarly conceived; spatially limited to roughly a locality or region and chronologically limited to a relatively brief interval of time.

physical anthropology: A subdiscipline of anthropology that views humans as biological organisms.

phytolith: Tiny silica particle contained in plants. Sometimes these fragments can be recovered from archaeologial sites, even after the plants themselves have decayed.

plant macrofossil: The preserved or carbonized plant parts recovered from archaeological sites.

pluralism: A theory that there are multiple kinds of ultimate reality. Pluralism is also commonly used to depict a society in which members of diverse ethnic, racial, religious, or social groups continue to participate in their traditional culture or special interest within today's nearly global culture.

polymerase chain reaction (PCR):   A laboratory technique for rapidly synthesizing large quantities of a given DNA segment. PCR methodology enables researchers to make millions (or even billions) of copies of a very small sample of mtDNA, so that this genetic material can be more readily studied.

postmodernist interpretivism: A philosophy with emphasis on empathetic approaches and multiple pathways of belief that sometimes produce indeterminate end products.

postmodernist thinking: A philosophy that embodies an emphathetic, playful, dissociated series of approaches, emphasizing multiple and sometimes fragmented pathways toward indeterminate, decentralized, transitory performances.

postprocessual critique: The strategy of postmodern interpretivism as applied to the past, emphasizing empathetic approaches and multiple pathways of belief, producing sometimes indeterminate end products. The postprocessual critique has fundamentally changed the way the world views archaeology and has shaped the direction of contemporary Americanist archaeology.

potassium-argon dating: An absolute dating technique that monitors the decay of potassium (K-40) into argon gas (Ar-40).

prehistoric: The time period before the appearance of written records.

primary refuse: Archaeological debris in the context where it was used and discarded.

processual agenda: The view that explains social, economic, and cultural change as primarily the result of internal dynamics (processes). Materialistic conditions are assumed to take causal priority over ideational factors in explaining change.

proton precession magnetometer: An instrument used to measure the strength of magnetism between the earth's magnetic core and the sensor, used in remote sensing.

provenience: In general, where an artifact came from. In the context of a specific site, it refers to the horizontal and vertical position of an object in relation to the established coordinate system.

quagga: A recently extinct zebra-like African beast.

racemization: See *amino acid racemization*.

radiocarbon (carbon-14) dating technique: A physiochemical method of estimating the length of time since the death of an organism.

ranked society: A society in which there is unequal access to the higher-status categories, and thus many people who are qualified for high-status positions are unable to achieve them.

reclamation process: The transition of cultural materials from the archaeological record back into the systemic context, such as the scavenging of archaeological artifacts for reuse by both nonindustrial and industrial peoples. The act of archaeological excavation is itself reclamation.

reflexive: Looking back on oneself. In anthropology, a reflexive approach explicitly recognizes the interaction between the anthropologist and the culture being studied.

relative date: See *dating, relative*.

remote sensing: The battery of nondestructive techniques used in geophysical prospection and to generate archaeological data without the need for excavation.

repatriate: To restore or return control to the rightful place of origin, allegiance, or citizenship.

residential group: A relatively permanent physical agglomeration of people, such as a domestic family or household, territorial band, or community-level village.

reuse process: The transformation of materials through successive states within the behavioral system. Potsherds, for example, are sometimes ground up to be used for manufacturing new vessels.

schlepp effect: The result of a butchering process in which the meat is piled on the skin and the lower limb bones are used to drag home the hide bearing the meat. When this is done, the upper limb bones are discarded at the kill site, and the lower limb bones are found more commonly at the habitation site.

science: The search for universals in nature by means of established scientific methods of inquiry.

scientific method: Accepted principles and procedures for the systematic pursuit of secure knowledge. Established scientific procedures involve the following steps: defining a relevant problem; establishing one or more hypotheses; determining the empirical implications of the above; collecting appropriate data through observation and/or experiment; comparing these data with the expected implications; and revising and/or retesting hypotheses as necessary.

seasonality: An estimate of when during the year a particular archaeological site was occupied.

secondary refuse: Artifacts, bone, shell, and other habitation debris discarded away from the immediate area of use.

sedimentary: In geology, rock formed by the accumulation and consolidation of mineral and particulate matter deposited by water action (or, less commonly, wind or glacial ice).

selectionist explanation: The view that human societies have evolved culturally in accord with the process governing biological evolution, namely *natural selection.* For instance, David Rindos has argued that the origins of agriculture are best understood by exploring the evolutionary forces affecting the development of domestication systems. Viewed this way, domestication is not seen as an evolutionary stage, but rather as a process; it is the result of interactions between humans and plants.

seriation: A temporal ordering of artifacts based on the assumption that cultural styles (fads) change and that the popularity of a particular style or decoration can be associated with a certain time period.

sex: The biological differences that distinguish between males and females.

shaman: One who has the power to contact the spirit world through trance, possession, or visions. On the basis of this ability, the shaman invokes, manipulates, or coerces the power of the spirits for socially recognized ends—both good and ill.

Shroud of Turin: A sheet of twill-woven linen cloth on which appears a pale sepia-tone image of the front and back of a naked man about 6 feet tall; pale carmine stains of blood mark wounds to the head, side, hands, and feet. The shroud was alleged to be the actual cloth in which Christ's crucified body was wrapped.

social Darwinism: The extension of the principles of Darwinian evolution to social phenomena. The implication is that conflict and competition between societies (and between classes of the same society) has a beneficial effect in long-term human evolution. Social Darwinism has three basic premises: (1) belief that rapid elimination of "unfit" individuals will benefit society; (2) confidence in laissez-faire economics, whereby a society's economic system functions best when the state keeps "hands off," allowing the fittest business enterprises to survive and the unfit to go under; and (3) reliance on warfare as the chief way in which natural selection operates on societies (thus warfare is seen as having had an enormous role in the rise of the state and various other social, political, economic, and religious organizations).

social organization: The structural organization of a society. It is first divided into smaller social units, called *groups.* Second, it has recognized social positions, or *statuses,* and appropriate behavior patterns for these positions, or *roles.*

social persona: The composite of the several identities maintained by a single individual. Which identity is currently operating depends on those with whom the individual is interacting. This all-encompassing social persona is reflected in the archaeological record, along with individual status categories such as sex and age.

soil resistivity: A remote sensing technique that monitors the degree of electrical resistance in soils—which often depends on the amount of moisture present—in a restricted volume near the surface. Buried features are usually detected by the differential retention of groundwater.

sondage: A test excavation unit.

Southeastern Ceremonial Complex: See *Southern cult.*

Southern cult: A ceremonial complex widely distributed throughout the American Southeast in Mississippian times, characterized by distinctive motifs such as the cross, the sun circle, the swastika, and the forked eye; also known as the Southeastern Ceremonial Complex.

specific evolution: The increasing adaptive specializations that improve the chances for survival of species, cultures, or individuals.

standard deviation: A statistical estimate of consistency (or the lack of it). When applied to radiocarbon dating, the standard deviation compares the various "counting runs" performed at the laboratory. Read as "plus or minus," the standard deviation (or "sigma") is a projection of the error of estimate. Because of their random, statistical nature, radiocarbon dates cannot be precise.

status: The rights and duties associated with a particular social position; sometimes called *social identities.*

status, achieved: Social rights and duties attributed to individuals through competition and individual effort, rather than inherited social position.

status, ascribed: Social rights and duties attributed to an individual at birth, regardless of ability or achievement.

stratigraphy: An analytical interpretation of the structure produced by the deposition of geological and/or cultural sediments into layers, or strata.

stratum: More or less homogeneous or gradational material, visually separable from other levels by a discrete change in the character of the material being deposited or a sharp break in deposition (or both).

stress: Any environmental factor that forces an individual or population out of equilibrium. Some effects of stress can be observed in human bone tissue.

structure: A domestic and political system assumed by the cultural materialist to be causally conditioned by infrastructure.

superstructure: The values, aesthetics, rules, beliefs, religions, and symbols assumed by cultural materialists to be causally conditioned by infrastructure.

symbiosis: The intimate living together of two dissimilar organisms.

systemic context: See *context, systemic.*

taphonomy: The study of processes that operate on organic remains after death to form fossil and archaeological deposits. The term combines the Greek word for "tomb" or "burial" *(taphos)* with that for "law" *(nomos).*

temporal type: A morphological type that has been shown to have temporal significance; also known as a *time-marker.*

tephra: Volcanic ash.

tephrochronology: Analysis of undisturbed beds of volcanic ash (tephra) with the aim of constructing a temporal sequence.

test pit: A small exploratory sounding designed to determine a site's depth and stratigraphy, preparatory to full-scale excavation.

testability: The degree to which one's observations and experiments can be reproduced.

time-marker: A temporally significant class of artifacts defined by a consistent clustering of attributes.

time slice: An analytical method for synthesizing the various ground-penetrating radar passes at a specific vertical level. Time slices can be made at various radar-scan depths, creating remotely sensed site plans for various depths below the ground surface—and all based strictly on nondestructive data.

transect sampling strategy: A research design in which investigators search for archaeological evidence within square or rectangular domains.

tree-ring dating: The use of annual growth rings in trees to date archaeological sites; also called *dendrochronology*.

type: A class of archaeological artifacts defined by a consistent clustering of attributes.

typology: The systematic arrangement of material culture into types.

uniformitarianism, doctrine of: See *doctrine of uniformitarianism*.

unilinear cultural evolution: The belief that human societies have evolved culturally along a single developmental trajectory. Typically, such schemes depict Western civilization as the most advanced evolutionary stage.

Upper Paleolithic: The last major division of the Old World Paleolithic, beginning about 40,000 years ago and lasting until the end of the Pleistocene (ca. 10,000 years ago). This is the period during which modern humans replaced Neanderthals.

wattle-and-daub: A building technique using a wooden framework (the wattle) that has been plastered (or daubed) with a mixture of mud, sand, and plant fibers.

Zinjanthropus: The now-abandoned term applied by Louis Leakey to a robust *Australopithecus* found at Olduvai Gorge in 1959.

Bibliography

◻ ◻ ◻

Abbott, James T., and Charles D. Frederick. 1990. Proton magnetometer investigations of burned rock middens in West-Central Texas: Clues to formation processes. *Journal of Archaeological Science* 17: 535–545.

Adams, William Y., and Ernest W. Adams. 1991. *Archaeological Typology and Practical Reality: A Dialectical Approach to Artifact Classification and Sorting.* Cambridge: Cambridge University Press.

Adler, Michael A. (Ed.). 1996. *The Prehistoric Pueblo World: A.D. 1150–1350.* Tucson: University of Arizona Press.

Adler, Michael A., Todd Van Pool, and Robert D. Leonard. 1996. Ancestral Pueblo population aggregation and abandonment in the North American Southwest. *Journal of World Prehistory* 10(3): 375–438.

Adovasio, J. M., and Ronald C. Carlisle. 1988. Some thoughts on cultural resource management archaeology in the United States. *Antiquity* 62(234): 72–87.

Adovasio, J. M., J. Donahue, and R. Stuckenrath. 1990. The Meadowcroft Rockshelter radiocarbon chronology 1975–1990. *American Antiquity* 55(2): 348–354.

Aitken, M. J. 1989. Luminescence dating: A guide for non-specialists. *Archaeometry* 31(2): 147–159.

———. 1990. *Science-Based Dating in Archaeology.* London: Longman.

Aldenderfer, Mark. 1993. Ritual, hierarchy, and change in foraging societies. *Journal of Anthropological Archaeology* 12(1): 1–40.

Anderson, E. N. 1995. Keeping the anthropological bird aloft. *Anthropology Newsletter* 36(9): 2.

Andresen, John M., Brian F. Byrd, Mark D. Elson, Randall H. McGuire, Ruben G. Mendoza, Edward Staski, and J. Peter White. 1981. The deer hunters: Star Carr reconsidered. *World Archaeology* 13(1): 31–46.

Anyon, Roger, and T. J. Ferguson. 1995. Cultural resources management at the Pueblo of Zuni, New Mexico, USA. *Antiquity* 69: 913–930.

Arden, H. 1989. Who owns our past? *National Geographic Magazine* 175(3): 376–392.

Arnold, Jeanne E. 1993. Labor and the rise of complex hunter-gatherers. *Journal of Anthropological Archaeology* 12(1): 75–119.

Avery, T. E., and T. R. Lyons. 1981. *Remote Sensing: Aerial and Terrestrial Photography for Archaeologists.* Washington, DC: National Park Service, Supplement 7.

Babcock, Barbara A., and Nancy J. Parezo. 1988. *Daughters of the Desert: Women Anthropologists and the Native American Southwest 1880–1980.* Albuquerque: University of New Mexico Press.

Bacus, Elisabeth A., Alex W. Barker, Jeffrey D. Bonevich, Sandra L. Dunavan, J. Benjamin Fitzhugh, Debra L. Gold, Nurit S. Goldman-Finn, William Griffin, and Karen M. Mudar (Eds.). 1993. *A Gendered Past: A Critical Bibliography of Gender in Archaeology*. Technical Report 25. Ann Arbor: University of Michigan, Museum of Anthropology.

Baillie, M. G. L. 1995. *A Slice Through Time: Dendrochronology and Precision Dating*. London: Batsford.

Bannister, Bryant. 1962. The interpretation of tree-ring dates. *American Antiquity* 27(4): 508–514.

—— 1970. Dendrochronology. In Don Brothwell and Eric Higgs (Eds.), *Science in Archaeology: A Survey of Progress and Research*. 2d ed. (pp. 191–205). New York: Praeger.

Barbour, Warren T. D. 1994, Spring. Musings on a dream deferred. *Federal Archaeology Report:* 12–13.

Barnett, William K., and John W. Hoopes (Eds.). 1995. *The Emergence of Pottery: Technology and Innovation in Ancient Societies*. Washington, DC: Smithsonian Institution Press.

Beaudry, Mary C. (Ed.). 1988. *Documentary Archaeology in the New World*. Cambridge: Cambridge University Press.

Beck, Charlotte (Ed.). 1994. *Dating in Exposed and Surface Contexts*. Albuquerque: University of New Mexico Press.

Beck, Lane Anderson (Ed.). 1995. *Regional Approaches to Mortuary Analysis*. New York: Plenum.

Behrensmeyer, Anna K., and Susan M. Kidwell. 1985. Taphonomy's contributions to paleobiology. *Paleobiology* 11(1): 105–119.

Bell, James A. 1994. *Reconstructing Prehistory: Scientific Method in Archaeology*. Philadelphia: Temple University Press.

Bender, Barbara. 1993. Cognitive archaeology and cultural materialism. *Cambridge Archaeological Journal* 3(2): 257–260.

Benedict, Ruth. 1948. Anthropology and the humanities. *American Anthropologist* 50(4, part 1): 585–593.

Bettinger, Robert L. 1980. Explanatory/predictive models of hunter-gatherer adaptation. In Michael B. Schiffer (Ed.), *Advances in Archaeological Method and Theory*. Vol. 3 (pp. 189–255). New York: Academic Press.

——. 1987. Archaeological approaches to hunter-gatherers. *Annual Review of Anthropology* 16: 121–142.

——. 1991. *Hunter-Gatherers: Archaeological and Evolutionary Theory*. New York: Plenum.

Bevan, Bruce W. 1983. Electromagnetics for mapping buried earth features. *Journal of Field Archaeology* 10(1): 47–54.

Bevan, Bruce W., and J. Kenyon. 1975. Ground-penetrating radar for historical archaeology. *MASCA Newsletter* 11(2): 2–7.

Bevan, Bruce W., David G. Orr, and Brooke S. Blades. 1984. The discovery of the Taylor house at the Petersburg National Battlefield. *Historical Archaeology* 18(2): 64–74.

Binford, Lewis R. 1962. A new method of calculating dates from kaolin pipe stem samples. *Southeastern Archaeological Conference Newsletter* 9(2): 19–21.

——. 1964. A consideration of archaeological research design. *American Antiquity* 29(4): 425–441.

——. 1967. Smudge pits and hide smoking: The use of analogy in archaeological reasoning. *American Antiquity* 32(1): 1–12.

——. 1968a. Archeological perspectives. In Sally R. Binford and Lewis R. Binford (Eds.), *New Perspectives in Archeology* (pp. 5–32). Chicago: Aldine.

——. 1968b. Post-Pleistocene adaptations. In Sally R. Binford and Lewis R. Binford (Eds.), *New Perspectives in Archeology* (pp. 313–341). Chicago: Aldine.

——. 1972. The "Binford" pipe stem formula: A return from the grave. *The Conference on Historic Site Archaeology Papers* 6: 230–253.

—— (Ed.). 1977. *For Theory Building in Archaeology*. New York: Academic Press.

——. 1978. *Nunamiut Ethnoarchaeology*. New York: Academic Press.

——. 1980. Willow smoke and dogs' tails: Hunter-gatherer settlement systems and archaeological site formation. *American Antiquity* 45(1): 4–20.

——. 1981. *Bones: Ancient Men and Modern Myths*. New York: Academic Press.

——. 1983. *In Pursuit of the Past: Decoding the Archaeological Record*. London: Thames and Hudson.

——. 1986. An Alyawara day: Making men's knives and beyond. *American Antiquity* 51(3): 547–562.

——. 1987a. Data, relativism, and archaeological science. *Man* 22(3): 391–404.

——. 1987b. Researching ambiguity: Frames of reference and site structure. In Susan Kent (Ed.), *Method and Theory for Activity Area Research: An Ethnoarchaeological Approach* (pp. 449–512). New York: Columbia University Press.

——. 1989a. Science to seance, or processual to "post-processual" archaeology. In *Debating Archaeology* (pp. 27–40). San Diego: Academic Press.

——. 1989b. [Review of Hodder, *Reading the Past: Current Approaches to Interpretation in Archaeology*]. In *Debating Archaeology* (pp. 69–71). San Diego: Academic Press.

Bintliff, John. 1991. Post-modernism, rhetoric, and scholasticism at TAG: The current state of British archaeological theory. *Antiquity* 65(247): 274–278.

Blakey, Michael L. 1995. Race, nationalism, and the Afrocentric past. In *Making Alternative Histories: The Practice of Archaeology and History in Non-Western Settings* (pp. 213–228). Santa Fe: School of American Research Press.

Blanton, Dennis B. 1995. The case for CRM training in academic institutions: The many faces of CRM. *Bulletin of the Society for American Archaeology* 13(4): 40–41.

Bohannan, Paul. 1965. *Social Anthropology*. New York: Holt, Rinehart and Winston.

Bohannan, Paul, and Mark Glazer (Eds.). 1988. *High Points in Anthropology*. 2d ed. New York: Knopf.

Bonde, Niels, and Arne Emil Christensen. 1993. Dendrochronological dating of the Viking Age ship burials at Oseberg, Gokstad, and Tune, Norway. *Antiquity* 67: 575–583.

Bonnichsen, Robson, and Alan L. Schneider. 1995, May/June. Ancient hair, and the DNA embedded in it, might reveal when and how the Americas were settled—but not if some Native Americans can help it. *The Sciences*: 27–31.

Bonnichson, Jim. 1990. Studying ancient American DNA. *Mammoth Trumpet* 6(1): 1, 3, 6.

Borofsky, Robert (Ed.). 1994. *Assessing Cultural Anthropology.* New York: McGraw-Hill.

Bowman, Sheridan. 1990. *Radiocarbon Dating.* Berkeley: University of California Press.

——. 1994. Using radiocarbon: An update. *Antiquity* 68(261): 838–843.

Boyd, Mark F., Hale G. Smith, and John W. Griffin. 1951. *Here They Once Stood: The Tragic End of the Apalachee Missions.* Gainesville: University of Florida Press.

Boyd, Robert, and Peter J. Richerson. 1985. *Culture and the Evolutionary Process.* Chicago: University of Chicago Press.

Braidwood, Robert J. 1959. Archeology and the evolutionary theory. In *Evolution and Anthropology: A Centennial Appraisal* (pp. 76–89). Washington, DC: Anthropological Society of Washington.

Braun, David P. 1985. Absolute seriation: A time-series approach. In Christopher Carr (Ed.), *For Concordance in Archaeological Analysis: Bridging Data Structure, Quantitative Technique, and Theory* (pp. 509–539). Kansas City: Westport.

Bray, Tamara L., and Thomas W. Killion (Eds.). 1994. *Reckoning With the Dead: The Larsen Bay Repatriation and the Smithsonian Institution.* Washington, DC: Smithsonian Institution Press.

Brew, John Otis. 1946. Archaeology of Alkali Ridge, Southeastern Utah. *Papers of the Peabody Museum of American Archaeology and Ethnology,* no. 21.

Brewer, Douglas J. 1992. Zooarchaeology: Method, theory, and goals. In M. B. Schiffer (Ed.), *Archaeological Method and Theory.* Vol. 4 (pp. 195–244). Tucson: University of Arizona Press.

Brody, J. J. 1990. *The Anasazi: Ancient Indian People of the American Southwest.* New York: Rizzoli.

——. 1991. *Anasazi and Pueblo Painting.* Albuquerque: University of New Mexico Press.

Bronitsky, G. (Ed.). 1989. *Pottery Technology: Ideas and Approaches.* Boulder, CO: Westview.

Brooks, A. S., P. E. Hare, J. E. Kokis, G. H. Miller, R. D. Ernst, and F. Wendorf. 1990. Dating Pleistocene archeological sites by protein diagenesis in ostrich eggshell. *Science* 248: 60–64.

Browman, David L., and Douglas R. Givens. 1996. Stratigraphic excavation: The first "new archaeology." *American Anthropologist* 98(1): 1–17.

Brown, James A. 1976. The Southern Cult reconsidered. *Midcontinental Journal of Archaeology* 1(2): 115–135.

Brown, Shelby. 1993. Feminist research in archaeology: What does it mean? Why is it taking so long? In Nancy Sorkin Rabinowitz and Amy Richlin (Eds.), *Feminist Theory and the Classics* (pp. 238–271). New York: Routledge.

Brown, Terence A., R. G. Allaby, K. A. Brown, and M. K. Jones. 1993. Biomolecular archaeology of wheat: Past, present and future. *World Archaeology* 25(1): 64–73.

Brown, Terence A., and Keri A. Brown. 1992. Ancient DNA and the archaeologist. *Antiquity* 66(250): 10–23.

Bruner, Edward M. 1994. Abraham Lincoln as authentic reproduction: A critique of postmodernism. *American Anthropologist* 96(2): 397–415.

Bryant, Vaughn M. Jr., and Stephen A. Hall. 1993. Archaeological palynology in the United States: A critique. *American Antiquity* 58(2): 277–286.

Burch, Ernest S. Jr., and Linda J. Ellanna (Eds.). 1994. *Key Issues in Hunter-Gatherer Research.* Oxford: Berg.

Burger, Richard L. 1992. *Chavín and the Origins of Andean Civilization.* London: Thames and Hudson.

Burger, Richard L., and Nikolaas J. van der Merwe. 1990. Maize and the origin of highland Chavín civilization: An isotopic perspective. *American Anthropologist* 92: 85–95.

Buurman, Janneke, and Jan Peter Pals. 1994. Palaeoethnobotany: What's in a name? [Review of "Phytoarchaeology" by Robert R. Brooks and Dieter Johannes, "New Light on Early Farming" by Jane M. Renfrew, and "Progress in Old World Palaeoethnobotany" ed. by Willem van Zeist, Krystyna Wasylikowa, and Karl-Ernst Bchre]. *Antiquity* 68: 471–473.

Carneiro, Robert L. 1970a. A quantitative law in anthropology. *American Antiquity* 35(4): 492–494.

——. 1970b. A theory of the origin of the state. *Science* 169: 733–738.

——. 1973a. Classical evolution. In Raoul Naroll and Frada Naroll (Eds.), *Main Currents in Cultural Anthropology* (pp. 57–121). Englewood Cliffs, NJ: Prentice Hall.

——. 1973b. The four faces of evolution: Unilinear, universal, multilinear, and differential. In John J. Honigmann (Ed.), *Handbook of Social and Cultural Anthropology.* Chicago: Rand McNally.

——. 1988. The circumscription theory: Challenge and response. *American Behavioral Scientist* 31(4): 497–511.

——. 1992. The role of natural selection in the evolution of culture. *Cultural Dynamics* 5(2): 113–140.

——. 1995. Godzilla meets new age anthropology: Facing the post-modernist challenge to a science of culture. *Europaea* 1(1): 3–22.

Carpenter, Edmund. 1991. Repatriation policy and the Heye Collection. *Museum Anthropology* 15(3): 15–18.

Carr, Christopher. 1982. *Handbook on Soil Resistivity Surveying: Interpretation of Data from Earthen Archaeological Sites.* Evanston, IL: Center for American Archeology Press.

Carr, Christopher, and Jill E. Neitzel (Eds.). 1995. *Style, Society, and Person: Archaeological and Ethnological Perspectives.* New York: Plenum.

Carrithers, Michael. 1990. Is anthropology art or science? *Current Anthropology* 31(3): 263–282.

——. 1992. *Why Humans Have Culture: Explaining Anthropology and Social Diversity.* Oxford: Oxford University Press.

Cashdan, Elizabeth (Ed.). 1990. *Risk and Uncertainty in Tribal and Peasant Economies.* Boulder, CO: Westview.

Cerroni-Long, E. L. 1996. Human science. *Anthropology Newsletter* 37(1): 50, 52.

Chaplin, R. E. 1971. *The Study of Animal Bones From Archaeological Sites.* London: Seminar.

Chase, A. F., D. Z. Chase, and H. W. Topsey. 1988. Archaeology and the ethics of collecting. *Archaeology* 41(1): 56–60, 87.

Childe, V. Gordon. 1951a. *Man Makes Himself.* New York: New American Library.

——. 1951b. *Social Evolution*. New York: Schuman.

Christenson, Andrew L. 1989. *Tracing Archaeology's Past: The Historiography of Archaeology*. Carbondale: Southern Illinois University Press.

Church, Tim. 1994. *Lithic Resource Studies: A Sourcebook for Archaeologists*. Special Publication no. 3: Lithic Technology. Tulsa, OK: University of Tulsa, Department of Anthropology.

Claassen, Cheryl (Ed.). 1992. *Exploring Gender Through Archaeology: Selected Papers From the 1991 Boone Conference*. Monographs in World Archaeology, no. 11. Madison, WI: Prehistory Press.

——. 1994. *Women in Archaeology*. Philadelphia: University of Pennsylvania Press.

Clark, Anthony. 1990. *Seeing Beneath the Soil: Prospecting Methods in Archaeology*. London: Batsford.

Clark, Donavan L. 1964. Archaeological chronology in California and the obsidian hydration method: Part 1. *Archaeological Survey Annual Report* (pp. 139–225). Los Angeles: University of California.

Clark, J. G. D. 1954. *Excavations at Star Carr, an Early Mesolithic Site at Seamer, Near Scarborough, Yorkshire*. Cambridge: Cambridge University Press.

——. 1972. Star Carr: A case study in bioarchaeology. *McCaleb Module in Anthropology*, no. 10. Reading, MA: Addison-Wesley Modular Publications.

Clarke, David L. 1979. *Analytical Archaeologist: Collected Papers of David L. Clarke*. Edited by his colleagues. New York: Academic Press.

Cleere, Henry (Ed.). 1989. *Archaeological Heritage Management in the Modern World*. London: Unwin Hyman.

——. 1993. Managing the archaeological heritage. *Antiquity* 67: 400–402.

Clifford, James. 1988. *The Predicament of Culture: Twentieth Century Ethnography, Literature, and Art*. Cambridge: Harvard University Press.

Clifford, James, and George E. Marcus (Eds.). 1986. *Writing Culture: The Poetics and Politics of Ethnography*. Berkeley: University of California Press.

Cobb, Charles R. 1993. Archaeological approaches to the political economy of nonstratified societies. In M. B. Schiffer (Ed.), *Archaeological Method and Theory*. Vol. 5 (pp. 43–100). Tucson: University of Arizona Press.

Cohen, Mark Nathan. 1977. *The Food Crisis in Prehistory: Overpopulation and the Origins of Agriculture*. New Haven: Yale University Press.

——. 1981. The ecological basis of New World state formation: General and local model building. In Grant D. Jones and Robert R. Kautz (Eds.), *The Transition to Statehood in the New World* (pp. 105–122). Cambridge: Cambridge University Press.

Cohen, Mark Nathan, and George J. Armelagos (Eds.). 1984. *Paleopathology at the Origins of Agriculture*. Orlando: Academic Press.

Colley, Sarah M. 1990. The analysis and interpretation of archaeological fish remains. In M. B. Schiffer (Ed.), *Archaeological Method and Theory*. Vol. 2 (pp. 207–253). Tucson: University of Arizona Press.

Conkey, Margaret W. 1991. Does it make a difference? Feminist thinking and archaeologies of gender. In *The Archaeology of Gender* (pp. 24–33). Proceedings of the 22nd

Annual Chacmool Conference. Calgary: University of Calgary Archaeological Association.

Conkey, Margaret W., and Janet Spector. 1984. Archaeology and the study of gender. In Michael B. Schiffer (Ed.), *Advances in Archaeological Method and Theory.* Vol. 7 (pp. 1–38). Orlando: Academic Press.

Conyers, Lawrence B. 1995. The use of ground-penetrating radar to map the buried structures and landscape of the Cerén site, El Salvador. *Geoarchaeology* 10(4): 275–299.

Cook, Karen. 1993. Bones of contention. *Village Voice* 38(18): 23–27.

Cordell, Linda S. 1984. *Prehistory of the Southwest.* Orlando: Academic Press.

——. 1994. *Ancient Pueblo Peoples.* Montreal: St. Remy Press; Washington, DC: Smithsonian Books.

Costin, Cathy Lynne, and Timothy Earle. 1989. Status distinction and legitimation of power as reflected in changing patterns of consumption in late prehispanic Peru. *American Antiquity* 54(4): 691–714.

Cotterell, Brian, and Johan Kamminga. 1990. *Mechanics of Pre-Industrial Technology.* Cambridge: Cambridge University Press.

Courty, M. A., P. Goldberg, and R. Macphail. 1989. *Soils and Micromorphology in Archaeology.* Cambridge: Cambridge University Press.

Cowan, C. Wesley, and Patty Jo Watson (Eds.). 1992. *The Origins of Agriculture: An International Perspective.* Washington, DC: Smithsonian Institution Press.

Crabtree, Don E. 1966. A stoneworker's approach to analyzing and replicating the Lindenmeier Folsom. *Tebiwa* 9: 3–39.

——. 1968. Mesoamerican polyhedral cores and prismatic blades. *American Antiquity* 33(4): 446–478.

——. 1979. Interview. *Flintknappers' Exchange* 2(1): 29–33.

Crabtree, Pam J. 1990. Zooarchaeology and complex societies: Some uses of faunal analysis for the study of trade, social status, and ethnicity. In M. B. Schiffer (Ed.), *Archaeological Method and Theory.* Vol. 2 (pp. 155–205). Tucson: University of Arizona Press.

Crader, Diana C. 1990. Slave diet at Monticello. *American Antiquity* 55(4): 690–717.

Cronyn, J. M. 1990. *The Elements of Archaeological Conservation.* London: Routledge.

Crown, Patricia L., and W. James Judge (Eds.). 1991. *Chaco and Hohokam: Prehistoric Regional Systems in the American Southwest.* Santa Fe: School of American Research Press.

Cullen, Tracey. 1995. Women in archaeology: Perils and progress [Review of the book *Equity Issues for Women in Archeology* ed. by M. C. Nelson, S. M. Nelson, and A. Wylie, and the book *Women in Archaeology* ed. by C. Claassen]. *Antiquity* 69: 1042–1045.

Dale, W. S. A. 1987. The shroud of Turin: Relic or icon? In H. H. Andersen and S. T. Picraux (Eds.), *Nuclear Instruments and Methods in Physics Research: Section B, Beam Interactions With Materials and Atoms.* Proceedings of the Fourth International Symposium on Accelerator Mass Spectrometry B29: 187–192.

D'Altroy, Terence N. 1992. *Provincial Power in the Inka Empire.* Washington, DC: Smithsonian Institution Press.

Dancey, William S. 1981. *Archaeological Field Methods: An Introduction*. Minneapolis: Burgess.

D'Andrade, Roy G. 1995. *The Development of Cognitive Anthropology*. Cambridge: Cambridge University Press.

Daniel, Glyn. 1962. *The Idea of Prehistory*. Baltimore: Penguin.

———. 1976. *A Hundred and Fifty Years of Archaeology*. Cambridge: Harvard University Press.

Daniel, Glyn, and Christopher Chippindale (Eds.). 1989. *The Pastmasters: Eleven Modern Pioneers of Archaeology*. London: Thames and Hudson.

Daniel, Glyn, and Colin Renfrew. 1988. *The Idea of Prehistory*. Edinburgh: University of Edinburgh Press.

Dark, K. R. 1995. *Theoretical Archaeology*. Ithaca: Cornell University Press.

Davis, Jonathan O. 1978. Quaternary tephrochronology of the Lake Lahontan area. *Nevada Archaeological Survey Research Paper,* no. 7.

———. 1983. Geology of Gatecliff Shelter: Sedimentary facies and Holocene climate. In "The archaeology of Monitor Valley: 2. Gatecliff Shelter" by David Hurst Thomas. *Anthropological Papers of the American Museum of Natural History* 59(1): 64–87.

Day, Petra. 1993. Preliminary results of high-resolution palaeoecological analyses at Star Carr, Yorkshire. *Cambridge Archaeological Journal* 3(1): 129–140.

Deagan, Kathleen. 1980. Spanish St. Augustine: America's first "melting pot." *Archaeology* 33(5): 22–30.

———. 1981. Downtown survey: The discovery of 16th century St. Augustine in an urban area. *American Antiquity* 46(3): 626–634.

———. 1982. Avenues of inquiry in historical archaeology. In Michael B. Schiffer (Ed.), *Advances in Archaeological Method and Theory*. Vol. 5 (pp. 151–177). New York: Academic Press.

———. 1987. *Artifacts of the Spanish Colonies of Florida and the Caribbean, 1500–1800*. Vol. 1, *Ceramics, Glassware, and Beads*. Washington, DC: Smithsonian Institution Press.

———. 1988. Neither history nor prehistory: The questions that count in historical archaeology. *Historical Archaeology* 22(1): 7–12.

———. 1991. Historical archaeology's contributions to our understanding of early America. In Lisa Falk (Ed.), *Historical Archaeology in Global Perspective* (pp. 97–112). Washington, DC: Smithsonian Institution Press.

——— (Ed.). 1995. *Puerto Real: The Archaeology of a Sixteenth-Century Spanish Town in Hispaniola*. Gainesville: University Press of Florida.

Deagan, Kathleen, and Darcie MacMahon. 1995. *Fort Mose: Colonial America's Black Fortress of Freedom*. Gainesville: University Press of Florida/Florida Museum of Natural History.

Dean, Jeffrey S. 1970. Aspects of Tsegi phase social organization: A trial reconstruction. In William A. Longacre (Ed.), *Reconstructing Prehistoric Pueblo Societies* (pp. 140–174). Albuquerque: University of New Mexico Press.

———. 1978a. Independent dating in archaeological analysis. In Michael B. Schiffer (Ed.), *Advances in Archaeological Theory and Method*. Vol. 1 (pp. 223–255). New York: Academic Press.

——. 1978b. Tree-ring dating in archeology. *University of Utah Miscellaneous Anthropological Papers,* no. 24, 99: 129–163.

Deetz, James. 1977. *In Small Things Forgotten: The Archaeology of Early American Life.* Garden City, NY: Anchor.

——. 1983. Scientific humanism and humanistic science: A plea for paradigmatic pluralism in historical archaeology. In R. W. Newman (Ed.), *Historical Archaeology of the Eastern United States: Papers From the R. J. Russell Symposium* (pp. 27–34). Baton Rouge: Louisiana State University.

——. 1991. Introduction: Archaeological evidence of sixteenth- and seventeenth-century encounters. In Lisa Falk (Ed.), *Historical Archaeology in Global Perspective* (pp. 1–9). Washington, DC: Smithsonian Institution Press.

Deloria, Vine Jr. 1992. Indians, archaeologists, and the future. *American Antiquity* 57(4): 595–598.

——. 1995. *Red Earth, White Lies: Native Americans and the Myth of Scientific Fact.* New York: Scribner's.

Del Pozzo, Giovanna. 1989. Mummy DNA fragment identified. *Nature* 339(June 8): 431–432.

Demarest, Arthur A. 1989. Ideology and evolutionism in American archaeology: Looking beyond the economic base. In C. C. Lamberg-Karlovsky (Ed.), *Archaeological Thought in America* (pp. 89–102). Cambridge: Cambridge University Press.

Demarest, Arthur A., and Geoffrey W. Conrad (Eds.). 1992. *Ideology and Pre-Columbian Civilizations.* Santa Fe: School of American Research Press.

DeNiro, Michael J., and S. Epstein. 1981. Influence of diet on the distribution of nitrogen isotopes in animals. *Geochimica de Cosmochimica Acta* 45: 341–351.

DeNiro, Michael J., and Margaret J. Schoeniger. 1983. Stable carbon and nitrogen isotope ratios of bone collagen: Variations within individuals, between sexes, and within populations raised on monotonous diets. *Journal of Archaeological Science* 10(3): 199–203.

d'Errico, Francesco. 1995. A new model and its implications for the origin of writing: The La Marche antler revisited. *Cambridge Archaeological Journal* 5(2): 163–206.

Deuel, Leo. 1969. *Flights Into Yesterday: The Story of Aerial Archaeology.* New York: St. Martin's.

Dickerson, James. 1993, August. Murders from the past. *Omni* 15(10): 50–54, 56–57, 82.

Dillehay, Tom D. 1989. *Monte Verde: A Late Pleistocene Settlement in Chile.* Washington, DC: Smithsonian Institution Press.

Dillehay, Tom D., and David J. Meltzer (Eds.). 1991. *The First Americans: Search and Research.* Boca Raton, FL: CRC Press.

Dillon, Brian D. (Ed.). 1989. *Practical Archaeology: Field and Laboratory Techniques and Archaeological Logistics.* Archaeological Research Tools 2. Los Angeles: University of California, Institute of Archaeology.

Doran, Glen H., David N. Dickel, William E. Ballinger Jr., O. Frank Agee, Philip J. Laipis, and William W. Hauswirth. 1986. Anatomical, cellular and molecular analysis of 8,000-yr-old human brain tissue from the Windover archaeological site. *Nature* 323: 803–806.

Douglass, Andrew Ellicott. 1929. The secret of the Southwest solved by talkative tree rings. *National Geographic* 56(6): 736–770.

Douglass, Frederick. 1950. The claims of the Negro ethnologically considered: Address delivered at Western Reserve College, July 12, 1854. In Philip S. Foner (Ed.), *The Life and Writings of Frederick Douglass*. Vol. 2, *Pre–Civil War Decade 1850–1860* (pp. 289–309). New York: International Publishers.

Doyel, David E. 1991. Hohokam exchange and interaction. In Patricia L. Crown and W. James Judge (Eds.), *Chaco and Hohokam: Prehistoric Regional Systems in the American Southwest* (pp. 225–252). Santa Fe: School of American Research Press.

Dunnell, Robert C. 1970. Seriation method and its evaluation. *American Antiquity* 35(3): 305–319.

——. 1971. *Systematics in Prehistory*. New York: Free Press.

——. 1979. Trends in current Americanist archaeology. *American Journal of Archaeology* 83(4): 437–449.

——. 1980. Evolutionary theory and archaeology. In Michael B. Schiffer (Ed.), *Advances in Archaeological Method and Theory*. Vol. 3 (pp. 35–99). New York: Academic Press.

——. 1985. Americanist archaeology in 1984. *American Journal of Archaeology* 89: 585–611.

——. 1986. Five decades of American archaeology. In David J. Meltzer, Don D. Fowler, and Jeremy A. Sabloff (Eds.), *American Archaeology Past and Future: A Celebration of the Society for American Archaeology 1935–1985* (pp. 23–49). Washington, DC: Smithsonian Institution Press.

——. 1989. Aspects of the application of evolutionary theory in archaeology. In C. C. Lamberg-Karlovsky (Ed.), *Archaeological Thought in America* (pp. 35–49). Cambridge: Cambridge University Press.

Dunnell, Robert C., and William S. Dancey. 1983. The siteless survey: A regional scale data collection strategy. In Michael B. Schiffer (Ed.), *Advances in Archeological Method and Theory*. Vol. 6 (pp. 267–287). New York: Academic Press.

Durham, William. 1981. Overview: Optimal foraging analysis in human ecology. In Bruce Winterhalder and Eric Alden Smith (Eds.), *Hunter-Gatherer Foraging Strategies: Ethnographic and Archaeological Analyses* (pp. 218–232). Chicago: University of Chicago Press.

——. 1992. Applications of evolutionary culture theory. *Annual Review of Anthropology* 21: 331–355.

Earle, Timothy K. (Ed.). 1991. *Chiefdoms: Power, Economy, and Ideology*. Cambridge: Cambridge University Press.

Earle, Timothy K., and Robert W. Preucel. 1987. Processual archaeology and the radical critique. *Current Anthropology* 28(4): 501–538.

Ebert, James I. 1984. Remote sensing applications in archaeology. In Michael B. Schiffer (Ed.), *Advances in Archaeological Method and Theory*. Vol. 7 (pp. 293–362). New York: Academic Press.

Echo-Hawk, Roger C., and Walter R. Echo-Hawk. 1994. *Battlefields and Burial Grounds: The Indian Struggle to Protect Ancestral Graves in the United States*. Minneapolis: Lerner.

Echo-Hawk, Walter (Ed.). 1992. Special Issue: Repatriation of American Indian remains. *American Indian Culture and Research Journal* 16(2): 1–200.

Eddy, Frank, Dale R. Lightfoot, Eden A. Welker, Layne L. Wright, and Dolores C. Torres. 1996. Air photographic mapping of San Marcos Pueblo. *Journal of Field Archaeology* 23(1): 1–13.

Ehrenreich, Robert M., Carole L. Crumley, and Janet E. Levy (Eds.). 1995. Heterarchy and the analysis of complex societies. *Archeological Papers of the American Anthropological Association,* no. 6.

Eichler, Margrit, and Jeanne Lapoint. 1985. *On the Treatment of the Sexes in Research.* Ottawa: Social Sciences and Humanities Research Council of Canada.

Elia, Ricardo J. 1993. U.S. cultural resource management and the ICAHM charter. *Antiquity* 67: 426–438.

Elkins, James. 1996. On the impossibility of close reading: The case of Alexander Marshack. *Current Anthropology* 37(2): 185–226.

Elliott, Melinda. 1995. *Great Excavations.* Santa Fe: School of American Research Press.

Ellis, G. Lain, Glenn A. Goodfriend, James T. Abbott, P. E. Hare, and David W. Von Endt. 1996. Assessment of integrity and geochronology of archeological sites using amino acid racemization in land snail shells: Examples from central Texas. *Geoarchaeology* 11(3): 189–213.

Elster, H., E. Gil-Av, and S. Weiner. 1991. Amino acid racemization of fossil bone. *Journal of Archaeological Science* 18: 605–617.

Elston, Robert G. 1992. Archaeological research in the context of cultural resource management: Pushing back in the 1990s. *Journal of California and Great Basin Anthropology* 14(1): 37–48.

Emerson, Thomas E., and Lewis R. Barry (Eds.). 1991. *Cahokia and the Hinterlands: Middle Mississippian Cultures of the Midwest.* Urbana: University of Illinois Press.

Engelstad, Ericka. 1991. Images of power and contradiction: Feminist theory and postprocessual archaeology. *Antiquity* 65: 502–514.

Ezzo, Joseph A., Clark Spencer Larsen, and James H. Burton. 1995. Elemental signatures of human diets from the Georgia Bight. *American Journal of Physical Anthropology* 98: 471–481.

Faegri, K., P. E. Kaland, and K. Krzywinski. 1989. *Textbook of Pollen Analysis.* 4th ed. New York: Wiley.

Fagan, Brian M. 1994. *Quest for the Past: Great Discoveries in Archaeology.* 2d ed. Prospect Heights, IL: Waveland.

Falk, Lisa (Ed.). 1991. *Historical Archaeology in Global Perspective.* Washington, DC: Smithsonian Institution Press.

Farnsworth, Paul, James E. Brady, Michael J. DeNiro, and Richard S. MacNeish. 1985. A reevaluation of the isotopic and archaeological reconstructions of diet in the Tehuacán Valley. *American Antiquity* 50(1): 102–116.

Fedick, Scott L. 1995. Indigenous agriculture in the Americas. *Journal of Archaeological Research* 3(4): 257–303.

Ferguson, Leland B. 1992. *Uncommon Ground: Archaeology and Early African America, 1650–1800.* Washington, DC: Smithsonian Institution Press.

Ferguson, T. J. 1996. Native Americans and the practice of archaeology. *Annual Review of Anthropology* 25: 63–79.

Findlow, Frank J., Victoria C. Bennett, Jonathon E. Ericson, and Suzanne P. De Atley. 1975. A new obsidian hydration rate for certain obsidians in the American Southwest. *American Antiquity* 40(3): 344–348.

Fisher, Deborah L., Mitchell M. Holland, Lloyd Mitchell, Paul S. Sledzik, Allison Webb Wilcox, Mark Wadhams, and Victor W. Weedn. 1993. Extraction, evaluation, and amplification of DNA from decalcified and undecalcified United States Civil War bone. *Journal of Forensic Sciences* 38(1): 60–68.

Fladmark, Knud R. 1978. *A Guide to Basic Archaeological Field Procedures.* Burnaby, British Columbia: Simon Fraser University, Department of Archaeology.

Flannery, Kent V. 1965. The ecology of early food production in Mesopotamia. *Science* 147(3663): 1247–1255.

——. 1969. Origins and ecological effects of early domestication in Iran and the Near East. In P. J. Ucko and G. W. Dimbleby (Eds.), *The Domestication and Exploitation of Plants and Animals* (pp. 73–100). Chicago: Aldine.

——. 1972. The cultural evolution of civilizations. *Annual Review of Ecology and Systematics* 3: 399–426.

——. 1973. The origins of agriculture. *Annual Review of Anthropology* 2: 271–310.

—— (Ed.). 1976. *The Early Mesoamerican Village.* New York: Academic Press.

—— (Ed.). 1986. *Guilá Naquitz: Archaic Foraging and Early Agriculture in Oaxaca, Mexico.* Orlando: Academic Press.

——. 1995. *Prehistoric Social Evolution: Research Frontiers in Anthropology.* Needham Heights, MA: Simon and Schuster.

Flannery, Kent V., and Joyce Marcus. 1993. Cognitive archaeology. *Cambridge Archaeological Journal* 3(2): 260–270.

Fleming, Stuart. 1977. *Dating Techniques in Archaeology.* New York: St. Martin's.

Flenniken, J. Jeffrey. 1978. Reevaluation of the Lindenmeier Folsom: A replication experiment in lithic technology. *American Antiquity* 43(3): 473–480.

——. 1981. Replicative systems analysis: A model applied to the vein quartz artifacts from the Hoko River site. *Laboratory of Anthropology Reports of Investigations,* no. 59. Pullman: Washington State University.

——. 1984. The past, present, and future of flintknapping: An anthropological perspective. *Annual Review of Anthropology* 13: 187–203.

Foley, Robert. 1981. Off-site archaeology: An alternative approach for the short-sited. In Ian Hodder, Glynn Isaac, and Norman Hammond (Eds.), *Pattern of the Past: Studies in Honour of David Clarke* (pp. 157–183). Cambridge: Cambridge University Press.

Ford, James Alfred. 1952. Measurements of some prehistoric design developments in the southeastern states. *Anthropological Papers of the American Museum of Natural History* 44(3).

——. 1954. The type concept revisited. *American Anthropologist* 56(1): 42–54.

——. 1962. *A Quantitative Method for Deriving Cultural Chronology.* Washington, DC: Pan American Union, Technical Manual, I.

Fowler, Don D. 1982. Cultural resources management. In Michael B. Schiffer (Ed.), *Advances in Archaeological Method and Theory.* Vol. 5 (pp. 1–50). New York: Academic Press.

——. 1986. Conserving American archaeological resources. In David J. Meltzer, Don D. Fowler, and Jeremy A. Sabloff (Eds.), *American Archaeology: Past and Future: A Celebration of the Society for American Archaeology 1935–1985* (pp. 135–162). Washington, DC: Smithsonian Institution Press.

Friedman, Irving, Fred W. Trembour, Franklin L. Smith, and George I. Smith. 1994. Is obsidian hydration dating affected by relative humidity? *Quaternary Research* 41: 185–190.

Frison, George C. 1989. Experimental use of Clovis weaponry and tools on African elephants. *American Antiquity* 54(4): 766–784.

———. 1993. North American high plains Paleo-Indian hunting strategies and weaponry assemblages. In Olga Soffer and N. D. Praslov (Eds.), *From Kostenki to Clovis: Upper Paleolithic-Paleo-Indian Adaptations* (pp. 237–249). New York: Plenum.

Frison, George C., and Bruce A. Bradley. 1980. *Folsom Tools and Technology at the Hanson Site, Wyoming*. Albuquerque: University of New Mexico Press.

Fritz, John M. 1978. Paleopsychology today: Ideational systems and human adaptation in prehistory. In Charles L. Redman, Mary Jane Berman, Edward V. Curtin, William T. Laughorne Jr., Nina M. Versaggi, and Jeffrey C. Wanser (Eds.), *Social Archaeology: Beyond Subsistence and Dating* (pp. 37–59). New York: Academic Press.

Gabriel, Kathryn. 1991. *Roads to Center Place: A Cultural Atlas of Chaco Canyon and the Anasazi*. Boulder, CO: Johnson.

Gaines, Patrice. 1995, August 3. Bones of forebears. *The Washington Post*.

Galloway, Patricia (Ed.). 1989. *The Southeastern Ceremonial Complex: Artifacts and Analysis*. Lincoln: University of Nebraska Press.

Gamble, C. S., and W. A. Boismier (Eds.). 1991. *Ethnoarchaeological Approaches to Mobile Campsites*. Ann Arbor: International Monographs in Prehistory.

Garrison, Ervan G., James G. Baker, and David Hurst Thomas. 1985. Magnetic prospection and the discovery of Mission Santa Catalina de Guale, Georgia. *Journal of Field Archaeology* 12(3): 299–313.

Gathercole, Peter, and David Lowenthal (Eds.). 1990. *The Politics of the Past*. One World Archaeology series. London: Unwin Hyman.

Geertz, Clifford. 1973. *The Interpretation of Cultures*. New York: Basic Books.

———. 1983. *Local Knowledge: Further Essays in Interpretive Anthropology*. New York: Basic Books.

———. 1984. Distinguished lecture: Anti anti-relativism. *American Anthropologist* 86(2): 263–278.

Gero, Joan M. 1983. Gender bias in archaeology: A cross-cultural perspective. In Joan Gero, David M. Lacy, and Michael L. Blakey (Eds.), *The Socio-Politics of Archaeology* (pp. 51–57). University of Massachusetts Department of Anthropology Research Report, no. 23.

———. 1985. Socio-politics and the woman-at-home ideology. *American Antiquity* 50(2): 342–350.

———. 1988. Gender bias in archaeology: Here, then and now. In Sue V. Rosser (Ed.), *Resistance of the Science and Health Care Professions to Feminism*. Elmsford, NY: Pergamon.

Gero, Joan M., and Margaret W. Conkey (Eds.). 1991. *Engendering Archaeology: Women and Prehistory*. Oxford: Basil Blackwell.

Gibbon, Guy. 1989. *Explanation in Archaeology*. Oxford: Basil Blackwell.

Gibbons, Ann. 1991. A "new look" for archaeology. *Science* 252: 918–920.

———. 1993. An array of science from mitochondrial Eve to EUVE. *Science* 259: 1249–1250.

Gibson, Alex M., and Ann Woods. 1990. *Prehistoric Pottery for the Archaeologist*. Leicester, England: Leicester University Press.

Gifford-Gonzalez, Diane. 1993. You can hide, but you can't run: Representation of women's work in illustrations of paleolithic life. *Visual Anthropology Review* 9(1): 23–40.

———. 1995. The real Flintstones? What are artists' depictions of human ancestors telling us? *Anthro Notes, National Museum of Natural History Bulletin for Teachers* 17(3): 1–9.

Gilbert, Robert I. Jr., and James H. Mielke (Eds.). 1985. *The Analysis of Prehistoric Diets*. Orlando: Academic Press.

Gilchrist, Roberta. 1991. Women's archaeology? Political feminism, gender theory and historical revision. *Antiquity* 65: 495–501.

———. 1994. *Gender and Material Culture: The Archaeology of Religious Women*. London: Routledge.

Gilman, Antonio. 1989. Marxism in American archaeology. In C. C. Lamberg-Karlovsky (Ed.), *Archaeological Thought in America* (pp. 63–73). Cambridge: Cambridge University Press.

Glover, I., and D. Griffiths (Eds.). 1989. Ceramic technology. *World Archaeology* 21(1).

Goldschmidt, Walter. 1960. *Exploring the Ways of Mankind*. New York: Holt, Rinehart and Winston.

———. 1983. [Review of the book *Beyond the Myths of Culture: Essays in Cultural Materialism*, ed. by Eric B. Ross]. *American Anthropologist* 85(3): 695–698.

Goldstein, Lynn, and Keith Kintigh. 1990. Ethics and the reburial controversy. *American Antiquity* 55(33): 585–591.

Goodenough, Ward H. 1965. Rethinking "status" and "role": Toward a general model of the cultural organization of social relationships. In Michael Banton (Ed.), *The Relevance of Models for Social Anthropology* (pp. 1–24). ASA Monographs, no. 1. New York: Praeger.

Goodman, Dean. 1994. Ground-penetrating radar simulation in engineering and archaeology. *Geophysics* 59(2): 224–232.

Goodman, Dean, and Yasushi Nishimura. 1993. A ground-radar view of Japanese burial mounds. *Antiquity* 67: 349–354.

Goodman, Dean, Y. Nishimura, T. Uno, and T. Yamamoto. 1994. A ground radar survey of medieval kiln sites in Suzu City, western Japan. *Archaeometry* 36: 317–326.

Gould, Richard A. 1966. Archaeology of the Point St. George site, and Tolowa prehistory. *University of California Publications in Anthropology*, vol. 4.

Gove, H. E. 1987. Turin workshop on radiocarbon dating the Turin shroud. *Nuclear Instruments and Methods in Physics Research* B29(1, 2): 193–195.

Graham, Martha. 1994. *Mobile Farmers: An Ethnoarchaeological Approach to Settlement Organization Among the Rarámuri of Northwestern Mexico*. International Monographs in Prehistory, Ethnoarchaeological Series 3. Ann Arbor, Michigan.

Grauer, Anne L. (Ed.). 1995. *Bodies of Evidence: Reconstructing History Through Skeletal Analysis*. New York: Wiley-Liss.

Grayson, Donald K. 1983. *The Establishment of Human Antiquity*. New York: Academic Press.

———. 1984. *Quantitative Zooarchaeology: Topics in the Analysis of Archaeological Faunas*. Orlando: Academic Press.

Grayson, Donald K., and David Hurst Thomas. 1983. Seasonality at Gatecliff Shelter. In "The archaeology of Monitor Valley: 2. Gatecliff Shelter" by David Hurst Thomas. *Anthropological Papers of the American Museum of Natural History* 59(1): 434–438.

Green, Ernestine L. (Ed.). 1984. *Ethics and Values in Archaeology.* New York: Free Press.

Greenfield, Jeanette. 1989. *The Return of Cultural Treasures.* Cambridge: Cambridge University Press.

Gryba, Eugene M. 1988. A Stone Age pressure method of Folsom fluting. *Plains Anthropologist* 33(119): 53–66.

Gulliford, Andrew. 1996. Bones of contention: The repatriation of Native American human remains. *Public Historian* 18(4): 119–143.

Gumerman, George J. (Ed.). 1991. *Exploring the Hohokam: Prehistoric Desert Peoples of the American Southwest.* Albuquerque: University of New Mexico Press.

Habermas, J. 1987. *The Philosophical Discourse of Modernity.* Oxford: Oxford University Press.

Hagelberg, Erika. 1993, August/September. DNA from archaeological bone. *The Biochemist:* 17–22.

Hammond, Philip C. 1974. Archaeometry and time: A review. *Journal of Field Archaeology* 1(3/4): 329–335.

Handsman, Russell G., and Mark P. Leone. 1989. Living history and critical archaeology in the reconstruction of the past. In Valerie Pinsky and Alison Wylie (Eds.), *Critical Traditions in Contemporary Archaeology: Essays in the Philosophy, History and Socio-Politics of Archaeology* (pp. 117–135). Cambridge: Cambridge University Press.

Handt, Oliva, Martin Richards, Marion Trommsdorff, Christian Kilger, Jaana Simanainen, Oleg Georgiev, Karin Bauer, Anne Stone, Robert Hedges, Walter Schaffner, Gerd Utermann, Bryan Sykes, and Svante Pääbo. 1994. Molecular genetic analyses of the Tyrolean ice man. *Science* 264: 1775–1778.

Harding, Sandra. 1991. *Whose Science? Whose Knowledge? Thinking From Women's Lives.* Ithaca: Cornell University Press.

Harp, Elmer Jr. 1975. *Photography in Archaeological Research.* Albuquerque: University of New Mexico Press.

Harrington, Jean C. 1954. Dating stem fragments of seventeenth and eighteenth century clay tobacco pipes. *Quarterly Bulletin: Archaeological Society of Virginia* 9(1).

Harrington, Spencer P. M. 1993, March/April. Bones and bureaucrats. *Archaeology* 46(3): 28–38.

Harris, Marvin. 1968. *The Rise of Anthropological Theory.* New York: Crowell.

——. 1979. *Cultural Materialism: The Struggle for a Science of Culture.* New York: Random House.

——. 1993. *Culture, People, Nature: An Introduction to General Anthropology.* 6th ed. New York: HarperCollins.

——. 1994. Cultural materialism is alive and well and won't go away until something better comes along. In R. Borofsky (Ed.), *Assessing Cultural Anthropology* (pp. 62–76). New York: McGraw-Hill.

Harris, Marvin, and Eric B. Ross (Eds.). 1987. *Food and Evolution: Toward a Theory of Human Food Habits.* Philadelphia: Temple University Press.

Harvey, David. 1989. *The Condition of Postmodernity: An Enquiry Into the Origins of Cultural Change*. Cambridge, MA: Blackwell.

Hastorf, Christine A., and Sissel Johannessen. 1991. Understanding changing people/plant relationships in the prehispanic Andes. In Robert W. Preucel (Ed.), *Processual and Post-processual Archaeologies: Multiple Ways of Knowing the Past* (pp. 140–155). Carbondale: Southern Illinois University, Center for Archaeological Investigations, Occasional Paper no. 10.

Hastorf, Christine A., and Virginia S. Popper (Eds.). 1988. *Current Paleoethnobotany: Analytical Methods and Cultural Interpretations of Archaeological Plant Remains*. Chicago: University of Chicago Press.

Haury, Emil W. 1950. *The Stratigraphy and Archaeology of Ventana Cave, Arizona*. Albuquerque: University of New Mexico Press; Tucson: University of Arizona Press.

———. 1962. HH-39: Recollections of a dramatic moment in Southwestern archaeology. *Tree-Ring Bulletin* 24(3–4): 11–14.

———. 1976. *The Hohokam, Desert Farmers and Craftsmen: Excavations at Snaketown, 1964–1965*. Tucson: University of Arizona Press.

Haviland, William A. 1994. *Anthropology*. 7th ed. Fort Worth: Harcourt Brace College Publishers.

Hawkes, Kristen, James F. O'Connell, and N. Blurton Jones. 1987. Hardworking Hadza grandmothers. In R. Foley and V. Standen (Eds.), *Comparative Socioecology of Mammals and Man*. London: Basil Blackwell.

Hay, Richard I., and Mary D. Leakey. 1982. The fossil footprints of Laetoli. *Scientific American* 246(2): 50–57.

Hayden, Brian. 1979. *Palaeolithic Reflections: Lithic Technology and Ethnographic Excavation Among Australian Aborigines*. Atlantic Highlands, NJ: Humanities Press.

———. 1987. *Lithic Studies Among the Contemporary Highland Maya*. Tucson: University of Arizona Press.

———. 1990. Nimrods, piscators, pluckers, and planters: The emergence of food production. *Journal of Anthropological Archaeology* 9: 31–69.

Hayden, Brian, and Aubrey Cannon. 1984. The structure of material systems: Ethnoarchaeology in the Maya highlands. *Society of American Archaeology Papers*, no. 3.

Hedges, R. E. M., and J. A. J. Gowlett. 1986. Radiocarbon dating by accelerator mass spectrometry. *Scientific American* 254(1): 100–107.

Henry, Donald O., and George H. Odell (Eds.). 1989. Alternative approaches to lithic analysis. *Archaeological Papers of the American Anthropological Association*, no. 1. Washington, DC: American Anthropological Association.

Herrmann, Bernd, and Susanne Hummell (Eds.). 1994. *Ancient DNA: Recovery and Analysis of Genetic Material From Paleontological, Archaeological, Museum, Medical, and Forensic Specimens*. New York: Springer-Verlag.

Hester, Thomas R., Harry J. Shafer, and Kenneth L. Feder. 1997. *Field Methods in Archaeology*. 7th ed. Mountain View, CA: Mayfield.

Hill, Andrew. 1979a. Butchery and natural disarticulation: An investigatory technique. *American Antiquity* 44: 739–744.

——. 1979b. Disarticulation and scattering of mammal skeletons. *Paleobiology* 5(3): 261–274.

Hill, James N. 1991. Archaeology and the accumulation of knowledge. In Robert W. Preucel (Ed.), *Processual and Postprocessual Archaeologies: Multiple Ways of Knowing the Past* (pp. 42–53). Carbondale: Southern Illinois University, Center for Archaeological Investigations, Occasional Paper no. 10.

Hodder, Ian. 1982. *Symbols in Action: Ethnoarchaeological Studies of Material Culture.* Cambridge: Cambridge University Press.

——. 1985. Postprocessual archaeology. In Michael B. Schiffer (Ed.), *Advances in Archaeological Method and Theory.* Vol. 8 (pp. 1–26). Orlando: Academic Press.

——. 1986. *Reading the Past: Current Approaches to Interpretation in Archaeology.* Cambridge: Cambridge University Press.

——. 1989a. Post-modernism, post-structuralism and post-processual archaeology. In Ian Hodder (Ed.), *The Meaning of Things.* One World Archaeology series, no. 6 (pp. 64–78). London: Unwin Hyman.

——. 1989b. Writing archaeology: Site reports in context. *Antiquity* 63(239): 268–274.

——. 1990. Archaeology and the post-modern. *Anthropology Today* 6(5): 13–15.

——. 1991a. Postprocessual archaeology and the current debate. In Robert W. Preucel (Ed.), *Processual and Postprocessual Archaeologies: Multiple Ways of Knowing the Past* (pp. 30–41). Carbondale: Southern Illinois University, Center for Archaeological Investigations, Occasional Paper no. 10.

——. 1991b. Interpretive archaeology and its role. *American Antiquity* 56(1): 7–18.

——. 1995. *Theory and Practice in Archaeology.* London: Routledge.

Hodder, Ian, Michael Shanks, Alexandra Alexandri, Victor Buehli, John Carman, Jonathan Last, and Gavin Lucas (Eds.). 1995. *Interpreting Archaeology: Finding Meaning in the Past.* London and New York: Routledge.

Holliday, Vance T. (Ed.). 1992. *Soils in Archaeology: Landscape Evolution and Human Occupation.* Washington, DC: Smithsonian Institution Press.

Hooton, Earnest Albert. 1930. *The Indians of Pecos Pueblo: A study of Their skeletal remains.* Papers of the Phillips Academy Southwestern Expedition 4. New Haven: Yale University Press.

Horai, Satoshi, Rumi Kondo, Yuko Nakagawa-Hattori, Seiji Hayashi, Shunro Sonoda, and Kazuo Tajima. 1993. Peopling of the Americas, founded by four major lineages of mitochondrial DNA. *Molecular Biological Evolution* 10(1): 23–47.

Horgan, John. 1996. *The End of Science: Facing the Limits of Knowledge in the Twilight of the Scientific Age.* Reading, MA: Addison-Wesley.

Howard, Hildegarde. 1929. The avifauna of Emeryville shellmound. *University of California Publications in Zoology* 32: 301–394.

Howells, W. W. 1960. Estimating population numbers through archaeological and skeletal remains. In R. F. Heizer and S. F. Cook (Eds.), *The Application of Quantitative Methods in Archaeology.* Viking Fund Publications in Anthropology, no. 28 (pp. 158–185). Chicago: Quadrangle.

Huss-Ashmore, Rebecca, Alan H. Goodman, and George J. Armelagos. 1982. Nutritional inference from paleopathology. In Michael B. Schiffer (Ed.), *Advances in Archaeological Method and Theory.* Vol. 5 (pp. 395–474). New York: Academic Press.

Hutchinson, Dale, and Clark Spencer Larsen. 1988. Determination of stress episode duration from linear enamel hypoplasias: A case study from St. Catherines Island, Georgia. *Human Biology* 60(1): 93–110.

Irwin-Williams, Cynthia. 1990. Women in the field: The role of women in archaeology before 1960. In G. Kass-Simon and Patricia Farnes (Eds.), *Women of Science: Righting the Record* (pp. 1–41). Bloomington: Indiana University Press.

Isaac, Glynn L. 1978. The food-sharing behavior of protohuman hominids. *Scientific American* 238(4): 90–108.

Jacobi, R. M. 1978. Northern England in the eighth millennium B.C.: An essay. In Paul Mellars (Ed.), *The Early Post-Glacial Settlement of Northern Europe* (pp. 295–332). London: Duckworth.

Jamieson, Ross W. 1995. Material culture and social death: African-American burial practices. *Historical Archaeology* 29(4): 39–58.

Johnson, Allen W., and Timothy Earle. 1987. *The Evolution of Human Societies: From Foraging Group to Agrarian State*. Stanford: Stanford University Press.

Johnson, Jay K. (Ed.). 1993. *The Development of Southeastern Archaeology*. Tuscaloosa: University of Alabama Press.

Johnston, R. B. 1961. Archaeological application of the proton magnetometer in Indiana (U.S.A.). *Archaeometry* 4: 71–72.

Joukowsky, Martha. 1980. *A Complete Manual of Field Archaeology: Tools and Techniques of Field Work for Archaeologists*. Englewood Cliffs, NJ: Prentice-Hall.

Jull, A. J. T., D. J. Donahue, and P. E. Damon. 1996. Factors affecting the apparent radiocarbon age of textiles: A comment on "Effects of fires and biofractionation of carbon isotopes on results of radiocarbon dating of old textiles: The Shroud of Turin" by D. A. Kouznetsov et al. *Journal of Archaeological Science* 23: 157–160.

Katzenberg, M. Anne, Henry P. Schwarcz, Martin Knyf, and F. Jerome Melbye. 1995. Stable isotope evidence for maize horticulture and paleodiet in southern Ontario, Canada. *American Antiquity* 60(2): 335–350.

Kelly, Robert L. 1995. *The Foraging Spectrum*. Washington, DC: Smithsonian Institution Press.

Kemeny, John G. 1959. *A Philosopher Looks at Science*. New York: Van Nostrand Reinhold.

Kidder, Alfred V. 1924. *An Introduction to the Study of Southwestern Archaeology*. New Haven: Yale University Press.

——. 1960. Reminiscences in Southwest archaeology, I. *Kiva* 25: 1–32.

Klesert, Anthony L. 1992. A view from Navajoland on the reconciliation of anthropologists and Native Americans. *Human Organization* 51(1): 17–22.

Klesert, Anthony L., and Alan S. Downer (Eds.). 1990. Preservation on the reservation: Native Americans, Native American lands and archaeology. *Navajo Nation Papers in Anthropology*, no. 26.

Klesert, Anthony L., and Shirley Powell. 1993. A perspective on ethics and the reburial controversy. *American Antiquity* 58(2): 348–354.

Koch, Christopher P. (Ed.). 1989. *Taphonomy: A Bibliographic Guide to the Literature*. Orono, ME: Center for the Study of the First Americans.

Kohl, Philip L. 1993. Limits to a post-processual archaeology (or, the dangers of a new scholasticism). In Norman Yoffee and Andrew Sheratt (Eds.), *Archaeological Theory: Who Sets the Agenda?* (pp. 13–19). Cambridge: Cambridge University Press.

Kosso, P. 1991. Method in archaeology: Middle-range theory as hermeneutics. *American Antiquity* 56(4): 621–627.

Kottak, Conrad Philip. 1991. *Anthropology: The Exploration of Human Diversity.* 5th ed. New York: McGraw-Hill.

Kouznetsov, Dmitri A., Andrey A. Ivanov, and Pavel R. Veletsky. 1996. Effects of fires and biofractionation of carbon isotopes on results of radiocarbon dating of old textiles: The Shroud of Turin. *Journal of Archaeological Science* 23: 109–121.

Krieger, Alex D. 1944. The typological concept. *American Antiquity* 9(3): 271–288.

Lamberg-Karlovsky, C. C. (Ed.). 1989. *Archaeological Thought in America.* Cambridge: Cambridge University Press.

Lambert, Patricia M. 1993. Health in prehistoric populations of the Santa Barbara Channel Islands. *American Antiquity* 58(3): 509–522.

Lambert, Patricia M., and Phillip L. Walker. 1991. Physical anthropological evidence for the evolution of social complexity in coastal Southern California. *Antiquity* 65(249): 963–973.

Landon, David B. 1996. Feeding colonial Boston: A zooarchaeological study. *Historical Archaeology* 30(1).

Lange, Charles H., and Carroll L. Riley. 1996. *Bandelier: The Life and Adventures of Adolph Bandelier.* Salt Lake City: University of Utah Press.

Lange, Frederick W., and Jerome S. Handler. 1985. The ethnohistorical approach to slavery. In Theresa A. Singleton (Ed.), *The Archaeology of Slavery and Plantation Life* (pp. 15–32). Orlando: Academic Press.

Larsen, Clark Spencer. 1987. Bioarchaeological interpretations of subsistence economy and behavior from human skeletal remains. In Michael B. Schiffer (Ed.), *Advances in Archaeological Method and Theory.* Vol. 10 (pp. 339–445). Orlando: Academic Press.

——. 1995. Biological changes in human populations with agriculture. *Annual Review of Anthropology* 24: 185–213.

——. 1997. *Bioarchaeology: Interpreting Behavior From the Human Skeleton.* Cambridge: Cambridge University Press.

Lathrap, Donald W. 1973. Gifts of the cayman: Some thoughts on the subsistence basis of Chavín. In Donald W. Lathrap and Jody Douglas (Eds.), *Variation in Anthropology* (pp. 91–105). Urbana: Illinois Archaeological Survey.

——. 1977. Our father the cayman, our mother the gourd: Spinden revisited, or a unitary model for the emergence of agriculture in the New World. In Charles A. Reed (Ed.), *Origins of Agriculture* (pp. 713–751). The Hague: Mouton.

——. 1985. Jaws: The control of power in the early nuclear American ceremonial center. In C. B. Donnan (Ed.), *Early Ceremonial Architecture in the Andes* (pp. 241–267). Washington, DC: Dumbarton Oaks Research Library and Collection.

Layton, Robert (Ed.). 1989. *Who Needs the Past? Indigenous Values and Archaeology.* One World Archaeology series. London: Unwin Hyman.

Leakey, Mary. 1984. *Disclosing the Past*. Garden City, NY: Doubleday.

Leakey, Mary, and J. M. Harris (Eds.). 1987. *Laetoli: A Pliocene Site in Northern Tanzania*. Oxford: Clarendon.

Lee, Richard B., and Irven DeVore. 1968. *Man the Hunter*. Chicago: Aldine.

Lees, Susan H. 1994. Irrigation and society. *Journal of Archaeological Research* 2(4): 361–378.

Legge, A. J., and P. A. Rowley-Conwy. 1988. *Star Carr Revisited*. London: University of London, Birkbeck College, Centre for Extra-Mural Studies.

Lekson, Stephen H. 1986. *Great Pueblo Architecture of Chaco Canyon*. Albuquerque: University of New Mexico Press.

Leonard, Robert D., and George T. Jones. 1987. Elements of an inclusive evolutionary model for archaeology. *Journal of Anthropological Archaeology* 6(3): 199–219.

Leone, Mark P. 1986. Symbolic, structural, and critical archaeology. In David J. Meltzer, Don D. Fowler, and Jeremy A. Sabloff (Eds.), *American Archaeology Past and Future: A Celebration of the Society for American Archaeology 1935–1985* (pp. 415–438). Washington, DC: Smithsonian Institution Press.

Leone, Mark P., Paul R. Mullins, Marian C. Creveling, Laurence Hurst, Barbara Jackson-Nash, Lynn D. Jones, Hannah Jopling Kaiser, George C. Logan, and Mark S. Warner. 1995. Can an African-American historical archaeology be an alternative voice? In Ian Hodder, Michael Shanks, Alexandra Alexandri, Victor Buehli, John Carman, Jonathan Last, and Gavin Lucas (Eds.), *Interpreting Archaeology: Finding Meaning in the Past* (pp. 110–124). London: Routledge.

Leone, Mark P., and Parker B. Potter Jr. 1992. Legitimation and the classification of archaeological sites. *American Antiquity* 57(1): 137–145.

Leone, Mark P., and Neil Asher Silberman. 1995. *Invisible America: Unearthing Our Hidden History*. New York: Henry Holt.

Leroi-Gourhan, Arlette. 1975. The flowers found with Shanidar IV, a Neanderthal burial in Iraq. *Science* 190(4214): 562–564.

Levine, Mary Ann. 1994. Creating their own niches: Career styles among women in Americanist archaeology between the wars. In Cheryl Claassen (Ed.), *Women in Archaeology* (pp. 9–40). Philadelphia: University of Pennsylvania Press.

Levy, Clifford J. 1993, August 13. Study to examine bones from blacks' burial site. *New York Times*.

Lewin, Roger. 1992. Mitochondria tell the tale of migrations to America. *New Scientist* 133(1809): 16.

Lightfoot, Kent G. 1995. Culture contact studies: Redefining the relationship between prehistoric and historical archaeology. *American Antiquity* 60(2): 199–217.

Little, Barbara J. (Ed.). 1992. *Text-Aided Archaeology*. Boca Raton, FL: CRC Press.

Little, Elizabeth A., and Margaret J. Schoeninger. 1995. The Late Woodland diet on Nantucket Island and the problem of maize in coastal New England. *American Antiquity* 60(2): 351–368.

Lofstrom, Ted, Jeffrey P. Tordoff, and Douglas C. George. 1982. A seriation of historic earthenwares in the Midwest, 1780–1870. *Minnesota Archaeologist* 41(1): 3–29.

Long, A., and Bruce Rippeteau. 1974. Testing contemporaneity and averaging radiocarbon dates. *American Antiquity* 39(2): 205–215.

Longacre, William A. (Ed.). 1991. *Ceramic Ethnoarchaeology.* Tucson: University of Arizona Press.

Longacre, William A., and James M. Skibo (Eds.). 1994. *Kalinga Ethnoarchaeology: Expanding Archaeological Method and Theory.* Washington, DC: Smithsonian Institution Press.

Lubbock, Sir John. 1865. *Pre-historic Times, As Illustrated by Ancient Remains, and the Manners and Customs of Modern Savages.* London: Williams and Norgate.

——. 1869. *Pre-historic Times.* 2d ed. London: Williams and Norgate.

——. 1870. *The Origin of Civilization and the Primitive Condition of Man: Mental and Social Conditions of Savages.* London: Longmans, Green.

Lukacs, John R., and Lori L. Minderman. 1992. Dental pathology and agricultural intensification from Neolithic to Chalcolithic periods at Mehrgarh (Baluchistan, Pakistan). In C. Jarrige, *South Asian Archaeology, 1989.* Monographs in World Archaeology, no. 14 (pp. 167–179). Madison, WI: Prehistory Press.

Lukacs, John R., D. H. Retief, and Jean-Francois Jarrige. 1985, Spring. Dental disease in prehistoric Baluchistan. *National Geographic Research* 1(2): 184–197.

Lukacs, John R., Michael Schultz, and Brian E. Hemphill. 1989. Dental pathology and dietary patterns in Iron Age northern Pakistan. In P. Sorensen and K. Frifelt (Eds.), *South Asian Archaeology 1985* (pp. 475–496). London: Curzon.

Lyman, R. Lee. 1994. *Vertebrate Taphonomy.* Cambridge: Cambridge University Press.

Lynott, Mark J., and Alison Wylie. 1995. *Ethics in American Archaeology: Challenges for the 1990s.* Special Report, Society for American Archaeology.

Lyon, Edwin A. 1996. *A New Deal for Southeastern Archaeology.* Tuscaloosa: University of Alabama Press.

Lyons, T. R., and T. E. Avery. 1984. *Remote Sensing: A Handbook for Archaeologists and Cultural Resource Managers.* Washington, DC: National Park Service, Department of the Interior.

Lyotard, Jean François. 1984. *The Postmodern Condition: A Report on Knowledge.* Translated by G. Bennington and B. Massumi. Minneapolis: University of Minnesota Press.

MacMahon, Darcie, and Kathleen Deagan. 1996, September/October. Legacy of Fort Mose. *Archaeology:* 54–58.

MacNeish, Richard S. 1967. A summary of the subsistence. In Douglas S. Byers (Ed.), *The Prehistory of the Tehuacan Valley.* Vol. 1, *Environment and Subsistence* (pp. 290–309). Austin: University of Texas Press.

——. 1992. *The Origins of Agriculture and Settled Life.* Norman: University of Oklahoma Press.

Majewski, Teresita, and Michael J. O'Brien. 1987. The use and misuse of nineteenth-century English and American ceramics in archaeological analysis. In Michael B. Schiffer (Ed.), *Advances in Archaeological Method and Theory.* Vol. 11 (pp. 97–210). New York: Academic Press.

Maples, William R., and Michael Browning. 1994. *Dead Men Do Tell Tales.* New York: Doubleday.

Marcus, George E. 1994. After the critique of ethnography: Faith, hope, and charity, but the greatest of these is charity. In Robert Borofsky (Ed.), *Assessing Cultural Anthropology* (pp. 40–54). New York: McGraw-Hill.

Marcus, George E., and Michael M. J. Fischer. 1986. *Anthropology as Cultural Critique: An Experimental Moment in the Human Sciences.* Chicago: University of Chicago Press.

Marcus, Joyce. 1992. *Mesoamerican Writing Systems: Propaganda, Myth, and History in Four Ancient Civilizations.* Princeton: Princeton University Press.

Marcus, Joyce, and Kent Flannery. 1996. *Zapotec Civilization.* London: Thames and Hudson.

Marquardt, William H. 1978. Advances in archaeological seriation. In Michael B. Schiffer (Ed.), *Advances in Archaeological Method and Theory.* Vol. 1 (pp. 257–314). New York: Academic Press.

Marshack, Alexander. 1976. Implications of the Paleolithic symbolic evidence for the origin of language. *American Scientist* 64(2): 136–145.

——. 1989. Evolution of the human capacity: The symbolic evidence. *Yearbook of Physical Anthropology* 32: 1–34.

——. 1991. *The Roots of Civilization: The Cognitive Beginnings of Man's First Art, Symbol and Notation.* Revised and expanded. Mount Kisco, NY: Moyer Bell.

——. 1995a, July/August. Images of the Ice Age. *Archaeology:* 28–36, 38–39.

——. 1995b. Methodology and the search for notation among engraved pebbles of the European Late Palaeolithic. *Antiquity* 69(266): 1049–1051.

——. 1996. A Middle Paleolithic symbolic composition from the Golan Heights: The earliest known depictive image. *Current Anthropology* 37(2): 357–365.

Marshack, Alexander, and Francesco d'Errico. 1996. The La Marche antler revisited. *Cambridge Archaeological Journal* 6(1): 99–117.

Martin, Debra L., Alan H. Goodman, and George J. Armelagos. 1985. Skeletal pathologies as indicators of quality and quantity of diet. In Robert I. Gilbert and James H. Mielke (Eds.), *The Analysis of Prehistoric Diets* (pp. 227–279). Orlando: Academic Press.

Martin, William A., James E. Bruseth, and Robert J. Huggins. 1991. Assessing feature function and spatial patterning of artifacts with geophysical remote-sensing data. *American Antiquity* 56(4): 701–720.

Maschner, Herbert Donald Graham (Ed.). 1996. *Darwinian Archaeologies.* New York: Plenum.

Matson, R. G. 1991. *The Origins of Southwestern Agriculture.* Tucson: University of Arizona Press.

Mayer-Oakes, William J. 1955. Prehistory of the upper Ohio valley. *Annals of the Carnegie Museum* 34.

Maynard Smith, J. 1978. Optimization theory in evolution. *Annual Review of Ecology and Systematics* 9: 31–56.

McEwan, Bonnie G. (Ed.). 1993. *The Spanish Missions of La Florida.* Gainesville: University Press of Florida.

McGuire, Randall H. 1992a. *A Marxist Archaeology.* San Diego: Academic Press.

——. 1992b. *Death, Society, and Ideology in a Hohokam Community.* Boulder, CO: Westview.

——. 1993. Archaeology and Marxism. In M. B. Schiffer (Ed.), *Archaeological Method and Theory*. Vol. 5 (pp. 101–157). Tucson: University of Arizona Press.

McGuire, Randall H., and Robert Paynter (Eds.). 1991. *The Archaeology of Inequality*. Oxford: Basil Blackwell.

McGuire, Randall H., and Michael B. Schiffer (Eds.). 1982. *Hohokam and Patayan: Prehistory of Southwestern Arizona*. New York: Academic Press.

McManamon, Francis P. 1984. Discovering sites unseen. In Michael B. Schiffer (Ed.), *Advances in Archaeological Method and Theory*. Vol. 7 (pp. 223–292). New York: Academic Press.

——. 1991. The many publics for archaeology. *American Antiquity* 56(1): 121–130.

——. 1992. Managing America's archaeological resources. In LuAnn Wandsnider (Ed.), *Quandaries and Quests: Visions of Archaeology's Future* (pp. 25–40). Carbondale: Southern Illinois University, Center for Archaeological Investigations, Occasional Paper no. 20.

——. 1994. Changing relationships between Native Americans and archaeologists. *Historic Preservation Forum* 8(2): 15–20.

McManamon, Francis P., Patricia C. Knoll, Ruthann Knudson, George S. Smith, and Richard C. Waldbauer (Comps.). 1993. *The Secretary of the Interior's Report to Congress: Federal Archeological Programs and Activities*. Washington, DC: National Park Service, Department of the Interior, Departmental Consulting Archeologist Archeological Assistance Program.

McMillon, Bill. 1991. *The Archaeology Handbook: A Field Manual and Resource Guide*. New York: Wiley.

McNutt, Charles H. 1973. On the methodological validity of frequency seriation. *American Antiquity* 38: 45–60.

Mehrer, Mark W. 1995. *Cahokia's Countryside: Household Archaeology, Settlement Patterns, and Social Power*. DeKalb: Northern Illinois University Press.

Mehringer, Peter J. 1986. Prehistoric environments. In Warren L. D'Azevedo (Ed.), *Handbook of North American Indians*. Vol. 11 (pp. 31–50). Washington, DC: Smithsonian Institution Press.

Mehringer, Peter J., Eric Blinman, and Kenneth L. Peterson. 1977. Pollen influx and volcanic ash. *Science* 198(4314): 257–261.

Meighan, Clement W. 1992. Some scholars' views on reburial. *American Antiquity* 57(4): 704–710.

Meltzer, David J. 1989. Why don't we know when the first people came to North America? *American Antiquity* 54(3): 471–490.

——. 1993, October. Coming to America. *Discover:* 90–97.

——. 1995. Clocking the first Americans. *Annual Review of Anthropology* 24: 21–45.

Meltzer, David J., Don D. Fowler, and Jeremy A. Sabloff (Eds.). 1986. *American Archaeology Past and Future: A Celebration of the Society for American Archaeology 1935–1985*. Washington, DC: Smithsonian Institution Press.

Messenger, Phyllis (Ed.). 1989. *The Ethics of Collecting Cultural Property: Whose Culture? Whose Property?* Albuquerque: University of New Mexico Press.

Michels, Joseph W. 1973. *Dating Methods in Archaeology*. New York: Seminar.

Miksicek, Charles H. 1987. Formation processes of the archaeobotanical record. In Michael B. Schiffer (Ed.), *Advances in Archaeological Method and Theory*. Vol. 10 (pp. 211–247). New York: Academic Press.

Miller, Daniel, and Christopher Tilley. 1984. *Ideology, Power and Prehistory*. Cambridge: Cambridge University Press.

Miller, George R., and Richard L. Burger. 1995. Our father the cayman, our dinner the llama: Animal utilization at Chavín de Huántar, Peru. *American Antiquity* 60(3): 421–458.

Miller, Gifford H., Peter B. Beaumont, A. J. T. Jull, and Beverly Johnson. 1992. Pleistocene geochronology and palaeothermometry from protein dia-genesis in ostrich eggshells: Implications for the evolution of modern humans. *Philosophical Transactions of the Royal Society of London* B337: 149–157.

Milner, George R., Eve Anderson, and Virginia G. Smith. 1991. Warfare in late prehistoric west-central Illinois. *American Antiquity* 56(4): 581–603.

Mithen, Steven. 1989. Evolutionary theory and post-processual archaeology. *Antiquity* 63(240): 483–494.

——. 1990. *Thoughtful Foragers: A Study of Prehistoric Decision Making*. Cambridge: Cambridge University Press.

——. 1995. Palaeolithic archaeology and the evolution of mind. *Journal of Archaeological Research* 3(4): 305–332.

Mobley, Charles M. 1980. Demographic structure of Pecos Indians: A model based on life tables. *American Antiquity* 45(3): 518–530.

Monastersky, Richard. 1990. Reopening old wounds. *Science News* 137(3): 40–42.

Monks, Gregory G. 1981. Seasonality studies. In Michael B. Schiffer (Ed.), *Advances in Archaeological Method and Theory*. Vol. 4 (pp. 177–240). New York: Academic Press.

Moore, P. D., J. A. Webb, and M. E. Collinson. 1991. *Pollen Analysis*. Oxford: Blackwell Scientific.

Morell, Virginia. 1994. An anthropological culture shift. *Science* 264: 20–22.

Morgan, Lewis Henry. [1877] 1963. *Ancient Society*. E. Leacock (Ed.), New York: Meridian Books; World Publishing.

Morris, Ann Axtell. 1933. *Digging in the Southwest*. New York: Doubleday, Doran.

Morris, Craig, and Adriana von Hagen. 1993. *The Inka Empire and Its Andean Origins*. New York: Abbeville.

Morris, Ian. 1991. The archaeology of ancestors: The Saxe/Goldstein hypothesis revisited. *Cambridge Archaeological Journal* 1(2): 147–168.

Murray, Tim. 1996. Coming to terms with the living: Some aspects of repatriation for the archaeologist. *Antiquity* 70(267): 217–220.

National Park Service. 1995, Fall/Winter. Special Report: The Native American Graves Protection and Repatriation Act. *Federal Archeology*.

Neff, Hector. 1992. Ceramics and evolution. In M. B. Schiffer (Ed.), *Archaeological Method and Theory*. Vol. 4 (pp. 141–194). Tucson: University of Arizona Press.

Nei, Masatoshi. 1992. Age of the common ancestor of human mitochondrial DNA. *Molecular Biology and Evolution* 9(6): 1176–1178.

Nelson, Nels C. 1914. Pueblo ruins of the Galisteo Basin, New Mexico. *Anthropological Papers of the American Museum of Natural History* 15(1).

——. 1916. Chronology of the Tano Ruins, New Mexico. *American Anthropologist* 18(2): 159–180.

Nelson, Margaret C., Sarah M. Nelson, and Alison Wylie (Eds.). 1994. Equity issues for women in archeology. *Archeological Papers of the American Anthropological Association,* no. 5.

Nelson, Sarah M., and Margaret C. Nelson. 1994. Conclusion. In M. C. Nelson, S. M. Nelson, and A. Wylie (Eds.), Equity issues for women in archeology. *Archeological Papers of the American Anthropological Association* 5: 229–235.

Nixon, Lucia. 1994. Gender bias in archaeology. In Leonie J. Archer and Susan Fischler (Eds.), *Women in Ancient Societies: An Illusion of the Night* (pp. 1–23). Basingstoke, England: Macmillan.

Noble, David Grant (Ed.). 1991. *The Hohokam: Ancient People of the Desert.* Santa Fe: School of American Research Press.

Noël Hume, Ivor. 1969a. *Archaeology and Wetherburn's Tavern.* Williamsburg: Colonial Williamsburg Foundation.

——. 1969b. *Historical Archaeology.* New York: Knopf.

——. 1976. *A Guide to Artifacts of Colonial America.* New York: Knopf.

Oakley, Kenneth P. 1968. *Frameworks for Dating Fossil Man.* 2d ed. Chicago: Aldine.

O'Brien, Michael J., and Thomas D. Holland. 1990. Variation, selection, and the archaeological record. In Michael B. Schiffer (Ed.), *Archaeological Method and Theory.* Vol. 2 (pp. 31–79). Tucson: University of Arizona Press.

O'Connell, James F., and Kristen Hawkes. 1981. Alyawara plant use and optimal foraging theory. In Bruce Winterhalder and Eric Alden Smith (Eds.), *Hunter-Gatherer Foraging Strategies: Ethnographic and Archaeological Analyses* (pp. 99–125). Chicago: University of Chicago Press.

——. 1984. Food choice and foraging sites among the Alyawara. *Journal of Anthropological Research* 40(4): 504–535.

Odell, George Hanley (Ed.). 1996. *Stone Tools: Theoretical Insights Into Human Prehistory.* New York: Plenum.

Orme, B. (Ed.). 1982. *Problems and Case Studies in Archaeological Dating.* Devon: University of Exeter.

Orser, Charles E. Jr. 1984. The past ten years of plantation archaeology in the southeastern United States. *Southeastern Archaeology* 3: 1–12.

——. 1991. The continued pattern of dominance: Landlord and tenant on the postbellum cotton plantation. In Randall H. McGuire and Robert Paynter (Eds.), *The Archaeology of Inequality* (pp. 40–54). Oxford: Basil Blackwell.

——. 1995. *A Historical Archaeology of the Modern World.* New York: Plenum.

Orser, Charles E. Jr., and Brian M. Fagan. 1995. *Historical Archaeology.* New York: HarperCollins.

Orton, Clive, Paul Tyers, and Alan Vince. 1993. *Pottery in Archaeology*. Cambridge: Cambridge University Press.

O'Shea, John M. 1984. *Mortuary Variability: An Archaeological Investigation*. Orlando: Academic Press.

Pääbo, Svante. 1993, November. Ancient DNA: Genetic information that had seemed lost forever turns out to linger in the remains of long-dead plants and animals. *Scientific American*: 87–92.

Palkovich, Ann M. 1983. A comment on Mobley's "Demographic Structure of Pecos Indians." *American Antiquity* 48(1): 142–147.

Parezo, Nancy J. (Ed.). 1993. *Hidden Scholars: Women Anthropologists and the Native American Southwest*. Albuquerque: University of New Mexico Press.

Parezo, Nancy J., and Susan Bender. 1994. From glacial to chilly climate: A comparison between archeology and socio-cultural anthropology. In M. C. Nelson, S. M. Nelson, and A. Wylie (Eds.), *Equity Issues for Women in Archeology* (pp. 73–81). Archeological Papers of the American Anthropological Association, no. 5.

Parker Pearson, Michael. 1982. Mortuary practices, society and ideology: An ethnoarchaeological study. In Ian Hodder (Ed.), *Symbolic and Structural Archaeology* (pp. 99–113). Cambridge: Cambridge University Press.

——. 1995. Return of the living dead: Mortuary analysis and the New Archaeology revisited. *Antiquity* 69(266): 1046–1048.

Patterson, Thomas C. 1990. Some theoretical tensions within and between the processual and postprocessual archaeologies. *Journal of Anthropological Archaeology* 9(2): 189–200.

——. 1995. *Toward a Social History of Archaeology in the United States*. Fort Worth: Harcourt Brace.

Paynter, Robert. 1989. The archaeology of equality and inequality. *Annual Review of Anthropology* 18: 369–399.

Pearsall, Deborah M. 1982. Phytolith analysis: Applications of a new paleo-ethnobotanical technique in archeology. *American Anthropologist* 84(4): 862–870.

Pearsall, Deborah M., and Dolores R. Piperno. 1990. Antiquity of maize cultivation in Ecuador: Summary and reevaluation of the evidence. *American Antiquity* 55(2): 324–337.

Peck, Mary. 1994. *Chaco Canyon: A Center and Its World*. Santa Fe: Museum of New Mexico Press.

Peebles, Christopher S. 1971. Moundville and surrounding sites: Some structural considerations of mortuary practices II. In James A. Brown (Ed.), *Approaches to the Social Dimensions of Mortuary Practices* (pp. 68–91). Society for American Archaeology Memoir 25.

——. 1977. Biocultural adaptation in prehistoric America: An archeologist's perspective. In Robert L. Blakely (Ed.), *Biocultural Adaptation in Prehistoric America* (pp. 115–130). Southern Anthropological Society Proceedings, no. 11. Athens: University of Georgia Press.

——. 1981. Archaeological research at Moundville: 1840–1980. *Southeastern Archaeological Conference Bulletin* 24: 77–81.

——. 1987. Moundville from 1000 to 1500 A.D. as seen from 1840 to 1985 A.D. In Robert D. Drennan and Carlos A. Uribe (Eds.), *Chiefdoms in the Americas* (pp. 21–41). Lanham, MD: University Press of America.

Peebles, Christopher S., and Susan M. Kus. 1977. Some archaeological correlates of ranked societies. *American Antiquity* 42: 421–448.

Pendleton, Michael W. 1983. A comment concerning testing flotation recovery rates. *American Antiquity* 48(3): 615–616.

Percy, George. 1976. The use of a mechanical earth auger at the Torreya Site, Liberty County, Florida. *Florida Anthropologist* 29(1): 24–32.

Perkins, Dexter, and Patricia Daly. 1968. A hunter's village in Neolithic Turkey. *Scientific American* 219: 96–106.

Phillips, Philip, and James A. Brown. 1978. *Pre-Columbian Shell Engravings From the Craig Mound at Spiro, Oklahoma. Part 1.* Cambridge, MA: Peabody Museum Press.

——. 1984. *Pre-Columbian Shell Engravings From the Craig Mound at Spiro, Oklahoma. Part 2.* Cambridge, MA: Peabody Museum of Archaeology and Ethnology.

Piperno, Dolores R. 1984. A comparison and differentiation of phytoliths from maize and wild grasses: Use of morphological criteria. *American Antiquity* 49(2): 361–383.

——. 1987. *Phytolith Analysis: An Archaeological and Geological Perspective.* San Diego: Academic Press.

Pitts, Mike. 1979. Hides and antlers: A new look at the gatherer-hunter site at Star Carr, North Yorkshire, England. *World Archaeology* 11(1): 32–42.

Podolefsky, Aaron, and Peter J. Brown. 1994. *Applying Anthropology: An Introductory Reader.* 3d ed. Mountain View, CA: Mayfield.

Powell, Mary Lucas. 1985. The analysis of dental wear and caries for dietary reconstructions. In R. I. Gilbert Jr., and J. H. Mielke (Eds.), *The Analysis of Prehistoric Diets* (pp. 307–338). Orlando: Academic Press.

——. 1988. *Status and Health in Prehistory: A Case Study of the Moundville Chiefdom.* Washington, DC: Smithsonian Institution Press.

Powell, Shirley, Christiana Elnora Garza, and Aubrey Hendricks. 1993. Ethics and ownership of the past: The reburial and repatriation controversy. In Michael B. Schiffer (Ed.), *Archaeological Method and Theory.* Vol. 5 (pp. 1–42). Tucson: University of Arizona Press.

Powledge, Tabitha M., and Mark Rose. 1996, September/October. The great DNA hunt. *Archaeology:* 36–44.

Preston, Douglas J. 1989, February. Skeletons in our museums' closets. *Harper's Magazine* 278(1665): 66–75.

Preucel, R. W. (Ed.). 1991. *Processual and Postprocessual Archaeologies: Multiple Ways of Knowing the Past.* Carbondale: Southern Illinois University, Center for Archaeological Investigations, Occasional Paper no. 10.

——. 1995. The postprocessual condition. *Journal of Archaeological Research* 3(2): 147–175.

Price, T. Douglas (Ed.). 1989. *The Chemistry of Prehistoric Human Bone.* Cambridge: Cambridge University Press.

Price, T. Douglas, and Gary M. Feinman. 1993. *Images of the Past.* Mountain View, CA: Mayfield.

—— (Eds.). 1995. *Foundations of Social Inequality.* New York: Plenum.

Price, T. Douglas, and Anne Birgitte Gebauer (Eds.). 1995. *Last Hunters–First Farmers: New Perspectives on the Prehistoric Transition to Agriculture*. Santa Fe: School of American Research Press.

Raab, L. Mark, and Albert C. Goodyear. 1984. Middle-range theory in archaeology: A critical review of origins and applications. *American Antiquity* 49(2): 255–268.

Ramenofsky, Ann F. 1987. *Vectors of Death: The Archaeology of European Contact*. Albuquerque: University of New Mexico Press.

Ramsey, Christopher Bronk. 1995. *OxCal Program 2.18*. Oxford Radiocarbon Accelerator Unit. Oxford: Oxford University.

Rankin-Hill, Lesley M., and Michael L. Blakey. 1994. W. Montague Cobb (1904–1990): Physical anthropologist, anatomist, and activist. *American Anthropologist* 96(1): 74–96.

Rapp, George, and John A. Gifford (Eds.). 1985. *Archaeological Geology*. New Haven: Yale University Press.

Rapp, George, and Susan C. Mulholland (Eds.). 1992. *Phytolith Systematics: Emerging Issues*. New York: Plenum.

Rathje, William L. 1984. The garbage decade. *American Behavioral Scientist* 28(1): 9–29.

——. 1991, May. Once and future landfills. *National Geographic* 25: 116–134.

Rathje, William L., and Wilson W. Hughes. 1975. The garbage project as a nonreactive approach: Garbage in . . . garbage out. In H. W. Sinaiko and L. A. Broedling (Eds.), *Perspectives on Attitude Assessment: Surveys and Their Alternatives*. Manpower Research and Advisory Services, Smithsonian Institution, Technical Report, no. 2.

Rathje, William L., W. W. Hughes, D. C. Wilson, M. K. Tani, G. H. Archer, R. G. Hunt, and T. W. Jones. 1992. The archaeology of contemporary landfills. *American Antiquity* 57(3): 437–447.

Reitz, Elizabeth J., and C. Margaret Scarry. 1985. Reconstructing historic subsistence with an example from sixteenth-century Spanish Florida. *Society of Historical Archaeology, Special Publication Series*, no. 3.

Renfrew, Colin. 1982. Explanation revisited. In C. Renfrew, M. J. Rowlands, and B. A. Segraves (Eds.), *Theory and Explanation in Archaeology* (pp. 1–23). New York: Academic Press.

——. 1992. Archaeology, genetics and linguistic diversity. *Man* 27: 445–478.

——. 1993. Cognitive archaeology: Some thoughts on the archaeology of thought. *Cambridge Archaeological Journal* 3(2): 248–250.

Renfrew, Colin, and Paul Bahn. 1996. *Archaeology: Theories, Methods, and Practice*. 2d. ed. London: Thames and Hudson.

Renfrew, Colin, and Stephen Shennan (Eds.). 1982. *Ranking, Resource and Exchange*. Cambridge: Cambridge University Press.

Renfrew, Colin, and Ezra B. W. Zubrow (Eds.). 1994. *The Ancient Mind: Elements of Cognitive Archaeology*. Cambridge: Cambridge University Press.

Reyman, J. E. (Ed.). 1992. *Rediscovering Our Past: Essays on the History of American Archaeology*. Brookfield, VT: Avebury.

Rice, Prudence M. 1987. *Pottery Analysis: A Sourcebook*. Chicago: University of Chicago Press.

——. 1996a. Recent ceramic analysis: 1. Function, style, and origins. *Journal of Archaeological Research* 4(2): 133–163.

——. 1996b. Recent ceramic analysis: 2. Composition, production, and theory. *Journal of Archaeological Research* 4(3): 165–202.

Rick, John W. 1987. Dates as data: An examination of the Peruvian pre-ceramic radiocarbon record. *American Antiquity* 52(1): 55–73.

Riding In, James. 1992. With ethics and morality: A historical overview of imperial archaeology and American Indians. *Arizona State Law Journal* 24(1): 11–34.

Ridings, Rosanna. 1996. Where in the world does obsidian hydration dating work? *American Antiquity* 61(1): 136–148.

Riley, D. N. 1987. *Air Photography and Archaeology.* London: Duckworth.

Rindos, David. 1984. *The Origins of Agriculture: An Evolutionary Perspective.* Orlando: Academic Press.

——. 1989a. Diversity, variation and selection. In R. D. Leonard and G. T. Jones (Eds.), *Quantifying Diversity in Archaeology* (pp. 13–23). Cambridge: Cambridge University Press.

——. 1989b. Undirected variation and the Darwinian explanation of culture change. In M. B. Schiffer (Ed.), *Archaeological Method and Theory.* Vol. 1 (pp. 1–46). Tucson: University of Arizona Press.

Roberts, Charlotte A., and Keith Manchester. 1995. *The Archaeology of Disease.* 2d ed. Ithaca: Cornell University Press.

Roberts, David. 1996. *In Search of the Old Ones: Exploring the Anasazi World of the Southwest.* New York: Simon and Schuster.

Rogers, Juliet, and Tony Waldron. 1989. Infections in paleopathology: The basis of classification according to most probable cause. *Journal of Archaeological Science* 16: 611–625.

Rose, Jerome C., Thomas J. Green, and Victoria D. Green. 1996. NAGPRA is forever: Osteology and the repatriation of skeletons. *Annual Review of Anthropology* 25: 81–103.

Rosenberg, Michael. 1994. Pattern, process, and hierarchy in the evolution of culture. *Journal of Anthropological Archaeology* 13: 307–340.

Rossignol, Jacqueline, and LuAnn Wandsnider (Eds.). 1992. *Space, Time, and Archaeological Landscapes.* New York: Plenum.

Rothschild, Bruce M., and Larry D. Martin. 1993. *Palaeopathology: Disease in the Fossil Record.* Boca Raton, FL: CRC Press.

Rothschild, Nan A. 1990. *New York City Neighborhoods: The 18th Century.* San Diego: Academic Press.

Rouse, Irving. 1960. The classification of artifacts in archaeology. *American Antiquity* 25(3): 313–323.

——. 1967. Seriation in archaeology. In Carrol L. Riley and Walter W. Taylor (Eds.), *American Historical Anthropology: Essays in Honor of Leslie Spier* (pp. 153–195). Carbondale: Southern Illinois University Press.

Rovner, Irwin. 1983. Plant opal phytolith analysis: Major advances in archaeobotanical research. In Michael B. Schiffer (Ed.), *Advances in Archaeological Method and Theory.* Vol. 6 (pp. 225–266). New York: Academic Press.

——. 1987. Plant opal phytoliths: A probable factor in the origins of agriculture. In Linda Manzanilla (Ed.), *Studies in the Neolithic and Urban Revolutions* (pp. 103–119). B.A.R. International Series 349.

——. 1988. Macro- and micro-ecological reconstruction using plant opal phytolith data from archaeological sediments. *Geoarchaeology* 3(2): 155–163.

Rowe, John Howland. 1965. The renaissance foundations of anthropology. *American Anthropologist* 67(1): 1–20.

Ruff, Christopher B. 1981. A reassessment of demographic estimates for Pecos Pueblo. *American Journal of Physical Anthropology* 54: 147–151.

Russell, Steve. 1995. The legacy of ethnic cleansing: Implementation of NAGPRA in Texas. *American Indian Culture and Research Journal* 19(4): 193–211.

Sabins, Floyd F. Jr. 1996. *Remote Sensing: Principles and Interpretation.* 3d ed. New York: Freeman.

Sahlins, Marshall D., and Elman R. Service. 1960. *Evolution and Culture.* Ann Arbor: University of Michigan Press.

Saitta, Dean J. 1992. Radical archaeology and middle-range methodology. *Antiquity* 66: 886–897.

Salwen, Bert, and Sarah T. Bridges. 1977. Cultural differences and the interpretation of archaeological evidence: Problems with dates. *Researches and Transactions of the New York State Archaeological Association* 17(1): 165–173.

Schiffer, Michael B. 1972. Archaeological context and systemic context. *American Antiquity* 37(2): 156–165.

——. 1976. *Behavioral Archeology.* New York: Academic Press.

——. 1987. *Formation Processes of the Archaeological Record.* Albuquerque: University of New Mexico Press.

Schiffer, Michael B., James M. Skibo, Tamara C. Boelke, Mark A. Neupert, and Meredith Aronson. 1994. New perspectives on experimental archaeology: Surface treatments and thermal response of the clay cooking pot. *American Antiquity* 59(2): 197–217.

Schulz, Peter D., and Sherri M. Gust. 1983a. Faunal remains and social status in 19th century Sacramento. *Historical Archaeology* 17(1): 44–53.

——. 1983b. Relative beef cut prices in the late 19th century: A note for historic sites faunal analysts. *Pacific Coast Archaeological Society Quarterly* 19(1): 12–18.

Scollar, Irwin. 1969. Some techniques for the evaluation of archaeological magnetometer surveys. *World Archaeology* 1(1): 77–89.

Scollar, Irwin, A. Tabbagh, A. Hesse, and I. Herzog (Eds.). 1990. *Archaeological Prospecting and Remote Sensing.* Cambridge: Cambridge University Press.

Scott, Elizabeth M. (Ed.). 1994. *Those of Little Note: Gender, Race, and Class in Historical Archaeology.* Tucson: University of Arizona Press.

Sebastian, Lynne. 1992. *The Chaco Anasazi: Sociopolitical Evolution in the Prehistoric Southwest. New Studies in Archaeology.* Cambridge: Cambridge University Press.

Seifert, Donna J. (Ed.). 1991. Gender in historical archaeology. *Historical Archaeology* 25(4).

Service, Elman. 1971. *Primitive Social Organization: An Evolutionary Perspective.* 2d ed. New York: Random House.

——. 1975. *Origins of the State and Civilization: The Process of Cultural Evolution.* New York: Norton.

Shackel, Paul A. 1996. *Culture Change and the New Technology: An Archaeology of the Early American Industrial Era.* New York: Plenum.

Shackley, Steven. 1995, March. Relics, rights and regulations. *Scientific American:* 115.

Shanks, Michael. 1992. *Experiencing the Past: On the Character of Archaeology.* London: Routledge.

Shanks, Michael, and Christopher Tilley. 1987a. *Reconstructing Archaeology: Theory and Practice.* Cambridge: Cambridge University Press.

——. 1987b. *Social Theory and Archaeology.* Albuquerque: University of New Mexico Press.

Shapiro, Gary. 1984. A soil resistivity survey of 16th-century Puerto Real, Haiti. *Journal of Field Archaeology* 11(1): 101–110.

——. 1987. Archaeology at San Luis: Broad-scale testing, 1984–1985. *Florida Archaeology,* no. 3.

Sheets, Payson D. (Ed.). 1983. *Archeology and Volcanism in Central America: The Zapotitán Valley of El Salvador.* Austin: University of Texas Press.

——. 1987. Dawn of a new Stone Age in eye surgery. In Robert J. Sharer and Wendy Ashmore (Eds.), *Archaeology: Discovering Our Past* (pp. 230–231). Mountain View, CA: Mayfield.

——. 1992. *The Cerén Site: A Prehistoric Village Buried by Volcanic Ash in Central America.* Fort Worth: Harcourt Brace Jovanovich.

Sheets, Payson D., and Donald K. Grayson. 1979. *Volcanic Activity and Human Ecology.* New York: Academic Press.

Sheets, Payson D., K. Hirth, F. Lange, F. Stross, F. Asaro, and H. Michel. 1990. Obsidian sources and elemental analyses of artifacts in southern Mesoamerica and the northern intermediate area. *American Antiquity* 55(1): 144–158.

Sheets, Payson D., and Brian R. McKee (Eds.). 1994. *Archaeology, Volcanism, and Remote Sensing in the Arenal Region, Costa Rica.* Austin: University of Texas Press.

Shreeve, James. 1992, September. The dating game. *Discover* 13(9): 76–83.

Singleton, Theresa A. (Ed.). 1985. *The Archaeology of Slavery and Plantation Life.* Orlando: Academic Press.

——. 1995. The archaeology of slavery in North America. *Annual Review of Anthropology* 24: 119–140.

Singleton, Theresa A., and M. Bograd. 1995. The archaeology of the African diaspora in the Americas. *Columbian Quincentenary Series Guides to the Archaeological Literature of the Immigrant Experience in America,* no. 2. Glassboro, NJ: Society for Historical Archaeology.

Skibo, James M., William H. Walker, and Axel E. Nielsen (Eds.). 1995. *Expanding Archaeology.* Salt Lake City: University of Utah Press.

Smith, Bruce D. (Ed.). 1990. *The Mississippian Emergence.* Washington, DC: Smithsonian Institution Press.

——. 1995. *The Emergence of Agriculture.* New York: Scientific American Library.

Smith, Charles C. 1994, Fall. In the presence of ancestors. *Massachusetts:* 10–13.

Smith, Eric Alden. 1983. Anthropological applications of optimal foraging theory: A critical review. *Current Anthropology* 24(5): 625–651.

——. 1985. On the logic and application of optimal foraging theory: A brief reply to Martin. *American Anthropologist* 87: 645–648.

Smith, Eric Alden, and Bruce Winterhalder. 1981. New perspectives on hunter-gatherer socioecology. In Bruce Winterhalder and Eric Alden Smith (Eds.), *Hunter-Gatherer Foraging Strategies: Ethnographic and Archeological Analyses* (pp. 1–12). Chicago: University of Chicago Press.

—— (Eds.). 1992. *Evolutionary Ecology and Human Behavior.* New York: Aldine de Gruyter.

Sobel, Mechal. 1987. *The World They Made Together: Black and White Values in Eighteenth-Century Virginia.* Princeton: Princeton University Press.

Sobolik, Kristin D. (Ed.). 1994. *Paleonutrition: The Diet and Health of Prehistoric Americans.* Carbondale: Southern Illinois University, Center for Archaeological Investigations, Occasional Paper no. 22.

Solecki, Ralph S. 1971. *Shanidar: The First Flower People.* New York: Knopf.

South, Stanley A. 1977a. *Method and Theory in Historical Archeology.* New York: Academic Press.

—— (Ed.). 1977b. *Research Strategies in Historical Archaeology.* New York: Academic Press.

——. 1994. The archaeologist and the crew: From the mountains to the sea. In Stanley South (Ed.), *Pioneers in Historical Archaeology: Breaking New Ground* (pp. 165–187). New York: Plenum.

Spaulding, Albert C. 1953. Statistical techniques for the discovery of artifact types. *American Antiquity* 18: 305–313.

——. 1960. The dimensions of archaeology. In G. E. Dole and R. L. Carneiro (Eds.), *Essays in the Science of Culture in Honor of Leslie A. White* (pp. 437–456). New York: Crowell.

——. 1977. On growth and form in archaeology: Multivariate analysis. *Journal of Anthropological Research* 33: 1–15.

——. 1985. Fifty years of theory. *American Antiquity* 50(2): 301–308.

——. 1988. Distinguished lecture: Archeology and anthropology. *American Anthropologist* 90(2): 263–271.

Spector, Janet D. 1983. Male/female task-differentiation among the Hidatsa: Toward the development of an archeological approach to the study of gender. In Patricia Albers and Beatrice Medicine (Eds.), *The Hidden Half: Studies of Plains Indian Women* (pp. 77–99). Lanham, MD: University Press of America.

——. 1993. *What This Awl Means: Feminist Archaeology at a Wahpeton Dakota Village.* St. Paul: Minnesota Historical Society Press.

Spencer, Charles. 1990. On the tempo and mode of state formation: Neoevolutionism reconsidered. *Journal of Anthropological Archaeology* 9(1): 1–30.

——. 1993. Human agency, biased transmission, and the cultural evolution of chiefly authority. *Journal of Anthropological Archaeology* 12: 41–74.

——. 1994. Factional ascendance, dimensions of leadership, and the development of centralized authority. In E. M. Brumfiel and J. W. Fox (Eds.), *Factional Competition and Political Development in the New World* (pp. 31–43). Cambridge: Cambridge University Press.

Spencer-Wood, Suzanne M. 1991. Toward a feminist historical archaeology of the construction of gender. In *The Archaeology of Gender* (pp. 234–244). Proceedings of the 22nd Annual Chacmool Conference. Calgary: University of Calgary Archaeological Association.

Spielmann, Katherine A. (Ed.). 1995. The archaeology of gender in the American Southwest. *Journal of Anthropological Research* 51(2): 91–191.

Spielmann, Katherine A., Margaret J. Schoeninger, and Katherine Moore. 1990. Plains-Pueblo interdependence and human diet at Pecos Pueblo, New Mexico. *American Antiquity* 55(4): 745–765.

Spier, Leslie. 1917. An outline for a chronology of Zuñi ruins. *Anthropological Papers of the American Museum of Natural History* 18(3): 207–331.

——. 1931. N. C. Nelson's stratigraphic technique in the reconstruction of prehistoric sequences in southwestern America. In S. A. Rice (Ed.), *Methods in Social Science* (pp. 275–283). Chicago: University of Chicago Press.

Stahl, Ann B. 1995. Has ethnoarchaeology come of age? *Antiquity* 69(263): 404–407.

Stahle, David W., and Daniel Wolfman. 1985. The potential for archaeological tree-ring dating in eastern North America. In Michael B. Schiffer (Ed.), *Advances in Archaeological Method and Theory*. Vol. 8 (pp. 279–302). New York: Academic Press.

Stallings, W. S. Jr. 1939. *Dating Prehistoric Ruins by Tree-Rings*. Santa Fe: Laboratory of Anthropology Bulletin no. 8.

Stark, Miriam T. 1993. Re-fitting the "cracked and broken facade": The case for empiricism in post-processual ethnoarchaeology. In Norman Yoffee and Andrew Sherratt (Eds.), *Archaeological Theory: Who Sets the Agenda?* (pp. 93–104). Cambridge: Cambridge University Press.

Steen-McIntyre, Virginia. 1985. Tephrochronology and its application to archaeology. In George Rapp Jr. and John A. Gifford (Eds.), *Archaeological Geology* (pp. 265–302). New Haven: Yale University Press.

Stein, Julie K. 1987. Deposits for archaeologists. In Michael B. Schiffer (Ed.), *Advances in Archaeological Method and Theory*. Vol. 11 (pp. 337–395). New York: Academic Press.

—— (Ed.). 1992. *Deciphering a Shell Midden*. San Diego: Academic Press.

Stephens, David W., and John R. Krebs. 1986. *Foraging Theory*. Princeton: Princeton University Press.

Steponaitis, Vincas P. 1983. *Ceramics, Chronology, and Community Patterns: An Archaeological Study at Moundville*. New York: Academic Press.

Steponaitis, Vincas P., and J. P. Brain. 1976. A portable differential proton magnetometer. *Journal of Field Archaeology* 3(4): 455–463.

Sterngold, James. 1993, May 24. Emperor's buried secrets: No digging allowed. *The New York Times:* A4.

Steward, Julian H. 1954. Types of types. *American Anthropologist* 56(1): 54–57.

Stiebing, William H. Jr. 1994. *Uncovering the Past: A History of Archaeology*. New York: Oxford University Press.

Stone, Anne C., and Mark Stoneking. 1993. Ancient DNA from a Pre-Columbian Amerindian population. *American Journal of Physical Anthropology* 92: 463–471.

Stoneking, Mark. 1994. In defense of "Eve"—a response to Templeton's critique. *American Anthropologist* 96(1): 131–141.

Straus, Lawrence G. 1990. Underground archaeology: Perspectives on caves and rock-shelters. In M. B. Schiffer (Ed.), *Archaeological Method and Theory*. Vol. 2 (pp. 255–304). Tucson: University of Arizona Press.

Struever, Stuart. 1968. Flotation techniques for the recovery of small-scale archaeological remains. *American Antiquity* 33(3): 353–362.

Stuiver, Minze, and Paula J. Reimer. 1993. Extended ^{14}C database and revised CALIB 3.0 ^{14}C age calibration program. *Radiocarbon* 35(1): 215–230.

Szathmary, Emöke J. E. 1993. Genetics of aboriginal North Americans. *Evolutionary Anthropology* 1(6): 202–220.

Tainter, Joseph A. 1983. Settlement behavior and the archaeological record: Concepts for the definition of "archaeological site." *Contract Abstracts and CRM Archaeology* 3(2): 130–132.

Taylor, R. E. 1985. The beginnings of radiocarbon dating in American antiquity: A historical perspective. *American Antiquity* 50(2): 309–325.

——. 1987. *Radiocarbon Dating: An Archaeological Perspective*. New York: Academic Press.

Taylor, R. E., Austin Long, and Rcncc S. Kra (Eds.). 1992. *Radiocarbon After Four Decades: An Interdisciplinary Perspective*. New York: Springer-Verlag.

Taylor, R. E., and Ian Longworth (Eds.). 1975. Dating: New methods and new results. *World Archaeology* 7(2).

Taylor, R. E., and Clement W. Meighan (Eds.). 1978. *Chronologies in New World Archaeology*. New York: Academic Press.

Taylor, Walter W. 1948. A study of archeology. *American Anthropological Association, Memoir*, 69.

Tello, J. C. 1943. Discovery of the Chavín culture in Peru. *American Antiquity* 9(1): 135–160.

Teltser, Patrice A. (Ed.). 1995. *Evolutionary Archaeology: Methodological Issues*. Tucson: University of Arizona Press.

Templeton, Alan R. 1993. The "Eve" hypotheses: A genetic critique and reanalysis. *American Anthropologist* 95(1): 51–72.

——. 1994. "Eve": Hypothesis compatibility versus hypothesis testing. *American Anthropologist* 96(1): 141–147.

Thomas, David Hurst. 1969. Great Basin hunting patterns: A quantitative method for treating faunal remains. *American Antiquity* 34(4): 392–401.

——. 1976. *Figuring Anthropology: First Principles of Probability and Statistics*. New York: Holt, Rinehart and Winston.

——. 1978. The awful truth about statistics in archaeology. *American Antiquity* 43(2): 231–244.

——. 1981. How to classify the projectile points from Monitor Valley, Nevada. *Journal of California and Great Basin Anthropology* 3(1): 7–43.

——. 1983a. The archaeology of Monitor Valley: 1. Epistemology. *Anthropological Papers of the American Museum of Natural History* 58(1): 1–194.

——. 1983b. The archaeology of Monitor Valley: 2. Gatecliff Shelter. *Anthropological Papers of the American Museum of Natural History* 59(1): 1–552.

——. 1986. Contemporary hunter-gatherer archaeology in America. In David J. Meltzer, Don D. Fowler, and Jeremy A. Sabloff (Eds.), *American Archaeology Past and Future: A Celebration of the Society of American Archaeology 1935–1985* (pp. 237–276). Washington, DC: Smithsonian Institution Press.

——. 1987. The archaeology of Mission Santa Catalina de Guale: 1. Search and discovery. *Anthropological Papers of the American Museum of Natural History* 63(2): 47–161.

——. 1988. Saints and soldiers at Santa Catalina: Hispanic designs for colonial America. In Mark P. Leone and Parker B. Potter (Eds.), *The Recovery of Meaning in Historic Archaeology* (pp. 73–140). Washington, DC: Smithsonian Institution Press.

——. 1993. The archaeology of Mission Santa Catalina de Guale: Our first 15 years. In Bonnie G. McEwan (Ed.), *The Missions of La Florida* (pp. 1–34). Gainesville: University Press of Florida.

Thomas, Kenneth (Ed.). 1990. Soils and early agriculture. *World Archaeology* 22(1).

—— (Ed.). 1996. Zooarchaeology: New approaches and theory. *World Archaeology* 28(1).

Tilley, Christopher. 1990. *Reading Material Culture*. Oxford: Basil Blackwell.

Torroni, Antonio, Theodore G. Schurr, Chi-Chuan Yang, Emöke J. E. Szathmary, Robert C. Williams, Moses S. Schanfield, Gary A. Troup, William C. Knowler, Dale N. Lawrence, Kenneth M. Weiss, and Douglas C. Wallace. 1991. Native American mitochondrial DNA analysis indicates that the Amerind and the Nadene populations were founded by two independent migrations. *Genetics* 130: 153–162.

Trigger, Bruce G. 1980a. *Gordon Childe: Revolutions in Archaeology*. New York: Columbia University Press.

——. 1980b. Archaeology and the image of the American Indian. *American Antiquity* 45(4): 662–676.

——. 1989a. *A History of Archaeological Thought*. Cambridge: Cambridge University Press.

——. 1989b. Comments on archaeology in the 1990s. *Norwegian Archaeological Review* 22(1): 28–31.

——. 1991. Post-processual developments in Anglo-American archaeology. *Norwegian Archaeological Review* 24: 65–76.

——. 1993. Marxism in contemporary western archaeology. In M. B. Schiffer (Ed.), *Archaeological Method and Theory*. Vol. 5 (pp. 159–200). Tucson: University of Arizona Press.

——. 1995. Expanding middle-range theory. *Antiquity* 69(264): 449–458.

Tringham, Ruth. 1991. Households with faces: The challenge of gender in prehistoric architectural remains. In Joan M. Gero and Margaret W. Conkey (Eds.), *Engendering Archaeology: Women and Prehistory* (pp. 93–131). Oxford: Basil Blackwell.

Tuohy, Donald R., and L. Kyle Napton. 1986. Duck decoys from Lovelock Cave, Nevada, dated by 14-C accelerator mass spectrometry. *American Antiquity* 51(4): 813–816.

Tuttle, Russell, D. Webb, E. Weidl, and M. Baksh. 1990. Further progress on the Laeotoli trails. *Journal of Archaeological Science* 17(3): 347–362.

Tyler, Stephen A. 1986. Post-modern ethnography: From document to the occult to occult document. In James Clifford and George E. Marcus (Eds.), *Writing Culture: The Poetics and Politics of Ethnography* (pp. 122–140). Berkeley: University of California Press.

Tylor, Edward Burnett. 1871. *Primitive Culture*. Vols. 1 and 2. London: Murray.

Upham, Steadman (Ed.). 1990. *The Evolution of Political Systems: Sociopolitics in Small-Scale Sedentary Societies*. Cambridge: Cambridge University Press.

van der Merwe, Nikolaas J. 1982. Carbon isotopes, photosynthesis, and archaeology. *American Scientist* 70: 596–606.

van der Plicht, Johannes. 1993. The Groningen Radiocarbon Calibration Program. *Radiocarbon* 35(1): 231–237.

van Gerven, Dennis P., and George Armelagos. 1983. "Farewell to paleodemography?" Rumors of its death have been greatly exaggerated. *Journal of Human Evolution* 12: 353–360.

van Gerven, Dennis P., Susan Guise Sheridan, and William Y. Adams. 1995. The health and nutrition of a medieval Nubian population. *American Anthropologist* 97(3): 468–480.

Verano, John W., and Douglas H. Ubelaker (Eds.). 1992. *Disease and Demography in the Americas*. Washington, DC: Smithsonian Institution Press.

Villablanca, Francis X. 1994. Evolutionary analysis: 3. Spatial and temporal aspects of populations revealed by mitochondrial DNA. In Bernd Herrmann and Susanne Hummel (Eds.), *Ancient DNA: Recovery and Analysis of Genetic Material From Paleontological, Archaeological, Museum, Medical, and Forensic Specimens* (pp. 31–58). New York: Springer-Verlag.

Vivian, R. Gwinn. 1990. *The Chacoan Prehistory of the San Juan Basin*. San Diego: Academic Press.

Vizenor, Gerald. 1990. *Crossbloods: Bone Courts, Bingo, and Other Reports*. Minneapolis: University of Minnesota Press.

von Frese, R. R. B., and V. E. Noble. 1984. Magnetometry for archaeological exploration of historical sites. *Historical Archaeology* 18(2): 38–53.

Wagner, Gail E. 1982. Testing flotation recovery rates. *American Antiquity* 47(1): 127–132.

Walde, Dale, and Noreen D. Willows (Eds.). 1991. *The Archaeology of Gender*. Proceedings of the 22nd Annual Chacmool Conference. Calgary: University of Calgary Archaeological Association.

Wall, Diane diZerega. 1994. *The Archaeology of Gender: Separating the Spheres in Urban America*. New York: Plenum.

Ward, R. G. W. (Ed.). 1987. Applications of tree-ring studies: Current research in dendrochronology and related subjects. *BAR International Series*, no. 333.

Waring, A. J. Jr., and Preston Holder. 1945. A prehistoric ceremonial complex in the southeastern United States. *American Anthropologist* 47(1): 1–34.

Waselkov, Gregory A. 1979. Zumwalt's Fort: An archaeological study of frontier process in Missouri. *Missouri Archaeologist* 40: 1–129.

Wason, Paul K. 1994. *The Archaeology of Rank*. Cambridge: Cambridge University Press.

Waters, Michael R. 1992. *Principles of Geoarchaeology: A North American Perspective*. Tucson: University of Arizona Press.

Watson, Patty Jo. 1974. Flotation procedures used on Salts Cave sediments. In Patty Jo Watson (Ed.), *Archeology of the Mammoth Cave Area* (pp. 107–108). New York: Academic Press.

——. 1976. In pursuit of prehistoric subsistence: A comparative account of some contemporary flotation techniques. *Midcontinental Journal of Archaeology* 1(1): 77–100.

——. 1986. Archaeological interpretation, 1985. In David J. Meltzer, Don D. Fowler, and Jeremy A. Sabloff (Eds.), *American Archaeology Past and Future: A Celebration of the Society of American Archaeology 1935–1985* (pp. 439–457). Washington, DC: Smithsonian Institution Press.

Watson, Richard A. 1991. What the New Archaeology has accomplished. *Current Anthropology* 33: 275–291.

Weberman, A. J. 1971. The art of garbage analysis. *Esquire* 5(456): 113–117.

Weiner, Daniel H. 1995, Spring. NAGPRA: Legal burden or historic opportunity? *The World of Tribal Arts.*

Welch, Paul D., and C. Margaret Scarry. 1995. Status-related variation in foodways in the Moundville chiefdom. *American Antiquity* 60(3): 397–419.

Weymouth, John W. 1986. Geophysical methods of archaeological site surveying. In Michael B. Schiffer (Ed.), *Advances in Archaeological Method and Theory.* Vol. 9 (pp. 311–395). Orlando: Academic Press.

Weymouth, John W., and Robert Huggins. 1985. Geophysical surveying of archaeological sites. In George R. Rapp Jr. and J. Gifford (Eds.), *Archaeological Geology* (pp. 191–235). New Haven: Yale University Press.

Whallon, Robert E. Jr., and James A. Brown (Eds.). 1982. *Essays on Archaeological Typology.* Evanston, IL: Center for American Archaeology Press.

Wheat, Joe Ben. 1972. The Olsen-Chubbuck site: A Paleo-Indian bison kill. *Society for American Archaeology Memoir* no. 26.

Wheeler, Mortimer. 1954. *Archaeology From the Earth.* Oxford: Oxford University Press; Clarendon.

Whelan, Mary K. 1995. Beyond hearth and home on the range: Feminist approaches to Plains archaeology. In Philip Duke and Michael C. Wilson (Eds.), *Beyond Subsistence: Plains Archaeology and the Postprocessual Critique* (pp. 46–65). Tuscaloosa: University of Alabama Press.

White, Leslie A. 1949. *The Science of Culture.* New York: Grove.

——. 1959. *The Evolution of Culture.* New York: McGraw-Hill.

——. 1975. *The Concept of Cultural Systems.* New York: Columbia University Press.

White, Randall. 1982. The manipulation of burins in incision and notation. *Canadian Journal of Anthropology* 2: 129–135.

——. 1992. Beyond art: Toward an understanding of the origins of material representation in Europe. *Annual Review of Anthropology* 21: 537–564.

——. 1994. [Review of the book *The Roots of Civilization* by Alexander Marshack]. *American Antiquity* 59(2): 392–393.

——. 1996. Comment. *Current Anthropology* 37(2): 218–220.

White, Theodore E. 1953. A method of calculating the dietary percentage of various food animals utilized by aboriginal peoples. *American Antiquity* 18(4): 396–398.

——. 1954. Observations on the butchering technique of some aboriginal peoples, nos. 3, 4, 5, and 6. *American Antiquity* 19(3): 254–264.

White, Tim D. 1991. *Human Osteology*. San Diego: Academic Press.

——. 1992. *Prehistoric Cannibalism at Mancos 5MTUMR-2346*. Princeton: Princeton University Press

Whittaker, John C. 1994. *Flintknapping: Making and Understanding Stone Tools*. Austin: University of Texas Press.

Willey, Gordon R., and Philip Phillips. 1958. *Method and Theory in American Archaeology*. Chicago: University of Chicago Press.

Willey, Gordon R., and Jeremy A. Sabloff. 1993. *A History of American Archaeology*. 3d ed. New York: Freeman.

Williams, Barbara. 1981. *Breakthrough: Women in Archaeology*. New York: Walker.

Wilshusen, Richard H., and Glenn D. Stone. 1990. An ethnoarchaeological perspective on soils. *World Archaeology* 22(1): 104–114.

Winterhalder, Bruce. 1981. Optimal foraging strategies and hunter-gatherer research in anthropology: Theory and models. In Bruce Winterhalder and Eric Alden Smith (Eds.), *Hunter-Gatherer Foraging Strategies* (pp. 13–35). Chicago: University of Chicago Press.

——. 1987. The analysis of hunter-gatherer diets: Stalking an optimal foraging model. In Marvin Harris and Eric B. Ross (Eds.), *Food and Evolution: Toward a Theory of Human Food Habits* (pp. 311–339). Philadelphia: Temple University Press.

Wintle, Ann G. 1996. Archaeologically relevant dating techniques for the next century. *Journal of Archaeological Science* 23(1): 123–138.

Wittfogel, Karl A. 1957. *Oriental Despotism: A Comparative Study of Total Power*. New Haven: Yale University Press.

Woodbury, Nathalie F. S. 1992, March. When my grandmother is your database: Reactions to repatriation. *Anthropology Newsletter:* 6, 22.

Woodbury, Richard B. 1960. Nels C. Nelson and chronological archaeology. *American Antiquity* 25(3): 400–401.

Wormington, H. M. 1981. Foreword to *Breakthrough: Women in Archaeology* by Barbara Williams. New York: Walker.

Wright, Henry T. 1977. Toward an explanation of the origin of the state. In James N. Hill (Ed.), *Explanation of Prehistoric Change* (pp. 215–230). Albuquerque: University of New Mexico Press.

——. 1986. The evolution of civilizations. In David J. Meltzer, Don D. Fowler, and Jeremy A. Sabloff (Eds.), *American Archaeology Past and Future: A Celebration of the Society for American Archaeology 1935–1985* (pp. 323–365). Washington, DC: Smithsonian Institution Press.

Wylie, Alison. 1991a. Feminist critiques and archaeological challenges. In *The Archaeology of Gender*. Proceedings of the 22nd Annual Chacmool Conference (pp. 17–23). Calgary: University of Calgary Archaeological Association.

——. 1991b. Gender theory and the archaeological record: Why is there no archaeology of gender? In Joan M. Gero and Margaret W. Conkey (Eds.), *Engendering Archaeology: Women and Prehistory* (pp. 31–54). Oxford: Basil Blackwell.

——. 1992. The interplay of evidential constraints and political interests: Recent archaeological research on gender. *American Antiquity* 57(1): 15–35.

Wynn, J. C. (Ed.). 1986. Special issue: Geophysics in archaeology. *Geophysics* 51(3): 533–639.

Yarnell, Richard A. 1974. Intestinal contents of the Salts Cave mummy and analysis of the initial Salts Cave flotation series. In Patty Jo Watson (Ed.), *Archaeology of the Mammoth Cave Area* (pp. 109–112). New York: Academic Press.

Yentsch, Anne Elizabeth, and Mary C. Beaudry (Eds.). 1992. *The Art and Mystery of Historical Archaeology: Essays in Honor of James Deetz.* Boca Raton, FL: CRC Press.

Yoffee, Norman. 1993. Too many chiefs? (or, safe texts for the '90s). In Norman Yoffee and Andrew Sherratt (Eds.), *Archaeological Theory: Who Sets the Agenda?* (pp. 60–78). Cambridge: Cambridge University Press.

Yoffee, Norman, and George L. Cowgill (Eds.). 1988. *The Collapse of Ancient States and Civilizations.* Tucson: University of Arizona Press.

Yoffee, Norman, and Andrew Sherratt (Eds.). 1993. *Archaeological Theory: Who Sets the Agenda?* Cambridge: Cambridge University Press.

Bibliographic Essay

□ □ □

Preface

Specific quotes and citations:
"Scientists are not mere . . ." (Horgan 1996: 5).
"Archaeology was not practiced . . ." (Spaulding 1985: 307).

Chapter 1 What Is Archaeology?

I strongly recommend Bruce Trigger's *A History of Archaeological Thought* (1989a), a theoretically informed overview of worldwide archaeology and its history. Additional important sources include *The Idea of Prehistory* by Glyn Daniel and Colin Renfrew (1988) and Donald K. Grayson's *The Establishment of Human Antiquity* (1983); see also Daniel (1976), Daniel and Chippindale (1989), and Stiebing (1994). For a glimpse of the major archaeological site discoveries throughout the world, see Fagan (1994) and Price and Feinman (1993).

A *History of American Archaeology* by Willey and Sabloff (1993) is a major synthesis. For a contrasting view, see Patterson (1995). I also recommend the papers in the Fiftieth Anniversary issue of *American Antiquity* (1985), as well as Christenson (1989), Johnson (1993), Lyon (1996), Meltzer et al. (1986), Reyman (1992), and Taylor (1948).

My use of "Americanist archaeology" follows Dunnell (1979).

The box titled "Archaeology's Unrecognized Working Women" is reproduced with permission from Levine (1994: 11–12).

Specific quotes and citations:
"I just like . . ." (quoted in Babcock and Parezo 1988: 131).
"The ancient Greeks . . ." (Rowe 1965: 2).
"We may perhaps . . ." (Daniel 1962: 19).
"People have a . . ." (Hill 1991: 45).

Chapter 2 Anthropology, Science, and the Humanities

This chapter relies on Trigger's (1989a) discussion of levels of theory in archaeology; see also Binford (1981), Clarke (1979), Raab and Goodyear (1984), and Spaulding (1960). Some general sources on anthropological theory include Bohannan and Glazer (1988), Borofsky (1994), Carrithers (1990, 1992), D'Andrade (1995), Geertz (1973, 1983, 1984), Harris (1968, 1993), Haviland (1994), and Kottak (1991).

The box titled "On Multiple Perspectives in Archaeology" is reproduced with permission from Preucel (1991: 14).

Science in archaeology: The best single source relating archaeology to its scientific framework is Bell's *Reconstructing Prehistory: Scientific Method in Archaeology* (1994). Gibbon's *Explanation in Archaeology* (1989) and Patty Jo Watson's (1986) synthesis are also important.

Humanistic approaches to anthropology and archaeology: See Benedict (1948), Carrithers (1990), Deetz (1983), and Spector (1983, 1993). A particularly informative dialogue on the interrelationship between scientific and humanistic approaches in anthropology can be found in the 1995 and 1996 issues of *Anthropological Newsletter* (published by the American Anthropological Association).

Cultural materialism: Marvin Harris named this approach, but the roots run much deeper; for a general introduction, see *The Rise of Anthropological Theory* (Harris 1968) and *Cultural Materialism: The Struggle for a Science of Culture* (Harris 1979); also see Harris (1994) and Harris and Ross (1987).

What's up with postmodernism? I like Harvey's *The Condition of Postmodernity* (1989). Other important works include Habermas (1987), Harding (1991), and Lyotard (1984).

Postmodern (interpretive) anthropology: Writing culture: See Clifford (1988), Clifford and Marcus (1986), Geertz (1983, 1984), Marcus and Fischer (1986), and Tyler (1986).

Critiques of postmodern approaches: Some good sources are Bruner (1994), Carneiro's "Godzilla Meets New Age Anthropology: Facing the Post-Modernist Challenge to a Science of Culture"(1995), and Harris (1994).

Archaeology's postprocessual critique: Ian Hodder has been the most vocal and prolific postprocessual critic. His more influential works include "Postprocessual Archaeology"(1985) and *Reading the Past: Current Approaches to Interpretation in Archaeology* (1986); see also Hodder (1989a, 1990, 1991a, 1991b, 1995) and Hodder et al. (1995). I also recommend Earle and Preucel (1987), Leone (1986), Patterson (1990), Preucel (1995), Shanks (1992), Shanks and Tilley (1987a, 1987b), and Tilley (1990).

Some critics of the postprocessual critique: Consult Binford (1987a, 1989a, 1989b), Bintliff (1991), and Watson (1991).

Some more balanced assessments of contemporary archaeological theory: See Bell (1994), Dark (1995), Lamberg-Karlovsky (1989), Preucel (1991), Skibo et al. (1995), Trigger (1989a, 1991), and Yoffee and Sherratt (1993).

Specific quotes and citations:

"Science and humanism . . ." (Anderson 1995: 2).

"The problem of creativity . . ." (Spaulding 1988: 264).

"a messy, bumbling . . ." (Cerroni-Long 1996: 52).

"No one is more convinced that I am . . ." (Benedict 1948: 587).

Chapter 3   Chronology Building: How to Get a Date

For a discussion of the theory behind chronological studies in contemporary archaeology, see Dean (1978a), Hammond (1974), Rick (1987), and Schiffer (1972). For a discussion of various new and innovative dating techniques, see Shreeve

(1992) and Wintle (1996); other solid general sources on chronology in archaeology include Fleming (1977), Michels (1973), Oakley (1968), Orme (1982), Taylor and Longworth (1975), and Taylor and Meighan (1978).

Dendrochronology: Important overviews include Baillie (1995), Dean (1978b), Stahle and Wolfman (1985), and Ward (1987). Classic discussions of dendrochronology can be found in Bannister (1962, 1970) and Stallings (1939); closing "the gap" is discussed by Douglass (1929), Haury (1962), and Morris (1933). The example from Betatakin is based on Dean (1970); the example of the Viking ship burial derives from Bonde and Christensen (1993).

Radiocarbon dating in archaeology: Bowman (1990) is a user-friendly and up-to-date introduction to the subject. Another useful overview is Taylor's (1987) *Radiocarbon Dating: An Archaeological Perspective,* emphasizing particularly the collaboration between archaeologist and radiocarbon lab; see also Adovasio et al. (1990), Aitken (1989), Bowman (1994), Taylor (1985), and Taylor et al. (1992). The statistics attached to radiocarbon dates are discussed by Long and Rippeteau (1974) and Thomas (1976, chapter 10).

Computer programs for calibrating radiocarbon dates: The OxCal program from Oxford University (Ramsey 1995), the CALIB program from the University of Washington (Stuiver and Reimer 1993), and the Groningen Radiocarbon Calibration Program (van der Plicht 1993) are all useful.

AMS dating: Hedges and Gowlett (1986) provide a readable summary of new developments in accelerator dating. AMS dating of the Lovelock Cave duck decoy is discussed by Tuohy and Napton (1986).

Dating the Shroud of Turin: See Dale (1987), Gove (1987), Jull et al. (1996), and Kouznetsov et al. (1996).

Obsidian hydration: The Government Mountain-Sitgreaves Peak study is based on research by Findlow et al. (1975). For a consideration of obsidian hydration and sourcing, see Clark (1964), Friedman et al. (1994), Michels (1973, chapter 13), Ridings (1996), and Sheets et al. (1990).

Protein dating of ancient ostrich egg shells: See Brooks et al. (1990), Ellis et al. (1996), Elster et al. (1991), and Miller et al. (1992).

Chapter 4 Chronology Building: Low-Level Archaeological Theory in Action

For a general overview of geoarchaeology, I highly recommend *Principles of Geoarchaeology: A North American Perspective* (Waters 1992). Other important sources include Courty et al. (1989), Holliday (1992), Rapp and Gifford (1985), Stein (1987, 1992), and Wilshusen and Stone (1990).

Some other general sources on the theory behind chronology building in archaeology include Adams and Adams (1991), Dunnell (1971, 1986), Spaulding (1977), Thomas (1981), and Whallon and Brown (1982). For some classical views of classification in archaeology, see Brew (1946: 44–66), Ford (1954), Krieger (1944), Rouse (1960), Spaulding (1953), and Steward (1954). For some guidelines to archaeological laboratory procedures, see Cronyn (1990) and Dillon (1989).

The box titled "Finding the Famous Fossil Footprints" is reproduced from Leakey (1984: 173) and Price and Feinman (1993: 11).

The box titled "Physical Stratigraphy at Gatecliff Shelter" is reproduced from Thomas (1983b: 55–56).

The Laetoli footprints: The stratigraphy at Laetoli is described in Leakey and Harris (1987); the footprints themselves are analyzed by Tuttle et al. (1990). For a popularized account, see Hay and Leakey (1982) and Leakey (1984).

Using volcanic ashes to date archaeological sites (tephrachronology): Consult Sheets and Grayson (1979) and Steen-McIntyre (1985). For specifics about the Mount Mazama eruption, see Davis (1978, 1983), Mehringer (1986), and Mehringer et al. (1977).

The index fossil concept in archaeology: Nelson's use of diagnostic artifacts and ersatz stratigraphy is discussed by Browman and Givens (1996); see also Kidder (1924: 94–129), Nelson (1914, 1916), Spier (1917, 1931), and Woodbury (1960).

Contemporary approaches for analyzing archaeological ceramics: See Barnett and Hoopes (1995), Bronitsky (1989), Gibson and Woods (1990), Glover and Griffiths (1989), Longacre (1991), Neff (1992), Orton et al. (1993), and Rice (1987, 1996a, 1996b).

Seriation in archaeology: See Braun (1985), Dunnell (1970), Ford (1962), Marquardt (1978), McNutt (1973), and Rouse (1967).

Pipe stem dating: The initial work was conducted by Harrington (1954), then refined by Binford (1962, 1972); see also Lofstrom et al. (1982), Majewski and O'Brien (1987: 170–172), Noël Hume (1976: 296–301), Salwen and Bridges (1977), South (1977a: chapter 7), and Waselkov (1979).

Specific quotes and citations:
"I performed this work . . ."(Nelson 1916: 165).
"We need more rather than fewer . . ."(Brew 1946: 65).
"*Discs*—Of the twenty-four . . ."(Haury 1950: 329).
"in making use of this dating device . . ."(Harrington 1954: 8).
"in all probability, therefore . . ."(Noël Hume 1976: 41).
"an archaeological unit possessing . . ."(Willey and Phillips 1958: 22).

Chapter 5   Fieldwork: Why Archaeologists Walk Straight Lines and Dig Square Holes

Several handbooks describe current approaches to archaeological fieldwork. Among the best sources are *Practical Archaeology: Field and Laboratory Techniques and Archaeological Logistics* (Dillon 1989), *The Archaeology Handbook: A Field Manual and Resource Guide* (McMillon 1991), and *Field Methods in Archaeology* (Hester et al. 1997); see also Dancey (1981), Fladmark (1978), and Joukowsky (1980). Although thoroughly dated, Wheeler's *Archaeology From the Earth* (1954) provides the flavor of what digging was like in the good old days of archaeological imperialism. Elliott's

Great Excavations (1995) details several important digs in the American Southwest. Stanley South (1977a, chapter 8) draws on his extensive experience to provide some guidelines for excavating historic-period sites; Noël Hume (1969) covers the same ground, but with a different emphasis. Straus (1990) discusses the archaeology of caves and rock shelters around the world.

The importance of regional archaeology and sampling at a regional level is discussed by Beck (1994), Binford (1964), Dunnell (1985), Dunnell and Dancey (1983), Rossignol and Wandsnider (1992), and Thomas (1978, 1986).

Weymouth (1986) provides an important overview of remote sensing in archaeology; see also Avery and Lyons (1981), Clark (1990), Ebert (1984), Gibbons (1991), Lyons and Avery (1984), Martin et al. (1991), Sabins (1996), Scollar et al. (1990), and Wynn (1986). For discussions on the overall potential of noninvasive archaeology, see Binford (1980: 9), Dunnell and Dancey (1983), Foley (1981), Tainter (1983), and Thomas (1987). Gibbons (1991) discusses how remote sensing technology has been used to look for early hominid remains.

The box titled "What Archaeological Survey Was Like in 1907" is reproduced from Kidder (1960: 12).

The search for Mission Santa Catalina: See Thomas (1987); some results and interpretations also appear in Garrison et al. (1985) and Thomas (1988a, 1993). For more on the archaeology of the mission system in Spanish Florida, see McEwan (1993). For discussions of power auger survey in archaeology, see Deagan (1980, 1981), McManamon (1984), Percy (1976), and Shapiro (1987).

Proton magnetometers in archaeology: See Abbott and Frederick (1990), Johnston (1961), Scollar (1969), Steponaitis and Brain (1976), von Frese and Noble (1984), and Weymouth (1986).

High altitude imagery: General sources include Deuel (1969), Harp (1975), and Riley (1987). Lindberg's early aerial surveys are discussed by Ann Axtell Morris (1933). Eddy et al. (1996) discuss use of air photography for archaeological site mapping.

Ancient roads of Chaco Canyon: See Crown and Judge (1991), Gabriel (1991), and Lyons and Avery (1984).

More on the archaeology of ancestral Pueblo people: Good sources include Adler (1996), Adler et al. (1996), Brody (1990, 1991), Cordell (1984, 1994), Lekson (1986), Peck (1994), Roberts (1996), Sebastian (1992), and Vivian (1990).

Soil resistivity in archaeology: See Bevan (1983), Carr (1982), Shapiro (1984), Weymouth (1986), and Weymouth and Huggins (1985).

The Cerén site: Refer to Conyers (1995) and Sheets (1983, 1992); the Arenal project is described in Sheets and McKee (1994).

Ground-penetrating radar studies of Japanese burial mounds: See Goodman (1994), Goodman and Nishimura (1993), and Goodman, Nishimura, and Yamamoto (1994); also see Sterngold (1993). Bevan and Kenyon (1975) provide a detailed discussion for archaeologists, outlining the theory behind ground-penetrating radar surveys; see also Bevan et al. (1984) and Weymouth (1986).

Flotation techniques in archaeology: Some useful sources include Flannery (1976: 104–105), Reitz and Scarry (1985: 12–13), Struever (1968), Wagner (1982), Watson (1974, 1976), and Yarnell (1974).

Specific quotes and citations:

"began to perceive . . ." (Sheets 1992: 12).

"When I excavate . . ." (Spector 1993: 1).

"My fieldwork . . ." (quoted in Babcock and Parezo 1988: 143).

Chapter 6   Middle-Range Research: Ethnoarchaeology and Experimental Archaeology

Specific case studies considered here can be found in Chaplin (1971), Frison (1989), Gould (1966), Hawkes et al. (1987), Perkins and Daly (1968), and White (1953, 1954).

The box titled "Why I Began Doing Ethnoarchaeology" is quoted with permission from Binford (1983: 98, 100–101).

The box titled "Garbage and Our Future" is quoted with permission from Rathje (1991: 134).

Formation processes: Michael Schiffer has been a driving force behind the recognition and explicit study of formation processes; *Behavioral Archaeology* (1976) remains critical to an understanding of modern archaeology, and *Formation Processes of the Archaeological Record* (1987) synthesizes the basic principles.

Middle-range research in archaeology: The basics were set out by Lewis Binford (1977, 1981, 1983, and 1987b); see also Hayden and Cannon (1984), Kosso (1991), Raab and Goodyear (1984), Thomas (1983a, 1986), Trigger (1989a, 1995), and Willey and Sabloff (1993).

Ethnoarchaeology: See Binford (1986), Graham (1994), Hayden (1979, 1987), Longacre (1991), Longacre and Skibo (1994), Saitta (1992), Stahl (1995), Stark (1993), and Wilshusen and Stone (1990).

Archaeology's Garbage Project: An overview of the Garbage Project is provided by Rathje (1984, 1991) and Rathje et al. (1992).

Experimental archaeology: See Cotterell and Kamminga (1990) and Schiffer et al. (1994).

The experimental replication of stone tools: John Whittaker's *Flintknapping: Making and Understanding Stone Tools* (1994) has been called the new "bible"on the subject, and I agree. Odell's *Stone Tools* (1996) presents several new, theory-based approaches to lithic analysis and its relationship to human behavior. For more on flintknapping, see also Church (1994), Crabtree (1966, 1979), Flenniken (1978, 1981, 1984), Frison and Bradley (1980), Gryba (1988), Henry and Odell (1989), and Sheets (1987).

Specific quotes and citations:

"Behavior is the first thing . . ." (quoted in Monastersky 1990: 41).

"Them old-timers never put . . ." (Gould 1966: 43).

"the focus on fauna . . ." (Binford 1978b: 451).

"the many rock magazines . . ." (Weberman 1971: 114).
"a rip-off, a threat . . ." (Rathje and Hughes 1975: 154).
"everybody's favorite villain . . ." (Rathje 1991: 122).
"They take a stick . . . " (quoted in Crabtree 1968: 449).

Chapter 7   How People Get Their Groceries: Reconstructing Human Subsistence and Ecology

Olsen-Chubbuck is discussed by Wheat (1972). The faunal remains from Smoky Creek Cave are presented by Thomas (1969). The California Gold Rush example comes from Schulz and Gust (1983a, 1983b).

The box titled "Ancient Bison Hunting at Olsen-Chubbuck" is reproduced with permission from Wheat (1972: 1–2).

Some general sources on zooarchaeology: Grayson (1984) reviews the basic assumptions, procedures, and analytical techniques of zooarchaeology in detail. A special issue of *World Archaeology* (Thomas 1996) contains several papers about contemporary zooarchaeology; see also Brewer (1992), Colley (1990), Crabtree (1990), and Reitz and Scarry (1985).

Taphonomy: The best single source is Lee Lyman's *Vertebrate Taphonomy* (1994); another highly useful source is *Taphonomy: A Bibliographic Guide to the Literature* (Koch 1989); see also Behrensmeyer and Kidwell (1985) and Hill (1979a, 1979b).

Studying ancient plant remains from archaeological sites: See Buurman and Pals (1994), Hastorf and Popper (1988), Pearsall and Piperno (1990), Reitz and Scarry (1985), and Smith (1985).

Some general sources on palynology: References include Bryant and Hall (1993), Faegri et al. (1989), and Moore et al. (1991).

Palynology at Star Carr: Consult Clark (1954, 1972), Day (1993), and Legge and Rowley-Conwy (1988).

Palynology of Shanidar Cave: See Leroi-Gourhan (1975), Miksicek (1987), and Solecki (1971).

Analysis of phytoliths from archaeological context: Some good sources are Pearsall (1982), Piperno (1984, 1987), Rapp and Mulholland (1992), and Rovner (1983, 1987, 1988).

Understanding seasonality: The chart from Guilá Naquitz is based on Flannery (1986: chapter 18). Howard (1929) discussed seasonality in the Emeryville Shellmound. Seasonality at Star Carr was first considered by Clark (1954), with subsequent critiques by Andreson et al. (1981), Jacobi (1978), and Pitts (1979); see also Day (1993). Some additional references on seasonality include Grayson and Thomas (1983) and Monks (1981).

"Reading the Fuel": See Hastorf and Johannessen (1991). For additional information on the Upper Montaro Valley Archaeological Project, see Costin and Earle (1989) and D'Altroy (1992).

Specific quotes and citations:

"Bones are documents . . ." (Wheeler 1954:192).
"Only a small part . . ." (quoted in Lyman 1994: 1).

"Wood and trees in the Andes . . ." (Hastorf and Johannessen 1991: 141).
"several dimensions of meaning . . ." (Hastorf and Johannessen 1991: 154).

Chapter 8   Some Bioarchaeological Perspectives on the Past

I strongly recommend Larsen's *Bioarchaeology: Interpreting Behavior From the Human Skeleton* (1997). The general field of bioarchaeology has also been recently reviewed by Grauer (1995), Larsen (1995), and White's *Human Osteology* (1991); see also Cohen and Armelagos (1984), Lambert (1993), Lambert and Walker (1991), Lukacs and Mindermann (1992), Martin et al. (1985), Milner et al. (1991), Sobolik (1994), and van Gerven et al. (1995).

The archaeology of ancient disease: See Roberts and Manchester (1995), Rogers and Waldron (1989), and Rothschild and Martin (1993).

The relationship of agriculture to human health: See Larsen (1987, 1995), Lukacs et al. (1985), Lukacs et al. (1989), and Lukacs and Minderman (1992).

Stable isotope analysis: For a relatively nontechnical general overview, see van der Merwe (1982); see also Ezzo et al. (1995), Katzenberg et al. (1995), Little and Schoeninger (1995), Price (1989), and Spielmann et al. (1990). The Tehuacán Valley study was conducted by DeNiro and Epstein (1981) and Farnsworth et al. (1985); see also DeNiro and Schoeniger (1983) and MacNeish (1967). The Chavín de Huántar study is reported by Burger and van der Merwe (1990).

Bioarchaeological investigation of "stress": Consult Huss-Ashmore et al. (1982), Hutchinson and Larsen (1988), Martin et al. (1985), and Powell (1985).

Paleodemography: Verano and Ubelaker (1992) is a particularly important source; see also Ramenofsky (1987) and Van Gerven and Armelagos (1983). Primary data and initial interpretations of the Pecos population are presented by Hooton (1930), Mobley (1980), Palkovich (1983), and Ruff (1981); see also Howells (1960). Spielman et al. (1990) report on stable isotope studies of this population.

Molecular archaeology: Pääbo (1993) provides an excellent and nontechnical overview of the potential for analyzing ancient DNA recovered in long-dead plants and animals; see also Brown and Brown (1992), Herrmann and Hummell (1994), and Powledge and Rose (1996). For some specific applications of molecular archaeology, see Del Pozzo (1989) on the subject of DNA fragments identified in mummified human remains. Handt et al. (1994) evaluate the DNA structure of the famous Tyrolean ice man; Doran et al. (1986) discuss the cellular and molecular composition of the 8,000-year-old human brain tissue recovered at the Windover site in Florida; see also Hagelberg (1993) and Villablanca (1994). Additional sources on molecular archaeology include Bonnichson (1990), Brown et al. (1993), and Grauer (1995). Bonnichsen and Schneider (1995) discuss the recovery of ancient hair from archaeological sites, and its potential for DNA analysis. Fisher et al. (1993) discuss DNA analysis of Civil War-era skeletal remains.

The African "Eve" hypothesis: See Gibbons (1993), Nei (1992), Stoneking (1994), and Templeton (1993, 1994).

The archaeology of DNA and the first Americans: Good sources include Dillehay (1989), Dillehay and Meltzer (1991), Horai et al. (1993), Lewin (1992), Meltzer (1989, 1993, 1995), Stone and Stoneking (1993), Szathmary (1993), and Torroni et al. (1991). On the relationship between archaeology, genetics, and linguistic diversity, see Meltzer (1995) and Renfrew (1992).

The case of the missing Russian czar: The best single reference is Maples and Browning (1994); see also Dickerson (1993).

Specific quotes and citations:

"I stood by . . . " (cited in Maples and Browning 1994: 243).

Chapter 9   Understanding the Social Systems of the Past

The definitions of social organization and social status are based on Bohannan (1965), Goldschmidt (1960, 1983), Goodenough (1965), and Service (1971). The sex-and-gender discussion follows Conkey and Spector (1984) and Gero (1988). The discussion of the Man-the-Hunter myth is based in part on Conkey and Spector (1984).

The box titled "Marxist Approaches in Anglo-American Archaeology" is reproduced with permission from McGuire (1992a: 1–2, 9, 83–84).

Engendering the human past: Two landmark sources are "Archaeology and the Study of Gender" (Conkey and Spector 1984) and *Engendering Archaeology: Women and Prehistory* edited by Gero and Conkey (1991); see also Brown (1993), Claassen (1992, 1994), Conkey (1991), Gero (1983, 1985), Gilchrist (1994), Nixon (1994), Seifert (1991), Spencer-Wood (1991), Spielmann (1995), Tringham (1991), Walde and Willows (1991), Whelan (1995), and Wylie (1991a, 1991b).

Moundville: Peebles and Kus (1977) provide the basic model distinguishing between ranked and egalitarian systems; see also Peebles (1971, 1977, 1981, 1987), Powell (1988), Steponaitis (1983), and Welch and Scarry (1995). For more on Mississippian archaeology, consult Emerson and Lewis (1991), Mehrer (1995), and Smith (1990). For more on the Southern Cult, see Brown (1976), Galloway (1989), Phillips and Brown (1978, 1984), and Waring and Holder (1945).

The archaeology of social status and inequity: McGuire and Paynter (1991) and Price and Feinman (1995) present diverse perspectives about the origins and operation of social inequality in the human past; see also Cobb (1993), Costin and Earle (1989), Ehrenreich et al. (1995), Flannery (1995), Gilman (1989), Paynter (1989), Renfrew and Shennan (1982), Upham (1990), and Wason (1994).

Life and death among the Hohokam: The discussion is based on Randall McGuire's *A Marxist Archaeology* (1992a); see also McGuire (1992b). For more on Hohokam archaeology, consult Crown and Judge (1991), Gumerman (1991), Haury (1976), McGuire and Schiffer (1982), and Noble (1991).

Marxist approaches in archaeology: See McGuire (1993) and Trigger (1993).

How archaeologists approach ancient mortuary behavior: Good resources include Beck (1995), McGuire (1992a: chapter 7), Morris (1991), O'Shea (1984), Parker Pearson (1982, 1995), and Peebles (1971).

The archaeology of power: For interesting perspectives, consult Costin and Earle (1989), Mehrer (1995), and Miller and Tilley (1984).

Specific quotes and citations:
"A consideration of ideology and power . . ." (Miller and Tilley 1984: vii).
"The structure of a society . . ." (Goldschmidt 1960: 266).
"The entire village . . ." (quoted by Eichler and Lapointe 1985: 11, and Wylie 1991b: 38).
"As long as we do not correct for . . ." (Isaac 1978: 102).
"There is also an important correlation . . ." (Thomas 1983b: 439–440).
"more the result of a false notion . . ." (Conkey and Spector 1984: 6).

Chapter 10   General Theory in Archaeology: Some Neo-Evolutionary Approaches

For a general overview of neo-evolutionary directions in archaeology, see Marcus and Flannery (1996), Maschner (1996), Spencer (1990, 1993, 1994), and Trigger (1989a, chapters 4 and 8). Other important references include Binford (1967, 1968a), Boyd and Richerson (1985), Carneiro (1970a, 1970b, 1973a, 1973b, 1988), Dunnell (1980), Durham (1992), Earle (1991), Ehrenreich et al. (1995), Flannery (1965, 1969, 1972, 1973), Johnson and Earle (1987), Lees (1994), Leonard and Jones (1987), Mithen (1989), Neff (1992), Rindos (1984), Rosenberg (1994), Trigger (1980a), Wright (1977, 1986), Yoffee and Cowgill (1988), and Yoffee and Sherratt (1993).

Some classic sources include Braidwood (1959), Childe (1951a, 1951b), Cohen (1977, 1981), Lubbock (1865, 1869, 1870), Morgan (1877), Sahlins and Service (1960), Service (1975), White (1949, 1959, 1975), and Wittfogel (1957).

Robert Kelly's *The Foraging Spectrum* (1995) is the best single source for understanding modern research on foraging populations. Other important sources include Aldenderfer (1993), Arnold (1993), Bettinger (1991), Burch and Ellanna (1994), Gamble and Boismier (1991), and Mithen (1990).

The box titled "Why Did People Domesticate Plants?" is quoted, with permission, from Flannery (1986: 5, 14, 16).

Optimal foraging approaches: Cashdan (1990) and Smith and Winterhalder (1992) include some important contributions, and Bettinger (1980) provides an early programmatic statement for archaeologists; see also Bettinger (1987), Durham (1981), O'Connell and Hawkes (1984), Smith (1983), Smith and Winterhalder (1981), and Winterhalder (1981, 1987). *Foraging Theory* (Stephens and Krebs 1986) is a general treatment of the subject; for a discussion of the concept of optimization, see Maynard Smith (1978). Alyawara foraging is discussed by O'-Connell and Hawkes (1981, 1984).

The origins of agriculture: See Binford (1968b), Cowan and Watson (1992), Fedick (1995), Harris (1994), Hayden (1990), MacNeish (1992), Matson (1991), Price and Gebauer (1995), Smith (1995), and Thomas (1990).

Selectionist approaches to neo-evolutionary archaeology: Good sources include Dunnell (1989), O'Brien and Holland (1990), Rindos (1984, 1989a, 1989b), and Teltser (1995).

Some cognitive and ideological approaches to evolution: For overviews, consult Demarest (1989), Flannery and Marcus (1993), Hodder (1982), and Marcus and Flannery (1996); for a concentrating view, see Carneiro (1992).

Neo-evolutionary theory: For critical perspectives, see Kohl (1993), Trigger (1989a: chapter 8), Yoffee (1993), and Yoffee and Sherratt (1993).

Specific quotes and citations:

"Any given system . . ." (Sahlins and Service 1960: 94–95).
"encouraged a major devaluation . . ." (Trigger 1989a: 24).
"[That] the discovery and cultivation . . ." (Morgan 1877: 23).
"The huntsman and his prey . . ." (Childe 1951a: 67–68).
"a question without real meaning . . ." (Rindos 1984: 141).
"They were neither inevitable . . ." (Rindos 1984: 141).
"The state is a type of very strong . . ." (Flannery 1972: 403–404).
"at some point in their history. . ." (Carneiro 1970a: 733).
"Why did many independent . . ." (Cohen 1977).
"there appears to be ample . . ." (Cohen 1981: 121–122).
"high population density . . ." (Johnson and Earle 1987: 270).
"It must simply be recognized . . ." (Renfrew 1982: 21).

Chapter 11 An Archaeology of the Human Mind

Key references include Mithen (1990), Renfrew (1982), Renfrew and Bahn (1996, esp. chapter 10), and Renfrew and Zubrow (1994); see also Bender (1993), Demarest and Conrad (1992), Earle (1991), Flannery and Marcus (1993), Fritz (1978), Marcus (1992), Mithen (1995), and Renfrew (1993).

The discussion of empathetic approaches, in some cases, follows the useful discussions by Bell (1994, chapter 8), Hodder (1989b), and Trigger (1980b). The notion of replacing the objective eye with the personal "I"comes from Marcus (1994: 45).

Marshack's work on the origins of iconography: The best general source is Marshack's revised edition of *The Root of Civilization: The Cognitive Beginning of Man's First Art, Symbol and Notation* (1991); see also Marshack (1976, 1989, 1995b, 1996) and Marshack and d'Errico (1996). A more popular overview is available in "Images of the Ice Age" (Marshack 1995a).

Some criticisms of Marshack's research: Elkins (1996) provides a literary critique, with important appended comments by a range of interested scholars; see also d'Errico (1995) and White (1982, 1992, 1994).

Exploring ancient Chavín cosmology: Burger's *Chavín and the Origin of Andean Civilization* (1992) is a key resource here, as is Morris and von Hagen (1993); see also Miller and Burger (1995). For earlier views on Chavín, see Lathrap (1973, 1977, 1985) and Tello (1943).

Specific quotes and citations:

"Humanists must cease thinking . . ." (Flannery 1972: 400).
"We would be *paleopsychologists* . . ." (Binford 1987a).
"To read what the 'ecologists' write . . ." (Flannery 1972: 400).
"purity of observation . . ." (R. White 1996: 219).
"At the level of technology . . ." (Marshack and d'Errico 1996: 110).
"I have never argued . . ." (Marshack and d'Errico 1996: 107).
"The paradox of Chavín . . ." (Miller and Burger 1995: 453–454).
"The ideology of Chavín de Huántar . . ." (Miller and Burger 1995: 454).
"Thus, the Chavín horizon . . ." (Burger 1992: 184).
"One message of Chavín . . ." (Miller and Burger 1995: 454).
"Progress is marked less . . ." (Geertz 1973: 29).
"Archaeology shows more clearly . . ." (Hodder 1991a:31).

Chapter 12   Archaeology in the Twenty-First Century

The phrase "unintended consequences" is taken from Wylie (1991b). The phrase "chilly climate" is taken from Parezo and Bender (1994).

The box titled "Why Are So Few African-Americans Doing African-American Archaeology?" is quoted with permission from Singleton (1995).

The box titled "Contrasting Views of 'Significance' at Zuni Pueblo" is reproduced with permission from Anyon and Ferguson (1995: 913–915).

Cultural resource management: See Adovasio and Carlisle (1988), Anyon and Ferguson (1995), Blanton (1995), Cleere (1989, 1993), Elia (1993), Elston (1992), Fowler (1982, 1986), Klesert and Downer (1990), Leone and Potter (1992), McManamon (1991, 1992), McManamon et al. (1993), and Podolefsky and Brown (1994). The Advisory Council on Historic Preservation has produced numerous manuals for resource managers (esp. 1988, 1989).

Women as working archaeologists: Good sources include Babcock and Parezo (1988), Claassen (1992, 1994), Cullen (1995), Irwin-Williams (1990), Nelson et al. (1994), Parezo (1993), and Williams (1981).

The relationship between postprocessual archaeology and feminist theory: See Engelstad (1991), Gilchrist (1991), and Wylie (1992).

Gender stereotypes in archaeology: The persistence of gender stereotyping is effectively and humorously addressed by Diane Gifford-Gonzalez (1993, 1995). Bacus et al. (1993) provide a critical bibliography of gender in archaeology. A special issue of the *Bulletin of the Society for American Archaeology* (1991) asks "Is Gender Still an Issue?"

Some key and relatively new contributions to historical archaeology: See the volume honoring the contributions of James Deetz (Yentsch and Beaudry 1992). Also see Leone and Silberman's *Invisible America* (1995) and Little's *Text-Aided Archaeology* (1992); other good sources include Beaudry (1988), Deagan (1988, 1991, 1995), Deetz (1977, 1991), Falk (1991), Handsman and Leone (1989), Landon (1996), Lightfoot (1995), Seifert (1991), Shackel (1996), South (1977a, 1977b, 1994), and Wall (1994).

African American archaeology: See Deagan and MacMahon (1995), Ferguson's *Uncommon Ground* (1992), Lange and Handler (1985), Leone et al. (1995), MacMahon and Deagan (1996), Scott (1994), and Singleton (1985, 1995); see also Barbour (1994), Blakey (1995), Jamieson (1995), Orser (1984, 1991, 1995), Orser and Fagan (1995), Rankin-Hill and Blakey (1994), and Sobel (1987). Singleton and Bograd (1995) have published a bibliographic guide to the literature of the African diaspora. Slave diets at Monticello are discussed by Crader (1990).

The archaeology of the African Burial Ground: Consult Cook (1993), Gaines (1995), Harrington (1993), Levy (1993), Rothschild (1990), and Smith (1994). For more on American slave life, see Douglass (1950).

Ethics in archaeology: The papers published by Lynott and Wylie (1995) cover a range of ethical concerns for the 1990s; see also Chase et al. (1988), Green (1984), and Messenger (1989).

"Who Owns the Past": Interesting perspectives are found in Arden (1989), Bray and Killion (1994), Gathercole and Lowenthal (1990), Goldstein and Kintigh (1990), Greenfield (1989), Layton (1989), Messenger (1989), Murray (1996), and Powell et al. (1993).

Native American Graves and Protection Act (NAGPRA): Some of the key sources include Carpenter (1991), Deloria (1992, 1995), Echo-Hawk and Echo-Hawk (1994), Ferguson (1996), Gulliford (1996), Klesert (1992), Klesert and Powell (1993), McManamon (1994), Meighan (1992), Morell (1994), Preston (1989), Riding In (1992), Rose et al. (1996), Russell (1995), Shackley (1995), Weiner (1995), and Woodbury (1992). Special issues of *American Indian Culture and Research Journal* (Echo-Hawk 1992) and *Federal Archeology* (National Park Service 1995) are devoted to NAGPRA discussions.

Specific quotes and citations:

"women could not withstand . . ." (Wormington 1981: v).

"Activities by many archaeologists . . ." (Wormington 1981: v).

"giving women their due . . ." (Nelson and Nelson 1994: 235).

"the cultural specific (emic) . . ." (Trigger 1989b: 31).

"for the comfort of the company's Negro men" (quoted in Harrington 1993: 30).

"the first European . . ." (quoted in Cook 1993).

"If it was an African . . ." (quoted in Harrington 1993: 34).

"We didn't include . . ." (quoted in Harrington 1993: 33).

"microcosm of the issues . . ." (cited in Harrington 1993: 30).

"very revolutionary . . ." (quoted in Harrington 1993: 38).

"If you desecrate a white grave . . ." (quoted in Vizenor 1990).

"It is most unpleasant work . . ." (quoted in Preston 1989: 70).

Illustration Credits

□ □ □

95   After Thomas (1983b: figure 22); drawing by the author and Nicholas Amorosi.

96   Table 4.1: After Thomas (1983b: table 3).

101   Table 4.2: After Nelson (1916: 166).

103   After Kidder (1924: figure 8).

106   Courtesy of the American Museum of Natural History; photograph by Craig Chesek.

107   After Mayer-Oakes (1955: figure 15); drawing by Dennis O'Brien.

108   After Ford (1952: figure 15). Courtesy American Museum of Natural History; drawing by Nicholas Amorosi.

110   After Harrington (1954); drawing by Dennis O'Brien.

112   After Deagan (1987: figure 6.2); drawing by Dennis O'Brien.

113 **(top)**   Courtesy of Museo del Prado, Madrid.

113 **(bottom)**   Courtesy of the Print Collection, Miriam and Ira D. Wallach Division of Art, Prints, and Photographs. The New York Public Library, Astor, Lenox, and Tilden Foundation.

116   Drawing by Dennis O'Brien.

Chapter 5   Fieldwork: Why Archaeologists Walk Straight Lines and Dig Square Holes

123   Courtesy of the American Museum of Natural History; photograph by Susan L. Bierwirth.

125   Courtesy of Faith Fuller Kidder and the School of American Research.

127   Courtesy of the American Museum of Natural History; drawing by Dennis O'Brien.

130   After Deagan (1980: 23); drawing by Dennis O'Brien.

131   Courtesy of Kathleen Deagan.

132   Courtesy of the American Museum of Natural History; photograph by Dennis O'Brien.

133   Courtesy of the American Museum of Natural History; photograph by Dennis O'Brien.

137   After Gabriel (1991); drawing by Dennis O'Brien.

139   Courtesy of the American Museum of Natural History; drawing by Dennis O'Brien.

142   Courtesy of Payson Sheets.

143   Courtesy of Payson Sheets.

146   After Goodman and Nishimura (1993: figure 2).

149   After Thomas (1983b: figure 8); drawing by Dennis O'Brien.

Chapter 6   Middle-Range Research: Ethnoarchaeology and Experimental Archaeology

165   Courtesy of James F. O'Connell.

169   Courtesy of William Rathje.

175   Courtesy of the American Museum of Natural History; photograph by R. Wanamaker.

178   Courtesy of Bruce Bradley and the Crow Canyon Archaeological Center.

180   Courtesy of the American Museum of Natural History; photograph by Anibal Rodriguez.

Chapter 7   How People Get Their Groceries: Reconstructing Human Subsistence and Ecology

185   Courtesy of Joe Ben Wheat and the University of Colorado.

191   After Thomas (1969: figure 1).

197   After Schulz and Gust (1983a, figures 1 and 2); drawing by Dennis O'Brien.

200   After Clark (1954: figure 2); drawing by Dennis O'Brien.

202   Courtesy of Ralph Solecki.

206   After Flannery (1986: Figure 18.1); drawing by Dennis O'Brien.

208   After Clark (1954: figure 5): drawing by Dennis O'Brien.

210   After Hastorf and Johannessen (1991).

211   After Hastorf and Johannessen (1991).

Chapter 8   Some Bioarchaeological Perspectives on the Past

218   After Gilbert and Mielke (1985: xiii); drawing by Dennis O'Brien.

220   After Farnsworth et al. (1985: figure 1); drawing by Dennis O'Brien.

226   After Martin, Goodman, and Armelagos (1985: figure 8.1); drawing by Dennis O'Brien.

228   After Mobley (1980: figure 1); drawing by Dennis O'Brien.

232   Courtesy of Corbis-Bettman.

233   Courtesy of William R. Maples.

Chapter 9   Understanding the Social Systems of the Past

249   Courtesy of the American Museum of Natural History.

255   Drawing by Diana Salles.

257   After Peebles and Kus (1977: figure 3); drawing by Dennis O'Brien.

261   After Doyel (1991); drawing by Dennis O'Brien.

Chapter 10   General Theory in Archaeology: Some Neo-Evolutionary Approaches

289   After Wright (1977: figure 7.1); drawing by Dennis O'Brien.

291   After Wright (1977: figure 7.3); drawing by Dennis O'Brien.

Chapter 11   An Archaeology of the Human Mind

305   Photograph by Alexander Marshack.

306   Courtesy of Alexander Marshack; drawing by Dennis O'Brien.

307   Courtesy of Alexander Marshack; drawing by Dennis O'Brien.

317   Drawing by Diana Salles.

Chapter 12   Archaeology in the Twenty-first Century

329   Courtesy of Lucasfilm Ltd; photograph by Keith Hamshere.

341 (top)   Courtesy of Theresa Singleton.

341 (bottom)   Courtesy of the Granger Collection.

343   Courtesy of the African Burial Ground and U.S. General Services Administration.

345   Courtesy of Chester Higgins Jr.

347   Courtesy of Barbara Mills.

Index

□ □ □

Abbott, James T., 368, 378, 411
Aborigines, Australian, 24, 165, 166, 276
Absolute date. *See* Dating, absolute
Accelerator Mass Spectrometry (AMS), 75–77, 355
Acheulean, 23, 355
Achieved status, 253–254
"Actualistic" research, 193
Adams, Ernest W., 368, 409
Adams, William Y., 368, 403, 409
Adaptive strategy, 33, 355
Adler, Michael, 368, 411
Adovasio, James M., 368, 409, 418
Advisory Council on Historic Preservation, 332, 418
Aerial photography, 15
African American archaeology, x, 337–346, 353
African Burial Ground (New York), 339–346, 353–354, 423
Agate Basin site (Wyoming), 177
Agee, O. Frank, 376
Aitken, M. J., 368, 409
Alabama Museum of Natural History, 255
Albers, Patricia, 399
Aldenderfer, Mark, 368, 416
Alexandri, Alexandra, 384, 387
Ali, Muhammad, 170
Allaby, R. G., 371

Alta Toquima (Nevada), 151, 204
American Anthropological Association, 69
American Indians, x, 7, 9, 215, 337, 346–348, 352. *See also Tribes by name*
American Museum of Natural History (New York), 13, 16, 62, 99, 126, 420, 421, 422
Americanist archaeology, viii–ix, 8–28, 355
Amino acid racemization, 83–85, 355
Amorosi, Nicholas, xii, 421
Anasazi, 136–138
Andersen, H. H., 374
Anderson, E. N., 30, 368, 408
Anderson, Eve, 391
Andresen, John, 208–209, 368, 413
Androcentrism, 247
Anthropological archaeology, 29–31
Anthropological linguistics, 31, 355
Anthropological Society of Washington, 18
Anthropology, 30, 355
Antiquarian, 4–5, 355
Anyon, Roger, 346–347, 368, 418
Apple Creek site (Illinois), 152
Applied archaeology, x, 329–333, 357
Arbitrary level, 150, 355
Archaeobotany, 198–215, 355

Archaeofauna, 188
Archaeological context, 158, 182
Archaeological Institute of America, 28
Archaeological site, 121, 355
Archaeological theory, 29, 34, 43–47, 157–183
  high-level, 29, 43, 48–55, 161, 320–321
  low-level, 29, 43–46, 161
  middle-level, 29, 43, 46–47, 157–183, 252, 279, 309–311
  neo-evolutionary, 271–299
  postmodern interpretivism, 51–57
Archaeology, 355
  American, father of, 8–10
  in antiquity, 3–4
  careers in, 154, 332–333, 336–337
  cognitive, ix, 300–327
  education in, 154–155
  ethno. *See* **Ethnoarchaeology**
  experimental, 157, 311–313
  goals of, vi–vii
  historical. *See* **Historical archaeology**
  minorities in, 337
  museum. *See* Museum archaeology
  noninvasive, 147, 153
  reflexive, 325–326
  science and, ix
  scientific. *See* Scientific archaeology